SHELLEYAN REIMAGININGS AND INFLUENCE

Through sensitive close readings, *Shelleyan Reimaginings and Influence: New Relations* brings out the imaginative and formal brilliance of Percy Bysshe Shelley's writing as it explores his involvement in processes of dialogue and influence. Shelley recognizes that poetic individuality is the reward of connectedness with other writers and cultural influences. 'A great Poem is a fountain forever overflowing with the waters of wisdom and delight', he writes, 'and after one person and one age has exhausted all its divine effluence which their peculiar relations enable them to share, another and yet another succeeds, and new relations are ever developed, the source of an unforeseen and an unconceived delight' (*A Defence of Poetry*). He is among the major Romantic poetic exponents and theorists of influence because of his passionately intelligent commitment to the onward dissemination of ideas and feelings and to the unpredictable ways in which poets position themselves and are culturally positioned between past and future.

The book has a tripartite structure. The first three chapters seek to illuminate Shelley's response to representative texts, figures, and themes that constitute the triple pillars of his cultural inheritance: the classical world (Plato); Renaissance poetry (Spenser and Milton); and Christianity—in particular, the concept of deity and the Bible. The second and major section of the book, explores Shelley's relations and affinities with, as well as differences from, his immediate predecessors and contemporaries: Hazlitt and Lamb; Wordsworth; Coleridge; Southey; Byron; Keats (including the influence of Dante on Shelley's elegy for his fellow Romantic); and the great painter J. M. W. Turner, with whom he is often linked. The third section considers Shelley's reception by later nineteenth-century writers, figures influenced by and responding to Shelley including Beddoes, Hemans, Landon, Tennyson, and Swinburne. A Coda discusses the body of critical work on Shelley produced by A. C. Bradley, a figure who stands at the threshold of twentieth-century thinking about Shelley.

Shelleyan Reimaginings and Influence

New Relations

MICHAEL O'NEILL

OXFORD
UNIVERSITY PRESS

Great Clarendon Street, Oxford, OX2 6DP,
United Kingdom

Oxford University Press is a department of the University of Oxford.
It furthers the University's objective of excellence in research, scholarship,
and education by publishing worldwide. Oxford is a registered trade mark of
Oxford University Press in the UK and in certain other countries

First published 2019
First published in paperback 2023

Published in the United States of America by Oxford University Press
198 Madison Avenue, New York, NY 10016, United States of America

British Library Cataloguing in Publication Data
Data available

Library of Congress Cataloging in Publication Data
Data available

ISBN 978–0–19–883369–7 (Hbk.)
ISBN 978–0–19–888425–5 (Pbk.)

'Arrivée de toujours, qui t'en iras partout'
Rimbaud, *Les Illuminations*

For Posy, Daniel, Melanie, and Millie

Acknowledgements

The present book was originally conceived as part of a longer work that would explore Shelley and influence from classical times to the present. In the event, the twentieth- and twenty-first-century aspects of that project were hived off and became part of a larger study of Romanticism's influence, *The All-Sustaining Air* (Oxford University Press, 2007), while the current book focuses more exclusively on Shelley and his relations with writers before 1900. I have incurred many debts in the decade and more on which I've been working on the book: to those who have invited me to give lectures and papers; to the audiences at such events; to those who have invited me to write chapters and essays, and have edited my work; to colleagues, students, and friends at Durham University and elsewhere who have encouraged and supported my endeavours; to all at Oxford University Press who have helped the book into print; to my wonderful family. The book was completed during a difficult year for me medically, and I owe thanks to many friends and colleagues who gave me the gift of their encouragement as well as many practical acts of assistance.

For all these foregoing forms of help, and at the risk of graceless if unintentional overlookings, I'd like to thank Anna Barton, John Barnard, Bernard Beatty, Andrew Bennett, Christoph Bode, Will Bowers, Audrey Bowron, Kostas Boyiopoulos, Ivan Callus, Madeleine Callaghan, Anna Camilleri, Robert Carver, Oliver Clarkson, James Corby, Richard Cronin, Nora and Keith Crook, Jack Donovan, the late Stephanie Dumke, Robert Douglas-Fairhurst, Kelvin Everest, Heather Ewington, Neil Fraistat, Tim Fulford, David Fuller, Marilyn Gaull, Stephen Gill, James Grande, Richard Gravil, Nicholas Halmi, Stephen Hebron, Sandra Heinen, Andrew Hodgson, Gavin Hopps, Anthony Howe, Paige Tovey Jones, John Kerrigan, Greg Kucich, Beth Lau, Angela Leighton, Norbert Lennartz, Gloria Lauri Lucente, Charles Mahoney, Michael Mack, Richard Marggraf Turley, Lucy Newlyn, Anita O'Connell, Catherine Paine, Adam Piette, Seamus Perry, Frank Pointner, Cecilia and Nick Powell, Lynda Pratt, Barbara Ravelhofer, Vidyan Ravinthiran, Alan Rawes, Gareth Reeves, Stephen Regan, Donald H. Reiman, Alastair Renfrew, Katharina Rennhak, Fiona Robertson, Nicholas Roe, Michael Rossington, Mark Sandy, Corinne Saunders, Maria Schoina, Matthew Scott, Kate Singer, Nanora Sweet, Fiona Stafford, Jane Stabler, Heidi Thomson, Peter Vassallo, Lisa Vargo, Alan M. Weinberg, Sarah Wootton, the late Jonathan Wordsworth, and Duncan Wu.

For their selfless, multifaceted forms of help, I am especially indebted to Mark Sandy and Sarah Wootton, best of colleagues. I owe a particularly large debt to Madeleine Callaghan, without whose invaluable and generous help the book would not have taken on publishable form. Jacqueline Norton has been a most encouraging and guiding presence at the Press. I am grateful to the two anonymous readers of my near-final typescript for their stimulating and positive reports. Daniel Norman has been principally responsible for compiling the index.

What I owe my wife Posy, my children Daniel and Melanie, and my granddaughter Millie is beyond words, though felt along the heart and in the soul. My conversations with Jamie McKendrick have sustained me throughout my adult life, never more so than in recent months. The encouragement and support of my parents, brothers and sisters, and their families, as well as that of my in-laws and their families, have been remarkable.

For permission to reprint published material in this book I am grateful to the following relevant editors and publishers: Cambridge University Press for material in *The Cambridge Companion to the Epic*, ed. Catherine Bates (2010). Oxford University Press for material in *Tennyson among the Poets: Bicentenary Essays*, ed. Robert Douglas-Fairhurst and Seamus Perry (2009), *The Oxford Handbook of Percy Bysshe Shelley*, ed. Michael O'Neill and Anthony Howe, with the assistance of Madeleine Callaghan (2013), and *Thinking Through Style: Non-Fiction Prose of the Long Nineteenth Century*, ed. Michael D. Hurley and Marcus Waithe (2018). Laterza for material in *Generi letterari: ibridismo e contaminazione*, ed. Annamaria Sportelli (2001). Ashgate (now Routledge) for material in the following: ' "Beautiful but Ideal": Intertextual Relations between Letitia Elizabeth Landon and Percy Bysshe Shelley', in *Fellow Romantics: Male and Female British Writers, 1790–1835*, ed. Beth Lau, 211–29 (2009); 'Emulating Plato: Shelley as Translator and Prose Poet', in *The Unfamiliar Shelley*, ed. Alan M. Weinberg and Timothy Webb, 239–55 (2009); ' "A Kind of an Excuse": Shelley and Wordsworth Revisited', in *Literature and Authenticity, 1780–1900*, ed. Ashley Chantler, Michael Davies, and Philip Shaw, 51–66 (2011), and ' "Stars Caught in My Branches": Swinburne and Shelley', in *Decadent Romanticism: 1780–1914*, ed. Kostas Boyiopoulos and Mark Sandy, 103–18 (2015). Wissenschaftlicher Verlag Trier for material in *Narratives of Romanticism*, ed. Sandra Heinen and Katharina Rennhak (2017). Palgrave for material in *English Romantic Writers and the West Country*, ed. Nicholas Roe (2010) and *Keats's Places/Placing Keats*, ed. Richard Marggraf Turley (2018).

Material is also reprinted by permission from the following journals: *The Cambridge Quarterly* 28 (1999); *Literature and Theology* 25 (2011); *Charles Lamb Bulletin* n.s. 154 (2011); *The Wordsworth Circle* 45 (2014); *Keats-Shelley Review* 19 (2005); *Romanticism* 14 (2008) and 17 (2011); *Byron Journal* 36 (2008); *Journal of Anglo-Italian Studies* 13–14 (2014); *Turner Society News* 109; 110 (2008); and *Women's Writing* 21 (2014).

Contents

Abbreviations

Each chapter indicates which edition of Shelley is being used. Prose works are set in italics, as are longer poems; shorter poems are set in roman.

BSM   *Bodleian Shelley Manuscripts*, gen. ed. Donald H. Reiman (22 vols.; New York: Garland, 1986–97): vol. I: *'Peter Bell the Third' [...] Bodleian MS. Shelley adds. c. 5 [...] and 'The Triumph of Life' [...] Bodleian MS. Shelley adds. c. 4, folios 18–58*, ed. Donald H. Reiman (1986); vol. II: *Bodleian MS. Shelley adds. d. 7*, ed. Irving Massey (1987); vol. III: *Bodleian MS. Shelley e. 4*, ed. P. M. S. Dawson (1988); vol. IV: *Bodleian MS. Shelley d. 1*, ed. E. B. Murray, 2 parts (1988); vol. V: *The 'Witch of Atlas' Notebook [...] Bodleian MS. Shelley adds. e. 6*, ed. Carlene Adamson (1997); vol. VI: *Shelley's Last Notebook [...] Bodleian MS. Shelley adds. e. 20 [...] with Bodleian MS. Shelley adds. e. 15 [...] and Bodleian MS. Shelley adds. c. 4, folios 212–46*, ed. Donald H. Reiman and Hélène Dworzan Reiman (1990); vol. VIII: *Bodleian MS. Shelley d. 3*, ed. Tatsuo Tokoo (1988); vol. IX: *The 'Prometheus Unbound' Fair Copies [...] Bodleian MSS. Shelley e. 1, e. 2, and e. 3*, ed. Neil Fraistat (1991); vol. X: *Mythological Dramas [...] Bodleian MS. Shelley d. 2 [...] with 'Relation of the Death of the Family of the Cenci' [...] Bodleian MS. Shelley adds. e. 13*, ed. Betty T. Bennett and Charles E. Robinson (1992); vol. XI: *The Geneva Notebook of [...] Shelley [...] Bodleian MSS. Shelley adds. e. 16 and adds. c. 4, folios 63, 65, 71, and 72*, ed. Michael Erkelenz (1992); vol. XII: *Shelley's 'Charles the First' Draft Notebook [...] Bodleian MS. Shelley adds. e. 17*, ed. Nora Crook (1991); vol. XIII: *Drafts for 'Laon and Cythna' [...] Bodleian MSS. Shelley adds. e. 14 and adds. e.19*, ed. Tatsuo Tokoo (1992); vol. XIV: *Shelley's 'Devils' Notebook [...] Bodleian MS. Shelley adds. e. 9*, ed. P. M. S. Dawson and Timothy Webb (1993); vol. XV: *The 'Julian and Maddalo' Draft Notebook [...] Bodleian MS. Shelley adds. e. 11*, ed. Steven E. Jones (1990); vol. XVI: *The 'Hellas' Notebook [...] Bodleian MS. Shelley adds. e. 7*, ed. Donald H. Reiman and Michael C. Neth (1994); vol. XVII: *Drafts for 'Laon and Cythna' [...] Bodleian MS. Shelley adds. e. 10*, ed. Steven E. Jones (1994); vol. XVIII: *The Homeric Hymns and 'Prometheus' Draft Notebook [...] Bodleian MS. Shelley adds. e. 12*, ed. Nancy Moore Goslee (1996); vol. XIX: *The Faust Draft Notebook [...] Bodleian MS Shelley adds. e. 18*, ed. Nora Crook and Timothy Webb (1997); vol. XX: *The 'Defence of Poetry' Fair Copies [...] Bodleian MSS. Shelley e. 6 and adds. e. 8*, ed. Michael O'Neill (1994); vol. XXI: *Miscellaneous Poetry, Prose and Translations [...] Bodleian MS. Shelley adds. c. 4, etc*, ed. E. B. Murray (1995); vol. XXII, *Part One: Bodleian MS Shelley adds. d. 6 [...]*; vol. XXII, *Part Two: Bodleian MS. Shelley adds. c. 5 [...]*, ed. Alan M. Weinberg (1997). See also vol. XXIII; *A Catalogue and Index of the Shelley Manuscripts in the Bodleian Library [...]*, ed. B. C. Barker-Benfield and Tatsuo Tokoo (London: Routledge, 2002).

CC	*The Journals of Claire Clairmont*, ed. Marion Kingston Stocking. Cambridge: Harvard University Press, 1968.
CPP	*Coleridge's Poetry and Prose*, ed. Nicholas Halmi, Paul Magnuson, and Raimonda Modiano. New York: Norton, 2004.
CPPBS	*The Complete Poetry of Percy Bysshe Shelley*, ed. Donald Reiman, Neil Fraistat, and Nora Crook. Baltimore: Johns Hopkins University Press. 3 vols to date: 2000, 2004, 2012.
H	*The Complete Poetical Works of Percy Bysshe Shelley*, ed. Thomas Hutchinson. Oxford: Clarendon, 1904. Issued 1905 and 1934 as Oxford Standard Authors edn.; corrected by G. M. Matthews, 1970.
Journals: MWS	*The Journals of Mary Shelley*, ed. Paula R. Feldman and Diana Scott-Kilvert. Oxford: Oxford University Press, 1987. 2 vols. Reprinted pbk as one volume by Johns Hopkins University Press, 1995.
Letters: MWS	*The Letters of Mary Wollstonecraft Shelley*, ed. Betty T. Bennett. Baltimore: Johns Hopkins University Press, 1980–8. 3 vols.
Letters PBS	*The Letters of Percy Bysshe Shelley*, ed. Frederick L. Jones. 2 vols. Oxford: Clarendon, 1964.
Longman	*The Poems of Shelley*, ed. Kelvin Everest and G. M. Matthews. London: Longman. 4 vols. to date: 1989, 2000, 2011, 2014.
Major Works	*Percy Bysshe Shelley: The Major Works*, ed. Zachary Leader and Michael O'Neill. Oxford: Oxford University Press, 2003, 2009 (corr.).
MYR	*Manuscripts of the Younger Romantics: Shelley*, gen. ed. Donald H. Reiman. New York: Garland, 1985–97. 9 vols. Relevant volumes: vol. I: *The Esdaile Notebook*, ed. Donald H. Reiman (1985); vol. II: *The Mask of Anarchy* (1985), ed. Donald H. Reiman; vol. III: *Hellas: A Lyrical Drama* (1985), ed. Donald H. Reiman; vol. IV: *The Mask of Anarchy Draft Notebook [...] Huntingdon MS. HM 2177*, ed. Mary A. Quinn (1990); vol. V: *The Harvard Shelley Poetic Manuscripts*, ed. Donald H. Reiman (1991); vol. VI: *Shelley's 1819–1821 Huntington Notebook [...] Huntington MS. HM 2176*, ed. Mary A. Quinn (1994); vol. VII: *Shelley's 1821–1822 Huntington Notebook [...] MS. HM 2111*, ed. Mary A. Quinn (1996); vol. VIII: *Fair-Copy Manuscripts of Shelley's Poems in European and American Libraries*, ed. Donald H. Reiman and Michael O'Neill (1997).
Norton	*Shelley's Poetry and Prose*, ed. Donald H. Reiman and Neil Fraistat. New York: Norton, 2002.
SC	*Posthumous Poems of Percy Bysshe Shelley* (London: John and Henry L. Hunt, Covent Garden, 1824).
Posthumous Poems (1824)	Cameron, Kenneth, Donald H. Reiman, and Doucet Devin Fischer, gen. eds. *Shelley and his Circle: 1773–1822*. 10 vols to date. Cambridge: Harvard University Press, 1961–.
Shelley's Prose	*The Prose Works of Percy Bysshe Shelley*, ed. E. B. Murray. 1 vol. published. Oxford: Clarendon, 1993.

Wolfe	*The Life of Percy Bysshe Shelley, As Comprised in 'The Life of Shelley' by Thomas Jefferson Hogg, 'The Recollections of Shelley and Byron' by Edward John Trelawny, 'Memoirs of Shelley' by Thomas Love Peacock,* intro. Humbert Wolfe, 2 vols. London: Dent, 1933.
Wordsworth: Major Works	*William Wordsworth: The Major Works, including* The Prelude, ed. Stephen Gill, Oxford World's Classics. Oxford: Oxford University Press, 2011.

Introduction

Throughout his career, Shelley followed in his own footsteps as well as those of others. In 'Hymn to Intellectual Beauty' (version A), his younger self appears as a figure 'with fearful steps pursuing / Hopes of high talk with the departed dead' (51–2).[1] The echo of James Thomson's 'There studious let me sit, / And hold converse with the mighty dead' is unignorable.[2] So, too, is the startling tonal change, 'studious converse' altered into the simultaneously loftier and less begowned 'high talk' and into a fearful, potentially hazardous, potentially sublime pursuit. For its part, 'departed' suggests that echoing others goes hand in glove with a process of self-echoing that is happening in the current poem; the word recalls and gains resonance from the threefold use of 'depart' in the previous stanza.[3] The Scrope Davies version of the poem (version B) is closer to Thomson, speaking of 'Hopes of strange converse with the storied dead' (52), but it still arrives at its own unsettling inflection through the collocation of 'strange' and 'storied', the former word undermining the narrative stability suggested by the latter.

Shelleyan allusions are sites of transformation, spaces in which metamorphoses originate. Discussing Dante, Shelley writes that 'His very words are instinct with spirit; each is as a spark, a burning atom of inextinguishable thought' (693), and his own ability to make a previous word 'a burning atom of inextinguishable thought' is apparent. The editors of the recent Penguin volume suggest that in choosing 'multitudinous' at the close of 'To Jane. The Invitation'—

> And the blue noon is over us,
> And the multitudinous
> Billows murmur at our feet
> Where the earth and ocean meet
> And all things seem only one
> In the universal Sun.—
>
> (64–9)—

Shelley is recalling Shakespeare's 'multitudinous seas' in *Macbeth* (II.ii. 60).[4] The allusive agility so often at work in the Romantic poet's writing is evident in the way

---

[1] Quoted from *Percy Bysshe Shelley: The Major Works*, ed. Zachary Leader and Michael O'Neill, Oxford World's Classics (Oxford: Oxford University Press, 2003). Hereafter *Major Works*. All quotations will be taken from this edition unless indicated otherwise.

[2] 'Winter' (1746), 431–2, quoted from James Thomson, *The Seasons*, ed. James Sambrook (Oxford: Clarendon, 1981).

[3] As I note in *CPPBS*, 3. 452.

[4] Percy Bysshe Shelley, *Selected Poems and Prose* (London: Penguin, 2017), 842. Shakespeare is quoted from *The Norton Shakespeare*, ed. Stephen Greenblatt and others (New York: Norton, 1997).

he transforms the bloody horror of the Shakespearean text, in which Macbeth nightmarishly sees his murderer's hand as able to 'incarnadine' the many seas. Shelley places the word suspensefully at the end of the line, but the enjambment ushers in a concluding vision of reciprocal harmony, of murmuring billows. The poem's trochaic 'feet', with a metapoetic pun coming into play, musically enact a state in which 'earth and ocean meet', a state that invites imaginative assent, even as the poet acknowledges that the oneness evoked at the close may involve a 'seeming'.

1

'My mind became the book through which I grew / Wise in all human wisdom' (5. 3100–1), asserts Cythna in Shelley's *Laon and Cythna.* The assertion may seem a shade unguarded, raptly self-centred. Yet Shelley's feminist heroine exhibits her creator's fascination with the relationship between discovery of one's own mental identity, depicted here as a 'book', something written, and responsiveness, some-times conflicted or critical, to previous cultural insights. That relationship bears centrally on the main topic of the present study, a topic whose theoretical and poetic implications will be delineated and explored in this Introduction. Cythna's self-education leads her to have access to a greater mind, 'One mind, the type of all, the moveless wave, / Whose calm reflects all moving things that are' (5. 3104–5), in a characteristic Shelleyan leap from self to a sense of larger significance, one made possible by immersion in the thought of others. As a result she 'grew / Wise in all human wisdom', the movement from 'Wise' to 'wisdom' less pleonastic than evocative of self-growth blending with a force both heterodox and collective ('all human wisdom') that enables, challenges, and is greater than the self.

If Cythna learns 'A subtler language within language wrought' (5. 3112), she does so by virtue of recovering through such language 'The key of truths which once were dimly taught / In old Crotona' (5. 3113–14), and through being the most inward of listeners to her fraternal soulmate Laon's 'songs' (5. 3118). Those 'truths' are likely to be Pythagorean intuitions of harmony and mathematical order, but Shelley's wording gives them an arcane, faintly subversive air.[5] If they were 'dimly taught', they were so for three reasons; they glimmer 'dimly' because no writings of Pythagoras have survived, reminding the reader of the fraught, hard-won nature of 'wisdom'; because of the obscuring perspective of aspects of the present age; and because more positive contemporary and future energies can shed light upon what has unfairly lost its lustre. The mercurial speed of suggestion is typical.

Shelley's most idealized conceptions of reimagining the past and the process of influence warrant a Dantean parallel. In John Flaxman's 1807 *Compositions from the Hell, Purgatory, and Heaven of Dante Alighieri,* published by Longman, Hurst, Rees, and Orme,[6] there is an engraved illustration (the image on the cover of the

---

[5] See Michael Neth's valuable commentary in *CPPBS,* 3. 810–11.

[6] The first publication appears to have occurred in Rome, 1802, though there may have been an 'pre-1802 edition...at least in Germany'; Robert Rosenblum, *Transformations in Late Eighteenth Century Art* (1967; Princeton: Princeton University Press, 1969), 169 n.16.

present book) of 'The Meeting with Statius', based on the encounter between Virgil and Dante, and the poet Statius.[7] Springing into their own bare visual space by means of Flaxman's neo-classical line, a line that is sharp-etched yet fluid, the three figures climb the stairs of Mount Purgatory, engrossed in conversation and thought. The steps look shallow rather than steep, as though poetic companionship is easing their ascent. There is both harmony and a pleasing fluency of movement as Flaxman implements what Robert Rosenblum calls a style of 'astonishing simplicity that leaps across the nineteenth century into the language of modern abstraction'.[8]

The figures are not locked in a rigidly masculinist geometry as in Jacques-Louis David's austere, republican *Oath of the Horatii* (1784), to which Flaxman's composition might even, with a transformative irony, allude.[9] They move independently, roughly parallel in their footing, yet with distinctness, too. The brothers in David stretch out their swords, looking from left to right. Flaxman's figures walk from right to left, the furthest figure, the chapleted Statius turning with sweet-featured, androgynous, even feminine concern to the fully gowned Virgil, who looks steadily ahead, flanked on his left, a stride behind, by Dante, wearing a cloak and hat, but, unlike his poetic confrères, sporting no poetic wreath.

The pictorial idiom is understated yet eloquent, itself an exemplary image of how great poetry continues to enjoy an ever-altering life in and through the work of a later artist. As discussed in Chapter 11, the meeting between the Augustan Roman poet (author of the *Aeneid*) who lived in the century before the birth of Christ, the Roman poet of the first century, AD (author of the *Thebeid*) and the medieval Italian poet (author of the *Divina Commedia*) acts as a paradigm of literary influence at its most fostering and enabling. Virgil's priority is allowed; he is the pilgrim's leader and Statius's poetic hero. Statius pays tribute to his influence in lines that acknowledge his predecessor's majestically 'divine flame' and quasi-maternal nurturing: 'the *Aeneid*...was like a mama / to me', he says, 'and nourished my poetry making; / without it I'd not weigh a gram'.[10] Awe and tenderness converge in an episode justly described by T. S. Eliot as 'affecting'.[11] Male and female figurations of 'poetic making' coalesce (the contrast with David's painting, in which male attitude-striking and female distress seem antithetical, is stark); the meeting is virtual, imagined, and takes place on Dante's terms and in his poetic text.

Dante depicts Statius as not initially realizing (in the lines just quoted, for instance) that the shade guiding Dante is indeed Virgil. When told the truth by Dante, Statius seeks to clasp his master's feet, only to be told by Virgil, 'Brother, / don't; you're a shade and a shade is what you see', a gentle rebuke that has a particular edge of pain when one recalls Eliot's remark that it is delivered by 'the lost

---

[7] A useful modern edition (with accompanying quotations from Longfellow's translation) of these engravings is John Flaxman, *Flaxman's Illustrations for Dante's Divine Comedy* (Mineola: Dover, 2007).
[8] Rosenblum, 171.
[9] For David and Flaxman, and the former's debt to the latter, see Rosenblum, 176–8, 182–3.
[10] The translation of lines from this canto (*Purgatorio* XXI) is my own from 'Meeting' in my collection of poems *Gangs of Shadow* (Todmorden: Arc, 2014).
[11] 'Dante' in *The Complete Prose of T. S. Eliot: The Critical Edition: Literature, Politics, Belief, 1927–1929*, ed. Frances Dickey, Jennifer Formicelli, and Ronald Schuchard (Baltimore: Johns Hopkins University Press, 2015), 700–45 (715). Online edition.

soul speaking to the saved'.[12] The canto ends by accepting 'our lack of power'; it conveys, at its close, a sense that the 'power' still to be actualized is that possessed by the living poet, even as he can actualize this power most richly by immersing his poetic selfhood in the companionship of former poetic shades. In so doing, Dante permits Virgil and Statius to speak back newly, in changed accents, to the present in ways that support David Hopkins's sensitive emphasis on 'the complexity of the processes of self-transcendence, self-discovery, meeting and mingling, both in and out of time, that are involved in all acts of literary reception'.[13]

Christopher Ricks writes of one piece in his *Allusion to the Poets* that 'The essay on loneliness has its bearing on allusion in that one thing allusion provides and calls upon is company (the society of dead poets being a living resource in its company)'.[14] Affirmation of influence's value embraces the latently plangent awareness that, in the end, the living poet is a separate individual, discovering a distinctive identity that borders on 'loneliness' in the act of imagining the 'company' of forebears. To be finally 'Allone, withouten any compaignye',[15] in the anguished words of Chaucer's Arcite, is always the potential fate and possibly subliminal wish of the allusive poet, even as, in Shelley's case, the fate and the wish coexist with the conviction that, in his greatest poems, 'the dead live there / And move like winds of light on dark and stormy air' (*Adonais*, 44. 395–6). The 'there', there, is the new poet's 'young heart' (44. 393) and the new poem's created world, imaged as a place where 'winds of light' compete, as in some conflation of the *Inferno* and *Paradiso*, with 'dark and stormy air'.

Shelley embraces the imagining of ultimate creative loneliness with different inflections: pride, sadness, defiant individuality. Refusing to be drawn into the controversy about the merits of Alexander Pope, he tells Byron his view that

> I certainly do not think that Pope, or *any* writer, a fit model for any succeeding writer; if he, or they should be determined to be so, it would all come to a question as to under *what forms* mediocrity should perpetually reproduce itself; for true genius vindicates to itself an exemption from all regard to whatever has gone before—and in this question I feel no interest.   (*Letters: PBS*, 2. 290)

This rejects uncompromisingly any unexamined idea of imitation and serves as a salutary reminder to Byron that, for all his high regard for Pope, his 'true genius' lay elsewhere, in the possibility that he '*will* write a great and connected poem, which shall bear the same relation to this age as the "Iliad", the "Divina Commedia", and "Paradise Lost" did to theirs' (*Letters: PBS*, 2. 309)—not that Byron, in composing this work, 'will imitate the structure, or borrow from the subjects, of

---

[12] 'Dante', 715.

[13] David Hopkins, *Conversing with Antiquity: English Poets and the Classics, from Shakespeare to Pope* (2010; Oxford: Oxford University Press, 2014), 36. For a superb discussion of how Shelley responded to Greek culture, see Timothy Webb, ch. 7 (191–227) in *Shelley: A Voice Not Understood* (Manchester: Manchester University Press, 1977).

[14] Christopher Ricks, 'Prefatory Note', *Allusion to the Poets* (Oxford: Oxford University Press, 2002), 1.

[15] Geoffrey Chaucer, *The Knight's Tale, 2779, in The Works of Geoffrey Chaucer*, ed. F. N. Robinson, 2nd edn (London: Oxford University Press, 1957).

any of these, or any degree assume them as your models' (*Letters: PBS*, 2. 309). For Shelley, *Don Juan*, much of which was composed after his death, was assuming the shape of such a poem, as is evident in his remark to Mary Shelley after Byron had read canto V to him: 'It may be vanity, but I think I see the trace of my earnest exhortations to him to create something wholly new' (*Letters: PBS*, 2. 323).

At the same time, the possibility of the 'wholly new' depends on dialogue with the past. Shelley will have seen Byron's own irreverent, impish way with previous epic literature, and, as for himself, his own way of being 'wholly new' does not preclude, but benefits from, his delight in Pope's poetry: in an early letter he speaks of a line from *An Essay on Man* ' "all are but parts of one tremendous whole" ' as something more than Poetry', before going on to assert, 'it has ever been my favourite theory' (*Letters PBS*, 1. 35), and in turn anticipating his later 'theory' in *A Defence of Poetry* of individual poems as ultimately composing 'that great poem, which all poets like the co-operating thoughts of one great mind have built up since the beginning of the world' (*Major Works*, 687). Patrick Story, moreover, has brought out the way in which a poem such as *The Dunciad* influences *The Triumph of Life*, the Augustan poet's 'Dullness' a terrifying forebear of Shelley's 'Life'.[16]

Shelley recognizes that individuality is the reward and cost of connectedness with other writers and cultural influences. 'A great Poem is a fountain forever overflowing with the waters of wisdom and delight', he writes, 'and after one person and one age has exhausted all its divine effluence which their peculiar relations enable them to share, another and yet another succeeds, and new relations are ever developed, the source of an unforeseen and an unconceived delight' (*Major Works*, 693). Thinking about Dante's *Commedia* sparks off these assertions, assertions that effortlessly link originating work with its onward developing and altering life. The sentence—shaped by and poetically attuned to an emerging series of 'successions'[17]—prompts and enters into a view of the nature of the 'great Poem' that emphasizes its ability to renew itself from 'one age' to the next, so that 'new relations are ever developed'.

Although the mood is joyously celebratory and the prose has a dynamic commitment to the value of redefined 'relations', the wording suggests, too, that a poem lives by swaying 'forward', to adapt Auden's lines from the close of 'August and their favourite islands', 'on the dangerous flood / Of history that never sleeps or dies'.[18] Poems must exult in and accept their inevitable openness to the 'new relations' proffered by different perspectives, and 'relations' itself, a key word in

---

[16] See Patrick Story, 'Pope, Pageantry, and Shelley's *Triumph of Life*', *Keats-Shelley Journal* 21–2 (1972–3): 145–59. See also Paige Tovey's discussion of Shelley's response to Pope in her share of our co-written chapter, 'Spenser and Pope', in *The Oxford Handbook of Percy Bysshe Shelley*, ed. Michael O'Neill and Anthony Howe, with the assistance of Madeleine Callaghan (Oxford: Oxford University Press, 2013), 504–12.
[17] For a discussion of the relationship between allusion and the topic of succession, see Ricks, 'Dryden and Pope', in *Allusion to the Poets*, esp. 19–42. The triple meanings that Ricks finds in Dryden's use of 'succeeds' in *The Medall*—'at once "ensures", "takes up the succession", and "effects success"' (20)—obtain in Shelley's passage, too.
[18] Quoted from *The English Auden: Poems, Essays and Dramatic Writings 1927–1939*, ed. Edward Mendelson (London: Faber, 1977).

A Defence of Poetry, veers between two senses recorded in the *Oxford English Dictionary*. The idea of relationship is to the fore (*OED* 2a: 'an attribute denoting or concept expressing a connection, correspondence, or contrast between different things; a particular way in which one thing or idea is connected or associated with another or others; a link, a correlation'); but just below it is the notion of something told, reported linguistically (*OED* 1a: 'The action of giving an account of something; narration, report'). In keeping with these definitions and the freedom they afford, Shelley's 'new relations' involve 'connection, correspondence, or contrast' and exist as they are 'reported linguistically'.

For his part, Auden's 'dangerous' is illuminating about a predicament to which Shelley finds creative solutions, since the word may well have commerce with what Walter Jackson Bate in *The Burden of the Past* calls 'its original, rather ominous sense'; that is, 'subjected to the tyranny of something outside one's own control as a free agent'.[19] Literary 'history' as a 'flood' that challenges the poet's sense of being 'a free agent' is a central theme of Bate's profound reflections, and, as he establishes, the burden of the past weighed on Shelley's immediate predecessors. In the final chapter of *The Burden of the Past*, Bate turns to a question which the present book wrestles with, the question 'why the Romantics—these children of the eighteenth century—were able to do what they did despite the apparent odds against them'.[20] Bate canvasses several answers, including the new way in which 'imagination was conceived as *noetic*, as an indispensable means for the apprehension of truth'.[21] But the suggestion which has most relevance to the current study is his emphasis on the Romantics' Longinian 'boldness of spirit' and their conviction, at their boldest, that 'the companionship, the support to the heart and spirit, of a direct and frank turning to the great' might be enabling rather than ambition-quelling.[22]

Shelley, this study contends, embodies such 'boldness' and engages in such 'turning to the great'. An attempted encouragement to Mary Shelley (in the midst of the muddle of arrangements meant to help Claire Clairmont in her complicated dealings with Byron) reads as pitiably close to self-exculpation from one perspective, as though Shelley were almost currying favour because he knew (in context) he was in some way in the wrong (his arrangements meant that Mary Shelley had undertaken a hasty journey with a sick child, Clara, who subsequently died). But that would be an over-cynical reduction of poetic 'genius' to shoddy husband.[23] The passage constitutes a strong restatement of a trust in human capabilities that makes him the most keenly sensitive critic of contemporary literary merit (and imperfection) in the Romantic period:

> Adieu my dearest love—remember remember Charles the Ist & Myrrha. I have been already imagining how you will conduct some scenes—The second volume of St. Leon

---

[19] W. Jackson Bate, *The Burden of the Past and the English Poet* (London: Chatto and Windus, 1971), 3.
[20] Bate, *The Burden of the Past*, 127.   [21] Bate, *The Burden of the Past*, 126.
[22] Bate, *The Burden of the Past*, 127, 129–30.
[23] For consistently perceptive reflections on 'Shelley's acute understanding of the fluid boundaries between poetry and biography', see Madeleine Callaghan, *Shelley's Living Artistry: Letters, Poems, Plays* (Liverpool: Liverpool University Press, 2017), 143.

begins with this proud & true sentiment, 'There is nothing which the human mind can conceive, which it may not execute'.—Shakespeare was only a human being.

(*Letters: PBS*, 2. 40)

The joke of the nursery rhyme phrase ('remember remember'); the artful if wryly redefining appeal to a fictional work by William Godwin, Mary Shelley's father, which could be read a cautionary tale about hubris; the defamiliarizing sentence about Shakespeare being 'only a human being', which de- and re-valorizes in the same utterance: all show Shelley's intense involvement in the bringing forth on Mary Shelley's part of something new.[24] That they had marital problems is incontrovertible; so, too, is the evidence that each valued highly if inevitably partially (in both senses of the adverb) the creative ability and potential of the other.

Shelley's understanding of canonicity is the reverse of reifying conservatism and has much in common with more recent interpretations of the canonical as precisely that quality in works of literature that makes them hospitable to endless interpretation.[25] He rejects the shrewd, ponderable yet relatively static understanding of literary merit implicit in Samuel Johnson's *Preface to Shakespeare* (1755) in which Johnson contends that 'Nothing can please many, and please long, but just representations of general nature'.[26] It is important not to caricature Johnson's prodigiously tenacious wisdom and balance of mind, or set up a simplistic antithesis between 'conservative' *Rambler* essayist and 'radical' Romantic progressivist. As Bate observes, Johnson's belief in the 'unchanging universal' accompanies a conviction that blind adherence to rules supposedly drawn from classical art was an error: imitation did not mean slavish copying but, rather, it involved awareness that 'the ancients were great partly because their sentiments and descriptions were derived from their own direct study of nature' (by 'nature' Bate appears to mean the wealth of data presented to the mind by its own thoughts and experiences of reality, including the physical world).[27]

Yet Johnson's limitations as well as his self-conflicted acuteness are evident in his famous *Rambler* essay 168, in which he quotes admiringly Lady Macbeth's lines starting 'Come, thick night! / And pall thee in the dunnest smoke of hell' as exhibiting 'all the force of poetry, that force which calls new powers into being', only to throttle his admiration for the emergent life of 'new powers' by objecting to the

---

[24] For a study of the relationship between the Shelleys that makes notable use of relevant manuscript materials, see Anna Mercer, *The Literary Relationship of Percy Bysshe Shelley and Mary Wollstonecraft Shelley* (London: Routledge, forthcoming).

[25] For a balanced critique of the notion that canonicity serves only 'some stupefying aesthetic ideology' and is 'subversive of justice', see Frank Kermode, 'Prologue', in *An Appetite for Poetry: Essays in Literary Interpretation* (London: Collins, 1989), 1–46 (13). Kermode argues in terms that recall Shelley's own wording in *A Defence of Poetry* that 'The point is that the value and the sense of canonical documents are not fossilized, for new values and meanings (still historically related to older ones) are, if you prefer to put it so, continually conferred upon them' (15).

[26] Samuel Johnson, 'Preface' to *The Plays of William Shakespeare*, in *The Major Works*, ed. Donald Greene (1984; Oxford: Oxford University Press, 2000), 420.

[27] Walter Jackson Bate, *From Classic to Romantic: Premises of Taste in Eighteenth-Century England* (Cambridge: Harvard University Press, 1946), 71, 70. For a recent discussion of a major Romantic poet's response to Johnson, see Anthony Howe, *Byron and the Forms of Thought* (Liverpool: Liverpool University Press, 2013).

lowness of 'dun' and 'knife' in the passage, and describing the 'risibility' produced in him by the thought of 'the avengers of guilt "peeping through a blanket"'.[28] Johnson, to his credit, notices the Shakespearean assault on subsequent ideas of taste, and, more generally, Freya Johnston argues cogently that 'Johnson strives not to bypass but to heighten consciousness of his audience's potential alienation, as well as endeavouring to persuade readers of the centrality of low and trifling subjects to their own lives'.[29] But Shelley, who is more freely ready to mix up his lexical choices between and even within poems, and highly alert to the opportunities afforded by different literary genres, does not have to sacrifice admiration on the altar of a partial view of 'decorum'.[30]

C. S. Lewis mounted a famous defence of Shelley by arguing that he was a more 'classical' writer, in part because of his adaptation of classical topoi and forms, than were Dryden or Pope, with their commitment to the relatively marginal genre, so far as classical literature is concerned, of satire.[31] Yet this compliment may seem limiting if thought of as trying to reclaim Shelley's work in elitist ways. For Lewis, Shelley's 'best poems...answer the demands of their forms, and they have unity of spirit'.[32] What he might have stressed more forcefully, however, is that, in obeying the claims of '*decorum* in the Renaissance sense of the word: that is, his disciplined production not just of poetry but of poetry in each case proper to the theme and the species of composition', Shelley is able to rise beyond imitation into original composition.[33] The difference between Johnson and Shelley is less that Shelley denies continuities between cultures, or disbelieves in 'general nature', but that his faith in the possibility of 'new relations' burns with an more evidently affirming if often self-qualifying ardour, a more energizing conviction that 'All high poetry is infinite; it is as the first acorn which contained all oaks potentially' (*A Defence of Poetry*, 693). That sentence closes with pointed openness on a suggestive adverb.

One way of understanding this difference is offered by Seamus Perry when he argues that Coleridge, in effect, revises Johnson's appeal to 'nature' to change it 'from a relationship with a reality outside the poem, to a justifying principle somehow internal to the poem'.[34] Shelley, too, engages in a renegotiation of Johnson's trenchant understanding of 'reality', since reality is always—initially, at

---

[28] Johnson, *Major Works*, 247–8. The lines from *Macbeth* are given as quoted by Johnson.

[29] Freya Johnston, *Samuel Johnson and the Art of Sinking 1709–1791* (Oxford: Oxford University Press, 2005), 76.

[30] For an eloquent exposition of Shelleyan range, see Alan Weinberg, 'Shelley's Diversity', *English* (66 (2017): 6–26, which argues that 'despite concerns (expressed by Keats, amongst others) about the dispersing of his talents, it served his artistic purposes perpetually to explore different avenues of expression' (6). See also Nora Crook, 'Shelley's Jingling Food for Oblivion: Hybridizing High and Low Styles and Forms', forthcoming in *The Wordsworth Circle* (2019).

[31] C. S. Lewis, 'Shelley, Dryden, and Mr Eliot' (1939), in C. S. Lewis, *Selected Literary Essays*, ed. Walter Hooper (1969; Cambridge: Cambridge University Press, 2013), 187–208 (for 'classical', applied to a critic's approach, see 194).

[32] Lewis, 199.

[33] Lewis, 194. It should be said that this awareness is at least implicit at the high points of Lewis's fine essay, as when he praises the final act of *Prometheus Unbound* as 'an intoxication, a riot, a complicated and uncontrollable splendour, long and yet not too long, sustained on the note of ecstasy such as no other English poet, perhaps no other poet, has given us', 208.

[34] Seamus Perry, *Coleridge and the Uses of Division* (Oxford: Clarendon Press, 1999), 8.

any rate—a more plastic, apparently malleable substance for the Romantic poet than for the eighteenth-century writer. Moreover, the debate between classical and Christian worldviews, forever threatening to take on adversarial shape in Milton, and to the fore in A. W. Schlegel's *Lectures on Dramatic Art and Literature* (translated by John Black in 1815 and read by Shelley in 1818), empowers Shelley's imaginings of past and future, and thus his sense of the 'new relations' that may lie in the wake of any return to classical origins. While Shelley would only, in part, endorse Schlegel's sense of the superiority of Christian over Grecian art and culture, the author of 'Hymn to Intellectual Beauty' and 'The Zucca' would not have been insensible to Schlegel's claim that, unlike the Greeks for whom 'human nature was in itself all-sufficient', in the Christian era 'every thing finite and mortal is lost in the contemplation of infinity'.[35] Shelley would reject the potential political quietism of this position, and he is a fierce critic of the view that true reality lies in a world beyond, not in the here and now, yet he would have recognized, too, in reading Schlegel, that his own predicament was unignorably that of the modern for whom 'the happiness after which we strive we can never here attain'.[36]

Shelleyan reimaginings and influences are marked by his version of what Anna Beer calls 'the consonances and dissonances between Milton's art and that of the other writers he invokes'.[37] There is, in Shelley's work, a remarkable awareness of that interplay with a precursor and an accompanying ability to turn it to his artistic advantage. Shelley displays originality by virtue of what he does to and with an originating text.[38] Lucretian atomistic materialism revives in Shelley's work, for example, and yet undergoes change, as Shelley plays, in a poem such as 'Ode to Heaven', with modes of understanding, including the Lucretian, as so many fictions.[39] In the 'Ode to Heaven', Shelley's lyrical mode, with its lilting, accelerating rhythm across six nine-line stanzas, allows for 'heaven' (almost an allegorical emblem of the literary canon) to be a permanent abode housing ever-changing 'Glorious shapes' (10) and proto-Lucretian 'Atoms of intensest light!' (18):[40]

> Generations as they pass
> Worship thee with bended knees.
> Their unremaining Gods and they

---

[35] A. W. Schlegel, *Lectures on Dramatic Literature and Art (1809–11)*, trans. John Black (London: Baldwin, Cradock, and Joy, 1815), 14.

[36] Schlegel, *Lectures*, 15. For a groundbreaking analysis of Schlegel's significance for Shelley, see the unpublished dissertation by my former postgraduate, the late Stephanie Julia Dumke, 'The Influence of Calderón and Goethe on Shelley in the Context of A. W. Schlegel's Conception of Romantic Drama' (Durham University, 2013).

[37] Anna Beer, *Milton: Poet, Pamphleteer and Patriot* (London: Bloomsbury, 2008), 315.

[38] This formulation owes a debt to John Kerrigan's brilliant discussion in *Shakespeare's Originality* (Oxford: Oxford University Press, 2018) of 'Shakespeare's use of his originals' (3).

[39] For Lucretius, see, for a pioneering study, Paul Turner, 'Shelley and Lucretius', *Review of English Studies* n.s. 10 (1959): 269–82. See, too, Hugh Roberts, *Shelley and the Chaos of History: A New Politics of Poetry* (University Park: Pennsylvania State University Press, 1997), especially the section 'Shelley's Lucretian Imagination', 411–86, and the discussion of how 'Shelley applies this Lucretian model of creativity to his own poetic practice' (439). See also Anthony John Harding, 'Shelley, Mythology, and the Classical Tradition', in *The Oxford Handbook of Percy Bysshe Shelley*, 427–43, esp. 433–5.

[40] For the Lucretian connection, see *Longman* 3, 178n.

Like a river roll away:
Thou remainest such—alway!
(23–7)

The triple rhyme concluding each stanza here holds in the same clasp the transient and the abiding; if 'they / Like a river roll away', 'Thou remainest such—alway!'. As that potentially ambiguous 'such' makes clear (it could mean that heaven remains unchanging, or that heaven always remains a place that has much in common with what always rolls away), the poem collocates perspectives with stunning rapidity and deftness; its three spirits offer contrasting perspectives, the first and third within as well as beyond their speeches. As suggested, the Ode implicitly allegorizes the view of cultural outlooks and future possibilities that lies behind the Shelleyan vision of the 'new relations' at poetry's potentially reorchestrating fingertips. So the last, coda-like stanza is spoken by the Third Spirit but has a resolving air, as though it represented a final position:

What is Heaven? a globe of dew,
Filling in the morning new
    Some eyed flower whose young leaves waken
On an unimagined world.
    Constellated suns unshaken,
Orbits measureless, are furled
    In that frail and fading sphere,
    With ten millions gathered there,
To tremble, gleam, and disappear!
(46–54)

The 'final' position is a vision of endless potential, of gleams and vanishings, of the infinite ('Orbits measureless') 'furled / in that frail and fading sphere': possibly an allusion to Andrew Marvell's 'On a Drop of Dew'.[41] Whereas Marvell's drop of dew is an emblem of the soul mournfully looking back to its celestial origins, Shelley's is 'Heaven' in liquid form, making possible the glimpse of an emergent, new, and previously 'unimagined world'.

The poem works with slyly graceful self-reflexive intent, the stanza itself a 'furled' shape opening up onto 'an unimagined world', full of an intoxicating plurality of visions, conveyed by the rapid run-on rhymes and rhythms, and the late change of the fair copy from 'million' to 'millions', which *Longman* assumes occurred in 'Mary [Shelley's] transcription'.[42] Yet there is, as noted above, disappearing as well as gleaming, a sense of the ephemeral at the heart of glimpses of the near-transcendent. Epiphanic revelation, or its possible simulacrum, is, in Wallace Steven's

[41] See *The Poems of Andrew Marvell*, ed. Nigel Smith (Harlow: Pearson, 2007); for an illuminating discussion of the poem, including a contrast between Marvell's and Shelley's use of the dewdrop image, see Christopher R. Miller, 'Shelley's Uncertain Heaven', *English Literary History* 72 (2005): 577–603, especially 590–6. See also the helpful editorial note in *Longman* III, 179–80n and, for a more general overview of Marvell's influence, see Michael O'Neill, 'Marvell and Nineteenth-Century Poetry: Wordsworth to Tennyson', in *The Oxford Handbook of Marvell*, ed. Martin Dzelzainis and Edward Holberton (Oxford: Oxford University Press, 2019).
[42] *Longman* III, 180n.

words, 'acutest at its vanishing'.[43] The poem spins a characteristic web of suggestions; it enacts its own valorizing of imaginative ranging, juxtaposition, and creative rethinking, and it does so, in part, because, while invoking Lucretius, it allows itself an inventive space between acknowledgement and surrender. It thrives on articulating, in its latently humorous and implicit way, what Christopher R. Miller terms the poet's 'ambivalent view of Lucretian materialism'.[44]

Elsewhere, in his consideration of classical culture, Shelley's position is less 'ambivalent' than double-sided. In the essay *A Discourse on the Manners of the Ancient Greeks Relative to the Subject of Love*, which he wrote to accompany and explain his translation of Plato's *Symposium* (central to this book's opening chapter), Shelley wrestles between the view that, 'should circumstances analogous to those which modelled the intellectual resources of the age to which we refer [immediately before and after the "government of Pericles"], into so harmonious a proportion, again arise', then even more remarkable achievements would occur in the future, and the more pessimistic concern that such betterment would require 'a universal and almost appalling change in the system of existing things'.[45] The essay, here, balances between celebration of the past and enduring relevance of Greek culture, and an elegy for its apparent near-irrecoverability, before it shapes a more positive way forward, committing itself, not to an simplistic idealization of the Greeks (the essay is critical of attitudes to slavery and women), but to a movingly eloquent sense that what the Greeks achieved is an earnest of hope: 'What the Greeks were, was a reality, not a promise. And what we are and hope to be, is derived, as it were, from the influence and inspiration of these glorious generations'.[46]

At times such casting of historical runes obeys anti-Christian polemic. Rhapsodic yet architecturally and descriptively acute reflections on Pompeii (for Shelley 'a Greek city') inspire the following comment in a letter to his classical friend, Thomas Love Peacock: 'O, but for that series of wretched wars which terminated in the Roman conquest of the world, but for the Christian religion which put a finishing stroke to the antient system; but for those changes which conducted Athens to its ruin, to what an eminence might not humanity have arrived!' (*Letters: PBS*, 2. 73, 75).[47] Shelley is, of course, preaching to the pagan-loving, unconverted Peacock, and he has already indicated in the letter his ability to 'conceive a great work, embodying the discoveries of all ages, & harmonizing the contending creeds by which mankind have been ruled' (*Letters PBS*, 2, 71). Such a great work, possibly in context a production of 'moral & political science' rather than of 'Poetry' (*Letters PBS*, 2.71), seems a goal towards which Shelley strives in his imaginative literature,

---

[43] 'The Idea of Order at Key West', in Wallace Stevens, *Collected Poems* (1954; London: Faber, 1955).
[44] Miller, 'Shelley's Uncertain Heaven', 595. For an acute philosophical discussion of Shelley's debt to and use of Lucretius, see Michael A. Vicario, *Shelley's Intellectual System and Its Epicurean Background* (London: Routledge, 2007).
[45] Text of *A Discourse* is taken from James A. Notopoulos, *The Platonism of Shelley: A Study of Platonism and the Poetic Mind* (Durham: Duke University Press, 1949), 406.
[46] Notopoulos, 407.
[47] For fine commentary on this letter, and on Pompeii as 'bodying forth the ideal city of the imagination', see Webb, *Shelley: A Voice Not Understood*, 193–4 (193).

yet any first steps in that direction involve necessary critique and antagonism rather than conciliation: whether Shelley is in often critique-driven dialogue with Aeschylus or Wordsworth.

Shelley's understanding of classical and Christian thought does not, by any means, work in simply oppositional terms. In *Hellas*, where he admittedly softens his view of historical Christianity for tactical purposes, he rises, through a dramatic gift that is increasingly apparent in work he produced after going to Italy in March 1818, to this riddlingly hypnotic speech by Ahasuerus:

> Mistake me not! All is contained in each.
> Dodona's forest to an acorn's cup
> Is that which has been, or will be, to that
> Which is—the absent to the present. Thought
> Alone, and its quick elements, Will, Passion,
> Reason, Imagination, cannot die;
> They are, what that which they regard appears,
> The stuff whence mutability can weave
> All that it hath dominion o'er, worlds, worms,
> Empires, and superstitions. What has thought
> To do with time, or place, or circumstance?
> Wouldst thou behold the future?—ask and have!
> Knock and it shall be opened—look and, lo!
> The coming age is shadowed on the past
> As on a glass.
>
> (792–806)

Arguably, Ahasuerus, with his lack of interest 'in the details of earthly history', in Hugh Roberts's phrase, is not Shelley.[48] Yet Shelley is close to Ahasuerus in this passage, and, for all the dismissal of 'time, or place, or circumstance', the allusion to 'Dodona's forest' keeps in play a particularizing energy of localized focus. 'Thought', twice placed out on its own at the end of the blank-verse line, must have something to think and a medium, language, through which to communicate its self-communings, as is evident in the final lines, with their reworking of Matthew 7:7, where Jesus says 'knock, and it shall be opened unto you' (namely, the kingdom of heaven).[49] Ahasuerus does not simply seek to 'obliterate the distinctions between temporal and eternal, past and present', as Bryan Shelley argues and Hugh Roberts suspects.[50] Rather, the poetry suggests that thought, withdrawing to its own still point of self-sustaining contemplation, can be a 'present' that brings an activity of mind to the absences that are to be woven into future forms by the agencies of 'mutability'; indeed, Shelley's syntax makes faculties of mind and imagination at once controlling and perilously vulnerable. 'They are', at the start of line 798, gives them almost god-like intransitive status, yet what they are turns out to be identical with that which 'they regard, / The stuff whence mutability can weave / All that it

---

[48] Hugh Roberts, *Shelley and the Chaos of History*, 480–1.
[49] The allusion is noted and discussed in Bryan Shelley, *Shelley and Scripture: The Interpreting Angel* (Oxford: Clarendon, 1994), 160.
[50] Bryan Shelley, *Shelley and Scripture*, 161.

hath dominion o'er'. Thought shapes its prophetic intuitions of insight out of a dynamic of control and surrender, one akin to a poet's dealings with his poetic forebears and legatees, dealings governed by the handling of form and sound, as when, to take one example, what is 'sha*dow*ed' forth is ushered in by the softly exclamatory 'lo', itself building on the awakening signalled by 'beh*old*' and '*o*pened': the passage is one where sound effects reinforce the suddenness of discovery which is part of the poetry's meaning.

Shelley's achievement in this passage is to make relevant to contemporary political struggle materials drawn from classical mythology, Platonic and neo-Platonic thought, and Christian scripture. He reminds the reader that the mind is the locus of freedom as it is of captivity, and that freedom is available precisely through creative interchanges with past works. His own lyrical drama *Hellas* senses and shares in that quality of canonical texts that Italo Calvino defines as follows: '*A classic is a book which with each rereading offers as much of a sense of discovery as the first reading*'.[51] 'Rereading' is what Shelley undertakes in a spirit of recreation as he seeks, in an anticipation of Rimbaud at the end of *Une saison en enfer*, to be 'absolutely modern'.[52]

2

'New relations', present in and kindled by Shelley, are this book's subject. There has been an increasing recognition in Shelley studies that his work involves what Jerrold Hogle calls 'transference' and Stuart Peterfreund identifies as 'intertextual and linguistic conceptions'.[53] Hogle's approach to Shelley is especially influential for my book. Ably and nimbly distinguishing his method from 'Some Affiliated Approaches', as an introductory sub-title has it, Hogle installs 'transference' or 'a rootless passage between different formations' as his central focus, even as he claims that it is 'the most decentered' of centres.[54] His work powerfully explores ways in which Shelley's poetry 'explodes the most established conventional thought-relations into interconnections with others that were rarely thought to be analogous before'.[55] My book does not so much disagree with Hogle's as wish to lay its emphasis on the poetry's modes of working, seeking the near-impossible goal of staging encounters with the poetry that are not in thrall to preconceived ideas about it. It is written in a different, less theorized idiom, though—inevitably—it will display influences, especially modes of critical attention associated with practitioners of so-called close reading from Empson to Ricks, and, indeed, the neo-Shelleyan view of Wolfgang Iser that 'Communication in literature' involves 'a mutually restrictive and magnifying interaction between the explicit and the implicit, between revelation

---

[51] Italo Calvino, *Why Read the Classics?*, trans. Martin McLoughlin (1999; London: Penguin, 2009), 5.
[52] See Arthur Rimbaud, *Collected Poems*, introd. and ed. Oliver Barnard (1962; rev. edn London: Penguin, 1997), 346.
[53] Hogle, p. vii; Stuart Peterfreund, *Shelley among Others: The Play of the Intertext and the Idea of Language* (Baltimore: Johns Hopkins University Press, 2002), p. ix.
[54] Hogle, 18, 15.   [55] Hogle, 27.

and concealment'.[56] It takes its cue from Shelley's invitation to his readers to generate new forms of poetic knowing from what their own 'peculiar relations' allow them to discern in past poetry. Its aim is to focus on Shelley's gift for creative dialogue with predecessors and contemporaries, and, more briefly, on his significance for later nineteenth-century poetry.

In exploring Shelley's significance for his 1820s and Victorian legatees, I have selected five authors with diverse talents, interests, and poetic temperaments: Thomas Lovell Beddoes; Felicia Hemans; Letitia Elizabeth Landon; Alfred, Lord Tennyson; and Algernon Charles Swinburne. Shelley is a point of origin for topics in their work that include death and reputation (Beddoes), spiritual intimations (Hemans), the literary career (Landon), elegy (Tennyson), and heterodoxy of various kinds (Swinburne). He inspires formal innovation in all these writers, ranging from the sprawling *Death's Jest-Book* of Beddoes, a lyrical drama that reworks *Prometheus Unbound* and *The Cenci* through the embittered prism of Byronic satire, to *Anactoria* by Swinburne in which the ecstatic couplets of *Epipsychidion* are remodelled for newly eroticized purposes. James Najarian, discerning a poetics of 'affection and devotion' in Victorian responses to Keats, asks a question relevant to all my chosen later nineteenth-century remodellers of Shelley: 'How do you love a poet?'[57]

The process of influence reminds us that poetic interchange subverts tidy ideas of literary periodization, yet inevitably returns one to meditation on the nature and fact of cultural history. This meditation can involve alienation, a sense of alterity, and difference.[58] If periodization itself is a form of a form, as Caroline Levine has argued recently, with periods serving as 'bounded containers', influence threatens to break through and down the good fences that academic love of order may seek to erect.[59] This complication is foreseen by Shelley, whose sense of futurity and the past is often a troubled one, as two sonnets, 'Ozymandias' and 'England in 1819', reveal. Both poems use a traditional genre, the sonnet, that fourteen-line structure that bewitches poetic questers after harmony, but each disturbs expectations through shifts and formal reversals (such as sestet preceding octave in 'England in 1819', and unexpected criss-crossing rhymes in 'Ozymandias').

---

[56] Wolfgang Iser, 'Interaction between Text and Reader', in *Norton Anthology*, ed. Leitch, 1455.

[57] James Najarian, *Victorian Keats: Manliness, Sexuality, and Desire* (Basingstoke: Palgrave, 2002), 10.

[58] Tom Mole's discussion of Robert Browning's 'Memorabilia' (concerned with Shelley) comments pertinently on the way in which the poem 'measures the distance separating its Victorian speaker from the Romantic poet of a previous generation who fascinates him': see Tom Mole, *What the Victorians Made of Romanticism: Material Artifacts, Cultural Practices and Reception History* (Princeton: Princeton University Press, 2018), 41. For an intricate and elegantly conceived reading of the living connections forged by Shelley's work with previous writing (such as Boccaccio) and with later writers (such as the Brownings), see Jane Stabler, *The Artistry of Exile: Romantic and Victorian Writers in Italy* (Oxford: Oxford University Press, 2013). And for lucid and penetrating readings of 'the common problem of wrestling with romanticism' in later nineteenth- and twentieth-century poets, see George Bornstein, *Poetic Remaking: The Art of Browning, Yeats, and Pound* (University Park: Pennsylvania State University Press, 1988), 7.

[59] Caroline Levine, *Forms: Whole, Rhythm, Hierarchy, Network* (Princeton: Princeton University Press, 2015), 54.

'Ozymandias' views the past as a heap of ruins bequeathed by time's erosions of a sculpture presumably commissioned by a long-dead tyrant; if it bears witness to the ultimate futility of earthly power, and holds out the hope that even an artist who is seemingly compliant with tyranny can through formal deftness unmask it, it questions too art's own desire for longevity: 'Nothing beside remains' (12) is a pungently truncated sentence that taunts and 'mocks', to use the poem's own verb (see line 8) with its double implications of 'deride' and 'imitate', both the 'King of Kings' (10) and the artist.[60] It is the 'traveller from an antique land' (1) and his addressee, the poem's 'I', who must participate in the process of sense-making enjoined on a subsequent and temporally remote culture: a weighty, tricky responsibility as well as an opportunity to give embodiment to that 'glorious Phantom' (13) which Shelley's self-aware projection of futurity conjures up at the close of 'England in 1819'.

Shelley's attitude to influence is linked with his suspicion of discrete identities even as he is also a poet who could not be mistaken for another writer. He is an author whom we meet through complex modes of self-presentation: the delayed entrance of the lyric 'I',[61] the use of near-personae, the reliance on dialectical structures—and above all the inveterate practice of allusion to and reworking of past literature. These formal techniques have philosophical correlatives and mirror his fascination with ways in which identity can seem transpersonal and yet obstinately particular. In his essay 'On Life', the 'existence of distinct individual minds' is ingeniously and with knowing contradictoriness found to be a 'delusion':

> The words, *I, you, they*, are not signs of any actual difference subsisting between the assemblage of thoughts thus indicated, but are merely marks employed to denote the different modifications of the one mind. [...] The words *I*, and *you* and *they* are grammatical devices invented simply for arrangement and totally devoid of the intense and exclusive sense usually attributed to them. It is difficult to find terms adequately to express so subtle a conception as that to which the intellectual philosophy has conducted us. We are on that verge where words abandon us, and what wonder if we grow dizzy to look down the dark abyss of—how little we know.   ('On Life', 635–6)

'Pursuing the same thread of reasoning'; 'questioning its own nature': thought is an active process, ongoing, living by and in the present participles that it generates. In proposing that 'the words *I* and *you* and *they* are grammatical devices invented simply for arrangement and totally devoid of the intense and exclusive sense usually attributed to them', Shelley intimates that 'life' is wholly different from the 'multitude of entangled thoughts' (635) which constitutes common-sense mental experience.

Instead, he uses the fiction of his own individuality to propose, through a style that questions the validity of 'grammatical devices', the truth of 'the one mind'. Here the fact that language is a common property rather than the possession of an

---

[60] For further commentary on 'Ozymandias', see my 'Sonnets and Odes' essay in *The Oxford Handbook of Percy Bysshe Shelley*, 329–31.
[61] See my note on 'Ode to the West Wind' in *Romantic Poetry: An Annotated Anthology* (Oxford: Blackwell, 2008), 377.

individual cleverly supports his argument, an argument that takes him with poetic rigour into a place where he contends that 'the existence of distinct individual minds similar to that which is employed in now questioning its own nature, is [...] found to be a delusion'. That 'delusion' is not exactly a falsehood, since without it the riddlingly and knowingly tangled exploration we are reading would not be possible. Comparably, as mentioned earlier, he writes in *A Defence of Poetry* of individual poems as 'episodes of that great poem, which all poets like the co-operating thoughts of one great mind have built up since the beginning of the world' (687). It is Shelley's distinction to produce poems that seem like such 'co-operating thoughts', even when they are at their most fiercely adversarial and conflict-ridden.

The 'one mind', like 'that great poem', is at once sweeping solution and an idea intimating an ongoing dilemma. In both cases, what we are offered is a duplicitously uncertain and suggestive notion. Thus, the 'one mind' may be related to 'the popular notion in critical works of the period of "the public mind" [...] an atmosphere of common opinion within which all think and act', which Timothy Clark suggestively offers as a gloss. At the same time, it points towards a concept that jars with any idea of 'common opinion'.[62] For Shelley, language imagines the abolition of distinctions which linguistic structures are required to sustain. His words perform a serendipitous trick: they convey the idea of a 'distinct individual mind' (which from a strictly philosophical perspective is 'a delusion') and they adumbrate an all-subsuming yet elusive 'one mind' from which the writer is debarred by his individuality and to which he is connected by language. Indeed, to the degree that language embraces, formulates, and refigures the idea of the 'one mind', it comes close to being its sole witness and guarantor. Again, 'that great poem' composed out of 'co-operating thoughts' posits a poem that never exists and can never be written, and yet the thought of its existence serves as a creative spur for Shelley.

Such overt questioning and latent sustaining of distinctions is fundamental to the way in which Shelley thinks about his relationship to other poets. All the Romantics conceive of themselves in a creative dialogue with tradition; moreover, their practice, as Susan Wolfson has argued, discloses a realization that 'authorial self-recognition takes shape as a reciprocal formation in a society of formations'.[63] In Shelley's case, 'self-recognition' is intimately connected to the self-reconfiguring that allusive strategies make possible, an 'unbuilding', to borrow (or adapt) from the last line of his process-praising lyric 'The Cloud', that keeps self, text, and imagination continually alert to change and re-description.

By comparison, with all their intertextual flair and command of the tricks and tropes of a poetry of allusion, the stance of other Romantics can seem more rootedly individualistic than Shelley's is. And yet Shelley shares in, even as he is especially sensitive to the dangers of poetic and ethical egotism, a Romantic awareness of the

---

[62] Timothy Clark, *Embodying Revolution: The Figure of the Poet in Shelley* (Oxford: Clarendon Press, 1989), 40.
[63] Susan J. Wolfson, *Romantic Interactions: Social Being and the Turns of Literary Action* (Baltimore: The Johns Hopkins University Press, 2010), 8.

balance that a writer needs to strike between the particular and the general, the individual and the communally shared. Even when Blake, or his poetic surrogate Los, asserts with pugnacious tenacity that he 'must Create a System or be enslav'd by another Man's. / I will not Reason & Compare: my business is to Create' (*Jerusalem*, 10: 20–1), his 'System' is not solipsistically enclosed.[64] It is devoted to the revelation and release of what it means, or might mean, to be fully human, and it is so, in part, because rhythmically Blake has departed from 'A Monotonous Cadence, like that used by Milton and Shakspeare & and all writers of English Blank Verse';[65] he has reasoned and compared his practice with predecessors and emerged with a new poetic sound, evident in the contrast he achieves in the two lines: the first proudly rejecting what it fears, enslavement at the hands of another, yet empathizing too with that state; the second trumping the long 'a' in 'enslav'd' as it returns, chiastically, to the 'business' at hand, the need to 'Create'.

Wordsworth, who summons Milton to his aid in sonnets and sees him in innumerable allusions as an epic precursor validating the Romantic poet's even more 'heroic argument' (*The Prelude*, 1805, III. 182), is, as Jonathan Wordsworth persuasively suggests, 'strongly aware of his own individuality…yet rests his claim for the new epic on a godlike capacity that we are assumed to have in common'.[66] The drama of poetic selfhood recorded in his poetry continually frees itself from egotism, however sublimely conceived, by virtue of this trust in a 'common' humanity, which includes the human capacity to sense and rejoice in cultural newness and transformation. John Livingston Lowes's virtuosic if arguably dated discussion of how Coleridge was inspired to create *The Rime of the Ancient Mariner* (and 'Kubla Khan') out of the 'scattered dust' of remembered and half-remembered reading still has value for its demonstration of how such 'dust' was 'fused by a flash of imaginative vision' into remarkable artistic life.[67] A youthful Coleridge commented perceptively, 'Poetry without egotism comparatively uninteresting'.[68] It is a remark that holds true of his work from the early conversation poems to the late 'Work without Hope'. At the same time, he is also the theorist who hymns a miraculous synthesis of opposites, a blending of, among other things, 'the individual, with the representative'.[69] Keats, most sensitively snail-horned of readers, can be uncompromisingly hostile to Milton, a poet, however magnificent, who may threaten his own creative genius: 'life to him would be death to me' puts at its starkest the belated author's sense of the threat posed by the precursor poet.[70] And yet his career beats witness to his trust in imitation as the ground of creative originality.

[64] *Blake: Complete Writings*, ed. Geoffrey Keynes (1966; corr. edn; Oxford: Oxford University Press, 1992).
[65] 'To the Public', *Jerusalem* 3, in *Blake: Complete Writings*, 621.
[66] Jonathan Wordsworth, *The Prelude*, in *A Companion to Romanticism*, ed. Duncan Wu (Oxford: Blackwell, 1998), 191–205 (192).
[67] John Livingston Lowes, *The Road to Xanadu: A Study in the Ways of the Imagination* (1927; London: Picador, 1978), 49.
[68] *Coleridge's Notebooks: A Selection*, ed. Seamus Perry (Oxford: Oxford University Press, 2002), 2.
[69] Samuel Taylor Coleridge, *Biographia Literaria*, ed. James Engell and Walter Jackson Bate, 2 vols. (Princeton: Princeton University Press, 1983), II. 15.
[70] John Keats, in *The Letters of John Keats 1814–1821*, ed. Hyder Edward Rollins, 2 vols. (Cambridge: Cambridge University Press, 1958), II, 212.

It is important, then, that Shelley's way with and understanding of influence participates in the uncomplacent, sometimes agonized, but creatively remarkable recovery of poetic intelligence, artistry, and courage that constitutes British Romanticism. If this book selects him as an exemplar, it also sees him, as Harold Bloom does, as a confederate of the visionary company, a phrase borrowed from 'The Broken Tower', Hart Crane's elegy-cum-affirmation for and of his own post-Romantic career.[71] It is firmly of the view that Romantic poetry, at its finest, represents an unexampled articulation of imaginative power, a power whose 'strength', in Shelley's work, often lies in the apparently paradoxical 'meekness' or even 'weakness' (see *Prometheus Unbound*, II. iii. 94, 93) of its hospitable if never uncritical welcoming of other writers' visions and modes.

Charles Larmore, in one of the most eloquent defences available of Romantic thinking, writes valuably, so far the current study is concerned, of the 'essential *temporalization* of the Romantic imagination'.[72] By this phrase he does not means that the Romantics engage in a self-dismantling of overt claims that betrays them to a De Manian collapse into 'temporality'. He means, rather, that they accept that 'the imagination can articulate a sense of ultimate reality only along the dimensions of past and future'.[73] Shelley is, at times, overt in his concern with 'ultimate reality': one thinks of assertions made in the 1816 poems, 'Hymn to Intellectual Beauty', or Demogorgon's tantalizingly Janus-faced pronouncement that 'the deep truth is imageless' (*Prometheus Unbound*, II. iv. 116), where 'imageless' may point to a truth beyond images or to a fiction unsustainable by images. But in such places 'the dimensions of past and future' make themselves felt, tremblingly alive in the very syntax and rhythms of the poetry. In his thinking about influence Shelley encourages both a remodelling engagement with the past and the 'kind of haunting of the present by the future', which Andrew Bennett has sensitively explored.[74]

Bennett's important work raises the question of Shelley's understanding of the reader's role in shaping 'new relations'. Bennett argues in post-Derridean vein that, for Shelley, 'reading is haunted by the unreadable' and comments on 'the unspeakable assertion in Romantic writing of the death of the reader, the dissolution, that is to say, of the reading subject, his or her inhabitation or possession by an other— an effect that we might call the ghosting of poetry'.[75] There is much in Shelley that supports Bennett's discovery of a writer who is 'haunted by the unreadable' and who haunts his readers as a poet not wholly 'readable'. This is not to make any concession to the poet's denigrators.[76] It is, though, to recognize that Shelley's

---

[71] For discussion of Crane in relation to Romantic poetry, see my essay '"Altered Forms": Romanticism and the Poetry of Hart Crane', *Romantic Presences in the Twentieth Century*, ed. Mark Sandy (Aldershot: Ashgate, 2012), 57–72.

[72] Charles Larmore, *The Romantic Legacy* (New York: Columbia University Press, 1996), 24.

[73] Larmore, *Romantic Legacy*, 24.

[74] Andrew Bennett, *Romantic Poets and the Culture of Posterity* (Cambridge: Cambridge University Press, 1999), 170.

[75] Bennett, 176.

[76] 'Anti-Shelleyans' (xlii) are succinctly consigned to six groups—'The school of "common sense"', 'The Christian orthodox', 'The school of "wit"', 'Moralists, of most varieties', 'The school of "classic" form', 'Precisionists, or concretists' (xliii)—and devastatingly seen off by Harold Bloom in his

tropes and techniques take his readers out of any place of comforting sureness and make them imagine a future yet fully to be realized; make them recognize, indeed, that, to adapt Rilke's phrase from the close of 'Archaic Torso of Apollo', they may need to change their lives.[77] Yet if Bennett is correct to argue that Shelley imagines subliminally the death of the reader, one would wish to add that the reader in question is constructed as limited by the constraints of 'time, or place, or circumstance'; the dead or dying reader is always the possibly resurrected reader (such as Bennett himself), one capable of 'new relations' with literary texts. Shelley imagines such a readerly process in *A Defence of Poetry* as he describes the effect of Bacon's 'language': 'it is a strain which distends, and then bursts the circumference of the reader's mind, and pours itself forth together with it into the universal element with which it has perpetual sympathy' (679). The distending and bursting of circumferential bounds is imagined as ultimately a mutual process ('pours itself forth together with it') that is capable of further extensions 'into the universal element' (that the antecedent of the final 'it' could be Bacon's language or the reader's mind makes the point that reading involves a neo-Pauline death to the old self and birth of a new one).

Of Shelley's readers, Harold Bloom remains among the most pre-eminently responsive to the challenge of the poetry. Bloom's work is of abiding significance for me in thinking about poetic interchange. This not because I necessarily agree with his insights and judgements, or endorse his scheme of interpretation, as set out in *The Anxiety of Influence*, in particular.[78] I often do not agree with that scheme, and would dispute (for example) his reading of lines from *The Triumph of Life*, lines saturated with echoes of Wordsworth's 'Ode: Intimations of Immortality', as showing a failed *apophrades*, by which term Bloom means poets' achievement of a 'style that captures and oddly retains priority over their precursors, so that the tyranny of time almost is overturned, and one can be believe, for startled moments, that they are being *imitated by their ancestors*'.[79] Shelley's references, at once echoic and allusive, to Wordsworth's Intimations Ode in the lines 'a gentle trace / Of light diviner than the common Sun / Sheds on the common Earth' (337–9), are read by Bloom as a tragically ineffectual 'yielding': Shelley 'yields to his precursor's "light of common day"'.[80] Even if one were disposed to win from that choice of 'yields' a counter-current of productive meaning in Shelley's favour, the reading seems

introduction to *Percy Bysshe Shelley: Selected Poetry*, ed. Harold Bloom (New York: Signet, 1966), pp. xlii–xlv. Over fifty years later, Bloom's taxonomy retains its satirical accuracy.

[77] See *The Selected Poetry of Rainer Maria Rilke*, ed. and trans. Stephen Mitchell (1980; London: Picador, 1987), 60–1.

[78] Hogle writes acutely about the difference between Bloom's scheme and Shelley's practice, arguing that 'There is less a restrictive, castrating father at the heart of what attracts a new poet to past writing and more a continual fecundity, a motherly bringing-to-birth out of earlier realms into different ones', 20. For sophisticated and sympathetic insights into the 'tangled, paradoxical predicament' facing both Romantic poets and Bloom, see Agata Bielek-Robson, *The Saving Lie: Harold Bloom and Deconstruction* (Evanston: Northwestern University Press, 2011), 36.

[79] Harold Bloom, *The Anxiety of Influence: A Theory of Poetry*, 2nd edn (1975; New York: Oxford University Press, 1997), 141.

[80] Bloom, *Anxiety*, 140.

falsely to posit a model of egotistical competitiveness. Shelley's allusions indicate, rather, his understanding that he and Wordsworth, for all their differences, share a 'common' predicament. 'These common woes I feel' (5), writes Shelley, even if he writes with a touch of hauteur, even if the sonnet in question 'To Wordsworth' is highly critical of the earlier poet.

The key value of Bloom's work for me is less a sense of the rightness of his judgements than gratitude for the stimulating brilliance of his engagement with the drama of 'how one poet deviates from another', especially as those deviations show in the handling of images, figures, metaphors.[81] His most recent meditation on the topic, *The Anatomy of Influence*, described by Bloom as his 'final reflection upon the influence process' (p. ix), 'deviates' from his earlier reflections in that it makes overt what was always an insistent if at times submerged under-presence in his work: the Pater-inspired belief that 'Literary criticism...ought to consist of acts of appreciation'.[82] The belief is one shared by the present book. Bloom's redefinition of 'influence simply as *literary love, tempered by defense*'[83] marks a return to the central Shelleyan value of 'Love; or a going out of our own nature, and an identification of ourselves with the beautiful which exists in thought, action or person, not our own' celebrated in *A Defence of Poetry* (682). There, in ways that tally with Shelley's conception of influence's workings, the self is both annulled and fulfilled through an 'identification of ourselves' with what lies beyond the self: wording that suggests a virtuous surrender that borders on a shrewd appropriation. Bloom's body of work stimulates future critics 'to think poetically about poetic thinking'.[84]

Shelley's dealings with other poets are marked less by the psychodrama mapped out in Bloom's earlier thinking about influence than by a constant sense of influence as a systolic or diastolic beat of the poetic heart, and a constant sense of it, too, as demanding the hard work of examining tradition, hard work evident in his labours as a translator: as Timothy Webb observes in a path-breaking study, translation was 'a poetic exercise which helped to ignite his creative faculties'.[85] If the poet is a 'nightingale', as *A Defence of Poetry* claims, he or she remains a poet surrounded by unknown 'auditors' (680), moved by the poet even if 'they know not whence or why' (681). Shelley anticipates Charles Taylor when the modern theorist of identity asserts that 'One is a self only among other selves. A self can never be described without reference to those who surround it', and yet he shows, too, an acute awareness of the poet's mysterious individuality as he contributes towards and participates in that 'great poem' written across the ages, a 'poem' which his best and most sensitive poetic heirs continue to sustain and rewrite.[86]

Fundamental to Shelley's understanding of influence is the idea that it is a form of recreation, a reimagining. In *A Defence of Poetry* the fear that language will grow

---

[81] Bloom, *Anxiety*, 11.
[82] Harold Bloom, *The Anatomy of Influence: Literature as a Way of Life* (New Haven: Yale University Press, 2011), pp. ix–x.
[83] Bloom, *Anatomy*, 8.   [84] Bloom, *Anatomy*, 13.
[85] Timothy Webb, *The Violet in the Crucible: Shelley and Translation* (Oxford: Clarendon, 1976), 48.
[86] Charles Taylor, *Sources of the Self: The Making of Modern Identity* (Cambridge: Cambridge University Press, 1989), 35.

'disorganized' and the need for poets to 'create afresh' weave in and out of one another, and they do so throughout his work. Because of this fear and need, the quality of what in *A Defence of Poetry* Shelley calls 'apprehension' in relation to poets' capacity to discover 'the before unapprehended relations of things' (676) must, in Ross Wilson's words, 'be alive'.[87] Language's very frailty and inadequacy provides the tinder which ignites his prose into eloquent, counter-active flame. That sense of language's deficiencies helps to explain why his prose is that of a poet, concerned, like Plato, 'to kindle a harmony in thoughts' (*A Defence of Poetry*, 679), aware both that 'harmony' involves a necessary awareness of the possibility of discord and a commitment to the imagination: 'there is a principle within the human being [...] which acts otherwise than in the lyre, and produces not melody alone, but harmony' (*A Defence of Poetry*, 675). Harmony involves responsiveness and adjustment, a thinking through the language being used, with a full recognition of its constraints and possibilities, and a strong awareness that meaning is being wrought into glowing but provisional being in the act of 'communicating and receiving intense and impassioned conceptions respecting man and nature' (701), as Shelley has it in his account of what poetry is towards the end of *A Defence of Poetry*.

His attunement to the literary quality of thinking is a major reason why, as James Donelan has it in a review, 'Shelley has long defied attempts to create a systemic account of his thought in criticism'.[88] In sympathy with this resistance to systematizing, whose temptations continually beckon the reader of Shelley, only tantalizingly to be given the slip by his work, the present book seeks to study him closely as he engages in that metamorphic process of becoming Shelley by surrendering himself to the influxes of possibility held out by the work of his predecessors. In turn, Shelley turns into an endlessly suggestive resource for later writers.

3

Shelleyan Reimaginings and Influence: New Relations seeks to trace what Bloom describes as 'the hidden roads that go from poem to poem',[89] allowing dialogues and influence to be explored in a series of case studies. It does not try to provide a complete list of poets and thinkers with whom Shelley interacts or of those who interact with Shelley: the gaps are many and range from major authors, including Homer, Shakespeare, Goethe, the Brownings, Emily Brontë, and Arnold, to minor ones, such as Hunt, Peacock, and a legion of other writers.[90] Shelley's responsive

---

[87] Ross Wilson, 'Poetry as Reanimation in Shelley', in *The Meaning of 'Life' in Romantic Poetry and Poetics*, ed. Ross Wilson (New York: Routledge, 2009), 131. See also the same critic's *Shelley and the Apprehension of Life* (Cambridge: Cambridge University Press, 2013).

[88] James Donelan, review of Wayne Deakin, *Hegel and the English Romantic Poets*, *Review of English Studies* (2015), advance access, first published 1 October 2015.

[89] Harold Bloom, *The Anxiety of Influence: A Theory of Poetry* (New York: Oxford University Press, 1973), 96.

[90] For thoughts on Shelley and Shakespeare, see my essays 'Shakespearean Poetry and the Romantics' in *The Oxford Handbook of Shakespeare's Poetry*, ed. Jonathan Post (Oxford: Oxford

openness to other poets and the diversity of his allusions precludes any hope of completion, as does the variousness of his significance for his poetic descendants. Still, establishing as its Alpha and Omega Shelley's response to Plato and A. C. Bradley's reflections on Shelley, the book attempts to convey the wide-ranging nature of his interactions and contributions to cultural and literary traditions.

It has a tripartite structure. The first three chapters seek to illuminate his response to representative texts, figures, and themes that constitute the triple pillars of his cultural inheritance: the classical world (Plato); Renaissance poetry (Spenser and Milton); and Christianity—in particular, the concept of deity and the Bible. The second and major section of the book, from Chapters 4 to 12, explores Shelley's relations and affinities with, as well as differences from, his immediate predecessors and contemporaries: Hazlitt and Lamb; Wordsworth; Coleridge; Southey; Byron; Keats; and the great painter J. M. W. Turner, with whom he is often linked. The third section considers Shelley's reception by later nineteenth-century writers, figures influenced by and responding to Shelley: the poets chosen, as noted above, are Beddoes, Hemans, Landon, Tennyson, and Swinburne. A Coda discusses the body of critical work on Shelley produced by A. C. Bradley, a figure who stands at the threshold of twentieth-century thinking about Shelley.

Chapter 1, 'Emulating Plato: Shelley as Translator and Prose Poet', reveals Shelley's immersion in Plato; it explores Shelley's impressive translations from and adaptations of his classical predecessor, especially his translation of the *Symposium*. Shelley's eloquence does justice to Plato's vision of love, while his figurative mobility is equal to the challenge posed by Platonic dialogue. Chapter 2, 'Shelley, Spenser, and Milton', considers Shelley's responses to two major Renaissance precursors. Chapter 3, 'A Double Face of False and True: Poetry and Religion in Shelley', views Shelley as a far more nuanced religious thinker than is often implied by critics, and by Shelley's own designation of himself as 'atheist'.

Chapters 4 to 7 read Shelley in dialogue with the older Romantic generation, from Lamb and Hazlitt to Southey. Chapter 4, 'Shelley, Lamb, Hazlitt, and the Revolutionary Imagination', offers a consideration of Shelley in relation to two major essayists of the Romantic period, Lamb and Hazlitt, who despite their apparent antipathy towards Shelley, offer original, jaggedly authentic views of the younger poet that display productive complexities. Chapter 5, '"A Kind of an Excuse": Shelley and Wordsworth Revisited', explores the intricacies of what is among Shelley's profoundest poetic relationships. Chapter 6, '"The Gleam of Those Words": Coleridge and Shelley', considers the relationship between the

University Press, 2013). 563–81, and 'Anatomizing Casuistry: Shelley's *The Cenci* and the Fate of Analysis', in *Romantic Ambiguities: Abodes of the Modern*, ed. Sebastian Domsch, Christoph Reinfandt, and Katharina Rennhak (Wissenschaftlicher Verlag Trier, 2017), 169–80. For aspects of Robert Browning's, Matthew Arnold's, and Emily Brontë's response to Shelley, see the following essays by me: '"Infinite Passion": Variations on a Romantic Topic in Robert Browning, Emily Brontë, Swinburne, Hopkins, Wilde, and Dowson', *Romantics Echoes in the Victorian Era*, ed. Andrew Radford and Mark Sandy (Aldershot: Ashgate, 2008), 175–89; 'The Romantic Bequest: Arnold and Others', in *The Oxford Handbook of Victorian Poetry*, ed. Matthew Bevis (Oxford: Oxford University Press, 2013), 217–34; and ' "Visions Rise, and Change": Emily Brontë's Poetry and Male Romantic Poetry', *Brontë Studies* 36 (2011): 57–63.

poets, from Coleridge's fond though potentially patronizing wish that he could have mentored Shelley,[91] to Shelley's fascinated responsiveness to Coleridge's work. Chapter 7, 'Southey and Shelley Reconsidered', brings out Shelley's career-long engagement with his older peer. Though Shelley would grow highly critical of what he perceived to be Southey's political 'tergiversation' (*Letters: PBS*, 1. 208), his ear was haunted by and attuned to the sinuous and hypnotizing rhythms of some of Southey's most ambitious poetry, the still underrated worth of which is brought out by the way in which it is reused by Shelley.

The following four chapters focus on Shelley's responses to Byron and Keats. Chapter 8, ' "The Fixed and the Fluid": Shelley and Byron', looks at Byron's and Shelley's literary relationship. Both poets write poetry aware of its status as poetry, but there are vital differences too, not least between Byron's narrative drive and Shelley's lyricism. Chapter 9 carries on with a consideration of Byron's and Shelley's relationship in 'Narrative and Play: Byron's *Beppo* and Shelley's *The Witch of Atlas*', seeing the two poets as parading their creative freedom even as they draw attention to its limits. Chapter 10, ' "The End and Aim of Poesy": Shelley and Keats in Dialogue', traces and differentiates between the two poets' evolving understandings of the place and value of art. Chapter 11, 'Turning to Dante: Shelley's *Adonais* Reconsidered', builds on the discussion of *Adonais* in the preceding chapter by considering Shelley's elegy for Keats in the light of his dialogue with Dante. Chapter 12, ' "The Inmost Spirit of Light": Shelley and Turner', considers the relationship between the work of the poet and the work of the artist, less in the light of influence than of affinity: the chapter's principal focus is on ways in which Shelley and Turner reimagine, through their respective mediums, concerns that often overlap. At this point the book turns to consider Shelley's influence on a select group of later nineteenth-century poets. Chapter 13, 'Shelley, Beddoes, Death, and Reputation', argues that Beddoes's motifs of death and resurrection bear on a concern with poetic reputation that he discerned in a poet he admired greatly. Chapter 14, ' "Materials for Imagination": Shelleyan Traces in Felicia Hemans's Later Poetry', analyses Hemans's engagement with Shelley's work in her poetry from 1822. Chapter 15, ' "Beautiful but Ideal": Intertextual Relations between Letitia Elizabeth Landon and Shelley', draws out the fluid responsiveness of Landon's relationship with Shelley.

The chapters (16 and 17) on Tennyson and Swinburne, respectively, dwell on Shelley's restless, haunting presence in Tennyson and on the intricacy with which Swinburne adapts and inherits Shelley's poetic thought, enabling the later poet to go far beyond being 'A sort of pseudo-Shelley'.[92] 'Coda: A. C. Bradley's Views of Shelley' considers Shelley's reception at the hands of A. C. Bradley, a critic distinguished by his tough-minded though sympathetically mobile readings of Shelley's poetry. How this fine critic shaped his own dialogue with Shelley offers a suggestive

---

[91] See Samuel Taylor Coleridge, *Table Talk*, ed. Carl Woodring, 2 vols (London: Routledge; Princeton: Princeton University Press, 1990), vol. 14 of *The Collected Works of Samuel Taylor Coleridge*, I, 574.

[92] Matthew Arnold, quoted in *Swinburne: The Critical Heritage*, ed. Clyde K. Hyder (London: Routledge, 1970), 116.

model to the reader who wishes still, in ways this book seeks to foster, to generate 'new relations' with the work of a major Romantic poet.[93]

4

The idea of Shelley as a purposefully dialogic writer is central to this book, even as it allows for the accidental mysteries of influence. I sympathize with G. Kim Blank in his disagreement with Bloom's view that 'if any poet knows too well what causes his poem, then he cannot write it, or at least will write it badly',[94] that a poet can never fully understand the processes of influence, since Shelley is evidently eager to embrace understanding of influence's workings. But Bloom's point is well taken, and a key word in his formulation is 'too' in 'too well'. Crucially, Shelley plaits so many strands of potential connection or contrast with previous works that his poetry seems to outstrip any 'determination of the will' (*Major Works*, 696) about orderly allusive procedure.

One critical method of response is to amalgamate previous influences so that they become a composite unified figure, one name made up of many names, typifying a common tendency that Shelley seeks to correct.[95] Another, preferred by the current book, is to allow for the different perspectives opened up on and by Shelley's poetry through its response to different precursor poets. Thus, in the fourth section of 'Ode to the West Wind', allusions to Wordsworth's 'Ode: Intimations of Immortality' and to the Psalms jostle productively, if one takes the word 'allusion' to imply a deliberate acknowledgement of a previous work, which is meant to be recognized as such by the reader. In Ricks's words, 'allusion is posited upon our calling the earlier work into play, whereas the one thing that plagiarism hopes is that the earlier work will not enter our heads'.[96] In the case of the Ode Shelley recalls with apparently conscious intent the Wordsworth who praises childhood: the younger poet writes longingly 'If even / I were as in my boyhood' (27–8), where 'even' aches palpably at the end of the line, and the Psalmist soliciting his creator 'in prayer in my sore need' (52). Yet it is surprisingly hard with Shelley to hold all allusive possibilities in a single act of critical response and judgement, and not only hard, one might add, but potentially misleading. It is part of his

---

[93] The word 'Reimaginings' in the present book's title draws, as does the title of my first book, *The Human Mind's Imaginings: Conflict and Achievement in Shelley's Poetry* (Oxford: Clarendon Press, 1989), on Shelley's mention, towards the close of 'Mont Blanc', of 'the human mind's imaginings'; the word and the idea it embodies might even be said to allude to that book, sometimes in an amplifying spirit, sometimes in one that is corrective, but it reaffirms even as it seeks to extend and explore the earlier book's sense of the unstable, often haunted, yet vitally creative value, for Shelley and his readers, of 'imaginings', conceived of as products of the imagination that require us to think of imagination as a ceaseless activity.

[94] Blank, 17, quoting Harold Bloom, *Poetry and Repression* (New Haven: Yale University Press, 1976), 3.

[95] For a related critique of any notion on Shelley's part of 'a reversion to a single past', see Jerrold E. Hogle, *Shelley's Process: Radical Transference and the Development of His Major Works* (New York: Oxford University Press, 1988), 168.

[96] *Allusion to the Poets*, 231–2.

poetic giftedness to have been able not only to design poems that are responsive to a near-bewildering array of critical approaches, but also to encourage his readers to undertake what might be called 'successive' and provisional if intense readings.

Such readings are at the heart of this book's approach to questions of allusion, reimagining, and influence in Shelley. As I do, Earl Wasserman sees Shelley as engaging in an allusive practice which differs from that of other poets. But, unlike the present book's emphasis, Wasserman's magnificent and monumentalizing study regards influence as serving a unified, totalizing, intellectual end. Whereas poets frequently want the reader to identify precisely the status of an allusion, Shelley, on Wasserman's reading, views myth as possessing 'components' that are 'indestructible and eternal mental possessions'.[97] It is less myths' reworking of previous fictional incarnations than their existence as 'actually or potentially true-beautiful organizations of thought' that matter; 'they are', in Wasserman's formulation, 'universal and eternal forms that become limited only insofar as they are thought of as specific myths; and any particular previous appearance of the myth is not a locus for literary allusion but merely another instance of the actual or potential archetypal form'.[98] Despite its downgrading of 'literary allusion', at odds with my own concerns, there is here a paradoxical clue to Shelley's allusive practices. Shelley's interest as a poet lies in specific details of original texts and ways in which they might be reconfigured in his own poetry; but the broader, more ambitious hope of realigning previous works with some new poem, 'though unimagined, yet to be' (*Prometheus Unbound* III. iii. 56), containing within itself 'A voice to be accomplished' (III. iii. 67), is to the fore in his understanding of influence's workings. The hope aligns itself with what, in relation to Julia Kristeva, has been described as 'The intertextual sense of the multiplicity of origins and meanings in language'.[99] The Shelleyan poem is at once purposefully allusive and conscious that poetic meanings often and intertextually exceed authorial intention.

Shelley is among the major Romantic poetic theorists of influence, partly because of his passionate commitment to the onward dissemination of ideas and feelings, and to the unpredictable ways in which poets position themselves and are culturally positioned between past and future, between being, as the thought-expanding close of *A Defence of Poetry* has it, 'the hierophants of an unapprehended inspiration' and 'the mirrors of the gigantic shadows which futurity casts upon the present' (701). Shelley's appositional syntax brings together two things: first, the role of poets in reviving what has gone before in the process of communicating an 'inspiration' that has hitherto been 'unapprehended', and may still not fully be apprehended by the communicator; and second, the role of poets in serving as 'mirrors' of what is to come.

---

[97] Earl R. Wasserman, *Shelley: A Critical Reading* (Baltimore: Johns Hopkins University Press, 1971), 272.
[98] Wasserman, 273.
[99] *The Norton Anthology of Theory and Criticism*, ed. Vincent B. Leitch (New York, Norton, 2018), 1939.

Shelley himself, as Blank has brought out, did not always feel buoyant about the possible alchemy wrought by the transformative imagination. Blank quotes from a prose passage in which Shelley writes:

> We do not attend sufficiently to what passes within ourselves. We combine words, combined a thousand times before. In our mind we assume entire opinions; and in the expression of those opinions, entire phrases, when we would philosophise. Our whole style of expression and sentiment is infected with the tritest plagiarisms. Our words are dead, our thoughts cold and borrowed.[100]

Shelley's answer is implicit in his diagnosis; it is the ability to recognize the treacheries which will be performed by words that are 'dead' and thoughts that are 'cold and borrowed' that inspires his countervailing poetic techniques, of which allusive self-awareness is one: techniques that seek to mark 'the before unapprehended relations of things', as *A Defence of Poetry* has it (676).

Earlier in his career, and as Blank notes in relation to the tricky question of 'contending with contemporaries, the Zeitgeist',[101] Shelley declares in his Preface to *Prometheus Unbound* that 'one great poet is a masterpiece of nature which another not only ought to study but must study' (231). One needs to recall that, in writing these words, Shelley is responding to a stinging attack in the April 1819 number of the *Quarterly Review*, composed by John Taylor Coleridge, in which Shelley was accused, in *The Revolt of Islam*, of plagiarizing Wordsworth. The reviewer states:

> Mr. Shelley indeed is an unsparing imitator; and he draws largely on the rich stores of another mountain poet [Southey has just been named], to whose religious mind, it must be matter, we think, of perpetual sorrow to see the philosophy which comes pure and holy from his pen, degraded and perverted, as it continually is, by this miserable crew of atheists or pantheists, who have just sense enough to abuse its terms, but neither heart nor principle to comprehend its import, or follow its application.[102]

In responding to the *Quarterly Reviewer's* gibes, Shelley, in the Preface to *Prometheus Unbound*, argues that a poet cannot avoid the influence of 'such writers as those who stand in the foremost ranks of our own' (230), and that 'A poet is the combined product of such internal powers as modify the nature of others, and of such external influences as excite and sustain these powers; he is not one, but both' (231). The recognition of 'anxious confinement', in Blank's words, may indeed be the 'necessary condition of poetic emancipation'.[103]

Blank's concept of 'poetic emancipation' accepts the initial fact of 'confinement' within a Shelleyan form, whether that confinement consists of generic or linguistic or cultural limitations, even as the subsequent work of the Shelleyan poem will be exhilaratingly to subvert, redefine and release 'new relations', as it conducts itself 'like a storm, bursting its cloudy prison / With thunder, and with whirlwind', energies

---

[100] Quoted from G. Kim Blank, *Wordsworth's Influence on Shelley: A Study of Poetic Authority* (Basingstoke: Macmillan, 1998), 18.

[101] Blank, 13.

[102] See Theodore Redpath, *The Young Romantics and Critical Opinion, 1807–1824* (London: Harrap, 1973), 337–47 (338–9).

[103] Blank, 17.

that emerge from 'the lampless caves of unimagined being' (*Prometheus Unbound*, IV. 376–7, 378). Yet 'confinement' can be enabling, if taken to refer to the work performed by poetic form; without the brilliantly handled six-line stanza form, rhyming *aabccb*, with iambic pentameters in all lines except for the alexandrines in lines 3 and 6, the Earth's vision of release and freedom would lack its full expressiveness. The stanza just quoted enjambs itself on a rhyme-word 'fleeing' that unsettles productively the idea of 'being' with which it rhymes.

By the time the *Quarterly Review* article appeared, William Hazlitt had published in *A Round Table* (1817) an essay on the topic 'Why the Arts are not Progressive?— A Fragment', in which he argues, in terms which are, in Bate's words, 'all the more persuasive because of his robust liberalism',[104] that 'Nothing is more contrary to the fact than the supposition that in what we understand by the *fine arts*, as painting and poetry, relative perfection is only the result of repeated efforts, and that what has been once well done constantly leads to something better'.[105] Liberal political views do not, in this instance, translate into an optimistic view of contemporary achievement. Yet among Shelley's most attractive gifts, as noted above, is his ability to detect and celebrate such achievement, an ability tied to the way in which, in David Duff's words, he 'asserts the collective and collaborative nature of poetry'.[106] But such an assertion depends—a central emphasis of the current study—on his own ways of shaping new poetic forms.

---

[104] Bate, *The Burden of the Past*, 108.
[105] William Hazlitt, *The Fight and Other Writings*, ed. Tom Paulin and David Chandler, introd. Tom Paulin (London: Penguin, 2000), 202.
[106] David Duff, *Romanticism and the Uses of Genre* (Oxford: Oxford University Press, 2009), 195–6.

1

Emulating Plato

Shelley as Translator and Prose Poet

This chapter explores how Shelley became Shelley through his immersion in Plato, a writer who influenced not only his thinking but also his style, and not only his poetic style, but his development of an original poetic prose. Although there have been many attempts to describe Shelley's distinctive poetic style, comparatively little energy has been spent on the effort to capture the impact of his prose. True, Jerrold Hogle opens his brilliant study of 'Shelley's process' by referring to and illustrating the poet's 'shifting, evanescent style, whether he is writing in verse or in prose'.[1] The passage he proceeds to discuss is the celebration in *A Defence of Poetry* of Dante, whose every word is said to be 'a burning atom of inextinguishable thought', a celebration which leads Shelley to assert that 'All high poetry' is 'infinite', 'the first acorn which contained all oaks potentially', and that a 'great Poem' is 'a fountain forever overflowing with the waters of wisdom and delight'.[2] In the passage's movement from image to image, Hogle finds what he calls 'a palimpsest of several figural levels and a deferral of figures towards later transformations of them'.[3] Helpfully he reads one sentence (that beginning 'Veil after veil' (*Major Works*, 693)) as 'an apt description of its paragraph's syntax', and he is alert to rhythm and sound: features close to the heart of good prose and the subject, among other things, of Tom Paulin's eye-opening study of Hazlitt.[4] Although Hogle asks pertinent questions about the passage's revelation and enactment of what seems to be 'radical discontinuity', I wish, without disagreeing with his analysis, to give greater stress than he does to the force and assurance of the writing.[5] The weighting of the phrases in the passage from *A Defence of Poetry* which Hogle cites makes us linger over each image, even as we are propelled forward to cross the gaps between images: 'His [Dante's] very words are instinct with spirit; each is as a spark, a burning atom of inextinguishable thought' (*Major Works*, 693). The idea unfolds sequentially there: the language conveys a sense of development involving both

---

[1] Jerrold E. Hogle, *Shelley's Process: Radical Transference and the Development of His Major Works* (New York: Oxford University Press, 1988), 3. For passages of sensitive commentary on Shelley's prose, see also William Keach, *Shelley's Style* (New York: Methuen, 1984).

[2] *The Major Works*, 693. Unless stated otherwise, this edition is used for quotations from Shelley's prose and poetry in this chapter.

[3] Hogle, *Shelley's Process*, 3.

[4] Hogle, *Shelley's Process*, 4. See Tom Paulin, *The Day-Star of Liberty: William Hazlitt's Radical Style* (London: Faber and Faber, 1998).

[5] Hogle, *Shelley's Process*, 4.

qualification and apposition, while the syntax ensures that a steady focus is brought to bear on each phrase and each argumentative phase.

For all its forward propulsion, the passage is typical of Shelley's prose in that each detail counts, rather as is the case in the Greek of the *Iliad*, where phenomena and events are sustained by the shifting, stream-like medium. It is a style which has something in common with Coleridge's description of the way a reader should be affected by 'a just poem':

> The reader should be carried forward, not merely or chiefly by the mechanical impulse of curiosity, or by a restless desire to arrive at the final solution; but by the pleasureable [*sic*] activity of mind excited by the attractions of the journey itself. Like the motion of a serpent, which the Egyptians made the emblem of intellectual power; or like the path of sound through the air; at every step he pauses and half recedes, and from the retrogressive movement collects the force which again carries him onward.[6]

Coleridge's 'pleasureable activity of mind' describes a less driving and intense experience than that represented and induced by Shelley's prose; the older poet's prose rocks backwards and forwards more sedately than is the case in *A Defence of Poetry*. But Coleridge's commitment to a use of words that allows, however implicitly, for pauses, half-recedings, and resumed onward momentum fits admirably Shelley's mode in *A Defence of Poetry*. For evidence of 'resumed onward momentum', one might look at the impact of Shelley's assertion that Dante's 'very words are instinct with spirit'. There, the phrase 'very words' galvanizes the allusion to the description in Book VI of *Paradise Lost* of the 'chariot of paternal deity, / Flashing thick flames, wheel within wheel undrawn, / It self instinct with spirit' (ll. 750–2).[7] For Milton's chariot of paternal deity (which is also alluded to in and acts as an influence on Panthea's vision in *Prometheus Unbound* IV, 236–61), Shelley gives us the exemplary poem, *The Divine Comedy*, driven onwards by its own god-like 'spirit'. His rhythm, one of assertion and revelation, brings out the life in Dante's language. Shelley begins with declarative statements full of short words, after which the polysyllabic 'inextinguishable' has an air of defiant affirmation, recalling the reawakening of 'Ashes and sparks' from 'the unextinguished hearth' at the close of *Ode to the West Wind* (ll. 67, 66), or, indeed, the 'inextinguishably beautiful' moon to which in *Epipsychidion* Emily is compared (in line 82). Nothing, Shelley at once asserts and hopes, can extinguish the spark of great poetry.

If *A Defence of Poetry* illustrates Shelley's prose at its most intellectually radiant and figuratively intricate, his rendering of Plato's *Symposium* in July 1818 shows it capable of changes of mood and conceptual acuteness. The *Symposium* gives evidence not only of Plato's 'surpassing graces of… composition' (as Shelley put it in a fragmentary Preface) but also of his dialogue's heterodox challenge to contemporary assumptions about love.[8] Primarily this challenge takes the form of

---

[6] Coleridge, *Biographia Literaria*, ed. James Engell and W. Jackson Bate. 2 vols (Princeton: Princeton University Press, 1983), vol. 2, Ch. 14, 13–14.

[7] Milton is quoted from *The Poems of John Milton*, ed. John Carey and Alastair Fowler (London: Longman, 1968).

[8] Quoted from the draft in *BSM* V, 124–5 (facsimile of Bodleian MS Shelley adds e. 6).

estimating homosexual love more highly than heterosexual love. Plato's conception of love also challenges the reader in suggestive ways. Even as the *Symposium* thrives on dualisms, it dismantles them. Flesh merges into spirit in a fashion at odds with many versions of Christian thinking. The tricky word 'love' is variously redefined in Plato's dialogue. In Diotima's reported speech to Socrates, it refers to a drive in humans that leads to the summit of intellectual understanding: knowledge of the nature of Beauty, which is an eternal Form virtually interchangeable with Truth and Good. In an essay written to accompany his translation, entitled 'A Discourse on the Manners of the Antient Greeks Relative to the Subject of Love', Shelley shapes his own ethos—and poetics—of love out of his response to Plato: he argues that the 'gratification of the senses'

> soon becomes a very small part of that profound & complicated sentiment which we call Love, which is rather the universal thirst for a communion not merely of the senses, but of our whole nature; intellectual, imaginative & sensitive & which, when individualised, becomes an imperious necessity only to be satisfied by the complete or partial, actual or supposed fulfilment of its claims.[9]

For Shelley, love is experienced as a 'universal thirst' (a phrase in which abstract and concrete terms fuse expressively). The pressure in Shelley's syntax is always towards a fusion or redefinition that will not allow words to sit back into comfortable semantic armchairs. The *Symposium*, too, dismantles oppositions between the sensuous and the spiritual in the act of creating them. In Shelley's version, the wording of Diotima's vision shapes, at its climax, a smooth glissade between the sensuous and the spiritual. Here is the prelude to that climax in Shelley's rendering: 'In addition he would consider the beauty which is in souls more excellent than that which is in form': 'more excellent'—the comparative allows the excellence of 'form' still to be acknowledged, and when the rhetorical wave of this paragraph reaches its topmost peak, Shelley restores a sense of the value of 'form' or 'forms':

> [...] contemplating thus the universal beauty, no longer like some servant in love with his fellow would he unworthily and meanly enslave himself to the attractions of one form, nor one subject of discipline or science, but would turn towards the wide ocean of intellectual beauty, and from the sight of the lovely and majestic forms which it contains, would abundantly bring forth his conceptions in philosophy: until strengthened and confirmed he should at length steadily contemplate one science, which is the science of this universal beauty.[10]

---

[9] 'A Discourse [...]' was drafted in Bodleian MS Shelley adds. e. 11 and Bodleian MS Shelley adds. e. 6. The title given in the text is Shelley's: see Jones, *BSM XV*, 19 (facsimile of Bodleian MS Shelley adds: e. 11). The quotation is taken from *BSM XV*, 36–9, with some minimal tidying-up.

[10] O'Neill, *BSM XX*, 402–5. Shelley's translation of the *Symposium* is quoted from *BSM XX* (facsimile of Bodleian MS Shelley adds. d. 8—the relevant manuscript in the case of the *Symposium*— and of Bodleian MS Shelley e. 6). Quotations in this chapter correct false starts and errors, restore censored cancellations made when the translation was prepared for its first publication by Mary Shelley in 1840 [1839], and introduce occasional punctuation. For discussion of Shelley's attempt 'to find language of his own that could communicate at least the echoes of Plato's persuasive music', see *The Symposium of Plato: The Shelley Translation*, ed. and intro., David K. O'Connor (South Bend: St Augustine's Press, 2002), p. xliii.

This sinuous eloquence illustrates Shelley's ability to find a language that rises to the challenge of, and serves as an aesthetic equivalent for, Platonic vision. Plotting its passage from subordinate to main clause and thence to the further expansion ushered in by 'until', the sentence-shape mimics the development and unfolding of the idea: an idea that allows, in Shelley's wording, 'forms' to return as 'lovely and majestic' when associated with the 'wide ocean of intellectual beauty', which, in a disciplined and affecting moment, the attention of the prose 'turns towards'. 'Forms' is Shelley's preferred single equivalent for what in Plato are different words (including 'bodies') for the object of the lover's attention; in its capacity to suggest both the physical and the spiritual, 'forms' shows an unsupine responsiveness to the Greek.[11] Again, 'intellectual' is not present in the Greek, nor in the Latin gloss of Ficino at the foot of Shelley's Bipont edition of the *Symposium*, and it was often used by him when he was gravelled by the Greek.[12] The adjective's insertion suggests that Shelley found in Plato a subject-rhyme with his own intuitions in his earlier *Hymn to Intellectual Beauty*, where such beauty, though supra-sensuous, is tangled up with the sensuous through the writing's figurative mobility.

Shelley's language, in his translation of Plato's *Symposium*, shows a reluctance simply to jettison the sensuous in favour of the idea. Some contemporary critics of Plato attribute the same reluctance to Plato himself. Christopher Gill writes that 'what the passage describes [that is, the whole account of Diotima] is not the replacement of interpersonal love by philosophy, but the deepening of interpersonal love by the lover's growing understanding of the true nature of beauty'.[13] Shelley is at his most responsive to Plato's Greek in the way that he captures this 'growing understanding' through the balance which his long sentences sustain: the way, for instance, the passage begins, for instance, with 'contemplating' and circles round to a repetition that marks an advancement in 'steadily contemplate one science'. The prose, pivoting on its verbs, seems itself to 'steadily contemplate'. A brief contrast with Benjamin Jowett's version of the same passage shows how the eminent Victorian thinks of the climactic insight as equivalent to a quasi-religious leading from above rather than a poetic intuition, earned and enacted, as Shelley's is, through steadily contemplative rhythms:

> [...] beholding the wide region already occupied by beauty, he may cease to be like a servant in love with one beauty only, that of a particular youth or man or institution, himself a slave mean and narrow-minded; but drawing towards and contemplating the vast sea of beauty, he will create many fair and noble thoughts and discourses in

---

[11] For Shelley's use of 'forms' where Plato has (the Greek for) 'bodies', see James A. Notopoulos, *The Platonism of Shelley: A Study of Platonism and the Poetic Mind* (Durham: Duke University Press, 1949), 583 and the notes on that page referring to 448, line 28, and 449, line 38, of Notopoulos's book.

[12] For Shelley's use of the Bipont edition of Plato's *Symposium*, with Ficino's Latin translation, see Notopoulos, *The Platonism of Shelley*, 41–2 and 398–9. For his insertion of the word 'intellectual', see Notopoulos, *The Platonism of Shelley*, 583. Shelley's 'Errors in Translation, Variants from the Greek, and Interpolations' in his translations of the *Symposium* and the *Ion* are gathered in Notopoulos, *The Platonism of Shelley*, 572–93.

[13] Plato, *The Symposium*, trans. with intro. and notes, Christopher Gill (London: Penguin, 1999), p. xxxi.

boundless love of wisdom, until on that shore he grows and waxes strong, and at last the vision is revealed to him of a single science, which is the science of beauty everywhere.[14]

In Shelley, the initiate 'steadily contemplates'; in Jowett 'the vision is revealed'. For Shelley, the interplay between the visionary standing on the edge of the wide ocean of intellectual beauty and the forms of beauty is fluid and ongoing in a way that it is not in Jowett, for whom the relationship between seeing and vision is more abrupt and unexplained. The result is a work that is quintessentially typical of Shelley and closer in spirit to Plato than virtually any other translation.

When Shelley moves on to translate the next section of Diotima's speech, in which she describes the supreme beauty that is 'wonderful in its nature', he again contrives in prose a rhythm suited to imaginative and intellectual encounter. By this stage, the translation has been through many twists and turns of mood and perspective. Now it evens out, having managed its ascent with great panache, breathing calmly and easily as it nears the summit. Shelley manages an effect of prolongation as he describes, in majestically sustained and balanced opposites, what this supreme beauty is not:

> it is not, like other things, partly beautiful and partly deformed; not at one time beautiful and at another time not; not beautiful in relation to one thing and deformed in relation to another; not here beautiful and there deformed; not beautiful in the estimation of one person and deformed in that of another; nor can this supreme beauty be figured to the imagination like a beautiful face or beautiful hands or any portion of the body, nor like any discourse or any science. Nor does it subsist in any other thing that lives or is, either in earth or in heaven or in any other place: but it is eternally uniform and consistent and monoeidic with itself.[15]

Shelley takes advantage of the power that lies in negation, as often in his poetry and prose. (Another example is the account in *A Defence of Poetry* of poetry as 'the source of an unforeseen and an unconceived delight' (*Major Works*, 693).) Here, negation works to negate the world of necessary imperfection. The phrases spin themselves out, spiralling towards the affirmation that 'it is eternally uniform and consistent and monoeidic with itself', 'monoeidic' being a Greek-derived term Shelley uses to convey the supreme beauty's self-consistency. The 'ands' in this last sentence and in the whole passage do not imply one thing after another, as is often the fate of 'and' to do; rather, they enact a turning of one term into its neighbour, until the writing evokes a succession of triumphantly reinforcing adjectives as Shelley discovers his own words for Plato's 'power of producing beauty in art', to borrow a phrase from a letter of August 1821 (*Letters: PBS*, 2. 322). Shelley would read Johann Joachim Winckelmann a few months after he translated the *Symposium*. Here his prose recreates the neo-classical theorist's emphasis on calm and repose. At such a moment Shelley's prose is Romantic in its belated recreation of a Platonic

---

[14] *The Dialogues of Plato: Translated into English with Analyses and Introductions* by B. Jowett, 4 vols, 4th edn (Oxford: Clarendon, 1953), vol. 1, 542. For the suggestion that Jowett's and Shelley's translations might usefully be contrasted, see *Shelley on Love*, ed. Richard Holmes (London: Anvil, 1980), 99–100.
[15] *BSM* XX: 404–5.

absolute, so that there is, just below the surface of the prose, a note of longing, but it is also Classical (or neo-classical) in its admiration for balance and poise. The passage (in Shelley's handling) enacts one of Winckelmann's dicta in his *History of Ancient Art* (1764): 'All beauty is heightened by unity and simplicity'.[16]

In a subsequent passage Shelley dwells on moving 'towards that which is beauty itself', a process which involves 'proceeding as on steps from the love of one form to that of two, and from that of two to that of all forms which are beautiful'.[17] Imagining the lover ascending the ladder of beauty 'as on steps', Shelley does justice to an element of beautiful fiction-making, one that anticipates his praise in *A Defence of Poetry* for the way, in the *Paradiso*, 'as by steps he [Dante] feigns himself to have ascended to the throne of the Supreme Cause' (*Major Works*, 691). There is a living link between those moments in Shelley and the more sceptical but still optimistic glimpse of meaning in Stevens's lines from *Notes Toward a Supreme Fiction*:

> Perhaps there are moments of awakening,
> Extreme fortuitous, personal, in which
> We more than awaken, sit on the edge of sleep,
> As on an elevation, and behold
> The academies like structures in a mist.[18]

The account, there, of 'moments of awakening' as those 'in which / We more than awaken' recalls Shelley's pressure of re-definition in his repeated use of the same word in a poem or passage of prose: a use which implies his self-awareness as maker of meaning. In the *Symposium* translation, 'as on steps' shows Shelley's fictionalizing self-awareness. There in the original Greek, it is brought out in the translation by a phrasing that shows accelerated confidence once the 'as if' is conceded. By contrast, Jowett has the relatively plodding, 'using these as steps only'.[19] The effect of Jowett's wording is of a narrowly defined logical ascent, lacking Shelley's deft consciousness of himself as engaged in aesthetic discovery and play.

If the *Symposium* offers Shelley an aesthetic vision, it also opens up an ethical one: one in which all things take their meaning from, and are measured by, the principle of beauty about which Diotima tells Socrates. This ethical vision explains, is tested by, and informs the final section of the work: Alcibiades's comic but moving account of his attempt and failure to seduce Socrates. Coming straight after Diotima's question-cum-exclamation, 'What must be the life of him who dwells with and gazes on that which it becomes us all to seek!', a life which ensures that one 'is in contact not with a shadow but with reality', this section occurs as an iridescent surprise. Diotima gives way to Alcibiades, the witty, self-mocking, glittering youth, who to the non-Platonist may seem to live among the realities of soldiery,

---

[16] *Winckelmann: Writings on Art*, selected and ed. David Irwin. London: Phaidon, 1972, p. 118. For Shelley's reading of Winckelmann, see *MWS Journals*, 246–7, 253, 267.

[17] *BSM* XX: 406–7.

[18] 'It Must Be Abstract', VII. Quoted from *The Collected Poems of Wallace Stevens* (London: Faber and Faber, 1955).

[19] Jowett, *Dialogues of Plato I*, 543.

drunkenness, partying, sexuality, Athenian politics, and 'those Silenuses that sit in the sculptors' shops' to which he compares Socrates.[20] However, it is Alcibiades who suggests that Socrates has access to a reality denied to him, and who sees behind Socratic 'irony' to the 'divine images which are within when he has been opened and is serious'.[21] In Shelley's version, Alcibiades presents Socrates as an implicit anticipated cognition of Wordsworth:

> [. . .] if any one will listen to the talk of Socrates, it will appear to him at first extremely ridiculous: the phrases and expressions which he employs fold around his exterior the skin as it were of a rude and wanton Satyr. He is always talking about great market asses and brass-founders, and leather-cutters, and skin-dressers; and this is his perpetual custom, so that any dull and unobservant person might easily laugh at his discourse. But if any one should see it opened, as it were, and get within the sense of his words, he would then find that they alone of all that enters into the mind of man to utter had a profound and persuasive meaning [. . .][22]

The Wordsworth who courts mockery but deals in fresh and disconcerting insights in poems such as 'The Idiot Boy' is a remote but real relation of this apparently self-mocking 'Satyr'. In *Peter Bell the Third* (written over a year after the translation of the *Symposium*), Shelley may see Peter as 'rude' (in the sense of 'coarse')—though not 'wanton' (in the possible senses of 'playful', 'irresponsible', or 'licentious'). His feelings about Wordsworth were more mixed than his feelings about Plato and Socrates, but in *Peter Bell the Third* one finds interest in Peter's capacity for meditative reflexivity and subsequent understanding: Shelley praises how, in Peter's (Wordsworth's) thinking, 'An apprehension clear, intense, / Of his mind's work, had made alive / The things it wrought on' (ll. 309–11). No poet engaged Shelley more deeply than Wordsworth did, even if, for Shelley, the latter's enclosed mode of self-consciousness differs from the imperturbable, near-Olympian alertness discernible in Plato's portrait of Socrates. Shelley's wording at this stage of the translation is alive to a blend of tones that makes it unsurprising when, in the closing paragraph, Socrates is found 'forcing' those still awake 'to confess [. . .] that the foundations of the tragic and comic arts were essentially the same'.[23]

In her introduction to her 1840 edition of Shelley's prose, Mary Shelley praises her husband's translation with eloquent perceptiveness:

> Shelley commands language splendid and melodious as Plato, and renders faithfully the elegance and the gaiety which make the *Symposium* as amusing as it is sublime. The whole mechanism of the drama, for such in some sort it is,—the enthusiasm of Apollodorus, the sententiousness of Eryximachus, the wit of Aristophanes, the rapt and golden eloquence of Agathon, the subtle dialectics and grandeur of aim of Socrates, the drunken outbreak of Alcibiades,—are given with grace and animation. The picture presented reminds us of that talent which, in a less degree, we may suppose

---

20   *BSM* XX: 408–9, 418–19.   21   *BSM* XX: 426–7.
22   *BSM* XX: 442–5.   23   *BSM* XX: 450–1.

to have dignified the orgies of the last generation of free-spirited wits,—Burke, Fox, Sheridan, and Curran.[24]

Mary Shelley reminds us of the work's conviviality (her manuscript transcription follows tradition and entitles the translation, *The Banquet*). Furthermore, she locates the translation's idiom and tone of debate in the oratory and speech of four very different writers of the revolutionary generation. The four writers share an avoidance of what Hazlitt calls in his 'Character of Mr Burke' the 'artificial' style, a style 'all in one key'. In such a style, according to Hazlitt, 'The words are not fitted to the things, but the things to the words. Every thing is seen through a false medium'. Hazlitt goes on to claim for his contemporaries (by contrast with classical writers such as Cicero) 'genius' or 'high and enthusiastic fancy'.[25] In his individual way Shelley shows himself to be a writer of 'genius' in the prose of his translation of the *Symposium*, able to move between idioms and registers, and to trace the curve of talk and thought. Indeed, he relishes Alcibiades's praise for Socrates's speech compared with that of Pericles: 'For when we hear Pericles or any other accomplished orator deliver a discourse, no one, as it were, cares any thing about it. But when any one hears you, or even your words, related by another, though ever so rude and unskilful a speaker, be that person a woman, man or child, we are struck and retained, as it were, by the discourse clinging to our mind.'[26] The two instances of 'as it were' catch the speaker's baffled admiration, while the seemingly casual uses of 'any' suddenly turn to Socrates's advantage at the start of the second sentence. The extract also brings out the dialogue's and Shelley's fascination with reported speech, with the effect of words being transmitted from speaker to listener to a third person. The writing is superbly equal to the challenge presented by Plato's dialogue of presence and absence, of glowing immediacy and dim, recessive mystery.[27] Mary Shelley's praise, quoted above, gives the lie to the notion that Shelley lacks a sense of humour. He does emphatic justice in the translation to Aristophanes's sardonic if intermittently tragic-comic explanation of the origins of love and desire: that in the beginning human beings existed in three forms (male, female, and androgynous), and that in each form they were round, 'the back and the sides being circularly joined... [with] two faces fixed upon a round neck, exactly like each other; one head between the two faces; four ears, and two organs of generation'.

Aristophanes goes on to explain that the gods feared the power of this creature, able when he 'wished to go fast' to make 'use of all his eight limbs'.[28] Zeus decided, literally, to cut him down to size, slicing each form into two halves 'as people cut eggs before they salt them', leaving each half perpetually longing to be reunited

[24] Percy Bysshe Shelley, *Essays, Letters from Abroad, Translations and Fragments*, ed. Mary Shelley. 2 vols (London: Moxon, 1840), I, pp. ix–x.
[25] William Hazlitt, *The Selected Writings of William Hazlitt*, ed. Duncan Wu (London: Pickering & Chatto, 1998), IV, 287, 289.
[26] *BSM* XX: 420–1.
[27] See *The Symposium of Plato* for pertinent discussion of Shelley's use of the word 'obscure' in his translation, esp. pp. xxxiv–xxv.
[28] *BSM* XX, 324–5.

with 'the other half of himself'. Shelley's prose captures the pungently physical quality of Aristophanes's flight of fancy, as in this version of Apollo's part in the operation: 'Apollo turned the face round, and drawing the skin upon what we now call the belly, like a contracted pouch and leaving one opening, that which is called the navel, tied it in the middle.' Short words, strong verbs, and a vigorous yet flowing syntax (shown in the chiastic arrangement of main verbs and participles) do justice to fantastical imaginings, which are paradoxically grounded in detail, as when Aristophanes asserts two sentences later: 'He left only a few wrinkles in the belly near the navel to serve as a record of its former adventure'.[29]

The body bears the trace of 'its former adventure': Shelley's translation is alert to the detail and to the larger picture of Plato's astonishing 'adventure' of thought and imagination, and this moment resonates in the context of the work as a whole. It is characteristic of Shelley to move through stages in a poem or piece of prose, to broaden or complicate perspectives, to reuse images with a new or deeper or more complex sense of their significance. As in sequences by Rimbaud or T. S. Eliot, or in symphonies by Mozart or Beethoven, Shelley's poems possess remarkable intra-textual memories. In his translation of the *Symposium*, he found a work whose internal relations have a subtlety and density of implication to which he is attuned: an attunement so finely balanced that it can accommodate potential discord, while hinting at a sub-textual role for his problematic literary mentor, Wordsworth. Aristophanes's parable touches on the sadness which surrounds love, as he half-jestingly imagines how 'these divided people threw their arms around and embraced each other, seeking to grow together, and from this resolution to do nothing with-out the other half they died of hunger and weakness'.[30] The mood is serio-comic, but the writing brings into the work the idea of love as bound up with seeking and longing, an idea to which Socrates will turn in due course. One keeps hearing, as the *Symposium* develops, a verbal 'record of its former adventure'.

Mary Shelley is correct to praise Shelley's dramatic grasp, his ability to do justice to 'The whole mechanism of the drama'. 'Mechanism' has a quasi-technical signifi-cance in literary criticism of the time; it means something like the 'adaptation of the parts' to the demands of a work's structure, or, to modify a further *OED* definition, 'the mode of operation of [the work's] process'. So, Shelley writes to Peacock of *Prometheus Unbound* with yet another echo of Milton, 'It is a drama, with characters & mechanism of a kind yet unattempted' (*Letters: PBS*, 2. 94).[31] 'Things unattempted yet in prose or rhyme' (*Paradise Lost* I, 16): the Miltonic original reminds us that prose has its own claims to deal with the 'unattempted'.[32] In his translation, Shelley values the 'mechanism' of Plato's dialogue, its interplay of different voices and perspectives, the journeying towards understanding:

[29] *BSM* XX, 328–9.   [30] *BSM* XX, 328–9.

[31] In the draft 'Preface' to the *Symposium*, Shelley calls the work a 'drama', 'for <so>', he writes, 'the lively distinction of the characters & the various & well wrought circumstances of the story almost entitl<e> it to be called', *BSM* V: 132–3.

[32] Shelley may also have in mind, as Alan Weinberg has suggested to me, Ariosto's
'Cosa non detta in prosa mai, né in rima', *Orlando Furioso*, I, ii, ii, the source of Milton's line, as noted in and quoted from *The Poems of John Milton*, 461n.

understanding which would not occur were it not for the qualifications and courteous disagreements that happen en route. Moreover, the *Symposium* translation plays a central part in the 'drama' of Shelley's career. It is as Shelley's imagination learns to dramatize and allow for opposing, shifting, or altering views that he becomes a great poet in Italy. A major poem begun a few months after the translation is *Julian and Maddalo*, which thrives on debate and conflicting perspectives, partakes, in places, of the Platonic dialogue's tone of urbane, civilized debate: it is subtitled 'A Conversation'.[33] The translation itself is alert to Jowett's point that, though the speeches 'are all designed to prepare the way for Socrates, who gathers up the threads anew, and skims the highest points of each of them', they 'are not to be regarded as the stages of an idea, rising above one another to a climax'.[34]

Each speech is alive with suggestions, and Shelley's responsiveness to all the interlocutors reveals his fascination with cultural relativism. If he idealized classical Greek culture, his egalitarian sympathies were troubled by the slavery to be found in it as well as by the inferior position of women. Part of the purpose of translating the *Symposium* was more fully to understand the relative nature of all cultures, although, typically, he uses acknowledgement of imperfection as a spur towards something better: 'When we discover how far', he writes in 'A Discourse', 'the most admirable community ever formed was removed from that perfection to which human society is impelled by some active power within each bosom, to aspire, how great ought to be our hopes, how resolute our struggles'.[35] When Phaedrus, in his attempt to prove how love inspires selfless devotion, searches for an example, he alights, to Shelley's palpable approval, on Alcestis: 'Not only men but even women who love, are those alone who willingly expose themselves to die for others. Alcestis, the daughter of Pelias, affords to the Greeks a remarkable example of this opinion; she alone being willing to die for her husband'.[36] The aloneness of her selfless love finds expression in Shelley's floated participial phrasing, which achieves a more poignant expressiveness than Jowett's sturdily rational, even Roman formulation: 'she was willing to lay down her life on behalf of her husband'.[37]

Throughout his translation of the *Symposium*, Shelley responds to Plato's drama-tizing imagination. At the heart of the work is the idea of eros as a desire for the beautiful and good, a desire which takes us out of ourselves, and in this sense the translation contains the germ of *A Defence of Poetry*, which sees off Plato's own objections to poetry by invoking the Platonic or *Symposium*-derived notion of 'Love; or a going out of our own nature, and an identification of ourselves with the beautiful which exists in thought, action or person, not our own' (*Major Works*, 682).[38] Such a process of 'going out' and 'identification' allows for negotiation between Pauline agape and Platonic eros, Shelleyan 'Love' seeking to work as a

---

[33] Ralph Pite argues that an influence on *Julian and Maddalo* may have been Peacock's novels 'which proceed via pseudo-intellectual conversation', in *Longman* 2, 659.
[34] Jowett, *Dialogues of Plato I*, 489.
[35] *BSM* XV, 30–3 (the comma after 'bosom' is Shelley's).   [36] *BSM* XX, 286–7.
[37] Jowett, *Dialogues of Plato I*, 511.
[38] See Notopoulos, *Platonism of Shelley*, 347: 'Poetry has for Shelley the same function as Eros in the *Symposium*'.

daimonic messenger between these cultural opposites; it also captures well the relationship between translator and original. The process of going out and iden-tification excites Shelley in *A Defence of Poetry* to sentences that mime the awakening and sustaining of imaginative effort. In the unfinished Preface to his translation, he praises Plato in these terms: 'Plato exhibits the rare union of close and subtle logic with the Pythian enthusiasm of poetry, [melted] by the splendour & harmony of his periods into one irresistible stream of musical [impressions] which hurry the persuasions onward as in a breathless career. His language is that of an immortal spirit rather than a man'.[39] That 'Pythian enthusiasm' associates Plato with Apollo, god of poetry, and alludes to the *Ion* which contains praise of poetry as inspiration; it also reclaims for Shelley's own creative project the transgressive possibilities of 'enthusiasm'. The prose itself in the Preface quotation is vibrant—especially in the comma-free draft—with a desire to convey a sense of speed, of having 'a breathless career'. At the same time, it wishes the reader to notice the connections and distinc-tions it is making. First, it offers a 'rare union' between 'close and subtle logic' and 'Pythian enthusiasm', but as if that were an achievement which, though rare, might seem in some way to be fixed or static, Shelley characteristically opens up the sentence to another refining thought: of the 'union' being '[melted]…into one irresistible stream of musical [impressions]'. Plato's thought aspires to the condition of music in this sentence, and is itself a period marked by its own 'splendour & harmony'.

In his translation of the *Ion* Shelley conveys Plato's 'persuasions' with comparable artistry. At the centre of the translation is Socrates's double-edged account of inspiration as 'a chain and a succession' of magnetic influence, and the result of 'a state of divine insanity': double-edged since he is determined to prove to Ion that the rhapsode, like the inspired poet, does not create out of stores of knowledge, but from 'his participation in the divine influence'. As he argues: 'In other respects, poets may be sufficiently ignorant and incapable. For they do not compose according to any art which they have acquired but from the impulse of the divinity within them'. But Shelley turns Socrates's eloquence to his own advantage and confers on the portrait of inspiration an ennobling power. His translation embodies in itself 'the rhythm and harmony' ascribed to 'composers of lyrical poetry' and their counterparts, 'the Corybantes', as the following passage reveals:

> For the souls of the Poets, as poets tell us, have this peculiar ministration in the world. They tell us that these souls, flying like bees from flower to flower and wandering over the gardens and the meadows and the honey-flowing fountains of the Muses, return to us laden with the sweetness of melody; and arrayed as they are in the plumes of rapid imagination they speak truth. For a poet is indeed a thing ethereally light, winged, and sacred, nor can he compose anything worth calling poetry until he becomes inspired and as it were mad; or whilst any reason remains in him.[40]

---

[39] *BSM* V, 126–9. (I have tidied up some readings in the light of Mary Shelley's published text of the work in Shelley, *Letters from Abroad, Translations and Fragments, I*, 71. For Carlene A. Adamson's comments on the text, including her reservations concerning the received reading 'melted' for a word which replaces the cancelled 'moulded', see *BSM* V, 387.)

[40] Notopoulos, *The Platonism of Shelley*, 472, 473, 472, 472–3. The textual state of Shelley's trans-lation of the *Ion* is complicated. I have taken as my copy-text the text in Notopoulos, *The Platonism of*

The flow of the prose in this version renders the 'peculiar ministration' of 'the souls of the poets'. There is, for one thing, a self-sealing yet onward-impelling circularity, caught in the momentary doubt whether 'arrayed as they are' refers to 'the souls of the poets' or to 'the poets' speaking about them. In fact, it is the latter, but the distinction dissolves, much as 'reason' passes into 'rapid imagination'. Notopoulos notes that the phrase 'arrayed as they are in the plumes of rapid imagination' was 'spun' by Shelley out of a Greek word meaning 'winging the air'.[41] The elaboration indicates a special pressure of interest on Shelley's part, a recreation whose Romantic eloquence is its own justification. The dazzling close of the second sentence in this later version has come a long way from the reading in MS Shelley e. l, '[?arrayed] as they are' with '[?clo]' written over 'arrayed' as though Shelley were about to write 'clothed'.[42] Yet, otherwise, the draft, beset as it is by cancellations and provisional solutions, is not far away from the achievement of the later version. In both, Shelley's enthusiasm for Plato's idea of inspiration is prominent. A version of the same passage in the draft reads:

> [...] for the souls of poets, as poets tell, have this peculiar ministration in the world; [...] that flying like bees from flower to flower, & wanderg [sic] over the gardens & the meadows & the honey flowing fountains of the Muses these souls return to us, laden with the sweetness of melody—and they speak truth. For indeed a poet is a thing aetherially light winged & sacred, nor is he capable of composing poetry until be becomes inspired & as it were mad, or whilst any reason remains in him.[43]

'Composing poetry' will become 'compose any thing worth calling poetry' in the final version, a revision that involves the injection of an almost colloquial note, a rationalizing voice at the heart of rapture. More generally, the particular success of the *Ion* translation lies in Shelley's ability to do justice to Socrates's complicated attitude to rhapsodizing inspiration.

Clearly *Ion* is, to some degree, the butt of Socrates's scepticism about the capacity of rhapsodes to be more than 'the interpreters of interpreters', an indictment given that the original interpreters (poets) are themselves often 'sufficiently ignorant and incapable'. Yet in Shelley's rendering Socratic scepticism goes hand in hand with wonder at the workings within poets and rhapsodes of 'the divine influence'. The prose never loses contact with logic and reason, even as it posits a force that puts reason and logic to flight and in the shade. In so doing, the translation typifies Shelley's response to Plato. When translating the passage about the poet and rhapsode as links in a magnetic chain of inspiration, Shelley's language is sharpened precisely by the sense that words can only come 'near to the truth':

> We call this inspiration and our expression indeed comes near to the truth; for the person who is an agent in this universal and reciprocal attraction is indeed possessed,

---

Shelley, which derives from Mary Shelley's 1840 [1839] edition of the prose. That text in turn, in part completed by Mary Shelley, derives from at least one missing manuscript, drafts for parts of which can be found in Bodleian MS Shelley e. 1; see Fraistat, *BSM* IX.

[41] Notopoulos, *The Platonism of Shelley*, 590.
[42] MS Shelley e. l, f. 45r, in *BSM* IX, 182–3.   [43] *BSM* IX, 178–9, 182–3.

and some are attracted and suspended by one of the poets who are the first rings in this great chain and some by another.

The brace of 'indeeds' serves as clarification of the speaker's sense that what he proposes—that those caught up in the chain of inspiration are 'possessed'—will bear emphasis. Moreover, the writing allows for agency in the midst of possession, since the 'possessed' person is an 'agent' engaged in a process that is 'universal and reciprocal'. Shelley captures how inspiration involves a possession which is at once beyond reason and yet intelligible to some degree in rational terms; his own prose participates in the 'universal and reciprocal attraction' it describes, as the translator emerges as one of those 'suspended from the Muse itself as from the origin of the influence'.[44]

In his rendering of the *Ion* Shelley discovers on the pulses of and reveals through his prose the truth he asserts in *A Defence of Poetry*: namely, that 'Plato was essentially a poet'. That moment comes straight after his dismissal of the distinction between 'poets and prose-writers' as 'a vulgar error' (*Major Works*, 679).[45] It is likely that he is adding his own insights to the debate begun by Wordsworth's claim in his Preface to *Lyrical Ballads* (present in 1800, though this chapter's copy-text is 1802) that 'there neither is, nor can be, any essential difference between the language of prose and metrical composition'. As Wordsworth remarks, 'the same human blood circulates through the veins of them both'. The older poet's prose thinks its way into 'the fluxes and refluxes of the mind when agitated by the great and simple affections of our nature', and has a movement in accord with the 'more subtle windings' of thought and feeling (*Wordsworth: Major Works*, 602, 598). It is clear that Shelley has doubts about aspects of Wordsworth's procedures, as when he writes to Leigh Hunt that the 'familiar style' is not 'to be admitted in the treatment of a subject wholly ideal' (*Letters: PBS*, 2. 108). Shelley's sense that prose can be poetry is never a celebration of the merely prosaic; rather, he is closer to the Coleridge who in *Biographia Literaria* declares, 'The writings of Plato…furnish undeniable proofs that poetry of the highest kind may exist without metre, and even without the contradistinguishing objects of a poem'.[46] In *A Defence of Poetry*, Shelley picks up Wordsworth's attempt to erase the difference between poetry and prose, and argues with Coleridge that great prose attains the condition of poetry. 'Plato was essentially a poet' for Shelley in terms that echo his praise for Plato in the Preface to the *Symposium* because 'the truth and splendour of his imagery and

---

[44] Notopoulos, *The Platonism of Shelley*, 473, 474, 474–5, 474. This section is based on the Claire Clairmont transcription of Shelley's translation of the *Ion*, a transcription known only as it appears in H. Buxton Foman's edition of the prose: for detailed accounts of a complex textual situation, see Notopoulos, *The Platonism of Shelley*, 462–7, Fraistat, *BSM IX*, pp. xxxiv–xliv, Murray, *BSM XXI*, 499–502, and Weinberg, *BSM XXII* (1), 20–1.

[45] See Fanny Delisle, *A Study of Shelley's 'A Defence of Poetry': A Textual and Critical Evaluation*, 2 vols (Salzburg: Institut fur Englische Sprache und Literatur, Universitat Salzburg, 1974), vol. 1, 217–20, for a synthesis of ideas about Shelley's sources for the statement that 'the distinction between poets and prose-writers is a vulgar error'.

[46] Engell and Bate, *Biographia Literaria 2*, 14 (Ch. 14). (I am grateful to Alan Weinberg for reminding me of this passage.)

the melody of his language is the most intense that it is possible to conceive'.[47] Shelley's prose sustains a discriminating precision in the midst of 'intense' celebration; it seems to erode the differences between nouns even as it sustains them and challenges what is 'possible to conceive'. Such prose has an energy that makes it the reverse of orotund. Shelley explains Plato's rejection of poetic forms in a manner that makes him sound like a Greek forerunner of Whitman or Lawrence or of *vers libre*: 'he sought to kindle a harmony in thoughts divested of shape and action, and he forebore to invent any regular plan of rhythm which would include, under determinate forms, the varied pauses of his style' (*Major Works*, 679). Once more the sound echoes sense, as the 'varied pauses' of Shelley's own rhythms flow past the barrier of that Latinate 'determinate' with its associations of something bounded, defined, or completed.

Indeed, the incompleteness that is part of Shelley's ideal of style—that is, the leaving open by one sentence or clause of something new to be said by the next— dominates this passage of *A Defence of Poetry*, as Shelley applies to Bacon's style a tribute that grows out of his admiration for Plato's: 'it [Bacon's language] is a strain which distends, and then bursts the circumference of the reader's mind, and pours itself forth together with it into the universal element with which it has perpetual sympathy' (*Major Works*, 679). This wording mimics a notion of prose as breaking down the dykes that exist between the 'universal' and the individual, of prose as expanding the experiencing 'mind'. Sentence after sentence in *A Defence of Poetry* 'bursts the circumference of the reader's mind'. Shelley concludes the third scene of Act III of *Prometheus Unbound* with a reference to the Lampadephoria, an Athenian ritual in which, in honour of Prometheus, a race was run by young men bearing torches: 'the emulous youths / Bore to thine honour through the divine gloom / The lamp which was thine emblem; even as those / Who bear the untransmitted torch of hope / Into the grave, across the night of life' (III.iii. 168–72). As Timothy Webb has pointed out, the image is precisely not that of 'a relay race'; life is a race towards the grave in which we bear a 'torch of hope' that cannot be 'transmitted'—and yet it can be rekindled by exemplary emulousness.[48] Something analogous happens with Shelley's prose; each sentence transmits its energy to the next precisely by behaving as though such transmission were not straightforward. The effect can be close to ardent improvisation. Or, to use the torch image a different way, the prose is aware of its complicated relationship with precursors, and its sentences often conduct themselves as though they were bearing a perilous torch of hope across the night of life.

Lest this chapter should suggest otherwise, it is important to remember that Shelley wrote different kinds of prose: these kinds include the polemical bite of the Notes to *Queen Mab*; the casuistical argumentative cunning of *A Refutation of Deism*; the political power and fervour of the *Address to the People on the Death of*

---

[47] *Major Works*, 679.
[48] Timothy Webb, 'The Unascended Heaven: Negatives in *Prometheus Unbound*', first published in *Shelley Revalued: Essays from the Gregynog Conference*, ed. Kelvin Everest (Leicester: Leicester University Press, 1983), 37–62; rpt. in *Norton*. See esp. 710: 'The crucial word is *untransmitted*, which limits the scope of optimism; this is not a relay race and each man has to carry the torch for himself.'

the Princess Charlotte; and the simultaneously hard-headed and libertarian persuasions of *A Philosophical View of Reform*. Yet, as it develops, Shelley's prose assumes a manner suited to the sophisticated revolutionary in politics, the hopeful sceptic in philosophical matters, the dogma-rejecting seeker after spiritual intimations, and the rhapsodizing lover conscious of his own compulsion to idealize. 'You know I always seek in what I see the manifestation of something beyond the present & tangible object', he writes to Peacock after reading Tasso's handwriting as 'the symbol of an intense & earnest mind exceeding at times its own depth' (*Letters: PBS*, 2. 47). One can see how Plato's *Symposium* would appeal to such a quester. But it is with one of the work's seemingly more self-contained speeches that I would like to end this chapter: Agathon's prose poem in praise of love, excerpted by Mary Shelley for separate publication.[49] Arguably (as Socrates, for one, will argue), the speech has philosophical flaws, but Shelley rises to the heights in his rendering of the passage and makes us feel how Agathon's errors in understanding the nature of love spring from his excusable poetic delight in its effect. These errors centre on his belief that love is beautiful rather than being, as Socrates points out, desirous of the beautiful. As a result, Agathon (from Socrates's perspective) talks about the impact of Love on those who experience it; he does not identify its true nature. This is left to Socrates, with Diotima's help. Still, as the following excerpt shows, there is great beauty in Agathon's description of Love.

> He is young therefore, and being young is tender and soft. There were need of some poet like Homer to celebrate the delicacy and tenderness of Love. For Homer says that the Goddess Calamity is delicate and that her feet are tender:—'Her feet are soft', he says, 'for she treads not on the ground, but makes her path upon the heads of men.' He gives as an evidence of her tenderness that she walks not upon that which is hard but that which is soft. The same evidence is sufficient to make manifest the tenderness of Love. For Love walks not upon the earth, nor over the heads of men, which are not indeed very soft, but he dwells within and treads on the softest of existing things, having established his habitation within the souls and inmost nature of Gods and men; not indeed in all souls—for wherever he chances to find a hard and rugged disposition, there he will not inhabit but only where it is most soft and tender.[50]

The command of repetition is remarkable, especially in the shifting changes rung on the two words 'tender' and 'soft'. Again, the chiastic frame is present: 'He is young therefore, and being young is tender and soft', the passage begins; it moves towards a close with the words, 'wherever he chances to find a hard and rugged disposition, there he will not inhabit but only where it is most soft and tender'. Shelley often produces fine verbal effects by restricting his diction and working words until their meaning is inseparable from the halo or aura which his rhythms and syntax have generated round them. In this, he responds to the Greek, but he also shapes something typical of his own sense that language 'has relation to

---

[49] Mary Shelley reprinted a slightly edited version of the speech in her article 'The Loves of the Poets', *The Westminster Review* (1829). Reprinted in *The Mary Shelley Reader*, eds Betty T. Bennett and Charles E. Robinson (New York: Oxford University Press, 1990), 365–71.
[50] *BSM* XX, 346–9.

thoughts alone' (*Major Works*, 678). By this stage 'tender and soft' have left behind their physical meanings, even as they stay in touch with the possible joke in the original at Socrates's expense (who may be teased by Agathon for not possessing a head which is 'soft').[51]

Shelley follows Agathon in his conversion of prose into poetry in the latter's final paragraph:

> Nor can I restrain the poetic enthusiasm which takes possession of my discourse, and, bids me declare that Love is the divinity who creates peace among men, and calm upon the sea, the windless silence of storms, repose and sleep in sadness. Love divests us of all alienation from each other, and fills our vacant hearts with overflowing sympathy; he gathers us together in such social meetings as we now delight to celebrate, our guardian and our guide in dances and sacrifices and feasts.—Yes—Love—who showers benignity upon the world, and before whose presence all harsh passions flee and perish; the author of all soft affections; the destroyer of all ungentle thoughts; merciful, mild, the object of the admiration of the wise and the delight of Gods; possessed by the fortunate, and desired by the unhappy, therefore unhappy because they possess him not; the father of grace, and delicacy, and gentleness, and delight, and persuasion, and desire; the cherisher of all that is good, the abolisher of all evil: our most excellent pilot, defence, saviour and guardian in labour and in fear, in desire and in reason; the ornament and governor of all things human and divine; the best, the loveliest: in whose footsteps every one ought to follow celebrating him excellently in song, and bearing each his part in that divinest harmony which Love sings to all things which live and are, soothing the troubled minds of Gods and men.[52]

Lavishing verbal attention on a passage whose attitudes and ideas Shelley knows will be superseded in the dialogue, the writing displays control in the midst of 'poetic enthusiasm': which is one reason why Shelley is an artist in prose as well as in poetry. The writing's rhythms, with their balance of poise and power, are central to its achievement. One source of this mingling of calm and buoyancy is the use of parallels and catalogues, as Love's qualities spill out in a series of augustly appositional phrases. An example is 'calm upon the sea, the windless silence of storms, repose and sleep in sadness', where the tranquillity does not exclude surprise and awareness of all that opposes love. By 'windless silence of storms', Shelley appears to mean that love brings windless silence to storms, but his precise wording says something more compelling: that at the eye of storms there is a windless silence locatable by love. Shelley also uses a technique one might call controlled chant, as when he celebrates love as 'the father of grace, and delicacy, and gentleness, and delight, and persuasion, and desire'. Brought together by the repeated employment of 'and', the abstractions join hands in an incantatory dance that confers new and renewed dignity on words we have met a thousand times, but which, because of the saraband-like stateliness of the wording, turn towards us semantic features we have ignored before. There is a secular sacredness about the

---

[51] See *Plato in Twelve Volumes*, '*Lysis*', '*Symposium*', '*Gorgias*', trans. W. R. M. Lamb (Cambridge: Harvard University Press, 1975), vol. 3, 155 n.

[52] *BSM* XX, 354–7.

writing, as Shelley achieves in his cadences and counterpoisings a heterodox rival to the heartenings and affirmations of the Authorized Version.

'[D]esired by the unhappy, therefore unhappy because they possess him not': Socrates will offer a critique of this view of unhappiness, seeing dispossession as the force that drives love. But the delicacy with which Shelley translates at this point, displaying a consciousness of unhappiness in the midst of joy, reveals the double-mindedness that pervades his work. Ultimately, one might gloss Agathon's speech, with its idealizing of love, rather as Shelley himself glosses his evocation of religious hope in 'On Christianity':

> All evil and pain have ceased forever [. . .] We see God, and we see that he is good. How delightful a picture even if it be not true! How magnificent and illustrious is the conception which this bold theory suggests to the contemplation, even if it be no more than the imagination of some sublimest and most holy poet, who impressed with the loveliness and majesty of his own nature, is impatient, discontented, with the narrow limits which this imperfect life, and the dark grave have assigned forever as his melancholy portion.[53]

The passage sets 'the imagination of some sublimest and most holy poet' against 'narrow limits', 'imperfect life', and 'the dark grave', explaining the former as shaped in compensating reaction against the latter. Shelley not only idealizes and delights in Plato's idealizing; he is aware of what is at stake in the act of idealizing. That blend of delight and awareness helps to account for Shelley's absorbed and absorbing response to Plato, a response that animates some of his finest prose.

---

[53] *The Prose Works of Percy Bysshe Shelley*, Vol. I, ed. E. B. Murray (Oxford: Clarendon Press, 1993), 256. Hereafter *Prose*.

2

'The Right Scale of that Balance'

Shelley, Spenser, Milton

1

Shelley learned from many other previous poets writing in English, including Dryden, Gray, and Thomson. But Milton and Spenser play a special role in Shelley's poetic development, as they do in different ways for Byron. If Spenser licenses Byron's complex reuse of the romance genre in *Childe Harold's Pilgrimage* and Milton prompts his highly individual form of satire in *Don Juan*, both writers are among the poetic predecessors who assist Shelley in fashioning a sophisticated vision of art and experience.

2

Spenser appeals to Shelley partly because of what Harold Bloom calls his 'power to project both the object of desire and the shape of nightmare with equal imaginative freedom'.[1] The older poet with his true and false Duessas, his archetypes of excellence and emblems of horror, often sponsors Shelley's visionary explorations. Spenser delighted Shelley's ear and imagination, but occasionally vexed his ideological intelligence. *A Defence of Poetry* manages to forgive the poet of *The Faerie Queene* for being 'a poet laureate' (*Major Works*, 699) since, along with other great poets on Shelley's circular argument, his 'errors have been weighed and found to have been dust in the balance' (*Major Works*, 699). For Shelley in *A Defence*, 'Posterity', like 'Time' in Auden's pre-self-censored elegy to Yeats, 'Pardons' Spenser 'for writing well'.[2] Moreover, Spenser was able, like many precursors, to inspire Shelley precisely by engaging the younger poet in that imaginative struggle in which he often engages, as a result of which poets, living and dead, even as 'they deny and abjure,...are yet compelled to serve, the Power which is seated on the throne of their own soul' (*Major Works*, 701).

---

[1] Harold Bloom, *The Best Poems of the English Language: From Chaucer through Robert Frost*, selected and with commentary by Harold Bloom (London: Harper, 2004), 61.
[2] 'In Memory of W. B. Yeats', *The English Auden*, 243.

Thomas Love Peacock glosses Shelley's allusion in a letter to 'the right scale of that balance which the Giant (of Arthegall) holds' in the following way:

> Shelley once pointed out this passage to me, observing: 'Artegall argues with the Giant; the Giant has the best of the argument; Artegall's iron man knocks him over into the sea and drowns him. This is the usual way in which power deals with opinion.' I said: 'That was not the lesson which Spenser intended to convey.' 'Perhaps not,' he said; 'it is the lesson which he conveys to me. I am of the Giant's faction'. (*Letters: PBS*, 2. 71n)

Spenser is clearly opposed to 'the Giant's faction', the Giant's speeches in favour of equality being treated as forms of rabble-rousing demagoguery: the assertion by the Giant that 'Tyrants that make men subiet to their law, / I will suppress, that they no more may raine' (5. 2: 38) prompts Arthegall's defence of kingship as divinely ordained: 'He maketh Kings to sit in souerainty' (5. 2: 41).[3] From *Queen Mab* to *Prometheus Unbound*, from 'Ozymandias' to 'Ode to Liberty', Shelley's opposition to kings for their usurpation of position and power, and their imposition upon their fellow-citizens, remains constant. But Spenser's dramatizing of a contest between an upholder of the status quo and a rebel against it appealed to Shelley since it furnished further grounds for his transformative critique of reactionary politics. The subsequent exploration of matters to do with justice and equity in Spenser's fifth book involves the encounter between Radigund the Amazon and Artegall, in which Artegall obeys Radigund, having been overcome by her, until she falls in love with him, as does her handmaiden, Clarinda, sent by Radigund to plead her mistress's suit. The resulting 'subtill nets' (5. 5: 52) humanize Artegall to the point where Spenser has to argue his case against readers who may find in him 'Great weaknesse' (5. 6: 1).

That a hero should be flawed and find gender relations a difficult area seems calculated to appeal to Shelley, whose own post-Spenserian epic *Laon and Cythna* (1817) has, as Greg Kucich notes, affinities with *The Faerie Queene* in its fascination with 'the drama of psychological collapse and renewal'.[4] Already in his 'Hymn to Intellectual Beauty' Shelley displays his productive compulsion to revise earlier canonical texts by Spenser, in this case his 'Fowre Hymns', along with responsiveness to the Platonic erotics of the Renaissance poet's vision. Spenser's 'An Hymne of Heavenly Beavtie' uses its stately seven-line stanzas of *rime royal* to establish a Christianized Platonic hierarchy at the top of which is God whose perfection induces the trope of inexpressibility to which Shelley also has recourse.[5] Yet by contrast with Spenser, Shelley is all glimpses and hurried fugitive intuitions; his Platonism is no settled scheme of understanding, but a dim background against which his own longings and yearnings flare into speech. There is poise, too, amidst Shelley's uncertainties, as is evident in his opening lines. Spenser appeals directly to God in the form of the Holy Spirit: 'O thou most almightie Spright' (8) 'To shed

---

[3] Spenser is quoted from *The Poetical Works of Edmund Spenser*, ed. J. C. Smith and E. De Selincourt (London: Oxford University Press, 1912).

[4] Greg Kucich, *Keats, Shelley, and Romantic Spenserianism* (University Park: Pennsylvania State University Press, 1991), 274.

[5] This is noted in Kucich, 263.

into my breast some sparkling light / Of thine eternall Truth' (10–11). Shelley states, enigmatically, authoritatively: 'The awful shadow of some unseen Power / Floats though unseen amongst us' ('Hymn to Intellectual Beauty', version A, 1–2). The idiom suggests a transaction with Christian and Platonic traditions. The poet is able to affirm the existence of something close to an absolute, while refusing to locate his intuition within a pre-existing framework of understanding. Shelley almost writes in the margins of Spenser's great Renaissance hymn, yet he does so in a way that finally seeks to reverse the places of text and commentary. The Shelleyan gloss establishes its own secular scripture, according to which revelation comes not from God but from the sceptical, questioning imagination present in 'Each human heart and countenance' (7) and embodied in the very workings of the poem we are reading, with its shifts, transitions, slumps, and rallying.

Spenser argues that 'we fraile wights' (120) are unable to discern 'The glory of that Maiestie diuine' (124) belonging to God; Shelley attacks as 'Frail spells' (29) orthodox Christian attempts to answer questions about the nature of reality, especially its changeableness: questions which provoke from religious believers answers that involve 'the name of God, and ghosts, and Heaven' (27). The same word points in different directions: humility for Spenser, an awareness of the limits that confront enquiry for Shelley, yet an awareness compatible with trust in the imagination. Addressing and blaming his 'hungry soule' (288) for feeding 'On idle fancies of thy foolish thought' (289), Spenser rejects 'vain deceiptfull shadowes' (291). Shelley finds in similes and comparisons possible analogues for an experience that has much in common with religious fervour save the belief in what Spenser calls 'that great *Deity*' (145) whose 'throne is built vpon Eternity' (152). Value, for Shelley, is conferred upon 'human thought or form' (15) by a 'Spirit of BEAUTY' (13) that agnostically refuses to declare its origins. As Kucich suggests, the difference between the Renaissance and the Romantic poets shows in the adjectives attached to 'beauty' in their titles: 'Heavenlie' in Spenser's poem, 'Intellectual' in Shelley's.[6] Spenser looks to a transcendently 'soueraine light' (295) to give meaning to existence; Shelley to poetic intimations of 'Thy light alone' (32), conveyed through similes that confess and affirm in the same breath that meaning is inseparable from 'fancies'.

With Harold Bloom as a forebear, Kucich uses the word 'revisionism' to explain Shelley's relationship with Spenser, and the word is helpful in its suggestion of purposeful re-orchestration by the later poet of the earlier writer's commitment to a vision of cosmic harmony founded 'Vpon the pillours of Eternity, / That is contrary to *Mutabilitie*' (*The Faerie Queene*, 8: 2). With their opposition between movement and stillness, change and rest, the Mutability cantos appear to have left a deep impression on Shelley's imagination.[7] In *Laon and Cythna*, Shelley explores the sardonically tragic view he takes in 'Mutability', a short poem in the *Alastor*

---

[6] Kucich, 262.
[7] See Kucich, 270, for an account of how Shelley was concerned 'with transferring Spenser's drama of mutability and transcendence to a modern, secular context' and *passim* for references to Bloom, especially 7n, where Bloom is praised for urging 'Spenser scholars to deepen their understanding of *The Faerie Queene* by reading it through the Romantics' revisionary criticism'.

volume, that 'Nought may endure but Mutability' (16).[8] The effect, there, of 'endure' suggests a bitter relish of paradox: all that lasts is the fact of change, with a sidelong glance at the human need to 'endure', in the sense of 'suffer'. Yet that poem suggests a latent exhilaration beneath its mask of sorrow in the fact that, whatever the feeling, 'The path of its departure still is free' (14). The surprising stress on 'its' may bring with it the implication that 'we' are not 'free' from the constraints of change, yet Shelley's embracing of revolution in *Laon and Cythna* brings with it an awareness of a fundamental commitment to change. These meanings are compacted in the poem's sub-title: 'The Revolution of the Golden City, A Vision of the Nineteenth Century, in the Stanza of Spenser'. Shelley seeks to imagine a 'revolution' in accord with his commitment to 'recommending…a great and important change in the spirit which animates the social institutions of mankind' (*Major Works*, 136–7). This commitment involves acceptance of, even a delight in, 'change'.

At the same time the poem wishes to recommend permanent ideals, to believe 'That virtue, though obscured on Earth, not less / Survives all mortal change in lasting loveliness' (*Laon and Cythna* 12. 37: 4781–2), locating this survival of 'virtue' in a post-mortal 'Temple of the Spirit' (12. 41: 4815), to which we have been introduced in the first canto, where the narrator is taken to 'a Temple, such as mortal hand / Has never built' (1. 49: 559–60). Laon and Cythna instigate a revolution in an imagined human city and Laon's is 'A tale of human power' (1. 58: 648). But, as Spenser's knights lose their way, or are embroiled in severe trials (Redcrosse's encounter with Despair, for example), so Shelley's hero and heroine must undergo challenges to their revolutionary virtue. The revolution is defeated; Laon and Cythna are burned at the stake; the voyage to the post-mortal Temple of the Spirit is at once a means of keeping alive dreams and hopes that, for Shelley's generation, had undergone historical defeat, and a confession that the poem's revolution is scarred by traumatic memories of the real-life events in France which Shelley sought to re-imagine and transform.

'Methinks, those who now live have survived an age of despair', writes Shelley in his Preface to the poem, in which he deplores the liberal defeatism of recent times, as a result of which 'gloom and misanthropy have become the characteristics of the age in which we live' (*Major Works*, 132). That Shelley can make two such contrary pronouncements in rapid succession, one optimistically proclaiming the political health of 'those who now live', the other accepting, even as it fights against, a less buoyant view of 'the age in which we live', prepares us for the swings between confidence and anxiety discernible in *Laon and Cythna*, as they are in *The Faerie Queene*. Indeed, Spenser gave Shelley the confidence to depict, through 'a succession of pictures' (as Kucich notes, a distinctly Spenserian procedure), the lineaments of 'a liberal and comprehensive morality' (*Major Works*, 131, 130).[9]

Part of the 'comprehensiveness' of this 'morality' is that it is conveyed in a work that 'is narrative not didactic' (*Major Works*, 131), allowing for narrative's ramifications to work on the reader's imagination. In Spenser's case this means that though, as a

---

[8] Quoted from *Longman* 1. Otherwise Shelley's poetry in this chapter is quoted from *Major Works*.
[9] Kucich, 274.

result of Una's upbraidings and heartenings, the Redcrosse Knight does not succumb to Despair's temptations, we still respond to those temptations in all their eloquent force, with their evocations of the desirability of death: 'Sleepe after toyle, port after stormie seas, / Ease after warre, death after life does greatly please' (1. 9: 40). The lines lull and seduce, despite the presence in the poem of a moral scheme urging the rejection of such lulling seductions. In Shelley's case, it means that Cythna's exhortations to welcome the coming political 'Spring' (9. 25: 3688) are allowed to pass into a deeply affecting confession of final existential uncertainty: 'All that we are or know, is darkly driven / Towards one gulf' (9. 35: 3779–80). The glimpses of 'Paradise' (9. 36: 3792) proffered by *Laon and Cythna* avoid the hack-neyed by virtue of the poem's ability to gaze into such a 'gulf' and still retain a sense of the revolutionary virtue embodied in a person such as Cythna, Laon's 'Fair star of life and love' and 'soul's delight' (9. 36: 3788), and Shelley's updated and remodelled version of Una, whose 'celestiall sight' (*The Faerie Queene* 1. 12: 23) fills Redcrosse with wonder at their wedding.[10] Cythna is a post-Wollstonecraftian feminist, full-blooded theological sceptic, and dauntless political agitator; Una is an allegorical type of the true Catholic Church supposedly recovered by the Reformed English religion. But Spenser's idealism (meaning his belief in ideals and his embodiment in words of an idea) is at work as a creative influence in Shelley's *Laon and Cythna*: the relations between the two heroines are not merely those of orthodox thesis and heretical antithesis.

Spenser lies behind *Laon and Cythna*'s 'conjunction of the theme of revolution with the language and form of romance', its highly original use of chivalric romance as the vehicle for Utopian quest.[11] Shelley points out in his sub-title that he is writing 'in the Stanza of Spenser', acknowledging one of the few English poets to have a form named after him. In the Preface Shelley writes that he has 'adopted the stanza of Spenser (a measure inexpressibly beautiful)', because, unlike the 'blank verse of Shakespeare and Milton', it provides some shelter for the 'aspiring spirit'. But he is also 'enticed . . . by the brilliancy and magnificence of sound which a mind that has been nourished upon musical thoughts can produce by a just and harmonious arrangement of the pauses of this measure' (*Major Works*, 135). That is an eloquent tribute to what Spenser's example and bequeathed 'measure' makes possible. Yeats quoted a stanza (6. 34) from *Laon and Cythna* to show how 'The rhythm is varied and troubled, and the lines which are in Spenser like bars of gold thrown ringing upon one another, are broken capriciously'. By contrast with the melodious self-sufficiency of *The Faerie Queene*, in which 'Spenser's verse is always rushing on to some preordained thought', Shelley's meaning 'is bound together by the vaguest suggestion'.[12] Yeats's ear is alert to real differences, and yet the opposition is cut too cleanly. Shelley's 'thought' may not be 'preordained', but it is consistently fascin-ated by the possibility of 'confounding' individuals 'into one / Unutterable power'

[10] For such remodellings, see Kucich, 274.

[11] David Duff, *Romance and Revolution: Shelley and the Politics of a Genre* (Cambridge: Cambridge University Press, 1994), 1.

[12] W. B. Yeats, 'Edmund Spenser', in *Selected Criticism and Prose*, ed. A. Norman Jeffares (London: Pan in association with Macmillan, 1980), 119.

(6. 35: 2641, 2642–3). David Duff is persuasive when he finds in 'the very sound of the poetry the idea of a developing harmony between the individual and the "universal life"'.[13] Spenser, for his part, is by no means averse to the 'inspiration of indolent Muses' which Yeats associates with Shelley.[14] P. C. Bayley comes closer than Yeats does to suggesting what Shelley derives from Spenser's poetic form when he writes of the Spenserian stanza, as handled by the Renaissance poet, that 'it is infinitely varied and intricate'.[15]

Similarly, Kucich is right to argue that Shelley and Byron seek 'to roughen a turbulence already there in Spenser'.[16] 'Turbulence' may not exactly fit the following stanza, one in Keats's mind when urging Shelley to '"load every rift" of your subject with ore'.[17] But the stanza shows how Spenser's style empathizes with his subject, here through an account of Mammon's Cave that demands an intuition of weight and covetous, massive strength, qualities that transmit themselves to and through the writing's patterns of stress:

> That houses form within was rude and strong,
> Like an huge caue, hewne out of rocky clift,
> From whose rough vaut the ragged breaches hong,
> Embost with massy gold of glorious gift,
> And with rich metal loaded euery rift,
> That heauy ruine they did seeme to threat;
> And ouer them *Arachne* high did lift
> Her cunning web, and spred her subtile net,
> Enwrapped in fowle smoke and clouds more blacke then Iet.
>
> (*The Faerie Queene*, 2. 7: 28)

'Bars of gold thrown ringing upon one another': Yeats may indeed have had this stanza in mind in making that formulation. Yet the sound-patterns intimate danger as much as wealth, and muffle and roughen their music, threading a short 'a' sound through 'ragged', 'massy', 'That', 'Arachne', and 'black' in a way that is less aureate than mimetic of a laboured, 'rude' strength. The caesurae here may seem well behaved and inconspicuous (only two strong medial pauses are present—in the second and eighth lines, and both in a predictable position). But the stanza is 'Embost' with heavy stresses, halting delivery, not permitting any easy way through to a 'preordained conclusion'. Spenser points up the surprising appearance of Arachne; her 'subtile net' conspires with Mammon yet is suggestive, too, of self-entrapment, serving in metapoetic fashion as an image of the very stanza we are reading.

---

[13] Duff, *Romance and Revolution*, p. 192, quoting *Laon and Cythna*, 6. 29: 2595.
[14] Yeats, 'Edmund Spenser', 119.
[15] Spenser, *The Faerie Queene: Book 1*, ed. P. C. Bayley ([1966] London: Oxford University Press, 1970 with corrections), 20.
[16] Kucich, 279. See also the same critic's observation that Leigh Hunt 'frequently adjured readers to hear the rhythm of passion in Spenser's modulations', 96.
[17] John Keats, *The Letters of John Keats 1814–1821*, ed. Hyder E. Rollins, 2 vols (Cambridge: Harvard University Press, 1958), II, 323.

A stanza in Shelley's poem that also describes a cave shows how he can be more harmoniously fluent, when he chooses, than Spenser himself. It occurs in canto 7, when Cythna, imprisoned by the tyrant in a 'cave / Above the waters' (7. 12: 2929–30), effectively turns Plato's myth of the cave (for Plato an image of benighted human consciousness) on its head. Long before Keats's advice, Shelley realized the significance of mining for poetic and political knowledge, as he has Cythna tell Laon. The introduction of this book suggested that these lines are partly about dialogues and influence:

> My mind became the book through which I grew
> Wise in all human wisdom, and its cave,
> Which like a mine I rifled through and through,
> To me the keeping of its secrets gave—
> One mind, the type of all, the moveless wave
> Whose calm reflects all moving things that are,
> Necessity, and love, and life, the grave,
> And sympathy, fountains of hope and fear;
> Justice, and truth, and time, and the world's natural sphere.
>   (7. 31: 3100–8)

Cythna, imprisoned in a cave, proves that a prison is not a prison when a metaphor can liberate it. 'Cave' is used to mean the stores of 'human wisdom' which she excavates; this 'mine' passes into her discovery of 'One mind, the type of all': an intuited Platonic absolute firmly rooted in rather than transcending the human condition, whose constituents are catalogued in the ensuing list. Spenser's Platonism is more explicitly in accord with traditional exposition; Shelley's is more individually inflected so as to take from Plato the idea of enduring value while implicitly calling into question, through the very display of metaphorical association in the stanza, any straightforward conceptual assent to 'the existence of a separate realm of abstract objects called "Forms"'.[18] Shelley's rhythms elsewhere are 'troubled'; here, they are in sympathy with a growth in wisdom and a world-reflecting 'calm', even as the stress-shift at the start of the alexandrine (in 'Justice') hints at a subliminal tension between 'things that are' and things as they ought to be. But as with Spenser's epic, *Laon and Cythna* deploys the space given by the roomy nine-line stanza to accommodate stillness and movement, being and becoming, desire and glimpses of fulfilment.

One of the older poet's greatest bequests to Shelley lies in what John Hughes, an early eighteenth-century editor of Spenser, described as his epic poem's 'surprizing Vein of fabulous Invention which runs thro' it, and enriches it every where with Imagery and Descriptions more than we meet with in any other modern Poem'.[19] It is in *Prometheus Unbound* that such a 'surprizing Vein' is most evident. A poem 'written in the merest spirit of ideal poetry' (*Letters: PBS*, 2. 219), the lyric drama abounds in scenes of 'fabulous Invention', where, drawing

---

[18] Richard Kraut, 'Introduction to the Study of Plato', in *The Cambridge Companion to Plato*, ed. Richard Kraut (Cambridge: Cambridge University Press, 1992), 8.
[19] Quoted in Kucich, 21.

on but also adapting to his own purposes classical and mythological stories, Shelley surprises and delights us through his 'Vein of fabulous invention', a vein that holds at bay the threat of 'Didactic poetry', his 'abhorrence', as he tells us in his Preface (*Major Works*, 232).

A figure illustrating this vein is Demogorgon, who serves to complicate in enhancing ways the poem's reflections on history. Demogorgon may derive from the first canto of *The Faerie Queene*, where he appears as 'Great *Gorgon*, Prince of darknesse and dead night' (1. 1: 37). Shelley recasts him as a less straightforwardly Stygian figure, one who is 'A living Spirit' (II. iv. 7) even as he has 'neither limb, / Nor form, nor outline' (II. iv. 5–6). As 'a mighty darkness' (II. iv. 2) Demogorgon represents the realm of potentiality rather than evil (or nightmare) and functions as the figure without whom tyranny cannot be deposed. It is he, not Prometheus, who drags Jupiter from his throne, possibly allowing Shelley to displace the problem of violent revolution from his newly forgiving hero to another character, but also allowing him to embody within the lyrical drama the suggestion that a desired change cannot happen simply because the forces of defiance (Prometheus) and love (Asia) combine, even though it could not happen without this combination. In the way allegorical thought entangles itself with concrete fabling and invention, Shelley shows himself to have learned much from Spenser's mythmaking, as Harold Bloom and Carlos Baker, among others, have argued.[20]

In his 'Letter to Maria Gisborne', Shelley depicts himself as a benign version of Spenser's wicked mage, Archimago, whose evil schemes are central to the first book of *The Faerie Queene*: 'And here like some weird Archimage sit I, / Plotting dark spells and devilish enginry' (106–7), where the second line mockingly ventriloquizes the paranoid suspicions evident in what Shelley calls sardonically 'our meek reviews' (110). In this poem, Shelley gestures towards an engagement with Spenser's inventiveness that flowers into individual being in *The Sensitive Plant* and *The Witch of Atlas*. In both poems, Spenser serves as spur and foil. In the former, a fable of seeming mutability and decay that is challenged by a 'modest creed' (Conclusion, 13) of idealist denial of such things, the Lady who tends the garden and dies at the close of Part Second is 'An Eve in this Eden' (116), but also brings to mind, as Jerrold Hogle suggests, 'Spenser's Una'.[21] The delicate interplay between loss and hope in the poem is distinctively Shelleyan in its ability to snatch a provisional affirmation from the jaws of steady-eyed scepticism. Yet the final lines evoke, even as they distinguish themselves from, a Spenserian movement from melancholy to dignified assurance.

---

[20] See Harold Bloom, *Shelley's Mythmaking* ([1959] Ithaca: Cornell University Press, 1969), where Spenser is said to be an exemplar of the 'visionary' school of poetry, and vital for the 'romantic mythmaking of Collins, Blake, Shelley, and Keats', 177; Carlos Baker, *Shelley's Major Poetry: The Fabric of a Vision* ([1948] New York: Russell, 1961).

[21] Hogle, *Shelley's Process*, 288. The Bower of Bliss and the Garden of Adonis also feature among the Spenserian archetypes stirred into remembered complementary and contrasting life by the poem's representation of the garden and its destruction. See Bloom, *Shelley's Mythmaking*, 178–80, for the poem's relationship to the Garden of Adonis in *The Faerie Queen* 3, 6.

The Witch of Atlas, Shelley's most exuberant tribute to 'the poetical faculty' (*Major Works*, 696), compares the poem being offered to a sceptical Mary to a 'silken-winged fly' (9), possibly alluding to Spenser's Clarion, chief of 'the race of siluer-winged Flies' (17), in *Muipotmos: or The Fate of the Butterflie*.[22] Writing, like Spenser, in *ottava rima* stanzas, Shelley mourns the ephemerality of his previous and present poems with deeply felt yet nonchalant good humour; now a lonely artist, expecting to be misunderstood, it would seem, he quietly bids farewell to his earlier self-image in the dedicatory stanzas to *Laon and Cythna* as a Spenserian 'victor Knight of Faery, / Earning bright spoils' for his Queen's 'enchanted home' (3–4). And yet the 'bright spoils' won by *The Witch of Atlas* include the recognition that a 'liberal and comprehensive morality' (Preface to *Laon and Cythna*, *Major Works*, 130) may be served best by an art that is bent on proclaiming its autonomy. The creation of the False Florimell in *The Faerie Queene* (3. 8: 6) mimics, in its blending of 'purest snow' and 'fine Mercury', a false art; Shelley's Witch creates Hermaphroditus from 'fire and snow' (321), but does so by 'tempering the repugnant mass / With liquid love' (322–3). Shelley's commitment to art and its condition of free and necessary play does not preclude—indeed, it entails—a wittily sharp-eyed view of art's limits, if we allegorize Hermaphroditus as a product and agent of artistic creativity.

By this stage of Shelley's career Spenser has emerged as an abiding presence in his imagination. He need not declare ideological war on the Renaissance poet because his swerving from his Christian Platonism is almost second nature. The more individual Shelley's voice is as he explores his sense of art's value and limits in a series of poems (*The Witch of Atlas* and *Adonais*, in particular), the more strongly he persuades the reader that he has absorbed Spenser deeply into his imagination's bloodstream. In *Adonais* he produces his most sustained and impressive poem in Spenserian stanzas and, arguably, in any measure. His recurrent concern with Spenser's twin theme of mutability and lasting significance finds memorable expression in an elegy that is indebted to Spenser's elegy for Sidney, *Astrophel*, and its incorporated lament, *The Lay of Clorinda*.[23] Clorinda's assertion of 'so diuine a thing' (66) as Astrophel's 'immortall spirit' (61), 'Ah no: it is not dead, ne can it die, / But liues for aie, in blissful Paradise' (67–8), underpins Shelley's pivotal movement from grief to affirmation in stanza 39: 'he is not dead, he doth not sleep—/ He hath awakened from the dream of life' (343–4). Shelley's version of 'blissful Paradise' is 'the abode where the Eternal are' (55. 495), an abode that is Platonic, knowingly fictive and secular, and a brave gesture towards transcendence: an abode that is the home of 'eternal' poets such as Keats and Spenser. It exists, in part, as a post-Christian response to Spenser's declarations of belief in eternity and represents Shelley's most significant revision of the older poet's work.

---

[22] See Bloom, *Shelley's Mythmaking*, 148–55 for an account of this poem's influence on *The Sensitive Plant* and 170–1 for commentary on the possible allusion in *The Witch of Atlas*.
[23] Spenser's influence on *Adonais* is discussed in Hogle, *Shelley's Process*, esp. 299–301, and Kucich, 326–45.

3

Shelley, in contrast with Wordsworth in *Lyrical Ballads*, does not in *Prometheus Unbound* 'begin *de novo* on a *tabula rasa* of poetry',[24] even if one might wish to argue that such a *tabula rasa* beacons from the abode where the deep truth beckons in all its imagelessness. As various critics have brought out, Shelley prefers to work with past genres in order to transform them. The famous epigraph to the volume containing the lyrical drama, 'Audisne haec Amphiare sub terram abdite?' (*Major Works*, 229), throws down the gauntlet to a number of formidable precursors, including Aeschylus, Milton, and Byron, whose magnificently gloomy *Manfred*, subtitled *A Dramatic Poem*, is one of Shelley's points of departure. One might adapt to his treatment of genre his discriminating reflections on originality in the Preface to his lyrical drama:

> As to imitation, poetry is a mimetic art. It creates, but it creates by combination and representation. Poetical abstractions are beautiful and new, not because the portions of which they are composed had no previous existence in the mind of man or nature, but because the whole produce by their combination has some intelligible and beautiful analogy with those sources of emotion and thought, and with the contemporary condition of them
>
> (Preface to *Prometheus Unbound*, *Major Works*, 231)

Shelley makes stronger claims for the newness of his work when he says in a letter that it includes 'characters & mechanism of a kind yet unattempted' (*Letters: PBS*, 2. 94), alluding, as my previous chapter noted, to Milton's assertion of originality at the start of *Paradise Lost*; it is written, he says in another letter, 'in the merest spirit of ideal Poetry, and not, as the name would indicate, a mere imitation of the Greek drama'—nor 'indeed', he continues, 'if I have been successful, it is an imitation of anything' (*Letters: PBS*, 2. 219). 'Ideal Poetry' suggests a drama that searches to idealize, to deal in its own non-propagandist way in ideas, and to set itself in relation to and shape historical events. Shelley's Romantic dislike of 'mere imitation' does not, however, prevent him from showing detailed knowledge of literary models, even as he attempts to unsay their high language and replace it with his own self-echoing and self-validating linguistic structure. When Shelley's lyrical drama opens with a flurry of echoes from Aeschylus and Milton, his poem positions itself between formal homage and ideological critique: Prometheus's description of an earth 'Made multitudinous' with Jupiter's 'slaves, whom thou / Requitest for knee-worship, prayer and praise, / And toil, and hecatombs of broken hearts, / With fear, and self-contempt and barren hope' (I. 5–8) recalls Satan's scorn for the 'Knee-tribute, yet unpaid, prostration vile' (*Paradise Lost*, V. 782) demanded, on his account by the newly crowned Messiah. Shelley, as is his custom, reads against the grain; his echo adapts what in *Paradise Lost* is overtly criticized—Satan's intransigent pride—to a context in which resistance to authority is morally admirable. At the same time, Shelley internalizes Milton's conflict. Whereas Satan wars with

---

[24] William Hazlitt, *The Spirit of the Age*, ed. E. D. Mackerness (London: Collins, 1969), 140.

God, Prometheus fights with himself, preserving—despite the Preface's assertions to the contrary—enough of Satan's faults to keep him dramatically compelling. In the lines that follow, Shelley again draws on a Miltonic source, this time *Samson Agonistes*. Prometheus compares his arch-foe—'eyeless in hate' (9)—to Samson as he languishes in Milton's poem 'Eyeless in Gaza at the mill with slaves' (41). Jupiter's eyeless hate broods over his slaves; Samson, literally blind, works 'in a common workhouse' (518), as the Argument to *Samson Agonistes* has it.[25] But the syntax of Shelley's lines blurs the identities of Samson and Jupiter, and triggers off some complicated equivalences. Prometheus is like Samson in being temporarily blind as a result of hatred; Jupiter is like Samson to the degree that he provokes pity. *Samson Agonistes* is prefaced by a prose disquisition 'Of That Sort of Dramatic Poem Which is Called Tragedy', in which Aristotle's cathartic notions are approvingly quoted: tragedy is said by Aristotle, according to Milton, 'to be of power, by raising pity and fear, or terror, to purge the mind of those and such-like passions' (517). Shelley's method is to place the cathartic moment—Prometheus's pity for Jupiter (53)—close to the start of his poem, and to show Prometheus both raising and purging 'pity' and such-like passions in and from his mind.

Echo and allusion tell us of Shelley's recreation in his own terms of central Miltonic effects. There is a telescoping of generic associations, epic and tragedy coming together, mingling, and giving up their Christian allegiances as Shelley begins his astonishing attempt to write a poem whose very hybridity speaks of his wish to combine poetical abstractions in a way that allows them to speak to a contemporary condition. The poetry in this section has, as well, a wholly original music, for all its debts to Milton and Aeschylus, a readiness to sound a lyrical note that anticipates the poem's subsequent wish to be, and float on, a stream of sound. So even in the second line, with its reference to 'those bright and rolling worlds / Which thou and I alone of living things / Behold with sleepless eyes' (I. 2–4), the writing looks ahead to the fourth act's lyric delight in the transformed physical creation. Prometheus's pain threatens to vanish into an exquisite dance of assonances and long-vowelled music in the famous lines, 'The crawling glaciers pierce me with the spears / Of their moon-freezing crystals, the bright chains / Eat with their burning cold into my bones' (I. 31–3).[26] Drama is giving way in such a passage to lyric; the lines conjure with piercing precision the effect of glacial cold, yet their beauty stirs in the reader an awareness, however subliminal, that ultimately the poetic world of the

---

[25] In this chapter, Milton is quoted from *Milton: Poetical Works*, ed. Douglas Bush (Oxford: Oxford University Press, 1966). For a valuable recent discussion of Shelley's response to Milton, see Madeleine Callaghan, 'Shelley and Milton', in *The Oxford Handbook of Percy Bysshe Shelley*, ed. Michael O'Neill and Anthony Howe, with the assistance of Madeleine Callaghan (Oxford: Oxford University Press, 2013), 478–94. For older work on the relationship between Milton and Shelley, still of considerable value, see perceptive comments (trackable via index) in E. M. W. Tillyard, *Milton* (1930; London: Penguin, in association with Chatto and Windus, 1968), including this remark on a passage from Milton's prose work *Animadversions upon the Remonstrant's Defence* (1641): 'Such lyrical fervour for a changed world joined with so blind a belief in its immediate possibility can be matched in English literature in Shelley alone' (106)—though I would wish to dissent from the view that *Prometheus Unbound*, the work Tillyard goes into mention, ever displays 'so blind a belief'.
[26] See the discussion in Peter Conrad, *The Victorian Treasure-House* (London: Collins, 1973), 18.

lyrical drama is a law unto itself. The poem is always travelling beyond conforming to generic expectations because its gaze is finally set on a Utopian realm beyond language. And yet, even as it concedes with Demogorgon that 'the deep truth is imageless' (II. iv. 169), it also relishes a vision of 'language' as 'a perpetual Orphic song, / Which rules with Daedal harmony a throng / Of thoughts and forms, which else senseless and shapeless were' (IV. 415–7). 'Orphic' indicates a power of enchantment that can be felt in the poem's treatment of power, and enchantment requires the cunning of Daedalus, the mythic artificer. Once these thoughts and forms have been clothed in daedal harmony, they are redeemed from senselessness and shapelessness.

The passage might describe the poem's treatment of literary 'forms'. By the fourth act, the lyrical drama has escaped the fetters of Miltonic/Aeschylean agon; it has proved itself to be the consummate example in Romantic poetry of what Curran calls 'composite orders'.[27] Yet one point needs to be added to Curran's discussion of how 'the mixture of genres implies an uncompromising multiperspectivism':[28] it is important to see how tensely Shelley wrestles with the implication of the genres to which he alludes or from which he borrows. The poem may, in its desire for change, embody within itself 'a perpetual Orphic song', but it is aware throughout of the danger that self-reflexive conversion of all genres into its new creation might turn into an empty narcissistic delight. To give just one example: in Act IV Panthea's depiction of the 'multitudinous Orb' (IV. 253) converts Milton's Chariot of Paternal Deity and Dante's paradisal wheelings (canto X of the *Paradiso*) into an account at once scientific and visionary that might serve as a paradigm of the work's relationship with genres; in the very movement of his blank verse Shelley enacts the process of spiritualizing the material:

> With mighty whirl the multitudinous Orb
> Grinds the bright brook into an azure mist
> Of elemental subtlety, like light;
> And the wild odour of the forest flowers,
> The music of the living grass and air,
> The emerald light of the leaf-entangled beams,
> Round its intense, yet self-conflicting speed,
> Seem kneaded into one aerial mass
> Which drowns the sense
>
> (IV. 253–61)

That drowning of the 'the sense' asserts an imaginative triumph over the sensory, the empirical. Yet the writing holds us partly because of the resistance to its wish to convert the external (a term which might be expanded to include generic norms) into its own image and likeness. The orb 'Grinds'—an expressively physical verb— 'the bright brook into an azure mist / Of elemental subtlety, like light'. Its speed may be 'intense' yet it is 'self-conflicting', too. What gives life to the passage is the

---

[27] Stuart Curran, *Poetic Form and British Romanticism* (New York: Oxford University Press, 1986), 180–203.
[28] Curran, 203.

implicit chastening of the imperious self-reflexive poetic imagination. It serves as an instance of how the perpetual Orphic song recognizes that its triumphs can only be provisional, occurring only within the poetic space carved out by the lyrical drama. Such triumphs are made possible by the very literary traditions they hope to supersede. When Demogorgon reminds us at the very end of the work that reversal of liberation is always possible, he reminds us, too, that Shelley's recreation of generic expectations can forever be undone: the joyful symphony of voices in Act 4 can turn back into the tragic note of epic defiance that the play begins with and transmutes.

As Lucy Newlyn has brought out in *Paradise Lost and the Romantic Reader*,[29] the Romantics were able to find in Milton a sponsor for switches of perspective, ambiguities of stance. It is no accident that while writing *Prometheus Unbound* Shelley broke off a number of times to explore in different generic experiments darker implications raised by the work, such as those that surround the overthrow of Jupiter. This overthrow is a combination of Asia's commitment to love and quest and Prometheus's initial act of pity, in conjunction with Demogorgon's ambiguous interventions. However, it is unclear how this overthrow translates into practical political terms. Shelley confronts the issue of action more directly in *The Cenci* in which his heroine, Satanically, refuses to obey Shelleyan principles of 'kindness and forbearance'. Still, as he points out, had Beatrice exercised such ideal virtues 'she would never have been a tragic character' (*Major Works*, 316). The play reanimates the genre of tragedy in order to set going a 'restless and anatomizing casuistry' (*Major Works*, 317) in its audience: our response to the heroine is linked to 'the pernicious casuistry' (*Major Works*, 230) that is brought into our minds when we reflect on Satan. Shelley is always conscious that each genre has its hour, and yet, for all its obedience to the form of tragedy, *The Cenci* resists easy explanation. The very emphasis on the difficulty of naming—'What are the words by which you would have me speak?' (III. i. 107), asks Beatrice after her rape by her father— extends, too, to the play's attitude to the heroine and to our view of the kind of work she inhabits. Is she a tragic figure whose fatal flaw was the determination to take revenge? Or is she a figure who alters or transcends moral judgements? Is Shelley turning tragedy into a new form that urges a transvaluation of moral (and generic) values?

Julian and Maddalo—which is saturated, like *The Cenci*, with echoes of *Prometheus Unbound*—develops dark possibilities lurking in the lyrical drama. At an early stage the narrator Julian compares his and Maddalo's talk with that of the fallen angels in Milton's hell:

> 'twas forlorn
> Yet pleasing, such as once, so poets tell,
> The devils held within the dales of Hell
> Concerning God, freewill, and destiny
> (39–42)

---

[29] Lucy Newlyn, *Paradise Lost and the Romantic Reader* (Oxford: Clarendon Press, 1993). Newlyn's work is relevant to the present book in its interest in 'defining allusion as a focus for indeterminacy', 5.

Shelley alludes gracefully in a spirit of free thought to Milton (who is subsumed within 'poets') and yet even as the next sentence begins a fresh passage of thought, the twisting couplets and their rhymes suggests that telling of Hell, and its endless complications, will be difficult to overcome. In particular, the richly double-sided attitude to the will in *Prometheus Unbound* converts itself in *Julian and Maddalo* into a cure for agonized psychodrama. In *Prometheus Unbound*, the evoking of different genres suggests that something greater is at work than the will of the individual poet. Different poetic achievements are called on as though they were heralds and forerunners of the lyrical drama, itself a gesture towards 'that great Poem', in Shelley's words in *A Defence*, 'which all poets like the co-operating thoughts of one great mind have built up since the beginning of the world' (*Major Works*, 687). In *Julian and Maddalo* we meet less 'the co-operating thoughts of one great mind' than a sharp debate between individuals, one (Julian) who is convinced that 'it is our will / That thus enchains us to permitted will' (171–2), and the other (Maddalo) persuaded that the best poets can do is to 'learn in suffering what they teach in song' (546). Milton inspires renewed and original visions of syncretic synthesis; he also stimulates Shelley's wish to accommodate debate and conflict, as in *Julian and Maddalo*, which teaches the exemplary moral lesson that human beings suffer, and that the reason for such suffering is often unfathomable.

Dreams of a renovated political or imaginative universe run like a crimson thread through the tapestry woven by Romantic dealings with epic. They are associated in Southey with one of his most influential generic modifications of epic, the intermittent lyricization of the form. There are moments of this kind in *Paradise Lost*, in a passage such as the address by Eve to Adam at IV. 639 ('With thee conversing I forget all time'); indeed, Keats sees such lyrical moments in Milton as portending the struggle in his own work between high seriousness and 'poetical Luxury', writing that Milton 'devoted himself rather to the Ardours than the pleasures of Song, solacing himself at intervals with cups of old song'.[30] But such lyrical 'pleasures' subsume themselves within 'Ardours', even as they play against them, in Romantic as well as Miltonic epic. Even if he does not vary his metrical scheme, Milton allows us to 'forget all time', as his figures perform their rhetorical dance to establish Eve's sense of complete 'converse' (meaning 'communion', *OED* 4) with Adam. The passage represents a still point in a turning and turbulent epic, the highpoint of an Edenic happiness that is about to be destroyed.

In *The Curse of Kehama*, the famous curse (II. 143–69) irradiates its terrifying, Medusa-like power. A curse arrests time, enchants it, bends it to its directive will: a form that is picked up by Byron in *Manfred* and Shelley in *Prometheus Unbound*, it serves as a compacted version of the central agon of the entire poem. Lyrics inserted in larger Romantic epic or quasi-epic forms serve less as escapist solace than

---

[30] 'Keats's Marginalia to *Paradise Lost*', quoted from *John Keats*, Oxford Authors, ed. Elizabeth Cook (Oxford: Oxford University Press, 1990), 336. This edition is used for all quotations from Keats's writings in this chapter. Wilkie suggests that Keats's words are 'clearly a projection of his own conflicts', see Brian Wilkie, *Romantic Poets and Epic Tradition* (Madison: University of Wisconsin Press, 1965), 162.

as thematic guide and distillation: in *Prometheus Unbound*, as suggested earlier, Shelley is manifestly intent on rivalling and outpacing Aeschylean drama and Miltonic and Dantean epic, but lyric frequently takes the reader to new depths or heights of apprehension. In Act II, 'Life of Life' (II. v. 48–71) crystallizes the work's intuition of transformation, suspending narrative description in favour of a privileged access to a visionary encounter. The lyric involves a dazzling series of redefinitions that induce a sense of joyously dizzy near-vertigo. A lilting trochaic metre and a nimble-footed syntax marry in an evocation of a presence that resists visualization, 'And all feel, yet see thee never, / As I feel now, lost forever!' (II. v. 64–5). The poem's epic labour of conveying 'beautiful idealisms of moral excellence' (*Major Works*, 232) into the reader's mind, heart, and imagination celebrates itself exultantly. The city that it founds is a community made up of 'the souls of whom thou lovest' (II. v. 68); that is to say, all those who are inspired by the poem.

Shelley's echoes of Milton reclaim as admirable the Satanic traits of pride and unalterable will that in *Paradise Lost* are critiqued: *Prometheus Unbound* internalizes Miltonic struggle. Whereas Satan fights an unwinnable battle against God, Prometheus wars with himself; there is a strong suggestion that the Furies, 'Crawling like agony' (I. 491) within Prometheus, represent his own doubts and inward temptation to despair. But epic agon, however reshaped, passes into a Shelleyan poetry that is impossible to assign a clear generic identity, even as it bears out, in its own heterodox fashion, Wordsworth's 'opinion in respect to epic poetry' as relayed to Southey in 1815:

> Epic poetry, of the highest class, requires in the first place an action eminently influ-ential, an action with a grand or sublime train of consequences; it next requires the intervention and guidance of beings superior to man, what the critics, I believe, call machinery; and lastly, I think with Dennis that no subject but a religious one can answer the demand of the soul in the highest class of this species of poetry.[31]

The main 'action' of *Prometheus Unbound*, the hero's expression of pity for his cruel, tormenting alter ego, Jupiter, and revocation of his former curse, occurs towards the end of the work's initial speech. This is the moment when in traditional epic the poet offers his poem's *initium*, setting out the poem's first action, and wonders about near-tragic trains of causality, as when Milton bids his muse, 'say first what cause / Moved our grand parents in that happy state, / Favoured of heaven so highly, to fall off / From their creator, and transgress his will' (I. 28–31). Shelley adapts the formula to a poem that is rewriting the epic rule-book; Prometheus (with Asia's help) will undertake an enquiry into causes, but only so as to release himself (and humankind) from one inexorable chain of events into an attempt to instigate another, one in which potential for good and the spread of happiness is fulfilled. The 'characters' include mythological figures given new, updated roles (Mercury is recast as the tyrant's sorrowful henchman, Prometheus himself as the

---

[31] *Letters of William Wordsworth: A New Selection*, ed. Alan G. Hill (Oxford: Oxford University Press, 1984), 185.

modern intellectual suffering agonies at the fate of institutional Christianity and political impasse after the seeming failure of the French Revolution). And a thronging choir of spirit voices, lyricizing desires and ideals, compose a 'mechanism' that tilts the poem in the direction of generic innovation.

The poem's subject is 'religious' (in Wordsworth's word) in that it addresses the relations between human beings and godship: both the false gods that belonged to the superseded 'dark and mighty faith' whose ruined memorials the Spirit of the Hour describes in the long speech that concludes Act III, and the new 'divinity in man', as Shelley will call it in *A Defence of Poetry* (*Major Works*, 683), that is celebrated in Act IV. That act's delight in the changed physical universe corresponds to jubilation that it can now define the human and the divine in terms of one another, as when the Earth evokes, 'Man, one harmonious soul of many a soul, / Whose nature is its own divine control' (IV. 400–1): there, the rhyme shows how the collective 'soul' of human kind bears witness to the 'divine' potential of the human by obeying its own self-sustaining, self-monitoring 'control'.

At the end, the lyrical drama may seem to have left behind Miltonic epic. Yet Shelley never completely ascends into an artistic heaven where genres (such as epic) and their histories are near-forgotten specks. When, at the work's close, Demogorgon addresses the dramatis personae, he offers 'spells' (IV. 568) that will permit the re-conquest of tyranny, should it return; in so doing, he reminds the reader that the triumph enacted in the play is a virtual poetic one, that the rapturously inspired cosmic choruses of Act IV may be silenced, giving way to the inflections of epic struggle with which the play began. Gyorgy Lukács argues that 'Any attempt at a properly utopian epic must fail because it is bound, subjectively or objectively, to transcend the empirical and spill over into the lyrical or dramatic; and such overlapping can never be fruitful for the epic'.[32] Shelley writes positively where Lukács reads negatively. In the lyrical drama of *Prometheus Unbound* epic gives way to the 'lyrical' and 'dramatic', even as Shelley never seals the compartments so tightly that generic 'spilling' is unlicensed, or regarded as an aesthetic flaw. Rather, true to his sense that the 'properly utopian' must ground itself in 'the empirical', he encourages dialogue, interplay, even the threat of reversibility. So, epic is a potently temporary absence from the play's close, a close that takes us back to the opening when Demogorgon enjoins future freedom fighters, 'Neither to change, nor falter, nor repent' (IV. 575). The line alludes to Satan's assertion, 'yet not for those, / Nor what the potent victor in his rage / Can else inflict, do I repent or change' (*Paradise Lost*, I. 94–6). The allusion tells us that we may need, we always may need, to wheel back to a start which was itself a redirection of earlier energies. Here, as elsewhere, Shelley readapts for his hero and presents in a provocatively positive light Satanic

---

[32] Gyorgy Lukács, *The Theory of the Novel: A Historic-Philosophical Essay on the Forms of Great Epic Literature*, trans. Anna Bostock ([1915] Cambridge: MIT Press, 1971), 46; quoted in Herbert F. Tucker, *Epic: Britain's Heroic Muse 1790–1910* (Oxford: Oxford University Press, 2008), 216 n. 33 and seen by Tucker as offering 'inadvertent commentary on [Shelley's] generic experiments'.

traits of which Milton officially disapproved. And yet, as Timothy Webb notes, 'Shelley was no Satanist, nor did he delight in overturning orthodoxies simply to hear the sound of broken glass'.[33] Shelley wants his poem and its readers to engage with subversive Miltonic energies, yet to adapt those energies to the humanist ideals of love, freedom, and justice advocated in the lyrical drama.

---

[33] Timothy Webb, *Shelley: A Voice Not Understood* (Manchester: Manchester University Press, 1977), 165.

3

'A Double Face of False and True'
Poetry and Religion in Shelley

1

Meditation on the absence or unknowableness of a transcendental signified abides in Shelley's work. Perhaps only a flamboyantly self-designating atheist would have had the 'Supreme Cause' (*A Defence of Poetry, Major Works*, 691) so much on the brain.[1] If that which is rejected always returns, then it is inevitable as well as slightly odd that someone thrown out of Oxford for refusing to disavow authorship of a pamphlet called *The Necessity of Atheism*, and who signed himself in Greek in the register of the Hotel de Londres, Chamonix, 23 July 1816 as 'a lover of mankind, democrat and atheist',[2] should spend a great deal of his time thinking about God and religion.

Indeed, the early Shelley is prompted to pinpoint the idea of 'a creative Deity' (Note to *Queen Mab*, VII. 13) as a major falsehood. Yet even when his thinking is most bluntly polemical, doubleness haunts his speculations. Of the exclamation 'There is no God!,' he writes in a note: 'This negation must be understood solely to affect a creative Deity. The hypothesis of a pervading Spirit coeternal with the universe, remains unshaken' (*Major Works*, 79). This formulation might have one eye on the orthodox thought-police, allowing the young revolutionary a queasily Deist or Spinozan bolthole. But it also expresses a deep conviction about the need not to have deep convictions when conviction is not present. Shelley does not mind leaving a 'hypothesis' 'unshaken'; he does mind the idea of being forced to believe. Hence he recycles material from *The Necessity of Atheism* to sustain the argument, derived from the empiricist notion that ideas emerge from reorganized sensations, that 'When a proposition is offered to the mind, it perceives the agree-ment or disagreement of the ideas of which it is composed. A perception of their agreement is termed *belief*.' Such a perception, Shelley contends, is 'passive', even if the mind is 'active in the investigation' that precedes the perception. He rejects the idea that 'belief is an act of volition' or that it is right to attach 'a degree of criminality to disbelief' (*Major Works*, 79).

---

[1] All quotations from Shelley's poetry and prose will be taken from *Major Works* in this chapter unless stated otherwise.
[2] See Gavin de Beer, 'An "Atheist" in the Alps', *Keats-Shelley Memorial Bulletin* 9 (1958): 1–15.

This may sound casuistical, or at best a form of logic-chopping designed to wrong-foot bigots and zealots, since Shelley's distinction between final 'belief' and the mind's preliminary work of 'investigation' seems specious. It is at odds with what occurs in his greatest poetry, in which the interplay between activity and passivity, investigation and final outcome is subtle, dynamic, and open to unexpected possibilities. And yet, if one grants the early Shelley his premise, it is evident from his poetry that the supposition of belief's very passivity means that disbelief, if it should operate at the level of the willed, cannot always be sustained. As Robert M. Ryan remarks, 'Observing a kind of Blakean dialectic, Shelley expresses the paradox that atheism allows religious speculation a kind of spontaneity and freedom that would be denied by any formal creed'.[3] Nowhere does this wavering of a premeditated stance show itself more than in the way that the language of the Bible, incessantly reorchestrated, sounds throughout his work. If this language undergoes secularized transformation, it often trails clouds of disconcerting sacredness. In 'Hymn to Intellectual Beauty' (version A), Shelley asserts that Intellectual Beauty 'Gives grace and truth to life's unquiet dream' (36), adapting for his own ends John 1:17, which rejoices that 'grace and truth came by Jesus Christ'. Christ may have given way to the poem's enigmatic 'thou' (14), but the need for 'grace and truth', and for mediating intercession ('Thy light alone' (32)), remains.

The question arises: what if your ideological foe is somehow your imagination's or your heart's ally? Or, phrased differently, can we assume that Shelley's reworking of Christianity always displays a rational, agnostic control over the original? By the time of *A Defence of Poetry* written in 1821, some sixteen months before his death—a death greeted with some ill-concealed gloating by the conservative press (*John Bull* noted that the drowned poet had been seeking to 'coalesce with some others of his own opinions to *write down* Christianity')[4]—Shelley was able to speak of 'religion' at least in terms which seem almost conciliatory: 'Poets', by whom he means 'those who imagine and express [an] indestructible order', include among their number 'teachers, who draw into a certain propinquity with the beautiful and the true that partial apprehension of the agencies of the invisible world which is called religion'. 'Hence', he continues, 'all original religions are allegorical or susceptible of allegory, and like Janus have a double face of false and true' (*A Defence of Poetry*, 677). 'Original religions' is a phrase that implies a Vico-like sense of history obeying cycles, a critique, perhaps, of religion as a supposedly time-transcending

[3] Robert M. Ryan, *The Romantic Reformation: Religious Politics in English Literature, 1789–1824* (Cambridge: Cambridge University Press, 1997), 221. See also Michael Scrivener, *Radical Shelley: The Philosophical Anarchism and Utopian Thought of Percy Bysshe Shelley* (Princeton: Princeton University Press, 1982); David Fuller, 'Shelley and Jesus', *Durham University Journal*, n.s. 54 (1993) 211–23; Bryan Shelley, *Shelley and Scripture: The Interpreting Angel* (Oxford: Clarendon Press, 1994); Martin Priestman, *Romantic Atheism: Poetry and Freethought 1780–1830* (Cambridge: Cambridge University Press, 2000); and Michael O'Neill, 'Cathestant or Protholic?: Shelley's Italian Imaginings', *Journal of Anglo-Italian Studies* 6 (2001): 153–68. Geoffrey Hartman has written perceptively on Shelley's 'atheism' as a refusal to name the unknown power he acknowledges in 'Gods, Ghosts, and Shelley's "Atheos"', *Literature and Theology* 24 (2010): 4–18, 4.

[4] Quoted in Sylva Norman, *Flight of the Skylark: The Development of Shelley's Reputation* (Oklahoma: University of Oklahoma Press; London: Reinhardt, 1954), 16.

body of truths, but also a tribute to 'religions' as a binding together of poetically generated 'apprehensions'. Indeed, Vico's comment that 'the origin of poetry' can be related to the fact that 'the proper subject of poetry is a believable impossibility' resonates with aspects of Shelley's paradoxical view of religion in *A Defence of Poetry*. Vico refers to 'a hidden sense that nations have of God's omnipotence'.[5] Shelley's position is more that poetry answers to, speaks of and from, and itself offers ways of imagining 'the divinity in man' (*A Defence of Poetry*, 698).

In his arresting phrase, 'a double face of false and true', Shelley suggests that what is 'true' about 'all original religions' links with their susceptibility to 'allegory'; that is, to some kind of non-literal mode of understanding, and with their 'partial apprehension of the agencies of the invisible world'. The formulation implies that there is 'an invisible world' with 'agencies' which religion does its best to apprehend, but does so only 'partially'. To grant as much is to concede a great deal, and shows how Shelley's career involves a constantly shifting view of the relationship between poetry and religion. Shelley is a pivotal figure for any reflections on poetry and belief because he emerges as a chief exemplar of that moment when Romanticism explicitly secularizes religion, when poetry discovers and celebrates its onerous, significant role as unmasker of the claims of dogma and metaphorically self-aware hierophant of the poetics of belief. In his work, Shelley poeticizes the nature of belief: belief turns into a crossroads where breakdown and breakthrough double up as one another, crisis and possibility exchange surreptitious glances, metaphor and fact engage in an endless arm-wrestle. Robert Browning thought that 'had Shelley lived he would have finally ranged himself among the Christians'.[6] In doing so, Browning indicates how Shelley lends himself to conservative or orthodox recuperation by those who wish to align the evident spirituality of his work with their own religious quests. If this recuperation can falsify the record of Shelley's intransigent opposition to Christian religion, it responds to the invitation, extended by the poet's work, for the scattered 'Ashes and sparks' ('Ode to the West Wind', 67) of his words to kindle a variety of inspirations in the minds of his readers.

That said, Browning's scenario of a poet ranging himself among his most explicit ideological foes would have difficulty in accommodating the evidence of a late letter (29 June 1822). This is Shelley writing some nine days before his death:

> It seems to me that things have now arrived at such a crisis as requires every man plainly to utter his sentiments on the inefficacy of the existing religions no less than political systems for restraining & guiding mankind. Let us see the truth whatever that may be. The destiny of man can scarcely be so degraded that he was born only to die; and if such should be the case, delusions, especially the gross & preposterous ones of the existing religion, can scarcely be supposed to exalt it. (*Letters: PBS*, 2. 442)

---

[5] Giambattista Vico, *New Science (1744)*, trans. David March (London: Penguin, 1999), 149.

[6] 'An Essay on Shelley' (1852), in *The Oxford Authors: Robert Browning*, ed. Adam Roberts (Oxford: Oxford University Press, 1997), 586. Browning finds Shelley 'everywhere taking for granted some of the more capital dogmas of Christianity, while most vehemently denying their historical basement', 587.

Even here, Shelley's objection to the 'delusions' of 'the existing religion' (presumably that of the Established Church of England) do not seem to come from the usual robustly hopeless quarter from which we learn that Death is 'The anaesthetic from which none come round', as Larkin phrases it with a soured melodiousness in 'Aubade'.[7] Rather, Shelley objects elusively to the notion that human beings were 'born only to die'. Yet the notion that we are born for something better can also seem a delusion. Commenting on Goethe's *Faust* some weeks earlier, he writes that the poem is 'an unfit study for any person who is a prey to the reproaches of memory, and the delusions of an imagination not to be restrained'. Those imaginative 'delusions', not wholly separable from the kinds of longing that lead others to construct transcendental absolutes, are, on reflection, worth entertaining. He goes on:

> Perhaps all discontent with the *less* (to use a Platonic sophism) supposes the sense of a just claim to the *greater*, and that we admirers of Faust are in the right road to Paradise. Such a supposition is not more absurd, and is certainly less demoniacal than that of Wordsworth—where he says
>
> > This earth,
> > Which is the world of all of us, & where
> > *We find our happiness or not at all.*
> > (*Letters: PBS*, 2. 406)

Shelley is misquoting lines excerpted from the *Prelude* in *The Friend* (26 October 1809) and in Wordsworth's 1815 *Poems*, under the title 'The French Revolution, As it appeared to Enthusiasts at its Commencement'. In those lines Wordsworth speaks of 'the very world which is the world / Of all of us, the place in which, in the end, / We find our happiness, or not at all' (*The Prelude*, 1805, X. 725–7).[8] This is strange: you would expect the rhapsodically Utopian poet of *Prometheus Unbound* to welcome such humanist urgency, but Shelley, by 1822, is on the side of those whom nothing will ever satisfy, searching for 'something evermore about to be' (*The Prelude*, 1805, VI, 542): potentially, one might wish to say, a quasi-religious state.

The upshot of Shelley's contemplations, as he surveyed what seemed to him to be the post-Enlightenment wreckage of the Christian system, was the capacity of human beings to create systems that would be wrecked. Echoing Milton's 'On the Morning of Christ's Nativity', his choral lyric in *Hellas* beginning 'Worlds on worlds are rolling ever' (197) laments in its third stanza that 'The Powers of earth and air / Fled from the folding star of Bethlehem' (230–1). On the Olympians 'killing Truth had glared' (234). The echo points up a dissimilarity. Milton, the Christian poet, surprises by elegizing the vanishing of Pagan gods. Shelley, the supposedly anti-Christian poet, identifies Christianity with 'killing Truth'. It may be that he is dramatizing the cultural predispositions of a chorus composed, after all, of 'Greek Captive Women' (*Major Works*, 551) with no love of Islam. And a

---

[7] Quoted from Philip Larkin, *Collected Poems*, ed. and intro. Anthony Thwaite (London: The Marvell Press and Faber, 1988).
[8] Quoted from *Wordsworth: The Major Works*.

note invites us to see the Chorus's view of religions as historically relativized: 'The popular notions of Christianity are represented in this chorus as true in their relation to the worship they superseded, and that which in all probability, they will supersede, without considering their merits in a relation more universal' (*Major Works*, 584).

Yet, as this note partly leads us to discover, the inflections of the lyric are antiphonal and complex. The chorus hails the triumph of Christianity over Islam—'The cross leads generations on' (224) while 'The moon of Mahomet / Arose, and it shall set' (221–2)—even as it is saddened by the vanishing of 'the golden years' (238); namely, the era associated with Hellenic myth. The lyric differs from the prose gloss of the note in that it cannot wholly sustain an intricately progressivist position. Its movement, as often in *Hellas*, begins as though seeking to trace a meliorist, even Utopian trajectory, but ends with a falling away from such a progressive construction of history. But the lyric's reference to Christ as 'A power from the unknown God' (211) brings into the reader's mind the possibility of an absolute ('the unknown God') removed from the endless coming and going of 'New gods' (208) mentioned in the chorus's first stanza. At the same time, such is the suggestive instability of the writing that the 'unknown God' may stand less for some ultimate reality than for human beings' persistent need to believe in such a reality. As Bryan Shelley has shown, *Hellas* swerves away from Christianity in the act of approaching it. It evokes as one of its analogues, not only Aeschylus' *The Persians* but also the Book of Daniel, yet the poem's differences from biblical apocalypse are real. In particular, '*Hellas* presents no overruling God superintending the revolutionary process'.[9]

Christianity and Shelleyan thought in *Hellas* run in swift, uneasy parallel lines. Ahasuerus, as Bryan Shelley notes, echoes the New Testament when he instructs the anxiety-ridden and power-shedding Mahmud: 'Wouldst thou behold the future?—ask and have! / Knock and it shall be opened' (803–4). For Bryan Shelley, the echo of Matthew 7:7 points up a sharp difference between Jesus characterizing 'the relationship between earthly man and his heavenly Father' and Ahasuerus who would 'obliterate the distinctions between temporal and eternal, past and present'.[10] But the fact that Shelley turns to such biblical language illustrates how profoundly such language presents itself to him as a medium for conveying the possibility of consciousness-altering apprehensions. At the poem's close the chorus imagines another turn of the cycle when 'Saturn and Love their long repose / Shall burst, more bright and good / Than all who fell, than One who rose, / Than many unsubdued' (1090–3). Shelley's note on the lines spells out his hostility to deities worshipped by various post-Saturnian creeds and cults, Christianity among them. Yet if the note serves to shock the orthodox, especially in its uncensored form in which the poet refers to the deity of Christianity as 'a Demon, who tempted, betrayed and punished the innocent beings who were called into existence by his sole will', the praise of 'the sublime human character of Jesus Christ' (587) bespeaks a need on Shelley's part to re-define Christianity in humanist terms.

---

[9] Bryan Shelley, *Shelley and Scripture*, 160.
[10] Bryan Shelley, *Shelley and Scripture*, 160, 161.

Praising the greatest Protestant and Catholic epics, Shelley wishes a plague upon their sectarian houses, but offers hosannas for their quality of poetic imagination:

> The *Divina Commedia* and *Paradise Lost* have conferred upon modern mythology a systematic form; and when change and time shall have added one more superstition to the mass of those which have arisen and decayed upon the earth, commentators will be learnedly employed in elucidating the religion of ancestral Europe, only not utterly forgotten because it will have been stamped with the eternity of genius.
>
> (*A Defence of Poetry*, 692)

This passage was reworked in *A Defence of Poetry* from an earlier prose work, *On the Devil, and Devils*, which is even more intransigent in its opposition to 'the popular creed'. If for Matthew Arnold, poetry was destined to replace religion, for Shelley, religion is always a form, albeit a distorted form, of poetry. Poetry, for the Shelley of *A Defence of Poetry*, does not usurp religion; it is what religion always was, a mode of imagining. And it is no small part of Milton's and Dante's achievement to bring this fact, however unconsciously on their part, to the fore: '[Dante's] apotheosis of Beatrice in Paradise, and the gradations of his own love and her loveliness, by which as by steps he feigns himself to have ascended to the throne of the Supreme Cause, is the most glorious imagination of modern poetry' (690–1). 'As by steps he feigns himself': in this passage, discussed in the first chapter in relation to Shelley's dealings with Plato, what lends energizing tension to the Romantic poet's understanding of religion is a dual sense that we can see at work. Feigning is what we do to understand; we cannot know save through 'the human mind's imaginings' ('Mont Blanc', 143). Yet this fact does not mean that reality is the sum of those imaginings by which we seek access to it.

2

It is tempting but over-simplifying to see Shelley as a child of Enlightenment thought, scoffing at the superstitious follies of religion. Here is the poet in 1817, hitting his rationalist, shrewdly evocative stride in *Laon and Cythna*, as Cythna asks:

> What then is God? Some moon-struck sophist stood
> Watching the shade from his own soul upthrown
> Fill Heaven and darken Earth, and in such mood
> The Form he saw and worshipped was his own,
> His likeness in the world's vast mirror shown;
> And 'twere an innocent dream, but that a faith
> Nursed by fear's dew of poison, grows thereon,
> And that men say, God has appointed Death
> On all who scorn his will, to wreak immortal wrath.
> (*CPPBS* 3. *Laon and Cythna* VIII: 6. 46–54)[11]

---

[11] All quotations from *Laon and Cythna; or the Revolution of the Golden City: A Vision of the Nineteenth Century in the Stanza of Spenser*, are taken from *CPPBS* 3.

Cythna's Enlightenment instruction uses the sinuous rhymes and rhythms of the Spenserian stanza to convey ideas that entwine an Enlightenment critique of superstition with Romanticism's own form of deconstruction. Such deconstruction involves an undeceived awareness of the role played by imaginative projection in all human constructions of meaning, an awareness found, for example, in Coleridge's 'Dejection: An Ode' ('we receive but what we give', 47).[12] Volney, too, in *The Ruins of Empire* is one of a number of Enlightenment sceptics (others are Holbach, Condorcet, and, closer to home, Paine) who would have influenced Cythna's sceptically nominalist perspective. Volney writes of primitive man that, 'substituting a phantastical world to [sic] the real one, he peopled it with imaginary beings, to the terror of his mind and the torment of his race'.[13] From this perspective, 'God' is just a word, corresponding to no objective reality; it names something to which 'moon-struck' mortals give meaning, solipsistically making the world a 'vast mirror' reflecting only their projected 'likeness'. This 'likeness' forgets its origin and nature, mistakenly supposing that the 'Form' it assumes has an independent reality.

Richard Dawkins might applaud such resolute agnosticism. Yet where do our best hopes derive? God might be an 'innocent dream', we notice, were it not for the uses to which He can be put. Later in the poem, Cythna, anticipating the imagery and argument of 'Ode to the West Wind', speaks of the way in which hope is sustained: 'In their own hearts the earnest of the hope / Which made them great, the good will ever find' (9. 27. 3703–4). Hope, the sense that the world can be bettered, seems to grow in the same place, 'their own hearts', as God, the product of the distorting aspirations projected by 'his own soul'. The stanza goes on to assert the ever-present functioning of Necessity, which will ensure that any 'envious shade' (3706) that comes between the 'effect' (3705) of such an 'earnest' and itself will be rendered null and void. Necessity allows Shelley to believe that 'Evil with evil, good with good must wind / In bands of union' (3709–10).

This trust in the adamantine chain of causal links caused by human 'good' (and 'evil') accompanies tenaciously, while bearing a flicker of contradictoriness mockery, the Christian idea that 'the cause of life could think and live' (VIII. 5. 3237), which is rejected as illicit anthropomorphism in such works as *A Refutation of Deism* (1813). In this early work, which stages a dialogue between an orthodox believer, Eusebes, and a deist, Theosophus, Shelley adeptly undercuts rational arguments in favour of Christianity, leaving the outcome to be a choice between blind faith and atheism. And yet among the arguments that are used to discredit belief in God is one that threatens to boomerang against Shelley's own atheism: it is the contention that because we cannot, following Hume, have knowledge of 'causation', 'it would be inadmissible to deduce the being of a God from the existence of the Universe'. Shelley adds, and here he is speaking his own view, that

---

[12] Quoted from *CPP.* Unless stated otherwise, this edition is used for all quotations from Coleridge's work; page numbers are supplied parenthetically for quotations from the prose.

[13] Kenneth Neill Cameron, 'A Major Source of *The Revolt of Islam*', *PMLA* 56 (1941): 175–206 (Volney quotation is from 194).

'If Power be an attribute of existing substance, substance could not have derived its origin from power'.[14] But in 1817, Shelley would publish 'Hymn to Intellectual Beauty', in which he hails 'The awful shadow of some unseen Power' (1). The same year, he published 'Mont Blanc', at the close of which (version A) he asserts that 'the power is there, / The still and solemn power of many sights' (127–8). The addition of the definite article makes it hard to avoid the view that this 'power' is the attribute of 'being', and not necessarily a 'being' bestowed by human projection, even though the 'human mind's imaginings' make possible its suppositious existence.

We require almost a new term for Shelley's fluidity of attitude: believing unbelief, or unbelieving belief. Much critical writing on Shelley's religion tries to claim the poet for a hard-headed rational scepticism, which is often only almost true, as the critic, albeit reluctantly, will admit. An example is Kenneth Neill Cameron who asserts in successive paragraphs about the 'Hymn to Intellectual Beauty' that 'The experience in the poem is neither mystical nor Platonic', but that 'the language of the poem conveys a sense of hope and feeling beyond scepticism, as do some prose passages in the *Essay on Christianity* and "A Defence of Poetry"'. This, Cameron explains, is because 'in impassioned creative writing, the emotions tend to take over and to force the writer's language beyond what he may rationally believe'.[15] Such an assertion is radically misleading about the function of poetic language, which is heuristic and exploratory in a way that Cameron ignores.

Shelley can express views that anticipate an 'as if' outlook. So, in the Conclusion to *The Sensitive Plant*, he rounds out his parable of beauty destroyed, fairy tale turned into Gothic nightmare, with the wryly and yet triumphantly consoling reflection that in this life

> Of error, ignorance, and strife,
> Where nothing is, but all things seem,
> And we the shadows of the dream,
>
> It is a modest creed, and yet
> Pleasant if one considers it,
> To own that death itself must be,
> Like all the rest, a mockery.
>
> (9–16)

If Shelley mocks himself as he mockingly discovers meaning in the fact or supposition that all is mockery, his language contrives to remain yieldingly open to the solicitations of desire: 'the shadows of the dream' give a sudden, intensified ontological stability to *the* dream, with an underlying hint that there is an awakened state beyond it.[16]

---

[14] *Prose* I, 121.

[15] Kenneth Neill Cameron, *Shelley: The Golden Years* (Cambridge: Harvard University Press, 1974), 242, 243.

[16] See my chapter on the poem in my *Romanticism and the Self-Conscious Poem* (Oxford: Clarendon, 1997).

This Shelley is engaged in what Zygmunt Bauman refers to as 'the "re-enchantment" of the world after the protracted and earnest, though in the end inconclusive modern struggle to dis-enchant it'.[17] But it is a desperate gamble at the same time, albeit a gamble that differs in its *modus operandi* from the act of self-consciously and self-protectively offering always and only 'fictions'. Instead, Shelley occupies an imagined state, seeing what emerges in the process of writing: he was conscious that such stanzaic unfurling might provide, in Keats's phrase, 'a regular stepping of the Imagination towards a Truth': perhaps the only 'Truth' available to both poets.[18]

One idea or desperate hope that Shelley could never relinquish finds expression in a number of places. It is the idea expressed in some fragmentary stanzas ('Frail clouds arrayed in sunlight lose their glory') that were 'apparently intended to serve as a meditative opening to *Laon and Cythna*'. Here is the third and crucial stanza:

> There is a Power whose passive instrument
> Our nature is—a Spirit that with motion
> Invisible and swift its breath hath sent
> Amongst us, like the wind on the wide Ocean—
> Around whose path the tumult and commotion
> Throng fast—deep calm doth follow, and precedeth.
> This Spirit, chained by some remote devotion,
> Our choice or will demanded not nor heedeth
> But for its hymns doth touch the human souls it needeth.
>
> (19–27)[19]

Wasserman writes of the 'quasi-theological myth' developed in the passage,[20] and from the opening assertion, 'There is a Power', the writing gleams with an unanswerable authority. This is more than a naming; it is also a conjuration. Through the fleet, hushed, controlled movement of the verse, there is the sense of an assured intuition that is too subtle for rational disquisition and too self-aware to be dismissed as homespun religious enthusiasm. Shelley is affected by the thought that we are the 'passive instrument' of 'some Power', that human souls are the trumpet of a prophecy that originates beyond them. This Power or Spirit sounds like a cross between a revelation of Godhead and a muse; it can be secularized, humanized, but it articulates a sensed connection between poetic inspiration and what is difficult not to term religious experience. In 'Frails clouds arrayed in sunlight like the glory', there is a rich, syntactical ambiguity in Shelley's assertion that the Spirit is 'chained by some remote devotion': the chaining devotion is the Spirit's to us or ours to it.

In 'Ode to the West Wind', Shelley both celebrates and confronts the Spirit, and reconsiders the question of reciprocal influence. The poem tries to net the Spirit through metaphors, continually raiding the religious word-hoard: 'hear, O, hear!' (14) concludes the first of the couplets transforming each section's *terza rima* into

---

[17] Quoted by Arthur Bradley in '"Until Death Tramples It to Fragments": Percy Bysshe Shelley after Postmodern Theology' in *Romanticism and Religion: From William Cowper to Wallace Stevens*, ed. Gavin Hopps and Jane Stabler (Aldershot: Ashgate, 2006), 191.

[18] *Letters: John Keats* I, 218.   [19] Comment and poem are quoted from *Longman* 2, 3.

[20] Wasserman, *Shelley: A Critical Reading*, 188.

a sonnet and echoing Psalmic modes of entreaty (see Psalm 61: 1, for example). The couplet acts as a stay against the onward momentum of the wind, the holy spirit turned into uncanny others. The 'breath of Autumn's being' (1), and an 'unseen presence' (2), it reminds the reader of different theologies and theodicies when named as simultaneously 'Destroyer and Preserver' (14), Siva as well as Vishnu.[21] Beyond that, the wind manifests itself as an Orphic storm that not only threatens corrupt regimes but recalls through its operations in the upper air 'the bright hair uplifted from the head / Of some fierce Maenad' (20–1), bringing to mind the legendary followers and ecstatic slayers of the archetypal poet.[22]

Shelley does what Eliot does in 'What the Thunder said', the fifth and final section of *The Waste Land*: he enters his own phantasmagoria, in which religious and mythic images swim into his mind rather as they will do in Rimbaud's prose poem from 'A Season in Hell': 'Jesus walked on the troubled waters. The lantern showed us him standing, in white and with brown tresses, on the flank of an emerald wave [...]'.[23] There is a kinship between this visionary blurring and collapsing of gospel and reverie, between the rehearsed proto-Christological humiliation of 'I fall upon the thorns of life! I bleed!' ('Ode to the West Wind', 54), and Eliot's 'agony in stony places / The shouting and the crying' (*The Waste Land*, 324–5).[24] Rimbaud, for his part, makes explicit the freedom to engage in hallucinatory recollection of Christianity and other religions when he asserts, with calculated bravado, 'I am about to unveil all mysteries: mysteries religious or natural, death, birth, future, past, the cosmogony, the void. I am a master of phantasmagoria'.[25] All three poets arrive at the recognition, and feel on the pulses of their poetry the fact that the poet is a seer, privileged and condemned, in his person, to reinvent the world's myths. Through the notion of agency involved in his active verbs, Shelley forestalls the idea that he is in some histrionic, self-deceiving way sealed off from suffering, as Michael Hofmann obliquely suggests in his allusion to this moment from the Ode in a review essay on Lauren Groff's *Florida*. Hofmann writes that Groff's obsession with fear ends up as 'the sort of delirium of loss—withdrawal of safety net, abandonment, insecurity, weekend survivalism, "I fall upon the thorns of life! I bleed!"—that feels like nothing so much as a perverse reassertion of ownership and invulnerability'.[26] Groff may be guilty of 'weekend survivalism'; Shelley is still able to write a poetry where what survives is both poetry as an event in itself, a way of happening, and the cultural burdens that have accrued to it in the wake of religious

---

[21] See Stuart Curran, *Shelley's Annus Mirabilis: The Maturing of an Epic Vision* (San Marino: Huntington Library, 1975), 163. Curran notes that in this pairing, as in the absence (at the poem's start) of Christ, 'what is missing – and indeed demanded by the poet – is the creative power of Brahma and of Christ', 165.

[22] See James Rieger, *The Mutiny Within: The Heresies of Percy Bysshe Shelley* (London: George Braziller, 1967), 180, where he writes in relation to this allusion: 'If mourner and murderess are identical, so are priest and victim'.

[23] Arthur Rimbaud, *A Season in Hell and Other Poems*, trans. Norman Cameron (London: Anvil, 1994), 155.

[24] T. S. Eliot, *The Complete Poems and Plays* (London: Faber, 1969).

[25] Rimbaud, *A Season in Hell*, 155.

[26] Michael Hofmann, 'The State with the Prettiest Name', *London Review of Books* 40: 10 (24 May 2018): 33–4 (at 34).

crisis and the indefeasible hope that art will sustain awareness of significance, including the possibly tragic inability of a poet to be the means through which such art persists. All this in a line which 'owns' the poet's pain, certainly, but which makes clear that any healing of the wound cannot depend on a pre-emptive or lazy assumption of 'invulnerability'. The emergence from abasement into pained authority will drive the poet's figurations throughout the superb final section.

Shelley in 'Ode to the West Wind' negotiates with belief systems; the poem contrives to be, in Harold Bloom's terms, 'Jobean' in its quality of struggle and deeply humanist in its 'affirmation of images and image-making power'.[27] Bloom's conjunction of suggestions is helpful, and yet the poetry's re-engagement with Christ's crucifixion, in 'I fall upon the thorns of life! I bleed!', is remarkable for its momentary but decisive destruction of cordoned-off categories such as 'religious' and 'humanist'. 'Ode to the West Wind' moves recklessly, dangerously and exhilaratingly, between personal confession, mythologizing, and constructing something upon which to rejoice. Shelley clings to prayer, even as his conviction of his powers undergoes a transitional crisis, and his prayer is, ultimately, to a force both within and without: 'Make me thy lyre, even as the forest is' (57), the last stanza begins, sounding the first notes of its post-Passion recovery. The poet, who had been striving, Jacob-like, in the previous section with the 'unseen presence' of the Wind, gradually offers us a present-tense re-enactment of such strife, as he bends the Power to his own will: 'Be through my lips to unawakened earth / The trumpet of a prophecy!' (68–9). The relations between poet and wind are endlessly locked in intimate and mutually inspiring struggle. In James Chandler's memorably riddling words, 'The Wind makes Shelley make the Wind make Shelley make the Wind and so on'.[28] The poem can be read in more or less secular terms, as involving the translation of motifs drawn from religion into a new and post-religious idiom. But it is best read as destabilizing the difference between the sacred and the secular, the religious and the non-religious. Above all, the Ode re-enacts, in its very form and onward rushing quasi-Pentecostal movement, the poet's identification of some ultimate power with his own recovery of inspiration.

3

Shelley's religious prose, prose which has as its main theme the ultimate spiritual destiny of human beings, reveals a double rhythm. Often its finest moments involve a turn, or a redefinition, a mobile life in the process of writing that is equivalent to that 'living by ideas' which Arnold praises in 'That return of Burke upon himself' in Burke's *Thoughts on French Affairs*.[29] Examples occur in *On Christianity* (1817), a work that is at once critical of 'the gross imaginations of the vulgar relatively to

    [27] Bloom, *Shelley's Mythmaking*, 84.
    [28] 'History's Lyre: The "West Wind" and the Poet's Work', quoted from *Norton*, 721.
    [29] Matthew Arnold, 'The Function of Criticism at the Present Time', in *Matthew Arnold*, The Oxford Authors, ed. Miriam Allott and Robert H. Super (Oxford: Oxford University Press, 1986), 324.

the ruling Power of the universe' and surprisingly, if one thinks of Shelley as authoring *The Necessity of Atheism* (1811), interested in trying to define 'God' as 'the interfused and overruling Spirit of all the energy and wisdom included within the circle of existing things'.[30] That 'acceptation' of the term keeps in play various possibilities:[31] 'the circle of existing things' sounds a materialist note, while 'interfused and overruling Spirit' balances the pantheist and spiritual. Other definitions in the work swing between the humanist and the quasi-transcendental, before a perilous harmony emerges. The humanist perspective shines through the comment that the person who 'only aspires to that which the divinity of his own nature shall consider and approve…he, has already seen God'.[32] This emphasis, with its reworking of traditional usages, immediately passes into shifts and reconsiderations: 'We live and move and think, but we are not the creators of our own origin and existence… There is a Power by which we are surrounded, like the atmosphere in which some motionless lyre is sustained, which visits with its breath our silent chords at will'.[33] Beginning with a complex echo of Acts 17:28 that acknowledges dependence on a higher power, even if that power may be internal, it seems no accident that this different sense of God (Shelley will go on to say 'This power is God') is inextricable from an account of poetic inspiration.[34] Later Shelley will shift into a more conceptual mode, as he brings humanity and God into alignment, asserting that 'The perfection of the human and the divine character is thus asserted to be the same', though at this stage he is paraphrasing his sense of Jesus's teaching.[35] In offering an account of Christ's teaching, the essay gives itself room to explore Shelley's own thinking, while allowing for a gap between the two. And not just Shelley's thinking, since thought here is deeply entangled with hope and desire:

> We die, says Jesus Christ; and, when we awaken from the languor of disease, the glories and the happiness of Paradise are around us. All evil and pain have ceased for ever… Our happiness also corresponds with and is adapted to, the nature of… what is most excellent in our being. We see God, and we see that he is good. How delightful a picture even if it be not true! How magnificent and illustrious is the conception which this bold theory suggests to the contemplation, even if it be no more than the imagination of some sublimest and most holy poet, who, impressed with the loveliness and majesty of his own nature, is impatient, discontented, with the narrow limits which this imperfect life, and the dark grave have assigned forever as his melancholy portion.[36]

The passage plays the delights of hope against a sober sense of likely reality in the exclamatory 'How delightful a picture even if it be not true!' A doubleness and subtlety of feeling course through phrases such as 'no more than the imagination of some sublimest and most holy poet', and beneath sadness at the sway exercised by the reality principle is a final twist that suggests that the matter is seen as it is because

---

[30] Qtd from *Prose Works of Shelley*, ed. Murray, 250.   [31] *Prose Works of Shelley*, 249.
[32] *Prose Works of Shelley*, 251.   [33] *Prose Works of Shelley*, 251.
[34] *Prose Works of Shelley*, 252.   [35] *Prose Works of Shelley*, 259.
[36] *Prose Works of Shelley*, 256.

of 'narrow limits'. The reader is pulled between melancholy and a recognition of the value of the 'imagination of some sublimest and most holy poet'. The final effect, that is, of 'the narrow limits which this imperfect life, and the dark grave have assigned forever as his melancholy portion' is as much protesting rejection as acquiescence. Gavin Hopps is persuasive when he argues that 'What we can see here, then, is the poet yearning in spite of himself for something he can't quite allow himself to believe in, which in turn won't allow his disbelief sovereignty either'.[37] If the writing bears witness to a residually conflicted aspect to Shelley's view of Christianity, it makes for prose that engages us in ways that theological and philosophical argument often fails to do. The text is knowingly scored through with longing and struggle.

Shelley might seem to smuggle back into his discourse a wish to honour what Wallace Stevens calls, albeit in a poem denying transcendental aspirations, 'the voice that is great within us'.[38] Yet the Romantic prose poet can pitilessly dissect the workings of desire, as at the close of *A Future State* (1818) where the possibility of life after death is examined by a side of Shelley he must at least in part overcome in writing *Adonais*:

> This desire to be forever as we are, this reluctance to a violent and unexperienced change, which is common to all the animate and inanimate combinations of the universe, is indeed the secret persuasion which has given birth to the opinion of a future state.
>
> (*BSM* XV: 132–3)

It is because of 'the desire to be forever as we are' that we entertain the idea of what we cannot know; it is because of dislike of a 'violent and unexperienced change' that we play Pascalian wagers in the hope of experiencing what is unimaginable when confronted by what our senses tell us. The rough draft has more material after this, all of which is crossed out, as though Shelley realized that further investigation would destroy the 'rondo', to borrow Coleridge's word,[39] of an essay which opens, 'It has been the persuasion of an immense majority of human beings in all ages and nations that we continue to live after death—that apparent termination of all the functions of sensitive and intellectual existence'.[40] Yet the word 'apparent', which ushers in 'all the functions' as an annulling antithesis to 'all ages and nations', undermines scepticism as much as it critiques credulity. A view is put forth which is at once unanswerable and finally inadequate, so that the topic feels unexhausted, ready to be reapproached.

Shelley could not be more explicit about his wish to 'bring the question to the test of experience and fact' or to establish clearly what we understand 'By the word death'.[41] But this practice of careful examination wars with sudden eruptions of latent feeling: 'When you can discover where the fresh colours of the faded flower

---

[37] Gavin Hopps, 'Religion and Ethics', in *The Oxford Handbook of Percy Bysshe Shelley*, 129.

[38] 'Evening without Angels', in *Wallace Stevens: Collected Poetry and Prose*, sel. with notes, ed. Frank Kermode and Joan Richardson (New York: Library of America, 1997).

[39] *Coleridge's Poetry and Prose*, ed. Nicholas Halmi, Paul Magnuson, and Raimonda Modiano (New York: Norton, 2004), 122–3.

[40] *A Future State*, 156–7 (rev.).   [41] *A Future State*, 152–3 (rev.), 148–9 (rev.).

abide, or the music of the broken lyre, seek life among the dead.'[42] The sentence behaves as though it were describing an absurdity, but it rehearses one of the functions of literary imagination, its drive to relocate 'The light that never was, on sea or land', as Wordsworth calls it in 'Elegiac Stanzas, Suggested by a Picture of Peele Castle'.[43]

4

It would be hard to hear any traces of the Hound of Heaven gambolling down the byways of the *terza rima* of *The Triumph of Life*. Yet the poem has a powerful sense of life as a place where and state in which ideals are brutally conquered, and energies are cruelly consumed, and of the imagination, deluded or otherwise, as exercising itself most compellingly in the presence of questions and enigmas: 'Show whence I came, and where I am, and why— / Pass not away upon the passing dream' (398–9), cries Shelley's double, confrère, and familiar compound ghost, the root-resembling Rousseau—nature's Savoyardian vicar, down on his uppers, sounding for all the world like his creator as he undergoes some kind of shattering experience in the presence of a 'shape all light' (352) who is at once emblem of transformation and a purveyor of disenchantment.[44] As so often in Shelley, Milton lurks behind the text as a complex prompter. So Rousseau's questions to the shape echo an Adamic state of disorientation when he wakes to self-consciousness: 'My self I then perused', 'But who I was, or where, or from what cause, / Knew not' (*Paradise Lost*, VIII. 267, 270–1).[45] He then undergoes a dream in which he meets 'Presence divine' (314) that says to him, 'Whom thou sought'st I am, / ... author of all this thou seest' (316–17): a sublime response that is intransitively echoic of the God who asserts 'I AM THAT I AM' (Exodus 3:14).[46] Rousseau and, indeed, Shelley have no dream from which they awaken to visions of truth. Rather, their state is permanently to know the despair which temporarily afflicts Adam when in a further waking dream he imagines and loses an embodiment of Eve: 'She disappeared, and left me dark, I waked / To find her, or for ever to deplore / Her loss, and other pleasures all abjure' (VIII. 478–80). He does find Eve, but briefly figured there is a scenario which recurs in the Romantic poet's work: 'She disappeared, and left me dark'. And yet if the imagination deceives, it can create.

---

[42] *A Future State*, 144–7 (rev.).   [43] *WW*, 15.

[44] Relevant to Rousseau's experience is Hartman's account of Shelley's aspiration (in 'Mont Blanc') 'to express a metareferential presence, a transcendental signified, the obscure object of desire', where the fluid contiguity of the appositional phrasing is itself highly expressive of the indeterminacy yet tenacity of the Shelleyan pursuit: see Hartman's 'God, Ghosts, and Shelley's "Atheos"', 13.

[45] Quoted from *The Poems of John Milton*. In *Shelley and the Chaos of History* (University Park: Pennsylvania State University Press, 1997), Hugh Roberts suggests an allusion to Eve's dream in Book IV, 449–65, in which Eve wonders 'where / And what I was, whence thither brought, and how' (451–2): see 212–13.

[46] Echo pointed out in *The Poems of John Milton*, 831n.

Rousseau is taken into a state which might be glossed as 'unknowing'. The writing switches into the third person, as the mental or psychic transformation he undergoes in the shape's presence takes us into a labyrinth of 'as ifs' and similes:

> And still her feet, no less than the sweet tune
> To which they moved, seemed as they moved, to blot
> The thoughts of him who gazed on them, and soon
>
> All that was seemed as if had been not,
> As if the gazer's mind was strewn beneath
> Her feet like embers, and she, thought by thought,
>
> Trampled its fires into the dust of death,
> As Day upon the threshold of the east
> Treads out the lamps of night, until the breath
>
> Of darkness re-illumines even the least
> Of heaven's living eyes—like day she came,
> Making the night a dream [...]
>
> (382–93)

The passage, at the heart of this book's understanding of Shelley, will be encountered again in later chapters. Rousseau experiences the very passivity that Shelley associates with belief, only here neither seeming nor reality, believing or disbelieving, seem somehow to matter; what does matter is the evocation of a state akin to mystical annihilation that is wrought by what might be, probably is, but possibly is not, a delusion. If day extinguishes some higher power of intuition or vision, there is always the hope that 'the breath / Of darkness' will renew inspiration, allow access to some different mode of seeing. Momentarily snuffed out as it is awakened here, this hope is poignantly reanimated when the shape—figured as day extinguishing night—soon becomes like a star extinguished by the day (see lines 412–15), glimmering, like so many hopes in Shelley, 'forever sought, forever lost' (431). The poem's Dantean parallels similarly shimmer, glimmer, and grow dimmer throughout the poem, ultimately indicating roads not taken or takeable, baffling the would-be finder of a system; but they, too, stay in the poem's subconscious as wandering cultural ghosts, straying in and out of a Christian belief-system that is never wholly abandoned or forgotten.

All that Shelley has to follow is the winding path of poetry itself: he is sure, in the words of Les Murray's poem 'Poetry and Religion', that 'Religions are poems' and that the 'only whole thinking' is 'poetry'; and sure, too, that 'Nothing's said till it's dreamed out in words / and nothing's true that figures in words only'. One imagines that Shelley would be more doubtful than Murray is whether 'poetry', let alone 'God', can be 'caught in any religion'.[47] Through its awareness that 'nothing's true that figures in words only', however, Shelley's poetry at its most compelling holds open a fine-spun hope that it seems right to call poetic and religious. Murray swithers between 'figures' as meaning 'making sense' and as 'serving as a figure for

---

[47] Quoted from Les Murray, *Collected Poems* (Manchester: Carcanet, 1991).

some prior reality', and Shelley anticipates him here, since his poetry never wholly disallows the possibility that 'the realm without a name' (*The Triumph of Life*, 396) is itself a potentially numinous space. *The Triumph of Life* tempts its reader to think that one day, in another poem, when 'Figures ever new / Rise on the bubble' (248–9) once more, poetry will or might or should embody its own 'apprehension', albeit 'partial', of 'the agencies of the invisible world'.

4

Shelley, Lamb, Hazlitt, and the Revolutionary Imagination

1

The relations between Shelley and two Romantic-period essayists, Charles Lamb and William Hazlitt are fascinating and still under-investigated. Surely it has to be conceded that Lamb's letter on Shelley's death shows an unrelenting dislike of Shelley. Or does it? Lucas says that 'Lamb's prejudiced attitude to Shelley was extreme, and his comment on Shelley's death in the letter to Barton of 9 October 1822 shows him, I think, in perhaps his least admirable moment'.[1] Yet Lamb thrives on being 'prejudiced', where that word means having the right to bring to bear on a situation a settled body of deeply held feeling, and since there is always some instinct in him half-wanting us to see him in less than a wholly 'admirable' light ('Confessions of a Drunkard' is only the most startling example), let us examine this letter in which Lamb is responding to Bernard Barton's 'Verses on the Death of P. B. Shelley'. The letter turns out to be rather more complicated than Lucas allows, and to have a plague on both houses aspect to it. 'I do not think', Lamb says of Barton's poem, that 'it will convert the club at Pisa, neither do I think it will satisfy the bigots on our side the water. Something like a parody on the song of Ariel would please them better:

> Full fathom five the Atheist lies,
> Of his bones are hell-dice made.—

I want time, or fancy, to fill up the rest'.[2] This, of course, is whimsy with a vengeance, and Lamb might be relishing the mockery. His 1799 poem, 'Living without God in the World', a reference to Joseph Priestley's criticism of the 'nominal believer', as David Chandler points out, distinguishes two kinds of people who dwell in an Atheistical or Deistical state.[3] The first group is defined thus: 'Some braver spirits of the modern stamp / Affect a Godhead nearer: these talk loud / Of mind and independent intellect, / Of energies omnipotent in man, / And man of his own fate

[1] Edward Verrall Lucas, *The Life of Charles Lamb*, 2 vols (London: Methuen, 1921), I, 488.

[2] *The Letters of Charles and Mary Anne Lamb*, ed. Edwin W. Marrs, 3 vols (Ithaca: Cornell University Press, 1975-8), 2, 338.

[3] Poem is quoted from *Romanticism: An Anthology*, 3rd edn ed. Duncan Wu (Malden: Blackwell, 2006); see the footnote on 740 for the reference to David Chandler, 'A Study of Lamb's "Living without God in the World"', *Charles Lamb Bulletin* n.s. 99 (July 1997): 86–101.

artificer' (23–7). This group must surely include Godwin, and it seems probable that Lamb would have put Shelley into this group as well. The second group is comprised of those who 'By word or deed deny a God': 'They eat / Their daily bread, and draw the breath of heaven, / Without or thought or thanks' (39–41), rather like those whom Shelley, in the Preface to *Alastor*, calls 'the morally dead', who are, as Shelley puts it with a sense of what should be said for his poetic alter ego, 'deluded by no generous error, instigated by no sacred thirst of doubtful knowledge, duped by no illustrious superstition'.[4]

That impulse of sympathy towards 'generous error', 'doubtful knowledge', and 'illustrious superstition' should have awakened Lamb's interest did he ever read it, but, according to Thomas Noon Talfourd, Lamb's early editor and biographer:

> Shelley's poetry [. . .] was icy cold to him; except one or two of the minor poems, in which he could not help admiring the exquisite beauty of the expression, and the 'Cenci', in which, notwithstanding the painful nature of the subject, there is a warmth and passion, and a correspondent simplicity of diction, which prove how mighty a poet the author would have become had he lived long enough for his feelings to have free discourse with his creative power.[5]

Talfourd records a response that is familiar in Mary Shelley's notes to the poems, published in 1839 after Lamb's death, but possibly discussed between the two of them. *The Cenci* is a work which may owe a considerable amount to Lamb's *Specimens of English Dramatic Poets*; one wonders, for example, whether Shelley's interest in the restless and self-anatomizing casuistry with which we respond to Beatrice draws its inspiration from Lamb's comment on Vittoria's 'innocence-resembling boldness' in *The White Devil*.[6] 'If you be my accuser, / Pray cease to be my judge', says Vittoria, rather as Beatrice will say, 'Who stands here / As my accuser? Ha! wilt thou be he, / Who art my judge?' (V. ii. 172–4).[7] Both men are fascinated by deceptions that are not all deceptions: both are moved by the courage of women who face down their accusers and judges.

Lamb did like *Rosalind and Helen*, and Shelley for his part greatly admired *Rosamund Gray*, which he read in the two-volume works of 1818, published by Charles Ollier (the two authors shared a publisher). Shelley wrote praisingly of *Rosamund Gray* to Hunt, regretting in a later letter that he had lost Lamb's 'society' through 'the calumny of an enemy' (*Letters: PBS*, 2. 111–12, 123). A work of 1798, *Rosamund Gray*, as Jonathan Wordsworth points out, responds strongly to Wordsworth's *The Ruined Cottage*, a poem that Shelley knew from its reworked form in Book I of *The Excursion*.[8] Lamb and Shelley draw close to one another in and through the text of *Rosamund Gray* in various ways. Shelley may seek (via Hunt's mediation) to play Lamb's texts against him, since one of Elinor's letters—slowing down the story, allowing it to branch off in different directions,

---

[4] *Major Works*, 93, 92–3.
[5] *Lamb as Critic*, ed. Roy Park (London: Routledge & Keegan Paul, 1980), 240.
[6] *Lamb as Critic*, 127.   [7] See *Major Works*, 758.
[8] See Jonathan Wordsworth's Introduction to *Rosamund Gray 1798* (Oxford: Woodstock, 1991), n.p. The work is quoted from this edition, though the long form of 's' has been modernized.

and foregrounding the narrative's stylishly elegant formal sense—recalls the fate of Elinor's and Alan's father:

> You know something of his story. You know, there was a foul tale current—it was the busy malice of that bad man, S----, which helped to spread it abroad—you will recollect the active good nature of our friends W---- and T----; what pains they took to undeceive people... but there was still a party, who shut their ears. You know the issue of it. My Father's great spirit bore up against it for some time,... but that spirit was broken at the last.   (*Rosamund Gray*, 72–3)

Perhaps Lamb did quietly recognize the relevance of his text to Shelley's own experiences of 'busy malice': in a letter to Barton he speaks admiringly of 'a sonnet' by Shelley 'conceived and expressed with a witty delicacy. It is that addressed to one who hated him but who could not persuade him to hate *him* again. His coyness to the other's passion (for hate demands a return as much as Love, and starves without it) is most arch and pleasant. Pray, like it very much'.[9] The poem 'Lines to a Reviewer' reads as follows:

> Alas, good friend, what profit can you see
> In hating such a hateless thing as me?
> There is no sport in hate when all the rage
> Is on one side. In vain would you assuage
> Your frowns upon an unresisting smile
> In which not even contempt lurks to beguile
> Your heart, by some faint sympathy of hate.
> O conquer what you cannot satiate!
> For to your passion I am far more coy
> Than ever yet was coldest maid or boy
> In winter noon. Of your antipathy,
> If I am the Narcissus, you are free,
> To pine into a sound with hating me.

The poem (published in Shelley's *Posthumous Poems* in 1824 from where it is quoted here) touches on Lamb's and the period's preoccupation with sympathy as well as its opposite, 'antipathy'. The last few lines suggest that the other can turn into an Echo pining away into a sound that means that the 'me' of the poem triumphs through refusing to reciprocate. It takes as its theme the very conditions of writing in the context of a reviewing culture which preoccupied writers of the period, playing deft variations on 'hate' as an emotion that reifies the stance of the hater. The hater's only and pitiful freedom is 'To pine into a sound with hating me', fixated on his victorious because emotionally dexterous foe.

Shelley as Narcissus triumphing over the Echo who is the reviewer intrigues and even charms Lamb, one suspects, because of the urbane social tone. The witticism is like one of Lamb's puns in its effect, and Lamb handsomely allows Shelley to score a point, however obliquely, at Lamb's expense. But for Lamb Shelley fails as a poet who is too much preoccupied with theories and nostrums, ringing with

---

[9] *The Letters of Charles Lamb*, ed. Edward Verrall Lucas, 3 vols (London: Dent, 1935), 2, 437.

their own 'emptiness' (themselves failed Echoes falling into vacancy because of the reader's indifference). 'Many are wiser and better for reading Shakspeare', he quotes Hazlitt as saying, but 'nobody was ever wiser or better for reading Sh--y'.[10] The judgement seems damning, but the sense, evident in Hazlitt too, of wishing to be rid of a troublesome contemporary voice, pays a backhanded compliment to Shelley's capacity to provoke; the very irritability of the put-down suggests a not fully acknowledged awareness of imaginative power.

2

In 'the outset of life', William Hazlitt muses, tellingly more than half way through 'My First Acquaintance with Poets', 'our imagination has a body to it'.[11] Hazlitt's imagination vividly embodies his 'first acquaintance' with Coleridge and Wordsworth, bathing it in an unsentimental glow of affection, even rapture, even as his later disillusion finds expression. The result is a remarkable account of an affective and intellectual trajectory central to the Romantic period: bliss at the 'outset' before subsequent disenchantment. In the essay Hazlitt writes with the subdued passion of the principled dissenter, who has not sold his political soul for a mess of Tory pottage, but he also writes with real and brilliant empathy: 'the sense of a new style and a new spirit in poetry came over me' (ix. 104), a 'new style and a new spirit' imprinted on the lineaments of the countryside round Alfoxden.

Romantic and revolutionary dawns broke in the west for Shelley, too, whose *Queen Mab*, first mentioned by the young poet in December 1811, seems to have taken a major step towards final completion in the summer of 1812 when he spent July and August in Lynmouth, near Barnstaple in Devon. The Shelley party, including Elizabeth Hitchener, left Lynmouth in haste on 28 August, after Shelley's Irish servant Daniel Healey (or Hill) had been arrested at Barnstaple (on 19 August) for distributing the poet's *Declaration of Rights*. Shelley could not pay the £200 fine, which meant that Healey had to spend six months in prison. During his stay at Lynmouth, Shelley wrote to Thomas Hookham: 'I enclose also by way of specimen all that I have written of a little poem begun since my arrival in England. I conceive I have matter enough for 6 more cantos...The Past, the Present, & the Future are the grand and comprehensive topics of this Poem. I have not yet exhausted the second of them' (*Letters: PBS*, 1. 324). By then, following his 'arrival in England' from Ireland to Wales in early April 1812 (or from Wales to England in late June), Shelley appears to have drafted, in the view of Donald H. Reiman and Neil Fraistat, 'approximately four of a projected ten cantos' (*CPPBS* 2, 492). Clearly the stay at Lynmouth was poetically productive. Edward Dowden asserted many years ago: 'The poetical mood was not likely to pass away when Shelley found himself at Lynmouth, still amid hills and rushing brooks [as when he was in

[10] *Letters of Charles Lamb*, 2, 437.
[11] William Hazlitt, *Selected Writings of William Hazlitt*, ed. Duncan Wu, 9 vols (London: Pickering & Chatto, 1998), 9, 104. Hereafter cited parenthetically.

Wales], and now in presence of the ever-changing sea'.[12] Belletristic this may now sound, but Shelley's time in Lynmouth was a crucial phase during a period of intense speculation and poetic experimentation; the effect of the West Country scenes leaves its impression on Shelley's poetry of the time. *Queen Mab* still remains a work ripe for attention to its imaginative and explosive attempt to reignite revolutionary fires, the extinction of which so disheartened Hazlitt.

No poet among the Romantics was more conscious of a 'new spirit in poetry' than Shelley. In his greatest shorter poem, 'Ode to the West Wind', he prays that the wind might 'Drive my dead thoughts over the universe / Like withered leaves to quicken a new birth' (63–4), while he writes in his peroration to *A Defence of Poetry*: 'It is impossible to read the compositions of the most celebrated writers of the present day without being startled with the electric life which burns within their words' (*Major Works*, 701). Here the wording repeats the phrasing used in the earlier *A Philosophical View of Reform*, except that Shelley now depicts himself as 'startled with' rather than 'startled by' (*Major Works*, 647), as though pointing up the involuntary 'startling' induced by 'the electric life' of the writings produced by his contemporaries, a life unsentimentally celebrated in Hazlitt's *Spirit of the Age*. Shelley's readiness to respond to the 'compositions' of others is at the centre of his own creativity and aligns him with the capacity for creative and critical relishing that Hazlitt calls 'Gusto'; that is, the 'power or passion defining any object' (II. 79).

With a Proustian subtlety, Hazlitt gives us a picture of the complex of feelings induced in him by reflecting on his first, unforgettable acquaintance with poets. Hazlitt's celebration of a 'new style and a new spirit', if linked, as below, with Shelley's Lynmouth-based explorations, involves parallels and suggestive comparisons rather than the tracing of a direct influence. Hazlitt and Shelley make a piquant pairing: they should have been allies, but Hazlitt reserves some of his most dazzling scorn for Shelley's own pyrotechnics. Leigh Hunt, who took principled exception to Hazlitt's first major attack on Shelley—in the *Table Talk* essay 'On Paradox and Common-Place' where the poet features as a 'philosophic fanatic' (VI. 130)—later recalled, as Nicholas Roe reminds us, 'someone telling him that Shelley had "cut up" Hazlitt at Godwin's'.[13] But Hazlitt's hostility seems to run more deeply than personal grudge will allow, and this chapter will finish with a brief coda on the final lack of concord between the two men.

Final lack of concord is almost a guarantee of authenticity in and for Hazlitt. Hazlitt's arguments '*in favour of the Natural Disinterestedness of the Human Mind*', to quote the subtitle of his 1805 work *An Essay on the Principles of Human Action*, bear most impressive fruit in Keats's notion of '*Negative Capability*', that is when man is capable of being in uncertainties, Mysteries, doubts, without any irritable reaching after fact & reason'.[14] They may have influenced Shelley's account of the sympathetically outgoing work performed by the imagination in *A Defence of*

---

[12] Thomas Jefferson Hogg, *The Life of Percy Bysshe Shelley*, ed. Edward Dowden (new edition, London: Kegan Paul, 1909), 143.
[13] Nicholas Roe, *Fiery Heart: the First Life of Leigh Hunt* (London: Pimlico, 2005), 331.
[14] *Letters: John Keats*, I. 193.

Poetry. Yet Hazlitt's practice as an essayist criss-crosses between being carried out of himself into the feelings of others and decisively complicating that negatively capable process by refusing to quiet the restless, aggressive impulse to impose his own perspective. Hazlitt's disinterestedness is a complex process that does not claim a superhuman ability to transcend personal feeling. The author who speaks, however wryly, of a 'secret affinity, a *hankering* after evil in the human mind' in 'On the Pleasure of Hating' (VIII. 118) was never likely to fall in love with a Utopian politics. Hazlitt's very ability to admire an ideological foe, such as Edmund Burke, strikes Tom Paulin as illustrating 'the disinterested ability to appreciate the arguments of an enemy', 'one of the fundamental values', according to Paulin, that Hazlitt 'acquired from his Unitarian upbringing'.[15] Yet Hazlitt's admiration for Burke is less a question of appreciating an argument than of responding to the power of a personality. His prose relishes Burke's performance rather than his paraphrasable point. For Hazlitt in 'On the Prose-Style of Poets', Burke's style has:

> the solidity, and sparkling effect of the diamond: all other *fine writing* is like French paste or Bristol-stones in the comparison. Burke's style is airy, flighty, adventurous, but it never loses sight of the subject; nay, is always in contact with, and derives its increased or varying impulse from it. It may be said to pass yawning gulfs 'on the unstedfast footing of a spear:' still it has an actual resting-place and tangible support under it—it is not suspended on nothing. It differs from poetry, as I conceive, like the chamois from the eagle: it climbs to an almost equal height, touches upon a cloud, overlooks a precipice, is picturesque, sublime—but all the while, instead of soaring through the air, it stands upon a rocky cliff, clambers up by abrupt and intricate ways, and browzes on the roughest bark, or crops the tender flower. The principle which guides his pen is truth, not beauty—not pleasure, but power.   (VIII. 7–8)

Paulin reminds us, apropos those colourless 'Bristol-stones' (quartz crystals found near Bristol), that the West Country allusion serves to recall the fact that Burke was MP for Bristol, but lost his seat when asserting 'the principle that a member of parliament must vote according to his conscience, not according to the wishes of his constituency'. Paulin notes, too, both the overt allusion to *Henry IV, Part 1* (I.iii.193), where the 'unstedfast footing of a spear' evokes Hotspur's and, by implication, Burke's 'wildly impolitic' nature, and the covert allusions to Godwin's *St Leon* and Caesar's encomium on Antony in *Antony and Cleopatra* when 'the barks of trees thou brows'd' (I.iv.66). This latter allusion serves, as Paulin argues, to remind us that there is 'a mighty general shadowing' Hazlitt's symbol of the chamois (Napoleon).[16] One might read these allusions as Hazlitt's refusal to conceal his own complicated view of Burke: that is, his prose is not simply a negatively capable medium through which the 'airy, flighty, adventurous' force of Burke's writing makes itself felt. David Bromwich has ingeniously argued for a reconciliation of Hazlitt's belief in disinterestedness and his understanding of the mixed motives at

[15] From 'Introduction', *William Hazlitt, The Fight and Other Writings*, ed. Tom Paulin and David Chandler, intro. Tom Paulin (London: Penguin, 2000), p. xvii.

[16] 'Introduction', William Hazlitt, *The Plain Speaker: The Key Essays*, ed. Duncan Wu and intro. Tom Paulin (Oxford: Blackwell, 1998), pp. x, xi, xii–xiii.

work in human beings, especially the contest that can take place between the admiration for power and the impulse towards sympathy.[17] And, like Burke's, Hazlitt's own style 'has an actual resting-place and tangible support'; yet that 'resting-place' and that 'support' can often seem to be nothing other than his own convictions and determination that others should appear as he wishes them to appear. Like Burke's prose, Hazlitt's 'never loses sight of its subject', yet that 'subject' is not necessarily to see the person as he was but as he appeared to Hazlitt to be. Thus, the allusion to Antony that Paulin points out works, as Paulin does not observe, to explain the tenacious hold that Burke has over Hazlitt: if Antony fleetingly brings Napoleon to mind, the effect is to remind us of Hazlitt's admiration for the French Emperor, while Caesar's praise—itself at odds with his antagonism towards Antony elsewhere in the drama—might prove 'disinterestedness' or it might suggest, rather, the reluctant yet inevitable admiration that Antony/Burke inspires. Above all, the passage brings out the strong drive in Hazlitt's portraits to make his subjects affirm a leading characteristic, a drive that is of the first importance in considering his account of the major Romantic poets.

There is in Hazlitt a recoil from abstraction that suggests he will find it difficult to devote his writing to the espousal of libertarian ideals. It is easier for him to mock Wordsworth's apostasy, for example, than to articulate a new or updated Declaration of Rights. What evokes his finest prose is an embittered nostalgia, expressed in his essay on Wordsworth's *The Excursion*, for the 'glad dawn of the day-star of liberty[...]' when France called her children to partake her equal blessings beneath her laughing skies'. This passage betrays in its very idiom a sharp recognition that 'that season of hope... is fled with the other dreams of our youth, which we cannot recal' (II. 120). Those 'equal blessings' beneath the 'laughing skies' convict themselves in their very utterance of something idealized, pastoral, and literary. This is not to deny the affective power of Hazlitt's longing for that 'day-star of liberty', nor the edge of his contempt for those (such as the author of *The Excursion*) who have taken to the penning of 'Birth-day and Thanksgiving odes, or the chaunting of *Te Deums* in all the churches of Christendom' (II. 120).

Yet Hazlitt is a writer in whom different feelings twist round one another. The very image of the 'day-star of liberty', for example, suggests a steady permanence, the light of the sun. But it also intimates the fate of stars in daylight, namely, that they will fade and be seen no more. That 'day-star', along with the 'dawn' in which it manifested itself, has both 'fled' and 'left behind it traces, which are not to be effaced' (II. 120), a sequence of ideas and images that bears acutely on the way in which Shelley words the central experience of *The Triumph of Life*. In Shelley's elegy for the fate of Romantic desire, stars—like ideals—pass into an all too common light of day, but they bequeath traces of their presence. Rousseau, who is central to Hazlitt, too, appears as the quintessential representative of Romantic desire, and is haunted by a beautiful 'shape all light' (352), his own 'day-star of liberty', a figure already met in the previous chapter. Like Hazlitt's day-star, Shelley's

---

[17] See David Bromwich, *Hazlitt: The Mind of a Critic* (New Haven: Yale University Press, 1983), esp. 101.

shape offers the promise of a new 'day': 'like day she came, / Making the night a dream' (392–3); like Hazlitt's day-star, she is eclipsed by an effacing, destructive light that turns her into a waning star, traces of whom are not utterly effaced: 'And the fair shape waned in the coming light / As veil by veil the silent splendour drops / From Lucifer' (412–14), and yet Rousseau is able to go on to say, 'So knew I in that light's severe excess / The presence of that shape' (424–5), even if it is a 'presence' that borders on the verge of absence, 'The ghost of a forgotten form of sleep' (428). Shelley might almost be writing his poetic gloss on Hazlitt's prose elegy for revolutionary ideals and even speaks the same or a similar language of 'traces' (see 337) and 'erasure' (see 406).

Neither Hazlitt nor Shelley deplores the failure of the Revolution in naively emotional terms. For one thing, *The Triumph of Life* never allows its dream-vision to be interpreted as a point-by-point allegory of recent history. For another, it evokes the bafflement of understanding and mimes the bewilderment of disillusion, but it does not supply an absolutely sure explanation. Attempts to explain seem only to raise more questions than they solve; questions themselves, with their air of striking to the heart of things, only catalyse further visions, new uncertainties. Hazlitt, too, asserts his allegiance to 'the day-star of liberty', but he associates it in the same sentence with the 'airy, unsubstantial dream' and the near-absoluteness of Wordsworthian loss, quoting the lines from the *Intimations Ode* that begin 'What though the radiance, which was once so bright, / Be now for ever taken from my sight' (quoted II. 120). Yes, those lines will turn into an assertion that finds 'Strength in what remains behind' (183),[18] but Hazlitt knows the near-tragic quasi-fact that human beings are destined always to lose their dearest dream. The pull towards this conviction shows itself throughout his prose in its many moments of recollection of past happiness, with their concomitant, implicit sense of present loss, redeemed only by the reclaiming work done by his prose. It shows, too, in such passages as the wry, sad, hilarious lament for lost friendships in 'On the Pleasure of Hating'. The sustaining of revolutionary ideals has somehow to occur in a world in which human beings are not equal to their best and brightest speculations, since they occupy a sphere in which, as if ruled by a gravitational law, emotions obey a cyclical and dispiriting rule as each heavily punctuated clause begets its hating neighbour: 'We hate old friends: we hate old books: we hate old opinions; and at last we come to hate ourselves' (VIII. 120–1). Keats's 1819 flare of distaste for perfectibilinarian notions has, one might feel, a grounding in his reading of Hazlitt: 'in truth I do not at all believe in this sort of perfectibility', he writes to the George Keatses; 'the nature of the world will not admit of it—the inhabitants of the world will correspond to itself' (2. 101). 'The inhabitants of the world will correspond to itself': the 'world', being what it is, makes us who we are, Keats asserts in a pointed rebuke to those who believe that they might transcend what even Shelley at his most enthusiastically Godwinian recognizes as obstacles: 'chance, and death, and mutability' (*Prometheus Unbound*, III.iv.201). This idea is not the premise for reactionary conservatism on Keats's part, who will go

---

[18] Quoted from *William Wordsworth: The Major Works*.

on to commend the notion of the 'world' as ' "The vale of Soul-making" '. 'Intelligences' come into existence and are made souls 'by the medium of world like this' (II. 102). But it reveals a robust dislike of facile optimism, an optimism that affects to transcend or ignore or annul the presence in life of 'Pains and troubles' (II. 102).

Hazlitt, along with Keats, dislikes in Shelley, not wholly fairly, the traces of such optimism, but before considering Hazlitt's response to Shelley further it is relevant to note that in his subtly entangled response to Wordsworth and Coleridge he is addressing former friends who have shaped his identity and with whom he quarrels the more intensely because of their influence over him. From the first word of its title, 'My First Acquaintance with Poets' speaks of personal experience. The essay's structure and tone balance between initial stirrings and the long vistas of retrospection that beguilingly refuse to overwhelm its subject. Cunningly, the essay begins with origins and primal allegiances: 'My Father was a Dissenting Minister at Wem in Shropshire; and in the year 1798 (the figures that compose that date are to me like the "dreaded name of Demogorgon") Mr Coleridge came to Shrewsbury, to succeed Mr Rowe in the spiritual charge of a Unitarian Congregation there' (9. 95). The seemingly factual sentence plays the part of a prologue to a swelling theme. It brings on to the essay's stage the *dramatis personae* of Hazlitt's imaginative awakening, the central theme of the essay. They include Hazlitt's father, the poetically, personally, and politically revolutionary year 1798,[19] the *ur*-figure of Demogorgon (possibly brought to Hazlitt's attention by Shelley's *Prometheus Unbound* as well as by *Paradise Lost*, II. 964–5), and the mentor par excellence, Coleridge, as poetry displaces theological zeal. An essay that is 'so conscious of its operations of allusion as to produce a typology of allusiveness',[20] in Susan Wolfson's words, it will end with a comic but telling allusion to Wordsworth's 'Hart-Leap Well', 'But there is matter for another rhyme, / And I to this may add a second tale' (quoted IX. 109), to which Shelley may also refer at the close of his witty epyllion *The Witch of Atlas* (669–70). In both essay and epyllion the allusion forges a link with Wordsworth and opens a gap between his work and his successors; in both cases, it asserts an ongoing creative energy. Hazlitt has just turned the tables on armchair, Utopian radicalism by way of an anecdote involving Lamb:

> It was at Godwin's that I met him [Lamb] with Holcroft and Coleridge, where they were disputing fiercely which was the best—*Man as he was, or man as he is to be*. 'Give me,' says Lamb, 'man as he is *not* to be.' This saying was the beginning of a friendship between us, which I believe still continues (IX. 109).

Holcroft and Coleridge stage the classic argument of the times: between conservative and Utopian perspectives. Lamb, puncturing pretension, takes us into the carnivalesque, anarchic realm of comedy where a turn of phrase annihilates the fixities of ideology. Discipleship (where Coleridge was the master) has passed into undemanding but vigilant friendship. Yet if the friendship with Lamb seems won

---

[19] See Paulin, *The Day-Star of Liberty*, 133–5, for the suggestion that 1798 here alludes to the Irish Rising.
[20] Susan J. Wolfson, *Romantic Shades and Shadows* (Baltimore: Johns Hopkins University Press, 2018), 73.

at the cost of estrangement from Wordsworth and Coleridge, the final quotation from 'Hart-Leap Well' functions in a complex way. It concludes the first part of Wordsworth's poem, and Wordsworth does, indeed, 'add a second tale', or, at any rate a 'Part Second' which concludes with an admonitory 'lesson' (173) that twines itself round the trellis of modified millenarianism as Wordsworth speaks of 'the coming of the milder day' (171). Concealed in Hazlitt's closing allusion, then, is the possibility of such a 'coming'. Wordsworth is quoted to serve Hazlitt's ends. Wordsworth's 'milder day' might have been at a remove from his earlier, more democratic aspirations, but it will suffice as an unmentioned vanishing point towards which Hazlitt's essay streams.

This is not to suggest that the essay effects some sentimentalizing rapprochement. But, true to the essay's fascination with 'likeness' and its endorsement of a fisherman's remark that 'we have a *nature* towards one another', which was seen by Coleridge as illustrating Hazlitt's 'theory of disinterestedness' (IX. 108), affinity as well as difference inheres in Hazlitt's subsequent as well as first acquaintance with the poets. Coleridge, too, earns an allusive salute at the close of the essay's penultimate paragraph, preparing us for the final reference to Wordsworth. In a delicately worked *mise-en-abîme*, Hazlitt writes with what might be termed meta-mnemonic subtlety:

> The next day we had a long day's walk to Bristol, and sat down, I recollect, by a well-side on the road, to cool ourselves and satisfy our thirst, when Coleridge repeated to me some descriptive lines from his tragedy of Remorse; which I must say better became his mouth and that occasion better than they, some years after, did Mr Elliston's and the Drury-lane boards,—
>> Oh memory! shield me from the world's poor strife,
>> And give those scenes thine everlasting life.
>
> (IX. 108)

The scene shifts between literary recollection and symbolic suggestions, as the two pedestrians sit 'by a well-side on the road, to cool ourselves and satisfy our thirst'. Holcroft had been found guilty by Coleridge (with Hazlitt's evident approval) of 'barricading the road to truth' (IX. 100), yet Coleridge himself betrayed 'instability of purpose' 'by shifting from one side of the foot-path to the other' (IX. 100–1, 100). In the essay's final return to Coleridge, the two men seek to 'satisfy' their 'thirst' beside the 'road', Hazlitt once again divining a common desire for meaning and significance, and reaffirming the value of 'memory' in giving early 'scenes' 'everlasting life' in his own prose. As he quotes Coleridge's invocation to memory, he may imply, too, the impossibility of being shielded from 'the world's poor strife'. Coleridge, like Hazlitt's father, lives a life that is a dream, even if 'No two individuals were ever more unlike than were the host and his guest' (IX. 98). Indeed, the father's 'glimmering notions', produced in response to the 'Bible, and the perusal of the Commentators', have a distinctly millenarian tinge: they may seem strange, arcane, even religiose, but they serve as veiled 'types, shadows' of the revolutionary epoch and the mental experience they bear witness to has value denied to ordinary modes of perception: 'though the soul might slumber with an hieroglyphic veil of inscrutable mysteries drawn over it, yet it was in a slumber ill-exchanged for all the sharpened realities of sense, wit, fancy, or reason' (IX. 98). Here Hazlitt seems to offer a parallel to *The Triumph of Life*, which begins with an account of the Poet experiencing a visionary trance whose indefinability is carefully defined, a 'strange trance' 'Which was not slumber, for the shade it spread // Was so transparent that the scene came through / As clear as when a veil of light is drawn / O'er evening hills they glimmer' (29, 30–3). Yet both writers set 'trance' and dream against 'the sharpened realities' that come in the wake of what both refer to as 'life'.

If Coleridge is both the medium towards realizing and a siren-voice luring away from an awareness of such 'realities', Hazlitt's relationship with him is a voyage of self-discovery. At the outset of this essay about 'the outset of life', Hazlitt cuts across factual narration with a powerful tribute to Coleridge, who is held gratefully responsible for ensuring that the younger man's 'understanding' 'did not remain dumb and brutish' and 'found a language to express itself' (IX. 96). In Hazlitt's *Great Gatsby*-like mode of narration, where the older Carraway voice evokes and judges his former self, the 'outset of life' is a liminal stage when 'We are in a state between sleeping and waking, and have indistinct but glorious glimpses of strange shapes' (IX. 104). That last phrase might easily slip, if metrically regularized, into a Shelleyan poem, and serve there as a speculative beacon of ultimate hope. In Hazlitt's case, these glimpses are the more tantalisingly impermanent because they were of realities, but realities that have now vanished into a temporal virtuality which can be recovered only through prose evocation. His essay sways between moods and perspectives. On the one hand, it delights in anticipation: so, Hazlitt is buoyed up by the thought '*I was to visit Coleridge in the Spring*' (IX. 102). On the other hand, it is heavy with retrospection, sometimes expressing itself as a general law of the human mind ('As we taste the pleasures of life, their spirit evaporates, the sense palls; and nothing is left but the phantoms, the lifeless shadows of what *has been!*' (IX. 104)), sometimes related to the practice of writing ('I can write fast enough now. Am I better than I was then? Oh no!' (IX. 101)). Superbly resistant to ideological pigeonholing, the essay holds possibilities and limits in suspension; adverse judgements marry grateful recognitions, and the essayist himself is at the centre of the experiencing process. By the close, the West Country, with its '*Valley of Rocks*', arbours, inns with delicious breakfasts, and 'dark brown heaths overlooking the channel', with sights recalling Coleridge's 'spectre ship in the *Ancient Mariner*' (IX. 107, 106), is both real and allegorical of the imagination's right to possess a kingdom of its own: one that, Hazlitt suggests through his tenaciously recollecting and arranging art, ought to extend its sway over society at large.

3

The young Shelley distributed a *Declaration of Rights* during his stay in Lynmouth; a copy was found floating in a bottle near Milford Haven, one of the 'Vessels of Heavenly medicine', no doubt, which Shelley apostrophizes in his 'Sonnet: On Launching Some Bottles Filled with *Knowledge* into the British Channel'. Shelley in the West Country brings us face to face with what might be called the *ur*-principles of the Romantic revolutionary imagination. There is the uncompromising sense that reason, art, and eloquence exist for the betterment of humanity. In *Declaration of Rights*, released in August 1812 though printed in Ireland in March of that year, Shelley rehearses the fundamental tenets of his thinking, thinking that draws on Godwin and Paine for its views of government as at best a necessary evil, for its commitment to 'unrestricted liberty of discussion' since 'falsehood', as Shelley says in a flashingly incisive use of a metaphor found also in Byron's *The Giaour* (first edition 1813), 'is a scorpion that will sting itself to death', and for its dismissal of any Burkean notion of society as a contract between the living and the dead (*Shelley's Prose*, 57). For Shelley, 'The present generation cannot bind their posterity' (*Shelley's Prose*, 58).

What is keenly evident and, indeed, quasi-Hazlittean is the courage which Shelley displayed in asserting his revolutionary ideals at a time when those ideals were hugely out of fashion. A nation engaged in war with Napoleon was in no mood to tolerate dissent or libertarianism. Shelley not only defied such intolerance in his own person; he also defended the right of others to publish heterodox opinion, sending in July and August 1812 various printed copies of his *Letter to Lord Ellenborough*, in which he mounts an impassioned attack on the decision by Lord Ellenborough to sentence the bookseller Daniel Isaac Eaton to eighteen months' imprisonment (including time in the pillory) for publishing *The Age of Reason: Part the Third*, attributed to Tom Paine and deemed blasphemous. Experiencing the '*perilous pleasure of becoming the champion of an innocent man*' (*Shelley's Prose*, 62), as he puts it in his Advertisement, Shelley was putting himself in the way of peril (the pamphlet would be used against him during the Chancery trial in 1817 over custody of his children by Harriet). The *Letter*, read by E. B. Murray as 'the first sustained example of Shelley's mature style' (*Shelley's Prose*, 356), has in common with Hazlitt's fiercest productions an uncompromising readiness to pick up the gauntlet thrown down by the poet's adversaries. Its cadences support its conviction of the right and duty to speak out:

> Falsehood skulks in holes and corners, 'it lets I *dare not* wait upon I *would*, like the poor cat in the adage,' except when it has power, and then, as it was a coward, it is a tyrant; but the eagle-eye of truth darts thro' the undazzling sunbeam of the immutable and just, gathering thence wherewith to vivify and illuminate a universe!
>
> (*Shelley's Prose*, 64)

The opposition between skulking falsehood and eagle-eyed truth allows of no shade of grey. Yet the same essay refers to the need to be guided 'thro' the labyrinth of life' (*Shelley's Prose*, 65), and the passage above anticipates Shelley's lament in *A Defence of Poetry* that 'we "let I *dare not* wait upon I *would*, like the poor cat in the adage" ', Lady Macbeth's taunt again drawn on, this time to regret the fact that 'We want the creative faculty to imagine that which we know' (*Major Works*, 695). The Shelley of 1812 is less preoccupied by the gulf between imagining and knowing, a gulf which his greatest work explores and seeks to span. But even in the passage quoted above, the mental processes associated with 'truth' are active and engaged, and make us aware of the need to experience and convey it: to gaze at the 'immutable and just', and to gather from that gaze 'wherewith to vivify and illuminate a universe!' The unspecific nature of 'wherewith' suggests less that the gazer will emerge from the encounter with the 'immutable and just' as some bearer of encoded absolutes than that he or she will incorporate into his or her thinking and feeling materials and energies which can be used, first, to revive, then to 'illuminate', 'a' rather than 'the' universe. Truth, we might extrapolate from Shelley's imagery, will be a dynamic process, one involving many cooperating minds, each recreating the world in the light of new insights and recognitions.

More generally, if Hazlitt in 'My First Acquaintance with Poets' looks back, the Shelley of 1812 anticipates. His mode at this time is essentially apocalyptic rather than elegiac, even when retrospection is at work. These summer months, when he was in the West Country, are deeply significant in poetic terms. Linked to the work on *Queen Mab* are reflections in the blank verse poem 'To Harriet' ('It is not blasphemy to hope'), which Dowden speculated was written in Lynmouth, partly because the poem contains strong echoes of 'Tintern Abbey', the scene of which the Shelleys would have passed on their way to Devonshire. Dowden enjoined himself to 'Note the traces' of Wordsworth's poem,[21] and the poem is derivative of Wordsworth in its syntax and phrasing, but strikingly Shelleyan in its concern with lyric subjectivity. The revolutionary self, not for the last time in Shelley's work, is cast as a 'lone spirit' (7) and subject to the 'Dark Flood of Time' (58), even as he hopes it will whirl him on to 'the space / When Time shall be no more' (9–10) (quoted from *CPPBS*). Above all, he appeals for a sustaining of 'the dear love / That binds our souls in soft communion' (46–7), a sustaining that requires 'the stretch of fancy's hope' (30), as though it might, in fact, not be possible. Love and politics mirror one another: the perfect society will, the poem implies, reflect the lovers' 'soft communion', and yet tensions that drive Shelley's later poetry may already be present: after all, the emotional 'binding' he longs for also sounds confining; the poem's cumulative and seemingly rhetorical questions, about, for example, whether the poet may ever 'learn to doubt / The mirror even of Truth' (57–8), tangle themselves up in self-doubting phrases that suggest the possibility of doubt, if not of 'Truth', then of Shelley's capacity to apprehend it, or of Harriet's readiness to support his pursuit of it.

In 'A retrospect of Times of Old' (quoted from *CPPBS* 2), probably written during his stay in Devon, Shelley produced a poem that, as Dowden noticed, has 'much in common with those earlier pages of "Queen Mab," which picture the fall of empires, and celebrate the oblivion that has overtaken the old rulers of men and lords of the earth'.[22] The poem fast-forwards through history with Shelley's characteristically millenarian eagerness; of the horrors that went into the composing of 'gore-emblazoned Victory' (57), Shelley writes, despatching them with rhythmic verve: 'All, all have faded in past time away! / New Gods, like men, changing in ceaseless flow, / Ever at hand as antient ones decay' (67–9). The prospect of eternal recurrence just glimmers here, in an anticipation of the closing chorus of *Hellas*,

---

[21] Quoted in Percy Bysshe Shelley, *The Esdaile Notebook: A Volume of Early Poems*, ed. Kenneth Neill Cameron (London: Faber and Faber, 1964), 217.

[22] Hogg, *Life of Percy Bysshe Shelley*, 143.

but the poem puts its faith in hope for a better future. Hope itself begins to take on a degree of complex uncertainty in 'The Voyage' (quoted from *CPPBS* 2), a poem in which narrative complicatedness captures the angularity of revolutionary perspectives: the poem is especially fine for the way in which it balances the 'Spirit's visioned solitude' (61), and the dignified trust attributed to 'seafaring men' in Necessity (or 'the Soul of Nature', 108) as 'Blind, changeless and eternal in her paths' (109), against the grim realities of human cruelty (recorded in the visionary's dream) and the horror of conscription visited upon a sailor.

In its vehemence of contempt for those who 'have appropriated human life / And human happiness' (267–8), 'The Voyage' reasserts a conviction in the essential rights deriving from the fact of being 'human'. *Queen Mab*, in the four cantos that Shelley seems to have drafted by 18 August 1812, probably including cantos 2 to 4, blends evocations of West Country seascapes, 'the wild ocean's echoing shore' (2. 2), with indictments of 'human pride', figured in the collapse of empires (canto 2) and the transience of tyrannical power (canto 3), and of 'War [...] the statesman's game, the priest's delight' (4. 168). The writing's pointedness about how political wrongs are abetted by the abuse of language is formidable, anticipating both the nominalist scepticism of 'Hymn to Intellectual Beauty' and the way in which rings are run round orthodoxy in *Prometheus Unbound*: 'They have three words:—well tyrants know their use, / Well pay them for the loan, with usury / Torn from a bleeding world!—God, Hell, and Heaven' (IV. 208–10). These, the opening lines of a passage (up to 220) which was one of four extracts from the poem 'specified in the indictment for blasphemous label…against Clark's original piracy' (*CPPBS* 2, 557) in 1821, illustrate Shelley's sense of tyranny as an interlocking mechanism in which state religion bolsters policies based on inequality, greed, and violence. The cold-eyed ferocity of the writing, its iambic rhythms steely with purpose as they register a voice intent on having its anti-establishment say, is impressively sustained. Things as they are in contemporary political terms contrast with things as they might be in a world whose only constant is dynamic process: 'Throughout this varied and eternal world / Soul is the only element, the block / That for uncounted ages has remained. / The moveless pillar of a mountain's weight / Is active, living spirit' (4. 139–43).[23] Such an 'active, living spirit' recalls the beliefs of 1790s radicals for whom spirit and matter are interfused in a truly active universe, one on which human institutions might model themselves. A virtual voice in the wilderness, Shelley sought to reaffirm this vision, steeped in Enlightenment values yet vibrant with Romantic revolutionary ardour, in his 1812 West Country writings.

4

Hazlitt was critical of contemporary poets for their self-centredness. Wordsworth displayed 'a systematic unwillingness to share the palm with his subject' (II. 328), where 'systematic' suggests that he did so out of settled conviction. Southey 'bows

---

[23] This edition retains the full stop after 'remained' in Shelley's first 1813 printing.

to no authority: he yields only to his own wayward peculiarities' (VII. 216). Byron, 'who in his politics is a *liberal,* in his genius is haughty and aristocratic' (VII. 135–6). Thus, Hazlitt's criticisms of Shelley, principally in 'On Paradox and Common-Place' and in his review of *Posthumous Poems,* are not *sui generis*; they reflect an abiding mistrust on Hazlitt's part against a wilfulness he sees as part of poetic genius. In 'On Paradox and Common-Place' he asserts that poets 'make bad philosophers and worse politicians' since 'They live, for the most part, in an ideal world of their own' (VI. 132). Such an 'ideal world' is for Hazlitt where Shelley, above all other poets, conducts us, and it is all the worse for being an 'ideal world' or Utopia that emerges from the 'metaphysical crucible' (VI. 130) of the poetry, a crucible in which Shelley puts everything about which he wishes to speculate. 'He is clogged', writes Hazlitt sardonically, by 'no dull system of realities' (VI. 130). Or again, 'Spurning the world of realities, he rushed into the world of nonentities and contingencies, like air into a *vacuum.*' Lurking beneath these firework displays of virtuoso brilliance lies ego; Shelley 'became the creature of his own will', 'wasting great powers by their application to unattainable objects' and leaving us with a poetic style that affects as 'a passionate dream,[...] a confused embodying of vague abstractions'.[24]

Hazlitt puts the case against his fellow revolutionary Romantic with ruthless one-sidedness. Leigh Hunt sought to redress the balance, and landed some shrewd blows, bringing into the open the gap between Hazlitt's professed belief in disinterestedness and the production of 'twenty articles to show that the most disinterested person in the world [Shelley] is only a malcontent and fanatic', and defending Shelley's use of 'will' to embody the fact 'the hope of reformation is not everywhere given up'. These are fine insights, as is Hunt's shrewd and delicate understanding of the relationship between the 'real' and the 'ideal' in Shelley. As Hunt notes, his friend's poetry can be read as an attempt to 'do the whole detail of the universe a sort of poetical justice, in default of being able to make his fellow-creatures attend to justice political'.[25] Shelley was more various in his poetic endeavours, more dynamic in his vision, and more wide-ranging and far-seeing in his political and spiritual vision than Hazlitt was able to discern. But if it is the essence of the revolutionary imagination to engage in permanent contest, yet to transform the terms of contestatory debate in the light of an imaginative drive for betterment, we can only be grateful for the intersecting legacies bequeathed by both Hazlitt and Shelley: legacies brooded over and kindled into being through their encounters with the West Country.

---

[24] Quoted from Hazlitt's unsigned review of Shelley's *Posthumous Poems* (1824) in *The Edinburgh Review,* July 1824, in Theodore Redpath, *The Young Romantics and Critical Opinion, 1807–1824* (London: Harrap, 1973), 390, 389, 388.
[25] From Leigh Hunt's *Lord Byron and Some of his Contemporaries* (1828), in Redpath, *The Young Romantics,* 407, 408, 409–10, 410.

5

'A Kind of an Excuse'
Shelley and Wordsworth Revisited

1

On 8 May 1820, Shelley sent Maria Gisborne 'An Exhortation', a poem which he included in the 1820 *Prometheus Unbound; with Other Poems* volume. It is a lyric dependent on analogies of the kind that Shelley found in Calderón, and has a tripping, trochaic lightness as it suggests why poets may be chameleonic: the analogical trap of the poem is sprung in the second stanza: 'Where light is, chameleons change: / Where love is not, poets do: / Fame is love disguised: if few / Find neither, never think it strange / That poets range' (15–18).[1] There is an arresting knot woven into the parallel strands. Chameleons thrive on light; poets on love. Therefore, one is lulled into thinking, both will respond in similar ways to positive stimuli. But the simple analogy allows itself to collapse. Love makes a poet true to himself; a lack of love, false. The chameleon is true to itself by changing; the poet is false by changing. And yet such is the elusive nature of fame that it seems almost inevitable that poets will 'range'. By 'range' Shelley means 'stray', but he also has already complicated his argument; the chameleon's changes are hard to view negatively, so the idea that a poet is the poorer for changing is itself being held up for inspection, is itself changing, even as it is being affirmed.

Shelley glossed the lyric as 'a little thing about Poets...a kind of an excuse for Wordsworth' (*Letters: PBS*, 2. 195), and its fleet-footed wit is characteristic of one aspect of the mature Shelley's response to a precursor poet of great significance throughout his career, as in different ways critics such as Harold Bloom, G. Kim Blank, and Vincent Newey have established. G. Kim Blank inserts the very distinction that Shelley withholds in 'An Exhortation' when he writes that, for Shelley, 'Wordsworth is...a chameleon turned lizard—a turncoat. He has lost the power of positive mutability'.[2] The same critic returns to this passage later, arguing that 'the ideal poet should be like a chameleon, capable of adapting not only to change, but also *with* change', but that the 'only changing Wordsworth performed was in

---

[1] Quoted from *Major Works* (as will be all poetry and prose in this chapter, unless cited otherwise). Wordsworth's poetry and prose will be quoted from *Wordsworth: Major Works*, unless indicated otherwise.

[2] G. Kim Blank, *Wordsworth's Influence on Shelley: A Study of Poetic Authority* (Basingstoke: Macmillan, 1988), 76.

his diminishing poetic and revolutionary zeal'.[3] Yet, in relation to 'An Exhortation', this is to impute too much censorious zeal to Shelley; it is the strength of the poem that it sees the proximity between 'positive mutability' and less positive change as connected. Vincent Newey, in a significant discussion of Shelley's interactions with Wordsworth and Byron, notes the presence of 'ambivalence' and underscores the 'creative dimension of the relationship'.[4] His nuanced sense of the ways in which Shelley enters into 'relationship' with other poets provides this chapter with an inspirational spur as it seeks to reconsider Shelley's intertextual relations with Wordsworth, mainly with regard to the poetry of the younger man's years in Italy.

Certainly these relations twine complex feelings of admiration and reproach, as 'Verses Written on Receiving a Celandine from England' reveals. As various critics, notably Mary Quinn and Timothy Webb, have shown, the poem dwells on what Webb calls 'the difference between then and now', his parenthetical rider '(in itself a characteristic Wordsworthian subject)' reminding us of the inward nature of even this poem, possibly the severest of Shelley's 'corrective tributes' to the older poet.[5] Its final vision of the withered celandine as emblematic of Wordsworth's apostate decline, and thus of 'Love sold, hope dead, and honour broken' (72), cannot eradicate the permanent value of 'his divine and simple song' (59). Wordsworth has 'overlived' himself (see 56), but he has lived and the best of his work will go living. Satire, polemic, and elegy tie an intricate knot in 'Verses', as its complicated ending bears witness: the 'priest of Nature's care' (67) must be Peacock who sent Shelley the celandine, and yet it must be Wordsworth, too, the reader senses, the Wordsworth addressed in an earlier elegizing sonnet as 'Poet of Nature' ('To Wordsworth', 1). Irony turns into belated praise; recollection of former greatness transforms itself into embittered irony. The rhetorical wheel spins round and round the poem's nine eight-line stanzas, until it almost seems that Shelley addresses himself and his severed relationship with Wordsworth when he speaks to the celandine of 'The stem whence thou wert disunited' (65).

'An Exhortation' seeks to restage the debate. 'Yet dare not stain with wealth or power / A poet's free and heavenly mind' (19–20): Shelley moves, in its third and final stanza, to the exhortation promised by his poem's title. The addressee is more society than the poet; and the language of 'staining' aligns the exhortation with a number of suggestions in later Shelley that imply the almost inevitable way in which something of enduring value will suffer 'staining' in the sublunary sphere. One thinks of the image in *Adonais* of 'Life' as 'a dome of many-coloured glass' that 'Stains the white radiance of Eternity' (52. 462–3), or of Rousseau's protest in *The Triumph of Life* against the staining 'disguise' which he 'still disdains', Farinata-like,

---

[3] Blank, *Wordsworth's Influence on Shelley*, 191.

[4] Vincent Newey, 'Shelley and the Poets: *Alastor*, "Julian and Maddalo", *Adonais*', *Durham University Journal* n.s. 54 (1993): 257–71 (258), 'Shelley Special Issue', guest editor Michael O'Neill.

[5] Mary A. Quinn, 'Shelley's "Verses on the Celandine": An Elegiac Parody of Wordsworth's Early Lyrics', *Keats-Shelley Journal* 36 (1987): 88–109; Timothy Webb, 'The Stiff Collar and the Mysteries of the Human Heart: The Younger Romantics and the Problem of *Lyrical Ballads*', 'A Natural Delineation of Human Passions': The Historic Moment of 'Lyrical Ballads', ed. C. C. Barfoot (Amsterdam: Rodopi, 2004), 216, 215.

to 'wear' (204–5). Such 'staining' imagery in Shelley is complexly at a remove from straightforward pessimism. It implies a disfiguring, but also the possibility of a pure, bright essence, as well as a more subliminal sense of a tainted beauty of its own. As 'An Exhortation' re-kindles belief in such an essence, it turns from society to poets, particularly Wordsworth, to conclude: 'Children of a sunnier star, / Spirits from beyond the moon, / O, refuse the boon!' (25–7). Shelley may allude, as Webb has suggested, to the fourth line of Wordsworth's anti-commercial sonnet, 'The world is too much with us': 'We have given our hearts away, a sordid boon!'[6] He characteristically angles the allusion to turn Wordsworth's fire against himself. If in the sonnet Wordsworth laments that we betray what is best about ourselves, by embroiling our lives in 'Getting and spending' (2), in the lyric Shelley exhorts Wordsworth not to accept the bribes of 'wealth or power'.

This tactic of the boomeranging allusion is one that Shelley has employed in relation to Wordsworth in earlier poems such as *Alastor*, a poem 'whose tacit transformation of Wordsworth's story of Margaret [in Book I of *The Excursion*]' was noted by Wasserman.[7] That 'transformation' shows in the quotation from Wordsworth that concludes the Preface to *Alastor*: 'The good die first, / And those whose hearts are dry as summer's dust, / Burn to the socket!' (*Major Works*, 93).[8] Shelley applies to Wordsworth lines that Wordsworth's Pedlar applies to Margaret, and his application of the allusion is Janus-featured, dividing Wordsworth into two poets, the 'good' poet who had died and the Tory Wordsworth whose heart is dry as dust and burning to the socket. Shelley's Narrator in *Alastor* appears to spurn the consolations of elegy (see 710–13), but, as Newey notes shrewdly, 'the quality of the poetry of *Alastor* as a whole…snatches plenitude from the jaws of negation'.[9] In his relationship with Wordsworth, Shelley 'snatches plenitude from the jaws of negation'. Just as the poem shimmers between perspectives, so that the Poet is both guilty of 'self-centred seclusion' (Preface, *Major Works*, 92) and a 'surpassing Spirit' (714), and just as its rhythms and music are unimaginable without the example of the older poet and are yet entirely its own, its involvement with Wordsworthian poetry is simultaneously an act of homage and a form of critique.

Alastor is no crude polemic. Rather, it recognizes that the loss which is its central theme, the seemingly inevitable destruction of desire through frustrated quest or the limitations of mortality, is one which Wordsworth has addressed in poems such as 'Ode: Intimations of Immortality'. Shelley's poem concludes by framing its elegiac insights in terms that consciously acknowledge Wordsworth's priority: 'It is a woe too "deep for tears"' (*Alastor*, 713), asserts Shelley or his Narrator, alluding to the closing line of the Intimations Ode and confronting the fact that the Poet's departure has left us with what a deep and possibly cross-grained reading of Wordsworth tells us is always there even for the older poet: 'Nature's vast frame, the web of

⁶ *Percy Bysshe Shelley: Poems and Prose*, ed. Timothy Webb (London: Dent, 1995), 409.
⁷ Wasserman, *Shelley: A Critical Reading*, 21.
⁸ For the original, which reads 'they' for 'those', see William Wordsworth, *The Excursion*, ed. Sally Bushell, James A. Butler, and Michael C. Jaye, with the assistance of David García (Ithaca: Cornell UP, 2007), I, 531–3.
⁹ Newey, 'Shelley and the Poets', 260.

human things, / Birth and the grave, that are not as they were' (719–20). This, the Wordsworthian cadences announce, is the fear at the back of Wordsworth's poetry: that Nature is a 'vast frame', not a loving parent, that we are entangled in 'the web of human things' rather than sustained by 'something far more deeply interfused' ('Lines Written a Few Miles above Tintern Abbey' ('Tintern Abbey'), 97), that we are always on the brink of unknowable origins and termini and of endless loss. With eerie empathy, Shelley latches on to the Wordsworthian anxieties held at bay, but only just, in a poem such as 'Tintern Abbey', where affirmations about our capacity to 'see into the life of things' (50) pass immediately into concern lest 'this / Be but a vain belief' (50–1).

Worry about vain beliefs is central to Shelley's work, and no belief is vainer to him than some supposed alliance between self and world. Such apprehensions of a one life or a near-pantheist unity recognize themselves as likely illusions in Shelley, or as emerging from 'the human mind's imaginings' (143), as he puts it in 'Mont Blanc' (version A). This poem, haunted by Wordsworthian diction, as when 'the life of things' ('Tintern Abbey', 50) turns into 'the secret strength of things' (139) towards the close, strongly senses that Romantic metaphysics are inseparable from metaphorical 'imaginings'. To that degree it serves as a rewriting of 'Tintern Abbey' that recognizes the earlier poem's achievement, but ousts Wordsworth's trust in memory's recuperative powers in favour of commitment to an ever-altering present tense, one in which the poet simultaneously presents and inspects his own 'human mind' as it engages in 'an unremitting interchange / With the clear universe of things around' ('Mont Blanc', version A, 39–40).

In 'An Exhortation', Shelley's 'excuse' for Wordsworth accompanies the suggestion in 'Children of a sunnier star' that Wordsworth is in danger of forgetting his own view that 'Our birth is but a sleep and a forgetting', that 'The Soul that rises with us, our life's star, / Hath had elsewhere its setting, / And cometh from afar' ('Ode: Intimations of Immortality', 58–61). Yet Wordsworth's 'forgetting' of his own best insights is a reminder of their value. When Shelley came to write the enigmatic and powerful lyric 'The Two Spirits—An Allegory', Wordsworth's lines from *The Excursion*, quoted at the close of the Preface to *Alastor*, returned to his mind. Above the poem's title he wrote 'The good die first—',[10] then below those words the cancelled line 'Two genii stood before me in a dream'. Wordsworth was clearly in his thoughts, and the twinning that is a disjunction of the 'Two genii' again reprises the Shelleyan sense of a covert bond with as well as difference from the older poet. Wasserman takes the view that the line ('The good die first') 'must have struck Shelley as an extraordinarily compressed formulation of man's paradoxical involvement in both moral life and afterlife'. I read it more as indicating Shelley's tragic awareness that, in Stuart Sperry's words, 'all are consumed by the fire of life within them'—which applies to Shelley as much as it does to Wordsworth.[11]

---

[10] See *BSM* XVIII, 14–15. It should be said that any reading text of 'The Two Spirits' must be speculative because of the condition of the manuscript.

[11] See Wasserman, *Shelley: A Critical Reading*, 42, and Stuart M. Sperry, *Shelley's Major Verse: The Narrative and Dramatic Poetry* (Cambridge: Harvard UP, 1988), 26.

Wordsworth's poetry haunts Shelley's figurations and imaginings, but their author appears to him, on occasions, to be like the First Spirit as described by the Second Spirit, tied to 'thy dull earth slumberbound' (30). The use of 'thy', there, shows that, for the Second Spirit, 'earth' may have an apparently objective reality, but such reality is a subjective impression, the product of a 'slumberbound' imagination. 'Slumberbound' in turn implies a deep sleep from which waking is nevertheless possible, and it seems distantly to recall Wordsworth's 'A slumber did my spirit seal', a poem in which the poet implicitly rebukes himself for having allowed such 'slumber' to 'seal' his 'spirit', and yet to regard it as state in which he might have been vouchsafed a true vision of Lucy's identity. To be 'slumberbound' is not wholly a negative thing, even if the coda's first stanza, depicting a circling chase involving 'storm' (37) and 'winged spirit' (38), feels as though it is rewriting Wordsworth's sense of Lucy as 'Rolled round in earth's diurnal course' (7). Awakening from slumber occurs, or is imagined as occurring, at the close of 'The Two Spirits', when the intimations-gifted traveller experiences a twinned sense of recovery and discovery:

> ...a shape like his early love doth pass
> Upborne by her wild and glittering hair,
> And when he awakes on the fragrant grass
> He finds night day.
>
> (45–8)

The poem can be read as being concerned with the differences and affinities between Shelley and Byron. Charles Robinson stresses the former rather than the latter: 'Because Shelley must have recognized the similarity between *The Two Spirits* and his long debate with Byron, the first four stanzas stand as an appropriate epilogue to the two poets' antagonism in 1818.'[12] But Shelley negotiates with Wordsworth, too, in the intertextual interstices of the poem, almost identifying the older poet with that 'shape like his early love', rediscovering his significance through a simplicity of diction that recalls the daring experiments of *Lyrical Ballads*. The passage alludes obliquely as well to the Wanderer's admonition of the Solitary in Book IV of Wordsworth's *The Excursion* to take note how

> Ambition reigns
> In the waste wilderness: the Soul ascends
> Towards her native firmament of heaven,
> When the fresh Eagle, in the month of May,
> Upborne, at evening, on replenished wing,
> This shady valley leaves
>
> (396–401)[13]

---

[12]   Charles E. Robinson, *Shelley and Byron: The Snake and Eagle Wreathed in Fight* (Baltimore: Johns Hopkins University Press, 1976), 111.
[13]   Qtd from Sally Bushell, James A. Butler, and Michael C. Jaye, ed., with the assistance of David García, *The Excursion* (Ithaca: Cornell University Press, 2007).

Wordsworth's 'Eagle' gives way to Shelley's 'shape'; but Shelley, who clearly read this book of Wordsworth's poem closely (there are evident echoes of it in *Alastor*),[14] adapts Wordsworth's understanding of the soul's ascending 'Ambition' to his own lyric's grappling with themes of desire and hope.

Wordsworth's 'Note to *The Thorn*' anticipates Shelley's practice of weighing repeated words such as 'night' and 'day' in 'the balance of feeling' (*Wordsworth: Major Works*, 594). To read Wordsworth as an admonitory First Spirit warning the exultant younger Shelley, 'who plumed with strong desire / Would float above the Earth' (1–2), is, in part, to respond to the suggestive invitation in the lyric's sub-title, 'An Allegory'. It is also to acknowledge the force and generosity of Shelley's response to the older poet, one with whose work he 'dosed' Byron 'even to nausea'.[15] The First Spirit is a father-figure more than half in love with the daring rashness of the son-like Second Spirit, and affects Judith Chernaik, for one, as speaking 'like a good friend, reluctantly abandoning a position once held by both': very much, one imagines, how Shelley might have wished to idealize so complex a poetic parent.[16] For him, as for the Second Spirit, 'It were delight to wander there' (7), and for the Second Spirit, the warning that 'A shadow tracks thy flight of fire' (3) serves as stimulus and goad rather than as impediment or barrier. It would be reductive to suppose that Shelley wrote the lyric as a *poeme à clef*, but it takes a new and revitalized life when read in the light of his career-long engagement with Wordsworth.

Wordsworth, in works such as 'Resolution and Independence', himself writes dialogic poems, albeit in that case implicitly so. In it he confronts and seeks to overcome the self that experiences chilling 'thoughts': 'the fear that kills; / The hope that is unwilling to be fed; / Cold, pain, and labour, and all fleshly ills' (120–2). The spondaic stress that opens the final line brings out Wordsworth's deliberating strength of feeling and analytical insight into the psychic and material enemies of promise and achievement. Shelley likely recalls the phrase 'all fleshly ills' (itself an echo of Hamlet's 'To be or not to be' soliloquy) when in *The Triumph of Life* his Rousseau tells the Poet that had he heard the music in the valley, 'Thou wouldst forget thus vainly to deplore / Ills, which if ills, can find no cure from thee' (327–8). Characteristically, Rousseau insinuates a Shelleyan uncertainty that is memorably glossed by A. C. Bradley:

> The words may imply a doubt on Shelley's own part about the ills that haunted him. Life, he may have felt, is so inexplicable, and so much ill seems to spring from what we once thought good and even superlatively good, that we can have no certainty as to the ultimate ill of what seems, and even haunts us as, ill.[17]

Rousseau is unsure whether what seem ills really are ills; we are unsure whether the poem ratifies or disputes his message of forlorn hopelessness. Wordsworth, in his

---

[14] Compare, for example, *Alastor*, 350–1, and *The Excursion*, IV, pp. 512–13.

[15] Quoted in Thomas Medwin, *Conversations of Lord Byron* (London: Colburn, 1824), 237.

[16] Judith Chernaik, *The Lyrics of Shelley* (Cleveland: The Press of Case Western Reserve University, 1972), 142.

[17] A. C. Bradley, 'Notes on Shelley's "Triumph of Life"', *Modern Language Review* 9 (1914): 441–56 (453). For further discussion, see Coda to this book.

poem, will take courage from the indomitable courage and perseverance of the Leech Gatherer. In 'The Two Spirits—An Allegory', Shelley allows for genuine debate, but he keeps in play the possibility of transcendental hope. Wordsworth alludes to 'A leading from above, a something given' (51) as a possible explanation for the Leech Gatherer's appearance, and if he lays his emphasis squarely on the Leech Gatherer's earthiness, he also implies the way in which his imaginings work trans-formatively on the earthly: of the famous slow dance of similes in which the Leech Gatherer participates, Wordsworth writes that 'the aged Man' is 'divested of so much of the indications of life and motion as to bring him to the point where the two objects unite and coalesce in the comparison' (Preface to *Poems* (1815), 633).

Both poets in these lyrics dramatize the resources and resourcefulness of the imagination. Wordsworth draws comfort from the example of the Leech Gatherer. But he is able to do so only after the Leech Gatherer's being has elicited from him a process of imagining that displays what he will call the imagination's 'endowing or modifying power' (Preface to *Poems* (1815), 633). Vital in a not wholly fathomable way for the poet's emergence from despondency is the way in which 'the lonely place, / The Old Man's shape, and speech, all troubled me' (134–5). Indeed, he is so 'troubled' that in ensuing lines he perceives the Old Man as a spectral wanderer in what appears to be as much mindscape as landscape: 'In my mind's eye I seemed to see him pace / About the weary moors continually, / Wandering about alone and silently' (136–8): lines where the adverbs and repetition of 'about', along with the drawn-out syntax, mimic a labyrinthine 'Wandering'.

Here the ordinariness of the Old Man turns into something extraordinary through the operations of the poet's troubled imagination. Wordsworth makes explicit these operations and their distance from a reality beyond them in the stanza's final couplet ('While I these thoughts within myself pursued, / He having made a pause, the same discourse renewed', 139–40), and it is part of the poem's odd persuasiveness that it allows for the jolts and disconnections between inner and outer. In chapter XXII of *Biographia Literaria*, which may have contributed to Shelley's maturing thought about Wordsworth, Coleridge regretted the poem's 'incongruity',[18] but it is among the poem's merits that it allows for the overpowering force of internal feeling without permitting the external to be simply overpowered. Wordsworth situates related forms of awareness within the same consciousness; Shelley divides them between his two speakers, and the third voice which enters the poem in what appears to be the coda of the final two stanzas. In 'The Two Spirits' the Second Spirit may initially sound naively ardent: 'Within my heart is the lamp of love / And that is day' (11–12), as though the 'lamp of love' can dispel the First Spirit's alarm-cry, 'Night is coming!' (8). But Shelley's lyric art devotes itself to the questioning of categories. Does 'Night is coming!' assert a fact or express a fear? The Second Spirit's very response would suggest that it does both; it refers to

---

[18] *Samuel Taylor Coleridge: The Oxford Authors*, ed. H. J. Jackson (Oxford: Oxford University Press, 1985), 390. Mary Shelley records Shelley reading and finishing 'Coleridge's Liteerary [*sic*] life' on 8 December 1817: see *MWS Journals*, 186.

'the shade of night' (10) as though it were at least a likely or proximate reality, yet it asserts that 'the lamp of love' can convert 'night' to 'day'.

The replay of their positions in stanzas three and four intensifies the initial difference, much as Wordsworth's 'My former thoughts returned' (120) in 'Resolution and Independence' 'returns' to earlier despondent 'blind thoughts' (28), but lends them a sharpened edge of near-unendurability. In stanza three, the First Spirit's quickened anxiety finds expression through an unfinished 'But if' clause which passes into a moment of seeing that has its own visionary exaltation: 'But if the whirlwinds of darkness waken / Eclipse and Lightning and stormy rain— / See, the bounds of the air are shaken, / Night is coming' (17–20). The inflections here suggest comparisons and contrasts with the troubled gravity of Wordsworth's sombre transitions: 'But there's a Tree, of many one, / A single Field which I have looked upon' ('Ode: Intimations of Immortality', 51–2, for example). Wordsworth locates the emotion in the objects of his contemplation and memory: tree and field 'speak of something that is gone' (53); Shelley catches natural objects up in a pre-existing force-field of feeling.

Wordsworth's 'emotions'—Leavis was surely right—'seem to derive from what is presented'. Shelley's emotions seem to precede the object and to exist in a complex relationship with 'Eclipse and Lightning and stormy rain'. Leavis was wrong to assert that 'Shelley, at his best and worst, offers the emotion in itself, unattached, in the void'.[19] But his hostile observation brings us up sharply against the need to account for the interplay between subject, object, and feeling in Shelley's poetry. It is part of of the impressive rapidity of Shelley's work (his intellect and emotions in affecting, intelligent interplay) to sense the ways in which figures refuse solely to obey the dictates of the pre-linguistic or to serve as obedient objective correlatives. Such a sense is crucial to the poem: thus, the command to 'See, the bounds of the air are shaken' (19) recognizes that 'seeing', visionary apprehension, is central to the way in which perception constructs reality. The command is half in love with the menace it officially deplores, because such menace speaks eloquently of the ways in which feeling acts as a shaping spirit. The Second Spirit's retort—'I see the glare and I hear the sound; / I'll sail on the flood of the tempest dark / With the calm within and light around / Which makes night day' (25–8)—positively glories in the shaping made possible by subjectivity. 'I see' decisively faces down the First Spirit's command to 'see', while the reference to 'the glare' and 'the tempest dark' implies that the Second Spirit accepts the First Spirit's account of the symbolic weather, but not its fear in the face of that weather-system. Rather the commitment to the potentially dangerous—in 'I'll sail'—not only anticipates the scorn and defiance of the closing stanza of *Adonais*, as Chernaik notes,[20] but it also shows a joyous confidence in the capacity for transformation of the 'calm within and the light around'. And yet even this confidence momentarily destabilizes itself; 'makes' in line 28 (the manuscript's probable reading) may be one of Shelley's false agreements

[19] F. R. Leavis, 'Shelley', *Revaluation: Tradition and Development in English Poetry* ([1936] Harmondsworth: Penguin, 1972), 200, 201.
[20] Chernaik, *The Lyrics of Shelley*, 143.

(one would expect 'make' following the two governing nouns, 'calm' and 'light'). Yet it may also show the Spirit's awareness that it cannot rely on inner calm; it depends, too, on 'the light around'.

2

Such dialogic delicacy is at work within Shelley's poetry and in its relations with Wordsworth, and subtly so in his response, as suggested already, to *The Excursion*. In this section, I discuss that poem and suggest how Shelley (and Keats) derives imaginative sustenance from its oscillations of mood and purpose. Much as Milton could be regarmented in indeterminate robes, so could Wordsworth, through the lens offered by the allusive practice of the younger Romantics, appear less decided and settled than at first sight seems possible. This-worldly at its most yearningly transcendental, *The Excursion* is a congeries of paradox: a narrative poem suspicious of narrative, a dialogue poem that seems to question the very nature of dialogue, a poem that continually swerves away from and returns to the discover of 'painful and discreditable shocks / Of contradiction' (V, 358–9), where sound effects knit themselves into waves of chiastic shock. Distinguished work in recent years has recognized in the poem a tale that is far from the unreadable monolith of critical tradition.[21] It is a poem of heights and depths, hope and despair, the private and the public, in many ways the quintessential Romantic long poem, as, in their different ways, Shelley and Keats were quick to see. Harold Bloom finds a 'very bitter rhetorical irony' in Keats's response at the start of *The Fall of Hyperion* to the spirit of lines from Book IV of Wordsworth's poem, lines that conclude, in Bloom's extract, thus: 'The words he uttered shall not pass away / Dispersed like music that the wind takes up / By snatches, and lets fall, to be forgotten.'[22] Bloom is quoting from a—beautifully—revised version that seems to recover an original readiness to mediate between opposites.[23] He might have shown more explicit admiration for the way in which Wordsworth's words imagine and enact their own musical dispersal in the act of denying that such dispersal will happen. The very movement from 'Dispersed' to 'like music' typifies the gentle shocks of mild surprise delivered by Wordsworth's rhythms and diction; musical dispersal is a very different thing from mere dispersal.

Keats responds to the poem's ability to convey the ebb and flow of feelings as among its chief distinctions. Whatever Shelley's overt polemical view of the poem, as indicated in the comment written by Mary Godwin in her journal in which she records the household's collective response to *The Excursion*, 'much disappointed. He is a slave', echoes in *Prometheus Unbound* suggest that he responded

---

[21] See Alison Hickey, *Impure Conceits: Rhetoric and Ideology in Wordsworth's 'Excursion'* (Stanford: Stanford University Press, 1997) and Sally Bushell, *Re-reading 'The Excursion': Narrative, Response, and the Wordsworthian Dramatic Voice* (Aldershot: Ashgate, 2002).

[22] Harold Bloom, *Poetry and Repression: Revisionism from Blake to Stevens* (New Haven: Yale University Press, 1976), 125.

[23] For the textual detail, see Bushell et al., ed. 165.

with a similar artistic appreciativeness to Keats.[24] One occurs in the first act, when the Fury taunts Prometheus with the 'emblem' of Christ on the cross: 'Behold, an emblem: those who do endure / Deep wrongs for man, and scorn and chains, but heap / Thousandfold torment on themselves and him' (I, 594–6). The Fury recalls the Solitary's gloomy moralizing over the expiring ashes of 'A gypsy fire' (IX, 528): 'Behold an emblem here / Of one day's pleasure, and all mortal joys!' (IX, 554–5). Shelley's poetry will frequently seek to rekindle those ashes, to advance beyond admonitory emblems. Still, the Solitary's words have struck home. Such, too, at the other end of the emotional spectrum, is the case with the Poet's words about the longevity of the Wanderer's words quoted above: 'The words he uttered shall not pass away' (IV, 1280). Shelley, whose Rousseau pleads with the shape all light in *The Triumph of Life*, 'Pass not away upon the passing stream' (399), is alert to the manner in which 'the passing stream' bears human hopes with it. At the close of his lyrical drama, a work preoccupied with the concern to find a language that will last without congealing into fixities and definites, Shelley hearkens back to the Poet's resolute assertion (with its distinctly optative undernote) when his dramatis personae address Demogorgon thus: 'Speak: thy strong words may never pass away' (IV, 553).

Shelley has learned from Wordsworth's poem, so his allusions indicate, how to convey different feelings within as well as across passages. This Wordsworthian ability relates to *The Excursion*'s dialogic form, even if Hazlitt's discrediting of Wordsworth's ventriloquism in his review of *The Excursion* still has force: 'An intense intellectual egotism swallows up everything. Even the dialogues introduced in the present volume are soliloquies of the same character, taking three different views of one subject'. He goes on effectively to annul the concession implied in 'different views': 'The recluse, the pastor and the pedlar, are three persons in one poet. We ourselves disapprove of these interlocutions between Lucius and Caius as impertinent babbling, where there is no dramatic distinction of character'.[25] Despite the valiant attempts of recent criticism, Hazlitt surely has the last word here, except one would wish to add a proviso. The wittily Trinitarian 'three persons in one poet' is better described as a psychomachia of struggling inflections; the result is an overall voice that blends movements towards resistance, instruction, acceptance, and resilience, and yet continually threatens to fracture into one of these stances.

For the inflections are stances, attitudes, achieved and sustained through rhetorical devices that foreground awareness of themselves as rhetorical devices. Question, apostrophe, rhapsodic flight, interjection, rumination, and analogy are among the means through Wordsworth both maintains a conversation and ensures that it is often univocal. And yet this univocality is neither tyrannous nor dull, as is evident when in Book IV, praising and illustrating the intuition of 'a SPIRIT hung' (731) in ancient Greece, the Wanderer evokes a thought

---

[24] *MWS Journals*, I. 25.
[25] William Hazlitt, review of *The Excursion*, in *William Wordsworth: A Critical Anthology*, ed. Graham McMaster (Harmondsworth: Penguin, 1972), 116.

Of Life continuous, Being unimpaired;
That has been, is and where it was and is
There shall be,—seen, and heard, and felt, and known,
And recognized,—existence unexposed
To the blind walk of mortal accident;
From diminution safe and weakening age;
While Man grows old, and dwindles, and decays;
And countless generations of Mankind
Depart; and leave no vestige where they trod.
(IV, 751–9)

Another poet would have concluded the passage after the first line, but not Wordsworth, a writer here as so often attracted by the possibilities of drawn-out sense, of taking his blank-verse line for an apparently rambling yet ultimately terrifying walk. That walk begins with near-mystical affirmation and leads itself and the reader, by the end, close to the gates of tragedy's mansion. Or to change the metaphor, appositional lines float on a sea of near-wayward suggestion. Two strong negative epithets bring to mind the conditions of impairment and exposure that they seek to outlaw. The effect is intensified by Wordsworth's manuscript revision from 'Of Being unimpaired, continuous life'.[26]

The impression is of assertions fending off anxiety. Wordsworth defines 'Life' and 'Being' through various modes of the verb 'to be' that chase one another across time (and the line-ending) like dots on an optometrist's visual screen tester. Being 'has been'; it 'is'; and 'where it was and is / There shall be'; the final future tense almost accidentally opposes the present tense which is being's preferred dimension—'almost accidentally' because there is, in *The Excursion*, something that does not love an unqualified assertion. The effect of 'There shall be' may mean to be lordly, to proclaim continuity, but the phrasing comes across as calculatedly over-emphatic, substituting imagined fiat for certainty.

Moreover, the lines roughen anything too fluent through jagged punctuation—dashes propel the thought sideways as much as forward. Abrupt caesurae, such as the pause after 'Depart' in the final line, impart point and edge to what might else risk complacency. So, too, does the collision between meaning and word order in 'From diminution safe and weakening age', where 'safe' does not safeguard the poetry from the threat of the 'age' with which it assonantally rhymes and over which it seeks to assert control. That control gives way to its opposite as Wordsworth imagines old age in a series of verbs that have a mind of their own. The very sounds in 'diminution' and 'age' refuse to be silenced, gaining a paradoxically 'weakening' momentum in 'dwindles', 'decays', 'generations', 'vestige', and 'they'.

That the passage inspired two of the most affecting moments in two of Keats's most affecting poems—he imagined the tread of 'hungry generations' in 'Ode to a Nightingale' (62) and the wasting effect of 'old age' on 'this generation' in 'Ode on a Grecian Urn' (45)—is itself a tribute to Wordsworth's elegiac achievement here. The Wanderer's verse and voice half-answer to Christopher Ricks's tribute to

---

[26] See Bushell et al., ed., 729.

Wordsworth's 'commitment to those ample relationships which yet do not swamp or warp the multiplicities which they accommodate'. Ricks sums this commitment up as follows: 'No fragmentation into separateness; but also no dissolution within a greedily engrossing unity'.[27] 'Half-answer' because the Wanderer's speech here and elsewhere does not occupy the benign via media between extremes that Ricks's elegant formulations articulate. Instead, 'greedily engrossing unity' slugs it out with threatened 'fragmentation into separateness' within the very texture of the poetry. Within a moment the recognition that 'Man grows old, and dwindles, and decays' has passed into lines that quell fear and yet raise further questions:

> We live by admiration, hope, and love;
> And even as these are well and wisely fixed,
> In dignity of being we ascend.
> But what is error?—'Answer he who can!'
> The Sceptic somewhat haughtily exclaimed,
> 'Love, Hope, and Admiration—are they not
> Mad Fancy's favourite Vassals?...'
>   (IV, 760)

The Solitary recognizes the dangers of Imagination in the spirit of one only too conscious of Imagination's lure. Here he seems to voice the Wanderer's own doubt, 'But what is error?' That is a good question to pose to one who engages in 'wandering'. It is the question that haunts Wordsworth's (and, one might add, Romanticism's) elevation of 'admiration, hope, and love'. Shelley will write of *Epipsychidion* that 'the error, and I confess it is not easy for spirits cased in flesh and blood to avoid it, consists in seeking in a mortal image the likeness of what is perhaps eternal' (*Letters: PBS*, 2. 434). Indeed, the 'generous error' (92) of which Shelley's Preface to *Alastor* speaks suggests empathy with the Solitary. What, indeed, is 'error?' The Wanderer's doubly abrupt turn is striking: first on his own expression of sadness at the human lot, then on his attempted advocacy of positive principles. It is in these moments when Wordsworth threatens to expose his fabric of belief in imagination and nature as based on performative rhetoric that *The Excursion* seems the forerunner, not only of Shelley's *Adonais* or Keats's *The Fall of Hyperion*, but also of a poem such as Stevens's *Notes Toward a Supreme Fiction*. So, a section such as IX from 'It Must Be Abstract', the opening part of *Notes*, mocks imagination as the supposed vehicle of a lightly derided 'apotheosis', apparently rejected in favour of reason's 'applied / Enflashings'.[28] Yet that way of describing 'reason' brings it close to imagination's gaudy, gorgeous brocade, and in a series of enjambed, appositionally redefining lines that modernize Wordsworth's handling of blank verse in *The Excursion*, Stevens starts to blur the distinctions round which his meditation is structured; so, 'reason' is 'lighted at midnight by the studious eye, / Swaddled in revery, the object of / The hum of thoughts evaded in the mind, / Hidden from other thoughts'. Stevens's syntax swaddles reason 'in revery', turns it (this revery-swaddled thought)

---

[27] 'Wordsworth: "A Pure Organic Pleasure from the Lines"', in McMaster, ed., 507.
[28] Wallace Stevens, *Collected Poems* (London: Faber, 1955).

into 'The object of / The hum of thoughts evaded in the mind'. Stevens is clear in his elegantly at-a-remove way about 'thoughts evaded in the mind'; Wordsworth gives the reader access to the specific pressures generating such evasions. But in both poets the 'hum of thoughts' or the still, sad music of reflection is audible in the very carriage of the poetry, in its intricately modulated melody.

'Imagination itself is the illness. It is also, of course, the strength of man', wrote Geoffrey Hartman in an incisive couple of sentences whose context (he is discussing Margaret's hope in Book 1 of *The Excursion*) makes it clear that 'man' is used inclusively.[29] Variations on this conflicting view of imagination constitute the real centre of the poem and provide something close to the 'poem of true spiritual debate' that Hartman senses as an only intermittent possibility.[30] The structure in Books II to IV attempts to envelop the Solitary in understanding: so, the Wanderer tells the tale of the Solitary, before the Solitary tells his own tale, and the Wanderer responds in would-be despondency-correcting mode. But the poem's effectiveness is to disrupt anything too pat or moralizing. Indeed, it is striking how the poetry is less interested in didactic point-scoring than in exploring 'the passages / Through which the Ear converses with the heart' (IV, 1148–9), moments when the answer is 'yes' to the Wanderer's question, 'Has not the Soul, the Being of your Life / Received a shock of awful consciousness…?' (IV, 1150–1). The question revolves on itself like so many formulations in the poem: to talk of 'Soul' receiving 'a shock of awful consciousness' is as though 'consciousness' were something done to 'Soul' when it seems also to be a mode of the soul's 'Being'. Tucked away in the lines is a Wordsworthian sense of 'Being' as a continuum interrupted by heightenings, interjections of awe-inspired and awe-inspiring awareness. From that amplitude of suggested sounds and effects, Shelley was able to imagine his own responses, in works as different from one another as *Prometheus Unbound* and *The Witch of Atlas*, to his age's challenges to the poet. Productive disagreement is sponsored by Shelley's inwardness with what Eric Lindstrom perceptively describes as 'how the thinking that takes place in Wordsworth's poetry actually sounds'.[31]

3

Or was Shelley, in the end, unable to free himself from Wordsworth's influence? Harold Bloom, with *The Triumph of Life* in mind, views Shelley's relationship as conforming to one of the sombre scenarios dictated by his revisionary ratios: even in the midst of some of his finest writing, Shelley, for Bloom, comes close to rehearsing a Wordsworthian *ur*-plot: 'Here, at his end', writes Bloom, 'Shelley is open again to the terror of Wordsworth's "Intimations" ode, and yields to his precursor's

---

[29] Geoffrey H. Hartman, *Wordsworth's Poetry, 1787–1814* (Cambridge: Harvard University Press, 1971), 301.
[30] Hartman, 300.
[31] Eric Lindstrom, 'Mourning Life: William Wordsworth and Percy Bysshe Shelley', *Romanticism* 23.1 (2017): 38–52 (45).

"light of common day" '.[32] Such an example of *apophrades*, the return of the dead, is, for Bloom, ambivalent: evidence of poetic defeat or of the strength that lies in yielding, and though he seems to imply that Wordsworth's return in *The Triumph of Life* is an example of the former, he leaves the door ajar to the view that it is evidence of the latter.

As Bloom goes on to remark: '*How* they [the dead] return is the decisive matter.'[33] Shelley echoes 'Ode: Intimations of Immortality' in his account of the 'shape all light' (352) in *The Triumph of Life* to haunting effect. If she comes trailing clouds of Wordsworthian allusion, associated as she initially is with 'a gentle trace / Of light diviner than the common sun / Sheds on the common Earth' (337–9), her role is not simply to show that all lights 'fade into the light of common day' ('Ode', 76), or that they can be retrieved only through memory, 'the philosophic mind' ('Ode', 189) and the suffering 'human heart by which we live' ('Ode', 203).[34] It is to rehearse a scene of imaginative seduction and desire, the poet's imagination conjuring an objective correlative of its dazzling capacity to shape scenarios of quest and encounter, even if the result is to take us into the peculiarly and purely Shelleyan realm where the object of poetic pursuit is 'forever sought, forever lost' (431). To depict with such radiant menace so ultimately enigmatic a meeting between poet and implicit muse is to criss-cross one's voice with a precursor's to original and compelling effect.

Wordsworth's return in Shelley's late poetry follows the swaying between mockery and reluctant admiration in *Peter Bell the Third*, the fifth section of which drew from Leavis the concessionary praise that it bears witness to a 'fine critical intelligence'. Leavis points out, too, that Shelley's reflections on Wordsworth involved a sense that 'the recognition of affinities is at the same time the realization of differences'.[35] That 'realization' is more the poetry's than the poet's. Leaving to one side for a moment the poem's 'avowedly skittish' nature, in Leavis's phrase,[36] it is fascinating to observe how Shelley, for all his sense of Peter's limits ('as much imagination / As a pint-pot', 298–9), ascribes to his satirical target a capacity for transcendental longing that seems more distinctive of the poem's author: Peter, writes Shelley, would make songs on 'the universal sky— / And the wide earth's bosom green;— / And the sweet, strange mystery / Of what beyond these things may lie / And yet remain unseen' (408–12). 'The "bosom" and the "sweet" there are not Wordsworth', says Leavis sniffily.[37] But what is perhaps even less Wordsworthian is the concern with what 'may lie' 'beyond' the natural 'And yet remain unseen'. Wordsworth's domain is the mind of man, or 'that blessed mood, / In which the burthen of the mystery . . . / Is lightened' ('Tintern Abbey', 38–42), or 'the mighty world / Of eye and ear' ('Tintern Abbey', 106–7).

---

[32] Harold Bloom, *The Anxiety of Influence: A Theory of Poetry* ([1973] New York: Oxford UP, 1975), 140.

[33] Bloom, *The Anxiety of Influence*, 141.

[34] The poem's light imagery has received much attention. For an illuminating recent discussion, see Mark Sandy, ' "Lines of Light": Poetic Variations in Wordsworth, Byron, and Shelley', *Romanticism* 22.3 (2016): 260–8, which comments on 'Shelley's desire to draw out the scepticism within Wordsworth's poetry' (267).

[35] Leavis, 'Shelley', 182, 182–3.   [36] Leavis, 'Shelley', 181.

[37] Leavis, 'Shelley', 183.

Shelley's wish to portray Wordsworth as a poet of the 'unseen' suggests a desire to free him the '*matter-of-factness*' or 'laborious minuteness and fidelity to the representations of objects, and their positions, as they appeared to the poet' to which Coleridge objects in *Biographia Literaria*.[38] But it also involves an element of conscious projection, Wordsworth proleptically anticipating the thirst for the 'unseen' which is at work in the poetry of one of his major poetic descendants. Shelley's 'universal sky' may take its cue from Wordsworth's account of 'Love, now an universal birth, / From heart to heart is stealing' (21–2) in 'Lines Written at Small Distance from My House'. But the universality of 'feeling' (24), which Wordsworth lyricizes with such keenly displaced millennial feeling, involves movement 'From earth to man, from man to earth' (23), as the chiastic phrasing has it. Shelley makes Peter an apostle of the 'universal sky', a phrase not without this-worldly or possibly pantheist implications, but one calculated to send the gaze soaring, much as Shelley's skylark, 'soaring still doest sing, and singing ever soarest' (10) fills the onlooker with a sense of 'hidden want' (70). Wordsworth's skylark certainly prompts the poet with admiration for the 'madness about thee, and joy divine / In that song of thine' ('To a Sky-Lark', 12–13). But, for all his command to come 'Up with me! up with me into the clouds' (1), a command that shows how any ascensions are on the poet's terms, Wordsworth concludes the poem with his feet firmly on the ground: 'Hearing thee, or else some other, / As merry a Brother, / I on the earth will go plodding on, / By myself, cheerfully, till the day is done' (26–9). Shelley, by contrast, does not suppose that, in any simple way, Wordsworth's hope that 'Joy and jollity be with us both!' (25) can be fulfilled. For all the poet's desire to be inspired as the skylark is, Shelley's lyric affects us most deeply as a confession of estrangement from and longing for the spirit-bird's undivided rapture. Even if we could do away with negative emotions, 'I know not how thy joy we ever should come near' (95), he says, which is a pointed rejoinder to Wordsworth's concluding trust in the fitness of things.

And yet Shelley's poem takes flight through the very acuteness of its desire. Wordsworth boisterously declines to compete with the bird he depicts as a 'Happy, happy Liver! / With a soul as strong as a mountain River!' (22–3), the feminine rhyme delighting in the bird's happiness and linking its 'soul' firmly with the strength of a 'mountain river'. Shelley ties the bird to his favourite image of idealistic ascent, once again adapting Wordsworth's image from 'Ode: Intimations of Immortality' to his less appeasable quest: 'Like a star of Heaven, / In the broad daylight / Thou art unseen,—but yet I hear thy shrill delight' (18–20). The simile works both to confirm the reality of that 'star of Heaven' (significantly given pride of place in the syntactical ordering) and its inability to make itself visible 'In the broad daylight'. And the poet's capacity to 'hear thy shrill delight' mixes up sense and intuition so that the skylark's audibility warrants, through the not wholly logical sleights of argumentative hand at which Shelley's poetry is adept, belief that the senses, though inadequate, can support the mind's and heart's best 'imaginings'.

[38] *Samuel Taylor Coleridge: The Oxford Authors*, ed. H. J. Jackson (Oxford: Oxford University Press, 1985), 391.

The phrasing reveals how 'scorn of the narrow good we can attain in our present state' wins the upper hand towards the close of Shelley's career. The letter of April 1822, from which those words are taken, views Wordsworth as a poet who has removed himself from 'emotions' (which evidently Shelley has experienced) 'known only to few' that 'derive their sole charm from despair & a scorn of the narrow good we can attain in our present state'. Indeed, the letter goes on to present the rather remarkable spectacle of Shelley taking Wordsworth to task, not for his alleged political conservatism, but because of his insufficiently robust otherworldly longing:

> Perhaps all discontent with the *less* (to use a Platonic sophism) supposes the sense of a just claim to the *greater*, & that we admirers of Faust are in the right road to Paradise.
> —Such a supposition is not more absurd, and is certainly less demoniacal than that of Wordsworth—where he says—
>
>
>
> This earth,
> Which is the world of all of us, & where
> *We find our happiness or not at all.*
>
>
>
> As if after sixty years of suffering here, we were to be roasted alive for sixty million more in Hell, or charitably annihilated by a coup de grace of the bungler, who brought us into existence at first.[39]
>
> (Letters: PBS, 2. 406, 406–7)

Meditating on *Faust*'s impact on him, Shelley concedes the sophistical nature of the quasi-Platonic arguments that the imperfect presupposes the existence of the perfect, but he refuses to detach himself from the wish that such a presupposition should be the case. Wasserman describes how Shelley 'succeeded, with the aid of "the intellectual philosophy," in transforming scepticism into a probabilism'.[40] But his 'probabilism' depends on no support from any 'intellectual philosophy', and seems, so the concluding sentence suggests, to have no truck with Christian dogma. But it also decisively rejects Wordsworth's complicated ventriloquizing of this-worldly hope expressed in the lines that Shelley slightly misquotes from 'The French Revolution, As It Appeared to Enthusiasts at its Commencement', a section of *The Prelude* (X. 725–7), printed in the older poet's collected *Poems* of 1815 (and attended to earlier in this book). Shelley sees as 'low-thoughted' (see *A Defence of Poetry*, 700) a view of 'happiness' that deems it locatable only in this world. Again, he seems to draw on Wordsworth's 'Ode: Intimations of Immortality' for confirmation that his precursor's best works speak against their creator. The 'Ode' locates 'Our destiny, our nature, and our home' with 'infinitude', as indeed Wordsworth also does in *The Prelude*, VI. 538–9. Shelley's dealings with Wordsworth in his later poetry hold the older poet to that intuition in the belief that 'it is the province of the poet to attach himself to those ideas which exalt and ennoble humanity' (note to line 197 of *Hellas*, 585), and that his great precursor is pre-eminent among those contemporary

---

[39] See also my discussion in *The All-Sustaining Air: Romantic Legacies and Renewals in British, American, and Irish Poetry since 1900* (Oxford: Oxford University Press, 2007), 110–11.
[40] Wasserman, *Shelley: A Critical Reading*, 176–7.

poets who 'even whilst they deny and abjure,…are yet compelled to serve, the Power which is seated on the throne of their own soul' (*A Defence of Poetry*, 701). When Shelley writes of his hope that 'we admirers of Faust are in the right road to Paradise', he engages with what David Luke notes as 'the motif of striving (*Tätigkeit, Streben*)' that is evident in the so-called ' "third phase" additions' of Goethe's work (*Faust: Part One* was published in 1808).[41]

What Shelley's triangulation of himself, Goethe, and Wordsworth bears witness to is a longing for affirmation borne out of near-desperation, a conjunction of impulses behind and at the heart of the final assertions of *Adonais* (1821). And as he sets himself to quest for 'a more sublime and far-distant *telos*' than Byron articulates as the final goal of *Childe Harold's Pilgrimage*,[42] Shelley summons as spur and stimulus to his voyage the figure of Wordsworth. Wordsworth appears in the draft as the likely prototype of one of the procession of mourners: 'And next came a spirit beautiful & strong / Wrapt in the guise of an uncomely form / He sometimes like a pedlar limped along / With packs upon his back';[43] tellingly, the language used in the draft attaches itself in significantly revised form, in the final version, to the self-portrait of the poet himself who appears as 'A pardlike Spirit beautiful and swift' (32. 280) and as 'a Power / Girt round with weakness' (32. 281–2). Wordsworth as a Shelleyan shadow self oddly ghosts the self-portrait, though Shelley assumes a Dionysian 'Power' not developed in his draft account.

Towards the poem's end Shelley nerves himself for a final voyage in pursuit of 'The soul of Adonais' which 'like a star, / Beacons from the abode where the Eternal are' (55. 494–5), and the stellar influences include Wordsworth's 'Ode' as well as the sestet of his sonnet to Milton ('Milton! thou shouldst be living at this hour') in which he asserts, 'Thou soul was like a star, and dwelt apart' (7).[44] This is not to agree with the pessimism implicit in Harold Bloom's severe judgement that Shelley had the greatness to recognize that 'Wordsworth will legislate and go on legislating for your poem, no matter how you resist or evade or even unconsciously ignore him'.[45] In his elegy for Keats, Shelley draws sustenance from Wordsworth, while retaining his own restless turbulent individuality, much as *Adonais*, in Newey's fine insight, 'valorizes transcendence' yet 'nowhere cuts us off from life'.[46] That Shelley does not cut us or himself off from life connects with the elegy's belated discovery of life's value, since the imagination demands that life must be more than material existence. Physical death cannot prevail over Keats's persistent poetic life. Asserting the reality of Keats's post-mortal being, Shelley, as Jonathan Wordsworth has observed, invokes a 'pantheism' in stanza 42 that cannot but recall the rhythms and

---

[41] See Johann Wolfgang von Goethe, *Faust: Part One*, trans. David Luke (Oxford: Oxford University Press, 1987), p. xxxii. For valuable conversations about Shelley and Goethe, I am grateful to the late Stephanie Dumke.
[42] Newey, 'Shelley and the Poets', 266.
[43] Quoted (in cleaned-up form) from the transcription in *BSM* XIV, 22–3.
[44] For this sonnet's significance for Shelley's sonnet 'To Wordsworth', see Graham Allen, 'Transumption and/in History: Bloom, Shelley and the Figure of the Poet', 'Shelley Special Issue', *Durham University Journal* n.s. 35 (1993): 247–56, esp. 250–1.
[45] Harold Bloom, *Poetry and Repression* (New Haven: Yale University Press, 1976), 111.
[46] Newey, 'Shelley and the Poets', 268.

diction of 'Tintern Abbey'. Thus, as Jonathan Wordsworth notes, Wordsworth has '*"felt | A presence* that disturbs [him] with the joy / Of elevated thoughts"' (94–6), while 'Adonais is himself "*a presence to be felt* and known"' (emphases are Jonathan Wordsworth's).[47]

Adonais is the name that Shelley has given to Wordsworth's 'something far more deeply interfused'. That a poet should emerge as an abiding presence is right for this poem that asserts the power and significance of poetry, and in doing so reminds us that *A Defence of Poetry* builds on the claims for poetry made by Wordsworth's Preface to *Lyrical Ballads*. But *Adonais* asserts poetry's significance and power with its eyes open. It explicitly notes the inadequacy of language, 'words' being among those frail material elements that 'are weak / The glory they transfuse with fitting truth to speak' (52. 467–8). It implicitly disclaims the role of poetry as guide to philosophical or metaphysical knowledge, unashamedly conceding its metaphorical nature in its final stanza's spirit-voyage and its readiness to draw clashing ideas together in its images and imaginings, the Platonic and Gnostic jostling with the humanist and pantheist. And yet in such concessions lies Shelley's final refusal to allow Wordsworth to legislate for him. What legislates for Shelley is what legislated for Wordsworth: the poetic 'Power' 'seated on the throne of [his] own soul'.

---

[47] Jonathan Wordsworth, 'Introduction', *Percy Bysshe Shelley: Adonais 1821* (Oxford: Woodstock, 1992), pp. v–vi, p. vi.

6

'The Gleam of Those Words'

Shelley and Coleridge

'When Coleridge met Shelley': it is a bewitching scenario, that, unlike the aldermanic poet's meeting with a credulous, sceptical Keats, who took away memories of words about 'Nightingales, Poetry [...] single and double touch', among many other things, and above all of an incessant voice, never happened.[1] But it was not for want of trying on Shelley's part. As a young firebrand, he visited Keswick in late 1811 to have it out with the Lake poets. In the event, he met Southey, former Pantisocratic zealot and now the subject of oscillating feelings on Shelley's part (feelings that will be explored more thoroughly in the next chapter). In a letter of December 1811 the older man is viewed with some sympathy as 'an advocate of liberty and equality', but also seen with considerable astringency as 'an advocate for existing establishments; he says he designs his three statues in Kehama to be con-templated with republican feelings—but not in this age'. For his part, in the same letter, Shelley reports that Southey informed Shelley that the latter was 'not an Atheist but a Pantheist' (from the perspective of some stanzas in *Adonais*, this com-ment was among Southey's more suggestive critical insights). Touchingly, since it implies a mingled sense of identification and loss, Southey confided to Grosvenor Bedford that Shelley 'acts upon me as my own Ghost would do', and that he had told Shelley that 'all the difference between us is, that he is nineteen, and I am thirty-seven'.[2] By mid-January 1812, Shelley had decided that 'Southey the Poet whose principles were pure & elevated once, is now the servile champion of every abuse and absurdity' and he remarks coolly that he does 'not feel the least disposition to be Mr. S's proselyte' (*Letters: PBS*, 2. 211, 212, 219, 2l9n, 231).

According to Thomas Jefferson Hogg's entertaining if unreliable biography of Shelley (to be revisited in the next chapter), one thing Shelley learned from Southey was a love of 'buttered tea-cakes' ('tea and toast' are lovingly praised in *Letter to Maria Gisborne*, 303).[3] After abstemiously watching Southey wolf down his grub, Shelley exclaimed, according to Hogg, 'It is awful, horrible, to see such a man as you are greedily devouring this nasty stuff', a phrase which Mrs Southey, the 'lovely Edith', did not care for: 'Nasty stuff! I like your impertinence!' Hogg narrates how Shelley then 'put his face close to the plate, and curiously scanned the cakes', pacifying

---

[1] *Letters: John Keats* II, 88, 89.
[2] *The Life and Correspondence of Robert Southey*, ed. Charles Cuthbert Southey, 6 vols (London: Longman, Brown, Green, & Longmans, 1850), 3, 325–6.
[3] Shelley's poetry and prose will be quoted from *Major Works* in this chapter.

Mrs Southey by beginning to 'eat as greedily as Southey himself'.⁴ It is possible to view the tale as a comic parable illustrating Shelley's fascination with the work of writers whom, at some level, he found guilty of producing 'nasty stuff'.

> Coleridge, in later life, regretted that he had not met Shelley in 1811–12. *Table Talk* records his views thus:

>> Shelley was a man of great power as a poet, and could he only have had some notion of order, could you only have given him some plane whereon to stand, and look down upon his own mind, he would have succeeded [...] He went to Keswick on purpose to see me and unfortunately fell in with Southey instead.

>> [...] Southey had no understanding or toleration of such principles as Shelley's. I should have laughed at his Atheism. I could have sympathised with him and shown him that I did so, and he would have felt that I do so. I could have shown him that I had once been in the same state myself, and I could have guided him through it. I have often bitterly regretted in my heart of hearts that I did never meet with Shelley.⁵

Coleridge sees Shelley here as another case for sympathetic 'mentoring', a process whose involvement with the construction of masculinity and the dynamics of power has been teased out by Anthony John Harding.⁶ It is fair to say that Coleridge underestimates the task he imagined himself performing. He echoes an Archimedean precept, which, ironically, Shelley quotes in support of fiercely republican ends as an epigraph to *Queen Mab* and *The Revolt of Islam*.⁷ Coleridge turns Shelley's activist wish to 'move the earth' into a more inward 'look down upon his own mind', but when Shelley looks 'down upon his own mind' in 'Mont Blanc' he experiences 'a trance sublime and strange' (version A, 35), and one might argue, against Coleridge, that such a process of vertigo-like self-exploration often occurs in the younger poet's best work. But Southey's dealings with Shelley brought Coleridge to the younger poet's notice. If he sends Elizabeth Hitchener Wordsworthian pastiche ('She was an aged woman') one day from Keswick (7 January 1812), the next week he posts her 'The Devils Walk', his version of Southey's and Coleridge's jointly composed anti-establishment ballad (*Letters: PBS*, 1. 224–6 and 235–7).

Steven Jones points out shrewdly in connection with Shelley's ballad that its ' "derivativeness" is precisely the point... Shelley declares himself to be derived— from [...] the best in the earlier work of the elder poets'.⁸ He simultaneously learns from Coleridge and Southey, and turns against his teachers the lessons of their former practice in a poem that has its own ways of upsetting the status quo, as when the parson hypocritically 'Bawled out that if the devil were [there] / His presence he couldn't abide' (*Letters: PBS*, 1. 236), lines where Shelley catches both bawling

---

⁴ *Wolfe*, I, 293, 294.

⁵ *Table Talk*, 2 vols, ed. Carl Woodring (London: Routledge; Princeton, NJ: Princeton University Press, 1990), vol. 14 of *The Collected Works Samuel Taylor Coleridge*, I, 574.

⁶ Anthony John Harding, 'Coleridge as Mentor and the Origins of Masculinist Modernity', *European Romantic Review* 14 (2003): 453–66.

⁷ See *Major Works*, 10, 130: 'Give me a place to stand, and I will move the earth' is the precept in question.

⁸ Steven E. Jones, *Shelley's Satire: Violence, Exhortation, and Authority* (DeKalb: Northern Illinois UP, 1994), 41–2.

greed and unctuousness. The poem's rhetorical strategies are double-edged. This is a signature of Shelley's response to Coleridge. The *locus classicus* for studying this response is 'Mont Blanc', evidently written with Coleridge's 'Hymn before Sun-rise, in the Vale of Chamouny' in mind. Most commentators stress Shelley's polemical reaction against Coleridge's theistic raptures. 'Who *would* be, who *could* be an Atheist in this valley of wonders!', exclaimed Coleridge in his poem's first printing in the *Morning Post* of 1802.[9] 'Me for one', Shelley appears to reply (though he may not have read those words since he appears to have read Coleridge's poem elsewhere). His poem invests the Alpine Mountain with a voice that repeals 'Large codes of fraud and woe' (version A, 82), including, it would seem, the codes associated with Mosaic law and the Christian dispensation. By contrast, famously or notoriously (via Fredericke Brun's 'Ode to Chamouny'), Coleridge persuades the natural world to identify its maker as God in a thunderous chorus.

However, before we settle for this now standard reading, according to which Shelley the atheist nimbly outwits Coleridge the plagiarizing believer, it is worth adding two qualifications. First, as Angela Esterhammer has pointed out, 'Hymn before Sun-rise' is, very much and in a highly self-conscious way, about poetic voice and its performance, and 'betrays his doubts that the Logos might finally be nothing but a projection of fallible human voice'.[10] Coleridge, in fact, pleads with natural elements to 'Utter forth GOD, and fill the Hills with Praise' (69).[11] There, 'Utter' has something of the force of 'give *outness* to', in this case a giving that involves a willed projection of voice.[12] Second, Shelley does something characteristically multiple and contrary in the last two sections of his poem, where, in effect, he offers two endings, each designed to show that assumptions dictate perception. Section 4 is Shelley at his most gruellingly and intransigently materialist. The descent of the glaciers leads first to ruin and destruction, then results in a river that is 'The breath and blood of distant lands' (124). None of this cares for us, though humans are the beneficiaries in that the river Rhone makes possible life, trade, and culture. Before he finishes the section, though, Shelley inserts an allusion to 'Kubla Khan', which he must have known via Southey (there is an echo in *Queen Mab*) or Byron.[13] Straight after depicting the glaciers' work of destruction—'The race / Of man flies far in dread; his work and dwelling / Vanish, like smoke before the tempest's stream, / And their place is not known' (117–20), where the final phrase's echo of Job 7:10 deepens its sombre tone—Shelley shifts into a different gear: 'Below, vast caves / Shine in the rushing torrents' restless gleam, / Which from those secret chasms in tumult welling / Meet in the vale' (120–3). The 'caves', 'chasms', and 'tumult' recall the arcane, variously symbolic progress of Coleridge's 'sacred

[9] Quoted from *The Poems of Samuel Taylor Coleridge*, ed. Ernest Hartley Coleridge (London: Oxford UP, 1912), 377n.
[10] 'Coleridge's "Hymn before Sun-rise" and the Voice Not Heard', *Samuel Taylor Coleridge and the Sciences of Life*, ed. Nicholas Roe (Oxford: Oxford University Press, 2001), 226.
[11] Quoted from *CPP*. Unless stated otherwise, this edition is used for all quotations from Coleridge's work; page numbers are supplied parenthetically for quotations from the prose.
[12] See *Samuel Taylor Coleridge: The Oxford Authors*, 543.
[13] For the echo of 'Kubla Khan' in *Queen Mab*, see A. C. Bradley, 'Coleridge-Echoes in Shelley's Poems', in his *A Miscellany* (London: Macmillan, 1929), 174.

river' ('Kubla Khan', 3; see also 34, 12, and 29). The dual nature of Shelley's vision hinges on and is caught by the rhyming, 'welling' pulling the poem into a positive dimension in a way that the ruination of 'dwelling' had seemed to deny.

Coleridge's presence in these lines brings into play possibilities of an upward turn. The echoes may mark an implicit concern, on Shelley's part, with creativity, with building domes in air. If Coleridge's river is 'sacred', Shelley's 'chasms' are 'secret', and that local pararhyme suggests Section 5's larger tangential approach to and movement from Coleridge's ambivalent ecstasy about creativity. Here at his poem's close Shelley nudges his 'secret strength of things' (139) in a numinous direction, but only by underscoring the operations of the 'human mind's imaginings' (143). Without these 'imaginings', themselves a deliberately curtailed version of Coleridge's 'shaping spirit of Imagination' ('Dejection; An Ode', 86), there would be no sense of meaning or even of meaninglessness (itself a meaning). Shelley returns for his emphatically excited ending, in which the limits of a materialist view of reality are glimpsed, to the hushed potency of Coleridge's 'silence'. Vital in Coleridge's poetry (vital as in vitalist)—one thinks of 'The Eolian Harp' or of 'Frost at Midnight'—silence allows for a Logos-mimicking emergence into creative voice.

It is characteristic of Shelley's inward response to Coleridge that he seizes on the potential that coils within the older poet's use of 'silence': 'The Arve', writes Coleridge in 'Hymn before Sun-rise', 'and Arveiron at thy base / Rave ceaselessly; but thou most awful Form! / Risest from forth thy silent Sea of Pines, / How silently!' (4–7). Coleridge's exclamation indicates how his imagination is fascinated by silence. It is Shelley's awareness that the human mind's imaginings can turn 'Silence and solitude' into states distinguishable from 'vacancy' (144), which, beautifully if momentarily and still guardedly, releases his poem from the rigorous sceptical grasp in which it has been held. He imparts this awareness through a reworking of the Coleridgean lines just quoted: 'Winds contend / Silently there, and heap the snow with breath / Rapid and strong but silently' ('Mont Blanc', 134–6). 'Silently', the twice-spoken adverb, lends 'silence' the status of an agent, and the echo of Coleridge is neither submissive nor usurpatory, but courteous, as though Shelley, at his poem's end, shows himself aware of ground shared with an ideological opponent. As Stuart Curran argues: 'Shelley's concluding question is subtler in its extensions, but otherwise is essentially the same as that with which Coleridge began his hymn ["Hast thou a charm to stay the Morning-Star / In his steep course"?]. Both mountains and morning-stars are accorded their charms by poets' imaginations.'[14] Curran's phrasing may too genially reconcile the two poems; Coleridge is, after all, intent on a 'blending' of mountain and 'Thought' (19); Shelley stresses the difficulty of such a blending. What is sub-text in Coleridge is suddenly urgent priority in Shelley. The overall effect produced by the interplay between the two poems corroborates Sally West's discovery in her fine study of 'a more dialectical relationship between the two writers' work' than is allowed for by the notion of a 'linear

---

[14] Stuart Curran, *Poetic Form and British Romanticism* (New York: Oxford UP, 1986), 62.

movement where forms, figures and ideas pass in a rather unreconstructed manner from Coleridge to Shelley'.[15]

That is one example of Shelleyan interaction with Coleridgean poetry. There is, in Shelley's use in the poem of 'Kubla Khan', a responsiveness to Coleridge's fascination with wholeness and coherence, and it is possible to contend that Shelley diverges from Coleridge by emphasizing the gap between poetic utterance and non-linguistic reality. Coleridge, the theorizing idealist, on this account, seeks to use language to mediate between word and thing, consciousness and being; his power shows itself 'in the balance or reconciliation of opposite or discordant qualities' (*Biographia Literaria*, 14, 495). Shelley, the very sceptical idealist, seems, on James Engell's reading and that of others, to allow a shadow or veil always to fall between idea and experience.[16] And yet, we need to recall, with Seamus Perry, that, for Coleridge, the poet 'struggles to idealize and to unify' (*Biographia Literaria*, 13, 488), where 'struggles' warrants a long look; indeed, much in the poetry that is of value struggles against the impulse to idealize and unify.[17] For his part, Shelley can sound like the unifying Coleridge of critical tradition when he argues in *A Defence of Poetry* that poetry 'transmutes all that it touches' and that 'every form moving within the radiance of its presence is changed by wondrous sympathy to an incarnation of the spirit which it breathes' (*Major Works*, 698). Admittedly, this sounds like more like a process of alchemical wizardry than a vision of poetry as symbolic; that is, as 'characterized by a translucence of the Special in the Individual or of the General in the Especial or of the Universal in the General' (*The Statesman's Manual*, 360). But, Shelley might retort, does poetry always partake 'of the Reality which it renders intelligible' (360) when, in fact, what it brings out is that the reality which it renders is not intelligible? From a perspective established by the more oracular moments in *The Statesman's Manual* and *Biographia Literaria, A Defence of Poetry* trades in paradoxical minglings of affirmation and doubt; from a perspective offered by *A Defence,* Shelley exposes the subjectivist implications, which Coleridge seeks to outflank, of believing, as he argues in *The Statesman's Manual*, that 'That, which we find in ourselves, is...the substance and the life of *all* our knowledge' (368). What follows is a shadow vision of a reality divested of 'substance' and 'life', which seems to be a recurrent Coleridgean nightmare, rendered with panache: 'Without this latent presence of the "I am," all modes of existence in the external world would flit before us as colored shadows' (*The Statesman's Manual*, 368). Shelley in *A Defence* overrides as inconsequential the dual possibility that poetry 'spreads its own figured curtain or withdraws life's dark veil from before the scene of things'; what matters is that poetry 'creates for us', in either mode, 'a being within our

---

[15] Sally West, *Coleridge and Shelley: Textual Engagement* (Aldershot: Ashgate, 2007), 14. See also Dewey Hall, ' "From Steep to Steep": Poetic Indebtedness in Coleridge and Shelley', *Coleridge Bulletin* 31 (2008): 102–11.

[16] James Engell, *The Creative Imagination: Enlightenment to Romanticism* (Cambridge: Harvard UP, 1981). Engell writes: 'The final paradox for Shelley is that the creation of a diffuse, even abstract higher world—one that can never be accurately expressed in words—places a hazy and receding goal before the poet' (264).

[17] Seamus Perry, *Coleridge and the Uses of Division* (Oxford: Clarendon P, 1999), 152.

being' (*Major Works*, 698). For Coleridge the absence of the 'I am' renders reality substanceless and confirms a gulf between 'Knowing' and 'Being' (*The Statesman's Manual*, 369); he also fears a state in which discovery within the self of analogues and evidences of reality gives way to solipsism. For Shelley, in some moods, poetry may either project or discover its meanings without sacrificing its gift of newly created being; in other moods, he fears or bravely accepts that the only validation of projected desire is desire itself.

The two most Janus-faced poets of their respective generations thus engage, as incited by Shelley, in remarkably intricate intertextual conversation. To stay for a moment with passages surrounding the just-quoted passage from *A Defence*, one notes that Shelley here echoes twice Coleridge's phrase 'film of familiarity'. In *Biographia Literaria* (chapter 14) Coleridge described how Wordsworth

> Was to propose to himself as his object, to give the charm of novelty to things of every day [...] by awakening the mind's attention from the lethargy of custom, and directing it to the loveliness and the wonders of the world before us; and inexhaustible treasure, but for which in consequence of the film of familiarity and selfish solicitude we have eyes, yet see not, ears that hear not, and hearts that neither feel nor understand. (490)

Shelley argues that poetry 'strips the veil of familiarity from the world', then in the next paragraph he asserts that poetry 'purges from our inward sight the film of familiarity which obscures from us the wonder of our being. It compels us to feel that which we perceive, and to imagine that which we know' (*A Defence of Poetry*, 698). The first reworking imagines decisive agency as it translates Coleridge's 'film' into Shelley's favoured 'veil' image; the second reworking looks hard at Coleridge's implied ocular image and makes clear that poetry performs a kind of 'inward' cataract operation. Elsewhere in *A Defence* Shelley has deplored obsession with the self, but here he drops the older poet's moralizing about 'selfish solicitude' and focuses on a mode of vision that is not identifiable with straightforward seeing. The relationship established is mobile and respectful, just possibly carrying with it an inflection of implied reproach when one recalls that within a few paragraphs Shelley almost certainly—in another image involving poetry's compulsion—has Coleridge in mind when he speaks of those contemporary poets who 'even whilst they deny and abjure...are yet compelled to serve, the Power which is seated on the throne of their own soul' (*A Defence of Poetry*, 701).

This 'Power' promotes and depends on 'Hope'. In the fifth number of the 1809–10 *The Friend* Coleridge writes, 'What an awful Duty, what a Nurse of all other, the fairest Virtues, does not hope become! We are', he goes on, 'bad ourselves, because we despair of the goodness of others'.[18] There are occasions when Coleridge writes as he had lost 'hope'; indeed, the early 'O! there are spirits of the air!' by Shelley seems to recognize, even sardonically to recommend, this hopeless state. 'Addressed in idea to Coleridge', according to Mary Shelley's Note, the poem sees Coleridge as a version of the defeated quester after ideals with whom Shelley demonstrates an

---

[18] Coleridge, *The Friend*, ed. Barbara F. Rooke, 2 vols (London: Routledge, 1969), 2, 70.

entangled sympathy in *Alastor*.[19] In the lyric, Shelley addresses the 'thou' with astringent if severely tender mockery: 'Ah! wherefore didst thou build thine hope / On the false earth's inconstancy?' (19–20). This may seem a bit rich since it is Coleridge who would have taught Shelley that 'we receive but what we give' ('Dejection: An Ode', 47), but it is possible that Shelley deploys in his critique of the older poet one of the latter's own phrases. Coleridge's manuscript correction to 'The Rime of the Ancient Mariner' in a copy of *Lyrical Ballads* (1798) between lines 503–4 reads, 'Then vanish'd all the lovely lights, / The spirits of the air, / No souls of mortal men were they, / But spirits bright and fair'.[20] Did Shelley know this? At any rate, he and the 'thou' share knowledge of 'spirits of the air, / And genii of the evening breeze' (1–2). 'Such lovely ministers to meet / Oft hast thou turned from men thy lonely feet' (5–6), Shelley continues, the pentameter consolidating the turn towards loneliness which elicits a sympathy that is unsparing, even lacerating. The poem is eerily diagnostic in the way it suggests that the speaker, for all his apparent aloofness, has undergone a similar disillusion. It turns Coleridge's image of a 'frightful fiend' from 'The Rime of the Ancient Mariner' (450) against him in the last stanza, where fiends mirror and multiply. Coleridge's lines (446–51) mimic in their turns across the line-endings a terrified compulsion to 'turn' and not to 'turn'; Shelley catches a similar pull between feelings since it is as though in his last stanza the speaker of Shelley's lyric cannot bear Coleridge not to bear his fate: 'Be as thou art. Thy settled fate, / Dark as it is, all change would aggravate' (35–6). 'Change', the motive for poetic figuration in Shelley, the lifeblood of his poetry, here would 'scourge thee to severer pangs' (34).

Shelley was, one senses, all the more responsive to Coleridge's celebration of 'hope' as a duty because of his sense that Coleridge's poems are aware of the difficulty of sustaining hope. In 'Dejection: An Ode' Coleridge refers with affecting restraint to a time when he could endure 'misfortunes': 'For hope grew round me, like the twining vine' (80); in 'To a Gentleman [William Wordsworth]', he magnifies hope until it takes on a larger political resonance, as he evokes the onset of the French Revolution, 'When from the general heart of Human kind / Hope sprang forth like a full-blown Deity!' (36–7), before that 'Hope' undergoes a sacrificial undoing in the next line: 'Of that dear Hope afflicted and struck down' (38). This is the condition that Shelley alludes to in his Preface to *Laon and Cythna*, where he regrets that 'many of the most ardent and tender-hearted of the worshippers of public good, have been morally ruined by what a partial glimpse of the events they deplored appeared to show as the melancholy desolation of all their cherished hopes' (*Major Works*, 132). 'To a Gentleman [William Wordsworth]' looks ahead to later lyric masterpieces such as 'Work Without Hope' when Coleridge speaks of how Wordsworth's reading of *The Prelude* awoke in him 'Fears self-will'd, that shunned the eye of Hope; / And Hope that scarce would know itself from Fear' (67–8). Allegorical abstractions tie themselves into an emotional knot that is hard to disentangle in those lines. Coleridge, then, may have helped Shelley to compose

---

[19] Quoted in *Longman* I, 448.   [20] *The Poems of Samuel Taylor Coleridge*, 205n.

the final lines of *Prometheus Unbound*, when Demogorgon recommends that, should tyranny return, human beings will need 'to hope, till Hope creates / From its own wreck the thing it contemplates' (IV, 573–4), where 'creates' saves 'contemplates' from passive acquiescence. The rhyme recalls but revises Christabel's acquiescence in Geraldine's evil power when she 'passively did imitate / That look of dull and treacherous hate' (593–4). Shelley's lines, like the lyrical drama as a whole, fight against the circularity of 'revolution' in the pessimistic sense of endless revolvings.

More indirectly, Coleridge's emphasis on hope may underpin 'Ode to the West Wind'. It is noteworthy that Shelley quotes from the passage about hope in the fifth number of the 1809–10 *The Friend* during the month (October 1819) when he composed the Ode. 'Let us believe in a kind of optimism in which we are our own gods', he writes, with good-humoured yet impassioned raillery; '[...] it is best that we should think all this for the best even though it be not, because Hope, as Coleridge says is a solemn duty which we owe alike to ourselves & to the world' (*Letters*: *PBS*, 2. 125). The Ode's blend of sadness and affirmation builds on the concern with what Coleridge in *Biographia Literaria* calls 'the mind's self-experience in the act of thinking' (7, 432), or, rather, praying, the activity with which 'To a Gentleman [William Wordsworth]' ends. Behind the plea in Shelley's final stanza to the god-like wind to 'Make me thy lyre, even as the forest is' (57) lies a Coleridgean sophistication concerning the workings of simile, about which Susan Wolfson has written, as well as an image—of the Eolian harp—which so far as the Romantics are concerned, Coleridge can be said to have patented.[21] Shelley uses the image of the Eolian harp with an inflection, one of affecting restraint, that recalls the first line of the last stanza of 'Dejection: An Ode': ''Tis midnight, but small thoughts have I of sleep' (l. 126). For Shelley, the stress induced by the effort to identify human and natural, a stress apparent in the phrase 'even as', will prove too great. Recovery from the depression of the Ode's previous section cannot erase the cause for that depression: namely, that the poet cannot be part of the natural cycle, as can leaf, cloud, wave, and wood. The curse and ambiguous blessing of human consciousness is that it permits the poet, in rhythms mimetic of struggle, to 'have striven / As thus with thee in prayer in my sore need' (51–2), where 'As thus', emphasized across the tercet's break, quickens the poem's pulse by making clear that its reference is to the poem we are currently experiencing. The final section of the Ode tests to the very limits the possibility of identification between wind and poet, before the lyre image is found wanting. The consequence is not despair, but a reaffirmation of poetic power, as by 'the incantation of this verse' (65) Shelley commands the wind to 'Scatter' (66) his 'words among mankind' (67). Coleridge, too, in 'The Eolian Harp', flirts with a fiction of universal harmony, 'And what if all of animated nature / Be but organic Harps diversely fram'd [...]?' (36–7) and concedes that to do so is to give way to 'idle flitting phantasies' (32), to mistake a metaphor for reality. The inflections of the two poems differ, but their self-awareness is comparable. Both poems do not mime their crises; they actively experience them.

---

[21] Susan J. Wolfson, *Formal Charges: The Shaping of Poetry in British Romanticism* (Stanford: Stanford University Press, 1997), see chapter 3, 'The Formings of Simile: Coleridge's "Comparing Power" '.

That said, Coleridge's preference for the return, the 'rondo',[22] the voyage back to the harbour, or to the 'COT' ('The Eolian Harp', l. 56), is not shared by Shelley whose lyric trajectory tends to be away from the concept of 'home', towards the 'intense inane' (*Prometheus Unbound*, III. iv. 204).

Both poets wrestle with evil, the chief challenge to their official, if very different, modes of optimism about the human condition. 'The Eolian Harp', especially in an earlier version sought to subsume 'Shrill Discords' within 'Creation's vast concent'.[23] Shelley respects Coleridge's attunement to those discords, and his own poetic music shows how attentively he listens to Coleridge's poetic compositions. Famously, the divesting by Geraldine in *Christabel* when 'she unbound / The cincture from beneath her breast' (242–3) caused Shelley to run shrieking from a room in Geneva; so wrought up by Coleridge's lines was he that he 'suddenly thought of a woman he had heard of who had eyes instead of nipples'.[24] It is intriguing how a frisson of horror in *Christabel* haunts a moment in one of Shelley's finest, though unfinished, short poems, 'The Two Spirits—An Allegory'. Composed after Coleridge's strictures on 'Allegory' in *The Statesman's Manual* as 'but a translation of abstract notions into a picture-language' (360), the poem, with its dual perspectives and coda of surmise and uncertainty, may concede and, indeed, affirm that poetry cannot render reality into intelligible form. Shelley's lyric suggests, that is, that poetry is always engaged in the potentially fruitless pursuit of 'empty echoes which the fancy arbitrarily associates with apparitions of matter' (360) that Coleridge mocks yet evokes with sympathy in his account of allegory in *The Statesman's Manual*. 'The breathless stars are bright above / If I should cross the shade of night' (9–10), asserts Shelley's second spirit, the optimistic one. There is a subliminal recollection, there, of the line in *Christabel* where Geraldine tells Christabel, 'And once we cross'd the shade of night' (l. 86). The spirit's optimism is shaded by the transgressive murk in Coleridge which it transforms to its own aspiring purposes.

Both poets see evil as coiling round the will. *The Cenci* and the first act of *Prometheus Unbound* are full-scale meditations on these lines in Coleridge's *The Dungeon*, excerpted from *Osorio* (*Remorse*): 'So he lies [the prisoner] / Circled with evil, till his very soul / Unmoulds its essence, hopelessly deformed / By sights of evermore deformity!' (16–19). Coleridge's syntax captures the mixedly passive and active nature of evil influence: passively 'Circled with evil'—here circles are not welcomed by Coleridge—the soul actively 'Unmoulds its essence'. The idea of becoming what you behold is, for Shelley, double-sided, leading either to spiritual betterment or to corruption. For a medico-spiritual version of the former view, one might cite the lines in *Prometheus Unbound*, Act II Scene iv, which contend that women who gaze during pregnancy on beautiful sculptures 'drank the love men see / Reflected in their race' (II. iv. 83–4). For an example of the latter view, one might

---

[22] See *CPP* for Coleridge's use of the term 'rondo' in explaining why he revised the end of 'Frost at Midnight': 'The six last lines I omit because they destroy the rondo, and return upon itself of the Poem', p. 123n (a photograph of the original is printed on 122).

[23] See *Poems of Samuel Taylor Coleridge*, 42, 43, 520.

[24] Quoted from John Buxton, *Byron and Shelley: The History of a Friendship* (London: Macmillan, 1968), 15.

turn to Prometheus' lines when confronted by the Furies: 'Whilst I behold such execrable shapes, / Methinks I grow like what I contemplate, / And laugh and stare in loathsome sympathy' (I, 449–51). The notion parodies the belief in poetry as seeking, say, to 'familiarize the highly refined imagination of the more select classes of poetical readers with beautiful idealisms of moral excellence' (*Major Works*, 232).[25]

The Cenci, too, is fascinated by the way in which the soul may unmould its essence through the exacting of vengeance, as is hinted by Coleridge in his deceptively light-hearted 'The Raven', which offers the parodic moral: 'They had taken his all, and REVENGE IT WAS SWEET!' (44).[26] 'Revenge', for Shelley, is a particularly dangerous form of 'loathsome sympathy'. *The Cenci* broods on Beatrice's decision to take revenge on her father for his incestuous rape of her. But that rape was not his only crime, since he proposes to 'teach [her] will / Dangerous secrets' (II. ii. 110–11), in Orsino's phrase, as when he asserts: 'She shall become (for what she most abhors / Shall have a fascination to entrap / Her loathing will) to her own conscious self / All she appears to others' (IV. i. 85–8). Shelley's language diagnoses psychological processes in a way that may owe a debt to Coleridge's insights in 'The Dungeon'. Again, in 'The Pains of Sleep' Coleridge dramatizes with agonizing and generalizing power a sense of 'the powerless will / Still baffled, and yet burning still!' (21–2). The poem seems to have impressed itself on Shelley, who not only borrows for his 1819 *Rosalind and Helen* volume the apologia for metrical licence claimed by Coleridge's Preface to *Christabel, Kubla Khan, and The Pains of Sleep* (1816),[27] but also refers in that *Rosalind and Helen* collection to a depressed state, at the start of 'Lines Written Among the Euganean Hills', of 'Longing with divided will, / But no power to seek shun' (22–3).

In 'The Pains of Sleep' Coleridge's response to his 'Sense of intolerable wrong' (19) is to have 'wept as I had been a child' (40). In 'Stanzas written in Dejection— December 1818, near Naples', the title of which declares a debt to Coleridge's 'Dejection: An Ode', Shelley demonstrates a Coleridgean ability to move between emotions. In the second-to-last stanza, encapsulating this mixture, he writes: 'Yet now despair itself is mild / Even as the winds and waters are; / I could lie down like a tired child / And weep away the life of care / Which I have borne and yet must bear' (28–32). Coleridge wept 'as I had been a child'; Shelley 'could lie down like a tired child'. In both cases, the longing for a simplified condition is recognized for what it is. Coleridge emerges from his nightmare with this harrowing declaration of 'need', 'To be beloved is all I need, / And whom I love, I love indeed' (51–2), which movingly compacts bewilderment self-exculpation, and distress. The lines trace a circle, but do not close the gap between their two assertions. Shelley, more

---

[25] These 'classes' may derive their existence from, and yet compose a liberal alternative to, the 'Higher Classes of Society', addressed by Coleridge in *The Statesman's Manual*, 354.

[26] Quoted from *The Poems of Samuel Taylor Coleridge*.

[27] Shelley writes in his Advertisement of his use in *Rosalind and Helen* of 'a measure, which only pretends to be regular inasmuch as it corresponds with, and expresses, the irregularity or the imaginations which inspired it', *Longman* 2, 269. More circumspectly, yet influentially, Coleridge writes of 'the metre of the Christabel' in his Preface to his 1816 volume that the 'occasional variation in the number of syllables is not introduced wantonly, or for the mere ends of convenience, but in correspondence with some transition in the nature of the imagery or passion' (in *CPP*, 162).

guardedly, presents himself, at his poem's close, as 'one / Whom men love not, and yet regret' (41–2). As in 'Dejection: An Ode', Shelley conveys a sense in 'Stanzas Written in Dejection' of seeing, but not wholly feeling, how beautiful natural objects are: 'I see the waves upon the shore / Like light dissolved in star-showers, thrown; / I sit upon the sands alone: / The lightning of the noontide Ocean / Is flashing round me, and a tone / Arises from its measured motion' (12–17). The word 'I' hangs like a millstone round the neck of these lines, with their attempted goings out of the self through synaesthestic comparisons that may recall Coleridge's dance of elements in 'The Eolian Harp' where he discerns 'A Light in sound, a sound-like power in Light' (see 18n)—phrasing which influences the opening of *Julian and Maddalo*. There, Shelley celebrates the fact that 'sound like delight broke forth / Harmonizing with solitude' (25–6), even as the poem discovers painfully that intimations of harmony are a hazardous guide to the sad realities of human life, embodied most disturbingly in the Maniac's soliloquy. Shelley's perception of 'measured motion' in 'Stanzas Written in Dejection' alludes to the 'mazy motion' (25) and 'mingled measure' (33) of 'Kubla Khan'; the younger poet's dejection is the more acute for occurring when glimpses of something approaching the paradisal offer themselves.

Shelley's response to Coleridge the 'subtle-souled Psychologist', as he is described in *Peter Bell the Third* (379), also reveals itself in the fine account of hypocrisy's complications in *Prometheus Unbound*, Act III, Scene iv. There is in Shelley's lines a creative reworking of the Conclusion to *Christabel*, Part 2. Coleridge describes how a father, through 'excess of love', speaks to his child 'With words of unmeant bitterness' (652–53). Shelley, describing his Utopia through negations of things as they are, asserts: 'None talked that common, false, cold, hollow talk / Which makes the heart deny the *yes* it breathes, / Yet question that unmeant hypocrisy / With such a self-mistrust as has no name' (III. iv. 149–52). Shelley puts Coleridge's acutely perceptive lines under great syntactical pressure, twisting and turning from clause to clause, as he seeks to communicate the semi-conscious, self-mistrusting workings of 'unmeant hypocrisy', getting close here to the psychic processes that constitute oppression or lack of freedom. Something comparable happens in his adaptation of a line from the close of *Remorse* ('Desolation is a beautiful thing'),[28] itself a full-bloodedly unexpected turn, in *Prometheus Unbound*, Act I: 'Ah, sister! Desolation is a delicate thing' (I. 772). In Shelley's hands, the line empathizes in an uncannily mocking way with those who (like Coleridge from Shelley's perspective) had succumbed to disillusion following the apparent failure of the French Revolution.

In more evidently political ways Shelley draws on, yet takes issue with, Coleridge in *Prometheus Unbound*, Act I, and 'Ode to Liberty' to convey the nature of oppression and freedom. Coleridge's 'France: An Ode' expresses the conviction that 'the great *ideal* of Freedom' does 'not belong to men, as a society, nor can possibly be

---

[28] Quoted from Cyrus Redding with A. & M. Galignani, *The Poetical Works of Coleridge, Shelley and Keats 1829* (Otley: Woodstock, 2002), intro. Jonathan Wordsworth, 95 [of the Coleridge section]. The echo in *Prometheus Unbound* or the line from *Remorse* is noted by Bradley, 'Coleridge-Echoes in Shelley's Poems', *A Miscellany*, 175.

either gratified or realised, under any form of human government' (116n.). Attesting
to Shelley's admiration, copies survive in Mary Godwin's hand of 'France: An Ode'
(and of 'Fire, Famine, and Slaughter').[29] Shelley would have responded, however
ambivalently, to the Ode's true radicalism, its insistence that no society could
accommodate the ideal of Liberty, and he would have been alert to the implication
that, ultimately, this ideal could only be realized in a poem. 'France: An Ode' uses
an intricate stanza form and rhyme scheme as a counterpoint to its belief that
nature's 'pathless march no mortal may control' (2). Shelley will have quarrelled
with Coleridge's glorification of 'the love and adoration of God in nature' (116n)
and devotes much space in his 'Ode to Liberty' to the view that liberty can, if only
partially, be embodied in particular societies. Adapting an image from Wordsworth's
'Elegiac Stanzas Suggested by a Picture of Peele Castle' to a sense of imperilled survival, he writes of Athens as a local habitation of Liberty: 'Within the surface of
Time's fleeting river / Its wrinkled image lies, as then it lay / Immovably unquiet,
and forever / It trembles, but it cannot pass away' (76–9). There is covert pathos in
that final phrase; one cannot but recall Rousseau's agonized plea to the shape all
light in *The Triumph of Life*, 'Pass not away upon the passing stream!' (399). And
yet Shelley locates Liberty in time, but sees it as having a transhistorical existence.
He would have admired Coleridge's ability to bring himself as a poet into relation
with the abstraction Liberty, and his poetry reflects, too, his admiration for
Coleridge's diagnosis of historical events: 'The sensual and the dark rebel in vain, /
Slaves by their own compulsion' (85–6): these lines from stanza 5 of Coleridge's
poem ('a *Dilatation*', in Coleridge's words, 'of those *golden* Lines of Milton—
"Licence they mean, when they cry—Liberty!" ' (119n.)) are the cornerstone of
Shelley's ethics of freedom: one might compare Coleridge's lines to the definition
of 'slavery' in *The Mask of Anarchy*: 'Tis to be a slave in soul / And to hold no strong
control / Over your own wills, but be / All that others make of ye' (184–7), where
the rhyme between 'soul' and 'control' clinches Shelley's obsessive meaning.

   When one returns to *Prometheus Unbound* Act I, one can see how Shelley has
more or less repeated Coleridge's diagnosis of the causes for the French Revolution's
failure. 'See, a disenchanted nation / Springs like day from desolation' (567–8),
cries the first Semichorus, knowing of the disillusion to come, but recalling Coleridge's
own initial siding with France against the Alliance of England and the continental
powers: 'And when to whelm the disenchanted nation', writes Coleridge, 'Like
fiends embattled by a wizard's wand, / The monarchs march'd in evil day.../ Yet
still my voice unaltered sang defeat / To all that brav'd the tyrant-quelling lance'
('France: An Ode', 28–30, 36–7). Among the proudest and bravest lines Coleridge
ever wrote, they bequeath the epithet 'tyrant-quelling' to Shelley's dream of a
redeemed society in *Prometheus Unbound* Act IV (see line 272). In both Coleridge
and Shelley, 'disenchanted' means freed from a spell, not disillusioned. But disenchantment, in the modern sense, sets in as Shelley notes how 'kindred murder kin'
(573) and deplores the fact that 'Despair smothers / The struggling world' (576–7).

---

[29] See SC 569 in *SC* 7, 1–12. The editors speculate that 'Mary either wrote them [the poems] down
from memory or took them down as Shelley recited them', 9.

It is here, in their interpretation of the aftermath of the Revolution, that they diverge; Shelley's main objection to Wordsworth, Coleridge, and Southey was their support for the post-Waterloo reconstruction of Europe on ultra-conservative lines. But *Prometheus Unbound*, Act I, shows intertextual commerce with what might loosely be called 'Jacobin Coleridge'. So, the Furies have about them more than a smack of the brilliantly ventriloquized voices in 'Fire, Famine, and Slaughter'— which was, for Shelley, one imagines, among the great poems of political protest in the language. These voices satirically exaggerate, and in so doing, bring into exposed view the consequence of conservative political perspectives, content (from Coleridge's viewpoint) to unleash destruction and death. Shelley's Furies, in a comparable way, crowd together at the prospect of 'Shipwreck and Famine's track' (*Prometheus Unbound*, I. 501).

Coleridge's final stanza in 'France: An Ode', in which he 'shot [his] being thro' earth, sea, and air, / Possessing all things with intensest love' (103–4), sponsors the erotic climax of *Epipsychidion*, where Shelley expresses the wish that he and Emily will be 'Possessing and possessed by all that is / Within that calm circumference of bliss, / And by each other, till to love and live / Be one' (549–52). As always with Shelley, circles of happiness contain within themselves the germs of their own undoing, and that 'till' ushers in the poem's climax in which the poet confronts the twin facts of desire's unattainable nature and the limits of expression. More generally, one might argue that the two poets differ in their attitude to poetic coherence. At his greatest, Coleridge achieves 'a dance of thought' ('Fears in Solitude', 217). His poetry aspires to the condition of perfected aphorism: moments of local distillation, crystallizing feather-touches, in George Eliot's phrase.[30] Examples include the following: 'At once the soul of Each, and God of all' ('The Eolian Harp', 40); 'a miracle of rare device' ('Kubla Khan', 35); 'Their life the eddying of her living soul' ('Dejection: An Ode', 136). The first and third examples show Coleridge's predilection for concurrent mergings that still allow for distinctness: the second example displays his ability to bring together opposites in a new synthesis (here, he mingles 'miracle', with its suggestion of something beyond contrivance, and 'rare device', with its admiration for a designer). Indeed, the pathos of Coleridge's poetry lies in its compulsion to move beyond such glimpses of perfection. In a Notebook entry, he asks: 'If a man could pass thro' Paradise in a Dream, & have a flower presented to him as a pledge that his Soul had really been there, & found that flower in his hand when he awoke—Aye? And what then?'[31] He attains the Holy Grail of complete verbal resolution, and is still discontented. So, in the final section of 'Kubla Khan', the climber who has reached the peak is back in the foothills: 'A damsel with a dulcimer / In a vision once I saw' (37–8). It is the poetry's movement round these moments—its swellings and decrescendos, its transitions and returns— that make it so fine, but it has, the reader is convinced, a centre round which to circle. Coleridge's poetic being urges its miscellaneous, divided awareness of complexity towards brief, miraculous moments of definition, where nature and

---

[30] George Eliot, *Middlemarch (1871–72)*, ed. W. J. Harvey (Harmondsworth: Penguin, 1965), 355.
[31] *Coleridge's Notebooks: A Selection*, ed. Seamus Perry (Oxford: Oxford UP, 2002), 127.

imagination still themselves into harmony, 'Quietly shining to the quiet moon' ('Frost at Midnight', 79). Shelley rarely aims at this wholeness of utterance; his words are quickened always by being the shadows of the words they want to be. Even when summation looms, the metre and syntax leave a loophole, an incentive, a spur. His poetry hastens relentlessly onwards. Coleridge's symbolic triumphs leave nothing to be said; Shelley's language suits a poetry of quest. Coleridge finds himself 'Alone, alone, all, all alone, / Alone on a wide wide sea!' ('The Rime of the Ancient Mariner' (1834), 232–3): there is something quintessential here, in the becalmed, motionless centring of the verse on a moment of stasis; the nightmare flipside of a state of blessing and being blessed. In *Adonais* Shelley commits himself at the close to the sea, but gives over his verse to surges that bear him onwards, 'darkly, fearfully, afar' (55. 492). Shelley will return to origins in poems, but never without a sense of wanting to avoid entrapment within a turning cycle.

Generally, Shelley's response to authors who mean a great deal to him is marked by independence and thoughtful awareness, and it is clearly over-simplifying to read Shelley's response to Coleridge in the polemical or ideological terms sometimes encouraged by the younger poet's remarks. The tapestry of response is richly woven, as is revealed by the two portraits of Coleridge which appear in Shelley's writings between 1819 and 1820. The first occurs in *Peter Bell the Third*. Initially, one needs to observe that Peter, primarily Wordsworth, has Coleridgean touches. The lines from Wordsworth about his pre-conversion attachment to 'the world / Of all of us', which Shelley quotes mockingly in his Preface (*Major Works*, 416), originally appeared in Coleridge's *The Friend*, where they are introduced as illustrating 'the state of thought and feeling [...] when France was reported to have solemnized her first sacrifice of error and prejudice on the bloodless altar of Freedom, by an Oath of Peace and Good-will to all Mankind'.[32] In Part Sixth, admittedly not working to Coleridge's advantage, Peter is said to read Kant, and to assume a pusillanimous subtlety: 'He was no Whig, he was no Tory: / No Deist and no Christian he,— / He got so subtle, that to be / Nothing, was all his glory' (565–8). These lines describe a posture not often associated with Wordsworth by his ideological opponents and one which Shelley imagines with a certain empathy and recoil, partly, one suspects, as a result of his reading of Coleridge. One notes, too, that, just a few stanzas later, Shelley observes that 'The old Peter—the hard, old Potter— / Was born anew within his mind: / He grew dull, harsh, sly, unrefined, / As when he tramped beside the Otter' (580–3), and appends a note: 'A famous river in the new Atlantis of the Dynastophylic Pantisocratists' (770): it is a jibe at political tergiversation that fuses Wordsworth and Coleridge (the author of an early sonnet to the river Otter) into a single subject.

It is in Part Fifth that Shelley offers his most sustained depiction of Coleridge (378–97), or of a figure meant to be identified with Coleridge. There is forthright critique here—of Coleridge's trust in 'shadows undiscerned' (386)—but troubled admiration, too. Shelley composes a version of 'tragic Coleridge', his inspired words somehow failing to save him from madness, but leaving on those who hear them

---

[32] *The Friend*, 2, 148, 147.

an indelible impression, a reflected 'gleam' (396). Arguably, *A Defence of Poetry* launches itself from the stanza beginning, 'He spoke of poetry, and how / "Divine it was"' (388–9). As Alan Weinberg puts it in a fine essay, 'Coleridge fails, but his potential for transformation...elevates him as well'.[33] The image Shelley uses to imply Coleridge's lack of self-understanding ('But his own mind—which was a mist', 382) derives from *The Rime of the Ancient Mariner* ('And now there came both mist and snow', 51). This wry reflex of poetic tribute receives support from the fact that the stanzas celebrating Coleridge's eloquence come after those offering critique. As a result, the reader is left with the effect on herself or himself that the words have on Peter—and indeed Coleridge: 'And when he ceased there lay the gleam / Of those words upon his face' (396–7). Of course, if there is admiration, there is mockery, too, as Shelley mimics the tones of effortless oratory. The description of poetry as 'A spirit which like wind doth blow / As it listeth' (390–1) is close to calculated commonplace, and crying out for the reworking which Shelley gives it in the prose poetry of *A Defence:* 'its footsteps are like those of a wind over the sea, which the coming calm erases, and whose traces remain only as on the wrinkled sand which paves it' (*Major Works*, 697). There, Shelley breathes into the figure of poetry as a sea a fugitive rarity of heightened perception.

In *Letter to Maria Gisborne*, Coleridge appears amidst a gallery of pen-portraits. Shelley depicts him in terms that recall his portrait of Maddalo in *Julian and Maddalo*. For Julian, Maddalo's sense that 'he was greater than his kind / Had struck, methinks, his eagle spirit blind / By gazing on its own / exceeding light' (50–2). In the *Letter* Coleridge

> sits obscure
> In the exceeding lustre, and the pure
> Intense irradiation of a mind
> Which, with its own internal lightning blind,
> Flags wearily through darkness and despair—
> A cloud-encircled meteor of the air,
> A hooded eagle among blinking owls.—
>
> (201–7)

The balance of admiration and criticism is expertly calibrated; there is a hint of Miltonic deity in the opening, and a tragic awareness of thwarted power pervades the writing. Empathy extends to the rhythm which itself 'Flags wearily'.

It is less Shelley's tragic awareness of Coleridge's fate with which one might wish to finish this discussion than the older poet's spur towards celebration, however productively conflicted. Two examples occur in 'To a Gentleman [William Wordsworth]'. First, Coleridge provides Shelley with the basis for his discovery in *A Defence of Poetry* of 'that great poem, which all poets like the co-operating thoughts of one great mind, have built up since the beginning of the world' (*Major Works*, 687). The subtlety with which Shelley stays inside temporal bounds, even

---

[33] See Alan Weinberg, ' "Yet in its Depth What Treasures": Shelley's Transforming Intellect and the Paradoxical Example of Coleridge', *Romanticism on the Net* 22 (May 2001) <http://id.erudit.org/iderudit/005979ar>.

as he surmounts them, owes much to the Coleridge who argues that: 'The truly Great / Have all one age, and from one visible space / Shed influence! They, both in power and act, / Are permanent, and Time is not with *them*, / Save as it worketh *for* them, they *in* it' (50–4); there, the final clause readmits 'the truly Great' into the workings of time as cooperative agents of 'permanence'. Again, the same poem's praise for *The Prelude* as 'An orphic song indeed, / A song divine of high and passionate thoughts, / To their own Music chaunted!' (45–7) underpins Shelley description in *Prometheus Unbound*, Act IV, of 'Language' as 'a perpetual Orphic song, / Which rules with daedal harmony a throng / Of thoughts and forms, which else senseless and shapeless were' (415–17). Shelley extends Coleridge's understanding of a poetry that is no less interested in 'high and passionate thoughts' for being in touch with its own 'music'. All 'language' in Shelley's redeemed universe aspires self-consciously to the condition of Coleridgean 'orphic song', even as it moves selflessly outwards to empower 'a throng / Of thoughts and forms'.

Those 'thoughts and forms' that would 'senseless and shapeless' be without language might alert us to the significance for Shelley's poetry of Coleridgean 'shaping' and 'shapes'. In 'The Rime of the Ancient Mariner', there is a passage which haunted Shelley, and which he turns to his own different and indeterminate ends, describing the arrival of the spectre-bark: 'At first it seemed a little speck, / And then it seemed a mist; / It moved and moved, and took at last / A certain shape, I wist' (149–52). Shelley echoes this passage in the first canto of *Laon and Cythna*: 'the hue / Of the white moon, amid that heaven so blue, / Suddenly stained with shadow did appear; / A speck, a cloud, a shape, approaching grew, / Like a great ship in the sun's sinking sphere / Beheld afar at sea, and swift it came anear' (1. 175–80). Here, Shelley places in the foreground the work of interpretation demanded of the readers of history, poetry—and this poem. In *The Mask of Anarchy*, too, Shelley inverts the nightmare scenario of 'The Rime of the Ancient Mariner' when the words of the 'maniac maid' (86) serve as prelude to the emergence of 'a Shape arrayed in mail' (110). This 'Shape', in turn, heralds the overthrow of 'Anarchy' (the chain of causality at this point is intricate).

Shapes of various degrees of benignity feature in Shelleyan poems as diverse as 'The Two Spirits—An Allegory' and *The Triumph of Life*, always testifying to Shelley's fascination with the ambivalent (to him), but all-important work of the 'shaping spirit of Imagination'. That ambivalence reveals itself in the use he makes in *The Triumph of Life* of the image at the start of 'Dejection: An Ode' of the old moon in the new moon's lap, 'foretelling / The coming on of rain and squally blast' ('Dejection: An Ode', 13–14): a gloomy prospect which Coleridge welcomes, since it 'might startle this dull pain, and make it move and live!' (20). Shelley introduces the shape within the car of life with the image of the old moon in the young moon's arms (79–85). This moment, Coleridge transfused with Dante, as it were, balances itself on 'the sunlit limits of the night' (80), exhibiting Shelley's sense of Coleridge as a poet of the liminal, of crossings between states. Not for nothing are these two poets the finest translators among the Romantics.

Coleridge inspires Shelley to some of his most affirmative moments. Behind the 'one Spirit's plastic stress' (43. 381) in *Adonais*, and allowing for difference (the greater pressure and urgency of Shelley's syntax is one key to this difference), is the momentarily pantheist Coleridge of 'The Eolian Harp', surmising the presence in nature of 'one intellectual Breeze' that is 'Plastic and vast' (39). Shelley pointedly rejects Coleridge's theistic solutions, but he shares his desire to affirm. So, the blessing of the water-snakes in 'The Rime of the Ancient Mariner' animates an epiphanic moment in *Prometheus Unbound*, when it is said of the Spirit of the Earth that 'as it moves, / The splendour drops in flakes upon the grass' (III. iv. 4–5), recalling the Mariner's sense of how when the water-snakes 'reared, the elfish light / Fell off in hoary flakes' (275–6). Again, one of the most terrifying (and already cited) stanzas in 'The Rime of the Ancient Mariner' (446–51), describing the feeling of being pursued by a frightful fiend (450), undergoes jubilant transformation in Shelley's complexly millennial anticipation of change in *Prometheus Unbound*, II. iv, where Asia sees 'cars drawn by rainbow-wingèd steeds' (130): 'Some look behind, as fiends pursued them there, / And yet I see no shapes but the keen stars' (133–4).[34] This passage might be read reflexively as describing Shelley's backward glance at Coleridge: his rejection of his more hag-ridden experiences of 'darkness and despair', and his delight in his imaginative power. To say this, though, would be to simplify a relationship of extreme intricacy and significance. Shelley's relationship with Coleridge, a poet who produced Conclusions to both parts of *Christabel* that conclude nothing, refuses all attempts at pre-emptive closure.[35]

---

[34] For these Coleridgean echoes in *Prometheus Unbound*, see *Shelley's 'Prometheus Unbound': A Variorum Edition*, ed. Lawrence J. Zillman (Seattle: University of Washington Press, 1959), 547, 482.

[35] For the application of Johnson's *Rasselas* to Coleridge's poem, see Stuart Curran, *Poetic Form*, 146.

7

Shelley and Southey Reconsidered

1

Shelley's visit to Southey in the winter of 1811–12 elicited the following story told by Thomas Jefferson Hogg in his *The Life of Shelley*:[1]

> Southey was addicted to reading his terrible epics—before they were printed—to any one who seemed to be a fit subject for the cruel experiment. He soon set his eyes on the newcomer, and one day having effected the caption [*sic*] of Shelley, he immediately lodged him securely in a little study upstairs, carefully locking the door upon himself and his prisoner and putting the key in his waistcoat-pocket. There was a window in the room, it is true, but it was so high above the ground that Baron Trenck himself would not have attempted it. 'Now you shall be delighted,' Southey said; 'but sit down.' Poor Bysshe sighed, and took his seat at the table. The author seated himself opposite, and placing his MS. on the table before him, began to read slowly and distinctly. The poem, if I mistake not, was *The Curse of Kehamah*. Charmed with his own composition, the admiring author read on, varying his voice occasionally, to point out the finer passages and invite applause. There was no commendation; no criticism; all was hushed. This was strange. Southey raised his eyes from the neatly-written MS.; Shelley had disappeared. This was still more strange. Escape was impossible; every precaution had been taken, yet he had vanished. Shelley had glided noiselessly from his chair to the floor, and the insensible young vandal lay buried in profound sleep underneath the table. No wonder the indignant and injured bard afterwards enrolled the sleeper as a member of the Satanic school, and inscribed his name, together with that of Byron, on a gibbet![2]

For Hogg, the encounter was paradigmatic of the poets' relations: Southey badgering his young visitor with all the thoroughgoing egotism of self-admiring mediocrity, Shelley outdoing Baron Trenck (whose adventurous *Life* had been translated by Thomas Holcroft in 1792) and escaping the boredom of one of Southey's 'terrible epics' through the time-honoured and nonchalantly well-bred expediency of falling asleep. Amusing as ever in his construction of a potent literary mythology, Hogg surely sacrifices fact to effect. All that we know about Shelley's initial response to Southey, a mixture of fervent admiration and critique, suggests that Hogg was deeply mistaken in his anecdotal impulse. 'The Curse of Kehama which you will have is my most favorite poem—yet there is a great error, *faith* in the character of the divine Kailyal' (*Letters: PBS*, 1. 101). So Shelley wrote on 11 June 1811 to

---

[1] For helpful comments on an earlier draft of this chapter, I am grateful to Madeleine Callaghan and Lynda Pratt.
[2] *Wolfe*, I, 292.

Elizabeth Hitchener, recipient of wide-ranging and metaphysical letters from the young poet. The qualifying criticism—'yet there is a great error, *faith* in the character of the divine Kailyal'—alerts us to the strain of dissent in Shelley's response to Southey, dissent which is imaginatively productive for the younger poet.

By '*faith*' Shelley is likely to have in mind disempowering trust in tyrannical powers beyond the self rather than in, say, a neutral power which is indifferent to human beings, floated as a hypothesis in poems such as 'Mont Blanc'. In *Laon and Cythna*, in a reprise of the scene involving three statues at the close of *The Curse of Kehama*, Shelley chooses as one of his three exemplary revolutionary figures an emblematic 'Image' 'dressed / In white wings':

> Beneath his feet, 'mongst ghastliest forms, repressed
> Lay Faith, an obscene worm, who sought to rise
> While calmly on the Sun he turned his diamond eyes.
> (*Laon and Cythna*, V. 2165–6, 2167–9)[3]

As is noted in the Longman edition, the image, 'recalling both the archangel Michael's defeat of Satan and St George's slaying of the dragon, is a traditional image of religious victory', but one that is here 'turned against *Faith*' (*Longman* 2, 153n).[4] By this stage of his career, after the disillusion that came quickly in the wake of meeting Southey in Keswick in the winter of 1811–12, Shelley rewrites the scene from *The Curse of Kehama* to express a critique of Southey's growing orthodoxy. In *The Curse of Kehama* the three statues, who condemn themselves as emblems of 'avarice, tyranny and religious fraud' (*Longman* 2, 152n), sustain a vacant 'Golden Throne' (*Kehama*, XXIV. 87) before Yamen, the Lord of Hell.[5] In the poem's final compelling twist Kehama, the tyrant, and Kailyal, the heroine, both drink the 'Amreeta-cup of immortality' (*Kehama*, XXIV. 131) and earn quite different rewards. Kehama becomes the fourth of the throne-bearers, Kailyal ascends to the Swerga Bowers, to enjoy everlasting bliss with her father, Ladurlad (who had been cursed by Kehama), her dead mother Yedillian, and her lover-protector Ereenia, the Glendoveer.

Kehama 'did not know the awful mystery / Of that divinest cup, that as the lips / Which touch it, even such its quality, / Good or malignant: Madman! and he thinks / The blessed prize is won, and joyfully he drinks' (*Kehama*, XXIV. 214–18): these clipped, half-Miltonic lines have that succinct direct address to the ethical implications of narrative easy to underestimate in Southey's verse. The drink's essence is its ambivalence, its fulfilment of the nature of the drinker. This aspect is pointed up by the way in which the writing takes us into Kehama's deluded mindset. 'The blessed prize is won' are words that shift with insidious skill into the present

---

[3] Since they are not included in *Major Works*, these lines are cited from *Longman* 2.

[4] It is also noted in *Longman* that one source for Shelley's 'diamond eyes' may have been 'the idol of Jaggernaut, described as having the shape of a serpent with seven heads in the notes to Southey's *The Curse of Kehama* ...XIV (JagaNaut)'. *Longman* 2, 153n).

[5] Southey is quoted from two relevant volumes in the Pickering & Chatto edition, *Robert Southey: Poetical Works, 1793–1810*, gen. ed. Lynda Pratt, 5 vols. (London: Pickering and Chatto, 2004), namely vol. 3, *Thalaba the Destroyer*, ed. Tim Fulford with the assistance of Daniel E. White and Carol Bolton, and vol. 4, *The Curse of Kehama*, ed. Daniel Sanjiv Roberts.

tense as they manifest the tyrant's thinking. More subliminally, Southey offers an internal rhyme ('touch' and 'such') that links character and event.

The lines seem to have lingered in Shelley's imagination to reappear, in transformed fashion, in *The Triumph of Life*, where Rousseau is told by the 'shape all light' (352) to drink,[6] and subsequently experiences a vision that involves her mourned-for vanishing and his immersion in the destructive element of life. Southey's 'Amreeta-cup of immortality' mirrors the disposition of the drinker, and Shelley may have remembered that detail but enlarged its cultural scope as he describes Rousseau's re-enactment of a pattern that is typical of *The Triumph of Life*. The pattern is one that involves partial obliteration of the past and renewed immersion in a continuous realignment of experience:

> I rose; and, bending at her sweet command,
>   Touched with faint lips the cup she raised,
>   And suddenly my brain became as sand
>
>   Where the first wave had more than half erased
>   The track of deer in desert Labrador,
>   Whilst the fierce wolf from which they fled amazed
>
> Leaves his stamp visibly upon the shore
>   Until the second bursts—so on my sight
> Burst a new Vision never seen before [...]
>   (*Triumph of Life*, 403–11)

Shelley owes much to Dante as he relies on simile to communicate Rousseau's movement through phases of consciousness. Rousseau tumbles through states that come alive through delicate adjustments of wording, as in the uses of 'first' and 'half' in the initial two tercets, or the extension of the simile of 'sand'. When the simile opens into the scenario of 'fierce wolf' and 'track of deer', suggestions, hard to divorce from erotic and visionary contexts, of hunting and flight, enter the verse. But narrative parallelisms do not correspond to causal explanations. The 'so' of line 410 does little to clarify why the 'new Vision' bursts upon Rousseau's sight; it gestures merely towards the enigmatic nature of its occurrence. The meaning of the changes that Rousseau experiences remains tantalizingly obscure. Yet the changes haunt us. Shelley's method of offering us the experience but denying us explanation of its final significance invites and, indeed, obliges us to take upon ourselves Rousseau's own bewildered subjective exposure to, and all-consuming awareness of, loss. From now on, the shape will, for Rousseau, be like 'A light from Heaven, whose half-extinguished beam // Through the sick day in which we wake to weep / Glimmers, forever sought, forever lost. —' (*Triumph of Life*, 429–31). Shelley's passage 'Glimmers' with possible ideas—Rousseau may be rehearsing the personal, imaginative, and historical disappointments of a generation—but the poetry does not underscore any allegorical message. Rather, it provides access to processes of feeling and thought.

[6] Quotations from Shelley's poetry and prose will come from *Major Works*, unless noted otherwise.

Kailyal experiences a change which may appear to be all outcome. Yet Southey explores somatic process too. As his heroine is shown 'Feeling her body melt', she undergoes an alteration that is also a reassertion of her moral being:

> Like one entranced she knelt,
> Feeling her body melt
> Till all but what was heavenly past away:
> Yet still she felt
> Her Spirit strong within her, the same heart [...]
>   (*Kehama*, XXIV. 271–5)

The triple rhyme gives emphasis to what 'she felt': a sturdily Anglo-Saxon Protestant assurance is at work, for all the poem's Orientalism. Such assurance is more than 'half erased' in Shelley's poem. In *The Triumph of Life*, feeling is no longer in any intuitive correspondence with what in Southey's poem is termed 'the will of Fate' (*Kehama*, XXIV. 223).

2

In 1822, Shelley's poetry adopts towards Southey's the blend of half-disillusioned intimacy and haunted near-estrangement which characterizes its dealings with precursors, particularly during the last few years of the poet's life. That Southey stayed in Shelley's thoughts is a testament to the impression made by the older poet's work and personality. Not that the impression was one-sided. Southey described the Shelley he met in 1811 to Grosvenor Bedford as a young man who 'acts upon me as my own Ghost would do'.[7] At this early stage Shelley detected affinities along with differences, as is clear from a letter of Boxing Day 1811 to Elizabeth Hitchener:

> You may conjecture that a man must possess high and estimable qualities, if with the prejudice of such total difference from my sentiments I can regard him great and worthy—In fact Southey is an advocate of liberty and equality; he looks forward to a state when all shall be perfected, and matter become subjected to the omnipotence of mind; but he is now an advocate for existing establishments; he says he designs his three statues in Kehama to be contemplated with republican feelings—but not in this age.—Southey hates the Irish, he speaks against Catholic Emancipation, & Parliamentary reform. In all these things we differ, & our differences were the subject of a long conversation [...] Southey thinks that a revolution is *inevitable*; this is one of his reasons for supporting things as they are.
>   (*Letters: PBS*, 1. 211–12, 213)

Even allowing for Shelley's Godwinian inflections (clear in that last phrase), it seems likely that his account of Southey's opinions is, in essentials, accurate, especially the insight it gives into Southey's management of apparent ideological contradictions. Frederick L. Jones noted that in a letter of 30 November 1814, Southey wrote to

---

[7] Letter of 26 January 1812, *The Life and Correspondence of Robert Southey*, ed. Charles Cuthbert Southey 6 vols. (London: Longman, Brown, Green, & Longmans, 1850), 3, 325–6.

Dr Gooch as follows: 'I am fully convinced that a gradual improvement is going on in the world, has been going on from its commencement, and will continue till the human race shall attain all the perfection of which it is capable in this mortal state. This belief grows out of knowledge; that is, it is a corollary deduced from the whole history of mankind' (*Letters: PBS*, 1. 212n). It is fascinating to hear, in that reported quotation, Southey, the arch-conservative so far as the liberal poets of the next generation were concerned, still employing the accents of perfectibility.[8] For the mature Shelley, in fact, Southey may have been among those to whom a Fury in the first act of *Prometheus Unbound* refers in acidic but empathizing terms, 'The good want power, but to weep barren tears' (*Prometheus Unbound* I. 625).

Viewed in the context of Shelley's correspondence with Hitchener, which includes agonized debate on the nature of virtue following Hogg's attempted seduction of Harriet, Southey appears in 1811 as the latest exemplar of that 'tergiversation' (*Letters: PBS*, 1. 208) about which the younger poet speaks in a letter of 15 December. Here, as elsewhere, idealistic projection discovering its folly is often the mainspring for Shelley's most affecting as well as most self-righteous writing. Shocked by Hogg's behaviour, Shelley seeks to argue himself into renewed assurance by drawing a clear line between 'This passion of animal love', that is in turn shaped by 'the false refinements of society [...] into an idol to which its misguided members burn incense', and '*friendship*' which is 'worthier of a rational being' in that it retains 'impassionateness' but also 'judgement, which is not blind tho it may chance to see something like perfections in its object' (*Letters: PBS*, 1. 208). The ecstatic tragedy of idealizing quest will emerge as one of Shelley's major subjects in his late poems (certainly from *Epipsychidion* onwards). But he is already seeking to come to terms with the demands of such a quest. Hogg has shown himself to have feet of sensual clay, to behave in a way that has converted him from a Hamlet-like 'celestial angel', into 'one of those mad votaries of selfishness' (*Letters: PBS*, 1. 207).

Before meeting Southey, Shelley had, then, been meditating on themes of importance both for himself and the older poet. *The Curse of Kehama* sets inflamed social passions and the will to power against the courageous goodness shown by Kailyal and her Glendoveer. Immediately after making his distinction between 'animal love' and '*friendship*', Shelley speaks of Southey in terms that might have been borrowed from *Kehama*: it is as though Southey were part of the manic 'death-procession' watched by 'Master and slave, old age and infancy' (I. 50. 6) with which *Kehama* opens, a passage that left a deep impression on Shelley's imagination, as is apparent in *The Triumph of Life* and that poem's early vision of the driven 'multitude' (49) made up of 'Old age and youth, manhood and infancy' (52):

> Southey has changed. I shall see him soon, and I shall reproach him of [for] his tergiversation—He to whom Bigotry Tyranny and Law was hateful has become the votary of these Idols, in a form most disgusting.—The Church of England it's Hell and all has become the subject of his panygeric.—the war in Spain that prodigal waste of

---

[8] For relevant discussion of the way in which *The Curse of Kehama* 'legitimizes its populist and revolutionary rhetoric by situating it in an imagined Orient', see Nigel Leask, *British Romantic Writers and the East: Anxieties of Empire* (Cambridge: Cambridge University Press, 1992), 96.

human blood to aggrandise the fame of Statesmen is his delight, the constitution of England with its Wellesley its Paget & its Prince are inflated with the prostituted exertions of his Pen.

(Letters: PBS, 1. 208)

In these reflections on 'falling off', Shelley experiences, as already noted, a Hamlet-like 'sickening distrust when I see all that I had considered good great & imitable fall around me into the gulph of error' (*Letters: PBS*, 1. 208). He prizes 'disinterestedness', 'that which seeks the good of all', the capacity to feel and respond in a way that has in mind always the interests of 'pure simple unsophisticated Virtue' (*Letters: PBS*, 1. 173). He continually explains a falling away from the right in terms that imply a staining of what is still fundamentally good, and these are terms he applies to Southey. 'I grieve at human nature' he writes to Hitchener on 26 January 1812, 'but am so far from despairing that I can readily trace all that is evil even in the youngest to the sophistications of society' (*Letters: PBS*, 1. 237). 'Even in the youngest' is inserted as a prelude to an attack on belief in original sin, belief, that is, in 'some original taint of our nature' (*Letters: PBS*, 1. 237).

For Shelley, echoing Wordsworth in 'Tintern Abbey', the culprit is not innate depravity, but 'The dreary intercourse of daily life' (*Letters: PBS*, 1. 238). Southey, for Shelley, is a near-tragic figure, whose *hamartia* was susceptibility to worldly corruption, social influence. '*Once* he *was*…everything you can conceive of prac-tised virtue', the italicized words tense with awareness of loss. 'Now he is corrupted by the world, contaminated by Custom; it rends my heart when I think what he might have been' (*Letters: PBS*, 1. 223). This judgement may sound patronizing, even dismissive, but it is indicative of a number of entwined responses to Southey on Shelley's part, responses that include the view that the older poet was or had been an exemplar, whose former conduct (and, presumably, poetry) offers a type of 'practised virtue', and that his falling off disturbs the younger poet in a way that is marked by an emotional distress similar to that evoked by a tragic scene. Shelley may sound close to blithe dismissal, but a brooding preoccupation with the mean-ings of Southey's career was the upshot; it did, indeed, 'rend [his] heart' to think of what Southey 'might have been'. If Southey saw Shelley as a ghost of his former self, Shelley saw in Southey a shadowy proleptic glimpse of selves both to aspire towards and to shun.

The peculiar hurt for Shelley arising out of his subsequent controversy with Southey has to do with a feeling that Southey had betrayed a trust earned by the example of his poems up to and including *The Curse of Kehama*. Shelley's creed of forbearance was ultimately the product of his diagnosis of what went awry with the French Revolution when it turned from Utopian dreams to internecine and inter-national violence. It finds a Southey-centred subject in the struggle to articulate, in poems such as 'To _____ (Lines to a Reviewer)' and 'Fragment of a Satire on Satire', the best way to avoid being drawn into a relationship with the older poet based on what the former poem calls 'some faint sympathy of hate' (7). Southey, it is evident, becomes a central theme for Shelley. The target of near-paranoid projec-tion, his antagonistic presence in Shelley's mind spurred on the younger poet to construct the final sublimities inhabited by *Adonais*. 'The abode where the Eternal are' (55. 495) takes on verbal form as a necessary fiction that will silence the slurs of the 'most base and unprincipled calumniator', probably the Reverend Henry Milman, but a phrase haunted by Shelley's suspicion of Southey Preface (*Major Works*, 530).[9]

That Southey remained as a productive if conflicting presence in the Shelleyan *imaginaire* has much to do with the poets' shared interest in cultural difference. As Tim Fulford observes, 'For Shelley, Southey also opened the possibility of questioning the orthodoxies of religious and political Britain by dramatizing the belief-systems of eastern cultures'.[10] Crucial to those 'belief-systems' is the question of fatalism. Fulford quotes Southey writing, in connection with the hero of *Thalaba the Destroyer*: 'Fatalism is the corner-stone of Mahometry, the hero of the Islamic romance was to act therefore under the impulse of Destiny'.[11] Fulford argues persuasively that *Thalaba* falls 'short of a full endorsement either of fatalism or rationalism',[12] and that this ambivalence is a clue to its power. Shelley will recast obedience to destiny as an aspect of the imaginative quest which dominates *Alastor* and later poems. More optimistically, he recasts eastern fatalism as quasi-Godwinian Necessity in *Queen Mab*. The political radicalism that is implicit in *Thalaba* (and *The Curse of Kehama*), and led Southey to write in his Common-Place Book, 'Cannot the Dom Danael be made to allegorise those systems that make the misery of mankind?',[13] appealed to Shelley.

Such radicalism is only one element in Southey's many-faceted romances-cum-epics, but it is an element on which Shelley was able to alight. A fundamental point of contact between the two writers is belief in the power of goodness to withstand evil (however those terms are construed), and a disbelief in innate badness, original sin. 'Southey {is} no believer in original sin: he thinks that which appears to be a taint of our nature is in effect the result of unnatural political institutions—there we agree' (*Letters: PBS*, 1. 216). Shelley's approving comment shapes a dialogue with Southey that persists. That Shelley heard in Southey's rhythmic measures impulses towards freedom seems likely. Southey invoked the notion of 'freedom' in attributing his style in *Thalaba* to the influence of Frank Sayers: 'The reason why the irregular rhymeless lyrics of Dr. Sayers were preferred for Thalaba was, that the freedom and variety of such verse were suited to the story' (Preface to *The Curse of Kehama*, 1838).[14] In the opening of *Queen Mab* ('How wonderful is Death'), there is, as has often been noted, a direct echo of the opening of *Thalaba* ('How beautiful is night'). Mary Shelley in her note on the poem wrote that 'the rhythm of *Queen Mab* was founded on that of *Thalaba*, and the first few lines bear a striking resemblance

---

[9] For the likely reference to Milman, see *The Poems of Shelley, Volume Four, 1820–1821*, ed. Michael Rossington, Jack Donovan, and Kelvin Everest (Abingdon: Routledge, 2014), 281.
[10] Robert Southey, *Poetical Works: 1793–1810*, gen. ed. Lynda Pratt 5 vols (London: Pickering and Chatto, 2004), 3, pp. xxiv–v.
[11] Quoted in Southey, *Poetical Works III*, p. xxx.   [12] Southey, *Poetical Works 3*, p. xxxi.
[13] Southey, *Poetical Works 3*, p. xxiii.
[14] Southey, *Poetical Works IV*, 4. For more information about Dr Frank Sayers, a Norwich physician and man of letters, see the note in *CPPBS* 2, 506–7. This volume contains valuable information about Southeyan echoes in *Queen Mab*.

in spirit, though not in idea, to the opening of that poem'.[15] But one 'idea' shared by the poems was that of the 'freedom' of the authorial imagination, freed, as it were, from any taint of influence's 'original sin', for all both poets' acknowledgement of literary debts. Writing to Hogg, Shelley invokes as 'authority' for the 'singularity' of his style 'Miltons Samson Agonistes, the Greek Choruses, & (you will laugh) Southeys Thalaba' (*Letters: PBS*, 1. 352). In both poems, style bespeaks an audacious readiness, on the part of the two poets, to go their own ways. Both open by drawing inspiration from a power or force—'night' in Southey, 'Death' in Shelley—that suggests the poets' visions are equal to the ultimate terms of human experience and the natural cycle.

David Duff argues that in *Queen Mab* Shelley uses the 'Thalaba style' to a double end: both to reclaim for his own purposes the 'inherently "revolutionary" quality of Southey's style' (a quality recognized, as Duff notes, by Hazlitt) and to 'subvert his source'.[16] That Southey's style in *Thalaba* offended conservative judges is clear from Francis Jeffrey's long discussion of the poem in the first issue of the *Edinburgh Review*. This review, which Southey disliked for its 'attempt at Thalabicide', took the opportunity to attack Southey for belonging to 'a *sect* of poets' who, among other things, adhered to 'The antisocial principles, and distempered sensibility of Rousseau'. Jeffrey, who is alert to some of the poem's merits, commenting favourably on the 'solemn and composed beauty' of the opening, for example, is unimpressed by the 'singular structure of the versification, which is a jumble of all the measures that are known in English poetry'.[17] The versification, that is, is a site for heterogeneous mixing and levelling. It affronts Jeffrey's neo-classical tenets as it parades a perplexing originality, and one senses that Jeffrey has glimpsed, in his own terms, the poem's lawless openness to interpretation.

Duff writes of *Thalaba*'s abrupt transitions as serving 'simply as a way of creating surprise and excitement in the narrative' as opposed to their function in *Queen Mab* where they startle 'the reader into political consciousness'.[18] One can add to his fine discussion by emphasizing that in *Thalaba* abrupt transition is one with a driving momentum, a momentum designed to show that the hero can display a dauntless courage and virtue in not succumbing to the dominion of the Dom Daniel. Shelley's creative responses to *Thalaba* show that he detected in the older poet's resistance to evil an energy cognate with his own conviction in *Queen Mab*, and embodied in the poem's obstacle-overbearing rhythmic movement, that the

---

[15] Mary Shelley is quoted from *H*, 837. Contemporary reviewers of *Queen Mab* (in the main, the pirated edition of 1821) noticed Southey's stylistic influence: in a piece that sought to 'do justice to the writer's genius, and *upon* his principles', *The Literary Gazette and Journal of Belles Lettres*, 19 May 1821, commented that 'The rhythm is of that sort which Mr. Southey employed so forcibly in his *Thalaba*, and other poems; and it is no mean praise to observe, that in his use of it, Mr. Shelley is not inferior to his distinguished predecessor' (*Shelley: The Critical Heritage*, ed. James E. Barcus (London: Routledge & Keegan Paul, 1975), 75).
[16] David Duff, *Romance and Revolution*, 77.
[17] *New Letters of Robert Southey*, ed. Kenneth Curry, 2 vols. (London and New York: Columbia UP, 1965), I, p. 306; Francis Jeffrey, unsigned review, *Edinburgh Review*, October 1802, in *Robert Southey: The Critical Heritage*, ed. Lionel Madden (London: Routledge & Keegan Paul, 1972), 68, 69, 87, 78.
[18] David Duff, *Romance and Revolution*, 78.

progressive direction of history is inseparable from the 'will' of the 'Spirit of Nature', addressed in the following terms at the close of canto III:

> Man, like these passive things,
> Thy will unconsciously fulfilleth:
> Like theirs, his age of endless peace,
> Which time is fast maturing,
> Will swiftly, surely come;
> And the unbounded frame, which thou pervadest,
> Will be without a flaw
> Marring its perfect symmetry.
>   (*Queen Mab*, III. 226, 233–40)

'Thoroughly Holbachian in both thought and diction'[19] this may be: and Holbach has certainly influenced Shelley's view of 'Nature' as, in the words of the French *philosophe*, 'an active living whole, whose parts necessarily concur, and that without their own knowledge, to maintain activity, life, and existence'.[20] But Shelley's rhythmic energy, with its strong forward-leaning, anticipatory bias, is at once his own and an advanced, more ideologically dynamized version of Southey's implicitly millenarian cadences. Shelley positions the phrase 'unconsciously fulfilleth' to suggest how 'Man' is the instrument of 'Thy will'. At the same time, 'Like theirs' is a wording that allows a smidgen of difference between the natural and human worlds; we have shifted from literal to analogous necessitarianism. The slight friction between 'swiftly' and 'surely', even between two senses of 'surely' (definitely and probably), acts as a foretaste of larger Shelleyan uncertainties about the operation of Necessity played out in *Prometheus Unbound*. Southey's own invocation of 'Destiny' in *Thalaba* is more theistic, even as the eastern clothing of his story means that the 'all-knowing Mind' in question cannot be straightforwardly identified with the Christian God. Book XI of the poem opens thus:

> O fool to think thy human hand
> Could check the chariot-wheels of Destiny!
> To dream of weakness in the all-knowing Mind
> That his decrees should change!
> To hope that the united Powers
> Of Earth, and Air, and Hell,
> Might blot one letter from the Book of Fate,
> Might break one link of the eternal chain!
>   (*Thalaba*, XI. 1–8)

Southey made this 'all-knowing Mind' even more indifferent to human desire in his 1838 revision of 'his decrees' to 'its decrees'.[21] His anaphoric infinitives and 'Mights' expose to scorn the folly of the ostensible addressee, Okba. This 'miserable, wicked, poor old man' (*Thalaba*, XI. 9) is momentarily Lear-like in his grief for his daughter, Laila, slain by his own hand when she saved Thalaba from the

---

[19] *CPPBS* 2, 549.   [20] Quoted in *CPPBS* 2, 531.
[21] See Southey, *Poetical Works 3*, 162n.

'deadly blow' (*Thalaba*, X. 440). As Thalaba presses on, seeking the freedom that comes from recognition and active pursuit of a providential necessity, Book XI rises to some of the most exhilarating poetry in the work, poetry which influenced Shelley's practice in *Alastor*, among other places, as it evokes the onward impetus of a journey made 'Without an oar, without a sail' (*Thalaba*, XI. 376).[22]

Shelley says to the 'Spirit of Nature' that 'Man' 'Thy will unconsciously fulfilleth' (*Queen Mab* III, 226, 233, 234), yet passive acceptance of Necessity or Destiny in *Thalaba* is inseparable from a poetry of will. Shelley in *Queen Mab* and Southey in *Thalaba* share a poetry in which questions are scornfully rhetorical, similes are evocatively brisk, and much of the writing strives for declarative certainty. Herbert Tucker recovers the force of Southey's originality when he describes *Thalaba* as possessing qualities of 'manic fusion' and 'hell-bent coherentism', and reads the poem as the 'epic' of any 'deracinated individualism' supposedly placed on 'the throne of the Romantic ideology'.[23] The hero of Thalaba embodies the fundamental 'individualism' at the heart of the Romantic project, but his is an individualism, for the most part, rigorously, even puritanically remote from ambiguities. Thalaba pursues his destruction of the evil Domdaniel, region of evil and sorcery, with little or no 'tergiversation', spectacularly different in this respect from one of his evident literary forerunners, Spenser's Redcrosse Knight.[24] He falters once when he seeks happiness with Oneiza, but the Angel of Death quickly puts a stop to such faltering in an electrifying moment of arrest: 'Who comes from the bridal chamber? / It is Azrael, the Angel of Death' (*Thalaba*, VII. 406–7).

Foiling of the quest is itself checked, and in the remaining books Thalaba is more than ever a man on a mission. This mission operates in a world whose self-generating intensities bear witness to the rekindled energies of the genre of romance, a genre aspiring towards modernized epic. Scorning all temptations, Thalaba is an alter ego of the Southey who in his extensive notes simultaneously shows immersion in and a scholarly detachment from the Orientalist stories that he documents exhaustively. Even in his notes, an overriding impression is of an imagination hungering for the marvellous. Again, a Southeyan incitement to Shelleyan invention (the addition of long essay-like notes to *Queen Mab*) is evident: Southey cautiously quotes from sources concerning 'The Mohammedan tradition' about the torments visited upon the wicked;[25] Shelley intrepidly takes arms against a sea of theological traditions, 'All that miserable tale of the Devil, and Eve, and an Intercessor' (*Major Works*, 71). Both counterpoint poem and prose, but it is as though Shelley seeks imaginative freedom through ideological battle, Southey through an autotelic engagement with remodelled genres.

---

[22] Detailed commentary on Southeyan echoes in *Alastor* is provided by Neil Fraistat in vol. 3 of *CPPBS*.
[23] Tucker, *Epic*, 88.
[24] Stuart Curran has a suggestive discussion of Spenserian parallels in *Poetic Form and British Romanticism*, 134.
[25] Southey *Poetical Works 3*, 276.

3

If, as Tucker notes, 'Thalaban faith is a condition of simplicity costing not less than everything',[26] it is arguable that Southey's poem is less interested in fantasies of control than in modes of ordeal, less bound up with Enlightenment syncretism than with a dauntless submission to destiny which at once drains freedom from the protagonist and gives him a will-driven inexorableness. There are many twists and turns in the plot, but Thalaba—unlike Aeneas, say—permits himself few or no swervings from the course charted by fatality. In this he might be a version of the British state, the hero himself the juggernaut which is depicted in *The Curse of Kehama* with horrified fascination, as 'Through blood and bones it ploughs its dreadful path' (*Kehama*, XIV. 68), Southey's strong stresses enacting the 'dreadful' ploughing. But he might also allegorize the very Romantic imagination which rises at the same time as the emergence of British imperialism and has a relationship with imperialist drives that is often implicitly critical. Above all, *Thalaba* unleashes a near autonomous imaginative energy. The poem's form boasts a variety of line-lengths, delivers thrills and spills with each line, but the impact is curiously toneless, or rather, continually rapt (it amounts to the same thing). In Book V, we hear of Baghdad that 'The many-coloured domes / Yet wore one dusky hue' (*Thalaba*, V. 110–11), probably remembered by Shelley in *Adonais*'s climactic image of 'Life' as 'a dome of many-coloured glass' (*Adonais*, 52. 462), but also serving as a covertly metapoetic image for *Thalaba*'s impact.

For an author central to our own culture's revisionist accounts of Romanticism, Southey is strangely but accommodatingly averse to the expression of ideas. An apparent exception is the exchange between Thalaba and the evil enchanter Mohareb, in Book IX, in which the latter, in Tucker's words, 'twits the hero with his merely agential status'.[27] Even here, for all the allusion to a Manichean dispensation ('in Nature are two hostile Gods, / Makers and Masters of existing things', *Thalaba*, IX. 150–1) and the gesture towards a post-Satanic, pre-Nietzschean nominalist scepticism ('Evil and Good . . . / What are they Thalaba but words?', *Thalaba*, IX. 169–70), the central issue is Thalaba's steadfast dedication to his role. After Mohareb concludes with an injunction based on an appropriate response to being supposedly 'abandoned', Thalaba replies in lines that are uncannily close to the stance adopted by Prometheus at the start of Shelley's lyrical drama:

> The Captive did not, hasty to confute
> Break off that subtle speech;
> But when the expectant silence of the King
> Looked for his answer, then spake Thalaba.
> 'And this then is thy faith! this monstrous creed!
> This lie against the Sun, and Moon, and Stars,
> And Earth, and Heaven! Blind man who canst not see
> How all things work the best! who wilt not know
> That in the Manhood of the World, whate'er

---

[26] Tucker, *Epic*, 87.   [27] Tucker *Epic*, 87.

Of folly mark'd its Infancy, of vice
Sullied its Youth, ripe Wisdom shall cast off,
Stablished in good, and knowing evil safe.
Sultan Mohareb, yes, ye have me here
In chains; but not forsaken, tho' opprest;
Cast down, but not destroyed. Shall danger daunt,
Shall death dismay his soul, whose life is given
For God and for his brethren of mankind?
Alike rewarded, in that holy cause,
The Conquerors and the Martyrs palm above
Beam with one glory. Hope ye that my blood
Can quench the dreaded flame? and know ye not
That leagued against ye are the Just and Wise
And all Good Actions of all ages past,
Yea your own Crimes, and Truth, and God in Heaven?'
(*Thalaba*, IX. 199–222)

Sinewy with contempt, conflating exultant exclamation and derisive question, Thalaba's reply has that simplifying integrity that both dismays and compels a reluctant admiration. Edward Dowden thought that 'The word *high-souled* takes possession of the mind as we think of Southey's heroic personages'. But while he is right to speak of 'chivalric ardour' and lack of human 'sympathy', he misses the poetry's love affair with 'the chariot-wheels of Destiny', here reconceived in progressivist terms ('How all things work the best!').[28] As a result, Dowden underplays the degree of repressed potential struggle pointed up by Thalaba's reworking of the accents of Satanic resistance. Thalaba, that is, struggles, or hints at struggle, in his refusal to concede that true struggle is other than the search for alignment with a higher will. His echoes of Satan suggest an individualism training itself to strive and not to yield. Southey's 'buts', in 'In chains; but not forsaken, tho' opprest; / Cast down, but not destroyed', give highlighted prominence to a conjunction never far from Milton's lexicon when Satan is in his thoughts, the Satan who, for example, is heard 'Vaunting aloud, but racked with deep despair' (*Paradise Lost*, 1, 126).

Thalaba opposes the Satanic in an idiom that has commerce with Milton's language of dauntless, '*high-souled*' courage; the very want of self-pity or compassion lends a subterranean pathos to the words of Southey's hero, even if it is the pathos of the would-be martyr. Thalaba conceives of language as a weapon, an alliteration-studded engine of scorn wielded in support of a 'holy cause'. A means of parrying the ploys of 'subtle speech' with a forthright indignation, his words drive from the poem's field the 'monstrous lie' proposed by Mohareb, that his actions are the result of his credulous submission to an unreal power. Yet there is an echoic vacancy after Thalaba's speech. There is no 'all-beholding Prophet's aweful voice' (*Thalaba*, XII. 465), here, a voice heard towards the very end, and itself vanishing at Thalaba's 'death-hour' (*Thalaba*, XII. 496) to be replaced by a ghostly substitute: 'There issued forth no Voice to answer him, / But lo! Hodeirah's Spirit comes to see / His

[28] From Dowden's *Southey* (1879), in *Southey: The Critical Heritage*, 475, 476, 475.

vengeance' (*Thalaba*, XII. 490–2). In the above speech, Thalaba's stirring trust, his 'Vaunting aloud', may be far removed from any 'deep despair', to borrow Milton's phrasing. But it is its own brave warranty, and that effect prevents the speech from seeming simply an act of robotic yea-saying.

If the poem's onward propulsiveness attracted Shelley to *Thalaba*, he was also drawn to its enchantments because they embody the notion of poetry as a spell or charm. 'I have often heard him quote', wrote Medwin, 'that exquisite passage, where the Enchantress winds round the finger of her victim a single hair, till the spell becomes inextricable—the charm cannot be broken'.[29] Here are some central lines from it:

> And then again she spake to him
> And still her speech was song,
> 'Now twine it round thy hands I say,
> Now twine it round thy hands I pray,
> My thread is small, my thread is fine,
> But he must be
> A stronger than thee,
> Who can break this thread of mine!'
> (*Thalaba*, VIII. 332–9)

Repetition and incantation, as though the Witches of *Macbeth* were transmuted into a Romantic realm, give these lines, and the whole speech, a siren-like hold over the reader. Southey might be commenting self-reflexively on this hold when he writes, 'And still her speech was song'. The lines themselves are both insidiously taunting 'speech' and lyrical 'song'. It is as though such a spell, even when uttered by a 'bad' character (though Maimuna will experience 'repentance in the sight of God', *Thalaba*, X. 22), provides a model of poetry as a space where the false hypnoses of evil can be experienced in all their force and power, and be exorcised.

Shelley, who called his friend Mrs Boinville 'Maimuna', according to Peacock, because 'She was a young-looking woman for her age, and her hair was as white as snow',[30] would make his mature response to this scene in a passage from *The Witch of Atlas*. There, rewriting Maimuna's magic for benevolent purposes, he represents the Witch as seeking to protect others from her dazzling beauty thus: 'she took her spindle / And twined three threads of fleecy mist' in order to weave 'A shadow for the splendour of her love' (*Witch of Atlas*, 13. 145–6, 152). But, as a younger poet, a later and radically interrogative Thalaba, so to speak, Shelley takes over such spell-like power, attaches it to revolutionary virtue whose first command is reverence for the self, and sees it work visionary abracadabra:

> The chains of earth's immurement
> Fell from Ianthe's spirit;
> They shrank and brake like bandages of straw
> Beneath a wakened giant's strength.

---

29 Thomas Medwin, *The Life of Percy Bysshe Shelley* (London: T. C. Newby, 1847), 61.
30 Wolfe 2, 326.

She knew her glorious change,
And felt in apprehension uncontrolled
New raptures opening round [...]
(*Queen Mab*, I. 188–94)

Shelley depicts the dawning of insight into how things are and might be, insight made possible through 'apprehension uncontrolled', a mode of grasping realities and ideals made possible by poetry. Both *Thalaba*-like spell and counter-spell are at work here, since the passage echoes the aftermath of Maimuna's remorse, when she reverses her spell and Thalaba 'wakes as from a dream of Paradise / And feels his fetters gone, and with the burst / Of wondering adoration praises God' (*Thalaba*, IX. 539–41). Southey's brief, unexpected simile—'as from a dream of Paradise'—is ironic, but it may intimate the power that lies in the hands of such as Maimuna, including the poet.

Shelley's visionary transformations mingle directness and complexity too. By the time he was writing *Queen Mab* he was working in ironic revisionist ways with Southey. But he recognizes in *Thalaba* a literary model that allowed him to depict his rejection of 'original sin', for Shelley the cornerstone of theological orthodoxy and political pessimism. The religious outlook of *Thalaba*, the subject of debate, is certainly mobile, a mobility that permits Nigel Leask to read its hero as, in Tim Fulford's summarizing terms, 'essentially a dissenting Protestant (like Southey himself in the 1790s)' and Daniel E. White to observe (again as described by Fulford) that 'it was finally not *rationalist* Christian sects that Southey allegorised in the poem, but fatalist ones'.[31] Politically, a similar fluidity of interpretation is possible: Thalaba might be seen as having the selfless energy of a supposedly incorruptible Robespierre or even of an idealized Napoleon; he might be the very embodiment of imperialism past, present, and to-come; he might be a near-revolutionary force opposed to all tyrannies.

Shelley saw in *Thalaba* a form and style that he could adapt to his own purposes, those purposes involving Utopian imaginings on the one hand, and an assault on contemporary wrongs on the other. What one might call the 'How beautiful' *Thalaba* note, a note struck at the opening of Southey's poem, sustains itself in such Utopian imaginings in *Queen Mab*: 'How sweet a scene will earth become! / Of purest spirits a pure dwelling-place' (*Queen Mab*, VI. 39–40), Shelley writes in canto VI, echoing *Kehama*'s account of a 'Bower of Bliss' that is 'Pure dwelling-place for perfect mind' (*Kehama*, X. 113, 119) as well as the opening of *Thalaba*. His poem's conclusion reties the knot that both poets fasten, as already noted, out of the relationship between destiny and the individual will: 'bravely bearing on, thy will / Is destined an eternal war to wage / With tyranny and falsehood' (*Queen Mab*, IX. 189–91). The phrasing of 'thy will / Is destined' points to Shelley's attempt to square the circle of freedom and determinism. Yet the wording of 'eternal war' may hint ominously, below the optimistic surface of the verse, at a perpetual struggle. 'One only earthly wish have I, to work / Thy will' (*Thalaba*,

---

[31] Southey, *Poetical Works 3*, p. xxx.

XII. 474–5), cries Thalaba in response to 'The all-beholding Prophet's aweful voice' (*Thalaba*, XII. 465), anticipating the younger poet's emphasis.

4

Later poems by Shelley play more complex variations on themes inherited from Southeyan romance. As suggested above, *Alastor* thrives on the fact that *Thalaba* is not, as Stuart Curran points out, adapting Harold Bloom's phrase, an internalized quest romance.[32] It draws nourishment, too, from the ideological flux of Southey's poem, as it builds on and makes explicit, yet not didactically so, the doubts that threaten the older poet's shows of intrepid clarity. Such doubts include the question of whether quest involves inhuman indifference to the claims of others. To be marked out from mankind, as Thalaba is, seems for the poet of *Alastor* to involve a potentially dangerous, quasi-narcissistic, and yet tragically distinguished voyage that turns up nothing but endless ambiguities. *Alastor* inaugurates, by way of its creative debt to Southey, a tradition of the metapoetic boat-voyage that reaches its climax in poems by Baudelaire and Rimbaud. Like Baudelaire's 'Le Voyage', in which the poet flamboyantly urges himself and his readers to plunge 'Au fond de l'Inconnu pour trouver du *nouveau!*' (144),[33] Shelley in *Alastor* commits his Poet to a subtly ironized journey into the 'new'. The irony is subtle, as in Baudelaire, because it occupies the same space as empathy. In Southey, admiration outdoes any irony. 'Obedient to the call, / By the pale moonlight Thalaba pursued / O'er track-less snows his way' (*Thalaba*, XI. 49–51), but we are assured that he is accompanied by a 'blessed messenger' (*Thalaba*, XI. 52). In *Alastor* we read an evident homage to this moment in Southey: 'Obedient to the light / That shone within his soul, he went, pursuing / The windings of the dell' (*Alastor*, 492–4). Yet Shelley plays up and focuses on the all-important but intrinsically uncertain value of the 'light / That shone within his soul', an uncertainty hardly discernible in *Thalaba*.

As though re-examining the worth of quest, Shelley will return to the conun-drum of the alliance between humanity and history, will and necessity, in *Prometheus Unbound*. Here the descent to Demogorgon's gloomy abode resonates loudly with echoes from Southey's long poems. In *Thalaba* the refrain 'down down' dominates the hero's journey into the Domdaniel: 'Then Thalaba pronounced the name of God / And leapt into the car. / Down, down it sunk,... down, down...' (*Thalaba*, XII. 254–6), where the suspension points and weighted monosyllables are alive with a sense of danger. In *Prometheus Unbound*, Act II Scene iii, the Spirits chant as Asia, Panthea, and Ione descend to Demogorgon's throne: 'To the deep, to the deep, / Down, down!' (*Prometheus Unbound*, II. iii. 54–5). Other echoic parallels between the works include the revaluation of spells. For the Oceanides, 'A spell is treasured but for thee alone' (*Prometheus Unbound*, II. iii. 88), whereas

---

[32] Curran, *Poetic Form and British Romanticism*, 134.
[33] Charles Baudelaire, *Les Fleurs du Mal*, ed. Jacques Dupont (Paris: Flammarion, 1991): the line might translate as 'To the depth of the Unknown in order to find the *new!*'

for the forces against which Thalaba combats 'Vain are all spells!' (*Thalaba*, XII. 362). Such parallels suggest that, as Shelley explores the tension between desire, love, quest, and ultimate Power, he takes inspiration from his former near-mentor.

In *A Defence of Poetry* Shelley describes the imaginative power of his contemporaries as 'an electric life which burns within their words' (*Major Works*, 701). 'Electric' would have been associated in Shelley's mind with such scientific developments as the demonstrations made by Luigi Galvani that muscle-tissue could be made to twitch after the application of an electrostatic spark. These demonstrations, which fed into the plot of *Frankenstein*, provide him, in the peroration of *A Defence*, with a metaphor for the influence exerted by contemporary writers. In writing it, he was expressing his awareness of being galvanized by the 'electric life' which he found burning within Southey's long poems, among other contemporary works.

Southey's poems, for instance, helped him to lyricize the long poem, especially in *Prometheus Unbound*. Southey's practice in *Thalaba*, as already noted with Maimuna's spell, or in *Kehama*, with the famous curse, is at strategic points to bring into the foreground a notion of poetry as sorcery, a notion which exists in exhilarating counterpoint to plainer, more workmanlike views of language operative in the poems.[34] Medwin recalls how his cousin 'doted on Kehama, the Curse of which I remember Shelley often declaiming'.[35] In *Kehama* the curse irradiates its power throughout the poem. A curse arrests time, enchants it; a device picked up by Byron in *Manfred* and Shelley in *Prometheus Unbound*, it operates in these cases, as in *Kehama*, as a compacted version of the entire poem. The curse in *Kehama* deserves to be quoted in full, as one of the finest and most-neglected passages of first-generation Romantic poetry:

> I charm thy life
> From the weapons of strife,
> From stone and from wood,
> From fire and from flood,
> From the serpent's tooth,
> And the beasts of blood:
> From Sickness I charm thee,
> And Time shall not harm thee;
> But Earth which is mine,
> Its fruits shall deny thee;
> And Water shall hear me,
> And know thee and fly thee;
> And the Winds shall not touch thee
> When they pass by thee,
> And the Dews shall not wet thee,
> When they fall nigh thee:

[34] Marilyn Butler argues suggestively that such passages 'evoke the uncanny' ('Repossessing the Past: The Case for an Open Literary History', in Marjorie Levinson et al., *Rethinking Historicism* (Oxford: Blackwell, 1989), 76).
[35] Medwin, *Life of Shelley*, 61.

And thou shalt seek Death
To release thee, in vain;
Thou shalt live in thy pain,
    While Kehama shall reign,
With a fire in thy heart,
And a fire in thy brain;
And Sleep shall obey me,
And visit thee never,
And the Curse shall be on thee
For ever and ever.
                    (*Kehama*, II. 144–69)

Immediately powerful in its impact, at once incantatory and an act of measured, cumulatively intensifying psychic violence, the curse is complex in its significance. It speaks of Kehama's utter control of Ladurlad through a series of verbs of which 'thee' is the subjugated object and through rhymes which testify to Kehama's 'reign'. A stupefying terror mounts gradually as it becomes clear that Ladurlad is preserved from a variety of harms ('weapons of strife', 'the serpent's tooth') only to be eternally enslaved by the curse. The uses of 'shall' and 'shalt' imply that future reality will bend to the will of the speaker, as when Kehama asserts, 'And Sleep shall obey me'. Moreover, the chant suggests—above and beyond its ostensible theme— Southey's ability to enthral and control his readership; it speaks of his poetic power. This suggestion may explain its appeal to Shelley, who would have sympathized with Southey's assertion in his 1838 preface: 'It appeared to me, that here neither the tone of morals, nor the strain of poetry, could be pitched too high; that nothing but moral sublimity could compensate for the extravagance of the fictions [...] I endeavoured, therefore, to combine the utmost richness of versification with the greatest freedom'.[36]

   Southey paved the way for Shelley to offer comparable combinations through 'fictions' that allowed for pursuit and redefinition. Shelley even wished that the Glendoveer in *Kehama* had not been made 'a male'; 'these detestable distinctions will surely be abolished in a future state of being', he wrote in a letter of 26 November 1811, where he quotes the following couplet from *Kehama*: 'The *holy* flame forever burneth, from Heaven it came, from Heaven returneth' (X. 158–9; cited from *Letters: PBS*, 1. 195 as Shelley gives it, without marking the line-ending after 'burneth' and with the replacement of Southey's 'Its' by 'The' and the italicization of '*holy*'). It is evident that he was able to read in his own terms these lines, like the poem as a whole. Indeed, *Epipsychidion*'s flight into the 'height of Love's rare Universe' (589) might have its genesis in Southey's preceding assertion that 'Love is indestructible' (*Kehama*, X. 157). There was a parting of the ways between the two men after the Keswick meeting in the winter of 1811–12, and

---

[36] Southey, *Poetical Works IV*, 4.

much bitterness would ensue.[37] But Southey's long poems, especially *Thalaba* and *Kehama*, were tributaries whose waters enriched the deep-flowing river of Shelley's developing and mature poetry. To view Southey from a Shelleyan perspective is to recognize in the older writer's poetry a value which posterity may have been too quick to disallow.[38]

[37] For further discussion, see Kenneth Neill Cameron, 'Shelley vs. Southey: New Light on an Old Quarrel', *PMLA* 57.2 (1942): 489–512.

[38] Marilyn Butler's groundbreaking work has alerted us to the implications of Shelley's use of Southey for a revised view of the older poet; see her comment in 'Repossessing the Past' that, in Shelley's poetry, 'features' appear that 'are so stamped with Shelley's signature that few nowadays think of them as first Southey's' (*Rethinking Historicism*, 79).

8

'The Fixed and the Fluid'
Identity in Shelley and Byron

1

'What am I? Nothing' (*Childe Harold's Pilgrimage*, III. 6. 50), writes Byron. '*Self*, that burr that will stick to one', Shelley comments wryly (*Letters: PBS*, 2. 109). This chapter returns to the multifaceted question of 'identity', especially poetic identity, in a range of works by Byron and Shelley. Both poets convey tugs and pulls in relation to this theme. To his fingertips the poet who in *Lines Written among the Euganean Hills* hymns a 'universal light' (208) enveloping 'the towers of Venice' (212),[1] a light that is both identified with and 'like thought-winged Liberty' (207), Shelley is a poet of transference, process, change, movements out of the self. At the same time he is also the poet who brings us back from imagined ends to imaginative origins, the trochaic tetrameter couplets alighting here, with a sense of unveiling a creative source, on 'the mind which feeds this verse / Peopling the lone universe' (318–19).

As the deictically alert phrase 'this verse' reveals, Shelley has in common with Byron an awareness of being engaged in composition. The effect in both is of poetic identity as a float held in suspension, renewed and altered with every line that they write. In this case, the 'universe', previously evoked in its multiple richness and variety (including such details as 'the line / Of the olive-sandalled Apennine' (305–6)), emerges as 'lone', in need of befriending 'peopling' on the part of the poet's imagination. However, such imaginative 'peopling' is not painless or triumphantly self-delighting in any cavalier fashion. If Shelley delights in 'a going out of our own nature' (*A Defence of Poetry*, 682), he is alert to the intricate ways in which that 'nature' operates, including its expression of the desire for self-transcendence.

Again, Byron may downplay the significance of his mortal self in the terse, even despairing question-and-answer exchange with which this essay began. Yet an immediate 'but' launches canto III of *Childe Harold's Pilgrimage* in a different direction, one that imagines the self remodelled through poetry: 'but not so art thou, / Soul of my thought! With whom I traverse thought' (III. 6. 50–1).[2] If Byron fascinated and repelled contemporaries and later readers through 'His frequent allusions to his own private history',[3] as John Scott loftily put it in an essay for the

---

[1] Shelley's poetry and prose will be quoted from *Major Works* unless cited otherwise.
[2] Byron's poetry will be quoted from Lord George Gordon Byron, *Lord Byron: The Major Works*, ed. Jerome McGann, Oxford World's Classics (Oxford: Oxford University Press, 2000), unless specified otherwise.
[3] Quoted from Redpath, *The Young Romantics*, 266.

London Magazine of January 1821, he can be seemingly unegotistical as he exalts art: 'The beings of the mind are not of clay'; he asserts at the start of *Childe Harold's Pilgrimage*, canto IV, with Venice in his thoughts; 'Essentially immortal, they create / And multiply in us a brighter ray / And more beloved existence' (IV. 5. 37–9).

'In us'; here Byron presents himself as typical reader as well as sublime writer, and it is an enthralling part of his achievement in *Childe Harold's Pilgrimage*, canto IV, that he is able to be one with the Grand Tourist and a solitary poetic genius. Speaking of the imaginative fictions of Shakespeare and Otway as able to 'create / And multiply in us a brighter ray', Byron also does justice to the way in which the Romantic reader creates in the process of receiving. That 'brighter ray' might be a 'ray brighter' than the light we know in our quotidian lives, but it is part of the quickness and mobility of Byron's verse, for all its air here of offering a stately set-piece, to suggest that Shakespeare and Otway are enjoying a 'more beloved exist-ence' in the lives of those readers who take them into their minds and hearts. Characteristic of Byron's sense of poetic identity is a feeling that experiential and artistic selves are at once near and far. In the succeeding lines, thanks to the sways of feeling, we learn that it is our 'state / Of mortal bondage' (IV. 5. 41–2) which makes us yearn for 'beings of the mind': 'And this worn feeling peoples many a page; / And, may be, that which grows beneath mine eye' (IV. 6. 48–9). Byronic assertion is itself endlessly double: there is a sense in which 'The beings of the mind are not of clay' means the opposite of what it says, its towering hauteur making us think of what it faces down: the sense that, were it not for our imprisonment within 'our helpless clay' (*Don Juan*, I. 63. 499), where 'our' speaks eloquent volumes about Byron's identification with humanity's encasement in flesh and blood, we would not dream of 'beings of the mind' that are 'Essentially immortal'. Imaginative peopling in Byron is a way of 'replenishing the void' (*Childe Harold's Pilgrimage*, IV. 5. 45). In Shelley such peopling supports his conviction that 'Many a green isle needs must be / In the deep wide sea of misery' (*Lines Written among the Euganean Hills*, 1–2). In both poets the high value placed on art is compensa-tory, redemptive, always embattled. Both writers display a powerful poetic self-hood and a longing to 'Strip off this fond and false identity' (II. 392), as Byron puts it in *The Island*,[4] in lines which move swiftly between folly (incorporating fondness) and falsity.

The poem, which contains some writing that seems to be more than half in love with Shelleyan inflections, reprises the raptures of *Epipsychidion* when Byron's narrator speaks of

> all we know of heaven below,
> The other better self, whose joy or woe
> Is more than ours; the all-absorbing flame
> Which kindled by another, grows the same,
> Wrapt in one blaze.
>
> (II. 376–80)

---

[4] Lord George Gordon Byron, *The Complete Poetical Works*, ed. Jerome J. McGann and Barry Weller, 7 vols. (Oxford: Clarendon Press, 1980–93), 7. All quotations from *The Island* will be taken from this edition.

The 'flame/same' rhyme, as Charles Robinson has noted,[5] and, indeed, the idea of being rapturously 'Wrapt in one blaze', derives from the close of Shelley's poem, where the verse imagines

> One passion in twin hearts, which grows and grew,
> 'Till like two meteors of expanding flame,
> Those spheres instinct with it become the same,
> Touch, mingle, are transfigured; ever still
> Burning, yet ever inconsumable [...]
> (*Epipsychidion*, 575–9)

Both passages imagine a surrender to the inflammatory power of 'passion', but Byron's lines feel like an almost nonchalant rhetorical gambit, a narratorial excursus into his friend's eroticized Platonism when set beside Shelley's passage. Byron's 'other better self' is both the 'self' transformed through love for another and a new 'self', a state in which 'self' is annihilated, entered into as a result of love. Key to it, as so often in Byron, is the capacity for greater intensity of feeling, whether involving 'joy or woe'. It retains its link, as does the passage in Shelley, with an idiom of Christianized Platonism, in which 'this clog and clod of clay' (*The Island*, II. 390) unclasps its alliterative fetters, leaving the soul free. Yet this soul, in both poets, has not renounced, but merely altered, its connection with the body.

At the same time, there are differences between the poets. The passage from Shelley, with its driven rhythms, its 'Till', here as elsewhere the marker of a transformative longing, and its audible yearning that the lovers, like the enflamed meteors, will 'become the same', conveys a *ne plus ultra* air. Byron appeals to common experience; Shelley allows us to overhear an intensely intimate and exclusive call to his idealized and significant other. Byron may not be rattling on exactly as he talks, but he does not allow his redefining terms to soar beyond other inflections employed in *The Island*. To its advantage Shelley's poem has no escape route, save for an urbane descent into his Dantean envoi, and one might see Shelley as a lyrical poet and Byron as a narrative poet. Shelley's poetry, with notable exceptions, tends towards the condition of a lyricism which cannot but follow its own career, however lit up by qualifications and nuance, as at the end of *Adonais*. Byron's invocation of 'The other better self' is but a moment in a many-angled narrative process. His art is profoundly one of story-telling, stories which somehow lengthen when begun. And yet such stories are often themselves particular, even precarious, in ways that challenge any narrative line that, so to speak, thinks of itself as grander than others.

[5] Robinson, *Shelley and Byron*, 239 (on the same page Robinson argues suggestively that Byron would 'have thought of Shelley when he portrayed Torquil'). This work is indispensable for consideration of the relationship between Byron and Shelley. See also William D. Brewer, *The Shelley-Byron Conversation* (Gainesville: University Press of Florida, 1994), a work especially valuable for its critique of the 'wrongheaded conception...that Byron invariably stood for pessimism, skepticism, and despair, while Shelley, an impractical dreamer, was unwaveringly optimistic and melioristic, a confident advocate of hope and reform', 5. For a perceptive recent re-consideration, see Tony Howe, 'Shelley and the Development of *Don Juan*', *Byron Journal* 35.1 (2007): 27–39, and for an energizingly sceptical critique of the relationship, see Peter Cochran, 'Byron and Shelley: Radical Incompatibles', *Romanticism on the Net* 43 (August 2006) <http://id.erudit.org/iderudit/013589ar>.

In *The Island*, that perilously would-be grander narrative has to do with the Byronic hero's last stand; the fixed will's dauntless courage, born out of its own despair, the more impressive for its futility, the more futile, it might be added, for its impressiveness. Summoning the memory of Thermopylae as a point of comparison and contrast, the narrator opines: ''tis the *cause* makes all, / Degrades or hallows courage in its fall' (IV. 261–2). The section closes with lines that are shot through with the ambivalence inherent in the situational ethics producing that antithetical verbal doublet ('Degrades or hallows'):

> But now the die was to be thrown, and all
> The chances were in favour of his fall.
> And such a fall! But still he faced the shock,
> Obdurate as a portion of the rock
> Whereon he stood, and fix'd his levell'd gun,
> Dark as a sullen cloud before the sun.
> (IV. 275–80)

Here, with something of a valedictory air, Byron seems elegiacally to salute, as well as offer yet another version of, the Byronic hero. 'And such a fall!' almost mocks the post-lapsarian state of the hero, as though the repeated tragic 'fall' had been rehearsed many times earlier. Yet the words 'But still he faced the shock' make us aware of Byron's admiration for Christian's capacity to 'face' his fate, even if he seems virtually to be leading a posthumous existence; we recall that he 'stood / Like an extinct volcano in his mood; / Silent, and sad, and savage' (III. 139–41).

However, his poem has another story on the go, a story whose tidal pull is towards Torquil's and Neuha's idyll of young love, occurring in the midst of a fallen world from which it offers a kind of fictive refuge. If Christian is compared to an 'obdurate rock', Torquil and Neuha survive by taking shelter in their underwater 'rocky den' (IV. 181). Christian is the ego in prison; Torquil and Neuha suggest the possibility of creative re-birth in a womb-like cave, though they, too, almost stray into a recognizably Byronic story—one we encounter with Haidée and Juan—that of the fated nature of young love. Though the poem ends happily, so far as Torquil and Neuha are concerned, there are disturbing hints, as James McKusick points out, that all may not be entirely well in lines such as the following:

> What deem'd they of the future or the past?
> The present, like a tyrant, held them fast:
> Their hour-glass was the sea-sand, and the tide,
> Like her smooth billow, saw their moments glide.
> (II. 352–5)

McKusick writes that 'the present moment becomes a "tyrant" because it usurps all memory of the past and all desire for the future' and goes on to make the suggestive point that 'Byron seems to be suggesting that his recurrent idyllic fiction of a "language of nature" . . . must be relativized by juxtaposition with other linguistic elements in order to avoid stalling the narrative and cloying the reader'.[6] This process

---

[6] James C. McKusick, 'The Politics of Language in Byron's *The Island*', *ELH* 39 (1992): 851 (839–56). McKusick also makes the point, relevant to an earlier stage of my argument, that 'Cut from the same

of relativization has its formal counterpart, one might think, in the way in which Byron's couplets 'hold [the lovers] fast', and yet, counterpointing this effect of containment, is the effect of release from sombre foreknowledge that finds entrance into the writing, when Neuha leads Torquil into the ocean's depths:

> So smoothly, bravely, brilliantly she went,
> Leaving a streak of light behind her heel,
> Which struck and flashed like an amphibious steel...
>
> (IV. 108–10)

These and surrounding lines negotiate the couplet form with the ease of Neuha's movement, making it the vehicle of a mode of transport, one in which new life and energy are caught up in and enacted by the verse form. Byron's triple run of adverbs builds to a sense of Neuha's shining brilliance that subsumes her athletic smoothness and her courage. Stories fix and identify; but they are also the doorways towards novelty and escape. So, as they enter the 'spacious cave' (IV. 121), Byron breathes startling life into the bower of bliss topos. When Neuha is said to have 'Wiped with her hair the brine from Torquil's eyes, / And clapped her hands with joy at his surprise' (IV. 127–8), the moment carries a metapoetic freight of suggestion, to say something of Byron's delight in surprising his reader.

2

'I looked on him, / But the gay smile had faded in his eye. / "And such"—he cried, "is our mortality"' (*Julian and Maddalo*, 118–20). So Shelley's Julian speaks of Maddalo, his post-gaze couplet capturing the cessation of gaiety ('in his eye' marks this cessation more immediately than the expected 'from his eye'), and suggesting something fluid and mercurial about Maddalo. Maddalo is not quite Byron, but his portraiture reveals, on Shelley's part, a keen awareness of how Byron was about to fictionalize himself in the performative self-revelations of *Don Juan*, a poem to whose qualities and originality Shelley was remarkably, even empathetically, attuned. Amidst the disputatious accents of Julian and Maddalo, Kelvin Everest hears a shared gentlemanly style of speech, one contested, on his reading, by the vehement, passionate mode of speech heard in the Maniac's soliloquy.[7] It need not involve a concession to the more hostile aspects of Everest's shrewd critique (according to which Julian and Maddalo betray their privileged complicity in an unequal class structure) to acknowledge that Shelley does make his and Byron's surrogates express themselves in a poetic equivalent to 'the actual way in which people talk with each other whom education and a certain refinement of sentiment have placed above the use of vulgar idioms'. Shelley goes on immediately to

---

cloth as Manfred, Cain, and the Corsair (any mythically identifiable with Satan, Prometheus, and Napoleon), Christian thrives in struggle against impossible odds' (847), though he does not read the multi-registered nature of the poem's rhetoric in the way that the present chapter does.

    7 See 'Shelley's Doubles: An Approach to *Julian and Maddalo*', *Shelley Revalued: Essays from the Gregynog Conference*, ed. Kelvin Everest (Leicester: Leicester UP, 1983), 63–88.

concede or assert that he uses 'the word *vulgar* in its most extensive sense' and to acknowledge that 'the vulgarity of rank and fashion is as gross in its way as that of Poverty' (*Letters: PBS*, 2. 108). The letter, like the poem and its Preface, reveals Shelley's awareness of each individual's enmeshment in a web of lived social relations; and for both poets identity is never removed wholly from its social manifestation.

Indeed, both writers turn this fact into a recognition and one that works to the advantage of their poetry. Shelley's Utopian longings in *Prometheus Unbound* stay in touch with the ability to speak with the disarming candour of an idealistic, fearless heir to a large estate, that estate reconceived as nothing less than the universe. The Byron whose accents duplicate themselves in Maddalo's is recognizably kin to the Byron the aristocratic role-player; the dandy on his geographical and spiritual travels, the celebrity figure able to speak of himself as an erstwhile 'Napoleon of the realms of rhyme' (*Don Juan*, XI. 55. 440) who celebrates yet implies the cost of 'mobility' in his note to *Don Juan*, XVI. 97, who switches from tone to tone like a daring bareback rider vaulting from horse to horse, who impudently lays an extremely affecting sheet of sorrows on the shelf for fear of seeming rather 'touch'd' himself (*Don Juan*, IV. 74. 588), who flaunts his uncertainties, mixes up his registers, and is always about to taunt his reader with the question, 'and what know *you*…?' (*Don Juan*, XIV. 3. 18).

It is worthy of note that the iambic pressure in Shelley's lines obliges the reader's voice, once again, to sound out and to plumb the meaning of a small but potent word, the word 'such'. Julian, we recall, has already told us that he loves 'all waste / And solitary places' (*Julian and Maddalo*, 14–15), beginning with a general observation, before using the particular place to prove its applicability: 'And such was this wide ocean, and this shore / More barren than its billows' (18–19). Maddalo's use of 'such' also betrays his pursuit of emblems, sights, experiences that can be seized upon in support of a larger generalization. To the degree that experience is made to bend to his interpretative predispositions, this Byron, Shelley's poem suggests, is a figure of brooding preoccupations, of fixity, not mobility, of a heart half-turned to stone. Christian's 'Obdurate' stance, in which he displays a courage inextinguishable from despair, has nobler but related precedents in Byron's work. In his *Prometheus* the Titan is an exemplary figure one who teaches 'Man' (49) how to find in the very condition of his 'sad unallied existence' (52) the existential wherewithal from which to shape his' own concentred recompense' (57). Wordsworth's 'Abundant recompence' (89) in *Lines Written a Few Miles above Tintern Abbey* is buoyed up and weighed down by a tidal ebb and flow of a syntax that holds it in the most delicate of balances with 'such loss' (88).[8] Byron's 'concentred recompense' is a positive that his Titan and other associated heroes earn by virtue of their ability of their 'Spirit' (54) to be 'equal to all woes' (55) while retaining 'a firm will' (56).

Shelley is likely to have been able to raise at best only two cheers for such a concept of heroism. His own Prometheus needs to endure, yes, but also to love, to

---

[8] Quoted from *William Wordsworth: The Major Works, including* The Prelude, ed. Stephen Gill, Oxford World's Classics (Oxford: Oxford University Press, 2011).

move beyond his sense of suffering. From a Shelleyan perspective, Byron and Maddalo may be 'concentred' in ways that threaten constriction of range and vision, as is pointed up by the allusive reference in the Preface to *Julian and Maddalo* to the 'concentred and impatient feelings which consume him' (*Major Works*, 212). Yet Byron was also, as Shelley observes in a letter that wheels between criticism and praise, a 'great poet', a truth proved for his fellow-writer by 'the address to Ocean' (*Letters: PBS*, 2. 58) at the end of *Childe Harold's Pilgrimage*, canto IV. 'Time writes no wrinkle on thine azure brow—', Byron asserts of the Ocean, 'Such as creation's dawn beheld, thou rollest now' (IV. 182. 1637–8). Here Byron's 'Such' purposefully collapses the distinction between temporal dimensions as he depicts an oceanic force that is always the same and always changing: 'bound-less, endless, and sublime— / The image of Eternity—the throne / Of the Invisible' (IV. 183. 1643–5). Ocean dwarfs the human and yet corresponds with the longing for boundlessness, 'as we wish our souls to be' (17), in Julian's words. In his lower-keyed parallel at the start of *Julian and Maddalo* to Byron's address, Shelley makes us look hard at the element of half-conceded wish-fulfilment in Julian's 'wish', pointing up the fact that Byron reminds his reader that, ultimately, sublimity lies in the will and the vision of the imaginative beholder, who lays his 'hand upon thy mane—as I do here' (*Childe Harold's Pilgrimage*, IV. 184. 1656). Among the many places traversed by Byron's poetry, none is so important as that 'here': the locus of present composition, it represents a virtual space where the authorial self fully encounters itself in and as a process of becoming. Time may write no wrinkle, but without Byron's writing the unknowableness of Ocean will itself remain unknown, even as Byron captures himself in the act of making known the limits of human knowledge and, to that degree, triumphing over a sense of human beings as merely limited (there is a contrast, then, as well as a connection with, say, the treatment of this topic in Pope's *Essay on Man*).

Byron's emergent self plays a game of manifestation and vanishing in lines which otherwise might seem merely vaunting:

> I love not Man the less, but Nature more,
> From these our interviews, in which I steal
> From all I may be, or have been before,
> To mingle with the Universe, and feel
> What I can ne'er express, yet can not all conceal.
> (*Childe Harold's Pilgrimage*, IV. 178. 1598–602)

For Byron, identity, for all his fascination with self-fashioning, has an unWords-worthian haphazardness; it is equally expressible in relation to 'all I may be, or have been before'. That 'or' is a hinge that moves between the possible and the past but still persistent; it leaves open, or opens up passageways between, different ways for Byron to be himself. Adapted to the demands of the Spenserian stanza, any Wordsworthian ideas about 'Man' and 'Nature' are quickly Byronized. Even as one feels sense being wrenched in order to satisfy the demands of the Spenserian stan-za's tyrannical *c* rhyme, Byron makes us conscious of his only partial commitment to the role he is assuming; the effect of the rhyming and writing is to emphasize the struggle to define what it is that Byron may 'feel', even as he shies away from final definitiveness, as he speaks, in a very Shelleyan way, of 'What I can ne'er express'.

Byron and Shelley had a poetic relationship that changed who they were as poets. Their disputes, admiration and reworkings whizz backwards and forwards; the interchange sometimes seems to harden into opposition, but usually leads the one to be more like the other. Thus, *Julian and Maddalo* out-Byronizes its subject; everything here tends, not simply towards the condition of narrative, but of dramatic mono- and duologue. According to Medwin, Byron thought that Shelley 'does not make me cut a good figure' in *Julian and Maddalo*.[9] But the poem is almost Chekhovian in its even-handedness, its ability both to allow for our need to speak and for the silence that follows all we say. It is among the great achievements of Romantic negative capability. Throughout, the fixed and the fluid interact and question one another. Maddalo's anti-Utopianism stems not from indifference, but from a tragic sense of the human condition. Julian argues with him, but concedes the imperious force of his utterance and is haunted by his eloquence: 'I recall / The Sense of what he said, although I mar / The force of his expressions' (130–2), he says early on and later, after the encounter with the Maniac he singles out a specifically forceful and resonant 'expression':

> And I remember one remark which then
> Maddalo made. He said: 'Most wretched men
> Are cradled into poetry by wrong,
> They learn in suffering what they teach in song.'
> (543–6)

In these lines, lines that are at once epigrammatic and empathetic, bitterness and wry insight coalesce, mirroring the symbiotic relationship between 'suffering' and 'song'. The tender solicitude implied by 'cradled' coexists with the fact that the hand that rocks the cradle is 'wrong'. The fixity of epigram's form encounters a fluidity in the sense. The idea of a defined end, that of 'song' as the artistic yield of 'suffering', cannot preclude the possibility that cause and effect, as William Keach suggested, run the other way: what is taught in song may then be learned in suffering.[10] Shelley's fluid senses include the possibility of being fixed in an attitude by the very flux of uncontrollable emotion. The portrait of the Maniac, trapped in a prison of seemingly 'incommunicable woe' (343), may suggest how integrity, insistence on truthfulness to a supposedly authentic self, can harden into entrapment within self-pity.

'May suggest': my formulation is intentionally cautious since even though the Maniac concludes his soliloquy with an image of entombment within entombment (508–10), the reader's wish for fixity of moral judgement is foiled as much as encouraged. Certainly, Julian and Maddalo have to abandon their sense of the Maniac as an argumentative exhibit. Julian inhabits, as we all do, a variety of

---

[9] Thomas Medwin, *Journal of the Conversations of Lord Byron* (London: Colburn, 1824), 118.
[10] See William Keach, *Shelley's Style*, 202, for the suggestion of this secondary meaning; namely, that 'men learn in "suffering" what they have already taught in "song" '.

imagined lives, nor need it involve censure of him (or us) to say these 'imagined lives' include modes of existence finer or nobler than those that he (or we) currently experience. One such mode bases itself on an experience already known; it is one in which he 'might sit / In Maddalo's great palace, and his wit / And subtle talk would cheer the winter night / And make me know myself' (558–61). Self-knowledge, that is, would flow from interaction with another, almost a key to Shelley's deepest conviction about poetic identity and the need to be influenced by a poet such as Byron, since, as he puts it in the Preface to *Prometheus Unbound*, 'one great poet is a masterpiece of nature which another not only ought to study but must study' (*Major Works*, 231). In another and related mode of imagined existence, Julian would 'by patience find / An entrance to the caverns of [the Maniac's] mind' (572–3), as a result of which he 'might reclaim him from his dark estate' (574). That 'might' opens up into a virtual realm, one in which thought is free, talk is cheap, and action confines. 'What he now designed / Made for long years impression on my mind' (580–1): it has fixed itself, the 'impression', on his 'mind' (tellingly used again as a rhyme word); but without accusing Julian of insincerity or posturing, Shelley allows his dramatically poised poetic text to make the point that ideas are one thing, deeds another.

The poem concludes, in its coda, where an older Julian meets the grown-up daughter of Maddalo, with an affecting sense of our inability to know or control. Editorially it is hard to know when Maddalo's daughter starts to speak or the degree to which her supposed speech is, in fact, reported by Julian.[11] That moment of fluidity suggests intimacy but also, disturbingly, how hard it is to report anything accurately. The poem ends up by keeping its hard-won yet incommunicable secrets to itself: 'she told me how / All happened—but the cold world shall not know' (616–17). 'How' and 'know' half-rhyme in an act of self-mocking closure. The reader is shut out of a poem that itself clicks shut, a door thudding in our face, exiling us from its offer of participation in its dramatic enquiry, reminding us of the final fixity—and perhaps final unknowableness—of an imaginative text.

3

Byron seems resolutely opposed to final resolution, to wish to exist in the now of utterance: 'even as I do now' rounds out his identify-redefining quatrain in *Childe Harold's Pilgrimage*, canto III, on the impulse to 'create and in creating live / A being more intense…gaining as we give / The life we image' (III. 6. 46–7, 48–9). The ensuing lines, already discussed, 'What I am? Nothing; but not art thou, / Soul of my thought' (III. 6. 50–1), spurn and send packing identity as empirically fixed; it emerges as a 'Nothing' crying out for imaginative and aesthetic replenishment. The preferred self is to be found in that 'life we image' towards which he reaches, a 'being more intense' (III. 6, 47), gained in the act of giving (see III. 6. 48). The stanza takes its place among the canonical Romantic affirmations about creativity, but one that revels in its perilous impermanence. A stanza later, the 'I' who self-spurningly wishes to cede supremacy to 'Soul of my thought' (III. 6. 51) is again to the fore: 'Yet must I think less wildly: —I *have* thought / Too long and darkly' (III. 7. 55–6). That self, about to fall into a Gothic chaos, 'A whirling gulf of phantasy and flame' (III. 7. 58), is the necessary point of departure for Byron's imagined flights in *Childe Harold's Pilgrimage*.

Later, in canto III, Byron asserts, with calculatedly uncertain persuasiveness, 'I live not in myself, but I become / Portion of that around me' (III. 72. 680–1), but the 'I' becoming portion of something 'other' retains centre-stage in the poem. More generally, we meet the following paradox: commitment to flux becomes a fixed point for one of the 'wanderers o'er Eternity / Whose bark drives on and on, and anchored ne'er shall be' (*Childe Harold's Pilgrimage*, III. 70. 669–70), where 'on and on' nails its colours to the mast of endless process. Shelley, these lines in his mind, along with the opening of the second canto of Dante's *Paradiso*, ends *Adonais* with a boat-voyage that is rapturous and fearful, suicidal and self-assertive, his 'spirit's bark driven / Far from the shore' (55. 488–9), the poetic self 'borne darkly, fearfully, afar' (55. 492). The two poets deploy their Spenserian stanzas to different ends. Byron's lines theatrically occur; Shelley's erupt with a controlled incandescence. Byron's, with their typically contrary launch-pad 'But', have that air—half confession, half swagger, all embittered rhetoric—which make his assertions arresting in *Childe Harold's Pilgrimage*. Shelley's final stanza emerges from what has gone before; it subsumes, refines, exalts, and advances; it drives beyond, even as it contains within itself, what has preceded it. 'The One remains, the many change and pass' (*Adonais*, 52. 460) might be a Shelleyan aesthetic dictum as well as Platonic speculation. 'Yet let us ponder boldly' (*Childe Harold's Pilgrimage*, IV. 127. 1135): Byron's 'yets' pull back, refuse any headlong journey, here into the pessimism sounded by the previous stanza's 'Our life is a false nature' (IV. 126. 1126); Shelley's 'yets' coil in and out of a duplicitously celebratory dance in *The Triumph of Life*, when the shape all light is said to have 'moved in a measure new / Yet sweet' (377–8). Less deceptively, they participate in a process of millennial definition in *Prometheus Unbound* when the 'sphere, which is as many thousand spheres' (IV. 238) affects the viewer in multiplying ways: 'Solid as crystal, yet through all its mass / Flow, as through empty space, music and light' (IV. 239–40). In Byron we take a breath and start anew; in Shelley we simultaneously see the same object in two ways.

In both poets the desire for self-transcendence posits a self to be transcended; 'Love wants and does not possess beauty?'—these questioning words from Shelley's translation of Plato's *Symposium* cut to the heart of the matter.[12] The self that would love knows that it loves principally through its inability to possess what it loves: the more the other is longed for, the sharper the sense of a distinct self. At the end of *Epipsychidion*, the poet comes down to earth, a poised ecstatic Icarus spiralling out of the empyrean, a sudden fusillade of first-person pronouns announcing the journey homeward to habitual self: 'I pant, I sink, I tremble, I expire!' (591). In Shelley identity is inseparable from and irreducible to the

---

[12] Quoted from the text of the translation in Notopoulos, *The Platonism of Shelley*, 440.

smoothly evolving, endless complicating labyrinths of syntax and rhythm into which he enters in pursuit of the non-self. Whether trying to evoke and analyse 'The glory of her being' (91) in *Epipsychidion*, or whether seeking similes that convey the rebuking and wholly other beauty of the skylark's song, or whether engaged in tracking, stage by stage, in *The Triumph of Life*, Rousseau's loss of self confronted by the ego-shattering, even menacing dazzle of the shape all light, Shelley's poetry takes on a voyage beyond self that makes us aware always of the spirit's bark, its sails running before the wind of inspiration.

This is the archetypal Shelleyan posture. It gives his poetry a quality of complete submission to the work in hand. The Byronic self, by contrast, stages its elegiac disasters, its comic rallying, and its ironic sallies with an eye to effect; he trails the pageant of his bleeding heart with dash, élan, and ultimate superiority to any of his oh-so quotable assertions. *Beppo* is quintessentially Byronic in that it is at once a poem of infinite variety and unshakeably sure of itself, an endlessly iterable performance. This is a poetry to make you start and stare, that rains in upon you: it is a poetry of the half-slipping mask. Yeats is its heir. 'All things fall and are built again, / And those that build them again are gay' ('Lapis Lazuli', 35–6).[13] This arrogant Yeats derives from Byron, from the Byron who haunts us with a sense of the homelessness of existence. Even the home of poetry is no home, merely a wide oceanic tract, lit up with Kean-like lightning flashes of dramatic genius. If one restricts illustrative quotations to the last canto of *Childe Harold's Pilgrimage*— 'There woos no home, nor hope, nor life, save what is here' (IV. 105. 945); 'Of its own beauty is the mind diseased, / And fevers into false creation' (IV. 122. 1090–1); 'for they distract the gaze, / And send us prying into the abyss' (IV. 165–6. 1485–6)— one can see how all is always effect, and yet never merely effect. A partially redemptive factor here is the courage to present strong iambic assertions that hold themselves self aloof from, even as they are half-fevered by, the temptations of 'false creation' (IV. 122. 1091), existential melodrama, posturing.

After *Childe Harold's Pilgrimage*, and building on its achievement, as critics such as Alan Rawes have shown,[14] comes the comic muse, turning what 'was once romantic to burlesque' (*Don Juan*, IV. 3. 24), but more than half in love with self-display. More glitteringly than ever, syntax, phrase, and rhythm are equal to an astonishing self-fashioning that disarms analysis: either you throw the poem away from you as did the dying Keats on the Maria Crowther, or it has you in its coils, simultaneously fascinated and moved by the thought that the man who can write 'And if I laugh at any mortal thing, / 'Tis that I may not weep; and if I weep, / 'Tis that our nature cannot always bring / Itself to apathy' (*Don Juan*, IV. 4. 25–8) pushes his aristocratic features into our faces with the strangest blend of fellow-feeling and something close to disdain. Shelley in his own *ottava rima* comedy, *The Witch of Atlas*, delights in play, fiction, metaphor, evocations of the 'before unapprehended relations of things' (*Major Works*, 676), as he calls them in

[13] Quoted from *Yeats's Poems*, ed. and annotated. A Norman Jeffares with an Appendix by Warwick Gould ([1989] London: Macmillan, 1991 rev. edn). Line numbers have been supplied.

[14] See Alan Rawes, *Byron's Poetic Experimentation* (Aldershot: Ashgate, 2000), *passim*.

A Defence of Poetry. In the poem's dedicatory stanzas, Shelley warns against Wordsworthian over-kill, but hints at the dangers and fascinations of 'idolatry' (48): image-worship. Perhaps the unattached imagination, delighting only in itself, risks narcissism. Shelley's implicit retort to his own self-doubting question is that his poetic gambits mirror his revisionary political hopes. But if there is implicit comedy for Shelley in image-making, as imagination 'creates / From its own wreck the thing it contemplates' (*Prometheus Unbound*, IV. 573–4), there is the ever-threatening possibility of pathos and let-down, too: either when self-transcendence is no longer possible, and one returns, defeatedly self-aware to the 'still cave of the Witch Poesy' (*Mont Blanc*, 44), or when figuration turns into disfiguration, as in *The Triumph of Life*, when every image reappears, besmirched rather than meta-morphosed. Art's wonders can seem to fixate on ideal nothings, beautiful mon-sters, as when the Witch creates Hermaphroditus, 'A living Image, which did far surpass / In beauty that bright shape of vital stone / Which drew the heart out of Pygmalion' (*The Witch of Atlas*, 326–8). These dazzling lines, setting limits to a creation nominally superior to Galatea, but lacking the power to draw out the viewer's heart, achieve a fluidity of perspective in the poetic, syntactical act of intimating rigidity.

Shelley is close here to self-critique and to praise of Byron's own refusal, in his *ottava rima* poems, to settle for anything less than a sense of inexhaustible potential. Byron himself might be presented as a poet of arrest, the poet who would have us 'Stop!—for thy tread is on an Empire's dust' (*Childe Harold's Pilgrimage*, III. 17. 145). But he is often at his most artistically all-inclusive when confronting the fact of human limitation, as in 'So, we'll go no more a roving'. Yes, the 'heart must pause to breathe, / And love itself have rest' (7–8), and yet if Byron's positives can suggest negatives, his cessations are full of restless energy; if ever there were a poem that sent one 'a roving / So late into the night' (1–2) it is this poem, sparkling with lyric glitter on the dark lagoon-waters of melancholy, a poem in which, for example, the 'So's' that open the first two lines function in startlingly different ways: the first, acquiescing in the inevitable, the second caught up in what he describes. Shelley's sonnet to Byron ('Lines to —— ') 'Marks your creations rise as fast & fair / As perfect worlds at the creator's will' (6–7), lines that combine praise appropriate to the poetic identities forged in the work of both these remarkable poets, each capable of perfection and a surprising plurality of 'creations'.[15] The lines are emblematic of the way in which, for Byron and Shelley, an endless force of inspiration materializes itself, over and over, in an enabling cage of words.

---

[15] Quoted from *MYR* 8, 251.

9

Narrative and Play

Shelley's *The Witch of Atlas* and Byron's *Beppo*

1

Two epigraphs of a sort will help to highlight this chapter's concerns. One comes from Brian Nellist, in eminently sensibly Anglo-Saxon mode: 'Pontifications about "play" by academics are liable to make even a tolerant reader wince.'[1] Nellist makes this statement before articulating a fundamental if double-headed point about 'play': that it involves freedom—'[t]he play of mind', is Nellist's example—but also conformity to rules.[2] The second occurs in Hans-Georg Gadamer's *Truth and Method*, where, in the course of a meditation on 'play', he makes the gnomic but suggestively riddling statement that '[t]he movement of playing has no goal that brings it to an end; rather, it renews itself in constant repetition'.[3] This chapter's two main exhibits—Byron's *Beppo* and Shelley's *The Witch of Atlas*—weave and unweave their poetic imaginings in such a way that their narrative form 'renews itself in constant repetition'. As they deal with what elsewhere in the same work Gadamer terms 'the reality of play, which we call the play of art',[4] they envisage narrative mimeses of a mode of freedom.

At bottom, both poems address the 'question of how art can be justified'.[5] The historical meaning of their doing so has been read as a challenge to German intensities and earnestness in the wake of Waterloo and the apparent triumph of a high Protestant seriousness.[6] But it is the argument of this chapter that both poems exploit the freedom offered by the *ottava rima* form and comic Italian tradition to post an exhilarating, defiant trust in the poetic imagination; their interest in play is unduly circumscribed by attribution to them of 'the rational play of mind'.[7] Self-awareness and irony protect this trust in both poets; Byron and Shelley are

[1] Brian Nellist, 'Shelley's Narratives and "The Witch of Atlas"', *Essays on Shelley*, ed. Miriam Allott (Liverpool: Liverpool University Press, 1982), 170.
[2] Nellist, 170.
[3] Hans-Georg Gadamer, *Truth and Method*, trans. rev. Joel Weinsheimer and Donald G. Marshall, 2nd edn (London: Bloomsbury, 2013), 108.
[4] Gadamer, *Truth and Method*, 117.
[5] Hans-Georg Gadamer, 'The Relevance of the Beautiful. Art as Play, Symbol, and Festival', *The Relevance of the Beautiful and Other Essays*, trans. Nicholas Walker (Cambridge: Cambridge University Press, 1987), 3.
[6] See Marilyn Butler, *Romantics, Rebels and Reactionaries: English Literature and Its Background 1760–1830* (Oxford: Oxford University Press, 1981), 123.
[7] Butler, 124.

beforehand with their critics, yet pugnacious in their implicit contempt for forms of subjugation to hegemonic models and modes of knowledge and power. The particular historical shaping of narrative form in these poems of play emerges from earlier work. Shelley's *Prometheus Unbound*, a long-meditated work published the month (August 1820) that *The Witch of Atlas* was composed, declares in its Preface its 'abhorrence' for 'Didactic poetry' (*Major Works*, 232). The lyrical drama articulates and seeks to demonstrate its ideal of poetry as 'a perpetual Orphic song' (IV. 415), an activity committed to ceaseless transformation. For Byron's part, a famous passage from *Lara* (1814), delineating the hero's flawed, compelling development, allows us access to relevant issues, albeit in dramatic, even tragic rather than comic mode:

> His early dreams of good outstripp'd the truth,
> And troubled manhood followed baffled youth;
> With thought of years in phantom chase misspent,
> And wasted powers for better purpose lent;
> And fiery passions that had poured their wrath
> In hurried desolation o'er his path,
> And left the better feelings all at strife
> In wild reflection o'er his stormy life;
> But haughty still, and loth himself to blame,
> He called on Nature's self to share the shame,
> And charged all faults upon the fleshly form
> She gave to clog the soul, and feast the worm;
> 'Till he at last confounded good and ill,
> And half mistook for fate the acts of will:
> Too high for common selfishness, he could
> At times resign his own for others' good,
> But not in pity, not because he ought,
> But in some strange perversity of thought,
> That swayed him onward with a secret pride
> To do what few or none would do beside [...]
> (18. 35–54)[8]

The lines show Byron shaping from the heroic couplet a narrative form in love with mysterious fatalism. If this form displays a propulsive, even compulsive empathy, the empathy accompanies sharpened judgement. But sharpened judgement declines moral absoluteness, even as it uses the language of moral absolutes. The verse behaves as though it were engaged in Popean analysis; one might compare it with Pope's excoriatingly painful and ruthlessly all-seeing portrait of Atticus in the *Epistle to Dr Arbuthnot*, ready to:

> Damn with faint praise, assent with civil leer,
> And without sneering, teach the rest to sneer;

---

[8] All quotations from Byron are taken from *The Complete Poetical Works of Lord Byron*, ed. Jerome. J. McGann, 7 vols. (Oxford: Clarendon Press, 1980–93), here vol. 2.

Willing to wound, and yet afraid to strike,
Just hint a fault, and hesitate dislike […]
(201–4)[9]

These lines deftly evoke a master-hypocrite, one who is able to manipulate others through wordless deviations from apparent assertions. The passage depends for its effect on a shared set of norms about sincerity of thought and speech, on recognizing that the gap which exists between the two is the source of Atticus's power over others and of his reprehensible moral nature; the passage delivers its verdicts from an agreed socio-ethical viewpoint. Byron has the force, but not the ethical clarity of Pope, the admired forebear whom the Romantic writer chose, when defending, to 'take on his strong ground—as an *Ethical* poet'.[10] Pope's Atticus is an agent, in control, governor of his acts, able to teach, 'Willing to wound' and so on. As such, he is subject to a moral critique founded on the assumption of action's intentionality. Byron's Lara has things happen to him, 'things' even and especially including his 'secret pride' that 'swayed him'; 'fiery passions had poured their wrath / In hurried desolation o'er his path', as though they were external to him, foes intent on his undoing, thwarting and harrowing 'his path'.

To make this distinction is not to imply adverse criticism of Byron. It is precisely by venturing into areas where ethical clarity no longer operates—areas where 'strange perversity of thought' reigns—that Byron enthrals and challenges the reader. It may be, as Rolf P. Lessenich has argued, that this is a more general characteristic of 'the Romantic tragic hero and heroine', figures often characterized by 'helplessness and aimlessness of purpose'.[11] But Byron's hero is divided against himself with a concentrated energy of artistic and existential purpose. Indeed, the heroism of the Byronic hero often derives from the fact that his very individualism means he is reacting to or against rather than controlling circumstance, a thread that runs from the overthrown Napoleon to the eminently seducible Juan. So, here, bafflement and trouble spur Lara to call 'on Nature's self to share the shame' and, finally, lead him 'To do what few or none would do beside'. He acts, buts his actions seem bound up in a self-generated dynamic of reaction.

Even as they spurn the authority of traditional socio-ethical standards, Byron's lines display a newly authoritative tone. Displaying empathy with inwardness, this tone is bound up with the poetry's swiftly enjambed sound, a sound that mimics the psychic dynamics being described. The couplets, too, are 'swayed onward with a secret pride'. Byron deploys an unPopean use of antitheses that clash without resolving into or implying the harmony whose ultimate source is clarity of authorial judgement; his lines display a restless and questioning use of a traditional moral idiom, in which, for example, highfalutin 'dreams of good' give way to experience-based 'truth'; and they fashion an experimentally distinctive notion of heroism.

---

[9] All quotations from Pope, unless indicated otherwise, are taken from *Alexander Pope: The Major Works*, ed. Pat Rogers ([1993] Oxford: Oxford University Press, 2006).
[10] Byron, *Lord Byron: The Complete Miscellaneous Prose*, ed. Andrew Nicholson (Oxford: Clarendon Press, 1991), 148. Hereafter *Byron's Prose*.
[11] Rolf P. Lessenich, *Romantic Disillusionism and the Sceptical Tradition* (Bonn: Bonn University Press, 2017), 196.

Or, as Bernard Beatty phrases it in a sophisticated discussion of the Byron/Pope relationship, Byron's 'antitheses [...] reinforce disturbance and suffering rather than the poise Pope maintains'.[12] Turning away in sardonic self-contempt from 'early dreams of good', the writing implies, Lara fears 'good' almost the way others fear evil. But if he will only resign 'his own for others' good' out of 'some strange perversity of thought', the fact that he has 'confounded good with ill' seems like a difficult achievement rather than a category mistake. Byron, it is clear, is much concerned in the poem with his hero's transvaluation of 'good' and 'ill', and *Lara* involves a quasi-existential search for a code by which to live.

2

Beppo, in its quiet facetiousness, to adapt Byron's description of *Don Juan*,[13] may seem worlds away from the storm and stress of *Lara*. But a link that connects the two works is fascination with codes of understanding, their imperfectness and unreliability. In *Beppo* the *ottava rima* stanza houses a proliferation of stories criss-crossing the main story, that of Beppo and Laura. The digressive consciousness of the narrator emerges as the narrative's central spring and source of interest. Whether describing the Venetian Carnival, paintings of women, a gondola, the difference between Italy and England, or telling us about the 'Ridotto' (505), a place he intends to 'go myself to-morrow, / Just to divert my thoughts a little space, / Because I'm rather hippish' (506–8), the narrator spins digressive thread after thread, miniature story after miniature story, in the same breath as offering a mock apology for doing so in stanza 50. Throughout *Beppo* Byron conducts his narrative so that the reader has the sense of life passing into poetic art without the loss of life.

Byron asserts that he does not know his heroine's 'real name' (166) and decides, with winning arbitrariness, that 'we'll call her Laura, if you please, / Because it slips into my verse with ease' (167–8). This 'ease' only appears to court our approval ('if you please'). Byron chooses Laura, in part, as Drummond Bone suggests in '*Childe Harold IV, Don Juan* and *Beppo*' to make 'an ironic reference to the unattainable Laura of Petrarch's sonnets',[14] yet his irony is as double as ever; his Laura has her own ability to enchant. The poem is determined to proceed as it pleases the narrator-author, a figure who is often concerned with matters, or so he with arch self-reflexiveness suggests, other than writing poetry. It is as though a world of realities lies in reach of his creative sight (one of which is the 'real' prototype of his heroine), providing an abundance of stories on which to draw. Byron makes clear this strategic self-presentation in his narrator's contempt for 'an author that's *all author*' (593). There, his difference from such an author shows in his appeal to common prejudice in the

---

[12] Bernard Beatty, 'Continuities and Discontinuities of Language and Voice in Dryden, Pope, and Byron', *Byron: Augustan and Romantic*, ed. Andrew Rutherford (Basingstoke: Macmillan, 1990), 129.

[13] Lord George Gordon Byron, *Byron's Letters and Journals*, ed. Leslie A. Marchand, 13 vols. (London: Murray, 1973–1994), 6. 67. Hereafter *BLJ*.

[14] Drummond Bone, '*Childe Harold IV, Don Juan* and *Beppo*', *The Cambridge Companion to Byron*, ed. Drummond Bone (Cambridge: Cambridge University Press, 2004), 164.

italicized phrase, virtually the textual equivalent of a drawled emphasis or lift of the eyebrow. In the same stanza he secures our support through his calculated use of nonchalant slang: 'One don't know what to say to them' (596), he says, objecting to the self-importance of inky scribblers, always suggesting that if one writes one should do so because of the multiplicity of stories waiting to be told; after all, *Beppo* is itself living proof that 'stories somehow lengthen when begun' (792), as the poem's last line has it.[15]

From the word go, systems of value collide and cast an amused glance at one another, mostly in the interests of a genial, sharp-eyed tolerance. The epigraphs mock the traveller to Venice (quoting Rosalind's mockery of 'Monsieur Traveller' in *As You Like It*, IV.i.) and the English version of Venice as 'the seat of all dissoluteness' (this, the second epigraph, is taken from Ayscough). It is less that Byron will rebut this allegation of 'dissoluteness' and more that he makes dissolute Venice, as typified by the much-interrupted story of Laura, Beppo, and the Count, a cant-free zone, and therefore an improvisatory location of the provisionally, light-on-its-feet positive, a place, indeed, where 'dissoluteness' 'dissolves' into something less readily defined. Via Rosalind Byron gets his self-deprecation in first, and, anyway, he is going to deliver the goods, packing the poem with authenticating details. *Beppo* is, in fact, a celebration of all the particulars of otherness, all the signs of life vividly going on elsewhere: there (or here) the language is different, a 'soft bastard Latin, / Which melts like kisses from a female mouth' (346–7), erotically charged in Byron's liquid syllables, unlike, imitated with equal panache, 'our harsh northern whistling, grunting guttural, / Which we're obliged to hiss, and spit, and sputter all' (351–2). As for Rosalind's gibe about having 'swam in a GONDOLA', Byron reserves one of his finest set-pieces for the derided craft:

> Didst ever see a gondola? For fear
> You should not, I'll describe it you exactly:
> 'Tis a long covered boat that's common here,
> Carved at the prow, built lightly, but compactly,
> Rowed by two rowers, each called 'Gondolier',
> It glides along the water, looking blackly,
> Just like a coffin clapt in a canoe,
> Where none can make out what you say or do.
>
> (145–52)

The last three lines mingle suggestions in a way that is typical of *Beppo*: 'It glides along the water, looking blackly' is funny (what, the reader has been wondering, will be the word to rhyme with 'exactly' and 'compactly') and almost autologous. The gondola looks like itself, Byron seems to say; it is a thing that suffices unto itself and is therefore iconic, receiving from the narrator an act of recreating homage that is at once comic and high-spiritedly reverential. The gondola is a part of a relished locale. To borrow Wallace Stevens's lines from 'Local Objects', it is among 'The local objects of a world without a foyer' and also among the 'things / For which a fresh

---

[15] Material in these last two paragraphs draws on O'Neill's discussion in Michael D. Hurley and Michael O'Neill, *Poetic Form: An Introduction* (Cambridge: Cambridge University Press, 2012), 205.

name always occurred'. As in Stevens's poem, which disentangles itself from the present tense, Byron's poem is also in a state of 'approaching / As toward an absolute foyer beyond romance'.[16] There is always before and after, 'foyer' and 'beyond', in Byron's world. In these lines there is an immediate shift into simile ('Just like a coffin clapt in a canoe') where the funereal edge is taken off by the lightly skipping 'canoe', while the last line moves from its glance at death to mildly scandalous hints of gossip and sex ('what you say and do'). Travel focuses the eye and broadens yet nuances humour, including self-mockery about a process of representation that promises exactness but prizes secrecy.[17]

There is a tendency to think of *Beppo* as a trial run for *Don Juan*. But, cumulatively, its tones are very different in register, and one does wrong to scan the earlier poem for the riotous subversions of the later masterpiece. Relations more intriguing than those of opposition are forever being discovered, even as contrast seems to be the poem's preoccupation. On the one hand, the poem is shadowed, in its account of Beppo's return, by one of the master-narratives of Western literature, the *Odyssey*.[18] On the other hand, in jokey, complicating tension with this framework, the poem is continually opening up into byways, oblique alleys, the textual equivalents of Venetian *calli*; its narrative architecture imitates the city's design or resistance to design, its chance discoveries, unusual vistas, sudden changes of mood, colour, vision. In *Beppo* Byron will have nothing or little to do with the contrast of glorious past and ignoble present familiar in Romantic writing about Italy—and finding its way into his 'Venice. An Ode' or the opening stanzas of *Childe Harold's Pilgrimage*, canto IV. True, he does 'fix his story' (79) in the heyday of the past, but the past he evokes has vivid commerce with the narrator's present. His account of the 'pretty faces' (81) of modern Venetian women leads him to find a comparison with famous art:

> [...] And like so many Venuses of Titian's
> (The best's at Florence—see it, if ye will)
> They look when leaning over the balcony,
> Or stepp'd from out a picture by Giorgione [...]
> (85–8)

The take-it-or-leave-it relationship with the reader envisaged by 'see it, if ye will' is part of an easy, even miraculous movement between writing (or painting) and living envisaged and enacted in these lines. The temptation in reading aloud is to play that last rhyme for a broadly comic laugh, yet the *Oxford English Dictionary* gives *c.* 1825 as the date when the pronunciation of the Italian-derived 'bal*cony*', with the emphasis on the second syllable, changed to '*bal*cony', with the emphasis on the first syllable. That is, Byron is not trying for a ludicrous undercutting in his rhyme.

---

[16] Wallace Stevens, *Collected Poetry and Prose*, sel. Frank Kermode and Joan Richardson (New York: Library of America, 1997), 473 & 474.
[17] Mark Sandy, 'Reimagining Venice and Visions of Decay in Wordsworth, the Shelleys, and Thomas Mann', *Venice and the Cultural Imagination: 'This Strange Dream upon the Water'*, ed. Michael O'Neill, Mark Sandy and Sarah Wootton (London: Pickering and Chatto, 2012), 40.
[18] As Angela Esterhammer reminded the audience in the discussion-period after a version of this section of the chapter was delivered as a lecture at the German Society of Romanticism's annual conference on 'Narratives of Romanticism' at Wuppertal, 8–11 October 2015.

Certainly the feminine rhyme here lifts the poetry out of the cant or gush of connoisseur or tourist, but it is surely right to hear in the rhyme something of the romance of serendipity as well as the humour of incongruity.

The act of 'leaning over the balcony'—this is the art and beauty of *Beppo*—is at once humdrum and a gesture ready to be captured in the light, aesthetic net of rhyme. Although the poem is far too fleet-footed to be pinned down to a position, it deftly but firmly champions the virtue of the 'real'. Stanzas 13 and 14 take off from the stanza under discussion; in them Byron praises the Triple Portrait in Manfrini's palace because of its reality, and the stanzas take one close to the goal of the narrative sympathy which animates the poetry of *Beppo* as Byron praises 'Love, in full life and length, not love ideal, / No, nor ideal beauty, that fine name, / But something better still, so very real' (97–9). *Beppo* places its trust in that 'something better still', the 'very real'. Confronted by objections that this notion of the 'very real' is itself another construction of the mind, the poem, in effect, shrugs its shoulders, saying, in its own way, 'I know as much, but thus I refute it, or its reductive implications', as it goes on to show how the real underpins the ideal, the poet recalling 'One of those forms which flit by us, when we / Are young, and fix our eyes on every face' (105–6) and compares it to 'the lost Pleiad seen no more below' (112). The pathos achieved by the appeal to shared experience ('which flit by us') and elegiac cadencing works its spell. When we 'fix our eyes', we are reminded of our own stories in the context of a larger poetic moment when the poet chooses to 'fix my story'.

Lawgivers on aesthetics are among Byron's targets when he turns his attention fully on the English world from which he is exiled. Before he has slyly settled scores with the Princess of Parallelograms (see 624–8) and just after he has provokingly attacked contemporary female creators and consumers of polite culture or 'blues' (569–74), he turns his attention to 'bustling Botherbys' (575) who 'show 'em / "That charming passage in the last new poem"' (575–6). Such a figure is depicted as 'A stalking oracle of awful phrase, / The approving "*Good*" (by no means GOOD in law) / Humming like flies around the newest blaze' (585–7). Himself 'humming' round the word 'good', Byron, not for the only time in his poetry, takes on something of the features of a person whom he attacks. The word 'good', we might say, is subjected to mockery, but mockery in the service of a 'good' beyond vanity. Byron sets himself up as something of an 'oracle', laid back rather than 'stalking', as he proceeds to commend 'Men of the world, who know the world like men, / S[co]tt, R[oger]s, M[oo]re, and all the better brothers, / Who think of something else beside the pen' (602–4). In *Beppo* Byron is at once all author, albeit of a Shandean, digressive kind—'It was the Carnival, as I have said / Some six and thirty stanzas back' (441–2)—and intent on 'something else beside the pen'. In this latter guise, he seeks to gain access, by way of his narrative strategies, to a state posited as extra-linguistic. Yet the praise of 'Men of the world, who know the world like men' has, partly because of the chiastic circularity of the wording, a self-enclosed quality. Byron's friends and poetic rivals are safely enclosed within their own remit and circuit, the 'world' suggesting a particular English social realm, one that the narrator knows about but is able, through his knowledge of Italy, to transcend.

Byron may seem to praise a domain of masculine freedom; it is, contrarily enough, one open to appreciation of the feminine. Throughout, Byron's alertness to and delight in gendered as well as cultural difference is on display, finding expression in the poetry's continual hints of the endless story of the difference not only between men and women, but also between members of the same gender. Laura's initial response to Beppo's self-discovery is an instance:

> But where an Englishwoman sometimes faints,
> Italian females don't do so outright;
> They only call a little on their saints,
> And then come to themselves, almost or quite;
> (707–10).

There is a poker-faced drollness here, the half-truth of generalization knowingly offering itself as 'the truth'. The self-assurance makes the passage buoyantly resistant to critique; there would be little dent in the writer's self-confidence, one feels, were one able to say that one knew Italian women who do faint, since the writing turns the prospect of fainting into a social performance which the supposedly binary tribes of English and Italian women do very differently. The writing reveals a guardedly unguarded poise as it half-gently mocks 'an Englishwoman' and half-admiringly teases 'Italian females', the poem's style balancing adroitly between badinage and the claim to be offering trenchant observation.

Throughout *Beppo* Venice is a mirror in which Englishness is persuaded to discover a coolly quizzical alternative to itself: it is a stage where the narrated good of a life based on avoidance of pain and pursuit of pleasure rehearses itself. In making his cultural observations, Byron enjoins unpreachily the virtues of tolerance and curiosity, but his poem's power comes from depths deeper than liberal recommendations. In its responsiveness to living, its combination of delight, sardonic sharpness (normally at the expense of Tory-governed England), and existential awareness, it defeats our attempts at analysis, leaving Drummond Bone in his important essay '*Beppo*: The Liberation of Fiction' with a sense of 'radiant sadness',[19] and tempting Jerome J. McGann to believe that it is the 'corporeality [of words such as paradise, beauty and love] which imparts […] spiritual value'.[20] Both critics give their own twist to Shelley's insight, in a discarded stanza to *Adonais*, into the kind of heroism involved in Byron's *Beppo*-esque way of being:

> His life seemed one long Carnival, one merry
> Farewell to flesh, to which all must bid farewell
> Before they pass the melancholy ferry
> He laughed and as the arrow of laughter fell
> Wounding with sweet and bitter mirth, it well
> Distilled the balm from its fine point to heal
> The wounds which it inflicted […][21]

---

[19] Drummond Bone, '*Beppo*: The Liberation of Fiction', *Byron and the Limits of Fiction*, ed. Bernard Beatty and Vincent Newey (Liverpool: Liverpool UP, 1988), 124.
[20] Jerome J. McGann, *Fiery Dust: Byron's Poetic Development* (Chicago: University of Chicago Press, 1968), 291.
[21] My transcription assumes 'it' was deleted in error for 'had', as do Dawson and Webb. See *BSM* 14, 22–3.

What Shelley has caught is Byron's ability to dwell among the 'sweet and bitter' contraries of existence, and to produce a poetry that is simultaneously funny and serious, capable of wounding and of healing, transcending through its accomplishment the often destructive element in which it immerses itself. The way in which Shelley puts side by side 'the melancholy ferry' and 'he laughed' is compactly suggestive of what is involved in Byron's carnivalesque manner. Byron may praise Venice, but the narrator is not a Venetian, merely 'a nameless sort of person / (A broken Dandy lately on my travels)' (409–10). The self-description is disingenuous, since the possibility of this Dandy retaining his anonymity (for all the poem's initially anonymous publication) is remote. Yet the gap between Byron and his various narrated locales, English or Venetian, is the source of much of the poetry's concealed melancholy. The poem's narrative tantalizingly offers narrator as well as reader the possibility of entrance into worlds from which, discreetly, affectingly, it is implied that the poet is, in reality, at a remove, passing through them in imagination, an ordinary mortal, yes, but gifted with a capacity of response that makes the stuff of living seem, paradoxically, lasting and perishable.

The storytelling manner is at once all-embracing and yet wittily ready to wrong-foot, requiring, on the reader's part, for all its air of disarming candour, a continual vigilance. The Venetian Carnival may license 'Masks of all times and nations, Turks and Jews' (18), but as if joking at the expense of a caricature of Shelley, Byron points out that 'no one in these parts may quiz the clergy, / Therefore take heed, ye Freethinkers! I charge ye' (23–4). Here and in the next stanza, Byron's wit is even-handed, playing up the alleged intolerance and venality of Italian Catholicism, even as he suggests that the 'Freethinkers' are far more hidebound than they think. Carnivalesque Venice is proof for Byron of the way in which cultures construct themselves round assumptions and beliefs. Fashions in poetry are mocked in stanzas 51–2, where Byron amusingly feigns to be 'a nameless sort of person', who might, were he able to write, 'sell you, mix'd with western sentimentalism, / Some samples of the finest Orientalism' (407–8). The insight, impudence and self-reflexivity of that last couplet are dazzlingly self-conscious: Byron implies mockery of his audience for consumerist tastes which he has himself shaped—the phrase 'finest Orientalism', for example, makes *The Giaour, Lalla Rookh,* and so forth sound like so many lengths of carpet, the notion of successful poetry declining from 'finest' into a sentimental commodity. The moment abandons a past poetic self, but it does not express cynicism about poetry itself, as it glances back at a stylistic mode felt to be merely fashionable. Byron makes us aware that poetry and fashion have an uneasy alliance, and there is a twinkling suggestion that the current poem is also riding the crest of some new wave; but *Beppo*'s de-idealizing is at one with a renewed appetite for the possibilities of the poetic art.

The poetry takes its cue from its own homage to what might be termed experiential relish. It brims with a pleasure taken in pleasure: 'With all its sinful doings, I must say, / That Italy's a pleasant place to me' (321–2) is how Byron begins one excursus that will evolve into his backhanded professions of affection for England. '[D]oings' is at once suggestive, an innuendo, and free from moralizing, taking the sting out of 'sinful' (try putting 'vices' in its place). But this pleasure is justified as resulting in happiness: 'on the whole', Byron writes of the Count and Laura, 'they were a happy pair' (425). Here and elsewhere, Byron contrives, through the conduct of his words, to suggest a way of viewing life that has its own authenticity, and has its own virtue. In the stanzas about England, for example, he is virtuously sardonic about cant—'I like the Habeas Corpus (when we've got it)' (374)—but he is surprisingly even-handed and unpinnable-down in his attitudes: anti-Government satire coexists with his aloofness from popular struggle, 'Our little riots just to show we're free men' (387), while his mixed feelings about Waterloo result in a couplet whose mood is difficult fully to explain, where he claims to 'greatly venerate our recent glories', but regrets that they were 'owing to the Tories' (391–2). The lampooning of triumphalism raises the question of Byron's true allegiances, yet the poem's manner allows him to draw a teasing veil over the matter. William Keach responds to Byron's evident ventriloquism by hearing 'the narrator as a Tory, loyal to "Regent, Church and King" but a little ashamed as well as proud of "our recent glories"'.[22] Yet such a distinct narrative creation seems born of a critical will to clarify that Byron delights in muddying.

Narrative play in *Beppo* is alive to muddle and contradiction. The poem's dealings with romantic cliché are a case in point. In one sense, cliché is tolerated only for a second, and yet, as with Louis MacNeice, Byron's amused undercuttings of cliché accompany a tolerant homage: thus, 'The moment dusky night with mantle covers / The skies' (9–10) is undercut by what follows, 'and the more duskily the better' (10). Byron has learned from Frere and Casti how to strike a romantic attitude and whisper sardonically behind his hand at the same time, a 'poetic form', indeed, as Vassallo notes, that 'was the nearest poetry could come to mirroring the reality of life itself'.[23] Part of the poem's charm is how it still feels the eagerness of desire for what it sees as easily 'smokeable', in Keats's word (*Letters: John Keats* II. 174), easily made fun of. So, later describing the parting of Laura and Beppo, Byron strikes this note with consummate expressiveness:

'Tis said that their last parting was pathetic,
As partings often are, or ought to be,
And their presentiment was quite prophetic
That they should never more each other see,
(A sort of morbid feeling, half poetic,
Which I have known occur in two or three)
When kneeling on the shore upon her sad knee,
He left this Adriatic Ariadne.
(217–24)

That last line is not just knockabout fun; Laura as an 'Adriatic Ariadne' survives her 'sad knee'—and, remarkably, the pathos of the parting survives the comic puncturing. Again, the narratorial art is all. Byron purports to tell us what it is he has heard

[22] William Keach, *Arbitrary Power: Romanticism, Language, Politics* (Princeton: Princeton University Press, 2004), 65–6.
[23] See Peter Vassallo, *Byron: The Italian Literary Influence* (London: Macmillan, 1988), 60 (see 43–63 for further discussion).

('Tis said'), as though he is merely transmitting the report of others, before his second line brings into play a quick mobility to how things 'are, or ought to be', which in turn registers a flicker of amusement at cultural assumptions. Feminine rhyming sets going a syncopated buoyancy at odds with too morose an immersion in the 'pathetic'. The parenthetical lines, however, hint at personal knowledge of the sadness of partings, even as they distance themselves from anything too personal through the detachment of 'morbid feeling'. Byron half-jests at scars while making us conscious he, too, has felt the preceding wound; he winds up the stanza with a vignette both funny and touching, 'Ariadne' just about getting the upper hand in its tragicomic rhyming tussle with 'sad knee'. More generally, the poem provokes us to laughter, and yet its playfulness often leaves us 'so doubly serious shortly after' (632). Byron, in the guise of dandy, lover of life, cynic, political and cultural commentator, and poet discovering new forms of engagement with words, subjects categories to witty and profound appraisal, in a story which somehow lengthens when begun, and prompts digressions about the very nature of creativity, the freedoms and responsibilities of the artist.

3

Such 'freedoms and responsibilities' dance before us and dissolve in the 'visionary rhyme' ('To Mary', l. 8) that is Shelley's *The Witch of Atlas*. This is the phrase he uses to commend the poem to Mary Shelley, who had expressed a robustly Johnsonian objection to the work 'Upon The Score Of Its Containing No Human Interest' (*Major Works*, 486). 'Play' in this poem deals a severe blow to potential abstract paraphrase (for which process this chapter is using the contested term 'allegorizing'). If Byron's poem uses *ottava rima* to enact checks, doublings back, incursions of Dandyesque comment, Shelley deploys it to create effects of impudent near-magic; each stanza is a hat out of which fantastical yet 'visionary creations' are pulled. The poem's relations with Byron are nuanced and beyond competitiveness. As Stuart Sperry writes, Shelley uses the same measure as Byron employs, but does so 'with his own grace and facility even while [the measure] continuously invites comparison with the older poet'.[24] Shelley gracefully if implicitly pays tribute to Byron's achievement in *Beppo* and *Don Juan*, yet he moves away from Byron's blend of seriousness and laughter into a tonal composite made up of registers that are visionary, poignant, urbanely composed, lonely, and aesthetically sophisticated. Binding the poem is less commitment to what Jerrold Hogle, with adroit legerdemain, calls 'allegory in the literal sense of that word, "a formal discourse always becoming alien from itself" (*agoruein* plus *allos*)',[25] than a continual process of challenging its own 'self-awareness of limitations'.[26] Reluctant to formulate a conceptual poetics in the poem itself, Shelley shapes an aesthetic experience through control of mood, the play of attitudes.

---

[24] Sperry, *Shelley's Major Verse*, 145.   [25] Hogle, *Shelley's Process*, 215.
[26] Bloom, *Shelley's Mythmaking*, 198.

Shelley's strategy, from the dedicatory stanzas onwards, is initially to deprecate his poem's significance, then to affirm it. An example is stanza 27, when he finds an image that does justice to his poem's defamiliarizing vision:

> While on her hearth lay blazing many a piece
> Of sandalwood, rare gums and cinnamon;
> Men scarcely know how beautiful fire is—
> Each flame of it is as a precious stone
> Dissolved in ever-moving light, and this
> Belongs to each and all who gaze upon.
> The Witch beheld it not, for in her hand
> She held a woof that dimmed the burning brand.
> (27. 257–64)

Before discussing these lines, it is important to note how the narrative pauses at this point; it changes tack and tone after the farewell to the nymphs episode (stanzas 22–5) which shows how the poem deals with human experience as though viewing it deliberately through the wrong end of a telescope. The Witch, in effect, laments in this section that she cannot experience the mortality which afflicts all things. Even the mythological Forms are doomed to share in this general perishability: 'The boundless ocean like a drop of dew / Will be consumed—the stubborn centre must / Be scattered, like a cloud of summer dust' (23. 230–2). Momentarily, Shelley supplies a vision of necessary destruction that is comically terrifying: that strategically positioned 'must' is at once coquettishly dogmatic and gravely sombre as the world is blown away like dust from the poem's hand. The effect bespeaks a re-focalizing mastery, as the writing survives its gaze into an entropic abyss, and humorous pathos, as the Witch is moved by the thought of her own invulnerability to the fate that the nymphs must suffer, 'I cannot die as ye must [. . .] and so, farewell' (24. 238, 240).

Then, she retreats, after a deliciously precise description of her tears and the 'intertangled lines of light' (25. 245) they get caught up in as they fall—almost, one might think, an image for what happens to anything on which the poet's imagination seizes as he shapes his poem—before Shelley moves into the stanzas about the Witch reading and writing 'wrought poesy' (26. 256). She becomes a narrator in the magical narrative of which she is the heroine, and her auratic power enables us to see with new eyes, 'Men scarcely know how beautiful fire is— / Each flame of it is as a precious stone'. The movement here supports Hogle's sense of the poetry's 'joyous play of relations',[27] of its continual de-centring, as the Witch pauses over the beauty of fire, only immediately to challenge our sense of it, solidi-fying lambent flame into 'precious stone'. Momentarily the fire is made available to 'each and all who gaze upon', the syntactical looseness expressive of a trance-like enlargement of vision.[28] Yet the Witch 'beheld it not', removed from the spectacle she makes available to us: 'in her hand / She held a woof that dimmed the burning

---

[27] Hogle, 219.
[28] For the prompt to think further about this feature, I am grateful here to Mark J. Bruhn's comment in the discussion-period mentioned in footnote 18 above.

brand'. Her 'woof', the tapestry on which she reads and writes, eclipses the miracle of fire; she withdraws from the narrative.

And she is able to do this because the narrative grants her an exemption from representation: Shelley makes the point in the following transition from grotesque creatures who are summoned by the Witch's beauty to the lady herself:

> [...] and such shapes as haunt
> Wet clefts,—and lumps neither alive nor dead,
> Dog-headed, bosom-eyed and bird-footed.
>
> For she was beautiful—her beauty made
> The bright world dim, and everything beside
> Seemed like the fleeting image of a shade:
> No thought of living spirit could abide,
> Which to her looks had ever been betrayed,
> On any object in the world so wide,
> On any hope within the circling skies,
> But on her form, and in her inmost eyes.
>   (11 & 12. 134–44)

The writing shifts with exhilarating fleetness of foot from the grotesque account of 'lumps neither alive nor dead, / Dog-headed, bosom-eyed and bird-footed', proleptic parodies of Hermaphroditus in its state of suspended life, a state mimicked by the deadened rhyme between lines 135 and 136, to the intake of breath induced by the glimpse of the 'beautiful' across the stanza break. This beauty, with its dimming of 'The bright world', leads to no agonizing over language's adequacy as it might elsewhere in Shelley. Indeed, his own history as an idealizing poet is lodged in the mini-narrative, the capsule of the stanza that records the fate of any onlooker who 'to her looks had ever been betrayed'. That word 'betrayed' is glossed as 'discovered' in the *Shelley Concordance*,[29] but the word's more usual meaning hints at and ensures that we experience a confined moment of pathos. The moment is not allowed to take over the poem, a poem which has its own laws, so that it belongs with those other experiences that Shelley tells us, mimicking his heroine's clipped bossiness, are 'Not to be mirrored in a holy song' (62. 538). And yet explicit exclusion can only bring such experiences to mind: a cause of the poem's capacity to affect.

'Holy song' is provocatively secular, but a valuable generic clue, not usually discussed in generic guides, but one that Shelley associates with acts of imaginative worship, even as he wishes to avoid what in his dedicatory stanzas he calls 'idolatry' ('To Mary' 6. 48): 'If you unveil my Witch, no Priest or Primate / Can shrive you of that sin, if sin there be / In love when it becomes idolatry' ('To Mary' 6. 46–8), he writes. Each image produced by the poem is an 'idol' that warrants the poem's fixed attention, yet the poem's movement is at odds with the 'sin' of fixation on its own 'imaginative creations'.[30] Stuart Sperry links the assertion with Shelley's view, expressed in *A Defence of Poetry*, that 'true poetry' involves an endless unveiling.[31] The narrative movement shares in this process of creation and decreation, moments of contemplation and commitment, to a

---

[29] *Longman* 3, 578n.   [30] O'Neill, *The Human Mind's Imaginings*, 130.
[31] Sperry, *Shelley's Major Verse*, 146.

delighted, onward-sweeping process. The narrative cancels itself as narrative in terms of something close to virtuosic poetic display, a display that is neither narcissistic nor instrumentalist. Despite the best attempts of critics, and for all Shelley's humorous potshots at Wordsworth in the Preface and his intermittent jabs at orthodoxy, it is difficult to enlist *The Witch of Atlas* as a clear-cut statement of radical political protest.

However, the poem *is* radically subversive of the idea of shared literary purpose, even as it has affectionately loyal links with literary traditions. It subverts the notion that a poem should serve any power or cause other than itself, thus discomforting liberal allies as well as conservative foes. This judgement has something in common with Ronald Tetreault's opinion (he is commenting on 'A Summer Evening Churchyard') that Shelley 'writes his best poetry' when he is 'able to maintain [a] marvelous equilibrium of uncertainty'.[32] But Shelley's poetry in *The Witch of Atlas* does not need the crutch of canny ambivalence to prop itself upon; it flies with an insouciant ease born out of its artistic confidence. Shelley asks Mary why she is inclined to 'condemn these verses I have written / Because they tell no story, false or true?' ('To Mary' 1. 3–4). He gifts his well-meaning antagonist with an announcement of his refusal to tell a true or false story, as though he were opposing her own ambitions as a writer of narrative fiction with his request to be allowed to delight in self-discovering play: 'May it not leap and play, as grown cats do, / Till its claws come?' ('To Mary' 1. 6–7) Sperry notes the nod towards the 'unpleasant predatory habits of the grown cat' and sees the lines as asking, 'Is this really the kind of evolution Mary desires for his talent?'[33] Yet it is also the case that the question is, more grimly, self-directed, that Shelley knows about that side of his 'talent' that is intent on polemical destruction. His poem is alive to its own being, a being which is a series of playful becomings that fence deftly with other presuppositions; if we engage in the poem's play, it cannot be on anything like the 'critic-bitten' ('To Mary' 1. 1) terms which he reproves in Mary.

Throughout, Shelley's delights, dolphin-backed, show their back above the poetic element in which they immerse themselves. He turns ineffability into realized fictionalized treasure: in stanza 20, 'wondrous works of substances unknown' (20. 201) pass into 'Carved lamps and chalices, and phials which shone / In their own golden beams—each like a flower, / Out of whose depth a fire-fly shakes his light / Under a cypress in a starless light' (20. 205–8). As here, when two strong caesurae after the sixth syllable create a pressure demanding release, detail rushes in in metaphorical support of detail throughout the poem. In these lines, a mini-digression places the reader momentarily, unforgettably in an Italian landscape, the fire-fly more illuminated and illuminating for the 'starless night'. And, typically the image serves a displaced metapoetic function: Shelley's fire-fly of a poem asserts, with Utopian genius, the author's imaginative power in the starless night of post-Napoleonic Europe.

---

[32] Ronald Tetreault, *The Poetry of Life: Shelley and Literary Form* (Toronto: University of Toronto Press, 1987), 44.
[33] Sperry, *Shelley's Major Verse*, 144.

The poem radiates in and out of recollected sources of mythical energy; mythic figure after mythic figure is called up; makers of myth from Herodotus to Spenser are summoned up in a necromantic poetic pageant, yet at the heart of the poem is Shelley's surrogate, the Witch. Female, heterodox, she is a version of the poet, participating in his own 'strange art' (35. 321), as, creating her surrogate Hermaphroditus, 'she kneaded fire and snow / Together, tempering the repugnant mass / With liquid love' (35. 321–3). The humour, there of 'liquid love' is characteristic of *The Witch of Atlas*: love, an ideal that takes on rapturous majesty in the final act of *Prometheus Unbound*, materializes here as a glue. *The Witch of Atlas* mocks and reworks previous poems by Shelley, its heroine both participating in and immune from the limits of temporality, even as that immunity is itself a form of limitation. Bloom, indeed, reads the Witch as hinting at 'The limitations of art' in her rejection of 'the love of every mortal being',[34] and there are times when the poem is sorely tempted by such a stance of final aesthetic indifference, yet its sympathy with the human predicament is also evident, especially in the gap that opens up between 'our' perspective and the Witch's attitude towards 'strife' (62. 543). Yet again, however, the poetry overrides its sense of the Witch's limitations as, mimicking her rapidity of design and action, stanzas flow from one another but rarely in ways that indicate the passage of time. All is a question of creative repetitions that grow, towards the end, more superbly assertive, as when the Witch overcomes death, or expresses her contempt for it, when she

> unwound the woven imagery
> Of second childhood's swaddling bands, and took
> The coffin, its last cradle, from its niche.
> And threw it with contempt into a ditch.
>   (70. 605–8)

The poem's bravura as it unwinds traditional 'woven imagery' is compelling, the triple verbal work of 'unwound', 'took', and 'threw' a mimesis of compacted energy and agency. Imagination delivers mortality its own fatal blow, treating it 'with contempt'. But the fact that 'a ditch' is the final world almost subliminally suggests that the conquered will stage a return; indeed, all the time a fall awaits—''Tis said in after times her spirit free / Knew what love was, and felt itself alone' (68. 585–6). The earlier uses of 'felt' (9. 119, 120) in relation to 'Universal Pan' (9. 113) were comic. This moment is tinged with post-lapsarian longing for a state which the 'rapid, blind / And fleeting generations of mankind' (71. 615–16) are doomed never to recover, in a tragic narrative playing in the margins of the poem's determination to bring its materials under the rule of the imagination.

4

Byron revels in stories as endlessly multiplying tales, which one might, with Cheryl Fallon Giuliano, identify with 'the literary power of gossip to impel

---

[34] Harold Bloom, 'Introduction', *Percy Bysshe Shelley: Modern Critical Views*, ed. Harold Bloom (New York: Chelsea, 1985), 20.

plots'.[35] He revels, too, in the opportunities that story-telling gives for the play of narratorial digression and presence. Shelley draws attention less to stories than to the impulse to create stories, their origin in a fundamental principle to create, to respond, to adapt, to work on the world. For neither poet is play merely autotelic. Rather, it serves as an indication of how reader and writer might return to the freedoms implicit in finiteness of which the boundedness of the *ottava rima* stanza is an enabling emblem. There is a historical context, a desire to champion rebellion through the exploration of comic modes. These modes have, for both poets, their own pathos, Mozartian radiance, and sadness. For both poets, the change represented by *Beppo* and *The Witch of Atlas* is decisive; it fortifies them for the major work they will go on to produce, in which their engagement with socio-political realities is less oblique, if never straightforward: *Don Juan* for Byron, *Adonais* and *The Triumph of Life* for Shelley. Again, their literary legacies are complex and oblique, but the narrative play of these poems foreshadows postmodernist experimentation and provokes thought about the power, autonomy, and limits of art and the responsibility of the artist to ensure that language is maintained in what Shelley, in *A Defence of Poetry*, describes as a 'vitally metaphorical' (*Major Works*, 676) state.

---

[35] Cheryl Fallon Giuliano, 'Marginal Discourse: The Authority of Gossip in *Beppo*', *Byron's Poetry and Prose*, sel. and ed. Alice Levine (New York: Norton, 2010), 936.

10

'The End and Aim of Poesy'

Shelley and Keats in Dialogue

1

'Life's nonsense pierces us with strange relation', writes Wallace Stevens, invoking ideas of contingency, chance, and destiny.[1] This chapter explores the medleyed 'strange relation' between two great Romantic poets, and will involve reflections on their developing understanding of the imaginative and cultural place of poetry, the art to which they devoted their lives. Destined to be buried in the same cemetery in Rome, to be the very type of English Romantic lyricism—so much so that, as a hardboiled undergraduate, W. H. Auden advised a fellow poet, Stephen Spender, to drop the 'Kelley and Sheats' act—Keats and Shelley have enjoyed an extraordinary intimacy in the cultural imaginary.[2] This, despite the often narrated notion of the relative coolness of their friendship, a coolness that seems largely on Keats's side: 'Keats did not take to Shelley as kindly as Shelley did to him' was how the literary champion of both, Leigh Hunt, remembered the dynamic of their interactions: interactions kindled into being after their probable meeting at Hunt's Hampstead cottage, that site of creatively productive encounters for Keats.[3]

Keats never forgot Shelley advising him on Hampstead Heath against prematurely publishing his 'first blights' (see letter of August 1820, quoted in full below). There's an irony in the recollection: if Shelley put a dampener on the younger poet's ardent hopes (though he appears to have assisted with helping the printing of Keats's first volume),[4] he did so in a scene that was among Keats's most poetically enabling places. Perhaps, in James Bieri's words, glossing Hunt's views, Keats 'felt uncomfortable with Shelley's privileged background'.[5]

Yet Keats regarded Shelley as a serious rival for poetic honours: Haydon's diary for 7 April 1817 records the following: 'Keats said to me today as we were walking along "Byron, Scott, Southey, & Shelley think they are to lead the age, but [the rest of the sentence has been erased]. This was said with all the consciousness of Genius;

---

[1] 'It Must Be Abstract', III, Notes Toward a Supreme Fiction, The Collected Poems of Wallace Stevens ([1955] London: Faber, 2006), 333.
[2] Stephen Spender, World Within World ([1951] London: Faber, 1977), 62.
[3] Leigh Hunt, Autobiography, 2 vols. (New York: Harpers, 1850), 2, 36.
[4] Donald H. Reiman, 'Keats and Shelley: Personal and Literary Relations', SC V, 399–427 (408).
[5] James Bieri, Percy Bysshe Shelley, A Biography: Exile of Unfulfilled Reknown, 1816–1822 (Cranbury: Associated University Presses, 2005), 34.

his face reddened'.[6] As Donald H. Reiman glosses this entry in his superb essay on the poets' 'personal and literary relations', 'However much Keats hoped to surpass Shelley, he did not dismiss him lightly, or he would never have classed him with Scott, Byron, and Southey—three of the most prolific and popular major writers of the day'.[7] The two poets engaged in sonnet-contests and appear to have written major long poems (*Endymion* and *The Revolt of Islam*) in friendly competition.[8]

Keats's opening up and out of places to accommodate textual spaces, spaces that he imagines in relation to such locations as bowers, darkling or otherwise, rooms with their fascinatingly liminal casements, firmaments 'reflected in a sea' (*Endymion*, 1. 300), mirror Shelley's own spatial imaginings. These imaginings also involve a near-recursive imagery of seas mirroring heavens, of commerce between dimensions, of air and ether shot through with radiant or dark semblances. And the poets' own textual places are always eagerly on the lookout for the hospitable inclusion of other voices and other texts. Thus, their remarkable 1820 exchange of letters shows each poet revealing something like the hiding places of his own power and attempting to navigate, not uncritically, into the different world of the other poet.

In these letters each sets the terms by which the other would be criticized ever since: Shelley implies Keats's powers of invention but relative lack of discipline as he describes having 'lately read your Endymion again & ever with a new sense of the treasures of poetry it contains, though treasures poured forth with indistinct profusion. This, people in general will not endure, & that is the cause of the comparatively few copies which have been sold'—hardly the most stinging criticism from a man who goes on in the letter's next sentence to say 'I feel persuaded that you are capable of the greatest things, so you but will' (*Letters: PBS*, 2. 221), and who positively relished his inability to sell his own poems. The previous autumn, Shelley's fictitious persona Miching Mallecho had included in his Preface to *Peter Bell the Third* this sportively insulting gibe at Tom Moore: 'Your works, indeed, dear Tom, sell better; but mine are far superior. The public is no judge; posterity sets all to rights'.[9] More pointedly, and probably going back to his earlier sense of Keats as an ally of the Leigh Hunt of *The Feast of the Poets* and *The Story of Rimini*, Shelley remarks: 'In poetry *I* have sought to avoid system & mannerism; I wish those who excel me in genius, would pursue the same plan'.[10]

---

[6] Benjamin Robert Haydon, *Diary*, ed. Willard Bissell Pope, 5 vols (Cambridge: Harvard University Press, 1960–3), 2, 106–7.
[7] Reiman, 'Keats and Shelley: Personal and Literary Relations', 405.
[8] For evidence of one such sonnet competition, see the discussion of their and Hunt's sonnets on the Nile, in *MYR* 8, 165, 166–9, 178–80; for the source of the story that the two poets wrote *Endymion* and *The Revolt of Islam* in emulous mode, see Thomas Medwin: 'Shelley told me that it was a friendly rivalry between them, which gave rise to "Endymion" and the "Revolt of Islam" ', *The Shelley Papers* (London: Whittaker, Treacher, & Co, 1833), 45.
[9] *Major Works*, 416. All Shelley's poetry will be quoted from this edition unless cited otherwise. See also Reiman, 424 for a discussion of this passage.
[10] See P. M. S. Dawson, 'Byron, Shelley, and the "New School" ', in *Shelley Revalued: Essays from the Gregynog Conference*, ed. Kelvin Everest (Leicester: Leicester University Press, 1983), 89–108, especially 100–6 on Byron's and Shelley's objections to idea of 'system'.

With a mixture of wryness and wit allied to what Coleridge might call 'some little faulty admixture' of ungenerosity,[11] Keats summoned up his energies and produced an uncommonly pitched, startling, and deeply affecting letter:

My dear Shelley,

I am very much gratified that you, in a foreign country, and with a mind almost over occupied, should write to me in the strain of the letter beside me. If I do not take advantage of your invitation, it will be prevented by a circumstance I have very much at heart to prophesy—There is no doubt that an english winter would put an end to me, and do so in a lingering hateful manner, therefore I must either voyage or journey to Italy as a soldier marches up to a battery. My nerves at present are the worst part of me, yet they feel soothed that come what extreme may, I shall not be destined to remain in one spot long enough to take a hatred of any four particular bed-posts. I am glad you take any pleasure in my poor Poem; —which I would willingly take the trouble to unwrite, if possible, did I care so much as I have done about Reputation. I received a copy of the Cenci, as from yourself from Hunt. There is only one part of it I am judge of; the Poetry, and dramatic effect, which by many spirits now a days is considered the mammon. A modern work it is said must have a purpose, which may be the God—an *artist* must serve Mammon—he must have 'self-concentration' selfishness perhaps. You I am sure will forgive me for sincerely remarking that you might curb your magnanimity, and be more of an artist, and 'load every rift' of your subject with ore. The thought of such discipline must fall like cold chains upon you, who perhaps never sat with your wings furl'd for six Months together. And is this not extraordina[r]y talk for the writer of Endymion? whose mind was like a pack of scattered cards—I am pick'd up and sorted to a pip. My Imagination is a Monastery and I am its Monk—you must explain my metap^{cs} to yourself. I am in expectation of Prometheus every day. Could I have my own wish effected, you would have it still in manuscript—or be but now putting an end to the second act. I remember you advising me not to publish my first-blights, on Hampstead heath—I am returning advice upon your hands. Most of the Poems in the volume I send you have been written above two years, and would never have been published but from a hope of gain; so you see I am inclined enough to take your advice now. I must exp[r]ess once more my deep sense of your kindness, adding my sincere thanks and respects for Mrs Shelley. In the hope of soon seeing you, I remain

most sincerely [yours,]
John Keats—

'You must explain my metap^{cs} to your self': the letter has an intransigent originality. The idea of being a poet who deals in 'indistinct profusion' clearly rankles with the author of some of the most densely compacted poems in the language. Keats even seems to test Shelley's capacity to grasp metaphorical richness in the assertion, 'My imagination is a Monastery and I am its Monk'. The phrasing reveals to Shelley the kind of ore-loaded linguistic 'discipline' that the younger poet had made his own; it implies Keats's rejection of 'system' and his unique individuality. Yet that Keats challenges Shelley in this way is an appeal as well to the imagination

---

[11] Coleridge on Cordelia, quoted in *Coleridge on Shakespeare*, ed. Terence Hawkes, intro. Alfred Harbage (Harmondsworth: Penguin, 1969), 203.

of a brother in the mystery, and, for all the sharpness with which Jeffrey Cox teases out a fundamental quarrel between a Keatsian 'Mammon of formalism' and a Shelleyan positioning of 'poetry' as 'prior to representation', the epistolary exchange (and subsequent response by Shelley in *A Defence of Poetry*) is equally compounded of mutual understanding as of antagonism.[12] One senses that Shelley, like Keats, for all his originality, would understand the near-derisive use of 'modern' ('A modern work it is said'). Neither poet is happy with having his 'purpose' dictated to him by the ideological exigencies of others.

Keats's letter has a Shakespearean nobility and mobility of spirit (one thinks of soliloquies by Hamlet or Othello). When he writes, 'therefore I must either voyage or journey to Italy, as a soldier marches up to a battery', the strong active verbs seem a countervailing response to a situation where agency is tragically delimited: 'I shall not be destined to remain in one spot long enough to take hatred of any four particular bedposts'. Those 'four particular bedposts' haunt any visitor to Keats's final address, as they clearly haunt his proleptic imaginings, yet their matter-of-fact detail gives us the Keats who is tethered to the world of objects. It seems at least possible that when Shelley 'dipped his pen in consuming fire for [Keats's] destroyers' in writing *Adonais*, his elegy for the dead Keats, he remembered details from this letter (*Letters: PBS*, 2. 302).[13]

The words 'spot' and 'remain' (the former discussed below, the latter immediately) play a crucial role at a key stage in *Adonais*. 'The One remains, the many change and pass' (52. 460). Keats has shared in the fate of the many; now he is part of the 'One', a One that is not simply separate from the many but 'interfused' (97) with it, to borrow Wordsworth's word from 'Lines Written a Few Miles above Tintern Abbey'.[14] In fact, Shelley does not so much borrow as adapt Wordsworth's verb when he concludes the same stanza of *Adonais* with the lines, 'Rome's azure sky, / Flowers, ruins, statues, music, words, are weak / The glory they transfuse with fitting truth to speak' (52. 466–8). The material world, including 'words' and, by implication, the language of poetry, is said to 'transfuse' an original 'glory', albeit inadequately; the phrasing has less quasi-pantheist confidence than that deployed in 'Tintern Abbey', but it establishes a mode of communication between the realms of the 'One' and the 'many'.

The echoes of Wordsworth in *Adonais* remind us that when Shelley and Keats first met in 1816, they were both ingesting considerable quantities of what Byron would

---

[12] Jeffrey N. Cox, 'Keats, Shelley, and the Wealth of the Imagination', *Studies in Romanticism* 34 (1995): 365–400, at 388: Cox argues that Shelley's statement in *A Defence of Poetry* that 'Poetry, and the principle of Self, of which money is the visible incarnation, are the God and the Mammon of the world' is 'a covert riposte' to Keats's assertion that 'an *artist* must serve Mammon' (380).

[13] Madeleine Callaghan's *Shelley's Living Artistry: Letters, Poems, Plays* (Liverpool: Liverpool University Press, 2017) helpfully discusses *Adonais* in the light of Shelley and Keats's correspondence (see chapter 8, 236–64). For a discussion of Shelley's informed and generous responsiveness to Keats in *Adonais*, see Kelvin Everest, 'Shelley's *Adonais* and John Keats', *Essays in Criticism* 57 (2007): 237–64. For a reading of the elegy as exhibiting complicated feelings towards Keats, including 'fierce ambivalence', see Andrew Epstein, in his 'Shelley's *Adonais*, Keats, and Poetic Influence', *Keats-Shelley Journal* 48 (1999): 90–128 (91).

[14] Wordsworth, *Major Works*.

later call 'Wordsworth physic'.[15] In each case there is evidence of a responsiveness to Wordsworth's style and vision. Shelley's 1816 *Alastor* volume reveals a state of double-minded admiration for Wordsworth's earlier poetry and recoil from his current conservative politics: his sonnet 'To Wordsworth' uses the older poet's cadences and phrases in order to express homage and critique.

For his part, Keats's 1816 reading of Wordsworth testifies to a condition of ardent discovery (his concerns about Wordsworth's 'palpable design' upon his readers would surface later). Keats was beginning to turn from Hunt to Wordsworth, encouraged, ironically, by Hunt's own advocacy of Wordsworth in the 1815 version of *The Feast of the Poets* as 'the Prince of the Bards of his Time.'[16] His sonnet 'Great spirits now on earth are sojourning' conjoins Wordsworth with Hunt and Haydon. Hunt, wearing 'the chain for Freedom's sake' (6), just about holds his own with 'He of the cloud, the cataract, the lake' (2), but the natural sublimity associated with Wordsworth earns a prior position in the sonnet.[17] Wordsworth starts to figure as a type of influence in *Sleep and Poetry*, which wonders with the arch self-consciousness of unmisgiving youth about 'many a verse from so strange influence / That we must ever wonder how and whence / It came' (69–71), lines that not only echo, as Miriam Allott points out, Wordsworth's 'To the Daisy', in which the older poet celebrate 'A happy, genial influence, / Coming one knows not how, nor whence', but also capture, in 'ever', the older poet's commitment in the Intimations Ode to that 'Which having been must ever be' (185). In later letters and poems, Keats would express his own mixed feelings about Wordsworth, as Shelley already had in the subtle ambivalences of the *Alastor* volume, which, as noted above, opens itself to the current of Wordsworthian influence even as, with Shelleyan reserve, it turns those currents awry or into different channels.

To return to *Adonais*, in the spirit of shuttling between the Alpha of their 1816 meeting and the Omega of Shelley's poem, the word 'spot' to which Keats's earthly remains are consigned also attracts his elegist's notice. This is the gravest of Keatsian places in an evidently punning sense: it holds his corpse; and it brings his elegist up against the arrested, sealed-up condition of death, so like and so unlike the finished perfection of the achieved work of art. Moreover, it has its own beauty, to which Shelley's prose in his Preface, with its internal rhyme of 'space' and 'place', is attuned: 'The cemetery is an open space among the ruins, covered in winter with violets and daisies. It might make one in love with death, to think that one should be buried in so sweet a place' (*Major Works*, 529). There is a graceful nod towards stanza 6 of 'Ode to a Nightingale' there, and Shelley, almost in compliance with the force of Keats's poem, goes one step further than the dead poet: if the dead poet was 'half in love with easeful Death' (52), the surviving poet imagines himself wholly 'in love with death', and the terror of death is softened—though not sentimentalized—as

[15] Byron's phrase is reported by Thomas Medwin in his *Conversations of Lord Byron*, ed. Ernest J. Lovell Jr (Princeton: Princeton University Press, 1966), 194.
[16] Hunt is quoted from Beth Lau, *Keats's Reading of the Romantic Poets* (Ann Arbor: University of Michigan Press, 1991), 19.
[17] Keats's poetry is quoted from John Keats, *The Complete Poems*, ed. John Barnard, 3rd edn (London: Penguin, 1988).

Shelley, as in a Socratic thought-experiment, thinks of himself 'buried in so sweet a place'. Shelley takes Keats's death personally; he brings to his poem an intensely focused contemplation of place, even as he has his gaze trained on the 'One'. The grand injunction, 'Go thou to Rome,— at once the Paradise, / The grave, the city, and the wilderness;' (49. 433–4) naming four compass points linked to destiny and desire, moves into the command to 'Pass, till the Spirit of the spot shall lead / Thy footsteps to a slope of green access' (49. 438–9), to the place in which Shelley's son William had been buried. In the same poem Keats is Urania's son, and Shelley his grief-worn brother poet, 'companionless' (31. 272), partly because Keats is now dead, mainly because he recognizes his own loneliness. A Keatsian 'spot' (in his August 1820 letter) has become a Shelleyan 'Spirit of the spot', as though Keats has been reborn as a Shelleyan tutelary spirit, in an anticipation of the final stanza in which, in pursuit of Keats/Adonais, Shelley asserts: 'my spirit's bark is driven / Far from the shore, far from the trembling throng / Whose sails were never to the tempest given' (55. 488–90).

The temptation is to read Shelley as all unpunctuated rush, all air, fire, and spirit, and Keats as all compacted evocativeness, all earth, flesh, and blood, but Shelleyan metaphysics and Keatsian physics reach out to their opposite. *Endymion* may offer a critique of the 'too thin breathing' (IV, 650), 'cloudy phantasms' (IV, 651), and cheating 'airy voices' (IV, 654) of *Alastor*; indeed, the following lines appear to supply 'a deliberate rejection of Shelley's visionary idealism in *Alastor*', as Miriam Allott suggests:[18]

> There never lived a mortal man, who bent
> His appetite beyond his natural sphere,
> But starved and died. My sweetest Indian, here,
> Here will I kneel, for thou redeemed hast
> My life from too thin breathing: gone and past
> Are cloudy phantasms.
>
> (IV, 646–51)

The half-rhyme between 'lived' and 'starved' is potently suggestive; one who goes 'beyond' his natural sphere' undoes his living condition, until he risks a starving state. These lines might well have in their sights the Poet-figure in Shelley's poem, depicted with astringent sympathy as bending his desires 'beyond his natural sphere', as in the following passage, which offer their own version of Keats's concern with the effect of going 'beyond his natural sphere' and entering a place of 'too thin breathing':

> The spirit of sweet human love has sent
> A vision to the sleep of him who spurned
> Her choicest gifts. He eagerly pursues
> Beyond the realms of dream that fleeting shade;
> He overleaps the bounds.
>
> (*Alastor*, 203–7)

---

[18] *The Poems of John Keats*, ed. Miriam Allott (London: Longman, 1970), 272n. For acute discussion of Keats's response to *Alastor* see chapter 3 of William A. Ulmer, *John Keats: Reimagining History* (Cham, Switzerland: Palgrave MacMillan/Springer, 2017).

'He eagerly pursues' sounds a note that is ambiguous in its impact in *Alastor*: pursuit and quest display all the 'eager' energies of ardent enquiry, yet they involve a transgressive defiance of 'bounds' that recalls the Satan of Book 4 of *Paradise Lost*.

Keats may seem robustly this-worldly—placed and emplaced—in the passage quoted from *Endymion*. But Shelley had, at the very least, provided him with a warning and an alluring counter-plot—to the degree to which bending appetite beyond the 'natural sphere' is actively promoted in the poetry of the author of *Alastor*—and Endymion's self-admonition cannot disguise the longing to be freed of mortal constraints that drives the 'Ode to a Nightingale' and 'Ode on a Grecian Urn', along with aspects of 'La Belle Dame Sans Merci' (those 'starved lips in the gloom' (41) remember *Endymion*'s use of 'starved'), *The Eve of St Agnes, Lamia*, and even, in its visionary ambitions, *The Fall of Hyperion* in which the poet-dreamer senses 'appetite / More yearning than on earth I ever felt / Growing within' (I, 38–40). For his part, Shelley, attuned as he is to mental operations, can describe them with vivid metaphorical force; in *Adonais* the onset of inspiration is caught in what feels, frighteningly, akin to a literal shattering of earth's bounds: 'The massy earth and sphered skies are riven!' (55. 491). Both poets are tugged between dream and reality, poetry's transformations and what Keats in *Endymion* calls 'The journey homeward to habitual self' (II, 276). Keats's 'sense of real things' that comes 'doubly strong' (157) in *Sleep and Poetry*, after 'The visions all are fled' (155), is not wholly unlike the Poet's awakening from the dream of the 'veiled maid' (151) in *Alastor*, which he may have read at about the same time as he was finishing the poem.

2

One could have wished Keats had appreciated *The Cenci* more fully, rather than sending Shelley back to the drawing board and telling him to 'curb his magnanimity and be more of an artist'. Beth Lau notes that Fanny Brawne in 1848 said that she possessed 'the Cenci by Shelly [sic] marked with many of Keats notes'.[19] Would that the copy had survived or might re-surface! Did Keats feel the play was blemished by too many Shakespearean reminiscences, à la Leavis, or did he take Shelley at his face value when the latter announced in his Preface that he had foregone 'the introduction of what is commonly called mere poetry' (317)? How could Keats not admire the terseness and bareness of the opening, 'That matter of the murder is hushed up' (I.i. 1), the intricacy of the insight into the dangers of 'Self-anatomy' (II.ii. 110), the wild grief of Beatrice's sense of violation, 'The beautiful blue heaven is flecked with blood' (III.i. 13), the stilled pathos of the final speech? Having tried to write a play himself (*Otho the Great*), Keats could not but see that Shelley had succeeded in doing what no other Romantic writer managed to do: write a play that took on Shakespeare without being overwhelmed by him. Still the advice to 'load every rift with ore' seems to have stayed with Shelley in the composition of

---

[19] Lau, *Keats's Reading*, 156.

his elegy,[20] an elegy that returns in its choice of stanza form to a common ancestor for both poets, Spenser: an ancestral debt and finely discussed by Greg Kucich.[21] One notices that Keats pays Shelley the compliment of an allusion to the description of the Cave of Mammon (he knows his literary rival will keep up), almost inviting Shelley to recognize that they both are original enough poets to hold 'high talk with the departed dead' (Shelley, 'Hymn to Intellectual Beauty', version A, 52) in ways that the genius of each dictates.

But one can only be saddened that Keats may not ever have read the 1820 *Prometheus Unbound* volume. In the 16 August 1820 letter quoted above, he writes, as though subliminally worried by the speed with which the *Prometheus* volume has been composed: 'I am in expectation of Prometheus every day. Could I have my own wish for its interest effected you would have it still in manuscript— or be but now putting an end to the second act. I remember you advising me not to publish my first blights, on Hampstead heath I am returning advice upon your hands' (*Letters: John Keats* II, 323). A great poet put on his mettle by what he may have felt to be patronizing advice, Keats gives as good as he felt that he got, but he chooses for reprimand and reproof the volume in which Shelley emerges as one of the finest poetic artists of his age, in a volume simultaneously committed to visions of a libertarian spring and resistant to what Shelley in his Preface to the title poem calls 'Didactic poetry' (*Major Works*, 232).

If Keats did not live long enough to read Shelley's best work, it is a measure of Shelley's magnanimity and critical acumen that he recognized Keats's rapid development as a poet and praised *Hyperion* repeatedly in letters to Peacock and Byron, among others (see *Letters: PBS*, 2. 239, 244). It is still too little acknowledged that Shelley was among the keenest appreciative critical intellects of his time, possessing the rare gift of valuing precisely the achievement and, even rarer, this, the potential achievement of contemporary poets. Able to see the importance of Byron's *Don Juan*, and responsive to the remarkable poetic powers of Coleridge and Wordsworth, for all his adverse comments on their mid-life political tergiversation (as he saw the matter), he was equally quick to see that *Hyperion* was 'certainly an astonishing piece of writing', one that, he declares on 8 November 1820 to Peacock, 'gives me a conception of Keats which I confess I had not before' (*Letters: PBS*, 2. 244). The verb 'confess' lends support to the idea that Shelley himself was now conscious that his earlier view of Keats's development had been, in Reiman's words, 'slightly patronizing',[22] and in an unsent letter to the *Quarterly Review* he draws attention to three passages in *Endymion* which he sees as illustrating and embodying what he had the year before described as 'the highest & the finest gleams of poetry' (*Letters: PBS*, 2. 117).

In this unsent letter of 1820 to the editor of the *Quarterly Review* in which Shelley sought to defend *Endymion*—'with all its faults' he writes 'a very remarkable

---

[20] The point is made by, among others, Epstein, in 'Shelley's *Adonais*, Keats, and Poetic Influence', 93).

[21] Kucich, *Keats, Shelley, and Romantic Spenserianism*, *passim*; see especially the account of 'how *Adonais*, a poem in Spenserian stanzas about mutability and eternity, elaborates Keats's Spenserianism in that other great lyrical drama of reality and idealism, *The Eve of St. Agnes*' (327).

[22] Reiman, 411.

production for a man of Keats's age' showing 'a promise of ultimate excellence...such as has rarely been afforded even by such as have afterwards attained high literary eminence'—he singles out three passages (II, 833ff.; III, 113ff.; and III, 193ff.; see *Letters: PBS*, 2. 252). The middle passage leaves an impression on Act 4, lines 283–95 of *Prometheus Unbound*. Endymion finds

> things
> More dead than Morpheus' imaginings:
> Old rusted anchors, helmets, breast-plates large
> Of gone sea-warriors; brazen beaks and targe;
> Rudders that for a hundred years had lost
> The sway of human hand...
>   (*Endymion*, III, 122–6)

These lines and the passage from which they come 'probably' rework, as Allott notes,[23] Gloucester's dream in *Richard III* (I. iv. 22–8), and the description's Shakespearean descent was not lost on Francis Jeffrey, earning his applause: 'it comes of no ignoble lineage nor shames its high descent'.[24] They open with a wry parallel to an important rhyme at the close of Shelley's 'Mont Blanc', composed in 1816, but published at the close of 1817 (*Endymion* Book III was composed in September of the same year), in which the idea of a 'secret strength of things' (139) seems ultimately dependent on 'the human mind's imaginings' (143). They share in the fascination with relics of a 'gone' history which bears finely desolate fruit in Shelley's 'Ozymandias' (composed late 1817, and published in January 1818). Endymion 'might have died' (III, 139) at the sight, but the thought of his moon-goddess allows him to carry on with 'cheerèd feel' (III, 139), until he is greeted as the harbinger of change and life by Glaucus, echoing Nathan to David in 2 Samuel 12:7: 'Thou art the man!' (III, 234).[25] Shelley takes his cue from Keats's reworking of Shakespeare as he lists 'anchors, beaks of ships; / Planks turned to marble; quivers, helms, and spears' (*Prometheus Unbound* IV, 289–91) and other 'sepulchred emblems / Of dead destruction' (IV, 294–5) among the images of 'the melancholy ruins / Of cancelled cycles' (IV, 288–9) exposed to light by the 'multitudinous orb' (IV, 253), itself a symbol for *Prometheus Unbound* itself.[26] Shelley substitutes blank verse for Keats's springily thought-generating couplets, as though to announce his own inheritance of Milton's mantle, 'the sacred Milton' (*Major Works*, 231) whose blank verse dominates the first act, but is itself the target of sublime parody in the fourth where Shelley replaces the Christian myth with an envisioning of human— and humanist—possibilities. Milton's 'one greater man' (I. 4) from the opening of *Paradise Lost* passes,[27] in *Prometheus Unbound*, into the celebration of 'Man, one harmonious soul of many a soul' (IV, 400).

---

[23] Allott, *Poems*, 211n.   [24] Jeffrey quoted in Allott, *Poems*, 211n.
[25] For the biblical allusion, see Allott, *Poems*, 216n.
[26] For discussion of the differences between Keats's and Shelley's passages, see Catherine Boyle's fine paper, delivered in 4 May 2014 at a Keats Conference, entitled ' "The Types of Didot": John Keats and Percy Bysshe Shelley's Engagement with Enlightenment Ideas of the Self and Historical Progress', 1–7 (see esp. 2–4). Cited from academia.edu.
[27] John Milton, *The Complete Poems*, ed. John Leonard (London: Penguin, 1998).

Both poets rely on poetry itself as the image and instrument of metamorphosis. Shelley admired, too, the account later in the third book of *Endymion* of Glaucus's cloak of blue, on which objects would change in the act of being looked at: 'The gulfing whale was like a dot in the spell. / Yet look upon it, and 'twould size and swell / To its huge self' (III, 205–7). The lines anticipate the account of the Witch of Atlas 'Spelling out scrolls of dread antiquity' (*The Witch of Atlas*, 250) and her 'magic treasures' (154), 'Which had the power all spirits of compelling' (155), a magical compulsion used for the essentially virtuous purpose of awakening subtleties of feeling. Keats gives us the conjuring trick as it happens in the gusto-laden verbs, 'size and swell'; Shelley talks more figuratively about the ways in which the Witch's magic leaves an impression. But difference in idiom and sensibility can't conceal a shared fascination with the impact of poetry and a vein of nuanced meta-poetry running through both writers' work.

3

In his letter Shelley also singled out a passage in Book II of *Endymion*, about a poet hearing a song, 'And after, straight, in that inspirèd place, / He sang the story up into the air, / Giving it universal freedom' (II, 837–9), a song that awaits listeners 'with ears / Whose tips are glowing hot' (II, 840–1). This tale of transmitted influence, of a poetic incandescence kindling and rekindling, anticipates Shelley's vision of poetry in his *Defence of Poetry*. And it suggests that Keats played a part in Shelley's developing ideas about poetic influence and about the influence of poetry. In *Sleep and Poetry*, in a passage from which this chapter takes its title, Keats produces a fine apologia for poetry that is content to accept the inadequacies of 'consequitive reasoning' and be 'explorative', as Wordsworth was in 'Tintern Abbey', of the 'dark passages' leading out from 'the Chamber of Maiden Thought' (*Letters: John Keats* I, 281): 'though I do not know', he writes, in *Sleep and Poetry*,

> The shifting of the mighty winds that blow
> Hither and thither all the changing thoughts
> Of man: though no great minist'ring reason sorts
> Out the dark mysteries of human souls
> To clear conceiving—yet there ever rolls
> A vast idea before me, and I glean
> Therefrom my liberty; thence too I've seen
> The end and aim of Poesy.
> (*Sleep and Poetry*, 285–93)

Keats does not say what this 'vast idea' is, but the writing suggests a value in not knowing, if knowing is defined as 'clear conceiving'; the poetry proposes the merit of sensing the worth implicit in the interplay of 'all the changing thoughts / Of man'. This 'liberty' might seem personal and existential, a trust and belief that 'That which is creative must create itself' (*Letters: John Keats* I, 374), yet it tallies with Shelley's later intuition in *A Defence of Poetry* of the connection between poetry's libertarian aspiration and the way in which it 'awakens and enlarges the mind itself by rendering it the receptacle of a thousand unapprehended combinations of thought' (*Major Works*, 681). Poetry is a mode of knowing and the source of a new knowledge distinct from the findings of instrumental reason.

Or such is the ideal. Just lines before, Keats had ambitiously and hauntingly sketched the gap between what poetry might be and what it, in contemporary Regency England, was:

> [...] in truth we've had
> Strange thunders from the potency of song;
> Mingled indeed with what is sweet and strong
> From majesty: but in clear truth the themes
> Are ugly clubs, the poets Polyphemes
> Disturbing the grand sea. A drainless shower
> Of light is Poesy; 'tis the supreme of power;
> 'Tis might half-slumbering on its own right arm.
> The very archings of her eye-lids charm
> A thousand willing agents to obey,
> And still she governs with the mildest sway:
> But strength alone, though of the Muses born,
> Is like a fallen angel: trees uptorn,
> Darkness, and worms, and shrouds, and sepulchres
> Delight it; for it feeds upon the burrs
> And thorns of life; forgetting the great end
> Of Poesy, that it should be a friend
> To soothe the cares, and lift the thoughts of man.
>
> (*Sleep and Poetry*, 230–47)

The passage makes a major contribution to the genre of brilliantly improvised, on-the-hoof Romantic poetics. Keats is evidently in two minds about work that is all the rage; thus, that 'potency of song' employing 'themes' like 'ugly clubs', as though cudgelling the reader, is, according to his friend and champion Richard Woodhouse, a power abused by 'Lord Byron, & his terrific stile of poetry' and alludes as well, according to the same commentator, to 'Christabel by Coleridge &c' (a poem just published in 1816, when *Sleep and Poetry* was composed).[28] At the same time, 'potency' acknowledges the force of Byron's *Childe Harold's Pilgrimage*, Canto III, say, while 'strange' grants Coleridge's enigmatic atmospherics their due. By contrast with those whose wild thrashings succeed only in 'Disturbing the grand sea' of poetry (Hamlet's 'To be, or not to be' seems to be in the background of the writing's metaphorical thinking), Keats proposes a Hellenic ideal: 'A drainless shower / Of light is Poesy; 'tis the supreme of power; / 'Tis might half-slumbering on its own right arm'; 'power' (that word that keeps coming into play in Romantic conceptions of poetic imagination) raises, in Keats, only two cheers as a 'fallen angel' when unaccompanied by thoughts of 'the great end / Of Poesy, that it should be a friend / To soothe the cares, and lift the thoughts of man'.

---

[28] Woodhouse quoted from Keats, *Complete Poems*, ed. Barnard, 577.

Again, that's the ideal, but the fact that 'it should be' such 'a friend' may indicate Keats's awareness that it cannot always attain such a state. Shelley's eye and ear were evidently caught by Keats's account of contemporary poetry's mistaken practice of feeding 'upon the burrs / And thorns of life'. The latter is a phrase that re-appears in 'Ode to the West Wind', when—his hopes dashed, his life as man and poet seemingly in ruins—the idealistic poet hits something close to rock-bottom: 'I fall upon the thorns of life! I bleed!' (54). Shelley strives in his fifth section to write a poetry that will be the trumpet of a prophecy, and 'lift the thoughts of man': for Keats's intricate yet grandly interknitting couplets, he deploys an odic *terza rima* that continually emphasizes gaps and re-seedings as much as continual ties. And for Keats's poetry of admonitory statement, he writes a poetry of yearning entreaty and finally potent command; 'Drive my dead thoughts', he exclaims in pleading yet peremptory tones to the wind, 'over the universe / Like withered leaves to quicken a new birth! / And, by the incantation of this verse, / Scatter, as from an unextinguished hearth / Ashes and sparks, my words among mankind!' (63–7).

The ode is far more conscious of the need to create, in its own 'workings' (to use Keats's word from the penultimate line of 'Great spirits now on earth are sojourning'), its understanding of the poetic influence: 'Scatter', placed at the line's head, makes the voice bear down on a word that, for all its sparagmos-like intensity, has yielded up any attempt to control the reader's thoughts. If Keats's poetry is beautifully instructive about 'the great end / Of Poesy', Shelley is more actively engaged in involving us in the process by which that 'end' might be attained, doing so with full awareness, so his only semi-rhetorical final question suggests, that all his ode's seasonal images are open to construction from the reader, who may be disinclined to equate the literal and metaphorical meanings of 'spring' and 'winter'.[29]

In the Preface to *Prometheus Unbound* Shelley contrasts imaginatively efficacious and 'beautiful idealisms of moral excellence' (*Major Works*, 232) with 'reasoned principles of moral conduct' (*Major Works*, 232), the latter seen as 'seeds cast upon the highway of life, which the unconscious passenger tramples into the dust, although they would bear the harvest of his happiness' (*Major Works*, 232): the affectingly virtual use of 'would' making Shelley's point that the 'seeds' that might 'bear the harvest of... happiness' might well bear no fruit. Yet, in his ode's hope of a 'new birth' (64), Shelley—again—has a Keatsian phrase in mind, this time from the so-called 'Hymn to Pan', that 'Very pretty piece of Paganism', in Wordsworth's somewhat churlish phrase,[30] in Book I of *Endymion*, where Pan is asked to be 'be still the leaven, / That spreading in this dull and clodded earth / Gives it a touch ethereal—a new birth' (296–8), a quickening Keatsian etherealization of 'dull and

[29] As Ronald Tetreault, writes, 'Shelley knew that the analogy between the seasonal cycle and political renovation was rhetorical and not logical', quoted from 'The Dramatic Lyric [*Ode to the West Wind*]', in *Shelley*, ed. and intro. Michael O'Neill, *Longman Critical Reader* (London: Longman, 1993), 140–51 (149).
[30] Quoted from Keats, *Complete Poems*, ed., Barnard, 587. For his part, Shelley saw in the poem 'promise of ultimate excellence', ibid.

clodded earth'. Keats uses 'ethereal' as though it named a quasi-chemical form of poetic animation.[31]

We know from a comment in a letter by Keats that one 1816 poem of Shelley's that made an impression on him was 'Hymn to Intellectual Beauty', first published by Hunt in *The Examiner* of 19 January 1817 after a comic series of hapless mislayings on Hunt's part, confessed in his 'Young Poets' article of 1 December 1816. Keats quotes from the poem in a letter of 13 March 1818, in which he playfully admits doubts about poetry, described as 'a mere Jack a lanthern to amuse whoever may chance to be struck with its brilliance' (*Letters: John Keats* I, 242), only to use the phrase 'consecrates...all it dost shine upon' (see lines 12–13 of Shelley's 'Hymn') in defence, as Beth Lau puts it, of a shared 'belief in abstract ideals despite their lack of objective or empirical existence'.[32] Lau quotes Sidney Colvin's view that 'Keats would have felt [the Hymn's] strain of aspiration and invocation too painful, too near despair...and...Shelley's "Spirit of BEAUTY"...would have seemed to him something abstract, remote, and uncomforting'; she also quotes Robert Gittings as arguing that Keats 'disliked the poem's characterization of this world as "a dim vast vale of tears"',[33] and, alluding to a famous later letter by Keats, she supposes Gittings to believe that Keats rejects that 'common cognomen' in favour of his view of the world as a 'vale of soul-making'.[34] Yet Lau's reservations about these reservations are well judged. A vast idea of beauty rolls through Keats's concretizing acts of imagination; he doubtless sensed that Shelley uses rather than commits himself to the view of this world as a 'dim vast vale of tears' (17), and that in the 'Hymn' the phrase is no sooner spoken than the heartbroken sentiment to which it contributes in the lines 'Why dost thou pass away and leave our state, / This dim vast vale of tears, vacant and desolate?' (16–17) is rebuked as foolish and facile in the immediately ensuing lines: 'Ask why the sunlight not forever / Weaves rainbows o'er yon mountain river' (18–19). This is the first in a series of mock, yet—such is the intricacy of feeling—simultaneously genuine questions that culminate in the unanswerable interrogation, 'why man has such a scope / For love and hate, despondency and hope?' (19–20).

The lines quoted from this second stanza stayed with Keats, until he finely remodelled them in the fourth and most poignant stanza of 'Ode on a Grecian Urn', a poem that is richly involved in a dialectical relationship with Shelley's poem. At the close of the fourth stanza, Keats moves from question to statement as he addresses the 'little town': 'And, little town, thy streets for evermore / Will silent be; and not a soul to tell / Why thou art desolate, can e'er return' (38–40). The turn in the lines takes us back to Shelley's 'where art thou gone? / Why dost thou pass away and leave our state, / This dim vast vale of tears, vacant and desolate' (16–17). Keats seem to recall, too, in 'not a soul to tell' Shelley's back-straightening rejection of transcendental conversation at the start of his next stanza: 'No voice

---

[31] See chapter 2, 'Chemistry of the Poetic Process' in Stuart M. Sperry, *Keats the Poet* (Princeton: Princeton University Press, 1973), 30–71.
[32] Lau, *Keats's Reading*, 150.   [33] Lau, *Keats's Reading*, 150.
[34] Lau, *Keats's Reading*, 150.

from some sublime world hath ever / To sage or poet these responses given' ('Hymn to Intellectual Beauty', 25–6).

To make the link is to point up differences. Shelley is still half in love with some sublime world as his Platonic language ('The awful shadow of some unseen Power', line 1), however qualified by empirical scepticism, suggests; Keats mourns for a vanished actuality, a 'little town'. Beauty for Shelley transfigures pain and despair and supplies a cause for hope; for Keats it exists steadfastly alongside the unbeautiful truth that 'old age shall this generation waste' (46). Not that Shelley ignores the fear that life may be a 'dark reality' (48), nor does Keats wholly reject the aesthetic promise of art, even if for a climactic moment, the aesthetic seems only to be a 'Cold Pastoral' (45). But it is noticeable that Keats begins to use the word 'beauty' in poems and letters with far greater force in the months and years after encountering Shelley's 'Hymn': the poem in which Shelley takes the shopworn Burkean term and brings it into intimate contact with existential poetic quest.

From now on, Keats uses the word with high seriousness and sometimes moral suspicion, as the following famous examples—a few among many—illustrate:

(a) A thing of beauty is a joy for ever (*Endymion*, I. 1)

(b) 'What the Imagination seize as Beauty must be truth' (*Letters: John Keats* I, 184)

(c) 'A friend to man, to whom say'st, / "Beauty is truth, truth beauty, —that is all / Ye know on earth, and all ye need to know" ' ('Ode on a Grecian Urn', 48–50)

(d) 'She dwells with Beauty—Beauty that must die' ('Ode on Melancholy', 21)

(e) 'How beautiful, if sorrow had not made / Sorrow more beautiful than Beauty's self' (*Hyperion* 1. 35–6)

'For 'tis the eternal law / That first in beauty should be first in might' (*Hyperion* 2. 228–9)

(f) 'All is cold Beauty; pain is never done / For who has mind to relish, Minoswise, / The real of Beauty' (On Visiting the Tomb of Burns', 8–10)

(g) 'I met a lady in the meads, / Full beautiful—a faery's child' ('La Belle Dame Sans Merci', 13–14)

(h) In a letter of December 1817 this strangely suggestive collocation occurs: 'with a great poet the sense of Beauty overcomes every other consideration, or rather obliterates all consideration. Shelley's poem is out & there are words about its being objected too, as much as Queen Mab was. Poor Shelley I think he has his Quota of good qualities, in sooth la!!' (*Letters: John Keats* I, 194).

That laid-back allusion to Cleopatra in touchingly and incongruously domestic unflappable mood (responding to Antony's equally affecting semi-impatience with her attempts to arm him) suggests that Keats is distinguishing himself from any 'Shelley bashing' taking place in his circle.[35] One might submit that among Shelley's

---

[35] The allusion to *Antony and Cleopatra*, IV. iv. 8 is noted in *The Letters of John Keats*, I, 194n.

'good qualities', from Keats's perspective, was his rescuing of beauty from the domain of the decorative and the sanctifying of it as an idea, an ideal that required endless pursuit and figurative cunning (displayed in the Dantean portraits of Moneta in *The Fall of Hyperion* and the 'shape all light' (352) in *The Triumph of Life* at the ends of both poets' active writing careers): an idea and ideal that took its value from the mind of the pursuer, concerned to 'define', in Sperry's gloss on the lines quoted above from *Sleep and Poetry*, 'if not the final truths, at least "The *end* and *aim* of Poesy"' (emphases are Sperry's).[36]

4

Yet beauty must coexist with power, as will be explored in this final section's exploration of the stanzas opening Shelley's *Adonais*. 'The language of poetry naturally falls in with the language of power', wrote Hazlitt with republican disapproval in his essay on *Coriolanus*.[37] Among the challenges facing Shelley is how to celebrate poetic power without that power seeming to be a form of despotism. *Adonais* is about poetic power and warrants praise for its own demonstration of such power. At the same time, its valuing of poetic power leads Shelley into complex if implicit reconsiderations of his social and political hopes, even as the poem engages in a power struggle with a culture hostile to poetic achievement. Arguably, something of that power struggle is currently repeating itself in critical accounts of the poem. My use of the word 'power' includes in its meanings 'the power of communicating and receiving intense and impassioned conceptions respecting man and nature' of which Shelley writes in *A Defence of Poetry* (*Major Works*, 701); it is, moreover, obstinately lower-case. True, Shelley refers in stanza 42 to 'that Power [...] / Which has withdrawn his being to its own, / Which wields the world with never wearied love, / Sustains it from beneath, and kindles it above' (42. 375–8); true, too, that the alliance between the poetic power revealed by *Adonais* and Shelley's reference to a quasi-transcendent Power tempts one into the deconstructive pathways profitably explored by Angela Leighton and Peter Sacks, among others, for whom the poem dramatizes the endless deferral of contact with a 'pure voice of creative "Power" beyond the deceptive fictions of language'.[38] And yet, the poem dwells less on the necessary failures of language than on its endless potential; in it, the mind in creation represents itself less as a fading and more as an increasingly glowing coal. In a rejected passage in the Preface, Shelley writes with Keats in mind: 'But a young spirit, panting for fame doubtful of its powers & certain only of the aspirations is not [fitted] to assign its true value to the shews of this [deceitful] world' (*BSM* VII: 194–5). Shelley is the antithesis of this 'young spirit'; he is certain of his 'powers,' even if he is doubtful about his 'aspirations'.

---

[36] Sperry, *Keats the Poet*, 87.
[37] William Hazlitt, *Complete Works of William Hazlitt*, ed. P. P. Howe, 21 vols. (London: Dent, 1930–4), 4. 214.
[38] Angela Leighton, *Shelley and the Sublime* (Cambridge: Cambridge University Press, 1984), 162; Peter Sacks, 'Last Clouds: A Reading of "Adonais"', *Studies In Romanticism* 23.3 (1984): 379–400.

Shelley's friend John Taaffe, commentator on Dante, persuaded Shelley to cancel 'from the preface the whole passage relating to my private wrongs'. Thanking Taaffe for his advice, Shelley continues: 'You are right: I ought not to shew my teeth before I can bite, or when I cannot bite' (*Letters: PBS*, 2. 306). But 'bite' he is out to do. His preferred tactic is to present the reviewers as hypocrites, promulgating a conservative, supposedly Christian ethos in a manner wholly at odds with the tenets of Christianity: hence the flurry of mockingly turned Biblical allusions in the Preface. 'It may be well said, that these wretched men know not what they do', with its allusion to Christ's words on the Cross, is an example (*Major Works*, 530). Moreover, he represents the reviewers as wholly incapable of recognizing poetic distinction when it shows itself: 'As to *Endymion*,' he writes scornfully, 'was it a poem, whatever might be its defects, to be treated contemptuously by those who had celebrated with various degrees of complacency and panegyric' many works by a long list of the 'illustrious obscure' (*Major Works*, 530). Intriguingly, Shelley announces his intention to enter the critical fray and produce 'a criticism upon the claims of [the poem's] lamented object to be classed among the writers of the highest genius who have adorned our age' (*Major Works*, 529). In a sense, the poem itself serves as that 'criticism'. Shelley, an intelligent critic of his contemporaries, would have no truck with the view that poetic value is solely some sort of cultural construct, despite his recognition in *A Defence of Poetry* of the fact that perception of value is made possible by the 'peculiar relations' (*Major Works*, 693) which each person and age experience. In Romantic poetry, *Adonais* is among the most decisive imaginings of the value of poetry itself; it brooks no rejoinder to its claims for poetry; it asserts the primacy of canonical figures ('The splendours of the firmament of time' [44. 399] is, in effect, an image for the canon); and it seeks to establish the greatness of Keats's poetry and, by implication, that of his elegist. And yet, for all its emphasis on the figure of Adonais as 'gathered to the kings of thought' (48. 430), a phrase which, in Vincent Newey's words, 'makes of the poets an alternative and superior authority',[39] *Adonais* does not quite affirm that 'Poets are the unacknowledged legislators of the World' (*A Defence of Poetry*, 701). 'Thy hopes are gone before' (53. 470), says Shelley of and to himself close to the poem's end, and those 'hopes', one may surmise, include assurance that the law-giving potential of poetry will be actualized. What Shelley does assert, with desperate conviction, is that great poetry endures.

In a draft, Milton is not 'the third among the sons of light' (4. 36), but the 'tenth', after Homer, Sophocles, Aeschylus, Dante, Petrarch, Lucretius, Virgil, Shakespeare, and Calderón (*BSM* XIV, 30–1). This list, extractable from a footnote scribbled in the draft, might be Shelley's version of the canon. And in the draft—and the poem—Shelley meditates on the essence of poetic power in past and present poets. The draft has some remarkable lines on a figure who, as often noted, and as discussed in Chapter 5, bears an uncanny resemblance to a caricature of Wordsworth: 'And next came a spirit beautiful & strong / Wrapt in the guise of an uncomely

[39] Vincent Newey, *Centring the Self: Subjectivity, Society and Reading from Thomas Gray to Thomas Hardy* (Aldershot: Scolar Press, 1995), 175.

form / He sometimes like a pedlar limped along / With packs upon his back, & did deform / Clothed in the skirts of a Scotch puritan' (*BSM* XIV, 22–3). For all the satirical inflection here, there is also a brief sense of an alliance between this Wordsworthian figure and the Shelleyan self-portrait at the heart of *Adonais*, where we meet 'A pardlike Spirit beautiful and swift' (32. 280). In the draft lines, 'Beautiful & strong' sounds a note of power, but the suggestion is of power deformed and frustrated. In the poem, the self-portrait occurs at a key moment and draws into itself the observations about Wordsworth in the draft. The procession of poet-mourners not only allows Shelley his chance to comment on the contemporary scene, but also to present himself, or a version of himself, as composed of power and weakness, much as is Adonais/Keats. The self-portrait is on a knife-edge, somewhere in the space between self-pity and the almost horrified recognition that comes from seeing the self as other. Presenting himself as 'a Power / Girt round with weakness' (32. 281–2), Shelley constructs a self not only to be confronted but also transcended through the act of confrontation.

This figure's weakness contrasts with the strength of Byron, chief among the mourners, 'The Pilgrim of Eternity, whose fame / Over his living head like Heaven is bent, / An early but enduring monument' (30. 264–6). But the contemporary poet most manifestly commented on is Keats, a figure with whom Shelley engages, often through allusion, and in whom he discovers a symbol of 'unfulfilled renown' (45. 397): that is, real greatness and magnificent potential. Susan Wolfson has traced the baleful cultural power of Shelley's 'bad medical pathology',[40] his ascription of Keats's death to the impact on him of a wounding review, and one critical construction which commands ready acceptance these days is the view that in *Adonais* 'Shelley consumes as well as re-creates the personality of Keats'. Heffernan's article argues that in the Preface and elsewhere Shelley offers a picture of a 'pathetically vulnerable mind', leading the critic to question why Shelley contrives to 'slander' Keats in the very act of seeking to defend him against slander?'[41] Heffernan's strain of covert disapproval seems to me misjudged; but the point he makes about the consuming of identity in the poem is a valuable one.

Identity is a perilous notion in the poem, at risk for a number of reasons. For a start, there is the need to bear in mind, in reading the poem, the force of Shelley's comment in a letter about the poem that 'The poet & the man are two different natures' (*Letters: PBS*, 2. 310). This is not to say that Shelley simply uses Keats. Throughout 1820, Shelley intuits his fellow-poet's greatness. In May 1820, he writes, 'Keats, I hope, is going to show himself a great poet' (*Letters: PBS*, 2. 197). In November, in an unsent letter to Gifford, he expresses his much-mocked and medically incorrect view that Keats contracted 'consumption' through the 'dreadful state of mind' into which he was 'thrown' by a review (*Letters: PBS*, 2. 252). The same unsent letter to Gifford shows, however, that Shelley had been re-reading

---

[40] Susan Wolfson, 'Keats Enters History: Autopsy, *Adonais*, and the Fame of Keats', *Keats and History*, ed. Nicholas Roe (Cambridge: Cambridge University Press, 1995), 27.

[41] James A. W. Heffernan, ' "Adonais": Shelley's Consumption of Keats', *Studies in Romanticism* 23.3 (1984): 295–315 (295, 300, 301).

Endymion with fastidious care. But Heffernan's point about the consumption of
Keats's identity in *Adonais* reminds us that, for Shelley, such consuming is inseparable from the act of writing poetry. Poetry as a force that threatens the poet's identity
is a motif that runs through Shelley's work.[42] The Shelleyan poet is a medium, as
much as an origin, through whom earlier poetic voices pour, even as they are
reshaped, and through whom collective energies are channelled. The poet's going
out of the self involves an ideal of self-extinction and transcendence of self. At the
same time the poet needs an identity for that identity to imagine its own being or
that of others experiencing consumption. Jeffrey N. Cox's reading of the poem as
seeking 'to rescue Keats from a Wordsworthian poetry of self-concentration' and
establish him as an exemplar of a poetry opposed to 'the principle of self' is eloquently
argued and responsive to the drama of the poetry.[43] However, the poem moves
between self-awareness and self-transcendence more fluidly and less systematically
than Cox allows. Generally, interpretations which deplore Shelley's emphasis on
Keats's vulnerability to criticism ignore the plot of the poem, and find it hard to fit
the final section of the poem into their account of Shelley's supposedly having
'wrapped Keats in a self-invested version of his history'.[44] Such readings risk being
trapped, as the poem does not, in its Preface and opening section.

Each of the opening stanzas involves a contest between the power of words,
tradition and imagination, and the repression and apparent failure of these things.
The pastoral elegy struggles to deliver the generic goods, but the beauty of the
opening derives from admitted failure. The verse shows a repeating pattern of
building up, then running into, the sands. In stanza 2 questions sound an indig-
nant note, as though the elegist were, initially, demanding an answer. Yet the
answer, when it comes, is conflicted: the 'mighty Mother' (2. 10) is rekindling
Keats's 'fading melodies' (2. 16). There is a struggle here between the defiance of
the flowers and the seeming omnipotence of death; it is against that seeming
omnipotence that Shelley directs the power of poetry and his poem. If Shelley
offers a concealed allusion here to stanza 5 of Keats's 'Ode to a Nightingale', which
links flowers with an image of the night as, effectively, an 'embalmed' (5. 43)
corpse, he shatters the acceptance of natural cycles in Keats. Keats imagines both
'Fast fading violets' (6. 48) and 'The coming musk-rose' (6. 49), which, in turn, will
be subject to decay, when it is 'The murmurous haunt of flies on summer eves' (6. 50).
Shelley sees the poet's melodies as having 'adorned and hid the coming bulk of
death' (2. 18), a line where the word 'coming' exposes the action of the verbs as
ultimately ineffectual. In stanza 5, 'some yet live, treading the thorny road / Which
leads, through toil and hate, to Fame's serene abode' (5. 44–5).

The fightback has begun; death may be the end of life, but the heroic figure of
Milton, who 'went, unterrified, / Into the gulf of death' (5. 43–4), plus the likes of
Shelley and Byron who tread 'the thorny road' (5. 44) leading to fame's serene

[42] A central argument in Clark, *Embodying Revolution*.
[43] Jeffrey N. Cox, *Poetry and Politics in the Cockney School: Keats, Shelley, Hunt and Their School*
(Cambridge: Cambridge University Press, 1998), 216, 217.
[44] Wolfson, *Keats and History*, 37.

abode, signal the possibility, even at this early stage, of there being an 'abode where the Eternal are' (55. 495). Even the repetition of 'Most musical of mourners, weep anew!' in stanzas 4 and 5 (28 and 37) shows the onset of a new confidence. Implicitly, the poem trusts in its music of mourning to lead it in the right direction. The style grows wonderfully high: 'Not all,' writes Shelley in relation to Milton, 'to that bright station dared to climb' (5. 38). To show how the power of the poem relies on delayed detonations, one needs to look ahead to stanza 44: 'The splendours of the firmament of time / May be eclipsed, but are extinguished not; / Like stars to their appointed height they climb' (44. 388–90). These later lines are vibrant with implications, including the following: that poetic fame does not quite escape 'the firmament of time' which it adorns; and that great poets take their place in the 'firmament of time' as if obeying an inevitable process (Shelley's early flirtation with Necessity reappears in changed form).

To return to the opening, the syntax of stanza 9 is a complicated version of the way the poetry mimes a would-be assertion of poetic power, only for it, apparently, to fall away. The 'quick Dreams' (9. 73) are alive with creativity, and look as though they will sustain a posthumous existence, but after five lines the delayed main verb concedes their inefficacy: they 'wander not' (9. 77), before the following lines describe further what they will not do. The recollection of how they moved from 'kindling brain to brain' (9. 78) sponsors an awareness of present dwindling; the energy of kindled interplay has given way to a failure to 'gather strength' (9. 81). But the very effect of diminishment speaks also of the life once present in those 'quick Dreams': pastoral convention has been altered, so that here the poet is mourned by his own mental processes. Shelley is sometimes accused of being too remote from Keats; but, in a special sense, he is very close to him as he dwells on the imaginative processes which made Keats's achievements possible.

Giving up the *Hyperion* project, Keats seeks to distinguish between 'the false beauties proceeding from art' and 'the true voice of feeling' (*Letters: John Keats* II 167). Certainly, both he and Shelley write with impressive truth of feeling when they address, as they do, implicitly and explicitly, and always with intelligence and intensity, the question of the significance to be attached to the 'beauties proceeding from art', 'false' or otherwise. And it was all, this richly woven tapestry of thoughts and feeling about poetry's 'end and aim', begun in earnest in 1816, a year that in Keats's case began with the expression of poetic fraternal feeling towards George Felton Matthews but ended in a meeting—probably 'during Shelley's initial visit [to Hunt], December 10 through 13'—with a patrician, slim, serious-minded young man,[45] who possessed a poetic and critical gift at once antithetical and complementary to Keats's own. The rest is poetic history: a history that indicates that their ultimate 'place' was and is the endlessly changing and turbulent canon they re-shaped and go on shaping with such creative energy and genius.

---

[45] Reiman, 403.

11

Turning to Dante

Shelley's *Adonais* Reprismed

As often, if not always, in his agonistic creative relationship with Shelley, Byron just about got there first in terms of responding to the imaginative range offered by Dante's example.[1] In *The Prophecy of Dante*, composed in 1819 but published in 1821, Byron writes from the persona of Dante: a bold move that allows for a sense of veiled autobiography. In places we suspect we are dealing with the Noble Lord as much as the Florentine poet. 'For I have been too long and deeply wreck'd / On the lone rock of desolate Despair' (I. 138–9) catches the throwing-it-all-to-the-winds cadence of 'I *have* thought / Too long and darkly, till my brain became, / In its own eddy boiling and o'erwrought, / A whirling gulf of phantasy and flame' of *Childe Harold's Pilgrimage* (III. 7. 55–8).[2] Again, the first canto of *The Prophecy of Dante* rakes over the still-burning coals of the separation from Lady Byron as it closes with a sardonic reference to 'that fatal she' (I. 172), the mother of his children, 'who hath brought / Destruction for a dowry' (I. 173–4). The feelings of Byron's Dante are mixed: he has been 'taught / A bitter lesson' (I. 175–6), but he affirms his essential freedom: 'it leaves me free: / I have not vilely found nor basely sought, / They made an Exile—not a slave of me' (I. 176–8). The poem is saved from tame postures of deference by such acts of appropriation.

Ways in which Byron and Shelley overlap in their response to Dante include a sense that Dante puts the poetic self at the centre of a poem, not to indulge ego, but to record experience, especially experience that can be called visionary. At the same time, what is recorded in Dante is often the poet's at least half-admiring response to speakers who very much put their ego to the fore. Shelley's portrait of Rousseau in *The Triumph of Life* as someone preoccupied by the self is an instance of the Italian poet's influence here. Shelley catches Rousseau's conviction, one never wholly dismissed by the poem, that his is the exemplary fate of modern

---

[1] This chapter is in dialogue with ideas developed in previous essays of mine, notably 'Realms without a Name: Shelley and Italy's Intenser Day', in *Dante and Italy in British Romanticism*, ed. Frederick Burwick and Paul Douglass (New York: Palgrave Macmillan, 2011), 77–91, and three essays in the *Journal of Anglo-Italian Studies*: 'Cathestant or Protholic? Shelley's Italian Imaginings', 6 (2001): 153–68; 'Fashioned from His Opposite: Yeats, Dante and Shelley' 8 (2006): 149–71; '"Admirable for Conciseness and Vigour": Dante and Romantic Epic', 10 (2009): 15–27. For helpful comments on a draft, I should like to thank Alan Weinberg.
[2] All quotations from Byron are taken from *The Complete Poetical Works of Lord Byron*, ed. Jerome. J. McGann, 7 vols. (Oxford: Clarendon Press, 1980–8), here vols. 4 and 2, respectively.

subjectivity; he asserts that he 'was overcome / By my own heart alone' (*The Triumph of Life*, 241–2), and that 'I'—the word held in towering aloneness at the end of a line—'Have suffered what I wrote, or viler pain!' (279–80).[3] Byron and Shelley share, too, an artistic awareness that *terza rima* can be adapted to English poetry, especially in the service of onward flowing feeling, a stream of sensation being central to both poets' desire to leave behind custom and tradition even as they draw from them what they think is most valuable. Shelley, in particular, realizes that *terza rima* can be adapted to a vision of experience that is alive to possibility and resistant to closure. Moreover, they respond to Dante in a fashion that allows them to challenge British philosophical and cultural traditions: Dante charts a trajectory that to a Romantic-period reader looks like a move from seen to unseen, empiricism to idealism, a movement that Byron evokes in the opening of *The Prophecy of Dante*. It is typical of the poetry's ambivalence, however, that he recalls 'the base / Of the eternal Triad' (I. 12–13) from the perspective of being 'Once more in man's frail world!' (I. 1). Finally, the two poets evolve an awareness of Dante as a poet of liberty.[4] Indeed, in places in their work Dante emerges as a precursor of modern hope for unification. A long section in canto II of Byron's poem discusses the present-day ignominy and tyranny suffered by Italians and ends with the vision: 'we, / Her sons, may do this with *one* deed— Unite!' (II. 144–5).[5]

Shelley appears to have read Byron's poem in August 1821, after its publication in April of the same year, and admired it greatly. He told Byron that its poetry was 'indeed sublime' (*Letters: PBS*, 2. 347). *The Prophecy of Dante* certainly leaves an impression on *The Triumph of Life* in the lines about 'the sacred few, who could not tame / Their spirits to the Conqueror, but as soon / As they had touched the world with living flame / Fled back like eagles to their native noon' (128–31). The lines recall, as Charles Robinson notes, those 'birds of Paradise' (III. 169) 'form'd of far too penetrable stuff' (III. 170) in Byron's poem who 'long to flee / Back to their native mansion' (III. 169–70); 'soon they find / Earth's mist with their pure pinions not agree' (III. 170–1).[6] And Shelley would have been struck, as Robinson suggests, by analogues with his recent thinking about poetry in *A Defence of Poetry* and *Adonais*, works deeply concerned with Dante. The lines in question, Robinson comments, 'anticipated [Shelley's] own images in *Adonais* where earth's "mist" and "the contagion of the world's slow stain" were "outsoared" by Keats, who had also been formed of "penetrable stuff"', a phrase quoted in Shelley's Preface to his

---

[3] Quoted from *Major Works*. All quotations from Shelley's prose (apart from his letters) and poetry are taken from this edition (page numbers are provided in parenthesis for prose quotations).

[4] Lilla Maria Crisafulli quotes Luigi Rava as drawing attention to the 'Ode to Liberty' as evidence of Shelley's support for Italian 'political aspirations', 'Shelley's Afterlife in Italy: from 1822 to 1922', in *The Reception of Shelley in Europe*, ed. Suzanne Schmid and Michael Rossington (London: Continuum, 2008), 50n.

[5] For the view that 'When Byron and Shelley turn to Dante in Italy, they advertise an extreme self-consciousness about their position between two cultures and outside the orthodox faith of both', see Jane Stabler, *The Artistry of Exile: Romantic and Victorian Writers in Italy* (Oxford: Oxford University Press, 2013), 100.

[6] Robinson, *Shelley and Byron*, 180–1.

elegy.[7] Yet Shelley blurs distinctions between realms, as Greg Kucich comments in relation to *The Revolt of Islam*'s 'modifying'—a modifying that is, in Kucich's view only partly successful—of 'Spenser's dichotomous vision'.[8] He tugs this-worldly metaphor and figure in the dimension of an other-worldly eternity, and suggests not only that eternity must be shadowed forth through temporal means, but also that it is in time that visions of eternity can and must be experienced.

Adonais typifies Shelley's view of poetry as engaged in creative response to previous poetry. Again, Kucich is helpful, allowing us to grasp the complexity of Shelley's journey towards such a creative response, one that involves jettisoning judgements about a previous poet on solely ideological grounds.[9] This jettisoning is evident in the assertion that 'Didactic poetry is my abhorrence' in the Preface to *Prometheus Unbound* (*Major Works*, 232) and in the account in *A Defence of Poetry* of Dante and Milton as great poets whose explicit and 'distorted notions of invisible things' are 'merely the mask and the mantle in which these great poets walk through eternity enveloped and disguised' (*Major Works*, 691). *Adonais* achieves a capacious if often conflicted openness to tradition; it is steeped in classical elegiac conventions, drawing on Shelley's translation of Bion's elegy for Adonis. Its Spenserians pay graceful tribute to Spenser's 'Astrophel', an oblique tribute since Spenser does not use his nine-line stanza in that poem. They also bring to mind Byron's *Childe Harold's Pilgrimage*, which Vincent Newey sees as a spur to Shelleyan emulousness in the poem, the later stanzas in particular revealing for Newey a Shelleyan 'drive to *outdistance* Byron'.[10] The poem is full of allusions to Keats, as Kelvin Everest has demonstrated. As Everest writes, the poem 'deliberately celebrates Keats's claims to classic status, and honours in ceremonially formal terms the seriousness and scale of his achievement'.[11] And it shares with Byron's *The Prophecy of Dante* a fascination with creativity, of a kind for which Dante turns into an exemplar. Thus Byron, in the guise of Dante, writes:

> For what is poesy but to create
> From overflowing good or ill; and aim
> At an external life beyond our fate,
> And be the new Prometheus of new men,
> Bestowing fire from heaven, and then, too late,
> Finding the pleasure given repaid with pain,
> And vultures to the heart of the bestower […]
>   (IV. 11–17)

The lines have that quality of reflective, near-metaphysical surprise characteristic of some of Byron's best writing. They say fine things almost unintentionally, to adapt Keats on Shakespeare's sonnets (*Letters: John Keats* I, 188), driven by the imperatives of rhyme and rhythm as they move from imagining what it might be 'to create' to

---

[7] Robinson, *Shelley and Byron*, 180, 182.
[8] Kucich, *Keats, Shelley, and Romantic Spenserianism*, 283.
[9] See the discussion of Shelley and influence in Kucich, 285–9.
[10] Newey, 'Shelley and the Poets: *Alastor*, "Julian and Maddalo", *Adonais*', 266.
[11] Everest, 'Shelley's *Adonais* and John Keats', 238.

sensing 'An external life beyond our fate', before a further rhyme, 'too late', quenches aspiration in disillusion. The way in which the thought develops through the *terza rima* has a post-Dantean blend of cognitive assurance and capacity for novelty.

Shelley, by 1821, is close to and yet far from this position: close, in that he has asserted in *A Defence of Poetry*, that it is not a poet's duty to 'embody his own conceptions of right and wrong, which are usually those of his place and time, in his poetical creations, which participate in neither' (*Major Works*, 682); far, in that he would prefer still not to believe in the pessimism which clouds Byronic affirmation, the belief that, 'too late', unwelcome discovery lies in wait for the Promethean poet who would redefine our fate through his power to create.[12] Shelley still, in theory at any rate, emphasizes the collective benefit rather than the personal pain of poetry: 'It awakens and enlarges the mind itself by rendering it the receptacle of a thousand unapprehended combinations of thought' (*Major Works*, 681). Those 'combinations' include the way in which poet and predecessors combine in the process of producing new creations.

Dante increasingly had come to the fore of Shelley's mind as a type of the 'great poet' whom the younger poet has written 'another' poet 'must study' (*Major Works*, 231). He inspires Shelley's own tropes for influence and crystallizes his remarkable readiness to confront the process of influence head-on rather than merely to accept it as a practice not brought into full consciousness: 'Dante', writes Shelley in *A Defence of Poetry*,

> was the first awakener of entranced Europe; he created a language in itself music and persuasion out of a chaos of inharmonious barbarisms. His very words are instinct with spirit; each is as a spark, a burning atom of inextinguishable thought; and many yet lie covered in the ashes of their birth, and pregnant with a lightning which has yet found no conductor.
>
> (*Major Works*, 693).

The 'Ashes and sparks' (66) of 'Ode to the West Wind', along with the 'fire for which all thirst' (54. 485), the 'burning fountain' (38. 339) and 'fire' that 'outlives its parent spark' (46. 408) of *Adonais*, find their source in the burning atoms of Dante's 'inextinguishable thought'. 'Poca favilla gran fiamma seconda' (From a small spark / Great flame hath risen), writes Dante in *Paradiso* I. 34 and Shelley's work responds to this invitation to be influenced.[13] Cary's note to the line, or lines in translation, refers to Pindar's third Pythian Ode, lines 67–8, as if to point up the

---

[12] Robinson argues that, for all his admiration for *The Prophecy of Dante*, 'Shelley sensed that Byron once more condoned the immoral effects of...despair', 184.

[13] Dante original cited from Temple Classics edition of the *Commedia*, ed. Philip H. Wicksteed, 3 vols. (London: Dent, 1904). Translations into English are from *The Vision; or Hell, Purgatory, and Paradise of Dante Alighieri*. trans. Henry Francis Cary, 3 vols., 2nd edn corr. with the Life of Dante, Additional Notes, and an Index (London: Taylor and Hessey, 1819). There are problems with Cary's translation, but as the translation most widely used by second-generation Romantic poets it has considerable historical interest. Shelley, who appeared to read Cary, but soon began reading Dante in Italian, would, it is presupposed here, have viewed Cary's version as both invaluable and not wholly adequate. For further discussion of Cary and Shelley, see Antonella Braida, *Dante and the Romantics* (Houndmills: Palgrave Macmillan, 2004). Ch. 4, 95–127. For the influence of Dante's line, see Alan M. Weinberg, *Shelley's Italian Experience* (London: Macmillan, 1991), 195.

process of influence.[14] Pindar writes (in English translation): 'As from one fatal spark arise / The flames aspiring to the skies, / And all the crackling wood consume'.[15]

To re-read the first canto of the *Paradiso* alone is to be reminded of why Shelley exalted this *cantica*.[16] Echoes aside, one of which will be discussed later, it is the daring and radiance of the writing from which Shelley seems to have drawn inspiration and to which he is, of all poets writing in English, the most evidently attuned by poetic temperament. Dante's sense of the hardness of his task; his appeal to Apollo and the reminder of the god's flaying of Marsyas; the divine cosmology with Beatrice looking at the sun; the Glaucus-like moment of 'transhuman' apprehension (see l. 71); the concern to avoid, yet readiness to confront, 'falso imaginar' (false imagination, as Cary has it, or 'imagining') (l. 88); the rapturously fluent account of 'lo gran mar dell'essere' (the vast sea of being) (l. 113); the metaphysics of form and matter (ll. 127–9): to all these beautifully connected units of vision Shelley would have been uniquely responsive. When Rachel Jacoff writes of Dante's *Paradiso*, 'The impossibility of directly rendering that reality [that is, of Paradise] turns out to have its positive value in the ways it liberates the poet for "making signs" with increasing freedom from any purely mimetic imperative',[17] the reader of Shelleyan poems such as *Prometheus Unbound and Epipsychidion* will wish to redirect her comment as illuminating about the Romantic poet's practice, too. One might even be tempted to find in Dante, as in some Bloomian critical manoeuvre that would reverse linearity, a Shelleyan dimension. So, Richard Harter Fogle writes that 'the first experience of the Empyrean Heaven [in *Paradiso* 30] is clothed in a garb which considering my point of view I hope I may be pardoned for calling highly Shelleyan'.[18] Fogle's phrasing is attentive to ways in which a later writer can fulfil an earlier one, so that the earlier writer's achievement seems incomplete without the later writer's. It reminds us, moreover, of the truly comic dimension of the *Paradiso* in which wrongs are made right and true happiness discovered, and where poetic justice passes into moments that joyfully exceed human apprehension, as in the redemption of the Trojan Ripheus (Riphaeus, in Shelley's spelling). Shelley's purpose in singling out the surprising decision to include Ripheus (see *A Defence of Poetry*, 691) is to hint at Dante's imaginative capacity to exceed his poem's framework of beliefs; the truly comic nature of the *Paradiso* lies in the freedom it embodies within itself and imparts to others to escape the handcuffs of ideological conviction. The eagle declares to the pilgrim-poet:

> Chi crederebbe giù nel monde errante,
>   che Rifeo Troiano in questo tondo
>   fosse la quinte delle luci sante?

---

[14] *The Vision*, ed. Cary, vol. 3, 5n.

[15] *Pindar*, trans. C. A. Wheelwright (London: Colburn and Bentley, 1830).

[16] 'The acutest critics', he writes in *A Defence of Poetry*, 'have justly reversed the judgement of the vulgar and the order of the great acts of the "Divine Drama" in the measure of the admiration which they accord to the Hell, Purgatory and Paradise', *Major Works*, 691.

[17] Rachel Jacoff, ' "Shadowy Prefaces": An Introduction to *Paradiso*', *The Cambridge Companion to Dante*, ed. Rachel Jacoff (Cambridge: Cambridge University Press, 1993), 210.

[18] Richard Harter Fogle, 'Dante and Shelley's *Adonais*', *Bucknell Review* 15. 39 (1967): 11–21 (12).

> ora conosce che in aere si spazia
> veder non può della divina grazia,
> benchè sua vista non discerna il fondo
> (*Paradiso*, 20. 67–72)
>
> (Who in the erring world beneath would deem,
> That Trojan Ripheus in this round was set
> Fifth of the saintly splendours? now he knows
> Enough of that, which the world cannot see,
> The grace divine, albeit e'en his sight
> Reach not its upmost depth.)

Ripheus cannot understand the reach of 'grace divine', and Shelley might say, in thinking about the episode, that Dante extends a 'grace' towards subsequent readers. The strangeness of the decision to place Ripheus in Paradise acts as an analogue to the fact that a medieval Catholic poem can serve as a stimulus to a second-generation English Romantic poet, with little love of Christian hierarchies and orthodoxies—yet with a passion for similitudes and a reverence for processes of desire and longing that are honoured in Dante's subsequent tercets (73–8).

The genius of influence must work itself out in a poet in multiple ways. 'All high poetry is infinite' (*Major Works*, 693), Shelley declares, straight after his praise of Dante in *A Defence of Poetry*, and the *Commedia* is clearly in his mind; 'new relations are ever developed' (*Major Works*, 693), Shelley asserts, and an example is *Adonais*. The *Commedia* itself contains a number of encounters with previous poets. Dante depends on Virgil as his guide. In *Purgatorio* 21 he participates in a triangulated scene of poetic encounter when Statius is told by him that the figure in front of him is indeed Virgil. In *Purgatorio* 22 he listens to the poets talking 'ch' / a poetar mi davano intelletto' (that to my thoughts conveyed / Mysterious lessons of sweet poesy) (l. 129). In *Adonais* Shelley seems, as in some proto-Joycean Oxen of the Sun episode, to be running through a gamut of possible poetic styles—not in that there is any effect of continuous parody, but in that the poet seems, in his 'highly wrought *piece of art*' (*Letters: PBS*, 2. 294), as he calls it, to be assuming and then flamboyantly discarding or transforming styles of dealing with the world, with death and with what that grim fact makes of life. The 'unapprehended combinations of thought' (*A Defence of Poetry*, 681) include an attempt to redefine what elegy is capable of, as we move from Bion's *Lament* though echoes of Milton, Keats, Spenser, and others, towards the final ascent where Dante comes to the fore.[19]

Indeed, it is possible to make the poem's trajectory seem like a relatively smooth series of progressive revelations, as in Wasserman's account, or a blueprint for Shelleyan process, as in Hogle's reading.[20] Alan Weinberg suggestively sees the poem's three stages as 'conforming to the progressive structure of the *Commedia*:

---

[19] For more detail about these allusions, see *Longman* 4, 235–345.

[20] See Wasserman, *Shelley: A Critical Reading* and Hogle, *Shelley's Process*. Wasserman writes that the final movement of the poem 'will be the fulfilment of implications latent in the first two', 472, and Hogle argues that 'the stages of Shelley's *Adonais*...appear to rise through the levels of Christian allegory

the first (stanzas 1 to 17) corresponds to the *Inferno*; the second (stanzas 18 to 37) corresponds to the *Purgatorio*; and the third (stanzas 38 to 55) to the *Paradiso*.[21] These approaches helpfully adumbrate Shelley's realization of the triadic possibilities present in Dante's poem. They encourage one, too, to search out those moments when Shelley departs from Dante and works in ultimately unsystematizable ways; indeed, Weinberg comments that 'The Dantean framework is not rigidly defined' and he prefaces his description of the structural parallels by pointing out the all-important difference between the 'linear narrative structure' in Dante and 'the antithetical lyrical structure' in Shelley'.[22]

Even if the *Inferno* analogy prompts us to reflect that Dante's subject is sin and Shelley's mortality, it might prompt us also to detect unexpected continuities. Sin might be said to enter the poem explicitly when Shelley, picking up his con-demnation in the Preface of a reviewer's malignity, expresses his contempt for the 'envy, hate, and wrong' (*Adonais* 36. 321) which 'was howling in one breast alone' (36. 322). But when sin does enter the poem, Shelley treats it with a curious empathy. He condemns the reviewer to feel emotions of self-abhorrence: 'Remorse and Self-contempt' (37. 331) and 'shame' (37. 332). The fitting punishment is for the reviewer to 'be thyself, and know thyself to be!' (37. 328). He is condemned; that is, as Shelley adapts a Dantean severity of charity to his own ends, to a form of spiritual advancement. Even if it sounds uncannily close to Dantean *contrapasso*, the authorial imperative implicitly departs from Dante's 'distribution of rewards and punishments' (*A Defence of Poetry*, 691)—though one might argue that Dante's sinners 'are', without knowing fully why they are. A few stanzas later, Shelley will supply a paradisal redefinition of death as a space free from 'Envy and calumny and hate and pain, / And that unrest which men miscall delight' (40. 353–4), and throughout *Adonais* the paradisal and the potentially infernal or purgatorial are unstably in contact.

Shelley works, as Weinberg implies, by unpredictable leaps rather than precise steps, responding with liberal creativity to Dante's own invitation to operate through sublime poetic aspiration in *Paradiso*, canto 23:

> E così, figurando il Paradiso,
>   convien saltar lo sacrato poema
>   come chi trova suo cammin reciso.
> (61–3)

(And with such figuring of Paradise,
The sacred strain must leap, like one that meets
A sudden interruption to his road.)[23]

---

as listed and applied by Dante', though he sees Shelley's poem as being at odds with 'Catholic (or any official Christian) theology', 318.

[21] Weinberg, *Shelley's Italian Experience*, 183.   [22] Weinberg, 183.

[23] For a seminal essay on these lines and their importance for understanding Shelley's response to Dante, see Stuart Curran, 'Figuration in Shelley and Dante', *Dante's Modern Afterlife: Reception and Response from Blake to Heaney*, ed. Nick Havely (New York: St Martin's Press, 1998), 49–59.

Dante was there before Shelley, so Shelley must have delightedly discovered, reading these lines. Indeed, just preceding the passage, Dante speaks of himself thus:

> Io era come quei, che si risente
> di vision obblita, e che s'ingegna
> indarno di ridularsi alla mente
> (49–51)
>
> (I was as one, when a forgotten dream
> Doth come across him, and he strives in vain
> To shape it in his fantasy again)

Shelley manages, throughout *Adonais*, to shape in his 'fantasy again' the 'forgotten dream' of Dantean imaginings. In the lines about the 'sacred poem' (a phrase repeated in the first line of canto 25), Dante acknowledges that he is engaged in the process of 'figuring', shadowing forth, finding poetic equivalents. Shelley's own 'sudden leap' is in the direction of a 'sacred strain', but one that is sung by a modern poet who is, who must be, priest of his own imaginative religion, rather as Keats imagines himself to be in the second half of 'Ode to Psyche'. What happens is more than a Romantic raid on the medieval Catholic Thomist epic; it is also a matter of independent responsiveness, as Shelley both appropriates and honours Dante, and seeks resurgent consolation and existential encouragement through the act and fact of poetic creativity. Shelley is often most original at the very points where we most detect Dante's influence. What might be thought of as a still point round which the wheel of the elegy turns, namely stanza 21, is a case in point:

> Alas! that all we loved of him should be,
> But for our grief, as if it had not been,
> And grief itself be mortal! Woe is me!
> Whence are we, and why are we? of what scene
> The actors or spectators? Great and mean
> Meet massed in death, who lends what life must borrow.
> As long as skies are blue, and fields are green,
> Evening must usher night, night urge the morrow,
> Month follow month with woe, and year wake year to sorrow.
> (21. 181–9)

The writing bears witness to one of the lessons that Dante has taught Shelley: bareness. It is the point at which near-Baroque stylization drops away, but the bareness is subtly organized, as the outcry 'Woe is me!' settles into the more resigned 'Month follow month with woe'.[24] Dante's tercets are replaced by Shelley's Spenserians, yet, without denying the presence of the English Renaissance poet in *Adonais*, it might be borne in mind that Shelley's chosen stanza allows him to highlight for individualized significance effects which in Dante are caught up more swiftly in

---

[24] For discussion of the poem's 'Baroque' elements, see Bruce Haley, *Living Forms: Romantics and the Monumental Figure* (Albany: State University of New York Press, 2003), 215–16. See also Weinberg, *Shelley's Italian Experience*, 176, which speaks of the opening's 'baroque verbal embellishment, quaintly suggestive of Giambattista Marino's *Adone*'.

and by the regularly self-parcelling out of the *terza rima*. The grieving and the sardonic coexist, too, as in the unexpected introduction to the fact of suffering effected by the antepenultimate line. 'As long as skies are blue, and fields are green': as long as this, the reader might expect the poem to go on, 'all will be well'. But the line makes the unsettling point, already conveyed in the opening, that transience is the condition of what is best as well as worst about life. Above all, the stanza confronts ultimate questions: 'Whence are we, and what are we? Of what scene / The actors or spectators?'

The poem's challenge to itself is to find answers to those questions and to find a convincing mode and style in which to articulate those answers. It must first do so through a reversal of Dante's meeting with figures such as Brunetto Latini and Foresi Donati. As Erich Auerbach observes, Dante's Thomist view of the unity of soul and body, and of history and eternity, made it possible and 'necessary that the characters in Dante's other world, in their situation and attitude, should represent the sum of themselves; that they should disclose, in a single act, the character and the fate that had filled out their lives'.[25] Dante's encounters are confirmations of the reality of history, even as the 'other world' confers a sometimes terrible and terrifying permanence on character. The one character still undergoing change is Dante the pilgrim, always entering new and enlarged dimensions of understanding.[26] This understanding can be a question of grasping more firmly the mysteries of ethereal cosmology, and seeing that there is always more mystery that exceeds his grasp, as when Dante writes in the first canto of the *Paradiso*:

> S'io fui del primo dubbio disvestito
>   per le sorrise parolette brevi,
>   dentro ad un novo più fui irretito...
>   (94–6)
>
> (Although divested of my first-rais'd doubt,
> By those brief words, accompanied with smiles,
> Yet in new doubt was I entangled more...)

The tercet traces a movement forward that is also a circling back, and highlights 'new doubt' as a poetic motive and motor. But the poet-pilgrim's growth is also a matter of the heart as well as the head, and of moral apprehension, too. So, the encounter with Francesca da Rimini, which overwhelms the pilgrim with pity, is part of a process of education in the nature of love, which takes on its full meaning at the very end of the poem, when Dante acknowledges 'l'amor che move il sole e l'altre stelle' (translated imprecisely by Cary as the Love... / That moves the sun in heav'n and all the stars) (*Paradiso* 33. 145). There is a strong comparison here between this line's effect and the final line of *Adonais*, with its discovery of 'the

---

[25] Eric Auerbach, *Dante: Poet of the Secular World*, trans. Ralph Mannheim, intro Michael Dirda (1st pub. in German 1929; New York: New York Review of Books, 2007), 91.
[26] Auerbach, *Dante*, writes: 'In the *Comedy* all the characters are interpreted, their individual destinies have been fulfilled; only Dante himself, the wanderer, in a state of uncertainty, still unfulfilled and subject to interpretation', 171.

abode where the Eternal are' (55. 495).[27] Shelley's line gathers to itself the longing for ultimate meaning pervading his elegy and stands against its sometimes sorrowful, but often surprisingly rapt, engagement in 'becoming'.

Shelley, as he reflects on whom he is or has been in the process of reflecting on what Keats was and now is, must meet, among others, himself in the riddling, strange self-portrait where, among the mourners, there enters 'A pard-like Spirit beautiful and swift' (31. 271). John Taaffe, friend of Shelley and author of *A Comment on the Divine Comedy of Dante Alighieri* (1822), compares the line to Dante's enigmatic depiction of 'una lonza leggiera e presta molto' (a panther nimble, light) (*Inferno* I. 32).[28] Cary, along with other commentators, glosses the panther as 'Pleasure, luxury'.[29] Yet, reappearing as an image of the Shelleyan self, the pleasure-seeking panther has discovered much about poetic pains. Presenting 'one frail Form, / A phantom among men' (31. 271–2), Shelley meets a version of himself, a figure at once vulnerable and powerful, 'frail' yet holding a thyrsus, 'a light spear topped with a cypress cone, / Round whose rude shaft dark ivy tresses grew' (33. 291–2). Objectified, Shelley is like a Dantean personage encountered by the poet and the poet encountering such a personage; it is as if, in the process of objectifying himself, he is able to move beyond his sense of himself as 'a Power / Girt round with weakness' (32. 281–2), to confront and leave behind his feelings of potential limitation and failure, and to propel his poem's assault on the limits of definition.[30]

Shelley does so by turning on its head the meanings attaching to life and death as the poet magnificently relies on the sheer force of declarative utterance: 'he is not dead, he doth not sleep— / He hath awakened from the dream of life—' (39. 343–4). If these lines might, given a sardonic twist, describe many of the characters whom Dante meets, figures who have awakened from the dream of life, Shelley has less interest in the particulars of post-mortal living. His is a poignantly tormented see-sawing between animosity towards 'the contagion of the world's slow stain' (40. 356) and imagining of some other state or dimension. But this other state or dimension is less a sequel to or fulfilment of this life than this life's shadowy, imaginatively compelling other.

As Fogle notes, what is 'hierarchical' in Dante is imaginatively 'dialectical' in Shelley.[31] Answers to questions are rhetorical, not theologically grounded; they are part of a poetic dynamic that is enthralled by Dantean flights and tropes but cannot be governed by the medieval poem's overall law of development. Affirmations obey their own Shelleyan impulses, having about them a quality of prolonged

---

[27] I am indebted to Alan Weinberg for this suggestion.
[28] Richard Harter Fogle, 'John Taaffe's Annotated Copy of *Adonais*', *Keats-Shelley Journal* 17 (1968): 31–52 (45).
[29] *The Vision*, trans. Cary, vol. 1. 5n.
[30] This account has much in common with Alan Weinberg's pertinent observations in a footnote: 'What is sometimes taken to be self-pity on the part of the poet is really a dramatic representation of the limitations and inadequacies of the aspiring poet, or indeed of poetry itself. The speaker engages in an implicit act of self-confrontation. One thinks of Dante-pilgrim whose imperfections, as poet and pilgrim, are mirrored throughout Purgatory', 294–5n.
[31] Fogle, 'Dante and Shelley's *Adonais*', 15.

chant, and indeed ebbing confidence or resulting qualification, as is seen in the remainder of the stanza in question (the whole is quoted for convenience):

> Peace, peace! he is not dead, he doth not sleep—
> He hath awakened from the dream of life—
> 'Tis we, who lost in stormy visions, keep
> With phantoms an unprofitable strife,
> And in mad trance, strike with our spirit's knife
> Invulnerable nothings.—*We* decay
> Like corpses in a charnel; fear and grief
> Convulse us and consume us day by day,
> And cold hopes swarm like worms within our living clay.
>   (39. 343–51)

The 'dream of life' idea is what takes over here, as Shelley focuses on the survivors, named as 'we', for whom 'life' turns out with devastating appositeness to rhyme with 'unprofitable strife'. The first lines send their reverberations through the stanza, and their radiant music never wholly fades, yet something darker and more dissonant emerges from that radiant music as the stanza finds its way to its desolate, sardonic close: 'And cold hopes swarm like worms within our living clay'.

The Spenserian stanza is programmed to achieve different effects from those more suited to *terza rima*. As suggested earlier, it can highlight moments that are starkly individual, as in the just-quoted stanza's opening challenge to conventional understanding of death and life; at the same time it can intimate prolonged reverberations and internal qualification, as in the reworking here of the 'charnel' image; see, by contrast and connection, the earlier beautiful but sinister reference to the 'vault of blue Italian day' (7. 59) as Adonais's 'fitting charnel-roof' (7. 60). That said, the Dantean offer of paradise is potent. In the medieval poet's depiction, Aristotelian whatness informs Platonic idea. Shelley's stance depends on a post-Dantean combination of these great complementary, warring thinkers in the Western tradition in which the lure of the ideal takes fully on board the claims of the material. In Stanza 52, for instance, Shelley brings his own dramatizing involvement with shifting possibilities to the fore:

> The One remains, the many change and pass;
> Heaven's light forever shines, Earth's shadows fly;
> Life, like a dome of many-coloured glass,
> Stains the white radiance of Eternity,
> Until Death tramples it to fragments. —Die,
> If thou wouldst be with that which thou dost seek!
> Follow where all is fled!—Rome's azure sky,
> Flowers, ruins, statues, music, words, are weak
> The glory they transfuse with fitting truth to speak.
>   (52. 460–8)

The stanza might be difficult to assign with certainty to a Dantean original, yet it feels like one of those passages where Shelley has completely absorbed a Dantean mode of thinking, an absorption that coalesces with his own readiness to explore and allow for divagation and shifts. It begins with unadorned Platonic statement, 'The One remains, the many change and pass'; it passes into apparent illustration that, through the dynamism of the image, transforms our grasp of the opening statement, since the image leaves us caught between 'white radiance' and 'dome of many-coloured glass', and possibly flinching at the brutalism of 'Death tramples it to fragments'. Then, as in some speeded-up involvement of the pilgrim-poet's function in Dante, the emphasis becomes openly subjective, for all Shelley's use of an apparently other-directed imperative: 'Die, / If thou wouldst be with that which thou dost seek! / Follow where all is fled'. The 'thou' here is the self; the power of the poetry has to do with the poet's and the reader's impulse both to 'Follow' and to shrink from the virtually screamed-out imperative, 'Die'. At the stanza's end the poetry drives towards a glimpse of near-inexpressibility; yet the very Dantean word 'transfuse'—one might compare 'trasumanar' in the first canto of *Paradiso*—implies a moving between realms at odds with the absolute distinctions made earlier in Shelley's poem. Mediation between the mortal and the eternal may be possible, language not only strained beyond as 'weak' (52. 467), but able, despite its limitations, to gesture 'with fitting truth' towards 'glory' (52. 468).

Stanza 54 also exemplifies the way in which 'new relations are ever developed' (*Major Works*, 693) through Shelley's response to Dante:

> That Light whose smile kindles the Universe,
> That Beauty in which all things work and move,
> That Benediction which the eclipsing Curse
> Of birth can quench not, that sustaining Love
> Which through the web of being blindly wove
> By man and beast and earth and air and sea,
> Burns bright or dim, as each are mirrors of
> The fire for which all thirst, now beams on me,
> Consuming the last clouds of cold mortality.
>
> (54. 478–86)

As one responds to this passage, one is conscious of the reaction in the poetry against some of the more pessimistic accounts of the human condition that have preceded it. The vision here is hostile, yes, to 'the last clouds of cold mortality', and is able to speak in near-Gnostic terms of 'the eclipsing curse / Of birth', and, moreover in 'the web of being blindly wove', it implies something close to the sense of hapless hap typical of Thomas Hardy.[32] Yet this negative view of life does not erase the splendour of affirmation in the reference to 'That Light whose smile kin- dles the Universe, / That Beauty in which all things work and move, / That Benediction which the eclipsing Curse / Of birth can quench not; that sustaining Love': Light, Beauty, Benediction, and Love kindle and sustain the poetry, transfer our attention to the ideals they embody. Shelley encapsulates great swathes of beatific suggestion in the *Paradiso* in the noun 'smile'; Peter S. Hawkins even goes

---

[32] Weinberg sees the 'main body of the stanza' as qualifying its initial reference to 'Light' 'in terms of the very opening lines of *Paradiso* I', 199. My emphasis is more on the radically dark nature of Shelley's qualification.

so far as to comment that 'the smile is not only Dante's signature gesture but perhaps his most original and indeed useful contribution to medieval theology— and indeed to the Christian tradition itself'.[33] At the same time, the repeated use of 'That', splendidly affirmative in one way, seems, in another, at least subliminally, a symptom of over-insistence, as though Shelley were demanding that he and we believe in the real existence of abstract ideals which much in experience seems to negate. 'That Light' turns to Dante for support, while accepting that such a turn is a reconfirmation that poetry is, as Shelley phrases it in *A Defence of Poetry*, 'vitally metaphorical' (*Major Works*, 676): both life-giving and a question of fictions.

In *A Defence of Poetry* Shelley praises Dante for the way in which 'as by steps he feigns himself to have ascended to the throne of the Supreme Cause'; as embodied in the *Paradiso*, this feigning adds up, for Shelley, to 'the most glorious imagination of modern poetry' (*Major Works*, 691). It is indeed, the 'feigning' idealism at work in a stanza such as 54 that gives the lie to Bloom's persuasively if perversely elo- quent account of the stanza: 'In this straining upward', writes Bloom, 'the natural world that is given to us becomes only a darkness'.[34] Dante has provided Shelley with a vocabulary for the later poet's deep wish to believe that there is, ultimately, a guarantor of goodness and harmony. Dante will call this guarantor God; Shelley, through his use of multiple terms, uses words that, in one mood, that of the sceptical voice heard in the first half of stanza 3 of 'Hymn to Intellectual Beauty', he might regard as the records of humanity's 'vain endeavour' (25) to come up with answers to ultimate questions. But, in another mood, one that prevails, they seem like necessary fictions or imaginings that nourish hope.

Dante's presence in stanza 54 is pervasive and subtle. As the Longman editors of *Adonais* note (and before them Fogle and Taaffe), one analogue is provided by the opening lines of *Paradiso* 1:

> La gloria di colui che tutto move
>   per l' universo penetra, e risplende
>   in una parte più, e meno altrove.
>   (1–3)
>
> (His glory, by whose might all things are mov'd,
> Pierces the universe, and in one part
> Sheds more resplendence, elsewhere less.)

Dante commented on these verses in the *Letter to Cangrande* (if he was the author of the letter), arguing, as Robert Hollander glosses the matter, 'that we are to find the glory of God's Being reflected in all that exists in His secondary creation':[35] a philosophically nuanced account. Shelley is more rhetorically extreme, at a stretch, not beginning an ascent towards a vision of God with a masterly exposition, but ending an unstable, virtually post-Christian elegy with a hoped-for clutching at

---

[33] Peter S. Hawkins, *Dante: A Brief History* (Malden: Blackwell, 2006), 129.
[34] Harold Bloom, *The Visionary Company: A Reading of English Romantic Poetry*, rev. and enlarged edn (Ithaca: Cornell University Press, 1971), 349.
[35] Dante Alighieri, *Paradiso*, verse translation by Robert and Jean Hollander, intro and notes by Robert Hollander (New York: Doubleday, 2007), 13.

imperishable ideals he remembers from Dante. Shelley retains a stronger sense of all that resists his absolute, even as he allows it to act on him in a way that recalls St Bernard's prayer to Mary on behalf of Dante in the final canto of the *Paradiso*: 'perchè tu ogni nube gli disleghi / di sua mortalità' (that thou wouldst drive / Each cloud of his mortality away) (33. 31–2). Bernard asks this so that Dante might gaze on 'il sommo piacer' (the sovran pleasure, as Cary has it; the Hollanders prefer 'beauty' for 'piacer') (l. 33). Noting this echo, Weinberg comments that 'Shelley puts the emphasis on "self" ("beams on me"), whereas Dante stresses vision'.[36] Shelley does not intercede; he claims and asserts. It is the woven, sustaining force of imaginative will and power that will ensure the consumption of cold mortality.

And yet, true to his own originality, Shelley then segues into the next and final stanza with a re-emergence of the fear and uncertainty which track the poetry's flight of fire in this final section. He has already alerted us to this fear when in the triply 'shrinking' formulation of stanza 53, line 469, 'Why linger, why turn back, why shrink, my Heart?', he reprises Virgil's questions to Dante at the close of *Inferno* 2:[37]

> Dunque che è? perchè, perchè ristai?
> perchè tanta viltà nel core allette?
> perchè ardire e franchezza non hai...
> (ll. 121–3)
> (What is this comes o'er thee then?
> Why, why dost thus hang back? why in thy breast
> Harbour vile fear? Why has thou not courage there,
> And noble daring?)

Virgil's very manner, his advocacy of freedom enacted by the unusual enjambment at the end of the tercet, gives Dante new heart, as the subsequent simile of the fainting flowers renewing their life at dawn bears witness (ll. 127–9). Yet in Shelley's hands, in the context of what feels like deep personal sorrow, Dantean question sheds its exhortatory vigour to a degree, and we detect the poet's fear, a fear which persists in the remarkable final stanza:

> The breath whose might I have invoked in song
> Descends on me; my spirit's bark is driven
> Far from the shore, far from the trembling throng
> Whose sails were never to the tempest given;
> The massy earth and sphered skies are riven!
> I am borne darkly, fearfully, afar;
> Whilst burning through the inmost veil of Heaven,
> The soul of Adonais, like a star,
> Beacons from the abode where the Eternal are.
> (55. 487–95)

As commentators have noted, Shelley begins with a glance at the opening of *Paradiso*, canto 2.[38] There, Dante suggest that 'voi, che siete in piccioletta barca, / desiderosi

[36] Weinberg, *Shelley's Italian Experience*, 197.   [37] See Weinberg, 196.
[38] For a full discussion, see Weinberg, 197–8.

d'ascoltar' (ye, who in small bark have following sail'd, / Eager to listen) (ll 1–2) should 'tornate a rivider li vostri liti' (Backward return with speed, and your own shores / Revisit) (l. 4) lest they go astray. Dante asserts his originality: 'L'acqua ch' io prendo giammai non si corse' (The way I pass, / Ne'er yet was run—Cary's version does less than justice to 'L'acqua', rendered by the Hollanders as 'The seas') (l. 7). Shelley affirms a state of inspiration. It is common to note the gap between Dante and Shelley. As Weinberg writes: Dante 'has a structured universe and the company of Beatrice to guide his way. Between the bard and the soul of *Adonais*, on the other hand, there is the emptiness of space'.[39] And certainly, in turning to Dante, Shelley marks the points at which he and his great predecessor diverge. But it is also the case that being borne 'darkly, fearfully' is what makes possible the poet's fictions of some final exalted glory.

The very gap between quester and goal affirms the possible existence of the latter. Shelley will, one imagines, have responded strongly to lines in *Paradiso*, canto 3, in which the pilgrim views spiritual beings as though they were shadows. A beautiful simile concerned with mirroring and reflections explains itself thus:

> tali vid' io più facce a parlar pronte,
>   perch' io dentro all' error contrario corsi
>   a quell ch' accese amor tra l' uomo el il fonte.
> (ll. 16–18)

> (such saw I many a face,
> All stretched to speak, from whence I straight conceived
> Delusion opposite to that, which raised,
> Between the man and fountain, amorous flame.)

Cary glosses his word 'Delusion' as though Dante were saying: 'An error contrary to that of Narcissus; because he mistook a shadow for a substance, I, a substance for a shadow'.[40] Dante partly frees Shelley from his self-suspicion, dating back at least to the reflexive enigmas of *Alastor*, that he is mistaking 'a shadow for a substance', offering the Romantic poet an idiom to develop the optimism made possible by doubt and uncertainty: the belief that one might, after all, be mistaking 'a substance for a shadow'. *Adonais*, as it turns to Dante, hopes that the metaphorical has a reality, that, though the poet is 'borne, darkly, fearfully, afar', he is moving far from a world that has lost meaning towards a dimension where, as in the *Paradiso*, he can meet soul-fulfilling realities.[41] That this imagined movement remains a burning hope, a shadow-ridden aspiration, reminds us of the burden placed on the shoulders of this Romantic answer to Dante's 'sacrato poema'. Shelley captures the way in which Dante reappears in *Adonais* when he describes the workings of influence in these lines:

> When lofty thought
> Lifts a young heart above its mortal lair,

---

[39] Weinberg, 198.   [40] *The Vision*, trans. Cary, vol. 3, 22n.
[41] For insightful commentary on the 'rhetorical process' of *Adonais*, see Mark Sandy, *Politics of Self and Form in Keats and Shelley: Nietzschean Subjectivity* (Aldershot: Ashgate, 2005), 107.

And love and life contend in it, for what
Shall be its earthly doom, the dead live there
And move like winds of light on dark and stormy air.
(44. 392–6)

The 'dead' may be plural, but the noun might be applied to Dante's verses and images, the way in which they 'live' in Shelley's poem, one that continually, as in the last stanza, moves between 'the dark and stormy' and 'light'. The phrase 'winds of light' has a Dantean resonance, recalling innumerable image-patterns throughout the *Paradiso* (compare canto 25, 79–81). Yet 'winds of light' have an auto-poetic quality. They do not speak of an approach to the Empyrean; rather, they suggest the currents of Dante-illuminated inspiration available to a poet exiled from the medieval poet's belief-system. Shelley's lines here themselves 'move like winds of light on dark and stormy air', with their striving rhymes that draw attention to the operations of poetic desire: the unparaphrasable 'what' towards which 'lofty thought' aims in a suggestive off-rhyme, the 'there' that is brought into view by the poetry's own 'dark and stormy air'. But the dead verses of Dante live again in *Adonais*, resurrected with a creative flair that ensures originality embeds itself in a spirited and independent honouring of previous poetic achievement.

12

'The Inmost Spirit of Light'

Shelley and Turner

The Cambridge Companion to Shelley has a detail from Turner's incandescent watercolour, *The Burning of the Houses of Parliament, from the Palace Courtyard* (*c.* 1834) on its front cover.[1] Turner is used to illustrate anything and everything, of course, but it seems to me legitimate to view the choice of cover-image as evidence that many Shelleyans think of their poet as Turneresque. For a Shelleyan, the apocalyptic conflagration blazing forth from the cover of the *Cambridge Companion* bears more than a casual resemblance to moments such as Jupiter's overthrow in *Prometheus Unbound*, where Shelley evokes 'the last glare of day's red agony, / Which, from a rent among the fiery clouds, / Burns far along the tempest-wrinkled deep' (III. ii. 7–9).[2] Turner's river in his two oil paintings of the 1834 fire has ripples of cool-green quiet amidst the reflected inferno, while Shelley's 'deep' is 'tempest-wrinkled', but in the same scene Ocean speaks of 'the unpastured sea hungering for calm' (III. ii. 49). Painter and poet show affinities in their juxtaposition of serenity and turbulence. 'Some say the world will end in fire', wrote Robert Frost, mindful of the word's Shelleyan chime with 'desire'.[3] Shelley and Turner were among their number. Both were prone to welcome the resmelting of an old world in the furnace of words and paint; both knew such burning away might also induce regret.

Whether admirers of Turner see their painter as Shelleyan is perhaps a more questionable point. Some shun the comparison, as though to make out it delivers Turner over to an otherworldly Shelley, longing for 'some world far from ours' ('To Jane: "The Keen Stars Were Twinkling"', 22). But that longing coexists in Shelley with many this-worldly feelings and pulls. On the other side, there have always been those who wish to propose a link. A review in the *Athenaeum* of *Mercury*

---

[1] A. J. Finberg, *A Complete Inventory of the Drawings of the Turner Bequest* (London: Darling & son, 1909), CCCLXIV, 373.

[2] Quoted from *Major Works*. Shelley's poetry and prose will be quoted from this edition unless stated otherwise. This book also has a Turner image on its cover, a detail from his *Sunset*; the choice of image was designed to suggest the coexistence of light and shadow in the poet's vision. For a previous discussion of poet and painter, see J. Drummond Bone, 'Turner and Shelley: The Sense of a Comparison', *The Romantic Imagination: Literature and Art in England and Germany*, ed. Frederick Burwick and Jürgen Klein (Amsterdam: Rodopi, 1996), 202–22.

[3] Robert Frost, *Collected Poems of Robert Frost* (London: Cape, 1943).

and Argus (1836),[4] described Turner's painting as 'another of his rainbow-toned rhapsodies, a thing like much of Shelley's poetry, to be felt rather than understood: here, too, he has given full vent to his poetical imagination, and, we grieve to add, extravagant colouring'.[5] 'Extravagant colouring' (which one would want to see in a more positive light than the *Athenaeum*'s reviewer) binds the two artists, as does their awareness of the beauty and horror lit up by the sun's radiance. Turner's painting may seem pastoral, even idyllic. Yet its subject is sombre. It depicts Mercury, at Zeus's command, lulling the hundred-eyed Argus to sleep with his flute-playing; when asleep, Mercury will cut off his head and bear away Io, Argus's wife, changed to a cow because of the jealousy of Hera, Zeus's consort. The plot shadowing this canvas reminds us that, at his most apparently 'rainbow-hued' and rhapsodic, Turner, like Shelley, is alive to the potential illusoriness of beauty. Tellingly, in *The Triumph of Life*, Shelley's most disquieting work, the juggernaut-like car of life reappears with 'the vermilion / And green and azure plumes of Iris' (439–40) building 'A moving arch of victory over it' (439); what should be an image of beauty undergoes perversion into one of frightening power.

In a comparable way, the *Wreck Buoy*,[6] greeted by *The Literary Gazette* as 'A wonderful specimen of [Turner's] power in colours',[7] has been read by John Gage as 'essentially a pessimistic work', its rainbows 'emblems of fallacious hope'.[8] Such pessimism, Gage argues, also pervades *Light and Colour (Goethe's Theory)—the Morning after the Deluge—Moses Writing the Book of Genesis*,[9] which was exhibited in 1843, with these lines said to be from Turner's manuscript poem, *Fallacies of Hope*, as part of the caption:

> The ark stood firm on Ararat; th' returning sun
> Exhaled earth's humid bubbles, and emulous of light,
> Reflected her lost forms, each in prismatic guise
> Hope's harbinger, ephemeral as the summer fly
> Which rises, flits, expands, and dies.[10]

Yet, true to another quality shared by Shelley and Turner, a capacity for double-mindedness, nothing is one thing only in this painter's work. The prismatic lights of the *Wreck Buoy* may only seem to be illusory; they may betoken genuine hope and redemption. These paintings are as enigmatic in their overall vision as, say, Shelley's *Adonais* and, especially, *The Triumph of Life*, are. *Light and Colour* may take issue with Goethe's colour theory, or it may wish, especially when paired with *Shade and Darkness—The Evening of the Deluge* (1843),[11] to illustrate the co-presence of light and shade. On this interpretation, the painting finds a way out of pessimism by virtue of emphasizing the never-ending production of alternatives in life, nature,

    [4] Martin Butlin and Evelyn Joll, *The Paintings of J. M. W. Turner* (2 vols [1977] New Haven: Yale University Press, rev. edn 1984), 367. Catalogue numbers, as here, are given without 'p' in front of them; material quoted from the 'Texts' volume is preceded by 'p'.
    [5] Butlin and Joll, *Paintings of Turner*, 219.   [6] Butlin and Joll, *Paintings of Turner*, 428.
    [7] Butlin and Joll, *Paintings of Turner*, p. 273.   [8] Ibid.
    [9] Butlin and Joll, *Paintings of Turner*, 405.   [10] Butlin and Joll, *Paintings of Turner*, p. 230.
    [11] Butlin and Joll, *Paintings of Turner*, 404.

and experience, much as Shelley's questioning in *The Triumph of Life* means that the poem cannot simply be read as undermining his supposed earlier optimism.[12] 'Figures ever new / Rise on the bubble, paint them how you may' (248–9): Rousseau's words may warn the Poet that there is no escape from involvement in life, but they remind us, too, of the poem's own participation in the production of 'Figures', and might serve as a gloss on Turner's *Light and Colour*, at the heart of which is the presiding presence of Moses writing Genesis and acting as a surrogate of the ever-creative and transfiguring painter. Turner and Shelley hymn change and lament evanescence in a blink of a line-ending or swish of a brushstroke; to try to pin them down to either praise or lament is nearly always to simplify.

In developing this point, one might consider the passage from Shelley's *Julian and Maddalo* from which this chapter's title is adapted. Julian, optimistic, a believer in human perfectibility, perhaps a delicately ironized self-portrait on Shelley's part, describes in rapturous terms a Venetian sunset:

> [...] the hoar
> And aery Alps towards the North appeared
> Through mist, an heaven-sustaining bulwark reared
> Between the East and West; and half the sky
> Was roofed with clouds of rich emblazonry
> Dark purple at the zenith, which still grew
> Down the steep West into a wondrous hue
> Brighter than burning gold, even to the rent
> Where the swift sun yet paused in his descent
> Among the many-folded hills: they were
> Those famous Euganean hills, which bear
> As seen from Lido through the harbour piles
> The likeness of a clump of peakèd isles—
> And then—as if the Earth and Sea had been
> Dissolved into one lake of fire, were seen
> Those mountains towering as from waves of flame
> Around the vaporous sun, from which there came
> The inmost purple spirit of light, and made
> Their very peaks transparent.
>
> (67–85)

Here guidebook picturesque undergoes visionary transformation. Julian may note that the 'many-folded hills' were 'those famous Euganean hills', but his own swiftly unfolding couplets attune themselves to a scene which changes second by second, and is the very reverse of a static descriptive piece. The clouds are 'Dark purple at the zenith', but this is a 'purple' which 'still grew / Down the steep West into a wondrous hue / Brighter than burning gold'; 'still grew'—even as he speaks, Julian notices change, alert to the sky as a vertically slanting space in which a near-alchemical process is taking place, one that produces 'a wondrous hue / Brighter than burning gold', one, that is, to which 'burning gold', in all its aureate splendour, is only an

---

[12] For more on this approach to *The Triumph of Life*, see the last chapter of O'Neill, *The Human Mind's Imaginings*.

approximation. Julian has his eyes and senses open to the truth of 'appearances' and '*impression*', to borrow the terms of Barry Venning's gloss on Ruskin's praise of Turner,[13] an openness which shows in that strong image of 'the rent / Where the swift sun yet paused' (a phrase which allows adjective and verb to vibrate in a 'swift' tension).

What cries out to be described as 'Turneresque' is the simile of earth and sky 'Dissolved into one lake of fire'. Dissolution into flame means that water and light intermingle, while mountains tower as from 'waves of flame', a metamorphosis affecting and induced by 'the vaporous sun', which turns the solid mountains into forms that are 'transparent'. Typical of Shelley in its fascination with change ('I change, but I cannot die' (76), affirms the speaker of 'The Cloud'), with forms yielding up their separateness, the passage is among the strongest intimations of a shared affinity between poet and painter.

For all that affinity, Shelley never wrote of Turner. Mary Shelley records, in May 1817, a visit to view 'Turner's Landscape'; if this was *The Decline of the Carthaginian Empire*,[14] exhibited in 1817, Shelley would have encountered a further example of light as portent of menace rather than emblem of celebration, plus a caption that refers both to 'Hope's delusive smile' and to 'th' ensanguined sun [*sic*]';[15] however, Turner's *Dolbadern Castle, North Wales* (1800),[16] his Diploma Work for the Royal Academy, was also on view in the Academy and it may have been that work to which the journal entry refers.[17] At the same time, Turner's knowledge of Shelley seems at best scanty, even though it has been argued that there may be an allusion to *Lines Written among the Euganean Hills* in the lines appended to *The Sun of Venice Going to Sea*.[18] But it is probable that one should be speaking more of a parallel with (rather than debt to) the awareness of sadness and depression in Shelley. Turner's lines, clearly indebted to Gray's *The Bard*,[19] read: 'Fair Shines the morn, and soft the zephyrs blow, / Venezia's fisher spreads his painted sail so gay, / Nor heeds the demon that in grim repose / Expects his evening prey';[20] Shelley's lines imagine a time after Venice has sunk back beneath the waves, when 'The fisher on his watery way, / Wandering at the close of day, / Will spread his sail and seize his oar / Till he pass the gloomy shore' (134–7). Still, it is likely that Shelley would have known Hazlitt's review of Turner in the *Examiner*, which contains the infamous but suggestive comment that foreshadows the same critic's attack on Shelley's *Posthumous Poems*: Hazlitt does concede that Turner is 'the ablest landscape-painter now living', but he contends that his paintings are 'too much abstractions of aerial perspective, and representations not properly of the objects of nature as of the medium through which they were seen'. 'They are pictures', writes Hazlitt, characteristically sharpening his style towards piquant summary, 'of the elements of air, earth, and water ... All is without form and void. Someone said of his late images that they were *pictures of nothing*,

---

[13] Barry Venning, *Turner* (London: Phaidon, 2003), 271.
[14] Butlin and Joll, *Paintings of Turner*, 135.   [15] Butlin and Joll, *Paintings of Turner*, p. 89.
[16] Butlin and Joll, *Paintings of Turner*, 12.   [17] *MWS Journals*, 170 (and note).
[18] See John Gage, *Colour in Turner: Poetry and Truth* (London: Studio Vista, 1969), pp. 145–7; Butlin and Joll, *Paintings of Turner*, 402.
[19] Butlin and Joll, *Paintings of Turner*, p. 228.   [20] Ibid.

and very like.[21] Regardless of mutual influence or awareness, however, Turner and Shelley exhibit at times a startling similarity, both in thematic terms and in terms of their angles of vision and affective impact on viewer or reader.

One might set alongside the depiction of the Venetian sunset in *Julian and Maddalo* any number of Turner's representations of that 'strange Dream upon the water', as Dickens calls Venice.[22] Many show his fascination with the city's infinite play of reflections, meltings, architecture forming oneiric marriages with water and sky, effects of lucid transparency seen through washes of light that seem paradoxically to form a veil. One example might be *Sunset over Santa Maria della Salute and the Dogana* (1840).[23] Quieter than the Shelleyan vision in *Julian and Maddalo*, this watercolour reworks the Venetian sunset into a wash of pale yellows and lilac-blues. The spectator is plunged into a lake of colour, if not of fire, in which, without losing its identity as a real place (Turner, as Ian Warrell observes, does 'not destroy the illusion of depth within the image'), the Venetian scene becomes an iridescent dream.[24] The buildings both resist and succumb to a de-materializing weightlessness as they float above grey reflections that at once shimmer through and inscribe themselves on an underwater realm of opalescent yellow. Even to speak of an 'underwater realm' ignores how Turner melts boundaries; substance and reflection take on equal validity in the new world of his art. In a way, this satisfies the demands of realism since, as Warrell notes, 'Turner perfectly captures the eye's inability to pick out detail when looking at objects against the light'.[25] At the same time, as often in Romantic artistic productions, another kind of seeing is made possible by the shutting down of normal modes of perception. For a further metamorphic sunset, one might turn to another watercolour by Turner of the Dogana, one entitled *The Punta della Dogana at Sunset, with the Domes of Santa Maria della Salute* (1840).[26] Here, as we look towards the inmost spirit of light, the Dogana, in Warrell's memorable image, turns into the 'prow of an otherworldly boat, bearing down on the viewer through the hazy sunlight'.[27] Turner's colours are, as often, impossible to see separately; they blur, form a continuous and imperceptible series of fine gradations. They remind us by contrast and yet by connection that Shelley speaks of 'the inmost purple spirit of light'. Turner is unafraid of tints, as in this watercolour, that smoulder on the edge of turning into a purple brilliance. Shelleyan 'purples', in evidence in *Prometheus Unbound* where the 'mountains' are said to be 'purple' (II. i. 19) or in 'Stanzas Written in Dejection—December 1818, near Naples', in which he declares that 'Blue isles and snowy mountains wear / The purples noon's transparent might' (3–4), are in fluid contact with and run into other colours—here 'Blue', in the passage from *Prometheus Unbound* the 'orange light of widening morn' (II. i. 18)—and mark

[21] Quoted from *Complete Works of William Hazlitt*, ed. P. P. Howe, 21 vols. (London: Dent, 1930–4), 4. 76n.
[22] Charles Dickens, 'American Notes' and 'Pictures from Italy' ([1865] London: Macmillan, 1903), 293.
[23] Finberg, *Turner Bequest*, CCCXV, 14.
[24] Ian Warrell, with essays by David Laven, Jan Morris, and Cecilia Powell, *Turner and Venice* (London: Tate Publishing, 2003), 214.
[25] Warrell et al., *Turner and Venice*, 209.   [26] Finberg, *Turner Bequest*, CCCXV, 15.
[27] Finberg, *Turner Bequest*, CCCXV, p. 214.

his response to one intensified solar effect. The use of 'purple' is both objective and subjective in his poetry; it bears witness to an intense Italian light and to Shelley's participation in the scene, colouring it with his impressions. Indeed, 'Stanzas Written in Dejection' dramatizes in its own nuanced lyrical terms the poet's intense response to a natural world from which he is also an outcast.

Underpinning the connections to be made between painter and poet on the basis of this juxtaposition of Venetian scenes is Turner's own sense that 'Poesy & Painting, being sisters agree intirely', even if he also saw that practitioners of both arts worked '*by very different* means'.[28] The first connection is that, to use a word significant for Shelley, their work impresses us as 'imaginings' (see the penultimate line of *Mont Blanc*), as involving a tussle between self and reality. You feel that Venice is proof for Julian that Italy is a 'Paradise of exiles' (*Julian and Maddalo*, 57), with its 'temples and its palaces' seeming 'Like fabrics of enchantment piled to Heaven' (*Julian and Maddalo*, 91, 92). Here undercurrents come into play. We are exiled from paradise; the miraculous vision of Venice cannot last. It is on the point, this vision, not simply of capturing the dissolution of form by and into light, but of rendering its own disappearance. Shelley's submerged allusion to *The Tempest* reminds us of Prospero's sense that the 'baseless fabric of this vision' will 'Leave not a wrack behind' (IV. i. 151, 156).

At this point in the poem, too, the darkness that stands in sharp and jolting contrast to the light celebrated by poet and painter comes into view. Maddalo, based on Byron, but almost a Shelleyan alter ego, offers an altogether different Venice: he takes Julian to what ironically he calls 'A better station' (87):

> I looked, and saw between us and the sun
> A building on an island; such a one
> As age to age might add, for uses vile,
> A windowless, deformed and dreary pile,
> And on the top an open tower, where hung
> A bell, which in the radiance swayed and swung.
> We could just hear its hoarse and iron tongue.
> The broad sun sunk behind it, and it tolled
> In strong and black relief.
>
> (98–106)

This 'building' brings into the poem human suffering and cruelty, and ambiguity; it represents a madhouse, Maddalo says, interpreting it as 'the emblem and the sign / Of what should be eternal and divine' (121–2). Julian's rapturous vision now appears just that: a vision, one threatened by a different, darker, more broodingly pessimistic outlook, but an outlook that is itself partial, even theatrical in its self-mocking way. Maddalo, impresario of life as doom and disaster, is himself conscious that human beings see in fundamentally different ways.

Turner has more than his share of Maddalo-like moments: radiance wrestles with and might even serve to make visible portents of horror, as in *Snow Storm: Hannibal*

---

[28] Quoted in James A. W. Heffernan, *The Re-creation of Landscape: A Study of Wordsworth, Coleridge, Constable, and Turner* (Hanover: University Press of New England, 1985), 47.

Crossing the Alps (1812),[29] with its vortices of storm and cloud surrounding the sun's dismal spotlight. The anti-gravitational weightless shimmer of his late Venetian scenes cannot, as they almost seem to, conceal his awareness of Venice as not just an aesthetic playground for jaded Northern sensibilities in need of sunlight, but also as suggesting parallels with another maritime empire, Britain. Turner saw Venice through Byronic eyes as the elegiac memorial of former greatness as well as the scene of present wonder; he was alert to what Olivier Meslay calls the city's 'tragic impression of decay mingled with pride'.[30] Vanishing, mutability, process, the shifting relativism of our perspectives: these Shelleyan themes, brought to a focus in *Julian and Maddalo* and taking on (as that poem shows) both buoyant and depressive inflections, find their pictorial correlative in Turner's Venetian works, whose art seems itself heroically to win from evanescence its own mirror-image and stay. Sky and water, buildings and ships, stakes and gondolas: all tremble and quiver in wash after wash of oil or watercolour; forms simultaneously and miraculously assert themselves in the act of vanishing, even as they vanish in the process of leaving their memory-trace on paper or canvas. In *Venice: San Giorgio Maggiore—Early Morning* (1819),[31] the church holds its visible shape in the presence, but it also floats in the greens, greys, and yellows of a post-dawn sky and reflection-laden lagoon. The image is a quiet annunciation; the world of Venice, freighted by history (former greatness, subsequent decline), seems reborn, and yet even in so delicate a work as this, one senses that Turner's rapt attentive gaze knows of its own refusal to depict befores and afters of a more troubling kind.

Ruskin speaks of the Venetian work as 'secret in fulness, confused in symmetry, as nature herself is to the bewildered and foiled glance, giving out of that indistinctness, and through that confusion, the perpetual newness of the infinite, and the beautiful'.[32] Indistinctness may have been Turner's 'fault', but it is also his 'forte'. The same is true of Shelley in, say, *Epipsychidion*, bidding us 'See where she stands!' (112) after a description of such intricate visionary intensity that normal 'seeing' has been cancelled, replaced by a new mode of perception, intent on making us conscious that Emily is 'Scarce visible from extreme loveliness' (104).[33] What Ruskin refers to as the 'perpetual newness of the infinite, and the beautiful' haunts Julian, who loves 'all waste / And solitary places, where we taste / The pleasure of believing what we see / Is boundless, as we wish our souls to be' (15–18). There, the qualifying hints in 'taste', 'pleasure', 'believing what we see', and, above all, 'wish' intimate that Julian's words describe a Romantic yearning for the sublime, yes, but one that is open to inspection, possibly even irony.[34] Shelley and Turner converge

---

[29] Butlin and Joll, *Paintings of Turner*, 126.
[30] Olivier Meslay, *J. M. W. Turner: The Man Who Set Painting on Fire*, trans. from the French *Turner L'incendie de la peinture* by Ruth Sharman ([2004] London: Thames and Hudson, 2005), 78.
[31] Finberg, *Turner Bequest*, CLXXXI, 4.
[32] Ruskin, *Modern Painters* 1; quoted in Dinah Birch, *Ruskin on Turner* (London: Cassell, 1990), 125.
[33] See Harold Bloom, 'Visionary Cinema of Romantic Poetry', *The Ringers in the Tower* (Chicago: University of Chicago Press, 1971), 51.
[34] For valuable discussion of the sublime in Turner, see Andrew Wilton, *Turner and the Sublime* (London: British Museum Publications, 1980); Wilton quotes the lines discussed here as an epigraph on 104.

here; acutely alert as both are to the *Fallacies of Hope*, the title of Turner's most famous poem, surviving only in quotations. Each artist in his individual way sustains hope. Demogorgon's 'spells' (IV. 568) at the end of *Prometheus Unbound*, spells to use in the event of a return to the tyranny whose overthrow has been celebrated in Shelley's lyrical drama, include the affecting injunction 'to hope, till Hope creates / From its own wreck the thing it contemplates' (IV. 573–4). The rhyme brings out how hope is inseparable from the courage involved in artistic creativity, a creativity able to survive its own wreckage, and deeply attuned to a process by which the mind 'creates' out of what it 'contemplates'. Poet and painter often depict the process by which hope recreates, however precariously, an image of itself out of its own wreckage.

In *The Re-creation of Landscape*, James Heffernan has written insightfully about the ambivalences involved in Wordsworth's use of the word 'colouring' for 'imaginative transformation'.[35] On the one hand, Wordsworth dislikes poems that 'deviate from the real language of nature, and are coloured by a diction of the Poet's own'; on the other, he says that he has sought 'to choose incidents and situations from common life' and to 'throw over them a certain colouring of imagination', where 'colouring' is used more positively.[36] This Janus-faced behaviour of the word 'colouring' directs us to a tension at the heart of Romantic literature and painting, and, more especially, at the heart of Shelley's and Turner's work: do they play fast and loose with the real, so that we experience an inertly 'weak grasp upon the actual' (F. R. Leavis's hostile phrase in his all-too-influential attack on Shelley), or view '*pictures of nothing, and very like*' (in the words that Hazlitt reports)?[37] Or do they exalt the 'human mind's imaginings' (143), in Shelley's words from the close of *Mont Blanc*, in which he suggests that any sense of meaning or indeed of meaning-lessness is dependent on such imaginings? 'And what', he addresses the mountain in the poem's final twist, 'were thou and earth, and stars, and sea, / If to the human mind's imaginings / Silence and solitude were vacancy?' (142–4).

Turner's images of Venice make the viewer deeply aware of the work done by 'imaginings'; the painter seeks to establish the truth of things 'not as they *are*, but as they *appear*', to use Wordsworth's distinction.[38] His Venice in, say, the oil painting *Venice—Santa Maria della Salute* (1844),[39] is still recognizably a city of domes and spires, stakes, sailboats, and gondolas, but it is even more a cauldron or swimming mix of light and colour. To the left of the top centre, a moon hangs, while cloud, sky, structures, and water are flooded by and shine with an array of glints and tints, swept along by impetuous brushstrokes, impasto lending its own urgency to what is at once panorama, dream, and vision. If objects do not quite annul themselves, they suggest new existences as emblems and symbols. Even the church's domes have kinship with Coleridge's bewitching 'dome of pleasure' (31) in *Kubla Khan*, a

[35] Heffernan, *The Re-creation of Landscape*, 137.
[36] Quoted by Heffernan, *The Re-creation of Landscape*, 137.
[37] F. R. Leavis, *Revaluation: Tradition and Development in English Poetry* (Harmondsworth: Penguin, 1964), 206.
[38] Quoted in Heffernan, *The Re-creation of Landscape*, p. 139.
[39] Butlin and Joll, *Paintings of Turner*, 411.

poem which profoundly affected Shelley's imagination, making its most hauntingly reworked and ambivalent appearance in *Adonais*: 'Life, like a dome of many-coloured glass, / Stains the white radiance of Eternity, / Until Death tramples it to fragments' (52. 462–4). Just as the dome of light 'Stains', in the double sense of 'disfigures' and 'enriches', so, one might wish to argue, light is not only set against darkness in Turner, it is also at war with itself. Here, I think, we arrive at a major link connecting poet and painter. Both at times strain towards a 'white radiance' even as both are more than half in love with 'many-coloured' light. Ruskin accurately notes the transcendent quiver in Turner's *Juliet and her Nurse* (exhibited 1836),[40] set with maverick incongruity in Venice, in which 'Many-coloured mists', as Ruskin puts it, 'are floating above the distant city', mists that both 'rise up into the brightness of the illimitable heaven' and are still in touch with humanity, 'aetherial spirits, souls of the mighty dead breathed out of the tombs of Italy into the blue of her bright heaven'.[41] Down below in St Mark's Square, the living mingle and breathe a less rarefied, more eroticized breath.[42] The painting displays an equal commitment to the 'illimitable' and the 'this-worldly', and shares some of the mingled tonalities of Shelley's prismatic image from *Adonais*.

It is as creators fascinated by process and experiencing a pull towards potentiality, even as they keep their eye on present glories and imperfections, that Shelley and Turner meet most congenially. Jack Lindsay, adroitly and affectingly combining the near-Marxist and the quasi-idealist, defends Turner against the charge that he has 'discarded' the 'human aspect' in a way that defenders of Shelley against a similar allegation might welcome: '. . . from a deeper viewpoint we may claim that the form of vision itself represents a higher level of humanity, something which transcends the levels at which the fallacies of hope operate. Man can now be present only as a pure potentiality'.[43] Especially in their complication of spectatorial viewpoint, there are affinities between many of Turner's paintings and the noonday epiphany in *Lines written among the Euganean Hills*, in which Shelley imagines the noon as 'a vaporous amethyst, / Or an air-dissolvèd star' (288–9), an almost electrical fluid that 'Fills the overflowing sky' (293). Shelley's view is double throughout. It extends panoramically to take in the far Alps 'whose snows are spread / High between the clouds and sun' (308–9), but it does so hot on the heels of the sinuously abrupt close-up of 'a flower / Glimmering at my feet' (304–5). His tetrameters are alive with energy, alert to glimmering, vibrating with a sense of life, especially life 'Interpenetrated' (313) by a consciousness that knows it has 'Darkened this swift stream of song' (312). Here the word 'Darkened' is pictorial as well as metaphorical, and recalls the earlier description of Venice in colours that overwhelm but include the 'altar of dark ocean':

> Lo! the sun upsprings behind,
> Broad, red, radiant, half reclined

---

[40] Butlin and Joll, *Paintings of Turner*, 365.

[41] Ruskin, *Modern Painters* 1; quoted in Birch, *Ruskin on Turner*, 122, 125.

[42] Barry Venning, in *Turner*, suggests that the viewpoint high up over Venice gives us an 'overview of the city's decadence', 234.

[43] Jack Lindsay, *Turner: His Life and Work, A Critical Biography* ([1966] Frogmore: Panther, 1973), 266.

On the level quivering line
Of the waters crystalline;
And before that chasm of light,
As within a furnace bright,
Column, tower, and dome, and spire,
Shine like obelisks of fire,
Pointing with inconstant motion
From the altar of dark ocean
To the sapphire-tinted skies;
As the flames of sacrifice
From the marble shrines did rise,
As to pierce the dome of gold
Where Apollo spoke of old.
                    (*Lines written among the
                    Euganean Hills*, 100–14)

This evocative passage finds an emblem for the poetry's own impulse to transform. It re-imagines the Venetian scene as a 'furnace' in which the elements of 'Column, tower, and dome, and spire' are reforged into 'obelisks of fire'. Some of Turner's most dazzlingly refulgent works suggest themselves as comparisons. The hint towards the end of 'sacrifice' might even briefly recall the terrible radiance that burns at the centre of *Regulus* (reworked 1837).[44] Regulus will be blinded by the Carthaginians and Turner emerges here as a painter for whom the Sun is a fearful, unendurable God. Sir John Gilbert's account of Turner in the act of creation suggests his fury of involvement:

> [Turner] kept on scumbling a lot of white into his picture—nearly all over it [...] The picture was a mass of red and yellow in all varieties. Every object was in this fiery state. He had a large palette, nothing in it but a huge lump of flake-white: he had two or three biggish hog tools to work with, and with these he was driving the white into all the hollows, and every part of the surface. This was the only work he did, and it was the finishing stroke.[45]

'Finishing stroke', indeed, and one that clinches the point that Turner's sense of light can be ambivalent, much as Shelley's treatment of light can. *Regulus* pulls us towards terror, *Lines Written in the Euganean Hills* towards transcendent rapture, but in both works it is clear that what holds might hold only in an unstable, even reversible form. Noting Shelley's explicit but suggestive allusion to 'the mind which feeds this verse / Peopling the lone universe' (318–19), a reticent way of bringing himself centre-stage, one might be prompted to ask, of *Regulus*, a work in which light overwhelms, 'where is the artist?' It is as though the painting's creator, like Milton's God, is 'Dark with excessive bright' (*Paradise Lost*, III. 380).

It is fascinating that both Turner and Shelley conceive of darkness as having a quasi-divine original life, as if one part of their minds subscribed to the heterodox creed that 'In the beginning was darkness'. In *Prometheus Unbound* Demogorgon is almost an exemplification of ultimate sublimity, Shelley's non-theistic rival to God, the force without which Prometheus's will and endurance, and Asia's love and intelligent questing, will come to nothing. It is Demogorgon who presides over the fall of tyranny and the celebration at the close. Shelley's inventive reworking of Milton's Death (there is a strong echo of *Paradise Lost*, II. 666–70 at *Prometheus Unbound*, II. iv. 2–5), Demogorgon exceeds the power of words, and is associated with description-defeating gloom. To reach him, Asia and Panthea must descend into the bottom of a volcano, accompanied by spirits who guide them through 'the grey, void abysm, / Down, down! / Where the air is no prism' (II. iii. 72–4), a place remote from the 'many-coloured' 'dome' or the 'white radiance of Eternity' (*Adonais* 52. 462, 463). Light, so to speak, shadows this 'mighty Darkness' (*Prometheus Unbound*, II. iv. 2). Yet for all the echoes of Milton's Death, Demogorgon has something in common with Shelley's account of poetry in *A Defence of Poetry*; he is an oxymoronically disembodied embodiment of that force which 'subdues to union under its light yoke all irreconcilable things' (*Major Works*, 698). Turner, for his part, lecturing on what he calls the 'livid, watery, subjugated interval of light' in Poussin's *Deluge*, fiercely brushes aside the claims of 'all comparative theory'. He asserts: 'aerial perspective has her limits; and if theory dared to stipulate for aerial hues, peculiar colors or tones of color, she would step to self-destruction. It is here the utmost range of art that should tell. [The] imagination of the artist dwells *enthroned* in his own recess [and] must be incomprehensible as from darkness'.[46] The image of the artist '*enthroned* in his own recess' bears a striking resemblance to Demogorgon's 'veilèd form' on his 'ebon throne' (*Prometheus Unbound* II. iv. 1).

Such a regard for darkness reminds us that light can be terrifying in Romantic painting and a token of unfriendly menace in Romantic literature. The locus classicus of light's treacheries in Romantic poetry is Wordsworth's 'Ode: Intimations of Immortality',[47] in which we enter the world 'trailing clouds of glory' (64), where 'clouds' muffle anything too stridently bright, but as we move away from that original light-source we find ourselves enveloped by the 'light of common day' (76). When the quotidian and the transcendent clash in Romantic poetry, the contest often expresses itself as a clash between differing modes of light. Over and over, Shelley's imagination is possessed by a single image, that of the morning star, vanishing into or extinguished by the dawn. This can be thought of optimistically, as the melting into one another of the ideal and the real, as, for example, in Asia's speech at the beginning of *Prometheus Unbound*, Act II. But as Shelley's career progresses, one might generalize that he grows more aware of 'the contagion of the world's slow stain' (*Adonais*, 40. 356). In *The Triumph of Life*, radiance and treacherous illusion are almost inseparable. We may think that the title offers us something positive, but it does not; the poem gives us, not life triumphing over disaster and evil, but life itself is a terrifying and destructive form of light that triumphs over those who live.

---

[46] Quoted in Gage, *Colour in Turner*, 208–9.
[47] Wordsworth's poetry is quoted from *Wordsworth: Major Works*.

In fact, the sun emerges as an agent of mesmeric obliteration. When the Car of Life appears, it is ushered in by these lines: 'And a cold glare, intense than the noon / But icy cold, obscured with [ ] light / The Sun as he the stars' (77–9).[48] Life presents itself as a series of erasures, blottings out, vanishings, cancellations of a higher form of light by one that retains no memory of that higher form, or at best the ghostliest of traces. Perhaps there is nothing quite comparable in Turner, and, as throughout this chapter, we encounter the problem involved in seeking to make comparisons between artistic media, each of which uses its own particular stylistic idiom, an idiom that is not easily translatable. But there are ambiguities of light in Turner, as we have seen in *The Decline of the Carthaginian Empire*, where the sun that sets over a Claude Lorrain-like scene melts into a refulgent V, whose potential delusiveness is emphasized by the verse-caption that Turner appended. Portentous suns occur elsewhere in Turner, nowhere more so than in the deeply sombre *Slavers Throwing Overboard the Dead and Dying—Typhoon Coming On* (1840).[49] Here Turner depicts one of the atrocities associated with the slave trade, the throwing overboard of the dead and dying so that the slave trader could claim insurance for them. Shelley imagines in *Prometheus Unbound* a scene in which Proteus and his nymphs track the paths of human ships

> no more by blood and groans
> And desolation, and the mingled voice
> Of slavery and command; but by the light
> Of wave-reflected flowers, and floating odours,
> And music soft, and mild, free, gentle voices,
> That sweetest music, such as spirits love.
>   (III. ii. 29–34)

Shelley evokes things as they might and should be by reminding us forcefully of things as they are (for all Britain's abolition of the slave trade in 1807). At the same time, he offers the poem that we are reading as an earnest of the possibility of regeneration, for it is in *Prometheus Unbound* itself that we hear 'That sweetest music, such as spirits love'. In Turner's painting, exhibited twenty years after the publication of Shelley's lyrical drama, light performs a fascinating role; it shows in lurid highlight the horror of manacled limbs sinking beneath the waves. Ruskin, as glossed by James Heffernan, argued that the 'predominantly crimson and scarlet hues of the picture express a judgment on the guilty vessel',[50] and the swathe of swept-up orange and red following in the ship's wake supports this reading. Heffernan also draws attention to an extraordinary effect of Turner's use of light in the picture; namely, the cross that is formed by the shaft of sunlight that cuts vertically through the centre of the picture. There is an effect of waters parted by light, as 'the sun becomes an infinitely blazing cross on which—in effect—the slaves are crucified'.[51] The white sunbeam

---

[48] For the persuasive view that the cancelled word before 'light' is 'lancinating', see *Percy Bysshe Shelley: Opere Poetiche*, ed. Francesco Rognoni (Milan: Mondadori, 2018), 1136, 1529.
[49] Butlin and Joll, *Paintings of Turner*, 385.
[50] Heffernan, *The Re-creation of Landscape*, 180.
[51] Heffernan, *The Re-creation of Landscape*, 181.

is at once beyond and engulfed by the orange, yellow and red; the sunset colours of 'fire and blood' of which Turner speaks both blend and wrestle with an incandescent whiteness.[52]

Turner's ability to suggest light's multiform meanings is evident in other major works, such as *Apollo and Python* (1811),[53] which John Gage explicates via a reference to Richard Payne Knight (jokily alluded to by Shelley in his friendly if deadly serious contest with Peacock about the value of poetry; see *Letters: PBS*, 2. 275). Knight, as Gage notes, was fascinated by 'a wide range of sun cults'.[54] Here is Knight glossing the fable of 'Apollo and the Python': it 'seems [...] to have originated from the mythological language of imitative art; the lithe Apollo signifying [...] the destroyer as well as the deliverer [...] the lizard, being supposed to exist upon the dews and moistures of the earth, was employed as the symbol of humidity [...] the sun exhaling the waters'.[55] The gloss makes a difference: Apollo as 'destroyer as well as [...] deliverer' has something in common with the Destroyer/Preserver, Vishnu/Shiva composite figure that is Shelley's west wind. 'Destroyer and Preserver; hear, O, hear!' ('Ode to the West Wind', 14), cries Shelley to a wind addressed as an 'unseen presence' (2), known through its various manifestations: on the land where it drives 'the leaves dead' (2); in the air where it shakes from the 'tangled boughs of Heaven and Ocean' (17) 'Angels of rain and lightning' (18), where 'Angels' recovers its primary meaning of 'messengers', but keeps to itself a suggestion of radiance amidst terror or apocalypse such as is possessed by Turner's *The Angel Standing in the Sun* (1846);[56] and through the sea.

Ruskin saw *Apollo and Python* in near-Manichaean terms, and reminds us that Apollo's conquest was not 'slightly esteemed by the victor deity', as shown by the fact that 'He took his great name from it thenceforth—his prophetic and sacred name— the Pythian'. 'Apollo's contest with [the Python] is the strife', writes Ruskin, of 'purity with pollution; of life with forgetfulness; of love, with the grave'.[57] Knight would seem to see the struggle in less clear-cut terms, but what both writers valuably underscore about Turner's work is that it derives its power from incessant struggle and tension. Apollo may be victorious, but Python, sickening to behold in one way, in another contributes his share to the glory of Turner's achievement; it, too, is flooded with a golden radiance. If Turner 'is', in Ruskin's words, 'the painter of the loveliness of nature, with the worm at its root',[58] Shelley is a poet we prize because, in the words of his first spirit (in 'the Two Spirits – An Allegory'), 'A shadow tracks thy flight of fire' (3).[59] Both study the external world with the minutest attention to the colours of sunset, manifestations and vanishings, all that speaks of process and mutability, of life comprehended in a post-Newtonian universe as involving endless change;

---

[52] See Lawrence Gowing, *Turner: Imagination and Reality* (New York: Doubleday, 1966), 81.
[53] Butlin and Joll, *Paintings of Turner*, 115.
[54] John Gage, *J. M. W. Turner: 'A Wonderful Range of Mind'* ([1987] New Haven: Yale University Press, 1987), 207.
[55] Gage, *J. M. W. Turner*, 208.   [56] Butlin and Joll, *Paintings of Turner*, 425.
[57] Ruskin, *Modern Painters* V; quoted in Birch, *Ruskin on Turner*, 92.
[58] Ruskin, *Modern Painters* V; quoted in Birch, *Ruskin on Turner*, 93.
[59] For the significance of this line, see Harold Bloom, 'The Unpastured Sea: A Reading of Shelley', in *The Ringers in the Tower*: it should be noted that in Shelley's manuscript the first word is cancelled.

both value beauty for its suggestion of impermanence; both see it as constantly in a dialogue, struggle, or tension with pain, suffering, ugliness, the reality-principle.

Turner depicting the Houses of Parliament on fire; his having been here and fired a gun, in Constable's rueful words; his ability to convert what seemed 'like chaos before the creation' into a masterpiece like 'a magician, performing his incantations in public': all bespeak a kind of improvisatory genius, one that boldly asserts itself in his oils, as it does in many of Shelley's poems, *Epipsychidion*, for instance, where the couplets mime their own warming to life, their own imminent collapse.[60] The paintings of Turner and poems of Shelley are often at once about process and able to embody their own status as artistic products that involved a shaping process, to reflect on their condition of coming into being. In the Cleveland depiction of the burning of the Houses of Parliament (1835),[61] reflection serves to remind us that the artist's watching eye, attentive to detail, is also a transforming one, winning from the windswept orange and yellow combustion a dazzling chasm of reflecting light that irradiates through and across the cool greys and greens of the Thames. For Shelley, too, reflection bears witness to the artist's transformative powers.[62] This is, in part, because, for Shelley, 'Neither the eye or the mind can see itself, unless reflected upon that which it resembles' (*A Defence of Poetry*, 685). In *Prometheus Unbound*, Shelley's poet will

> watch from dawn to gloom
> The lake-reflected sun illume
> The yellow bees i' the ivy-bloom,
> Nor heed nor see what things they be;
> But from these create he can
> Forms more real than living man,
> Nurslings of immortality!
>   (I. 743–9)

This lyric suggests an indifference to 'what things they be' that is more absolute than is usually the case in Shelley's work and one would want to add the rider that the previous lines have compactly brought together elements of the physical scene; yet 'the lake-reflected sun' along with the 'yellow bees' and 'ivy-bloom' seek to shape themselves into 'Forms more real than living man'. Turner's paintings allow themselves freedom from naturalistic norms; such 'Forms' in both poet and painter speak less, perhaps, of the lure of some transcendent dimension associated with Plato's ideal forms (powerful as this idea, a supreme fiction for him, was for Shelley) than of a conviction that the artist can shape out of his experience designs that have an intrinsic beauty. Not that this aesthetic autonomy is indifferent to 'the real'. In Turner's oil, the political significance, at a time of deep social unrest, of the houses of government being engulfed by flames, is probable; indeed, Jack Lindsay has argued, 'he seized on the event as symbolically expressive of the fires of decay and

---

[60] For the Constable story and remark, see Gage, *J. M. W. Turner*, 89–90; for E. V. Rippingille's sense of Turner as a magician, see ibid, 92.

[61] Butlin and Joll, *Paintings of Turner*, 364.

[62] For a stimulating discussion of the 'revaluation' of 'reflection' in Romantic poetry and painting, see Heffernan, *The Re-creation of Landscape*, 201–24.

violence at work in English society and liable to burst out in general conflagration'.[63]
Such apocalyptic or Utopian fires rage in many of Shelley's poems; yet, just as
Shelley renounced didacticism, preferring appeals to his readers' imagination as a
way of reconfiguring things as they are (see his Preface to *Prometheus Unbound*, 232),
so Turner's social vision expresses itself with no polemical simplification. These oils
could be Burkean elegies as much as revolutionary forces of destruction, and the
lovingly rendered bridges and quiet presence of the Thames in both oils tell of
an impulse to cherish and preserve. What one can say is that the turbulent vision
of change is recorded with dramatic, imaginative power.

In Shelley and Turner, displays of imaginative power twine round a fascination
with process and provisionality. In Shelley, the all-presiding deity of a poet like
James Thomson has gone, leaving behind a sceptically challenged God-shaped
hole, but his poetry is made of air and fire, alive with motion. In it 'buds grow red
when snow-storms flee' (*Prometheus Unbound*, I. 791), 'Bright clouds float in heaven,
/ Dew-stars gleam on earth, / Waves assemble on ocean' (*Prometheus Unbound*, IV.
40–2); 'Men scarcely know how beautiful fire is— / Each flame of it is as a precious
stone / Dissolved in ever-moving light' (*The Witch of Atlas*, 259–61); 'the Earth and
Ocean seem / To sleep in one another's arms, and dream / Of waves, flowers, clouds,
woods, rocks, and all that we / Read in their smiles, and call reality' (*Epipsychidion*,
509–12); the poet himself is 'borne darkly, fearfully, afar' (*Adonais*, 55. 492), while
'Worlds on worlds are rolling ever / From creation to decay, / Like the bubbles on
a river' (*Hellas*, 197–9), even as the 'The flower that smiles today / Tomorrow dies'
('The flower that smiles today', 1–2), and if tragedy gathers its forces 'on the sunlit
limits of the night' (*The Triumph of Life*, 80), the ever-unforeseeable, hope-surrounded
future figures itself as 'the loftiest star of unascended Heaven, / Pinnacled dim in
the intense inane' (*Prometheus Unbound*, 3. 4. 203–4). Like Turner, Shelley imbues
mythological reference with astonishing power. Just as Turner makes *Ulysses derid-
ing Polyphemus* (1829) a painting that shows,[64] in Cecilia Powell's words, how he
'used colour expressively, as a vehicle of human emotion',[65] so Shelley's mention in
Ode to the West Wind of some 'fierce Maenad' (21) brings, as noted elsewhere in the
volume, a Dionysian cluster of suggestions into the poem, foreshadowing the *spa-
ragmos* of section IV in which the poet must 'fall upon the thorns of life' (54), before
rising up, in the final section, to reaffirm his imaginative power, as 'by the incantation
of this verse' (65), he bids the wind to 'Scatter, as from an unextinguished hearth /
Ashes and sparks, my words among mankind!' (66–7).[66]

Shelley hands over his poem; we are the legatees of his words. Turner, too, invites
our intent and intense participation in works which flame again in our imaginations.
In *The Fighting Temeraire, Tugged to her Last Berth to be Broken Up, 1838* (1839),[67]
Turner produces an elegy for the Britain which fought and won its long battles
against Napoleon that, one suspects, would win from Shelley and Byron only two

---

[63] Lindsay, *Turner: His Life and Work*, 238.   [64] Butlin and Joll, *Paintings of Turner*, 330.
[65] Cecilia Powell, *Turner* (Norwich: Pitkin, 2003), 27.
[66] See James Rieger, *The Mutiny Within: The Heresies of Percy Bysshe Shelley* (New York: Braziller,
1967), 179.
[67] Butlin and Joll, *Paintings of Turner*, 377.

cheers for its seeming ideological conservatism. For its composed pathos and dignity, expressed through colour and wheeling rays of light, they would surely have been full of admiration, especially for the way, in which celebration and elegy, the stoical and the magnificent, the funereal and the solemnly august intermingle and refuse to be disentangled, so that the vivid, dying orange-red reflections allow their troubled anguish to melt into the calm, the cold, the controlled desolateness and ability stead-fastly to endure that one senses in the painting's cooler colours and distant vistas. *Rain, Steam and Speed—the Great Western Railway* (1844),[68] its train hurtling towards the viewer, seems among the most Shelleyan of Turner's pictures because of its fas-cination with modern science and technology (one recalls how in *Prometheus Unbound*, the Earth's song in Act IV celebrates human control of the elements: 'The lightning is his slave; heaven's utmost deep / Gives up her stars, and like a flock of sheep / They pass before his eye, are numbered, and roll on!' (IV. 418–20). Yet, despite their passion for the dynamics of motion and speed, there is, for both, danger implicit in the exhilaration: for Turner, this awareness of danger shows in the image of the hare racing to outstrip the terrifying train and by the glimpses of rural life being changed for ever by the new machine; for Shelley, it shows, in his lament, foreshadowing the worries of Carlyle, Arnold, and Ruskin, about the mechanistic utilitarianism of an age in which, 'man, having enslaved the elements, remains himself a slave' (*A Defence of Poetry*, 696); 'we want', writes Shelley in the same paragraph of *A Defence*, where 'want' means both 'need' and 'lack', 'the poetry of life'.

It is such a poetry that Turner offers us in his *Norham Castle, Sunrise* (c. 1845–50) in which the painter's imagination re-baptizes the world,[69] steeping it in exquisite blues, browns, oranges, and golds, refusing easy symmetry, or a parade of mastery, indeed undoing the evidence of such mastery revealed by his own former pictures of the same scene, but inviting us to see the scene by virtue of a rare, imaginative light. To see the world as in a dream, but one revealing the sanity of true genius, a dream that awakens us in a sense of recognition and longing, as though a potential vision had been realized even as its potentiality is the more keenly admitted and delighted in: this is the great gift transmitted to us by the 'inmost spirit of light' at the heart of Turner's and Shelley's radiant and irreducible artistic visions. Carlyle suggests appropriate terms of continued praise in a passage from his 'Hero-Worship' in *Past and Present*:[70]

> For though fierce travails, though wide seas and roaring gulfs, lie before us, is it not something if a Loadstar, in the eternal sky, do once more disclose itself; an everlasting light, shining forth through all cloud-tempests and roaring billows, ever as we emerge from the trough of the sea: the blessed beacon, far off on the edge of far horizons, towards which we are to steer incessantly for life?

It is such a loadstar, such a beacon, that the art of Turner and the poetry of Shelley have still the power to be.

---

[68] Butlin and Joll, *Paintings of Turner*, 409.   [69] Butlin and Joll, *Paintings of Turner*, 512.
[70] Thomas Carlyle, *Past and Present* (New York: Colyer, 1843), 31.

13

Shelley, Beddoes, Death, and Reputation

Throughout the work of Thomas Lovell Beddoes, a disembodied spirit of poetry, for all its satisfying verbal incarnations, seems to wait to be shaped into a literary form as yet unavailable; at the same time his pages are peopled with very material ghosts that yearn for 'dishumation'. In using Beddoes's own word for the process of securing recognition for the literary achievement of the, in his view, unjustly neglected St John Dorset, I mean to suggest that Beddoes's work is best read reflexively, as being about its own ambitions and aspirations.[1] The major form that Beddoes tried to revive was poetic drama, though he was conscious of the dangers of the pseudo-Elizabethan and the fake Jacobean: 'With the greatest reverence for all the antiquities of the drama, I still think that we had better beget than revive—attempt to give the literature of this age an idiosyncrasy & spirit of its own, & only raise a ghost to gaze on, not to live with—just now the drama is a haunted ruin' (Donner, 595).

Yet Beddoes's own work is 'haunted' by the ghosts that it both gazes on and lives with; his success is bound up with failure, and with the difficulties of being born too late and too early. Beddoes (1803–49) would never experience, in H. W. Donner's words, 'the dazzling fame that his father, Thomas Beddoes, enjoyed during his lifetime'. Thomas Beddoes senior, who died when the poet was five, was an eminent physician, a friend of Coleridge and Humphry Davy, a pamphleteering sympathiser with the French Revolution, a poet, and a chemist fascinated by 'the medical uses of gas'. The poet's mother Anna Maria, sister of the novelist Maria Edgeworth, was described by Davy as possessing 'a fancy almost poetical in the highest sense of the word';[2] she died in 1824 when the poet was twenty, the year in which Shelley's *Posthumous Poems* was published, a conjunction of events which, with hindsight, appears fateful. If his mother's death appears to have crystallized in the young poet the fascination with Death which led Ezra Pound in Canto LXXX to call him 'prince of morticians' and to regret that 'none can speak his language', Shelley's volume gave a decisive turn to his lyric creativity.

Beddoes, as a mature writer, combines a 'poetical fancy' with a restless scientific curiosity into the nature and origins of life. His poetic vision is wrought from

---

[1] Quoted from Beddoes's essay on *Montezuma*, a tragedy by St John Dorset, in H. W. Donner, ed., *The Works of Thomas Lovell Beddoes* (London: Oxford University Press, 1935), 543. All Beddoes's writings are quoted from this edition, hereafter Donner; references to prose writings are given parenthetically in the text.

[2] H. W. Donner, *Thomas Lovell Beddoes: The Making of a Poet* (Oxford: Basil Blackwell, 1935), 35, 41, 55.

bleakly humorous, sometimes tragic life-weariness, outbursts of politically rebellious trust in some 'awakening world' (Donner, 97) and hopeless hope in what lies the other side of the grave. In 1829 he wrote in a letter, 'I am now already so thoroughly penetrated with the conviction of the absurdity & unsatisfactory nature of human life that I search with avidity for every shadow of a proof or probability of an after-existence, both in the material & immaterial nature of man' (Donner, 629–30.) From an early stage his writing was preoccupied by mortality, and its apparent morbidity may be one reason why he has remained obstinately unread over the years, despite the efforts of some notable apologists. Another reason is the fact that in his own lifetime he published very little. Though there is a good collected works, it is not widely available, and he is beginning to seem to be one of those minor writers on whose behalf certain critics periodically make large claims, which go virtually unnoticed. This is a great shame. Along with Letitia Landon, John Clare, and Felicia Hemans, Beddoes is a major figure of what might called 'Third-Generation Romantic Poetry'. Powerfully influenced by Shelley in particular, Beddoes at the same time makes something memorably his own out of an interiorizing and extension of Romantic motifs and a pervasive sense of alienation, expressed in his life through his self-exile from England to study anatomy and literature in Germany and Switzerland, an exile that would lead him into flirtations with political radicalism, scrapes with various authorities, and expulsion from Gottingen University. His work deserves the renewed attention it is receiving for its subtlety and power.[3] Gender-based approaches have revolutionized the study of Romantic poetry by women, and likewise, they have shed light on Beddoes's own secretive and, one senses, tormented sexuality.[4] One hopes Romantic and nineteenth-century studies will not allow Beddoes to languish in the cold of the very critical neglect that, this chapter will argue, generates some of his finest writing.

In two of the best pieces written on Beddoes's poetry, Northrop Frye sees the poet as anticipating the absurdism of Beckett and Christopher Ricks draws attention to Beddoes's tantalizing affinities with the new form of the dramatic monologue.[5] As Ricks points out, a form dependent on the eloquent presence of 'the silent interlocutor' has parallels with Beddoes's creation of a world in which, as H. W. Donner puts it, 'All the characters seem to declaim in a void'.[6] Ricks glosses Donner's (derogatory) comment with the saving remark that, in Beddoes's work, the void is 'truly a void' and 'the unutterability of an answer . . . as audible as a gong' (Ricks, 156, 157).

---

[3] See, for example, *The Ashgate Companion to the Work of Thomas Lovell Beddoes*, ed. Ute Berns and Michael Bradshaw (Aldershot: Ashgate, 2007) and Ute Berns, *Science, Politics, and Friendship in the Works of Thomas Lovell Beddoes* (Newark: University of Delaware Press, 2012).

[4] See, for example, Frederick Burwick, '*Death's Jest-Book* and the Pathological Imagination' in *Ashgate Companion*, 97–121 (especially 98–9), and Christopher Moylan, 'T. L. Beddoes's Terminable or Interminable End', *Ashgate Companion*, 229–39 (especially 234–5).

[5] Northrop Frye, 'Yorick: The Romantic Macabre', in *A Study of English Romanticism* (1968; Brighton: Harvester Press, 1983), 51–85, ('We are constantly in a twilight world between life and death, like the world of Beckett', 63); Christopher Ricks, 'Thomas Lovell Beddoes: "A Dying Start" ', in *The Force of Poetry* (Oxford: Oxford University Press, 1984), 135–62, hereafter Ricks (Ricks writes, in fact, that 'Beddoes wrote non-plays, but invented the dramatic monopollylogue', 157).

[6] Ricks, 150; quoted in Ricks, 156.

Much of Beddoes's eloquence derives from the vitality with which he imagines the difficulty of coming to life. In lines that open one of the poet's most famous lyrics, Isbrand (appearing explicitly in the character of a rhymester) sings:

> Squats on a toad-stool under a tree
> A bodiless childfull of life in the gloom,
> Crying with frog voice, 'What shall I be?...'
> (*Death's Jest-Book*, III. iii. 321–3)

The lines show in their zany inventiveness—their mouthfilling ability to give physical substance to the 'bodiless'—that Beddoes's poetry asks the question 'What shall I be?' with as much swank as anxious belatedness. Isbrand makes a good (and characteristic) joke at the close of his song when he says in response to Siegfried's praise ('A noble hymn to the belly gods indeed', III. iii. 368): 'I fear you flatter: 'tis perhaps a little / Too sweet and tender, but that is the fashion; / Besides my failing is too much sentiment' (III. iii. 370–2). 'A little', there, tentatively positioned at the end of the line, apes perfectly a shivering moue of critical disapproval. Beddoes knows that the last thing his great song can be accused of is being 'Too sweet and tender', and the moment illustrates how he made from exile, aloneness and apartness a poetry that debunks the clichés of literary 'fashion' and consequent reputation.

1

Beddoes's poetry and letters are, from an early stage, obsessed with the making of poetic reputation. In a letter of 25 August 1824, he writes:

> The disappearance of Shelley from the world seems, like the tropical setting of that luminary, (aside, I hate that word) to which his poetical genius can alone be compared with reference to the companions of his day, to have been followed by instant darkness and owl-season: whether the vociferous Darley is to be the comet, or tender, fullfaced L. E. L. the milk-and-watery moon of our darkness, are questions for the astrologers: if I were the literary weather-guesser for 1825 I would safely prognosticate fog, rain, blight in due succession for it's dullard months. (Donner, 589)

The idealization of Shelley is accompanied by dislike of puffing ('aside, I hate that word' he writes of 'luminary') and lack of enthusiasm for writers such as George Darley and Letitia Landon, intuitively sensed by Beddoes to be 'minor' authors.[7] In doing so he subscribes to a notion of literary excellence depicted in Shelley's *Adonais* in, say, Urania's pronouncements in the following stanza:

> 'The sun comes forth, and many reptiles spawn;
> He sets, and each ephemeral insect then
> Is gathered into death without a dawn,
> And the immortal stars awake again;

---

[7] In the case of Darley, at least, Beddoes revised his opinion in a more favourable direction; see his comments in a letter of 11 January 1825, Donner, 595.

> So is it in the world of living men:
> A godlike mind soars forth, in its delight
> Making earth bare and veiling heaven, and when
> It sinks, the swarms that dimmed or shared its light
> Leave to its kindred lamps the spirit's awful night.'
>   (*Adonais* 29, 253–61).[8]

Yet there is in Shelley a note of self-denigration at odds with the high claims for his poetic significance implicitly made by *Adonais*. The Preface to *Prometheus Unbound* seeks to ward off, in its concluding paragraph, the potential hostility of reviewers when Shelley argues that 'if a [writer's] attempt be ineffectual, let the punishment of an unaccomplished purpose have been sufficient; let none trouble themselves to heap the dust of oblivion upon his efforts; the pile they raise will betray his grave which might otherwise have been unknown' (*Major Works*, 232). Shelley imagines literary failure as a death, marked by a 'grave', images that help to illuminate Beddoes's death-obsessed imagination.

In fact, Beddoes was probably the most intelligently responsive reader of Shelley's lyrical drama (and other poetry) in the 1820s. In his 'Lines Written in a Blank Leaf of the "Prometheus Unbound"' he produced a remarkable celebration of Shelley's 'bright creations' (8). If Thomas Forbes Kelsall is right in his dating of the poem to assert that 'When Mr. Beddoes penned this fine extravaganza, the subject of its graceful idolatry was still living' (Donner, 796), the poem, when composed, was a proleptic elegy. The poem turns on the idea of Shelley as both 'human' (8) and akin to a 'providence' (16): 'a Spirit of the sun' (1), Beddoes writes, 'Was sphered in mortal earth' (6). 'Lines…' moves between a sense of Shelley as a transcendent 'Spirit' and a 'mortal' human; its own form of 'concentrate song' (5) seems itself to be 'centred and condensed in his one name / As in a providence—and that was SHELLEY' (15–16). The very title suggests that Beddoes sees his writing as subsidiary and supplementary to Shelley's lyrical drama. Writing on a blank leaf of the poem, Beddoes declares himself to be a disciple of Shelley and an authentic heir. The opening imperative—'Write it in gold' (1)—aspires to a permanence of memorializing. Yet, as in Beddoes's 'Pygmalion', it is the artist's life-giving but mortal gusto that holds the attention: in lines such as 'Angelic sounds / Alive with panting thoughts sunned the dim world', Shelleyan diction is taken over and made to serve a vision of poetry as ever newly 'Alive' and animating.

This motif of surprising resurgence crops up in a variety of guises in Beddoes's work. In 'Lines Written at Geneva; July 16 1824', for instance, scenic description passes sinuously into reflection on the after-life of sound that has been silenced; this is a poetry that confidently apprehends the inapprehensible. 'Or was there ever sound, or can what was / Now be so dead?' (10–11) are questions that provoke the notion of sound as a living thing whose 'echo' 'is its ghost' (19). At this point the poem could easily have continued to pirouette on the pin of a conceit, but

---

[8] Quoted from *Percy Bysshe Shelley: The Major Works*, ed. Zachary Leader and Michael O'Neill, *Oxford World's Classics* (Oxford: Oxford University Press, 2003). Hereafter *Major Works*. All quotations will be taken from this edition unless indicated otherwise.

Beddoes switches from metaphoric to literal dying, evoking a mood of calm entranced acceptance of the potentially bizarre or hideous: 'The earth is full of chambers for the dead, / And every soul is quiet in his bed' (22–3). 'For' in this couplet's first line suggests that the earth is concerned about the comfort of 'the dead' and 'quiet' in the second line represses and, in so doing, suggests the possibility of unquietness. There is a strong sense in the poetry of a poet looking into, without entering, a whirlpool of images that obscurely haunt him as central to his imaginative being. In *Death's Jest-Book* Beddoes will take the plunge.

Kelsall's introduction to the first publication of 'Lines Written in a Blank Leaf of the "Prometheus Unbound"' in the *Athanaeum*, 18 May 1833, frets that Beddoes is not better known, linking his relative lack of publications to Shelley's death: 'For aught, indeed, that our literature would have lost, he might have perished in the same fatal storm in the gulf of Spezia. How much longer is he contented to be un-known as the author of the Bride's Tragedy ...?' (Donner, 796). The phrasing is inadvertently suggestive of the way Beddoes may have been tempted to show allegiance to the dead Shelley—by suffering a form of the neglect that his poetic master had endured. Both poets share a comparable concern with reputation: Shelley affecting indifference to the reviews (as in 'Lines to a Critic' which Beddoes would have read in *Posthumous Poems*) but placing his trust in posterity; Beddoes lamenting in his final letter to Revell Phillips (26 January 1849) that 'I ought to have been among other things a good poet' (Donner, 683). Giving a positive spin to an insight of Judith Higgens—that Beddoes experienced 'a permanent veering in his nature between cynicism and arrogance on the one hand and a depressing sense of failure on the other'[9]—I would relate Beddoes' mixed attitudes towards his own literary merit to his admiration for Shelley. The obsession with death in Beddoes can suggest, by implication, a longing for absorption into the canonical body of English literature; at the same time it can also express a frightening sense of literary aloneness.

At times Beddoes brings to mind in his dealings with Shelley Harold Bloom's theory of the anxiety of influence: the very readiness to suffer neglect may suggest an act of 'kenosis', that '"undoing" and ... "isolating" movement of the imagination' which is the third of Bloom's revisionary ratios. Elsewhere, Bloom writes that 'Beddoes, in despair of his times and of himself, chose to waste his genius on a theme that baffled his own imagination'.[10] Yet more often Beddoes holds ghostly commune with the dead Shelley in ways that seek to pay tribute rather than express anxiety of influence and through imaginative modes that are at once stylishly and grotesquely productive. There are traces of anxiety in his response to Shelley, as when he writes mock-reproachfully to Kelsall, who, at Beddoes's request, had sent him a copy of Shelley's *The Cenci*: 'Why did you send me the Cenci? I open my own page, & see at once what damned trash it all is' (Donner, 619). But Beddoes,

[9] Judith Higgens, ed., *Thomas Lovell Beddoes: Selected Poems* (Manchester: Carcanet Press, 1976), 12.
[10] Harold Bloom, *The Anxiety of Influence: A Theory of Poetry*, 2nd edn (1975; New York: Oxford University Press, 1997), 87; Harold Bloom, *The Visionary Company: A Reading of English Romantic Poetry*, rev. and enlarged edn (Ithaca: Cornell University Press, 1971), 444.

who helped with the publication of Shelley's *Posthumous Poems* (1824), was engaged complexly in his writing with questions of reputation raised by Shelley's legacy. The ghosts that populate Beddoes's poetry are, among other things, images of poetic images, as in Shelley's 'Mont Blanc' where the poet imagines gazing within 'the still cave of the witch Poesy' at 'Ghosts of all things that are' (44, 46). Ghosts in Beddoes are the symptoms of a mind obstinately sure that its imaginings are significant yet sardonically aware that they will be regarded as nugatory by those for whom the 'sunny world' (*Death's Jest-Book*, IV. i. 50) is the true reality. Beddoes arms himself in his poetry against an audience and a reviewing clique he supposes will be unsympathetic.

In his Preface to *Death's Jest-Book* Beddoes offers a magisterial defence of his own dramatic practice, especially of its 'Gothic' use of 'a wild fancy, sometime slight and joyous, sometimes fearfully hideous—often satirical, grotesque or ludicrous' (Donner, 533, 534). This defence is conducted with a sure sense that his practice will not find favour. Ironically, he expresses his 'humble hope that the greater number of critics (or, to speak more properly) reviewers will be kind enough to find it guilty of almost every literary offence according to their critical judgement' (Donner, 534). Above all, Beddoes 'begs of these gentlemen, to spare him the vexation of being eulogized by them' (Donner, 534–5). His intransigent contempt for reviewers belongs to a more general reaction among early nineteenth-century writers to the disappearance of patronage relations and the growth of a reading public swayed heavily by a group of literary reviewers. However, Beddoes's dislike of reviewers and literary politics links with aspects of his creativity that are original and strange. Christopher Ricks has suggested that a poet 'obsessed... with the thousand ways in which the dead won't lie down, would have relished the grim comedy by which at intervals his art is exhumed' (Ricks, 137), and he comments later, in an image worthy of his subject, on Beddoes's 'always hanging by his finger-nails above literary history's *oubliette*' (Ricks, 141). Beddoes's language is suffused with a fore-knowledge, even a welcoming, of neglect. Uncannily he contrives a relationship with his reader that is intimate yet aloof, taunting us and himself with the transience attendant on 'painted clay'. That phrase comes from the end of the second of two early sonnets on 'A Clock Striking at Midnight', and while its close—distinguishing between 'clay' (13) and 'the glad spirit' (14)—is conventional enough, the scorn for poetry's aspirations has genuine lexical and syntactical energy. 'Can we think' (4), he asks, that 'our grovelling thoughts shall e'er be writ / In never-fading stars' (8–9). The answer implied by the contemptuous 'grovelling' is 'no', yet the note of yearning admitted by the concluding cadence lifts self-contempt into something more challengingly uncertain.

There is, throughout Beddoes, a powerful aversion to selling one's soul, as it were, for literary profit: 'to count one's fingers, and take the sweat of our Grub street brows for the true juice, the critical drops w^h the soul's struggles must press from our veins ere it be genuine: to pant for fame, to print & correct our tame frigid follies, to be advertised in the newspapers with the praise of the Lit. Gaz. is really abundantly pitiful' (Donner, 635). Part of what makes 'Dream Pedlary' typical of Beddoes is the mixture of the sardonic and the haunting in its (implicit) treatment of literary aspiration. As a pedlar of dreams, the poet is seeking to win a name for himself through selling his 'innermost' self (see Donner, 635): 'If there were dreams to sell, / What would you buy?' (1–2). The poem owes its impact to the fact that 'you' might be the poet addressing himself or the poet addressing the reader. Characteristically, the cost of producing what may be 'advertised in the newspapers' is brought home by the poet to himself and his reader in a fashion that is at once self-rebuking and rebuking: 'Some cost a passing bell; / Some a light sigh' (3–4). Playing taut variations on the notion of life as a dream (intermittently explored by Shelley), the poet in stanza 3 appears to denounce the buying and selling of dreams by suggesting their intimate connection with 'ghosts': 'Dreaming a dream to prize, / Is wishing ghosts to rise' (24–5). But better to 'prize' a dream, the poem surreptitiously hints, than 'Waking, to die' (23); in the dream-state of 'Life' (22), to prize a dream 'Is wishing ghosts to rise'. Beddoes searches for some way to validate the pursuit and expression of what Shelley calls 'Dreams and the light imaginings of men, / And all that faith creates or love desires' (*Prometheus Unbound*, I. 201–2), while retaining a sceptical distance from his poetic yearnings.

Yet part of 'Dream Pedlary' suggests that the poetic cost in terms of self-exploration is too great. As Beddoes presses on in stanza 4 to ask which ghost he should 'call' (30), he imagines his 'loved longlost boy' (33) in a gesture that is intimate yet impenetrably private. The stanza concludes that 'There are no ghosts to raise; / Out of death lead no ways; / Vain is the call' (35–7). This does not say that there are 'no ghosts'; rather, it says there are none that can be 'raised'. Such a 'call'—the word might suggest the 'calling' of a poet as well as the call of a necromancer—is 'Vain' because, the poem intimates, to buy and sell human dreams only transports one between the literary market-place and an impossibly private spiritual domain. And yet the poem's next twist implies that only the loveless have no 'ghosts to sue' (38). The poem's twists and turns, its blockings and swervings recall the workings of Shelley's *Alastor*, a poem which begins with an attempted conjuration. The Narrator speaks there of 'forcing some lone ghost' 'to render up the tale / Of what we are' (27, 28–9). Beddoes inherits from Shelley the idea that 'what we are' is a 'tale' that can be told by a 'ghost'. But he gives the Shelleyan quest his own self-divided inflections.

2

Northrop Frye argues that 'The root of the conception of the grotesque is the sense of the simultaneous presence of life and death. Ghosts, for example, are at once alive and dead, and so inspire the kind of hysteria that is expressed equally by horror and by laughter'.[11] 'Ghosts' in Beddoes are images of ideas, feelings, and perceptions that the poet seeks to bring back to life. Or, rather, he contrasts their half-life with that of living human beings in ways that imply the desirability of the ghost-world. This can be read as representing an escapist flight from reality. But Beddoes's ghosts have a life that mocks (in both senses) the life of the living. Here Shelley's

---

[11] Frye, 'Yorick: The Romantic Macabre', 60.

influence is strong. On receiving a copy of Shelley's *Posthumous Poems*, Beddoes wrote: 'Shelley's book! This is a ghost indeed, and one who will answer to our demand for hidden treasure' (Donner, 590). The book is described as a 'ghost' 'who' will respond to 'our demand for hidden treasure', as if only a 'ghost' can supply the cultural 'treasure' needed by Beddoes and his friends. The rest of this postscript laments the sad waste of Shelley's early death: 'What would he not have done, if ten years more, that will be wasted upon the lives of unprofitable knaves and fools, had been given to him' (Donner, 590). 'Unprofitable' defines 'profit' in immaterial terms, a clue to Beddoes's sense of the value of immaterial ghosts. Deploying the same image of the creative genius as a providence which he uses in 'Lines Written in a Blank Leaf of the "Prometheus Unbound"' (and which Shelley himself uses in several places about Byron), Beddoes goes on to depict the future 'glorious creations' made possible by Shelley's 'extinction': 'How many springs will blossom with his thoughts! how many fair and glorious creations be born of his one extinction!' (Donner, 590).

Death giving rise to life is the central Utopian metaphor of Shelley's poetry. In 'Dirge for the Year', singled out with other pieces in *Posthumous Poems* for special praise by Beddoes, Shelley's lilting trochaics quickly redefine the sombre note of grief with which the poem begins: 'Orphan hours, the year is dead, / Come and sigh, come and weep! / Merry hours, smile instead, / For the year is but asleep. / See, it smiles as it is sleeping, / Mocking your untimely weeping'.[12] This has an exuberant rejection of sorrow discernible in many places in Shelley's poetry, a rejection that is the more affecting for being alive to the possibilities of death, for displaying a care-laden wish to be carefree. Believing that death precedes rather than follows life—in the personal, spiritual, and political realms—is, as the end of 'Ode to the West Wind' well knows, ultimately a matter of faith. There, the seemingly rhetorical question, 'O, wind, / If Winter comes, can Spring be far behind?' (69–70), is keenly conscious that the analogy being established between seasonal and human cycles holds only to the degree that human beings can make it hold.

Beddoes exaggerates to the point of grotesquerie this swiftly redefining and tremor-ridden movement between hope and fear in Shelley. His use of 'ghosts' reacts in complicated ways to the ghost imagery of 'Ode to the West Wind'. In that poem, 'the leaves dead / Are driven, like ghosts from an enchanter fleeing' (2–3); each winged seed lives 'like a corpse within its grave' (8); yet the resurrecting drive of the poem reanimates the ghosts, exploiting the fact that the resemblance between dormant seed and corpse is only deceptive, and imagining a poetic self-renewal that can be compared with the driving by the wind of 'withered leaves to quicken a new birth' (64). Though Beddoes responded powerfully to Shelley's creative affirmations, his own deployment of Shelleyan imagery frequently has about it a self-questioning twist. In *The Brides' Tragedy* the death-haunted Hesperus requests the power of night to 'Teach my eager soul / Fit language for your ears' (II. vi. 57–8). As in *The Cenci*, admired greatly by Beddoes, the search for 'Fit language' cannot

---

[12] Quoted from Percy Bysshe Shelley, *Posthumous Poems 1824*, a facsimile reprint, introd. Jonathan Wordsworth (Oxford: Woodstock Books, 1991).

wholly avoid a Shakespearean intonation. But the peculiar originality of Beddoes's language is that it inhabits a border between life and death. Such a border-zone is not foreign to Shelley's imaginings, but it evokes in Beddoes a characteristically darker tone. At the close of *Epipsychidion*, Shelley seeks to create for himself and Emily 'One hope within two wills, one will beneath / Two overshadowing minds, one life, one death, / One Heaven, one Hell, one immortality, / And one annihilation' (584–7). Shelley's dream of 'union' thwarts itself in the recognition that only 'annihilation' can make it possible. Hesperus plays an ironic variation on this Shelleyan trope when he imagines a post-mortal wedding for himself and Olivia:

> For when our souls are born then will we wed;
> Our dust shall mix and grow into one stalk,
> Our breaths shall make one perfume in one bed…
> (II. iii. 76–8)

Death is imagined here, in Frye's words, 'as the real consummation of love as well as of life' (Frye, 54). Frye is also illuminating on the way in which, for Beddoes, 'Consciousness… is a kind of withdrawal from being, a death-principle which fulfills itself by possessing death' and 'birth is a shifting of the center from the universe to the individual ego'.[13] There are some affinities between this outlook and aspects of Shelley's late poetry, notably the envisaging of life as a form of dying in *Adonais* and the playing, in *Hellas*, with notions of reincarnation. But Beddoes's positives seem ironically self-cancelling: hence the attraction for him of Tieck's theory of Romantic Irony and, perhaps, an edgy mistrust of the processes of poetic communication, a mistrust which is the source of much of his finest work.

It is lyric utterance, however, with its brief intimations of a voice that transcends individual utterance, that show Beddoes's liking for an oblique, slanting connection with imagined auditors. Here the compositional history of *Death's Jest-Book* is revealing. In 1829 Beddoes submitted a manuscript of the poem to friends in England who recommended against publication. Beddoes, regrettably, took their advice: regrettably because the inability to get the work out of his life and mind undoubtedly depressed the poet and contributed to his sense of failure, and, thus, to his eventual suicide. At the same time the poem grew in length and stature (for details see Donner, xxxiv–xxxviii and his textual apparatus for the different versions of the poem): in November 1844, for example, Beddoes writes in a letter to Kelsall before transcribing 'In lover's ear a wild voice cried', 'I'll sing you another song, w^h I believe is new to you—I have stuck it into the endless J. B.' (Donner, 674). Throughout *Death's Jest-Book*, Beddoes inserts lyrics that rise up—like resurrected ghosts—from the mordantly witty tragi-comedy of the play. Ultimately, such resurrections serve to assert the indestructibility of a poetic impulse ignored, for the most part, by Beddoes's contemporaries. Frequently, as in 'As mad sexton's bell tolling', images occur of death and life interpenetrating and 'Ghostlily' mirroring each other (I. iv. 136, 139). The 'Song from the Waters' in I. iv.—'As sudden thunder' (204)—has, as a self-referential sub-text, the poetry's own claims to live on, to

---

[13] Frye, 'Yorick: The Romantic Macabre', 77.

enjoy a posthumous reputation: 'As wake the morning / Trumpets bright; / As snowdrop, scorning / Winter's night, / Rises warning / Like a sprite: / The buried, dead, and slain / Rise again' (220–7). Here the Shelleyan trope of rebirth protects itself against the surrounding irony by means of a cartoon-like supervividness, as though 'Ode to the West Wind' had been replayed at helter-skelter speed.

The great lyric sung at Wolfram's death—'The swallow leaves her nest' (I. iv. 259)—reworks beguilingly Shelleyan poems such as 'Remembrance' (entitled 'A Lament' in *Posthumous Poems* from which the poem is quoted here). Though Beddoes's stanza and metre differ from Shelley's in 'A Lament', the driving use of rhyme and what might be called analogous imagery calls Shelley to mind. 'A Lament' describes the coming and going of an unspecified 'thou' whose departure leaves the poet 'lone, alone' (8). The poem is the richer for not specifying the cause of its emotional condition. In the context of Shelley's career, however, it is not unduly fanciful to relate the poem's mood to its creator's feelings of literary neglect. Representing himself as a 'living grave' (21) —like and as a poet whose works are not read he is living out a state of 'death'—Shelley requests, 'Let no friend, however dear, / Waste one hope, one fear for me' (23-4). The formulation over-protests. The concealed thrust of the line is that the support of friends would be welcome, were it not for the writer's sense that such support would merely be wasteful. In 'The swallow leaves her nest' Beddoes may well respond to 'A Lament', with its rapid alternations between memory and longing, hope and fear, 'I' and 'thou'. For Shelleyan indeterminacy, however, Beddoes's lyric substitutes a brave, death-accepting optimism:

> The swallow leaves her nest,
> The soul my weary breast;
> But therefore let the rain
>   On my grave
> Fall pure; for why complain
> Since both will come again
>   O'er the wave?
>   (I. iv. 259–65)

The question—'for why complain . . . ?'—remodels the genre of complaint to which the poem seems to belong. In the second and final stanza the lyric draws on a Shelleyan wind to break out of natural imagery into an apocalyptic imagining of 'a storm of ghosts' shaking 'The dead, until they wake / In the grave' (I. iv. 270, 271–2). There is a suggestion that authentic living (made possible by the 'storm of ghosts') occurs 'In the grave', the poem's final words. Again, the motif of resurrection has a sardonic self-referentiality: the poetry will return in later ages, so the lyric's sub-text says, but as 'a storm of ghosts'.

A Shelleyan passage that must have stayed with Beddoes and influenced his thinking about death and the other forms of life it sustains—thinking related to his view of poetry and its survival—is Earth's famous imagining of a shadow-world in *Prometheus Unbound*. 'For know,' Earth utters with majestic authority, 'there are two worlds of life and death' (I. 195). In Shelley, the shadow world suggests a realm of ghostly possibilities, past, present, and future. Beddoes's characters in *Death's Jest-Book* imagine the other world as alive and kicking; once, Siegfried asserts,

The other world was cold
And thinly-peopled, so life's emigrants
Came back to mingle with the crowds of earth:
But now great cities are transported thither,
Memphis, and Babylon, and either Thebes,
And Priam's towery town with its one beech.
(III. iii. 390–5)[14]

The lines, with a grimly comic energy (playing through that last line), delight in thinking of death as a virtual mirror-world of life. Though Siegfried and Isbrand feel the increased number of the dead explains a decrease in 'haunting' (III. iii. 397), it is through dwelling on the kinship of the living with the dead that Beddoes, affectingly and ironically, establishes a relationship with literary tradition. The relationship is one that allows his own quirkily individual talent to thrive.

Death's Jest-Book is prescient about its likely reception. Isbrand's words in an early soliloquy might be Beddoes's to himself—and Beddoes's admirers to a poet who pushed Romantic dreams of canonical, individual greatness to a terrifying yet wittily vigorous extreme ('Cheer up' is superbly conversational in context): 'Isbrand, thou tragic fool, / Cheer up. Art thou alone? Why so should be / Creators and destroyers' (I. i. 314–16). Yet the feeling of 'aloneness' is linked to a responsiveness to previous literature (the final phrase remodels Shelley's 'Destroyer and Preserver' ('Ode to the West Wind', 14)) and an uncanny sensitivity to nineteenth-century developments of thought (Nietzsche waits in the wings). It is the relation with Shelley, however, that will help most in understanding Beddoes's ability to thematize an ironic link between poetic value and 'death', understood as a metaphor for literary neglect. When Wolfram comes back from the dead to woo Sibylla in *Death's Jest-Book*, IV. ii. she says to him in words that recall Asia's lyric, 'My soul is an enchanted boat' (*Prometheus Unbound*, II. v. 72): 'Do not go. / Speak as at first you did; there was in the words / A mystery and music, which did thaw / The hard old rocky world into a flood, / Whereon a swan-drawn boat seemed at my feet / Rocking on its blue billows' (46–51). These words might be read as describing Beddoes's initial response to Shelley. Yet Wolfram's response picks up other Shelleyan echoes: 'Listen not to me, look not on me more. / I have a fascination in my words, / A magnet in my look, which drags you downwards, / From hope and life' (64–7). The phrasing brings to mind various passages from *The Cenci* concerned with the evil power that one mind can possess over another (see *The Cenci*, II. ii. 82–8, and IV. i. 85–8); and Wolfram's subsequent image of a 'jutting stone / Which crumbles down the steeps of an abyss' (IV. ii. 69–70) evokes yet redirects the energies of a memorable speech by Beatrice about 'a mighty rock' like a 'wretched soul' (*The Cenci*, III. i. 247, 252).[15] Not only do these subtly deployed echoes show how inwardly Beddoes read Shelley, they also reveal that he refuses wholly to 'buy' the dream peddled by some of Shelley's poetry that poetry will be valued by readers for the ideals it communicates.

[14] For the suggestion that the line's verve might in part derive from its 'feisty' dealings with 'the Romantic obsession with singularity', see Michael O'Neill and Madeleine Callaghan, *The Romantic Poetry Handbook* (Hoboken: Wiley Blackwell, 2018), 321.
[15] See the discussion in O'Neill and Callaghan, *Romantic Poetry Handbook*, 322.

Yet the spectral beauty of Wolfram's and Sibylla's wooing reaffirms trust, however strained, in a medium—poetry—whose relationship with the language of reputation-making is, for complicated reasons, profoundly antagonistic. Moreover, in Beddoes's work this complicatedly antagonistic relationship between poetry and the processes of reputation-making colours poetry's relationship with any readership. What 'fascinates' is the imaginative energy to which this complex of difficulties gives rise. The reader of Beddoes's work is warned, with grace and tragic irony, as Wolfram warns Sibylla, 'Leave me, or you must fall into the deep' (IV. ii. 72). Beddoes enacts here, with tragic metapoetic awareness, his sense of himself as a dangerous poet for his virtually non-existent readers, so many Sibyllas imagined as ready to 'fall into the deep' of Beddoes's ghost-ridden, life-teeming poetry. It is a poetry that requires a form of praise keenly aware of chiaroscuro and interwoven paradox, such as Beddoes himself extended in 'Lines Written in Switzerland', where he depicts 'Shelley's dazzling spirit' (12) as 'Quivering like dagger on the breast of night' (13).

14

'Materials for Imagination'

Shelleyan Traces in Felicia Hemans's Later Poetry

The youthful Shelley admired the 1808 *Poems* of Felicia Dorothea Browne, as she then was. Thomas Medwin, who had showed him the volume, describes Shelley's reaction: 'with a prophetic spirit he foresaw the coming greatness of that genius, which under the name of Hemans afterwards electrified the world'.[1] According to Henry Fothergill Chorley, Hemans was, for her part, by 1828,

> long since... won from her early disinclination to enjoy or even admit any of Shelley's dreamy, but most inspired poems, by the elevation of thought they display, even at their wildest, and the exquisite charms of their imagery and versification. Her mind was as certainly accessible by the former as her fancy and her ear were open to the enchantment of the latter: one of the lyrics she loved best was his 'Ode to the West Wind'.[2]

Part, no doubt, of the process by which Hemans 'was won from her early disinclination' was the attempted unbesmirching of Shelley's reputation at work in Mary Shelley's 1824 edition of *Posthumous Poems*. This volume does not so much depoliticize Shelley as present a poet able to excel in different modes and, above all, to make self-conflict central to his work, as occurs in manifest or more covert ways in poems such as *Julian and Maddalo*, *The Witch of Atlas*, and *The Triumph of Life*, all appearing in print for the first time within it.[3] Again, lyrics such as 'Stanzas Written in Dejection—December, 1818, near Naples', a poem admired by Hemans (in a letter of 1831) as 'quite a union of music and picture in poetry', exhibit the suffering lyric self behind the radical tilter against orthodoxy. That poem points up, too, the link between the suffering lyric self and the capacity to respond to natural beauty in a poetry of inventive sound effects, enterprising verse form (the poem is composed in modified Spenserian stanzas, the first eight lines in tetrameters, the ninth an alexandrine), and image (mood is conveyed through sensitive notation of the external scene).

---

[1] Quoted from *Felicia Hemans: Selected Poems, Letters, Reception Materials*, ed. Susan J. Wolfson (Princeton: Princeton University Press, 2000), 526. Unless indicated otherwise, Hemans's poetry and prose is quoted from this edition, which, in such cases, is cited parenthetically, with line or page numbers, in the main text. References to other materials in the edition appear in the endnotes.

[2] Henry Fothergill Chorley, *Memorials of Mrs Hemans: With Illustrations of Her Literary Character from Her Private Correspondence*, 2 vols (London: Saunders and Otley, 1836) 1. 296.

[3] See my 'Trying To Make It as Good as I Can' Mary Shelley's Editing of Shelley's Poetry and Prose', in *Mary Shelley in Her Times*, ed. Betty T. Bennett and Stuart Curran (Baltimore: Johns Hopkins University Press, 2000), 185–97, 279–81.

Hemans's recollection of lines from the poem in this letter of 3 April 1831 is significantly if unconsciously intent on enhancing its subjective nature and metapoetic awareness: where Shelley writes, 'and a tone / Arises from its measured motion' (16–17), Hemans has, 'and I hear / The music of its measured motion'.[4] It is a subtle mishearing, betraying Hemans's awareness of Shelley's cultural presence and invitation to later writers to insert their own sense of self into poetic scenarios modelled on his own. Shelley is, in fact, in affecting ways absent from and present in his poem: if his opening stanza seems to comprise delighted notations of external things, the writing is imbued, too, as stanza 2 brings out, with feelings of isolation. After the lines misquoted by Hemans, Shelley exclaims, 'How sweet! did any heart now share in my emotion' (18). The poem is haunted by the ghosts of the companionship whose absence it laments. At the poem's end Shelley allegorizes imaginings of reception, and yet the writing is full of twists and turns: 'Some might lament' (37) the poet's death, 'for I am one', writes Shelley

> Whom men love not, and yet regret;
> Unlike this Day, which, when the Sun
> Shall on its stainless glory set,
> Will linger though enjoyed, like joy in Memory yet.
> ('Stanzas Written in Dejection—December 1818,
> near Naples', 42–5)

The lines dwell on the poet's sense of himself, a figure unloved by others, but in some way the object of their 'regret', either because, one might speculate, they feel that he has wasted his talents, or because, retrospectively, they recognize that they are unequal to the task of responding adequately to his achievement. Certainly they rouse in a poet such as Hemans a curiosity about what Shelley did have to offer. One gift he bequeaths to later writers here is a performed reticence, one that follows hard on the heels of something close to emotional display; the poem turns from self-preoccupied ego to the 'stainless glory' of the day, a day whose objective perfection, in a final turn, is an experience, 'like joy in memory yet'.

In a way that tallies with the poetic lessons taught by 'Stanzas Written in Dejection', Hemans's response to Shelley after his death in July 1822—this chapter's subject—is at once pervasive and almost secret. It allows us to study the complicated way in which Shelley's influence made itself felt in a writer of very different ideological persuasions in the aftermath of his death.[5] Hemans's inveterate reworking of Shelley's tropes and phrases seeks to acknowledge yet critique, to allow for

---

[4] Chorley 2. 194. Hemans also quotes the poem, in describing the appeal to her viewing Liverpool from the nearby Seacombe across the Mersey: 'The city's voice itself / Is soft as Solitude's'. *Memoir of The Life and Writings of Mrs Hemans, By Her Sister* (Philadelphia: Lea and Blanchard, 1840), 184. Shelley's ambitious alexandrine is broken into two lines and 'as' substituted for 'like'.

[5] For thoughts on the 'marking of Hemans within a particular religious context' and on the critical advantages of 'a "hermeneutics of advocacy"' in relation to her work, see David E. Latané Jr, 'Who Counts? Popularity, Modern Recovery, and the Early Nineteenth-Century Woman Poet', in *Teaching British Women Writers 1750–1900*, ed. Jeanne Moskal and Shannon R. Wooden (New York: Lang, 2005): 205–23; qted from *Volume 291: Nineteenth-Century Literature Criticism*, ed. Lawrence J. Trudeau (Farmington Hills, Mich: Gale/Cengage Learning, 2014), 132–43 (at 138, 136).

'enchantment' but to chasten and subdue. Shelley turns up in surprising places and ways in her work. In 'Woman and Fame', published in 1829 in *The Amulet, or Christian and Literary Remembrancer*, Hemans orchestrates enthralled, corrective references to 'Mont Blanc' and *Epipsychidion*: 'Thou hast a voice, whose thrilling tone / Can bid each life-pulse beat' (13–14). In 'Mont Blanc', Shelley asserts: 'Thou hast a voice, great Mountain, to repeal / Large codes of fraud and woe' (80–1). Hemans's work appears in a publication whose subtitle is at odds with Shelleyan heterodoxy, even as she mimics his note of authoritative assertion. In *Epipsychidion*, Shelley refers to 'looks, which dart / With thrilling tone into the voiceless heart' (562–3). Hemans redefines Shelleyan eroticism as the lure of duplicitous reputation. As elsewhere, her poetry's allusive, echoic resonances mingle admiration for and distancing from a Shelleyan original. Hemans draws on Shelleyan concerns with voice and voicelessness to articulate her own rejection of a voice, that of fame, which attracts and repels her. It is possible to hear in 'Woman and Fame' the adroit practice of a poet who eats her cake and has it, too, professing rejection of meretricious fame while evoking the 'thrilling tone' of its 'trumpet's note' (15). Such ambivalence gives life to work which may exalt its supposed indifference to fame, but is still captivated by it.

In discussing Hemans's response to Shelley, it is difficult not to triangulate that response, at least briefly, with her attitude to Byron. 'She wrote in his voice, quoted him in letters, sounded his phrases in his poems, summoned his verse for epigraphs': Susan Wolfson captures well the uncanny empathy which Hemans felt for Byron, an empathy that made possible 'oppositional' and 'canny' readings.[6] As Wolfson's annotations to her edition of Hemans's writings bring out, Hemans was also acutely aware of Shelley, sometimes seeing him as an alternative to Byron as well as ally. Hemans is sensitive to the different accents of longing in the two poets: bitterly frustrated in Byron, yearningly unrealized in Shelley. An interplay between these different, allied accents, adapted to Hemans's own capacity for dramatic monologue, takes place in *The Forest Sanctuary*, part second, when the hero, fleeing Spain, looks at his wife Leonor, who loves him but regards his spiritual views as heretical. For the speaker, it is as though Leonor's melancholy were explicable in terms other than those that turn out to be true (that she is dying):

> I told my heart 'twas but the exile's woe
> Which press'd on that sweet bosom;—I deceiv'd
> My heart but half:—a whisper faint and low,
> Haunting it ever, and at times believ'd,
> Spoke of some deeper cause. How oft we seem
> Like those that dream, and *know* the while they dream,
> Midst the soft falls of airy voices griev'd,
> And troubled, while bright phantoms round them play,
> By a dim sense that all will float and fade away!
> (II. xxxvi. 316–24)

---

[6] Susan J. Wolfson, 'Hemans and the Romance of Byron', *Felicia Hemans: Reimagining Poetry in the Nineteenth Century*, ed. Nanora Sweet and Julie Melnyk (Basingstoke: Palgrave, 2001), 155–80 (156).

This idiom tempers and transmutes Byronic and Shelleyan rhetorics of feeling. Indeed, the condition of being 'Midst the soft falls of airy voices griev'd' seems almost reflexive; it evokes the way in which Hemans, a poet aware of and alert to 'voice', as Diego Saglia has brought out, positions herself in relation to Shelley.[7] Often Hemans is 'griev'd' amidst the enchanting 'wandering voices' (*Prometheus Unbound*, III. iii. 57) which bring intimations of radical hope in Shelley's work; 'griev'd', in part, because of her abiding concern with mortality as an absolute check to any secularized vision of happiness. For his part, Byron had made 'the exile's woe' his special territory; he is, too, a poet who responds to the lure of 'bright phantoms', as in the stanza from *Childe Harold's Pilgrimage* which Hemans quotes as the epigraph to 'The Beings of the Mind'. In that stanza, Byron says of such 'beings' that they 'multiply in us a brighter ray / And more beloved existence' (*Childe Harold's Pilgrimage*, IV. 5. 39–40).[8] The possibility that they may be merely compensatory, a means of 'replenishing the void' (*Childe Harold's Pilgrimage*, IV. 5. 45), shadows Byron's high-sounding assertions, a possibility which is not lost on Hemans. In 'The Beings of the Mind' the idea of the mind as housing 'children of the soul' associates itself with the peril always attendant on the trope of domestic security in her work, while the declension of Byron's 'beings of the mind' into 'bright phantoms' in *The Forest Sanctuary* hands them over to an imagining of loss.[9]

That sense of loss communicates through the rhyme's passage from 'play' to 'fade away', as though to 'play' imaginatively were to 'fade away'. Hemans's form in *The Forest Sanctuary*, 'a variation of the Spenserian stanza (*ababccbdd* instead of *ababbcbcc*)', as Wolfson notes, adapts itself to what in her prefatory note the poet calls the 'mental conflict, as well as outward sufferings' of the speaker.[10] Employing an extra rhyme (four rather than the usual three), Hemans allows for a mid-stanza redirection, and here her prompter seems Shelley, whose interest in nuanced psychological states is at work in the evocation of semi-conscious awareness: 'I deceiv'd / My heart but half', for example, recalls the soliloquizing Orsino in *The Cenci*, offered by Beatrice an unflattering image of himself, 'To which I grow half reconciled' (III. ii. 118); and Hemans's phrasing evokes comments by the same figure about his operations of desire:

> [...] thus unprofitably
> I clasp the phantoms of unfelt delights
> Till weak imagination half possesses
> The self-created shadow
> (II. ii. 140–3)

Those last lines suggest the stealthy, feline links between Hemans's work and Shelley's. Where Shelley is, Byron may often be present too, and vice versa. Hemans's

---

[7] Diego Saglia, '"A Deeper and Richer Music": The Poetics of Sound and Voice in Felicia Hemans's 1820s Poetry', *English Literary History* 74.2 (2007): 351–70.

[8] Quoted from *Byron: The Major Works*, ed. Jerome J. McGann ([1986] Oxford: Oxford University Press, 2008).

[9] *The Poetical Works of Mrs Hemans* (London: Warne, 1897), 453–4.

[10] *Hemans*, ed. Wolfson, 269.

'How oft we seem / Like those that dream, and *know* the while they dream' might, for instance, bring to mind the Byron of 'The Dream' or indeed the Shelley for whom 'all things seem, / And we the shadows of the dream' (Conclusion, 11–12) in *The Sensitive Plant.* More specifically, the lines have caught a Shelleyan interest in the way in which dream seems a mode of liminal trespass, to have a vivifying or morbid intensity that threatens the validity of waking consciousness, as when Laon discerns 'A dim and feeble joy, whose glimpses oft / Were quenched in a relapse of wildering dreams' (*Laon and Cythna*, III. 33. 289–90).[11] But Hemans has given an individualizing twist to the difficult partnership between seeming and dreaming. Her speaker appeals to the idea of knowledge amidst 'dream', a knowledge less ratiocinative than made up of intimation and foreboding, what in 'The Spirit's Mysteries' she calls 'the strange inborn sense of coming ill': a characteristic locution that turns a nominal construction into a compounded 'sense'.[12]

Often this sense seems at work in her responses—explicit and oblique—to the figure of Shelley, who is surely, as Fiona Stafford has recently suggested, the hidden addressee of 'The Lost Pleiad'.[13] As in some Dantean love-poem, Byron acts as the screen figure in this lyric, which appears to be directed to him, given the title with its allusion to a famous stanza (15) from *Beppo*. Yet if 'The Lost Pleiad' evokes the Byron who was a 'forgotten celebrity in 1823', it reads, too, as a complex meditation on Shelley.[14] Wolfson discovers 'sly wit' and subversive intent (at Byron's expense), reading the poem as asserting that 'England's new constellation of poets can survive the loss of its most famous exile'.[15] Certainly Hemans constructs a poem whose five-lined rhyming pentameters have a beauty and majesty that survives the loss they lament. Yet the poem seems less to turn the tables on Byron than to find an answerable sublimity for the fate, a fate beyond pathos and fit speech, of the 'vanish'd' Shelley; poetry—the poem bears witness—can survive the loss of a poet who established himself in *Adonais* as the greatest elegist since Milton, but the survival seems at once slightly benumbed and astonished by its own calm. *Adonais* comes to mind with particular force in the final stanza:

> Why, who shall talk of thrones, of sceptres riven?—
> Bow'd be our hearts to think on what *we* are,
>   When from its height afar,
> A world sinks thus—and yon majestic heaven
> Shines not the less for that one vanish'd star!
>   (21–5)

---

[11] Quoted from *CPPBS* 3.   [12] *The Poetical Works of Mrs Hemans*, 432.

[13] 'Since some of the sentiments and imagery are reminiscent of *Adonais*, it seems more likely to have been inspired by Shelley', Fiona Stafford, *Reading Romantic Poetry* (Hoboken: Wiley-Blackwell, 2012), 197.

[14] Wolfson, 'Hemans and the Romance of Byron', *Felicia Hemans: Reimagining Poetry*, 175.

[15] Wolfson, 'Hemans and the Romance of Byron', *Felicia Hemans: Reimagining Poetry*, 176. See also Jerome McGann, *The Poetics of Sensibility: A Revolution in Literary Style* (Oxford: Clarendon, 1996), 160–4. McGann comments on the fact that, in correspondence, Nanora Sweet 'emphasizes both Shelley and Byron as important presences in the poem', 160 n. 4.

In the final stanza of *Adonais*, Shelley is

> [...] borne darkly, fearfully, afar;
> Whilst burning through the inmost veil of Heaven,
> The soul of Adonais, like a star,
> Beacons from the abode where the Eternal are.
>
> (55. 492–5)

To think on 'what *we* are' in a stanza that recalls the rhymes of the final stanza of *Adonais* seems less to subvert the arrogant male poet than to express a tangle of interrelated feelings about the loss of 'that one vanish'd star'. Hemans achieves a tonality utterly her own by opening the poem to the inrush of vanished magnificence. 'The Lost Pleiad' offers that vanished magnificence its own steadfast correlative. Recalling, but refusing wholly to endorse, Shelley's tactics in his revisionary sonnet 'To Wordsworth', Hemans neither mourns nor refuses to mourn. Her poem is sumptuously musical, yet carefully self-aware, attentive, sorrowful, courageous, equal to the challenge presented by 'glory from the heavens departed'. The 'majestic heaven', rhyming with 'sceptres riven', recalls a second set of rhymes in the final stanza of *Adonais*, where the 'inmost veil of Heaven' represents the goal of a quest in which 'The massy earth and spherèd skies are riven!' (55. 491). But whereas those 'riven' skies represent the intensity of Shelley's drive towards 'the inmost veil of Heaven', Hemans's poem removes quest from the picture. In her poem, earth is a place of 'sceptres riven', while the sky, discreetly allegorical locale of canonicity and artistic immortality, is a 'majestic heaven', seemingly untouched by human sorrows.[16]

The stanza, as quoted above, comes from the poem's first book-length publication of the poem, in the second edition of *The Forest Sanctuary* (1829). Different editors have noted that Hemans substituted 'Bow'd be our hearts' for 'It is too sad'—the reading in the poem's initial magazine publication in the *New Monthly Magazine*, 8 December 1823—the idea of bowed hearts working at one remove from the more hackneyed notion of bowed heads.[17] The bowing of hearts mixes recognition of comparative insignificance with the self-reverence frequently advocated by Shelley (as in the last line of 'Hymn to Intellectual Beauty'). As suggested above, the poem's poise, its implicit self-defence, is never simply readable as gendered retaliation. But if it ends, almost in a note of deferential tribute, with a reference to 'that one vanish'd star', it manipulates distance with skill, speaking now of an objectified 'star', not of the more intimate 'thou' or 'thee' addressed in previous stanzas (5, 8, 15, 16, 19) and placing a counteracting stress on the fact that 'yon majestic heaven / Shines not the less'.

---

[16] For related commentary, see Michael O'Neill 'Mournful Ditties and Merry Measures: Feeling and Form in the Romantic Short Lyric and Song', in *A Companion to Romantic Poetry*, ed. Charles Mahoney (Malden: Wiley-Blackwell, 2011), 18–19.

[17] See *Romantic Women Poets: An Anthology*, ed. Duncan Wu (Oxford: Blackwell, 1997); *Hemans*, ed. Wolfson; *Records of Woman, with Other Poems*, ed. Paula R. Feldman (Lexington: University Press of Kentucky, 1999); *Romantic Poetry: An Annotated Anthology*, ed. Michael O'Neill and Charles Mahoney (Oxford: Blackwell, 2008).

In a late, unfinished lyric, 'The Zucca', Shelley speaks in knowingly desirous terms of 'Thou, whom seen no where, I feel everywhere'.[18] Hemans uses the same device of vocative address at the close of her first stanza—'Thou, that no more art seen of mortal eye' (5)—but her sentence construction is passive, where Shelley's is active; indeed, she confers action on the 'starry myriads' (11) that continue to 'rise' and 'have not mourned for thee' (15). Shelley's addressee in 'The Zucca' is, typically, the 'Dim object of my soul's idolatry', 'idolatry' rhyming with 'thee' in a gesture of self-knowledge, as Shelley admits his subliminal fear lest 'sin there be / In love, when it becomes idolatry' ('To Mary' 6. 47–8), as he phrases the matter in the dedicatory stanzas at the head of *The Witch of Atlas* (stanzas that Hemans would not have known). Hemans, too, subjects 'idolatry' to question, though where Shelley suggests the dangers of aesthetic infatuation, Hemans implies the ethical peril of a 'wild and passionate idolatry', as her presumably self-created epigraph to 'Juana' has it, given that it must operate 'in the shadow of the grave'. Yet Hemans invites a sympathetic reading of Shelleyan 'idolatry' as itself typifying the 'generous error' (Preface to *Alastor*, *Major Works*, 92) that her epigraph's final lines articulate: 'too much we give / Unto the things that perish'. 'The Lost Pleiad' benefits from its withheld decorum, its restraint. Hemans moves between elegy and enforced or detached acceptance. It is the impression, however, that such a balance is difficult, that there may be powerful feelings of regret for the 'thou' that are deliberately not being expressed, which explains its affective potency.

The poem defies paraphrase; it marks the emergence of what might be called the fully mature Hemans. More remains to be written about the different phases of Hemans's precocious and productive career.[19] But Maria Jewsbury offers a valuable point of departure:

> Within the time specified [c. 1815–1831], Mrs. Hemans has differed as materially from herself as from any other writer; and not in minor points merely, but in very essential ones. Up to the publication of the 'Siege of Valencia', her poetry was correct, classical, and highly polished—but it wanted warmth; it partook more of the nature of statuary than of painting. She fettered her mind with facts and authorities, and drew upon her memory when she should have relied upon her imagination [...] But now this is no longer the case. The sun of feeling has risen upon her song—noon has followed morning the Promethean touch has been given to the statue—the Memnon yields its music. She writes from and to the heart, putting her memory to its fitting use—that of supplying materials for imagination to fashion and build with.

Jewsbury singles out, in particular (though not without misgivings), the later poetry's 'bias toward the supernatural of thought' and comments that:

> Most of her later poems breathe of midnight fancies and lone questionings—of a spirit that muses much and mournfully on the grave, not as forever shrouding beloved objects from the living, but as a shrine where high unearthly oracles may be won; and

---

[18] Quoted from *Posthumous Poems 1824* (Spelsbury: Woodstock, 1991).
[19] See the valuable comments in Julie Melnyk, 'Hemans's Later Poetry: Religion and the Vatic Poet,' in *Felicia Hemans: Reimagining Poetry*, ed. Sweet and Melnyk, 74–91, esp. 74–7.

all the magnificence of this universal frame, the stars, the mountains, the deep forest, and the ever-sounding sea, are made ministrants to this form of imagination.[20]

The analysis does much to capture a new note in Hemans's work, and, though Jewsbury does not invoke any interaction with male writers, her praise for Hemans borrows liberally from Shelley's *Alastor* (a key text for Hemans).[21] Jewsbury's 'lone questionings' recall Shelley's post-Wordsworthian 'obstinate questionings' (*Alastor*, 26), involving 'some lone ghost' (*Alastor*, 27); her 'universal frame' seems to have the Poet's now dead, once 'wondrous frame' (*Alastor*, 665) in mind; her 'magnificence' remembers the reference in Shelley's preface to 'The magnificence and beauty of the external world' (*Alastor*, 92). Jewsbury senses that Hemans operates with a post-Shelleyan dialectic between 'external world' and the 'high thoughts' (*Alastor*, 107) that, in different ways, propel the Poet of *Alastor*. Though she does not mention Shelley, it is revealing that her searching praise is interspersed by a gendered digression on the futility of ignoring 'the difference between the poetry of men and women', which segues into a more subtly mingled sense that if 'we discover that power is the element of man's genius' and 'beauty that of woman's', 'occasionally we reciprocate their respective influence, by discerning the beauty of power, and feeling the power of beauty'.[22]

Commenting on this elegantly turned passage, Gary Kelly remarks shrewdly that Jewsbury 'can accept the kind of gender distinction advanced by Jeffrey, while denying that this distinction is hierarchical, and arguing that the difference can be dialectical'.[23] Hemans herself is often artfully dialectical in her dealings with Shelley. Shelley's self-presentation subverts masculine stereotypes; he is unafraid to feminize the self, admit weakness, express a longing for the 'sister' of his soul in *Epipsychidion* in a way that threatens the notion of the self-contained male self: he addresses Emily thus: 'Ah me! / I am not thine: I am a part of *thee*' (51–2).[24] In 'A Spirit's Return' Hemans, as Wolfson observes, 'often deploys Shelleyan diction and imagery' in a poem that makes Shelley into a medium for Hemansesque longing.[25] Shelley in *Epipsychidion* asks Emily that she would 'blot from this sad song / All of its much mortality and wrong' (35–6), before going on to posit pre-existent 'fields of immortality' (133) where his 'spirit should at first have worshipped thine' (134). His tone is rhapsodic but composed, almost witty in its glance at a Wordsworthian Platonism, imagining an alternative, probably pre-existent state. Hemans's speaker uses similar diction as she longs 'for gifts more high! / For a seer's glance to rend

---

[20] *Hemans*, ed. Wolfson, 563–4, 564.
[21] See under 'Shelley, Percy Bysshe' in the index to *Hemans*, ed. Wolfson.
[22] *Hemans*, ed. Wolfson, 564.
[23] *Felicia Hemans: Selected Poems, Prose, and Letters*, ed. Gary Kelly (Peterborough: Broadview, 2002), 66.
[24] For class-coded constructions of Shelley as 'feminine' but not 'effeminate', see Susan J. Wolfson, *Borderlines: The Shiftings of Gender in British Romanticism* (Stanford: Stanford Univeristy Press, 2006), 248–9.
[25] *Hemans* ed. Wolfson, 445. See also Alan Richardson, 'Spiritual Converse: Hemans's *A Spirit's Return* in Dialogue with Byron and Shelley', in *Fellow Romantics: Male and Female British Writers, 1790–1835*, ed. Beth Lau (Farnham: Ashgate, 2009), 123–38.

mortality' (57–8). In one sense, this longing goes a step further than Shelley, wishing to transcend rather than erase the traces of 'mortality' and giving 'mortality' its full, existential significance. Hemans finishes on a note that is assertively confident, not passionately aware of imminent collapse, as is the case in Shelley when his 'wingèd words' (588) crash and burn. For Hemans, less disturbed by the potential failure of language, 'that glimpse of joy divine, / Proved thee for ever and for ever mine' (261–2).

Hemans writes in couplets in 'A Spirit's Return', as does Shelley in *Epipsychidion*, but hers bind whereas his threaten always to break: Shelley's final movement is away from the circles he seems intent on shaping into being; when he uses the same rhyme on 'divine' as that with which Hemans's poem concludes, it is at the sophisticated service of poetic deferral. In his Dantean envoi, he commands his 'Weak Verses' (*Epipsychidion*, 592) to 'kneel at your Sovereign's feet' (Love's) and ask 'What wouldest thou with us and ours and thine?' (592, 594), and go on to sing that:

> Love's very pain is sweet,
> But its reward is in the world divine
> Which, if not here, it builds beyond the grave.
> (*Epipsychidion*, 596–8)

Hemans claims to have heard a voice from 'beyond the grave'; Shelley offers such a voice as a poetic fiction. Hemans literalizes, with exalted, uncanny intensity, a Shelleyan metaphor. Hemans (or her speaker) asks the spirit and affirms, with the nimbly enjambed skill typical of her later poetry:

> Dost thou not rejoice,
> When the spring sends forth an awakening voice,
> Through the young woods?—Thou dost!
> (237–9)

Shelley, for all his uses of 'voice' in *Epipsychidion*, skips the full-bodied assurance that the rhyme of 'voice' and 'rejoice' suggests; Hemans brings him out of the sceptical shadows that surround his daring intuitions, even as her voice is interrogative as well as indicative. Hemans individuates religious experience; Shelley translates it into a series of analogues for a new version of the relations between men and women, the renovated political structures intimated by the descent of the spirit-like 'spring' of Asia's speech at the start of Act II of *Prometheus Unbound* (see especially 1–12). For Hemans, Spring's 'awakening voice' traverses boundaries between the living and the dead, serving as an earnest of spiritual hope; for Shelley, when 'a fountain' makes 'an awakening sound' (III. iii. 13, 14) in a cave where Prometheus and Asia dwell, the awakening serves as a portal onto a redeemed universe.

Hemans draws Shelley into her own spiritualizing dialogue and debate. The resulting interaction allows for considerable difference—Hemans is continually fending off the threat of Shelleyan heterodoxy—but also accommodates fellow-understanding, which enables her to refine her own tonalities. George Gilfillan saw Hemans in 1847 as 'less a maker than a *musician*', a not wholly thought-through distinction

glimmering through many accounts of Shelley, yet his sibling fantasy about the two
poets, albeit sentimentalized, is, in its own mid-Victorian manner, compelling:

> In many points, Mrs. Hemans reminds us of a poet [...] whom she passionately
> admired, namely, Shelley. Like him, dropping fragile, a reed shaken by the wind, a
> mighty wind, in sooth, too powerful for the tremulous reed on which it discoursed its
> music; like him, the victim of exquisite nervous organization; like him, verse flowed
> for and from her, and the sweet sound often overpowered the meaning, kissing it, as it
> were, to death [...] Mrs. Hemans, indeed, was not like Shelley, a vates; she has never
> reached his heights, nor sounded his depths, yet they are, to our thought, so strikingly
> alike, as to seem brother and sister, in one beautiful, but delicate and dying family.[26]

Gilfillan notes the lack in Hemans of Shelley's 'faithless despondency', writing that
'Her spirit was cheered by faith'.[27] But Hemans's interest in prophecy, the capacity
for vatic insight, is underplayed here; it frequently occurs in contexts where 'faith'
wrestles with a quasi-Shelleyan sense that 'we press upon the brink / Haply of viewless
worlds, and know it not', as 'The Spirit's Mysteries' has it.[28] Hemans's doubt is
attendant upon commitment to belief in our 'immortal being', as the same poem has
it, though a commitment that is consciously driven by will and desire: 'So let us
deem', she comments in this poem, consciously pointing up the will to believe—here,
that the spirit's mysteries serve as earnests of immortality. Shelley, in poems such
as 'Hymn to Intellectual Beauty', presents the struggle between scepticism and
self-generated belief with a lyric inwardness that differs from Hemans's practice of
spectatorial comment. Shelley relies on an image's possible ambivalence, intellectual
beauty, say, providing 'human thought' with 'nourishment / Like darkness to a
dying flame' (44–5); Hemans holds image and comment in a fine equilibrium in
'The Spirit's Mysteries', as though, in the act of sounding Shelley's depths, she is
refusing to be drawn into the rushing vortex of his doubled suggestions. This is less
dogmatic timidity than a means of staging her poetry's tensions; as she reimagines
a nineteenth-century precursor, to adapt the subtitle of Sweet and Melynk's edited
collection, she captures herself in the process of doing so.

Hemans's dealings with Shelley have a clandestine element. Shelley is a rare
source, for example, of epigraphs, Hemans's usual way of cueing influences, because
of his alleged 'follies and impieties'. These are the words of Blackwood, responding
to Hemans's 1828 request that a motto from Shelley be retained for her poem 'The
Broken Lute', though she asks that his 'name' should be 'omitted' on account of
friends who 'objected much to my having taken a motto from Shelley'. But Blackwood
was able to assure Hemans that Shelley 'was a true poet'.[29] The very concept of the
'true poet' is, indeed, at stake in consideration of Hemans's response to Shelley.
Gary Kelly sees her later 'turn to the personal lyric' as part of a change in 'her public
self-construction', one that involved alignment more with Wordsworth, now

---

[26] *Hemans*, ed. Wolfson, 593, 595.   [27] *Hemans*, ed. Wolfson, 595.
[28] In *Romantic Poetry*, ed. O'Neill and Mahoney, the editors comment that the word 'brink' 'is
placed deftly at the line ending, as it is in Shelley's *Adonais*, l. 423' (408n): the Shelleyan line in question is 'When hope has kindled hope, and lured thee to the brink'.
[29] *Hemans*, ed. Wolfson, 496, 495, 496.

regarded as an exemplar of the male poet, than with a 'transgressive' figure such as Shelley. Kelly's arrestingly inflected ideological argument is that Hemans's 'public standing enabled her to represent herself as victim of the contradictions of woman and fame, private and public identity, and thereby to represent herself as exemplary liberal subject in an as yet illiberal state'.[30] The double use of 'represent herself' argues for a performative calculatedness on Hemans's part that may do justice to one aspect of her art. Yet it ascribes to her a settled political outlook at odds with her poetry's 'turn', to use Kelly's word, towards exploration of subjectivity. Kelly's 'exemplary liberal subject in an as yet illiberal state' plays cleverly on the dual meanings of 'subject' (both an agent and one acted upon); but it turns subjectivity from process to static posture.

Hemans suggests the focus of her vocation as a poet and her interest in Shelley when she quotes Maddalo's line, 'They learn in suffering what they teach in song' (*Julian and Maddalo*, 546), as the epigraph to 'The Diver'. What validates 'suffering' and 'song', in Hemans's appropriation of these terms, is existential and verbal uniqueness. In a fascinating comparison between Hemans's 'The Image in Lava' and Shelley's 'Ozymandias', Isobel Armstrong finds that Hemans replaces the male poet's alleged 'dialectic of violence and mockery' with 'a *social* dyad of impassioned inter-subjective feeling'.[31] Yet Shelley often comes to Hemans's mind as a fraught ally when 'intersubjectivity', in the form of intertextual responsiveness, points up poetic aloneness. At the end of 'The Graves of a Household', for example, Hemans turns from celebratory lament to something disruptively transgressive, an apparent sentence failing to round itself out and breaking off into a near-questioning exclamation:

> They that with smiles lit up the hall,
>   And cheer'd with song the hearth,—
> Alas, for love! if *thou* wert all,
>   And naught beyond, oh, earth!
>
> (27–30)

The address to the italicized 'thou' seizes on and makes capital out of Shelley's question at the end of 'Mont Blanc':

> And what wert thou, and earth, and stars, and sea,
> If to the human mind's imaginings
> Silence and solitude were vacancy?
>
> (142–4)

In both works, the possibility of 'vacancy' surfaces: Shelley expresses his sense that what seems epiphanic from one perspective might, from another, appear emptied of significance, all depending on the 'human mind's imaginings'; Hemans stages a seeming breakdown of lyric fluency as she articulates the fear that the 'earth might

---

[30] *Hemans*, ed. Kelly, 59, 60, 59.
[31] 'Natural and National Monuments—Felicia Hemans's "The Image in Lava": A Note', in *Felicia Hemans: Reimagining Poetry*, 212–30 (225).

be all, / And naught beyond'.[32] This is Hemans at her most lyrically multi-vocal, not so much riven as alert to contradiction and ineradicable conflict: the celebrant of family recognizes the inevitability of familial disintegration in the face of death; the believer in some final heavenly happiness expresses her recognition that such envisaged happiness may be a cheat.

In the poem, Hemans subjects to keen inspection a rhyme (between 'hearth' and 'earth') which Shelley uses in support of hope towards the close of 'Ode to the West Wind'. There, Shelley commands the wind to:

> Scatter, as from an unextinguished hearth
> Ashes and sparks, my words among mankind!
> Be through my lips to unawakened earth
> The trumpet of a prophecy!
>
> (66–9)

The 'hearth' of poetic inspiration is only 'unextinguished'; it will give rise to 'Ashes' as well as 'sparks', but Shelley hopes that, though as yet 'unawakened', 'earth' will hear, as a result of his intervention, 'The trumpet of a prophecy!' The poem darts from figure to figure in the ardour of its half-desperate longing. As often in Shelley's work, as Walter Bagehot memorably put it, 'In the wildest of ecstasies his self-anatomising intellect is equal to itself'—able, here, to recognize that the wind's 'scattering' will involve dispersal as well as dissemination, able, too, to indicate that the poem's main warrant for its strain of affirmation is its own metaphor-dependent eloquence.[33] Whereas 'earth' will, for Shelley, be the beneficiary of what is scattered from the 'hearth', Hemans breaks the link promised by the rhyme. Instead, equally able to retain intellectual control amidst passionate feeling, she posits 'earth' as both the preserver and destroyer of the 'hearth', turned, in her hands from a locus of creativity to an image of desired familial stability.

In 'The Diver' Hemans addresses an alter ego of the explorative and suffering poet and a version of the Romantic quester who is described in terms that seem deliberately to echo Shelley's poetry. At the same time, Hemans's poem compacts the Shelleyan into its own tightly constructed formal design. Shelley's sonorities find themselves encased in Hemans's jewel-box stanzas. The Poet of *Alastor* speaks of the 'measureless ocean' (509) and 'oozy caverns' (510) as beyond understanding; Hemans invokes the diver as 'Thou searcher of ocean's caves!' (4), where the rhythmical lilt created by an extra syllable is buoyantly at odds with the mood of sadness. Indeed, the poem's tonal colouring blends sympathy with an air of anguished distance. In the following stanzas, Hemans summarizes the plot of *Alastor*:

> A wild and weary life is thine;
> A wasting task and lone,
> Though treasure-grots for thee may shine,

---

[32] See Anne K. Mellor, *Romanticism and Gender* (New York: Routledge, 1993), 129 for relevant discussion.
[33] Walter Bagehot, 'Percy Bysshe Shelley' (1856), *Literary Studies*, 2 vols (London: Dent, 1911), 1, 111.

> To all besides unknown!
> A weary life! but a swift decay
> Soon, soon shall set thee free;
> Thou'rt passing fast from thy toils away,
> Thou wrestler with the sea!
> (13–20)

The first stanza here recalls the way in which, in the devastating aftermath of the vision of the 'veilèd maid' (*Alastor*, 151), the Poet is depicted: 'wildly he wandered on, / Day after day, a weary waste of hours' (244–5); his 'lone' state dominates the poem, yet, cross-gendering, Hemans brings Shelley's Poet into connection with Wordsworth's Lucy who, in 'Song: "She dwelt among th' untrodden ways"', 'liv'd unknown' ('Song', 9).[34] Characteristically a Shelleyan energy of hopeless hope is redefined, twinned with a suffering passivity. The Poet's death in *Alastor* stems from the 'decaying flame' (*Alastor*, 247) of a life that consumes itself for want of satisfactory emotional nutriment, prompting the Narrator's sorrowing outrage at such a waste, an outrage that pre-empts and precludes the elegiac consolations of 'Art and eloquence' (*Alastor*, 710). The 'swift decay' experienced by Hemans's diver is the source of freedom. Hemans turns to death as to a finality that silences complaint.

And yet the rest of 'The Diver' complicates acceptance of suffering. As the poem spells out the comparison between 'the wrestler with sea' and those 'Who win for earth the gems of thoughts' (31), Hemans mingles pride and pain, suggesting 'the price of bitter tears, / Paid for the lonely power' (41–2). Shelley's *Epipsychidion*, a revisiting of *Alastor* and revitalization of its perished hopes, serves as a point of departure. Shelley wishes to plumb, in his rhapsodic address to Emily, 'The fountains of our deepest life' and for them to 'be / Confused in passion's golden purity' (570–1), where 'Confused' means 'fused together'.[35] Alluding to Shelley's impassioned project, Hemans writes of her intrepid explorers: 'Down to the gulfs of the soul they go, / Where the passion-fountains burn' (33–4). Hemans seizes on Shelley's phrasing, condenses and compacts it (one notices the hybrid formation of 'passion-fountains'), almost does violence to it, turning prolonged lyric excursus into packed formulation. Her diagnostic manner masks her involvement in the predicament she describes, even as she hints at her own knowledge of 'bitter tears'. Yet 'The Diver' leaves little room for doubt that Shelley is an exemplary figure of the poet for her, and she appropriates his image of disseminated words from the end of 'Ode to the West Wind' when she describes the effect of 'lonely power', one that is implicitly poetic:

> Like flower-seeds, by the wild wind spread,
> So radiant thoughts are strewed;
> The soul whence those high gifts are shed,
> May faint in solitude!
> (45–8)

---

[34] *Romantic Poetry*, ed. O'Neill and Mahoney, 123.
[35] *A Lexical Concordance to the Poetical Works of Percy Bysshe Shelley*, comp. and ed. F. S. Ellis (London: Bernard Quaritch, 1892).

Shelley wishes that the wind would 'Scatter [...] my words among mankind', where the final word, viewed from Hemans's perspective, takes on an anachronistically gendered tone; she implies a less willed process by which 'high gifts are shed', hinting at the lot of the woman poet, even though her poem's pronouns here are masculine.

At stake for Hemans, in her mid-career turn, is the question of subjectivity's nature and significance. In 'Arabella Stuart', Hemans takes one of her two epigraphs from Byron's *The Prophecy of Dante*: 'And is not love in vain / Torture enough without a living tomb?' (III. 147–8).[36] Her depiction of Arabella's mental torments, however, enters into dialogue with Shelley's rendering of a figure dwelling in a 'living tomb', the Maniac in his *Julian and Maddalo*. The Maniac endures 'a living death of agonies' (415). Indeed, Shelley's groundbreaking evocation of such 'agonies' warrants Paula R. Feldman's praise for Hemans's 'extraordinary imaginative reconstruction of the human psyche under almost unbearable stress'.[37] Shelley uses asterisks, Hemans mostly sections (as well as asterisks at the end of section v); but they both emphasize what Shelley, with the Maniac in mind, calls the 'unconnected exclamations' (213) of their speakers' hearts. Shelley captures a psyche audibly wounded by remembered words. He conveys distress through abrupt transitions and a syntax that twists and turns with a 'tortured' expressiveness, as in the lines:

> You say that I am proud—that when I speak
> My lip is tortured with the wrongs which break
> The spirit it expresses
>
> (408–10)

Hemans, also writing in couplets, is less visceral in her intensities than Shelley, but she is able to capture deftly in her monologue Arabella's rapid changes of feeling, through questions, short sentences, and eloquently pointed rhyme in the lines: 'Dost though forget me, Seymour? I am prov'd / So long, so sternly! Seymour, my belov'd!' (160–1). The lover's name is repeated, but with different emphases—anxiously then yearningly. The staccato phrasing builds on Shelley's striking ability to enact the rhythms of somatic disturbance. If both poems brood over the fact that the need, as the Maniac has it, 'To love and be beloved with gentleness' (*Julian and Maddalo*, 208), may be unrequited, both poems are troubled by the 'cold world'. Julian refuses to let this world 'know' (617) what Maddalo's daughter told him about the Maniac; Arabella, reversing the Maniac's not wholly unequivocal wish that 'Oblivion' should 'hide this grief' (508), requests that Seymour should 'send / Ev'n then, in silent hours a thought, dear friend! / Down to my voiceless chamber' (246–8), before she proceeds to say:

> [...] for thy love
> Hath been to me all gifts of earth above,
> Tho' bought with burning tears! It is the sting
> Of death to leave that vainly-precious thing
> In this cold world!
>
> (248–52)

---

[36] Epigraph traced in editions of Wu, Feldman, Wolfson, and Kelly.
[37] *Records of Woman*, ed. Feldman, p. xxiii.

The command of the couplet form here has a Shelleyan attentiveness to the movement of the speaking voice, as displayed in *Julian and Maddalo*, a self-described 'Conversation' (212). Hemans shapes a gap between 'send' and 'Down', the delay between the words allowing the speaker to dally with the desired 'thought', before the writing captures, in 'Down into my voiceless chamber', the dark descent of any such imagined 'thought' into the 'voiceless chamber' of the tomb. Arabella's 'Ev'n then' appears to allude to the time 'when I am with the dead!' (237). Yet the 'voiceless chamber' is also Arabella's existence and, indeed, the poem which Hemans has written, haunting us with the paradox of hearing a voice that is written. Shelley, too, suggests a speaking that is also a writing, an overhearing, an entombment of voice, an expression of feeling, a liberation of feeling and a silencing.

Thus, the Maniac wonders at his speaking and writing, almost a displaced version of that tension between 'heart and art' which Wolfson discerns in the next poem in *Records of Woman*, 'Properzia Rossi'. Wolfson's phrase is the 'calculus of heart and art', a term that suggests balancing, awareness, contrivance, in the face of all that resists equipoise, control, manipulation.[38] The monologue embodies and expresses that tension between empathy and understanding, feeling and intelligence, which Hemans developed the capacity to represent in later, Shelley-influenced, work. The poem's specular doublings have a Shelleyan depth. Just as Rousseau is and is not the Poet, who is and is not Shelley, in *The Triumph of Life*, so Properzia is and is not the sculptured 'Forsaken Ariadne' (37) to whom she gives 'my own life's history' (36), and is and is not the Felicia Hemans, who makes her say words that seem veiled autobiography in places, yet who controls her speech, stylizing it into an externalized, shaped script. Properzia begins less by sublimating her pain (stemming from unrequited love) into art than by consciously performing the work of sublimation, retaining a final distance from it:

> One dream of passion and of beauty more!
> And in its bright fulfilment let me pour
> My soul away! Let earth retain a trace
> Of that which lit my being, though its race
> Might have been loftier far.
>
> (1–5)

Energy leaks into loss, in the engineered enjambment at 'pour / My soul away'—not simply 'pour'. Pouring away is one mode that the poem captures, a process of loss, and yet a process that has its own self-vexing nobility. Hemans's wording at this point recalls Shelley's in *The Triumph of Life*: in the version Hemans would have known, that published by Mary Shelley in *Posthumous Poems* (1824), Rousseau blames his fate on the lack of 'purer sentiment' ('nutriment' in modern editions) with which 'the spark with which Heaven lit my spirit' had been 'supplied'. Properzia echoes yet modifies Rousseau's apologia; she confesses that she might have achieved 'loftier' successes, yet she affirms the value of that which 'lit my being'. Both express

[38] Susan J. Wolfson, ' "Domestic Affections" and "the spear of Minerva": Felicia Hemans and the Dilemma of Gender', *Re-Visioning Romanticism: British Women Writers, 1776–1837*, ed. Carol Shiner Wilson and Joel Haefner (Philadelphia: University of Pennsylvania Press, 2004), 128–66 (157).

a mixture of self-value and self-criticism, but Properzia brings a gendered inflection of longing to her expression of incomplete 'fulfilment', to employ a word used with affecting irony at the poem's beginning.[39] Byron's *Werner*, with its reference to 'my weary hope's unthought fulfilment' (I. ii. 249), may prompt Hemans's word-choice; so, too, may Shelley's lovers in *The Witch of Atlas* who, under the Witch's benign and bond-relaxing influence, would 'take sweet joy, / To the fulfilment of their inmost thought' (651–2).

More generally, the opening of 'Properzia Rossi', like the poem as a whole, has the composure of the artist rising free of her materials, even as she immerses herself in them. Such a composure marks Hemans's finest poetry like a signature or 'trace', to use Properzia's term, a word that carries a Shelleyan resonance. Like Shelley, Hemans makes poetry out of the search for a palpably lost, elusive 'trace / Of light diviner than the common Sun / Sheds on the common Earth' (*The Triumph of Life*, 337–8). She may have longed for Wordsworthian calm, but that very longing was more akin to Shelley's unsatisfied quests than, as Coleridge puts it, to Wordsworth's 'Bright healthful waves' ('To Wordsworth', 30). At the same time, Hemans continually reworks Shelleyan pursuit into a poetry of quasi-transcendental intimation that rarely settles for banal piety, but prompts us, rather, to see in her a poet grappling with the aesthetic challenge of constructing her own poetic habitation out of the 'materials for imagination' available in her culture. In her elegiac 'Felicia Hemans', Letitia Landon does justice to the contest between search and projection which animates Hemans's poetry, and to the fact that this contest has a Shelleyan colouring, when she poses a question in the form of an exclamation:

> What on this earth could answer thy requiring,
> For earnest faith—for love, the deep and true,
> The beautiful which was thy soul's desiring
> But only from thyself its being drew!
>
> (65–8)[40]

Shelley's 'Sensitive Plant', which 'desires what is has not, the beautiful!' (77), is one influence co-opted by Landon; so, too, is Shelley's confession in *Epipsychidion* that his pursuit of beauty involved questing after 'The shadow of that idol of my thought' (268). Landon honours as she articulates the nature of Hemans's poetic 'desiring'. As she does so, in a form that alternates feminine and masculine rhymes throughout, she pays tribute to Shelley, a poet of subtle though seemingly inexhaustible importance for herself and for Hemans.

---

[39] See the note in *Romantic Poetry*, ed. O'Neill and Mahoney, 402n.
[40] *Hemans*, ed. Wolfson, 583.

15

'Beautiful but Ideal'

Intertextual Relations between Percy Bysshe
Shelley and Letitia Elizabeth Landon

'With what enthusiasm do some set up Wordsworth for an idol, and others Shelley!
But this taste is quite another feeling to that which creates; and the little now written
possesses beauty not originality,' Landon remarks in 'On the Ancient and Modern
Influence of Poetry', her parallel to aspects of Shelley's *A Defence of Poetry* (unpublished in her lifetime). A little later, sustaining the note of lament for belatedness,
Landon asks: 'who could for a moment have hesitated as to whether a poem was
marked with the actual and benevolent philosophy of Wordsworth, or the beautiful
but ideal theory of Shelley?'[1] The essay's implications are various. Landon defines
her age as one that has lost the 'originality' of the heyday of Romantic poetry. But she
hints at the advantages as well as the disadvantages of belatedness: able to hold in
balance the relative merits of Wordsworth's 'actual and benevolent philosophy' and
Shelley's 'beautiful but ideal theory', Landon subtly implies that the poetry of her
predecessors opens itself to her own responsive appropriations. At the same time,
her ways of suggesting the impoverishment of the present indicate a profoundly intertextual imagination, one saturated in the dominant tropes of the Romantic poets.

My stress in this discussion is on her intricate relationship with Shelley, a poet
to whom Landon responds in a fluid and productive manner. If she sympathizes,
she qualifies, yet if she withholds total assent from his vision, she does not disavow
its hold over her imagination. In his *Life and Literary Remains* (1841) of Landon,
Laman Blanchard included her judgement of Shelley:

> Of all poets SHELLEY is the most poetical:
>
>> 'Love was born with him, so intense,
>> It was his very being, not a sense.'—
>
> The defect of his imagination was a want of being sufficiently balanced with the real;
> everything appeared to him through an exaggerated medium. He reasoned with is
> feelings; now feelings are the worst possible reasoners—they excite, and they mislead.
> He saw evil and sorrow, and believed too easily in redress: he was too young to make
> allowance—that first step in true philosophy—and fancied that to defy a system was

---

[1] Quoted from *Critical Writings by Letitia Elizabeth Landon*, ed. F. J. Sypher (Delmar: Scholars'
Facsimiles and Reprints, 1996), 64; hereafter referred to parenthetically as 'Sypher' in the main body
of the text.

to destroy it. It was a boy's error, who believes he is judging when he is only learning. Shelley's versification has a melody peculiarly his own. It can only be described by similitudes. It suggests the notes of some old favourite song—the sound of falling waters, or the murmurs of the wind among the branches. There is a nameless fascination in some sweet human voices, and there is the same in many of the shorter poems of Shelley.   (Quoted from Sypher, 175)

The prose pivots and poises itself round the key Landon term, 'learning'. Once she has delivered her measured and critically unremarkable rebuke of Shelley's 'want of being sufficiently balanced with the real',[2] Landon is able to give expression to her sense of the 'nameless fascination' Shelley exercises, a fascination which is bound up with her implicit admiration for his complete commitment to his 'poetical' vision. Illustrating such commitment, Landon cites, close to the start of her passage, a distinctly Shelleyan couplet, even if comes, in economically adapted form, from Byron's *Don Juan*, canto 4, where he describes the passionate intimacy between Juan and Haidée: 'Love was born *with* them, *in* them, so intense, / It was their very spirit—not a sense' (stanza 27).[3] Byron out-Shelleys Shelley, rhyming two words ('intense' and 'sense') which Shelley seems never to have rhymed himself, though the couplet makes us think he should have done and reminds us how his poetry verges always on a chime between acuteness of feeling and fully mobilized resources of human apprehension. 'Love' in Byron's lines—and, Landon suggests, in Shelley—seems at once to include and transcend 'sense'. Moreover, as Hemans applies the couplet in the above extract, it suggests that love appears to originate with Shelley, a thought whose boldness has implications for her sense of how an allusive poet may seek, paradoxically, to begin anew, to reclaim a point of origin.

An invocation in 'The Hall of the Statues'—'God of the West Wind, awake!' (58)—argues, in context, in favour of Landon's awareness of Shelley's 'Ode to the West Wind': the context being one in which praise is expressed for those who:

> have head and heart on fire
> With unquenchable desire
> Of those higher hopes which spring
> Heavenward on an eager wing
>   (44–7)[4]

If the 'fire'/'desire' rhyme is Byronic as well as Shelleyan, the 'spring'/'wing' rhyme recalls the second stanza of Shelley's 'To a Skylark,' a poem in which the poet seeks to create 'hymns' 'Till the world is wrought / To sympathy with hopes and fears it

---

[2] Something of the prevailing hostility to Shelley in Landon's milieu can be gauged by reviews carried in the *Literary Gazette*, edited by William Jerdan, Landon's mentor (and lover): see Susan Matoff, 'William Jerdan, Poetry, and *The Literary Gazette*', *The Wordsworth Circle* 47. 1 (2016): 40–7, esp. 42 and 45.

[3] See Michael J. Plygawko's discussion of the passage in connection with Byron's search 'in his own voice for a controlled core that synthesizes feeling and form', '"The Controlless Core of Human Hearts": Writing the Self in Byron's *Don Juan*', *Byron Journal* 42.2 (2014): 123–30 (at 129).

[4] Unless indicated otherwise, Landon's poetry is quoted from *Letitia Elizabeth Landon: Selected Writings*, ed. Jerome McGann and Daniel Riess (Peterborough: Broadview, 1997), hereafter *LSW*; quotations from the 'Introduction' are incorporated parenthetically in the main body of the text.

heeded not' (39–40).[5] These lines seem, in turn, to be in 'sympathy with and to underpin Landon's subsequent praise in 'The Hall of Statues' for 'Those wide aims which seek to bind / Man the closer with his kind— / By earth's most unearthly ties, / Praise, hopes and sympathies' (48–51). To be sure, Landon's responsiveness to Shelley in 'The Hall of Statues' has a guardedness in the midst of enthusiasm; and there is a spectatorial quality to the writing: 'Thankful should we be to those / Who disdain a dull repose' (42–3). Yet the responsiveness, however guarded, is evident, and affirmed by a further echo of Shelley in 'dull repose'. The phrase reminds us that in *Adonais* Shelley exhibits a comparable disdain for 'repose', as the elegy faces up to and faces down the grim possibility that consciousness of doomed to extinction, that 'th' intense atom glows / A moment, then is quench'd in a most cold repose' (179–80). 'The Hall of Statues' concludes in doubt and uncertainty, 'All the shapes I gaz'd upon, / Like the dream that raised them, gone' (168–9), allowing Landon the freedom to present her imaginings both as merely the products of a 'dream' and as possessing the truthfulness peculiar to poetic imaginings. She thus sustains her independence as a poet, preventing her admiration for ardent idealists such as Shelley from dominating the poem. But the hold over her imagination of Shelley's practice and example is apparent.

In 'On the Ancient and Modern Influence of Poetry', published a year after 'The Hall of Statues', Landon's prose seems imbued with Shelleyan tropes. We lack, she says, any 'voice that startles us into wonder, and hurries us forth to see whose trumpet is awakening the land' (Sypher, 64). Such a voice is Shelleyan, a voice akin to that imagined at the end of 'Ode to the West Wind' when Shelley implores or commands the wind to 'Be through my lips to unawaken'd earth / The trumpet of a prophecy!' (68–9). Landon takes the desire for the poetic deed. Shelley engages in anguished wrestling with the wind that momentarily subdues the wind to his will as a poet, until it, rather than he, is the trumpet rather than the trumpeter. By the time of Landon's tacit allusion, the trumpet is or ought to be the possession of a dominant poetic voice, and it is 'awakening the land' which remains obstinately 'unawaken'd' in the original Ode. Landon suggests the possibility of poetry going through cycles, drawing on the hopeful aspects of Shelley's final question in the Ode, as well as glancingly referring to the opening of Shakespeare's *Richard III*: 'Perhaps poetry too may have its atmosphere; and a long cold winter may be needed for its glad and glorious summer' (Sypher, 64). In terms that are uncannily like those used by Shelley

---

[5] Shelley is quoted from Redding and Galignani, *The Poetical Works of Coleridge, Shelley and Keats 1829*. The Galignanis' edition is both one possible source of Landon's knowledge of Shelley's poetry and gathers together poems published previously which Landon may have read in earlier publications. Along with poems published in Shelley's lifetime, the Galignanis' edition incorporates poems published in Mary Shelley's edition of Shelley's *Posthumous Poems* (1824). Landon would also have had access to Shelley's poetry in the various pirated editions of his work published in the 1820s and '30s, including *The Works of Percy Bysshe Shelley, with His Life*, 2 vols (London: Ascham, 1834). Landon would also have encountered poems placed by Mary Shelley and others such as Thomas Medwin in various annuals and periodicals; thus, 'To Edward Williams' ['The serpent is shut out from paradise'] was published in *Fraser's Magazine* in 1832. For essential information about the transmission of Shelley's texts, see Charles H. Taylor Jr, *The Early Collected Editions of Shelley's Poems: A Study in the History and Transmission of the Printed Text* (New Haven: Yale University Press, 1958). For convenience, line-numbers are provided from *Norton*, or are taken from *H*.

in *A Defence of Poetry*, Landon castigates the present. 'Selfishness is its principle,' she writes, 'indifference its affection, and ridicule its commonplace. We allow no appeals save to our reason, or to our fear of laughter' (Sypher, 64). Here Landon offers a parallel to Shelley's attack on the 'principle of Self' at work in the present, and to his attack on 'Comedy' in 'the reign of Charles II' when 'malignity, sarcasm and contempt, succeed to sympathetic merriment; we hardly laugh, but we smile'.[6]

The parallel indicates that we may be wise to take issue with the view that Landon, at her best, is most finely understood as an undermining critic of Romantic illusion, a view eloquently expressed by McGann and Riess, who say of her poetry that 'An imagination like hers has few illusions about illusory worlds, and least of all about that supreme Land of Cockayne, the romantic imagination' (*LSW*, 25–6). Landon as the pitiless unmasker of Romantic poetry is an attractive proposition, but her sympathy with the Romantic project—itself hardly ever undivided in aim—shows in her poetry and criticism. In 'On the Character of Mrs. Hemans's Writings,' she subscribes to an expressivist, confessional poetics, saying of poetry that 'Its haunted words will be to us even as our own. Solitude and sorrow reveal to us its secrets, even as they first revealed themselves to those "Who learnt in suffering what they taught in song"' (Sypher, 67). After that allusion to Shelley's *Julian and Maddalo*, in which Maddalo remarks of 'wretched men' (544) that, 'cradled into poetry by wrong' (545), 'They learn in suffering what they teach in song' (546), Landon continues: 'I believe that no poet ever made his readers feel unless he had himself felt' (Sypher, 67). Landon's allusion to *Julian and Maddalo* works in multiple ways. It reminds us, as McGann and Riess observe (*LSW*, 79), that her subject Hemans had used the line as an epigraph to her poem 'The Diver'; thus, Landon constructs a link connecting her with Hemans and both female poets with Shelley. Hemans's diver is a figure for the poet who pays a 'price of bitter tears' for 'the lonely power' won by diving 'Down to the gulfs of the soul'.[7] The wisdom afforded by the poem's metaphoric equivalences consists in comfortless but intense revelation: the poet is one 'that has been to the pearl's dark shrine' and is addressed as 'O wrestler with the sea!' Such a posture of heroic wrestling in Hemans's poem is Byronic as much as Shelleyan, and Landon's allusion to *Julian and Maddalo* points up the availability for her of Byronic as well as Shelleyan influence, since the line, as mentioned, is spoken by Maddalo, Shelley's representation of Byron. The glancing but rich intertextual nature of Landon's writing comes through in her play with the close of 'Mont Blanc', where Shelley asks of the mountain:

> And what wert thou, and earth, and stars, and sea,
> If to the human mind's imaginings
> Silence and solitude were vacancy?
>
> (142–4).

Landon's emphasis is less on 'Silence and solitude' than on 'Solitude and sorrow', but her concern with 'silence' and 'the human mind's imaginings' is prominent in

---

[6] *Norton*, 520, 521–2.
[7] Hemans is quoted from *The Poetical Works of Mrs Hemans, with Prefatory Memoir, Notes, Etc*, The 'Albion' Edition (London and New York: Warne, 1897).

one of her finest poems, 'Lines of Life', a poem which displays her covert yet strong responsiveness to Shelley.

That responsiveness, it should be acknowledged, entwines round Landon's reading of Byron. Like Scott, Byron stimulates Landon's narrative inventions; he also quickens her sense of the poet's life as fated, as involving deep feeling, and as inextricable from social dissimulation; Shelley is the poet on whose Utopian imaginings she draws when envisaging possibilities of transcendence.[8] In 'Lines of Life,' Landon begins rather as Shelley opens his 'To Constantia, Singing', in the version she would have known, with physiological evidence of emotion. Shelley concludes the first stanza in his ecstatic rendition of the experience of listening to the song of 'Constantia' (Claire Clairmont) with a couplet that at once confesses feeling and suggests further revelations kept in check: 'Even while I write, my burning cheeks are wet— / Alas, that the torn heart can bleed, but not forget!'[9] That alexandrine moves beyond the present tense of composition explored in 'Even while I write' to a generalized sense of emotion's explosive impact. 'Forgetfulness', so dearly prized by Byron in Canto III of *Childe Harold's Pilgrimage* (4. 35), is not easily possessed by Shelley's speaker. The burden of Shelley's lyric, in the version available to Landon, is a miniature drama centred on loss of self through rhapsodic identification with another, until, finally, the self imagines itself suspended by song in a net of otherness: 'I have no life, Constantia, now, but thee, / Whilst, like the world-surrounding air, thy song / Flows on, and fills all things with melody'. Landon, the role of the *improvisatrice* always uppermost in her thoughts, plays many variations on the theme of self surrendered and re-won through poetic song.

In 'Lines of Life,' we find the speaker of Shelley's 'To Constantia, Singing' transported to a cold climate. 'Well, read my cheek, and watch my eye' (1), she begins, echoing and half-mocking the conversational ingenuousness of Coleridge's opening to 'This Lime-Tree Bower My Prison'. The invitation to 'read my cheek, and watch my eye' is issued by one whose eyes are not wet with tears and whose cheeks are not 'burning'. 'Too strictly school'd are they', she continues, 'One secret of my soul to show, / One hidden thought betray' (2–4). Landon employs her near singsong stanzaic form, with its equable eight-six balance of syllables, to communicate dissonant, unlyrical sentiments. The poetry is intricately self-annulling. It speaks intimately of the poet's refusal to countenance intimacy. The failure to rhyme the stanza's first and third lines adds to a sense of repudiation. Yet Landon's relation to Shelley—the poet who in *The Triumph of Life* alludes to 'thoughts which must remain untold' (21)—is not merely one of ironic dissent from emotive outcry. Much in Shelley, in fact, concerns itself with the repression of feeling. Examples include the close of *Julian and Maddalo* ('she told me how / All happen'd—but the cold world shall not know' (616–17)) and the opening of *Lines Written among the Euganean Hills*, where plangent trochees meet in a triplet rhyme to ask: 'What, if there no

---

[8] For a reading of Felicia Hemans's response to Byron, a response which may have influenced Landon's, see Susan J. Wolfson, 'Hemans and the Romance of Byron', *Felicia Hemans: Reimagining Poetry in the Nineteenth Century*, 155–80.
[9] The poem's text and stanzaic order, as Landon would have known it, differs so much from the best contemporary texts that no attempt is made to supply line-numbers.

friends will greet; / What, if there no heart will meet / His with love's impatient beat' (27–9). Landon occupies a lyric space that makes her the centre of a drama, the first act of which is to state that her life has not permitted her any chance to display authentic emotion. Landon's is a song of negative experience, yet positives gleam through the wreckage of social conformity and submission, as is signalled by the first line and a half of the poem's epigraph (presumably composed by Landon herself): 'Orphan in my first years, I early learnt / To make my heart suffice itself, and seek / Support and sympathy in its own depths'. Landon touches here on a motif resonantly developed by Wordsworth in *The Prelude* (unpublished until 1850) in which Wordsworth speaks of 'The self-sufficing power of solitude' (*1805*, II. 79) while the impulse to seek out and trust in the heart's 'own depths' implies a limit to the speaker's cynicism.[10] Indeed, accounting for the pathos of 'Lines of Life' is a strong sense that the speaker has not wholly quelled her longing for emotional fulfilment.

What is offered is protest as much as analysis. 'I never knew the time my heart / Look'd freely from my brow' (5–6) Landon writes in stanza 2, half-voicing belief in what her lines deny: a 'time my heart / Look'd freely from my brow'. Indeed, the poem might be spoken by one of the inhabitants of Shelley's fallen world in *Prometheus Unbound*, whose mode of speech is one that we know as it is negated through the millennial transformation depicted by the Spirit of the Hour at the end of Act III. 'I live among the cold, the false', asserts Landon in her third stanza, 'And I must seem like them; / And such I am, for I am false / As those I must condemn' (9–12). In Shelley's altered world, 'None talk'd that common, false, cold, hollow talk / Which makes the heart deny the *yes* it breathes, / Yet question that unmeant hypocrisy / With such a self-mistrust as has no name' (III. iv. 149–52). 'Such a self-mistrust' is given a name and a local habitation in 'Lines of Life'. 'False' is a complex word in Shelley's poetry; it denotes both a state of being at odds with the truth and a condition of near-helpless complicity. Julian and Maddalo sympathetically diagnose the Maniac as having, for the sake of someone by whom he has been crossed in love, 'fix'd a blot / Of falsehood in his mind, which flourish'd not / But in the light of all-beholding truth' (529–31). In the just-quoted lines from *Prometheus Unbound*, 'false' joins hands with 'cold', 'common', and 'hollow' to establish itself as a potent parallel to and possible source for Landon's glancing hint at drawing-room insincerities and treacheries. Landon rhymes 'false' with itself in the usually unrhymed first and third lines of the stanza to convey the depth of her inescapable entrapment.

In her first ten stanzas, and intermittently thereafter, Landon uses a device—repetition of the first-person pronoun—which conveys a sense, not of agency, but of clear-sighted awareness of being caught in the coils of an unfeeling, cynical social world. There may even be a suggestion of poetic as well as social dependence at the close of stanza 4: 'I borrow others' likeness, till / Almost I lose my own' (15–16). Looking ahead to T. S. Eliot's posturing speaker in 'Portrait of a Lady,' and backwards to Byron's attacks on social dissimulation in *Childe Harold's Pilgrimage*, Landon 'borrows' a technique which she would have met in Shelley's 'Song of

----

[10] Quoted from *Wordsworth: The Major Works*.

Apollo', published as 'Hymn of Apollo' in *Posthumous Poems*. Apollo's self-centred rhetoric is glorious more than vainglorious: 'I am the eye with which the Universe / Beholds itself, and knows it is divine' (31–2). These lines, the start of the last stanza, have an eloquence that is proof against the would-be cynical interpreter. At the same time, we might recall, as Earl R. Wasserman points out, that the 'Song of Apollo' is countered by Shelley's 'Song of Pan'. In the latter poem, Pan, speaks, not of an 'entirely self-contained subjectivity', as does Apollo, but of 'lived experience'.[11] So in the last stanza of the poem, Pan turns to the personal 'sorrow' of which his sweet 'pipings' (36) finally tell: 'And then I changed my pipings, — / Singing how down the vale of Menalus / I pursued a maiden and clasp'd a reed: / God and men, we are all deluded thus!' (29–32). Metrical variations work expressively here, reinforcing the cry of distress in that last line. Shelley's poems, then, offer an object lesson in two ways of using the first-person pronoun: one that represents the self as all-sufficient and all-powerful, the other that represents the self as open to pain and suffering, but achieving an awareness of fellow-feeling ('*we* are all deluded thus'; emphasis added).

If Landon studied Shelley's differing uses of the first-person pronoun in his two Hymns, she might have derived lessons which bear on her practice in a poem which takes as its subject the question of self-presentation. 'Lines of Life' is aware that the idea of the self as unwoundable and in control is a social sham, even as it senses that the hurts inflicted by 'lived experience' open the door to sympathy with others.

Certainly Landon's recourse to a similar rhetorical method is part of her poem's subterranean drama, its deep conviction that 'L. E. L.'—idol and plaything of post-Romantic literary consumerism—has that within her which equals the significance claimed for himself by Shelley's Apollo, as well as the capacity for pain and sympathy shown by Shelley's Pan.[12] That composite conviction begins to surface in stanza 7. After the ironic 'learn to feel their way' (20) of stanza 6, the suggestion of incompletely successful repression is matter for hope, however minimalist:

> I check my thoughts like curbed steeds
>   That struggle with the rein;
> I bid my feelings sleep, like wrecks
>   In the unfathom'd main.
>
> (21–4)

The image of shipwreck is distinctly Shelleyan, and may derive from 'Time', which opens, 'Unfathomable Sea! whose waves are years, / Ocean of time whose waters of deep woe / Are brackish with the salt of human tears!' (1–3), and whose gloomy metaphorical waters themselves seem to react against Byron's more august address to the Ocean at the close of *Childe Harold's Pilgrimage*, canto IV. Certainly, Landon's sleeping 'feelings' do not trust what Shelley calls the 'inhospitable shore' (7) bordering the 'unfathom'd main' of her inner existence. Shelleyan, too, in a more

---

[11] 'The Poetry of Skepticism', in *Norton*, 573.
[12] For Landon's 'commodified life', see ch. 6 of Anne K. Mellor, *Romanticism and Gender* (New York: Routledge, 1993), 123.

uplifting sense is the use of a negative adjective ('unfathom'd) to point towards 'infinite potentiality,' in Timothy Webb's phrase.[13] And the image of 'the curbed steeds' conjures up a Shelleyan energy—of the kind at work in the description of the 'cars drawn by rainbow-winged steeds' in *Prometheus Unbound* (II. iv.130)—in the act of evoking the need to check it.

Ensuing stanzas indicate the extent to which Landon has not interiorized her society's values. Landon shares Shelley's dislike of those who 'Mock at all high and early truth' (27), and belongs to that line of poets, beginning with Blake and cul-minating in Yeats, who would 'Mock mockers after that' ('Nineteen Hundred and Nineteen', V. 108).[14] So her line 'high and early truth' asserts its superiority to those who would mock it. But the miserable fact, for Landon, lending her poem its unique timbre, is the confession of complicity, caught in the let-down quality of the stanza's last line: 'And I too do the same' (28). There, 'too,' more than a line-filler, concedes the speaker's herd-following conformity. Shelley, indeed, may be among the 'spiritual, the kind, / The pure, but named in mirth' (33–4) of stanza nine, and certainly that stanza exhibits a Shelleyan mournfulness as it imagines the consequences of cynical 'mirth': 'Till all of good, ay, even hope, / Seems exiled from our earth' (3–6). Landon might be describing the quasi-Dantean condition of the 'morally dead,' to borrow Shelley's phrase from his Preface to *Alastor*, even as she herself bids to be seen as 'a wonder of this earth, / Where there is little of transcendent worth', as *Julian and Maddalo* has it (590–1). 'Hope' is the funda-mental Shelleyan virtue, closely connected, at the close of *Prometheus Unbound*, to the creative energies that might undo the ill effects of tyranny's return, as Demogorgon admonishes his listeners 'to hope till Hope creates / From its own wreck the thing it contemplates' (IV. 573–4),

Before Landon's poem follows Demogorgon's advice, it has further depths of self-abasement to plumb. Tersely, Landon concludes the opening ten stanzas governed by the first person with an image, that of the sword of Damocles, used strikingly by Shelley in *Prometheus Unbound*. Landon uses it to describe her fear of 'withering ridicule' (37), 'A sword hung by a single hair / For ever o'er the head' (39–40). Shelley employs the image to depict what is at stake in Prometheus's resistance to Jupiter's reign:

> For what submission but that fatal word,
> The death-seal of mankind's captivity,
> Like the Sicilian's hair-suspended sword,
> Which trembles o'er his crown, would he accept,
> Or could I yield?
> (I. 396–400)

Landon brings Shelley's concern with power politics into the gendered realm of salon and ballroom, but her diagnosis of social paralysis suggests the need for change.

---

[13] 'The Unascended Heaven: Negatives in *Prometheus Unbound*,' in *Norton*, 703.
[14] W. B. Yeats, *The Variorum Edition of the Poems of W. B. Yeats*, ed. Peter Allt and Russell K. Alspach (New York: Macmillan, 1957), 432.

Her attack on 'a most servile faith' (41), that of conformity to social dictates, is hardly exceeded by Shelley's hostility to religious faith.

The breakthrough comes in stanza 13 where an assertive rather than a penitent 'I' takes over. In this stanza, and the next three, Landon articulates a visionary apologia, the more affecting for its apparent withdrawal in stanzas 17 and 18, when 'earth, and earth's debasing stain, / Again is on my soul; / And I am but a nameless part / Of a most worthless whole' (69–72). Internal rhyme reinforces the sense of a struggle taking place in the throes of composition, a practice often found in Shelley, as in Byron. But before the descent into savage mockery of a Romantic notion of life as a 'whole,' Landon has uttered sentiments that are distinctly Shelleyan, feeling 'a loftier mood / Of generous impulse, high resolve, / Steal o'er my solitude!' (50–2). She describes, too, a longing for a stellar light that recalls Shelley's sense, at the end of *Adonais*, of a star-like soul that 'Beacons from the abode where the Eternal are' (495). Her verse moves us by watching itself 'wish, so passionately wish, / A light like theirs on high' (55–6). She expresses 'eagerness of hope / To benefit my kind' (57–8) and, in a very Shelleyan rhyme, caps this eagerness with the conviction that 'immortal power / Were given to my mind' (59–60). Landon, too, is caught up in dreams of 'eternal fame' (61), momentarily allying herself, as she imagines 'the gloriousness of death' (63), with that 'best philosophy' (213) of which Shelley writes in *Epipsychidion*, 'whose taste / Makes this cold common hell, our life, a doom / As glorious as a fiery martyrdom' (213–14). Landon compares 'eternal fame' to 'The sun of earthly gloom' (62), a suggestive image, since if fame is a 'sun' that shines out in the midst of 'earthly gloom' it is part of and even derives its lustre from the very 'gloom' which it seems to transcend. The writing suggests a dialectic, both compensatory and creative, between the experience of 'earthly gloom' and the hoped-for attainment of 'eternal fame'. Shelley and Landon share a view of 'our life' as a 'cold common hell' that, for both, can be transfigured: for Shelley by that 'best philosophy', for Landon by 'eternal fame'. Landon's ideal, however, is distinctly perilous, where it seems the idealizing shadow of worldly gossip and censure, and it may be an implicit recognition of this fact that brings her poem tumbling down to earth.

When it recovers, a new tone emerges, one that links Landon unabashedly with Shelley and Byron as she asks the question central to poetic composition and articulates an answer at the heart of the Romantic project:

> Why write I this? because my heart
> Towards the future springs,
> That future where it loves to soar
> On more than eagle wings.
>
> (73–6)

'Why write I this?': the use of 'this' rather than, say, 'verse' defines Landon's question as being about the current poem, 'Lines of Life'. And the deferral of hope to the future is a characteristic Shelleyan posture of the spirit: 'my heart / Towards the future springs' might serve as an epigraph to Shelley's poetic oeuvre, close to whose heart lies a Utopian impulse. Mercury tortures Prometheus with a chilling vista of 'Eternity' as a place where all we can 'imagine' of time, 'age on age', 'Seems but a point'

(*Prometheus Unbound*, I. 417, 418, 419). Landon borrows Mercury's image as a point of departure for hope:

> The present, it is but a speck
> In that eternal time,
> In which my lost hopes find a home,
> My spirit knows its clime.
>
> (77–80)

Landon's succinct charting of 'futurity' as the 'home' for her 'lost hopes' implicitly passes a judgement on itself. The very language seems half to concede that its imaginings are compensatory. At this point, Landon draws a distinction between her quotidian self, rejected as 'worthless', and her inspired poetic self when 'song has touch'd my lips with fire,' a distinction which owes much to Byron's contrast in *Childe Harold's Pilgrimage*, canto III, stanza 6, between his ordinary self and the 'Soul of my thought', and to Shelley's movement, in 'Ode to the West Wind', from the self that falls upon 'the thorns of life' (54) to the empowered self inspired by the wind whose 'lyre' (57) he proposes to be. Landon's image of herself as 'a vile link / Amid life's weary chain' (89–90) adapts both Byronic and Shelleyan images to her own condition.[15] The image of the 'chain' seems especially to recall the moment in *Julian and Maddalo* when the Maniac cries out against dragging 'life on—which like a heavy chain / Lengthens behind with many a link of pain' (302–3). 'O do not say in vain!' (92) is Landon's exclamation after her proud assertion that she has spoken 'hallow'd words' (91) hoping to counteract the force of the Maniac's tersely enjambed 'How vain / Are words!' (472–3). Evidently Landon wears her chain with a difference; yet there is kinship as well as distance between the imprisonment of disappointed yet residually heroic souls in 'Lines of Life' and *Julian and Maddalo*. Just as the Maniac's conviction of the futility of words does not prevent him from speaking, so the element of creative self-doubt in 'Lines of Life' cannot wholly quell the poet's desire that her 'charmed chords' (94) will 'Wake to the morning light of fame' (95). Such, she confesses, qualifying her earlier outburst at lines 55–6, is 'My first, my last, my only wish' (93). The power of the poem lies in its compactly tensed gush of hope that the poet's 'words' (96) will survive, murmured and read by future readers. After these questions comes the final stanza:

> Let music make less terrible
> The silence of the dead;
> I care not, so my spirit last
> Long after life has fled.
>
> (105–8)

Landon concludes with a 'terrible' affirmation: her use of 'terrible' (placed resonantly at the end of the line) is strong enough to vibrate with the force of Pericles' 'A terrible childbed hast thou had, my dear' (*Pericles* III. i. 56) and yet in touch with the overlappings conjured up by Shelley in 'To Night', when he speaks of the 'Spirit of

---

[15] For the suggestion of an echo of *Childe Harold's Pilgrimage*, III. 72. 685 ('A link reluctant in a fleshly chain'), see *Romantic Poetry: An Annotated Anthology*, 465.

Night' as having 'wovest dreams of joy and fear, / Which make thee terrible and dear' (5–6). Landon's own music brings out how 'dear' her literary dreams of 'joy and fear' have been, and bravely allows 'The silence of the dead,' set apart in a line to itself, its 'terrible' and challenging authority. The 'silence' imagined here is that which will fall upon her in death, and the 'music' is perhaps that of a church-service, perhaps, more generally, composed of trumpet-blasts of fame. Such 'music' now, almost as though Landon were forsaking fame, the last infirmity of noble minds, seems not to matter. 'I care not', she writes, all her hopes pinned on the survival of 'my spirit'. The poem lays bare, affectingly, the hopes and fears that underpin Romantic assertions that spirit is indomitable, as in its different way does a poem like *Adonais*, whose positive declarations—'the pure spirit shall flow / Back to the burning fountain whence it came' (38. 338–9)—allow us to experience them as springing from the very human compulsion to find answers to formidable questions, in this case those broached earlier in Shelley's elegy: 'Whence are we, and why are we? of what scene / The actors or spectators?' (21. 184–5). A dramatized wildness and varied emotional turbulence fit themselves to the symmetrical neatness of Landon's stanzas, embodying the conflict between adherence to social norms and the wish to break free from such norms at the centre of her strangely 'terrible' poem.[16]

In response to a portrait of Keats, Landon sent some blank verse lines to a correspondent which were published in *The Examiner*, 1 September 1824. In them, she writes of Keats: 'thou dost hold communion with / Thoughts dark and terrible', lines which mimic their imagined 'communion' by loitering at the end of the line before the strong stresses that cluster in 'Thoughts dark and terrible' (Sypher, 183–4). Landon addresses Keats in Shelleyan terms: 'thou / Wert like the lovely presence of a dream', she writes, and one recalls how the Poet of *Alastor*, republished in *Posthumous Poems* in the same year as Landon's poem about Keats appeared in print, was 'driven / By the bright shadow of that lovely dream' (232–3). Landon, that is, conceives of Keats rather as the Poet shapes his imaginings of the lost 'veilèd maid' (151); in both Landon and Shelley the 'lovely' twines disquietingly round the 'terrible' (Landon) or the brightly shadowy (Shelley).

Landon responds most vividly to Shelley when she hears in his work the accents of transcendental seeker and anguishing elegist. In *A History of the Lyre* she plays her own gendered variation on the theme and mode of *Julian and Maddalo*. Like Shelley, Landon surrounds presentation of a figure at the edge of society—in her case not a Maniac, but an *improvisatrice*, Eulalie—with a narrative frame.[17] Like

---

[16] The poem is the more intriguing for complicating what Richard Cronin, in a very suggestive discussion, calls 'the relationship that remains central in all of Landon's poems, the relationship between herself and her reader'. Cronin's elegant formulation of this 'relationship' reads as follows: 'These are stories of "woman's tears", and tears, for Landon, dissolve the distinction between poet and character. Her characters weep, and she represents the verse that records their tears as itself a kind of weeping', *Romantic Victorians: English Literature, 1824–1840* (Basingstoke: Palgrave, 2002), 85. Landon's sobs are distinctly suppressed in 'Lines of Life'.

[17] For readings of 'A History of the Lyre', see, in particular, Angela Leighton, *Victorian Women Poets: Writing against the Heart* (New York: Harvester Wheatsheaf, 1992), who argues that the poem benefits artistically from 'a scepticism precisely against feeling', 68, and Angela Esterhammer, who, in 'The Improvisatrice's Fame: Landon, Staël, and Female Performers in Italy', in *British and European*

Julian, the narrator writes, at the opening, of remembered experience: 'This face, whose rudely pencill'd sketch you hold, / Recalls to me a host of pleasant thoughts, / And some more serious. —This is EULALIE' (5–7). And he proceeds later to a leave-taking—'I soon left Italy' (378)—that echoes Julian's 'The following morning, urged by my affairs, / I left bright Venice' (582–3), and to a subsequent return. Whereas Julian meets Maddalo's daughter, Landon's narrator, now married and with a child, meets Eulalie again, now virtually her own statue, an emblem of a creativity foiling anything approaching normal human life:

> Yon statue is my emblem; see, its grasp
> Is raised to Heaven, forgetful that the while
> Its step has crush'd the fairest of earth's flowers
> With its neglect
>
> (442–5)

Seeking to offer a sketch 'from that most passionate page, / A woman's heart', as her poem's epigraph tells us, Landon suggests that Eulalie is, in some way, a female descendant of Shelley's Poet in *Alastor*. Shelley's Poet, after a period in which he lives 'without human sympathy', 'seeks in vain for a prototype of his conception' (Preface to *Alastor*, 92) of an ideal partner. If he represents from one moralizing perspective a warning against poetic solitude, he also, more powerfully, suggests the tragic fate of a figure dedicated to his own exalted conceptions. Eulalie, too, 'would be beloved' (252), but she laments her inability to achieve love; like Shelley's Poet, Eulalie's commitment to the imagination seems to exile her from the world of ordinary feelings. When at the close, then, in lines 442–5, quoted above, she finds an 'emblem' for her life in an art-work, her own statue, she implicitly points up the life-stifling consequences of an artistic achievement that embodies transcendent yearning: the statue's 'grasp' may be 'raised to Heaven', but 'Its step has crush'd the fairest of earth's flowers / With its neglect'. Shelley's Poet, too, treats 'an Arab maiden' (129) with neglect, before developing an obsession with his at least partly self-created and idealized 'veiled maid'; moreover, in lines that Landon may be recalling, his own approaching physical dissolution inflicts a matching decay on the natural world: 'from his steps / Bright flowers departed' (536–7).

Unlike Shelley's Poet, Eulalie receives due fame: she is 'The centre of group, whose converse light / Made a fit element, in which her wit / Flash'd like the lightning' (99–101), where Landon may draw her imagery from Shelley's 'Letter to Maria Gisborne' in which the poet recalls feeling 'the transverse lightning linger warm / Upon my cheek' (149–50). But Shelley celebrates 'good will' (151); Eulalie is alone in the midst of company. Both poets unite in their admiration of 'the immortal dead' (*A History of the Lyre*, 136), yet both are troubled by the status of 'feeling'. Just as Shelley's Maniac mistrusts language and just as Rousseau in *The Triumph of Life* worries that his words have been the 'seeds of misery' (280), so in *A History*

Romanticisms: Selected Papers from the Munich Conference of the German Society for English Romanticism, ed. Christoph Bode and Sebastian Domsch, ed. (Trier: Wissenschaftlicher Verlag Trier, 2007), 227–38, explores 'what happens when the writing poet self-consciously re-casts her own experience as that of an *improvisatrice*', 233.

of the Lyre Landon stages an impasse faced by a poet driven by the intensity of her feeling to a confrontation with possible alternatives to Romantic intensities (suicidal despair or cynical indifference) which both seem untenable, and so reaffirms her commitment to a sensitivity which isolates her.[18] An earlier credo provoked by praise for Leigh Hunt's criticism—'in criticism as in everything else to feel is to understand' (Sypher, 184)—still abides. Eulalie's account of the unassuagable 'price' (216) paid by the inspired poet again echoes emphases in Shelley. In the fragmentary lyric 'The Zucca', Shelley's speaker uses sinuous yet halting (and uncompleted) *ottava rima* to communicate a sense that 'this low sphere, / And all that it contains, contains not thee' (20–1). 'Thee', there, is Shelley's version of Coleridge's Ideal Object, unlocatable for the younger poet in 'this low sphere' and deriving its value from its unlocatableness. The poet is left to 'weep / The instability of all but weeping' (9–10). In *The Triumph of Life*, Rousseau argues with fierce disdain that 'if the spark with which Heaven lit my spirit / Had been with purer sentiment supplied, / Corruption would not now thus much inherit / Of what was once Rousseau, — nor this disguise / Stain'd that which ought to have disdain'd to wear it' (201–5).[19] The complicated syntax keeps in play Rousseau's sense of being the victim of what was best about him, 'the spark with which Heaven lit my spirit', even as the last line concedes a subliminal degree of responsibility for his fall.

The lines feel like the last testament of a High Romantic posture of the spirit— and to involve an embattled defence of such a posture. Landon, too, through Eulalie's history of her poetic career, speaks of disappointment, but, finally, preserves a desperate faith in poetry. Eulalie's speech articulates mingled feelings of regret and longing. Like Shelley's speaker in 'The Zucca,' or like Rousseau, for her, 'gleams of heaven have only made me feel / Its distance from our earth more forcibly' (218–19). Yet to 'feel' is to retain a spiritual distinction that has it own worth, and forces one to qualify Leighton's reading of the poem as showing that 'To be sceptical is a new truth which L. E. L. learns towards the end of her poetic career'.[20] 'Learns', that powerful verb in Landon's vocabulary, passes over into the prose of one of her most distinguished critics, but whether the value of *A History of the Lyre* lies in a 'sceptical' lesson that it supposedly teaches is a view about which one might wish to be 'sceptical'.

The critical desire to rescue Landon from the tearful idiom of sensibility with which she is often associated and see her as developing into a maturer, sceptical reserve about feeling is understandable, but it risks overlooking her almost Blakean refusal to settle for the apparent truths of experience: hope and desire remain in the midst of clear evidence of their inevitable failure. Indeed, in the lines singled out by Leighton as marking a step towards a soberer truth, lines in which Eulalie describes how the increasingly disillusioned young poet 'has turn'd sceptic to the truth which made / His feelings poetry' (297–8), Landon comes close to describing the condition

---

[18] Leighton, *Victorian Women Poets*, 68.
[19] Mary Shelley's 1824 edition, the edition possibly used by Landon, uses 'purer sentiment' rather than 'nutriment', and 'Had' for 'Earth'; the latter readings are preferred by modern editors.
[20] Leighton, *Victorian Women Poets*, 68.

against which Shelley warns in *Prometheus Unbound*, Act I: 'Ah, sister! Desolation is a delicate thing' (772). It is by no means clear that turning 'sceptic to the truth which made / His feelings poetry' composes a stepping-stone towards some recompensing if disillusioned truth; indeed, poetic death is seen as the consequence of such scepticism: 'What can he do / But hang his lute on some lone tree, and die?' (303–4). Eulalie, in fact, turns from such end-stopped scepticism to reawaken awareness of what cradled her into poetry in the first place, and chiefly ascribes the originating impulse to 'Remembrance' (311), a sense at once Wordsworthian and Shelleyan that 'we must have known some former state / More glorious than our present' (305–6). Though such knowledge and remembrance are double-edged in that they bequeath a longing that takes away 'happiness' (321), their lure is still to be felt in the poetry, which demonstrates tugs to and from 'the actual world' (314): tugs of a kind often found in Shelley.

Eulalie says that it is remembrance 'that fills the actual world / With unreal likenesses of lovely shapes, / That were and are not' (314–16), a thought that comes close to simultaneous critique of and empathy with Shelleyan idealism. Landon calls to mind Shelley's warning admonition to:

> Lift not the painted veil which those who live
> Call Life: though unreal shapes be pictured there,
> And it but mimic all we would believe
> With colours idly spread'
>
> (1–4)

Eulalie speaks of 'unreal likenesses of lovely shapes', but she does not condemn the shapes as 'unreal', only their 'likenesses'; she is still persuaded that such shapes 'were', even if they 'are not'. Indeed, 'the actual world' uses 'actual' to suggest limitation; there must, she still implies, be more in heaven and earth than seem apparent in 'the actual world'. Shelley identifies 'Life' with 'unreal shapes' and 'colours idly spread'. In both poets the lure of the 'real', as opposed to the 'actual', can still be felt, for all their sense that disappointment lies in wait for the idealizing quester. Shelley's reversed sonnet features in its octave an account of one who 'sought, / For his lost heart was tender, things to love, / But found them not, alas! nor was there aught / The world contains, the which he could approve' (7–10). The attitudes are balanced between detachment (his 'heart' was 'lost' and there is a shade of something almost arrogantly superior in 'could approve') and sympathy (his heart was 'tender', the quest for 'things to love' sounds genuine). Shelley displaces the process on to a doubled other. Landon, too, uses Eulalie to depict a version of herself as poet. If the first-person narrative deployed by Landon makes Eulalie sound less guarded than Shelley in his sonnet, her confessions of fault are never unqualified: 'My thoughts were birds of paradise, that breathed / The airs of heaven, but died on touching home' (338–9). Rousseau's rejection of a world which failed to sustain his heaven-lit spirit again resonates in the background, and it is Landon's distinction to reawaken memories of Shelley's own divided views of idealism.

The price paid as a poet in Landon's work is heavy, and Landon frequently recounts it. But it is, in Eulalie's words, '*my* price' (216; emphasis added). Landon never wholly rejects the value of poetry, even as she can see how in her culture and career poems can be merely commodified. Landon's reflections on the poetic career and on the Shelleyan or High Romantic legacy articulate themselves with most persuasiveness in her elegy for her fellow female poet, Felicia Hemans. From its opening 'No more, no more—oh, never more returning, / Will thy beloved presence gladden earth' (1–2), Landon's poem alludes to other Romantic poems. As McGann and Riess note, she produces 'self-consciously quotational writing' (*LSW*, 23), almost annulling itself in the act of utterance. Here, one catches echoes of Byron's 'Dejection Ode' stanzas in the first canto of *Don Juan* which play on and play up a strain of plangency: 'No more—no more—Oh! never more on me / The freshness of the heart can fall like dew' (*Don Juan* I. 214. 1705–6). One hears, too, Shelley's lament in *Adonais*: 'He will awake no more, oh, never more!' (8. 64). As throughout her essay on Hemans, Landon is also alluding to the dead woman's poetry, especially her poem 'No More!', a poem which forms a lyric meditation on the 'dirge-like sound' of the two words. McGann and Riess would have us hear Landon as a pasticheur of genius who brilliantly exposes the hollowness of the poem as affect-commodity. This is more persuasive than John Constable's robust view that the opening echoes (he notes only the Byronic reference) expose Landon's threadbare lack of invention: 'who but the apologist' Constable asks scornfully, 'would care to distinguish the Byronism of Felicia Dorothea Hemans from that of Letitia Elizabeth Landon?'[21] The implication is that both are as bad as each other. But neither the consummate professional nor the artless amateur will quite suit as a label to define the elegist of 'Felicia Hemans'. The texture of the verse is less 'quotational' than subtly aligning itself with a Romantic company of poets, all of whom win artistic recompense from experiential loss. The very fact of beginning with multiple echoes associates Landon with poets who use words as a stay against the vanishing lamented by the content of the words. Thus, Landon invokes the visionary company of High Romantics, not as a simpering admirer nor as a gender-embattled critic, but as a fellow-traveller through the same regions of initial delight in poetry's promise of supplying, Wordsworth-like, 'A general bond of union' (21), and into the subsequent discovery of poetry's cost—'Was not his purchased all too dearly?' (33).

The power of this antistrophic turn in the poem where the original emphasis on what is 'known' passes into what we 'know not'—'We see the goal, but know not the endeavour' (35)—is immense. Landon's melodious, rhyming pentameters, with their alternating feminine rhymes, exist in affecting contrast to the 'sorrow' that emerges in stanza 3 as inseparable from 'song' (42). She plays a keenly individual variation on the Shelleyan discovery of the limits of knowledge, expressed in 'To a Skylark' in the question 'What thou art we know not' (31), or in *Julian and Maddalo* as Maddalo's sense that 'Our thoughts and our desires' 'pray' 'For what? they know not' (125, 126, 127).

The poem is sophisticated in its determination to tell the truth about what it is to be a female poet in Landon's culture. Landon employs dizzying double-takes: her

[21] John Constable, 'Romantic Women's Poetry: Is It Any Good?', *Cambridge Quarterly* 29 (2000): 133–43 (142).

elegy for Hemans is manifestly a poem in which the elegist dwells on her own concerns, much as the poet of *Adonais*, or his double, knows himself to be one 'Who in another's fate now wept his own' (34. 300). And what she shares with Hemans turns out to be a finally triumphant inability fully to break out of the very artistic work whose purpose is to tell us of 'the long sad hours' (45) lived beyond art. The poem retains its dignity and poise, teaching in song what it has learned in suffering, which is that 'song' and 'sorrow' are fated always to stay apart from one another, itself a source of suffering: 'We say, the song is sorrowful, but know not / What may have left that sorrow on the song' (41–2).

It is fitting that Landon uses Shelley to comprehend the nature of Hemans's (and her own) latent tragedies in two ways: she sees 'The fable of Prometheus and the vulture' (55) as revealing 'the poet's and the woman's heart' (56), implying the relevance of Shelley's most ambitious long poem; and she concludes by devising for Hemans an abode beyond this world that recalls Shelley's millennial imaginings in his lyrical drama. Asia is borne on by singing that is inspired by 'music's most serene dominions' (II. v. 86). Landon invites Hemans to 'Enter [...] that serene dominion, / Where earthly cares and earthly sorrows cease' (75–6), turning Shelley's journey towards transformation into a resting-place; but even as she imagines a world beyond poetry she finds solace and creative stimulus for her female poet in the 'fascination' still aroused in her by one of her most significant male forerunners.

16

The Wheels of Being

Shelley and Tennyson

Comparing Tennyson with Shelley, Walter Bagehot deemed the younger poet to be 'evidently inferior in general intensity of mind', but to be 'a first-rate *realiser*'. 'It is characteristic of Shelley', writes Bagehot, 'that he was obliged to abandon one of his favourite speculations, "dizzy from thrilling horror"'. Of this abstract intensity Mr. Tennyson has not a particle. He is never very eager about anything, and he is certainly not over-anxious about phantoms and abstractions'.[1] The fact that one might pass in virtually the same moment from agreeing readily with Bagehot to taking issue with him points towards a key feature of Tennyson's poetic relations with Shelley: that they are sinuously if murkily antithetical and covertly sympathetic, a matter of turning away and towards, the later poet's hand forever at his lips bidding adieu. Emergence and differentiation marry as Tennyson, the 'first-rate *realiser*', lingers in the chambers of a post-Romantic sea, amplifying and modulating the music typical of Shelleyan aspirations, crises, hopes, and fears.

'*Realise*' Tennyson does over and over in his dealings with the great idealizer among the Romantics. In *The Triumph of Life* Shelley's Rousseau locates his tale of menacing bewitchment in spring, a metaphorical season no longer far behind, but now entrancingly if treacherously alive with a sense of new birth and hope, a time 'When all the forest-tips began to burn / With kindling green' (309–10).[2] Tennyson rekindles the charge of Shelley's lines in duskier, gloomier mode when in *In Memoriam* he writes of the yew tree, with covert reference to the speaker's own

---

[1] Quoted in *Tennyson: The Critical Heritage*, ed. John D. Jump (London: Routledge & Kegan Paul, 1967), 234, 235, 234. Comparisons between Tennyson and Shelley effectively begin with A. H. Hallam's unsigned review in *Englishman's Magazine* 1 (August 1831), 616–28, of *Poems, Chiefly Lyrical* (1832), which emphasizes '[Tennyson's] original genius' while classing him with Keats and Shelley as 'Poets of Sensation' (*Tennyson: Critical Heritage*, 42). More recent notable contributions to comparative discussion include Margaret A. Lourie, 'Below the Thunders of the Upper Deep: Tennyson as Romantic Revisionist', *Studies in Romanticism* 18 (1979): 3–27, hereafter Lourie; and relevant sections of Herbert F. Tucker, *Tennyson and the Doom of Romanticism* (Cambridge: Harvard University Press, 1988), hereafter Tucker, *Tennyson*; Cronin, *Romantic Victorians*; and Aidan Day, *Tennyson's Scepticism* (Basingstoke: Palgrave, 2005), hereafter Day. Ricks's edition, *The Poems of Tennyson*, ed. Christopher Ricks, 2nd edn incorporating the Trinity College MSS, 3 vols (Harlow: Longman, 1987), hereafter *Ricks* (the edition used for quotations from Tennyson's poetry) and *In Memoriam*, ed. Susan Shatto and Marion Shaw (Oxford: Oxford University Press, 1982), offer invaluable help in tracing allusions and echoes.

[2] Quoted from *Major Works*. This edition, with some other modern editions, reads 'forest tops' rather than 'forest tips', the reading Tennyson would have encountered in Mary Shelley's editions. The echo of Shelley is noted by Ricks (XXXIX, 11n.).

passages of feeling: 'Thy gloom is kindled at the tips, / And passes into gloom again'.[3] 'Thy' serves almost as metapoetic self-address as Tennyson coaxes Shelley's lines into a distillation of mercurial if elegiac mood.

What Tennyson's compact allusion suggests is that gloom can be 'kindled'; grief can pass into song, perhaps even model itself on the evocation of a neo-Dantean 'Light whose smile kindles the Universe' in *Adonais* (54. 478), a 'Light' that seeks to render benign 'the eclipsing Curse / Of birth' (54. 480–1) with which the line containing it rhymes. With the hyper-dextrous speed typical of poetic allusion, Tennyson glances at *Adonais* in the act of recalling *The Triumph of Life*, and his glance expands, as can often happen with allusion, into a gaze that reads Shelley's elegy in a newly quickened and quickening fashion. As a reading of *Adonais*, it captures, in the terms and through the mode peculiar to literary allusion, the insight which A. C. Bradley expresses when he remarks that 'in *Adonais* [...] the impression of passionate rapidity in the transition from gloom to glory is essential to the effect'.[4]

Tennyson's 'realizations' engage with the ideal, even as Shelleyan ideals frequently remind us of their unreached location in some as yet 'unascended Heaven' (*Prometheus Unbound*, III. iv. 203). 'He is often too much in the clouds for me. I admire his "Alastor," "Adonais," "Prometheus Unbound," and "Epipsychidion" ',[5] Tennyson is reported to have said of Shelley, with no apparent sense of having selected four examples of his predecessor at his most magnificently cloudy. Such cloudiness, indeed, may betoken something dark, even tragic in Shelley, who is able to imagine, in a tone of severe lament, Venice and its sister cities as 'Clouds which stain truth's rising day' (161) in 'Lines Written among the Euganean Hills', or who speaks, in even more sombre mood, of 'the last clouds of cold mortality' (54. 486) towards the close of *Adonais*. Shelley comes trailing clouds of ardent aspiration for Tennyson, yes, but also he brings with him haunting traces of close encounters with 'sad reality' (*Major Works*, 314), as he calls it in his dedicatory letter to Leigh Hunt at the head of *The Cenci*.

In Memoriam thrives on discontinuities as well as links between its 'Short swallow-flights of song' (XLVIII. 15), and, despite the grief evident in many preceding poems, it is still with a frisson of shelving and deepening that one enters the slow-pulsed, depressive movement of section L:

> Be near me when my light is low,
>   When the blood creeps, and the nerves prick
>   And tingle; and the heart is sick,
> And all the wheels of Being slow.
>
> (L. 1–4)

---

[3] Quoted from *The Poems of Tennyson*, ed. Ricks, 296: XXXIX. 11–12. References are made not to page number, but to poem, canto and line numbers. Unless otherwise noted, quotations from Tennyson's poetry are from this volume.

[4] A. C. Bradley, *A Commentary on Tennyson's 'In Memoriam'* (London: Macmillan, 1901), 23.

[5] Hallam Tennyson, *Alfred, Lord Tennyson: A Memoir by his Son*, 2 vols (London: Macmillan, 1897), 2, 285. Hereafter *Mem*.

Tennyson's echoes and borrowings are remarkable for their blend of the unmisgiving and the canny. On the one hand, one imagines that he would dismiss abruptly the observation that these lines contain potent reminiscences (noted by Ricks) of Shelley's *The Cenci*, where the Count is in a state of chilling excitement at the thought of his imminent rape of his daughter—

> My blood is running up and down my veins;
> A fearful pleasure makes it prick and tingle:
> I feel a giddy sickness of strange awe—
> (*The Cenci*, IV. i. 163–5)

and of *Queen Mab*, IX. 151–2, in which it is stated that all things 'urge / The restless wheels of being on their way'. On the other hand, there seem good reasons why those Shelleyan phrases might have grouped themselves together in his memory. The lines spoken by Count Cenci belong to the drama's fascination with 'self-anatomy' (II. ii. 110), as Orsino describes it. They do not merely describe; they also imply the speaker's half-sickened view of his response to 'fearful pleasure', sparking off his subliminal recognition of the moral abyss that opens before him. Cenci about to rape Beatrice is a nightmarish double of the poet experiencing 'strange awe' in the face of sublime experience, as when the speaker of 'Mont Blanc' exclaims 'Dizzy Ravine!' (version A, 34) and seemingly enters a 'trance sublime and strange' (35). Tennyson, when his 'light is low', has an appalled knowledge of a shadow self and that knowledge is pointed up by the echo of Cenci's words. And, true to the deepest tendency of the *abba* rhyme scheme, 'all the wheels of Being slow', the powerful brake of the verb stills a stanza whose pulse has been beating both distinctly and with abnormal languor. It is understandable at this juncture that a moment of fiery exultation from *Queen Mab* should manifest itself, bringing to the fore a contrasting view in which 'the restless wheels of being' turn with accelerating hopefulness.

Tennyson's allusive art, at the close of this stanza, recalls a Shelleyan idea, then, one of millenarian hope, even as it re-adapts its language to a passage marked by intense psychological realization, to stay with Bagehot's term. In so doing, it typifies the dialectical subtlety of Tennyson's poetic commerce with Shelley, one that bears comparison with the way in which his great rival, Robert Browning, shaped his poetic selfhood out of a complex response to his sun-treading precursor. 'Browning's grotesque diction', Sarah Wood writes helpfully, 'is formed in reaction to the lyrical beauty of Shelley's, and Browning's poems display Shelleyan tropes in perverse and ingenious ways'.[6] 'Two in the Campagna' is not exactly 'grotesque' in its language. But its leaping, jumpy rhythms put to the test the incantatory couplets and idealizing longings of Shelley's *Epipsychidion*; their melody and ecstatic anguishing are replayed in a modern, puzzled consciousness haunted by the Romantic poet's desire for union, but able only and yet fully to 'discern— / Infinite passion, and the pain / Of finite hearts that yearn' (58–60).[7] If that sounds

⁶ Sarah Wood, *Robert Browning: A Literary Life* (Basingstoke: Palgrave, 2001), 117.
⁷ Quoted from *Victorian Poetry: An Annotated Anthology*, ed. Francis O'Gorman (Malden: Blackwell, 2004).

like a thwarting, it is strikingly Shelleyan in its ability to grasp acutely the link between erotic 'pain' and a 'yearning' for something 'Infinite', some absolute. That example might suggest that it is dangerous ever to try to cut antitheses too cleanly where Shelley's relations with Victorian poetry are concerned. So, when one returns to Bagehot's assurance that 'Tennyson is certainly not over-anxious about phantoms and abstractions', the phrasing seems a touch too gruffly sensible, even over-certain. The Shelley of 'England in 1819' (published posthumously in 1839), desperately hopeful that from the 'graves' of contemporary society 'a glorious Phantom may / Burst, to illumine our tempestuous day' (13–14), is one thing; and the Tennyson, whose post-nervous breakdown speaker in *Maud* sees 'the dreary phantom' of his 'old hysterical mock-disease' 'arise and fly / Far into the North, and battle, and seas of death' (316: III. 36, 33, 36–7), is another. But both deal in mental entities and projections; both convey duplicity of intent through adroit formal manoeuvres. Shelley places his emphasis with a calculatedly dithering firmness on the very unfirm auxiliary 'may'. Tennyson coalesces ideas of exorcism and persistence through the phrasing of 'arise and fly / Far into [...]': the 'dreary phantom', that is, is lost in and, therefore, an abiding part of 'the North, and battle, and seas of death', as though the speaker were unconsciously acknowledging that the embracing, through the Crimean War, of 'the purpose of God, and the doom assigned' (III. 59) derived from 'That old hysterical mock-disease'.

Tennyson's speaker apostrophizes his 'passionate heart' (III. 32) in a way that Yeats echoes at the start of 'The Tower', when he exclaims, 'O heart, O troubled heart' (I. 2).[8] There, the wording re-inserts the 'trouble' that Tennyson's speaker seeks to expel, bringing out an affinity between three poets—Shelley, Tennyson, and Yeats—in whom the troubled heart is the begetter of 'phantoms'. In Yeats's case, the sequence after 'The Tower', 'Meditations in Time of Civil War', concludes with a poem that bears the self-mocking yet grand title 'I See Phantoms of Hatred and of the Heart's Fullness and of the Coming Emptiness'. The title is self-mocking because the phantoms that promise occult knowledge vanish into a failed genie's bottle marked 'half-read wisdom of daemonic images' (VII. 39), but it is grand, or refuses wholly to dispel an aura of grandeur, because to 'see phantoms' may be, for the post-Romantic poet, the nearest approach to 'wisdom' that remains. In his turn, Shelley invokes and evokes Emily as 'High, spirit-wingèd Heart' (13) in *Epipsychidion*, one of Tennyson's favourite poems by his Romantic forebear.[9] He does so precisely because his own heart urges him to hear a projected voice telling him, ' "O Thou of hearts the weakest, / The phantom is beside thee whom thou seekest" ' (231–2). The grieving Tennyson of *In Memoriam* allows considerable licence to Sorrow's supposedly 'lying lip' when from it falls the following assertion: ' "And all the phantom, Nature, stands— / With all the music in her tone, / A hollow echo of my own,— / A hollow form with empty hands" ' (III. 4, 9–12). All delight is 'hollow' when shaped into a 'form' dominated by 'echo': Nature is but an echo

    [8] See Yeats, *The Variorum Edition of the Poems of W. B. Yeats*.
    [9] Tennyson is reported as saying in 1869, 'Nobody admires Shelley more than I once did, and I still admire him. I think I like his "Epipsychidion" as much as anything by him'. See *Mem.* 2, 70.

of human 'Sorrow', and 'tone' rhymes with 'own' in a solipsistic refusal to allow that Nature has her music, too.

But Tennyson's verbal recollections of Shelley show that the Romantic poet, 'the idol before whom we are to be short by the knees', as Arthur Hallam wittily put it in a letter of 1828, is, for the later poet, to be more than an empty vessel, more than 'A hollow echo' of his successor's concerns.[10] Tennyson's rhymes form a saddened counterpart to Shelley's rhapsodic attempt to assert, as he chants his way towards the climax of *Epipsychidion*, that 'every motion, odour, beam, and tone, / With that deep music is in unison: / Which is a soul within the soul' (453–5). That attempt to bring all tones into 'unison' will ultimately fail in Shelley's poem, and Tennyson rubs salt into the wounds of the failure. Sorrow whispers to the Victorian poet a post-Romantic lesson—that Nature always betrays the heart that loves her—which Romantic poets themselves frequently teach or learn in their different ways.

The centrality of *Alastor* to aspects of Tennyson's poetic vision and practice, noted by various critics,[11] is illuminating here, since in his dark romance Shelley anticipates a powerful sub-theme that runs through his later work; that is, the sense that idealistic quest may be fated only to find images of its own longing. Such reflex images may also bear witness to the imagination's seemingly all-sufficing power. Of it, as of Emily, Shelley might in ecstatic moods assert that 'All shapes look glorious which thou gazest on!' (*Epipsychidion*, 32). Shelley's ability to sustain a buoyant dialogue between positive and negative aspects of idealistic desire is central to the power of his poetry, and is extremely difficult to rival. Lionel Stevenson and Herbert F. Tucker have contended persuasively that 'The Lady of Shalott' engages in intertextual debate with Shelleyan poems.[12] The poem's very use of simile in part III serves, in Tucker's view, to caricature Shelley as 'a wild-eyed optimist'. Yet the subtlest aspect of Tucker's argument is his account of the poem's close, where he moves away from the notion that the poem is best read as 'an analysis of Romantic solipsism'. Instead, he implies that the poem rejects, as one of a number of 'beautiful delusions', 'the belief that the way out of solipsism requires nothing more than the will to love forthrightly'.[13]

The Lady of Shalott may be 'half sick of shadows' (*Ricks* 159: 72), but 'shadows', in the sense of endless poetic figurations and artful structures, prove difficult to dispel. The Lady, endlessly weaving images out of 'the mirror's magic sights' (65), seems ultimately to be an artistic Penelope condemned never to achieve any spousal consummation with the Ulysses of reality. Still, controlling the line and rhyme is the artist's potent and magical mantra, 'she delights' (64). And in this self-delight, she recalls Shelley's Witch of Atlas weaving 'A shadow for the splendour of her

[10] *The Letters of Arthur Henry Hallam*, ed. Jack Kolb (Columbus: Ohio State University Press, 1981), 245.

[11] See, for example, Lourie comparing Mariana with 'the desperate and driven *Alastor* youth, vainly seeking his epipsyche in the outer world' (15n.) and Day's discussion of parallels between Shelley's poem and *The Lover's Tale* in chapter 4 of his book.

[12] Lionel Stevenson, 'The "High-Born Maiden" Symbol in Tennyson', *PMLA* 63 (1948): 234–43, and Tucker, *Tennyson*, 103–5, 112–13. Lourie compares Tennyson's poem with 'Mont Blanc' (19) and *Prometheus Unbound* (21).

[13] Tucker, *Tennyson*, 113, 116, 117.

love' (13. 52). Yet, as so often between these poets, the dialectic of exchange and difference starts to dizzy. As the Platonizing glamour of the pentameter just quoted suggests, in Shelley's poem the Witch, elusive embodiment of art's aloof charity, protects the onlooker from being dazzled, as Shelley has it in *A Defence of Poetry*, by 'the inmost naked beauty' (*Major Works*, 693) of her 'love'. The Witch has unmediated access to some primary 'splendour', art's capacity for transforming vision. Recalling the *Alastor*-poet's development from 'self-possessed' (Preface to *Alastor*, 92) tranquillity to insatiable longing, as outlined in Shelley's 'Preface', the Lady 'weaveth steadily' (43). Initially she does so out of self-sufficing aesthetic pleasure before she is driven to attempt to capture a different kind of primary reality, that which lies the other side of art's structures, 'life' itself, to put in quotation marks a word which Shelley subjects to intermittent bursts of intricate speculation. 'Shadows of the world appear' (48) in the 'There' (49) of her 'mirror clear' (46). Tennyson's hypnotic, chanting rhythms and stanzas, each made up of two rounds of intoxicating monorhyme with wheeling bob and refrain, suit a poem that is mistrustful of, and ineluctably committed to, art's devices. Sir Lancelot, apparent breaker of art's curse and champion of mirror-cracking reality, is, in fact, just another masterful image, a flashing reflection affecting the Lady so strongly because, like the knight 'that kneeled / To a lady in his shield' (78–9), he is himself an objectified emblem of desire.[14]

Tucker argues that 'This Apollonian Lancelot is no presence, but pure representation'.[15] And yet representation assumes its own form of presence in Tennyson's poem, which, in the end 'Like some bold seër in a trance, / Seeing all his own mischance' (128–9), indirectly accepts that the fate and privilege of the artist is to be caught in the cold snows of a dream, doomed never fully to be understood, even when sympathetically responded to, as the Lady is by the puzzled, musing Lancelot. For Shelley, representation continually asserts the absence of presence ('What thou art we know not; / What is most like thee?' ('To a Skylark', 31–2)), as if to keep alive the possibility of a realm beyond words and poetry. The topos of inexpressibility is the key that unlocks the doors behind which potentiality waits. But Tennyson's reading of 'To a Skylark' (as evidenced by 'The Lady of Shalott') hears the note of conditional yearning in Shelley's final line, 'The world should listen then—as I am listening now' (105), where 'should' defers hope to an as yet unrealized future. And his response to 'The Witch of Atlas' is attentive to that poem's strains of wistful isolation and fear of self-idolatry.

In a related vein, Shelleyan eros and Tennysonian passion meet, criss-cross, and diverge. *Epipsychidion* seeks to give poetic immediacy to the visionary female-figure met in *Alastor* as a 'veilèd maid' (151), but it falls back on the solitary poetic self, tumbling out of his imagined heaven of union in a line tense with subjective rediscovery: 'I pant, I sink, I tremble, I expire!' (591). *Maud*, true to Tennyson's mode of suspending the forward momentum of Shelleyan desire, inhabits a place of longing that, like the heroine's dreamed and pallid face, is 'Growing and fading and growing, till I could bear it no more' (*Ricks* 316: 96). The intermittent, abrupt

---

[14] See the discussion in Tucker, *Tennyson*, 111–17.   [15] Tucker, *Tennyson*, 112.

inability to 'bear' the weight of suspended longing drives the monodrama's plot. That is, there are sudden changes and 'different phases of passion', in Tennyson's phrase (*Ricks* 316, headnote), yet always we are taken into a poetic present. Whatever the metre, its beat responds to the living pulse of feeling. *Epipsychidion* is formally different, a long, impassioned, lyric assault on ecstasies, ardours, and limits of over six hundred lines, whose discontinuities of mood and even mode (lyric passing into narrative and polemic without being anything other than lyric) are masked by the poem's sustaining of 'a continuous air' (146). But the poem's almost heroic refusal to be anything other than enthralled by its own feelings, even as it maintains a sharp intelligence about those feelings, links it with *Maud*. And Tennyson, too, through his reworking of the dramatic monologue, a reworking that allows him never wholly to be identified with his speaker, keeps formal control over feelings by which his poem is captivated.

Here, Hallam's insight, quoted already, that Tennyson, Keats, and Shelley were, for all their differences, 'Poets of Sensation', is borne out. At the same time, one recalls, not only Hallam's praise for Tennyson's 'luxuriance of imagination, and at the same time his control over it', but also his admiration for the poet's ability to hold his 'delineation of objects...*fused*, to borrow a metaphor from science, in a medium of strong emotion' (*CH*, 42). Shelley is more explicitly and metapoetically conscious than Tennyson that his images involve such fusions. Indeed, the result of such awareness can be to allow figure and object deliberately to fly apart, as when the poem converts Emily into 'A Metaphor of Spring and Youth and Morning' (120), a line that backs away from the previous comparison between Emily's bodily incarnation and 'The crimson pulse of living morning' (100) to suggest that the poet's imaginings are, at some level, only a way of talking, however beautifully. With his own potent control over 'a medium of strong emotion', and working in a space that his response to Romanticism has shaped, Tennyson fuses feeling and image throughout: examples are multiple, but might include proto-Freudian trauma and 'dreadful hollow' (I. 1), exquisite anxiety and the fear that the 'solid ground' will 'fail beneath my feet' (I. 398–9), rapture and the sea's 'purer sapphire' (I. 650), visionary, haunted imminence and 'ever so airy a tread' (I. 917), 'passion so intense' (II. 107), and 'one of his many rings' (II. 116), and a terror that recalls utterances made by Shelley's Maniac in *Julian and Maddalo* (compare 505–10 of that poem) and the longed-for refuge of 'some still cavern deep' (II. 236).

Again, part II of *The Lover's Tale* concludes by weltering, momentarily but powerfully, in a void conjured out of the poet's response to Shelley:

> I, groaning, from me flung
> Her empty phantom: all the sway and whirl
> Of the storm dropt to windless calm, and I
> Down weltered through the dark ever and ever.
> (*Ricks* 153: II. 202–5)

In his notes Ricks cites Cary's translation of the Ulysses episode in the *Inferno*, canto XXVI, as apposite to what Ricks calls the 'drowning vision'. Tennyson, however, emphasizes the lonely, single isolation of the experience, especially in the placement of 'I' at the end of the penultimate line. As quoted by Ricks, Cary translates the last line of Dante's canto in this way: 'And over us the booming billow clos'd' (II. 194–205n.). Tennyson has 'fused' various memories of Shelley to emerge with something uncannily his own in its suspension between the melancholy of loss and a brooding, self-reflexive pleasure in sustaining its verbal life: the Phantasm of Jupiter, who asks in the first act of *Prometheus Unbound*, 'Why have the secret powers of this strange world / Driven me, a frail and empty phantom, hither / On direst storms?' (I. 240–2; echo noted by Ricks: II. 203–4 n.), is both self and beloved other in Tennyson's reworking, each being converted into an 'empty phantom'. The 'I' that falls slowly 'through the dark' recalls Jupiter plummeting to his downfall, 'I sink / Dizzily down, ever, forever, down' (III. i. 80–1) in Shelley's lyrical drama, in its turn a parodic allusion to the ecstatic 'Life of Life' lyric (*Prometheus Unbound*, II. v. 65, 71). As with the echo of *The Cenci* discussed earlier, Tennyson has responded to and wrought an idiom for visionary depression out of what in Shelley reads as strangely empathetic satire. And the hope of happiness that haunts the speaker finds its way into the poem by means of a further Shelleyan scenario, this time the affecting moment in *The Witch of Atlas*, when the Witch's aloofness from human sorrow is the matter of an extended figurative contrast: 'But she in the calm depths her way could take, / Where in bright bowers immortal forms abide, / Beneath the weltering of the restless tide' (550–2). In the very evocation of 'windless calm' Tennyson imitates the Witch's detachment from sorrow, even as his hero is condemned to 'welter'.

Tennyson seems to have sensed intuitively that Shelley's 'sweetest songs' were those that told of 'saddest thought' ('To a Skylark', 90). Discussing 'The Palace of Art', Tucker finds in Shelley's *Alastor* the 'clearest of analogues' to the 'complex neurosis' exhibited by the speaker's Soul in Tennyson's work, and comments that Tennyson 'is an acute enough reader to follow Shelley's bleak poem rather than Shelley's melioristic preface'.[16] Indeed, in a stanza quoted by Tucker, Tennyson's Soul displays a terror at its helpless self-entrapment that reads as a gloss on the state of 'pale despair and cold tranquillity' (718) articulated three lines from the close of *Alastor* by that poem's Narrator:

> Deep dread and loathing of her solitude
>   Fell on her, from which mood was born
> Scorn of herself; again, from out that mood
>   Laughter at her own scorn.
> ('The Palace of Art', *Ricks* 167: ll. 229–32)

The Soul's private Hell suggests an aesthetic solitude turning in on itself and recalls but contrasts with the rendering of conversational interchange between Julian and Maddalo:

> Our talk grew somewhat serious, as may be
> Talk interrupted with such raillery
> As mocks itself, because it cannot scorn
> The thoughts it would extinguish
>   (*Julian and Maddalo*, 36–9)

---

[16] Tucker, *Tennyson*, 122.

The twisting syntax intimates discomfort on the part of Julian with 'raillery' (he is 'rather serious' (*Major Works*, 213), as the Preface notes in its poker-faced way). It invites an optimistic interpretation: in a 'raillery / That mocks itself', Julian chooses to discern the limits of any view of life that would place its faith in 'scorn'. Tennyson's Soul does succumb to 'Scorn of herself', and his own convoluted syntax does not mime, as such syntax does in Shelley's lines, an escape from 'scorn', but a discomforted writhing embrace of 'scorn', one that includes 'Laughter at her self-scorn'. Yet the passages exist in a finely balanced relationship. Tennyson's 'Soul' will learn the lesson that Apollo's torso teaches Rilke; she must change her life. Julian and Maddalo, too, confronted by the Maniac's sufferings, recognize in their different ways life's refusal to conform to ideas about life, whether optimistic or pessimistic. An even stronger bond between the poems is an impulse to warn against conclusions. We never quite learn in *Julian and Maddalo* what 'happened' to the Maniac: 'she told me how / All happened—but the cold world shall not know' (616–17). For all her wish to purge her guilt, the Soul feels more than a last-minute twinge of love for her 'palace towers, that are / So lightly, beautifully built' (293–4), pleading that they should not be pulled down.

Shelleyan pursuit and Tennysonian stasis also seem closer than might have been supposed when one links the poets in a dialectical reading. As a characteristic posture of the Shelleyan imagination under full sail, one might turn to Asia's vision of the chariots of the hours hurtling towards millennial redemption:

> The rocks are cloven, and through the purple night
> I see cars driven by rainbow-wingèd steeds
> Which trample the dim winds: in each there stands
> A wild-eyed charioteer, urging their flight.
> Some look behind, as fiends pursued them there,
> And yet I see no shapes but the keen stars;
> Others, with burning eyes, lean forth, and drink
> With eager lips the wind of their own speed
> As if the thing they loved fled on before,
> And now, even now, they clasped it. Their bright locks
> Stream like a comet's flashing hair: they all
> Sweep onward.
>
> (II. iv. 129–40)

Tennyson's imagination appears drawn more towards circlings back, slowed suspensions, yieldings up of desire, darkly sweet entrancements that tell us, as do his Lotos-eaters, that 'Surely, surely, slumber is more sweet than toil, the shore / Than labour in the deep mid-ocean, wind and wave and oar' (*Ricks* 170: 171–2). In the wake of Matthew Arnold, Ricks has attuned our ears to the 'reluctance' in 'Ulysses' 'to use the future tense', while Tucker discerns in the close of Tennyson's poem a complex dialogue with Shelley's *Adonais*, especially its penultimate stanza, made to seem, by contrast with Tennyson's evocation of 'a plurivocal, impersonal deep', 'hasty in both its matter and its manner'.[17]

---

[17] Christopher Ricks, *Tennyson* ([1972] London: Macmillan, 1978), 125; Tucker, *Tennyson*, 237, 238.

Was Shelley's deepest lesson for Tennyson, then, as Tucker half-implies, to do with the folly of questing 'toil' or the over-simplifying nature of 'the Shelleyan rush'?[18] One's answer will inevitably be modified by the sense that each poet shares the ability, in the midst of one emotion or mood, to glimpse the beckoning features of its opposite. If one looks at the lines from *Prometheus Unbound* just quoted, it is possible to trace what might be termed a high-spirited visionary mockery. Asia celebrates the 'speed' and 'eager' longing of the charioteers, who have sprung up from nowhere, 'Forms more real than living man' (*Prometheus Unbound*, I. 748), ephemeral, unforgettable embodiments of the lyrical drama's longing to 'see', to find, that is, a verbal equivalent for its transformative longing. But it is also the case that Shelley manages remarkably to infuse the scene with something close to an idealizing humour, as Asia reports the oncoming sweep 'through the purple night' of the chariots. As so often in Shelley, attention is focused on hope rather than attainment, on hope's endlessly various modes of coming into being. The passage's rhythms are in love with the chariots' headlong career; they might be heard as 'urging their flight'. Yet Asia is as much delighted spectator as participant; in the same act of mind and feeling she understands that 'Some look behind, as fiends pursued them there', and conveys her sense that this feeling of exalted terror, itself, as noted in Chapter 6, a reworking of nightmarish lines from Coleridge's *The Rime of the Ancient Mariner*, is a form of delusion. Her own gaze finds 'no shapes but the keen stars'. Has she advanced to a stage at which former terrors are but idle tales? Is she so intent on the triumph of the ideal that she can see only 'keen stars'? The poetry seems almost to play with these possibilities, able, such is the intensity of its delight, to withhold assent to a final statement. Something similar happens when Asia turns her gaze to those who look ahead, those who 'with burning eyes, lean forth, and drink / With eager lips the wind of their own speed, / As if the thing they loved fled on before, / And now, even now, they clasped it'. The verse both ratifies and does not commit itself to the vision of these burning-eyed ones, buoyed up by 'their own speed', their object of desire articulated by means of a typically Shelleyan 'As if' clause.

'In the wildest of ecstasies his self-anatomizing intellect is equal to itself':[19] no one has caught this side of Shelley more keenly than has Walter Bagehot. It is a side to which later poets are often subliminally drawn, even when they think that they are distancing themselves from Shelley. To set beside Asia's lines or stanza 53 of *Adonais* a passage such as the conclusion of 'Ulysses' is to see how Tennyson does, indeed, offer languorous slowness where Shelley imitates the rhythms of ardent impatience:

> The long day wanes: the slow moon climbs: the deep
> Moans round with many voices. Come, my friends,
> 'Tis not too late to seek a newer world.
> Push off, and sitting well in order smite
> The sounding furrows; for my purpose holds
> To sail beyond the sunset, and the baths
> Of all the western stars, until I die.
> (*Ricks* 217: 55–61)

[18] Tucker, *Tennyson*, 238.   [19] Bagehot, 'Percy Bysshe Shelley' (1856), I, 111.

Tucker hears echoes here of Shelley's 'The soft sky smiles,—the low wind whispers near: / 'Tis Adonais calls! oh, hasten thither, / No more let Life divide what Death can join together' (53. 475–7).[20] True to his conviction that, despite 'the sense of loss and that all had gone by... still life must be fought out to the end',[21] Tennyson resists the dissolution of division offered by Shelleyan 'Death'. But the effects are complicated in Shelley, too, since his stanza's final self-admonition implies, as noted earlier in the present book, on the speaker's part, that the opening question, 'Why linger, why turn back, why shrink, my Heart?' (53. 469), is far from being rhetorical. Tennyson, as so often, blunts the edge of a Shelleyan intensity that is never simply quite at one with itself, anyway. The Victorian poet both chastens Romantic longing and suggests that his own temperament's and era's would-be stoic awareness that 'that which we are, we are' (67) lurked in the poetry of a pre-cursor whose sight seemed forever set on what was 'yet to be' (*Prometheus Unbound*, III. iii. 56). Tennyson almost turns his back on the very goal on which his speaker directs his steady, near-exhausted gaze, as though it were 'too late to seek a newer world', and yet if his 'very faults, doubts, swervings, doublings upon himself, have been typical of our age', as Whitman thought, this is, in part, because Tennyson checks his own impulse to waver by recalling Shelleyan intensities, themselves interspersed with complexities and ambivalence.[22]

In a comparable manner, the echoes that implore Asia, Panthea and Ione to 'follow, follow' (in *Prometheus Unbound*, II. i. 159) re-resonate in *The Princess*, when the Prince, thinking of the Princess, has this experience:

> while I meditated
> A wind arose and rushed upon the South,
> And shook the songs, the whispers, and the shrieks
> Of the wild woods together; and a Voice
> Went with it, 'Follow, follow, thou shalt win.'
> (*Ricks* 286: I. 95–9)

As Ricks notes, Tennyson is recalling this passage from Shelley's lyrical drama—

> A wind arose among the pines; it shook
> The clinging music from their boughs, and then
> Low, sweet, faint sounds, like the farewell of ghosts,
> Were heard: O, FOLLOW, FOLLOW, FOLLOW ME!
> (II. i. 156–9)

—though like many poets before and since he protested his innocence of any indebtedness, writing to S. E. Dawson, 'I believe the resemblance which you note is just a chance one. Shelley's lines are not familiar to me, though of course, if they occur in the *Prometheus*, I must have read them' (*Ricks* 286: I. 96–9n).[23] Shelley's

---

[20] Tucker, *Tennyson*, 237.　　　[21] Quoted in *Ricks* 217 headnote.
[22] Walt Whitman, 'A Word about Tennyson', *The Critic*, 7 (I January 1887), 1–2; repr. in *Tennyson: The Critical Heritage*, 350.
[23] In the same note, Ricks notes that 'T[ennyson] wished P. M. Walker to delete a reference to this parallel passage from his edition of *The Princess*'.

music clings to Tennyson's poem, whose inspiring 'wind' arises from one of the most Utopian poems composed by Mary Wollstonecraft's son-in-law. Tennyson's poem will 'win' from his 'medley' of attitudes, tones, and restless intuitions about gender-roles a tempered, Victorian version of the more extreme union imagined by Shelley in *Epipsychidion*. Shelley imagines, and concedes his failure to attain, a state in which he and Emily are 'One hope within two wills, one will beneath / Two over-shadowing minds, one life, one death' (584–5), where 'death' slides in as if to sustain the rhyme-scheme but attests to the imminent end that will befall the poem's straining after abolition of identity. The Prince and Princess—after the failure of the latter to find that Archimidean 'POU STOU whence after-hands / May move the world' (III. 246–7) which Shelley invokes in epigraphs to *Queen Mab* and *The Revolt of Islam*—settle, or seem to settle (we hear little from the Princess), for a relationship whose guiding principle is that the partners should be 'Self-reverent each and rever-encing each, / Distinct in individualities, / But like each other even as those who love' (VII. 274–6). Here Tennyson modifies yet builds on Shelley's determination 'To fear himself, and love all human kind' (version A, 84) at the end of 'Hymn to Intellectual Beauty', a line in which 'fear' means 'revere'.

Not that Tennyson, here or elsewhere, evolves out of Shelley in some diagram-matic or uncomplicated fashion. But Tennyson's poetic identity develops in accordance with his response to Shelley's multi-faceted practice. A. C. Bradley commented that 'with the partial exception of Shelley, Tennyson is the only one of our great poets whose attitude towards the sciences of Nature was what a mod-ern poet's attitude ought to be'.[24] Recent work on Shelley might wish to query that 'partial', since he as much as Tennyson confronts the findings of geology (for example). Shelley, conscious of such findings' heterodox potential, asks code-repealing questions about the Alpine waste at which he gazes in section III of 'Mont Blanc'. Tennyson, in *In Memoriam*, is more anguished in his sense of the meaninglessness that may lurk at the back of creation, but his anguish is unimagin-able without Shelley's sense of the 'vacancy' (144) that would yawn, were it not for the imperilled 'human mind's imaginings' (143) that are dependent on and con-stitutive of the very materialist 'secret strength of things' (139) which his poetry has conjured into being.

The poets come together, too, not in their final attitudes to Christianity, but in their kindred readiness to subject orthodoxy to questioning, albeit of different kinds. Their great elegies turn post-mortal existence into a topic tense with imaginative urgency. If Shelley wishes to convert the real Keats into a poetic sym-bol, Tennyson wishes to prevent Hallam from vanishing too quickly into some all-consuming light. In 'On Life', Shelley suggests that it may be a 'delusion' to believe in 'the existence of distinct individual minds similar to that which is employed in now questioning its own nature', and that a contrary sense of 'unity' corresponds to that state known in 'childhood' (and re-experienced by some as 'reverie' in adulthood) when 'We less habitually distinguished all that we saw and felt from ourselves' (*Major Works*, 635). Tennyson seems almost to gloss the passage

---

[24] A. C. Bradley, 'The Reaction against Tennyson', in *A Miscellany*, 30–1.

in his evocation in *In Memoriam* XLV on the way in which 'The baby new to earth and sky' (*Ricks* 296: XLV. 1) 'Has never thought that "this is I" ' (4), but learns, with the passage of years, to differentiate himself from 'what I see' (7) and 'the things I touch' (8), until he develops a 'separate mind' (9) through which 'His isolation grows defined' (12). 'Defined' suggests identity as well as limits, and in its doubleness it corresponds to Tennyson's frail hope that death may represent a change into some different, higher mode of existence and that Hallam is, in some way, still the same.

Two poems later, in XLVII, this train of thought comes to a head as another of the poem's 'Short swallow-flights of song' poises itself on a coign of impermanent assurance. Here, while giving hesitant consent to a post-mortal notion of the 'general Soul' (4), Tennyson differs sharply from the side of Shelley that views Adonais as now 'made one with Nature' (42. 370). For Shelley, ringing the changes on 'change', Adonais transforms the very nature of transformation; he or his 'pure spirit' (38. 338) has become 'A portion of the Eternal, which must glow / Through time and change, unquenchably the same' (38. 340–1), demanding a poetry 'which must glow' in similar terms, at once deeply aware of 'time and change', and disbelieving in them as ultimate realities. Shelley's Spenserian stanzas, thus, progress towards a final revelation or goal, 'the abode where the Eternal are' (55. 495).

And yet, when in that moment of anguished self-questioning already quoted, Shelley asks, 'Why linger, why turn back, why shrink, my Heart?' (53. 469), he brings us close to characteristic ways in which Tennyson's wheeling stanzas conduct themselves. In XLVII, for instance, Tennyson flinches from, even as he faces up to, his earlier fear that 'I have lost the links that bound / Thy changes; here upon the ground, / No more partaker of thy change' (XLI. 6–8). Writing of 'the mood / Of Love on earth' (XLVII. 11–12), he says:

> He seeks at least
> Upon the last and sharpest height,
> Before the spirits fade away,
> Some landing-place, to clasp and say,
> 'Farewell! We lose ourselves in light.'
> (XLVII. 12–16)

'If we are to be finally merged in the Universal Soul, Love asks to have at least one more parting before we lose ourselves': Tennyson's gloss (*Ricks* 296: XLVII n.) spells out the explicit meaning of the lines, but cannot reproduce the fineness with which the moment of 'Farewell', in which he imagines himself and Hallam saying 'We lose ourselves in light', is conjured into existence. Its 'ave atque vale' brevity the more pointed for occurring in a sentence that is long and syntactically complex, the final line captures the most poignant of brief re-encounters.

Elsewhere in *In Memoriam*, true to his uncanny ear for Shelley's darker tonalities, Tennyson locates the unspeakable responses to his unanswerable questions 'Behind the veil, behind the veil' (LVI. 28). Rarely was the definite article so definite as in that line, as though Tennyson were allowing for the fact that he is making use of a, possibly *the*, central image in Shelley's poetry. Two examples in Shelley, which

Tennyson would have known, suggest the threads woven from hope and scepticism that tie round one another in the Romantic poet's use of the image, and help to explain the polyvalent nature of Tennyson's line. The first is from the sonnet which opens with the command 'Lift not the painted veil which those who live / Call Life' (1–2), a tongue-twistingly sardonic run of syllables that puts paid to any notion that Shelley employs the veil image in the spirit of a straightforward believer in Platonic forms. Plato's hold over Shelley is undeniable, but his response has a characteristic independence. So, here, he suggests that the 'veil', in its 'painted' form', is an ensnaring delusion. By 'painted' Shelley presumably means 'coloured so as to deceive' (OED 1b), even 'brightly coloured or variegated, as if painted' (OED 3). But if he anticipates his Coleridgean image of a life as a 'dome of many-coloured glass' (*Adonais*, 52. 462), his sonnet has nothing to say of 'the white radiance of Eternity' (*Adonais*, 52. 463), save to imply that there is no such thing. Rather, when the poem's exemplum of idealist folly (the speaker's surrogate) does lift the veil, he finds only, the poem's inverted sestet implies, a sickeningly vertiginous 'chasm, sightless and drear' (16).

Even in *Adonais*, the 'white radiance of Eternity' (52. 463) earns only two cheers; the poem hurtles towards transcendence and a self-consuming wish to die into a wordless ecstasy, yet *towards* (emphasis added) is indeed the preposition which dominates its trajectory. If 'the soul of Adonais, like a star, / Beacons from the abode where the Eternal are' (55. 494–5), the fact that it is glimpsed 'burning through the inmost veil of Heaven' (55. 493) is crucial. The poem stays, and it must stay, this side of those 'inmost veils', even as a beaconing and beckoning light offers itself to the poet as an image of his craving for some absolute. Tennyson, we may feel, wishes to dwell with a more prolonged gaze than Shelley does on that which lies this side of the veil. In his work, quest often mesmerizes itself into something close to imaginative reverie. But the yearning to know what lies 'Behind the veil' is by no means buried in the Victorian poet, who inherits from Shelley longings and despairs that are transmuted into his own lyric meditations. Tennyson may slow the wheels of his precursor's poetic being to a pace that suits his purposes, but the paths travelled by much of his greatest work often take their point of departure from Shelley.

17

'Stars Caught in My Branches'

Shelley and Swinburne

1

'A sort of pseudo-Shelley' was Matthew Arnold's response on first meeting Swinburne.[1] Yet Swinburne is eminently original precisely by following the precepts of Shelleyan influence: for him, to return again to Shelley's dictum in his Preface to *Prometheus Unbound*, 'one great poet is a masterpiece of nature which another not only ought to study but must study'.[2] Often Swinburne impels aspects of Shelley's poetry towards a Decadent uncovering of its various possibilities through intent and intense reworking. David G. Riede offers a compact summary of Swinburne's place in a post-Shelleyan lineage: 'Swinburne inherited his agnostic mythmaking from Shelley, modulated it, and passed it on in altered form—with a greatly increased realization of solipsism and man's dependence upon himself—to the greatest of his disciples, Thomas Hardy'.[3]

The degree to which Shelley engages in 'agnostic mythmaking' may be less of a commonplace after Jerrold Hogle's deconstruction of the idea that Shelley was a mythmaker (for Hogle he was more an unmaker of myth) than it was in 1978 when Harold Bloom's influential reading held sway.[4] But certainly Swinburne starts, conceptually, from the intersection between agnostic freedom and the fear of (or, perhaps, fascination with) autonomy shading into solipsism to be found in many of Shelley's works. Yet the conceptual is nothing without poetic and generic creation, and, after consideration of the quotation it takes as its title, this chapter will explore Swinburne's response to Shelley through readings of paired poems across a range of literary kinds: lyric, remodellings of classical drama, elegy, and extended metapoetic rhapsodies-cum-meditations. It will argue that Swinburne's poetry, with

---

[1] Matthew Arnold, *quoted in Swinburne: The Critical Heritage*, ed. Clyde K. Hyder (London: Routledge, 1970), 116. Hereafter *Swinburne: The Critical Heritage*.

[2] *Major Works*, 231. This edition is used for quotations from Shelley's poetry and prose, which Swinburne read in nineteenth-century editions deriving from Mary Shelley's editions of 1824 and 1839 (1840 for the prose). His interest in Shelley's text is apparent in his essay on William Michael Rossetti's editing of the poetry, 'Notes on the Text of Shelley', in *Essays and Studies* (London: Chatto and Windus, 1875), 184–237. Hereafter *NTS*.

[3] David G. Riede, *Swinburne: A Study of Romantic Mythmaking* (Charlottesville: University Press of Virginia, 1978), 217.

[4] See Hogle, *Shelley's Process*; Bloom, *Shelley's Mythmaking*.

its shifts of tone and stance, invites us to reanimate our understanding of Decadence, and accord it more purpose, power, and energy than is often allowed.

My title derives from a typical revision by Swinburne of a network of Shelleyan influences. It occurs in the following stanza from *Hertha*, a poem with Blakean inflections, but one whose speaker recalls the accents of Earth in Shelley's 'Written on Hearing the News of the Death of Napoleon':

> My own blood is what stanches
>   The wounds in my bark;
> Stars caught in my branches
>   Make day of the dark,
> And are worshipped as suns till the sunrise shall tread out their fires as a spark.[5]
>   (*Hertha*, 106–10)

The quoted third line echoes, with a purposeful, composite intricacy, the meta-phorically daring 'tangled boughs of Heaven and Ocean' (17) in 'Ode to the West Wind' and a desolately wintry image in *The Sensitive Plant* in which 'The birds dropped stiff from the frozen air / And were caught in the branches naked and bare' (III, 104–5). The anapaestic movement of *The Sensitive Plant* has found its way into the final line's bravura hexameter, which also recalls, as does the five-line stanza, Shelley's form in 'To a Skylark'. But whereas Shelley makes his lines sing and soar through trochaic trimeters in his four lines and an iambic alexandrine in his fifth line, Swinburne—responding, too, to the hero's long chant in Arnold's *Empedocles on Etna*—employs a more brooding if often agile movement, in which trochees, iambs, and anapaests arrange a meditative, lilting tune. Occasional spon-daic substitution, as in his third line, is among the devices that ensure Hertha's rejection of what Swinburne, with Arnold's *Empedocles* in mind, calls 'the futile forgeries of unprofitable comfort'.[6]

Already it is evident that Shelley is not Swinburne's only precursor. Arnold, Blake, Byron, Hugo, and many other authors all possess, for Swinburne, 'the life that lives for ever in the work of all great poets', a life that 'has in it the sap, the blood, the seed, derived from the living and everlasting word of their fathers before them'.[7] But for Swinburne, Shelley is an endlessly profitable source and origin. That the Shelley poems cited above suggest nature's creativity and capacity for destruction is germane to Swinburne's purposes, since his goddess is simultaneously one thing and its opposite. Sometimes she sounds like God's mocking voice from the whirlwind in *The Book of Job*, a text much meditated by Shelley: 'Who hath given, who hath sold it thee, / Knowledge of me? (*Hertha*, 51–2).[8] And yet Hertha

---

[5] Algernon Charles Swinburne, *Major Poems and Selected Prose*, ed. Jerome J. McGann and Charles L. Sligh (New Haven: Yale University Press, 2004). All subsequent quotations, unless indi-cated otherwise, are from this edition. Hereafter *MPSP*.

[6] Algernon Charles Swinburne, 'Matthew Arnold's New Poems', *Swinburne as Critic*, ed. Clyde K. Hyder (London: Routledge, 1972), 64.

[7] Algernon Charles Swinburne, *New Writings*, ed. Cecil Y. Lang (New York: Syracuse University Press, 1964), 70–1.

[8] Echo of Job suggested in *MPSP*, 482. See also Cecil Y. Lang, ed., *The Pre-Raphaelites and Their Circle*, 2nd edn (Chicago: University of Chicago Press, 1975), 516. Hereafter *TPR*.

spurns identification with 'the shadow called God' (93), a figure dismissed by her as a human-created projection, much as Cythna answers her question, 'What then is God?' (VIII: 6. 46), by describing how a 'moon-struck sophist' (VIII: 6. 46) mistook 'the shade from his own soul upthrown' (VIII: 6. 47) for an ultimate power.[9] If Hertha ascribes life to God, the ascription functions in the same breath as anticipation, on God's part, of his imminent demise: his 'hour taketh hold on him stricken, the last of his infinite year' (185). Shelley's Jupiter comes to mind, a phantasmagoric illusion yet a potent reality. Swinburne, like Shelley, is able to suggest that an ideology is defunct, even as he shows the dangerous vitality that defunct ideology can possess.

Before leaving the stanza quoted from *Hertha*, one might note how, in its final long line, Swinburne alludes to a central figuration in Shelley's *The Triumph of Life*, that of the sunrise treading out a star. He echoes the account by Shelley of the shape all light's effect on Rousseau's consciousness. She, as noted and discussed in earlier chapters,

> Trampled its fires into the dust of death,
> As Day upon the threshold of the east
> Treads out the lamps of night, until the breath
> Of darkness re-illumines even the least
> Of heaven's living eyes
>
> (388–92).

Swinburne writes that the stars 'are worshipped as suns till the sunrise shall tread out their fires as a spark', reminding the reader of Shelley's fondness for the image. The implication in Shelley is of an obliteration of higher vision, which his supple rhythms, rhymes, and syntax bring back into play. After the 'death' inflicted by the shape, there will be a renewing 'breath / Of darkness' which will help to reanimate and re-illumine the stars. For Shelley, danger and possibility inhere in the poetry's very being. For Swinburne, extinction, while painful, is necessary; false ideas and ideals are trodden out 'as a spark', part of a cycle.

2

That image of trapped and erased stars might also hint at a gloomy view of literary influence. But Swinburne generates a poetic vision that makes an imaginative continuum out of apparent opposites. Shelley's own dialectical poetry, destroying and preserving in the same breath, is, for all its differences of strategy and inflection, a frequent sponsor of Swinburne's work, especially its lyrical dimension. Each poet converts all genres into the condition of lyrical song. This conversion is partly a function of the ways in which, as Jerome McGann points out, 'the poetry [...]

---

[9] All quotations from *Laon and Cythna; or the Revolution of the Golden City: A Vision of the Nineteenth Century in the Stanza of Spenser* will be taken from *CPPBS* 3.

repeatedly echoes and mirrors itself'.[10] But in this section attention will be given to poems that are self-evidently lyrics. Swinburne's 'To a Seamew' rewrites Shelley's 'To a Skylark'. McGann (or 'Kernahan') sees Shelley as engaged in a 'breathless attack upon the transcendent world', one that 'ends in a failure' that is 'at once the proof of the goal's value and, paradoxically, the discovery of Shelley's identity with the lark'.[11] Yet whether that paradoxical 'identity' occurs is arguable. Shelley's stanza form, with its trochaic shorter lines and lilting alexandrine in the final and fifth line, may imitate the skylark's soaring beauty of song, but it is also suited to reflection on the poet's and humanity's divided consciousness. Presumably McGann means to imply that, in pursuing the lark's oneness with the 'transcendent', Shelley writes a poem that embodies in its harmony and beauty an 'echo of the eternal music', to borrow his own phrasing from *A Defence of Poetry* (*Major Works*, 679). Yet the poem refuses to confer such achieved status on itself, being the more affecting for such a refusal. Rather, it shifts between modes.

At first, figurative approximations pour out. So, the bird's springing ascension is 'Like a cloud of fire' ('To a Skylark', 8). This is a witty but pointed conflation of the dual forms in which, in the Book of Exodus, the Lord appears to the children of Israel: 'a pillar of a cloud' by day and 'a pillar of fire' by night (*Authorized Version*, Exodus 13:21). The longing to find a sign for what approximates to the 'transcendent' finds expression in that collapsing of the two forms into a single simile. But simile cedes its lack of representational stability. The bird and its song lie beyond sense apprehension. 'To a Skylark' chafes against, even as it relies on, material analogies; even for the bird to be likened to 'an unbodied joy' ('To a Skylark', 15) is to bring into play the idea of the embodied. At the heart of this stage of the poem is the concession and question in 'What thou art we know not; / What is most like thee?' (31–2). A flurry of further comparisons follows, until the poem seems, indirectly, to turn on itself as it moves into a recognizably different mode, that of reflection on human imperfection, the divisions of consciousness, the sense of feeling 'some hidden want' (70), the conviction that 'Our sweetest songs are those that tell of saddest thought' (90).

One such sadness-inducing thought is the following: the only way in which Shelley can write a lyric that matches, in the human sphere, that of the skylark in the natural realm is by conceding his non-identity with the skylark. The concession permeates even the last three stanzas of the poem, which imagine an overcoming of human limitation only to grant its reality. The poem's final stance involves the poet as present auditor and self-imagined creator. Shelley asserts how, were he to be inspired as the bird is, 'The world should listen then—as I am listening now' (105). As often in Shelley, the poem's dynamics are those of process and change; the poem itself behaves as though its 'race' were 'just begun' (10). It is a setting out, a brave assay, avoiding the melodrama implicit in McGann's diagnosis of 'failure'

---

[10] Jerome J. McGann, *Swinburne: An Experiment in Criticism* (Chicago: U of Chicago P, 1972), 74. Hereafter *SEC*. McGann devises the book as a structured debate between various critics of Swinburne; here the speaker is 'Coulson Kernahan'.
[11] McGann, *SEC*, 147.

and the certainty implied by his 'discovery of Shelley's identity with the lark'. Swinburne saw Shelley with gorgeous hyperbole as 'a son and soldier of light, an archangel winged and weaponed for angel's work':[12] a verdict that proleptically answers Arnold's largely adverse description (first published in 1881 in an essay on Byron) of Shelley as a 'beautiful and ineffectual angel'.[13] Yet Shelley's angelism, if that is what his lyric idealism amounts to, coexists with a recognition of incompleteness.

Indeed, Swinburne's praise for Shelley, 'He was alone the perfect singing-god', suggests a desire to turn the older poet into an idol or icon which is at odds with the self-chasingly temporal nature of the poetry itself.[14] It might better describe Swinburne's own poetic dream, embodied in the seamew, of what McGann calls 'an image of purified desire, beyond the dialectics of hopes and fear'.[15] And yet the poem contains a degree of unstilled energy. True, Swinburne's eight-line stanza, with its use of feminine and deferred rhymes, is less suited to the springing ascent accommodated by Shelley's than to a revisiting, a circling which never ceases. He picks up from Shelley the contrast drawn between the bounded nature of human beings and the seamew's exhilarating life. Yet he also insinuates a sense that the seamew and poet share qualities in common and that the seamew's superiority derives from something that anticipates a Yeatsian tragic joy. The first and last stanzas bring out the alliance, now lost and longed-for, between poet and bird: 'When I had wings, my brother, / Such wings were mine as thine' (1–2) is how the poem begins, a way of phrasing it that recalls Shelley's 'If even / If I were as in my boyhood' (47–8) from the 'Ode to the West Wind', yet refusing to locate the time of having wings simply in 'boyhood'. That refusal generates a stoic, unstated sadness, and Swinburne poises his stanza between such sadness and a responsiveness to the bird, as in the second stanza; there, picking up the phrase 'Such life' from the third line, he dispenses with a main verb:

> Such life as thrills and quickens
>   The silence of thy flight,
> Or fills thy note's elation
> With lordlier exaltation
> Than man's, whose faint heart sickens
>   With hopes and fears that blight
> Such life as thrills and quickens
>   The silence of thy flight.
>   ('To a Seamew', 9–16)

'He is a reed through which all things blow into music': Tennyson's remark combines praise and put-down, but Swinburne admires his seamew both for 'thy note's elation' and for 'The silence of thy flight'.[16] Swinburnean verbal music sometimes has about it a 'life' that 'thrills and quickens', but it seems often to be the auditor

---

[12] Swinburne, *NTS*, 216.
[13] Matthew Arnold, 'Shelley', *Poetry and Criticism of Matthew Arnold*, ed. A. Dwight Culler (Boston: Houghton Mifflin, 1961), 380.
[14] Swinburne, *NTS*, 215.   [15] McGann, *SEC*, 148.   [16] *TCH*, 113.

of a silence that compels it into being and yet chastens its mode of existence. McGann/Kernahan glosses the 'meaning of silence' in Swinburne as 'his condition for perfect speech'.[17] This might suggest an almost Platonic poet, comparable to the Shelley who sets the 'One' against 'the many' in *Adonais* (52. 460). But McGann's earlier account of 'a succession of vacancies and silences' is closer to what happens—albeit in different ways—in Shelley and Swinburne.[18] Both are poets who never quite believe in 'perfect speech', who enter the world of language, becoming, process, and politics. The crucial difference is that Shelley's handling of form and genre is itself alive to process and becoming: hymn turns into ode, elegy into visionary pilgrimage, quasi-Aeschylean sequel into post-Dantean interplay of jubilant lyrical voices.

Swinburne's counter-Shelleyan achievement is to fuse a poem's becomings with its essential being. 'Dolores', for example, celebrates its femme fatale as though she were the very principle of a Decadent 'twilight where virtues are vices' (185), and makes its twilight seem the apotheosis of the ages and a point beyond which further development is impossible. Swinburne's constant refrain-like references to 'Our Lady of Pain' (8 and *passim*) and his hypnotic rhythms do not elide the historical, but the 'goddess new-born' (336) of the poem's final line is, so the wheeling, recurrent stanzas say, one with a sexualized cyclical vision of 'The passion that slays and recovers' (165), one that pays homage to longing, satiety, and renewed longing. The poem is less harmoniously uniform and consignable to a smoothly thematic and rhythmic groove than is sometimes conceded in critical accounts of Swinburne. While 'To a Seamew' poises itself in a poetic space somewhere between resignation and acceptance, it is the entangling nature of Swinburne's language in the lyric that suggests his debt to the Shelley who allows irreconcilable realms to collide and mutually inflect one another. In the stanza from 'To a Seamew' (9–16) quoted above, enjambment allows for double meanings, as when we are told that men's 'hopes and fears' may 'blight / Such life as thrills and quickens / The silence of thy flight'. If 'hopes and fears' blight 'life', they also catalyse, and not only by contrast, awareness of 'Such life'. There is almost the suggestion that it is in the blighting that recognition of the seamew's 'life' comes into existence. The constant wheeling in each stanza works cunningly here, too, not merely to confirm, but also to cause the reader to readjust. 'Such life [...]' in the opening two stanzas follows on from 'Such wings were mine' (8). The repetition of the phrase opens a gap between poet and bird, but re-implies that there is a connection.

That gap is sharply apparent in Shelley, too, and in him it is more evidently a provocation to the trajectories of pursuit than it is in Swinburne, who manages both to be at one with bird and humanity. Certainly, as the poem develops, Swinburne echoes Shelley's 'To a Skylark', with its seemingly sharp division between the condition of the bird and that of human beings. But rebalancings occur, via other echoes, that make Swinburne appear more disillusioned than and yet as hopeful, in his way, as Shelley. When Echoes beckon Asia, Panthea and Ione to 'follow, follow' (*Prometheus Unbound*, II. i. 173), the upshot will be an encounter with the

---

[17] McGann, *SEC*, 189.   [18] McGann, *SEC*, 188.

unknowable figure of Demogorgon, but that encounter, with its agnostic resolutions, will, in turn, be part of the journey which enables Prometheus to carry the 'untransmitted torch of hope' (III. iii. 171) 'To this far goal of time' (III. iii. 174). Swinburne effectively condenses the lyrical drama's quest into an unconditioned state of human existence when he writes that:

> And we, whom dreams embolden,
>   We can but creep and sing
> And watch through heaven's waste hollow
> The flight no sight may follow
> To the utter bourne beholden
>   Of none that lack thy wing:
>   ('To a Seamew', 89–94)

The stanza reworks a number of Shelleyan texts. 'To a Skylark' is there, as the Romantic poet's 'We look before and after, / And pine for what is not' (86–7) serves as a point of departure for Swinburne's sense that 'we' are creatures of divided purpose. That sense leads him on to recall a just-noted rhyme and moment from *Prometheus Unbound*: 'O, follow, follow, / As our voice recedeth / Through the caverns hollow' (II. i. 173–5). That this command, sung by 'Echoes', finds its way into Swinburne's verse suggests a subliminally metapoetic awareness of Shelley's echoic presence. One notices the qualifications of too bleak a vision, in part a product of Swinburne's use here of 'we', with its awareness of multiple experience, even as it seems to generalize on behalf of all.

To 'creep and sing' is to carry out activities that are not straightforwardly compatible. Swinburne carefully avoids using 'song' or 'sing' in relation to the seamew, preferring 'note' (see 11) or 'clarion-call of joy' (42). The seamew's element is, oxymoronically, one of 'songless measure' (83), a rhythm beyond song. To some degree, however, the poet approaches it, his rhymes able to follow where 'no sight' may go. The pronoun used here is 'we', yet Swinburne's subjective investment is strong. In the final stanza, he restates the opening's indicative assertion as a conditional, yearningly impossible hope that materializes itself through the eloquence of the verse. Only in the poetry is the desirable transaction between bird and poet possible, the wish that the bird would:

> [...] change lives with me,
> And take my song's wild honey,
> And give me back thy sunny
> Wide eyes that weary never,
>   And wings that search the sea;
>   ('To a Seamew', 114–18)

The verbs endow the bird with agency, but enjambment and rhyme claim it back again for the poem, seeming to enact the desired conversion. Swinburne engages in dialogue with Shelley's 'Ode to the West Wind', in which desire for sameness breaks down through the very fierceness with which it is voiced. Swinburne is able to imagine a total transformation in which he would 'change lives', yet the poem does not, as Shelley's Ode does, undergo an expressive breakthrough from one state into another. Swinburne's lyricism is in singing unison with its own redefinitions, which include its rewriting of Shelleyan aspiration, as in the closing lines: 'Ah, well were I for ever, / Wouldst thou change lives with me' (119–20). In the impression it gives of imperturbable stylistic control, Swinburne's lyric occupies the imagined space named by 'for ever'. At its end, the poem reconfirms that it has entered its own domain, one that movingly expresses a desired aloofness from human hopes and fears. When Shelley uses the same adverb ('forever'), the effect is more of restless activity, of a poet whose creative and experiential selves are equally caught up in the tumult of pursuit. 'Heaven's light forever shines, Earth's shadows fly' (*Adonais*, 52. 461) is a line where 'forever' speaks less of eternal shining certitude than of a constant spur to agonizing hope.

3

Atalanta in Calydon provokes comparison with and draws inspiration from *Prometheus Unbound*. Cecil Y. Lang finds Swinburne far more Greek than Shelley, following Swinburne's own cue in a letter written after publication: 'I think it [*Atalanta*] is pure Greek, and the first poem of the sort in modern times, combining lyric and dramatic work on the old principle. Shelley's Prometheus is magnificent and un-Hellenic, spoilt too, in my mind, by the infusion of philanthropic doctrinaire views and "progress of the species".'[19] Terry L. Meyers quotes this letter in support of his view that 'Swinburne is reacting in *Atalanta* not only against the God that Shelley's Prometheus arraigns, but against Shelley's own faith that the God can be overcome'.[20] Acknowledging Meyers and quoting Swinburne's own comment, Kenneth Haynes, too, argues that Swinburne's 'dark antitheism contrasts with Shelley's "philanthropic doctrinaire views"'; he also makes the point that '[t]he Greek structure of his drama contrasts with acts and scenes of Shelley's drama in English form'.[21]

These are usefully succinct reports on difference. Shelley advances ideas that might be called 'doctrinaire' in places, such as Earth's speech in Act IV of his lyrical drama. But even when he does so, he offers figurative constructions of exhilarating intricacy; man as 'a chain of linkèd thought' (IV. 394) brings to mind what he seeks to banish into the past, the chain of references to chains in the poem, whether to the 'chained Titan's woeful doom' (II. ii. 93) or to 'the links of the great chain of things' (II. iv. 20) oppressing humanity. Implicit in this chain of references to chains is the poem's shadowing awareness that freedom is an imagined, Utopian, highly unstable condition, and that the imagining of freedom is taking place within a poetic structure.

---

[19] *The Swinburne Letters*, ed. Cecil Y. Lang, 6 vols. (New Haven: Yale UP; London: Oxford University Press, 1959–62), I, 115. See also *TPR*, 520.

[20] Terry L. Meyers, 'Shelley's Influence on *Atalanta in Calydon*', *Victorian Poetry* 14 (1976): 150–4 (150). Hereafter *SI*.

[21] Algernon Charles Swinburne, *'Poems and Ballads' and 'Atalanta in Calydon'*, ed. Kenneth Haynes (London: Penguin, 2000), 381. Hereafter *PBAC*.

Prometheus Unbound, that is, derives its true imaginative power from its interplay, at every moment, between optimism and pessimism. It is important not to under-estimate Swinburne's awareness of this interplay, evident in *Atalanta*, whatever his post-facto self-representation. *Atalanta* is keenly in touch with the darker aspects of Shelley's vision, most vividly articulated in Prometheus's torments in Act I. Althaea responds to the killing of her brothers by her son Meleager by speaking of the latter as 'in his ravin like a beast' (1690), echoing the Fury who asserts the terrible truth that 'In each human heart terror survives / The ravin it has gorged' (*Prometheus Unbound* I. 618–19). Shelley describes in his lyrical drama the way in which 'terror' lives on, consuming and reconsuming, an indigestible aftershock of the Revolutionary Terror. His aim is to diagnose an ideological malaise, to account for the refusal of those who should know better to reject 'Hypocrisy and custom' (I. 621), yet his poetry functions by empathizing with those of whom it speaks, entering their states of mind and heart with a strange near-neurological inwardness.

That inwardness will infuse itself in a benign way into the poetry's own self-sustaining idiom, looking less to history than to a poetic model of Utopian hope. Such a model depends for its effect on the reworking of images, on the poem applying the balm of figurative reflexivity to sites of conflict. In Act IV of *Prometheus Unbound* the Earth addresses the moon as a beloved other:

> [...] thy crystal accents pierce
> The caverns of my pride's deep universe,
> Charming the tiger Joy, whose tramplings fierce
> Made wounds which need thy balm
> (IV. 499–502).

The opening image characteristically converts words associated with the torment undergone by Prometheus into triumphal lyric signifiers; when Earth says, 'the crystal accents pierce', his words enter the lyrical drama's symphonic mesh of echoes as they recall, but redefine, the terms of Prometheus's suffering: 'The crawling glaciers piece me with the spears / Of their moon-freezing crystals' (I. 31–2). Again, gorging on ravin has turned into 'tiger Joy', a Blake-like energy metamorphosed from fear into happiness, but inevitably recalling, even as it seeks to redeem, earlier less hopeful 'tramplings'. Here the 'trampling' in question takes us back to a passage from Act I, a passage that is central to Swinburne's building on and departure from Shelley in *Atalanta*:

> Though Ruin now Love's shadow be,
> Following him destroyingly
>   On Death's white and wingèd steed,
> Which the fleetest cannot flee,
>   Trampling down both flower and weed,
> Man and beast, and foul and fair,
> Like a tempest through the air;
> Thou shall quell this horseman grim,
> Woundless though in heart or limb.
> (780–8)

The Chorus delivers this bleak vision of Love's accompaniment by Ruin as an equivocal incantation, something pointed up by the allusion in line 775 to the Witches' dark charm in the opening scene of *Macbeth*. They prophesy an end to fairness giving way to foulness in the penultimate line, yet 'Death', the adversary that Prometheus will 'quell', cannot, as the end of the third act concedes, be wholly vanquished; it is 'Woundless'.

What will allow Prometheus to 'quell' the fear of Death and put a stop to the inevitability of Ruin are the twinned forces of love and hope, the latter imaged at the very end of the lyrical drama as able to create 'From its own wreck the thing it contemplates' (*Prometheus Unbound* IV. 574). It is less that there are chinks in Shelley's armour of optimism than that his work bravely seeks to face up and face down the forces pitted against affirmation. Swinburne's *Atalanta* shows extreme sensitivity to this Shelleyan dialectic. He makes his poem's music out of the near-fatalistic sense that 'Ruin' will always 'Love's shadow be'; it is a music that delights in the convergence of divergences through the entwining of sounds as in Shelley's line, 'Whom the fleetest cannot flee', where the inability to 'flee' makes a mockery of the hopes of the 'fleetest'. Swinburne recalls those lines and their effect in *Ave atque Vale*, his elegy for Baudelaire, in which his 'flying song flies after, / O sweet strange elder singer, thy more fleet / Singing, and footprints of thy fleeter feet' (78–80). Yet it is Shelley's 'more fleet / Singing' which Swinburne pursues in *Atalanta* (and, arguably, as will be suggested in the next section, in *Ave atque Vale* as well).

Love as shadowed by Ruin or Pain is a Shelleyan topos after which his 'flying song flies' in his play. The Chief Huntsman addresses Artemis as 'Goddess whom all gods love with threefold heart, / Being treble in thy divided deity' (3–4), latently intimating divisive vexations attendant upon love: the implied need, that is, for the gods to love the goddess in 'divided' ways because of Artemis's potentially fearful nature. The first chorus, 'When the hounds of spring are on winter's traces' (65), addresses Artemis, in terms borrowed from Shelley, as 'The mother of months' (66), and associates, at least implicitly, Atalanta with her as 'Maiden most perfect, lady of light' (74), and picks up on the Romantic poet's fascination with 'fleetness'.[22] Pan and Bacchus are described as 'Fleeter of foot than the fleet-foot kid' (106) in a stanza that celebrates 'The god pursuing, the maiden hid' (112). Yet the very verse form, in its mixture of iambs and anapaests, combines both speed and slowness.[23] Delight in the fact that 'winter's rains and ruins are over' (89) cannot erase the reality of what is superseded, 'The days dividing lover and lover, / The light that loses, the night that wins' (91–2). As critics have noted, the idea of 'division' is central to Swinburne's play.[24] This should prevent us from seeing him too hastily as a pessimistic fatalist. *Atalanta* may end as tragedy, but it is capable of tragic resonance because of the lyric exaltation evident as one note in the work, as this choral lyric exemplifies.

---

[22] For the Shelleyan echo in 'mother of months', see *PBAC*, 387.

[23] For discussion of the chorus's scansion, see *PBAC*, 387–8.

[24] See, among others, Kenneth Haynes, *English Literature and Ancient Languages* (Oxford: Oxford University Press, 2007), 153.

It is not the case Swinburne relentlessly ironizes love. Nor is it simply the case that he 'makes clear his antipathy to Shelley's faith in love'.[25] It is truer to say that he wholly grasps the strength and validity of that faith to the degree that he sees that human beings cannot live with love and desire; at the same time, he makes far more explicit an awareness, often strongly implicit in Shelley, that love and desire are inextricable from error, transgression, and hatred. But it is vital to remember that the play is a drama. Swinburne enjoys the liberty that drama gives of voicing what might be felt at certain times, in response to certain situations. It is important that the imaginative energies of the work are not restricted as codified prejudice or ideological assertion. 'The supreme evil, God' (*Atalanta*, 1151), undoubtedly, bespeaks the youthful rebel trailing his anti-Christian coat. But Swinburne has his cake and eats it, too; the phrase works dramatically, put in the mouths of a Chorus that seeks relief from its sense of love as unknowable and enmeshed in contradiction, from its apprehension of a potentially all-powerful, seductive, and sinister 'lord of love and loathing and of strife' (1140). What the speed and fluency of the verse in the Chorus at 719, for example, allow us to experience, is a post-Shelleyan sense of Love as 'fair' and 'goodly' (719), but also, in a redirection that owes much to Shelley's practice in a lyric such as 'Ah, sister! Desolation is a delicate thing' (*Prometheus Unbound*, I. 772), as 'swift and subtle and blind as a flame of fire' (I. 723). Aphrodite is a 'mother of strife' (767) for this Chorus, yet the division she brings is both the source of suffering and the mainspring, Swinburne implies, of poetry such as the very speech we are reading: it may not simply be because of Aphrodite that men 'hear / Sweet articulate words / Sweetly divided apart' (750–2), but the sweetness and division are intensified by her birth.

Shelley hopes that 'language', the language of his lyrical drama in particular, might be 'a perpetual Orphic song' (*Prometheus Unbound*, IV. 415), yet like Swinburne he sees in the divisions of words from one another the impossibility of ever bringing any human utterance to a perfect point of completion. Language will have to be 'perpetual' and 'Orphic', *Prometheus Unbound* tells us in a sombre undertone, if the visions attained in the work are to be sustained. At any moment, new poetic 'spells' will need to 're-assume / An empire o'er the disentangled Doom' (IV. 568, 569). Swinburne's achievement in *Atalanta* is to take devices which Shelley uses to simulate the possibility of 'Orphic song' and complicate and remix them in a drama endlessly nourished by that which consumes it: the idea of love as shadowed by ruin.

4

Praising three elegies—Milton's *Lycidas*, Shelley's *Adonais*, and Arnold's *Thyrsis*—Swinburne writes: 'The least pathetic of the three is "Adonais," which indeed is hardly pathetic at all; it is passionate, subtle, splendid; but "Thyrsis," like "Lycidas," has a quiet and tender undertone which gives it something of sacred. Shelley brings

[25] Meyers, *SI*, 153.

fire from heaven, but these bring also "the meed of some melodious tear" '.²⁶ The declaration smacks a little of the misprision that Harold Bloom argues is central to poetic creation. Swinburne's *Ave atque Vale*, written when the poet mistakenly thought Baudelaire had died, owes much to Shelley's *Adonais*, as McGann and others have argued, and yet its deportment in relation to the earlier elegy is of a poem inclined to the 'pathetic', to a pathos of unillusioned recognitions. Taking his cue from the poem's covert self-representation, McGann sees Swinburne as sharing Shelley's sense that 'this life is a dream', but as differing from him in being unable to cherish 'illusions about an afterlife. Adonais has returned "Back to the burning fountain" whence he came, but Baudelaire has passed beyond the limits of Swinburne's initial vision'.²⁷ Such a reading is at once forceful and misleading to the degree that it fails to see how much pathos Shelley derives from his refusal to settle for mere pathos.

Shelley's poem achieves pathos through the courage with which it 'brings fire from heaven'. The questions at the start of stanza 53—'Why linger, why turn back, why shrink, my Heart?' (53. 469)—are not merely a form of self-exhortation; they realize that there is every reason why the poet's heart should linger, turn back, and shrink. Swinburne's elegy, like his critical comment, behaves as though it could not compete with Shelleyan affirmation and seeks instead to convey its quieter sense that Baudelaire is 'far too far for wings of words to follow' (89). Yet, as in 'To a Seamew', the assertion of an inability to follow seems to accompany, even catalyse a wish to do precisely that, and some of the poem's finest writing seeks a way out of its own cunningly organized self-foilings, as in the concluding lines of this stanza (9):

> What ails us gazing where all seen is hollow?
> Yet with some fancy, yet with some desire,
> Dreams pursue death as winds a flying fire,
> Our dreams pursue our dead and do not find.
> Still, and more swift than they, the thin flame flies,
> The low light fails us in elusive skies,
> Still the foiled earnest ear is deaf, and blind
> Are still the eluded eyes.
> *(Ave atque Vale*, 9. 92–9)

The passage finishes with 'the foiled earnest ear' and 'the eluded eyes', but Swinburne recalls Shelley's characteristic commitment to quest. The subtext of *Adonais* comes to the surface in the line, 'Dreams pursue death as winds a flying fire'. Shelley speaks of 'The fire for which all thirst' (54. 485), a way of putting it that suggests that thirst is unlikely to be quenched, and his poem's final beacon of light is located beyond 'spherèd skies' (55. 491), skies that are as 'elusive' as Swinburne's. *Ave atque Vale* involves readjustments of Shelley's writing in ways that imply Swinburne's greater awareness, as though his poem has foresuffered all the moves made by previous elegies, but it pays a strong if understated tribute to the multi-toned nature of Shelley's poem. So, here, 'The low light fails us in elusive skies' makes explicit a

---

²⁶ *MPSP*, 367.   ²⁷ McGann, *SEC*, 295.

feeling that haunts lines from the close of *Adonais*, stanza 53: 'The soft sky smiles, —the low wind whispers near: / 'Tis Adonais calls! oh, hasten thither' (53. 476–7). Swinburne snuffs out the hope still burning in Shelley's lines, yet he acknowledges too that Shelley's individual search has shaped the terms in which elegy's longing to contact the dead can be understood.

Questions are vital as Shelley half-concedes lack of ultimate knowledge while articulating his longing for communion with the supposedly happy dead: 'Who mourns for Adonais?' (47. 415); 'What Adonais is, why fear we to become?' (51. 459). These questions are, in effect, forms of self-address. Swinburne's tactic is to direct the questions, in a tone that glints with mockery, to the dead Baudelaire: 'Hast thou found any likeness for thy vision?' he asks the poet of works such as 'Le Voyage', with its bravura declaration 'O Mort, vieux capitaine, il est temps! levons l'ancre!' (section VIII) (O Death, old captain, it is time! Let us weigh anchor!).[28] As Seamus Perry notes, Swinburne's 'repeated questions grow practically jocular', and yet if there is a joke at the expense of poetic search it is one directed as much at Swinburne's own poem and finally gives way to mirthless humour the other side of the grave, 'Some dim derision of mysterious laughter / From the blind tongueless warders of the dead' (81–2).[29]

At such moments, Swinburne's Decadent difference from Shelley shows most clearly: beyond the 'last clouds of cold mortality' (*Adonais*, 54. 486) which the Romantic poet wishes to burn away lies, for Swinburne, nothing other than 'the solemn earth, a fatal earth' (*Ave atque Vale*, 191) or a glimpse of 'the under skies' (154). Both are let down by muse figures: Urania cannot follow Adonais; Baudelaire is lured by Venus/Proserpine 'Into the footless places once more trod, / And shadows hot from hell' (164–5). Yet Shelley suggests that the fault is that of a traditional poetry as he reconceives of elegy's role. In *Adonais* the elegist ends up as dauntless voyager, with all the riches of Spenserian music at his disposal as he announces his own inspired assault on limits: 'The breath whose might I have invoked in song / Descends on me' (55. 487–8). Swinburne's eleven-line stanza with concluding iambic trimeter seems almost to ironize Shelley's Spenserian splendours; it has a serpentine, coiling movement as its rhymes fold back in the *abba* pattern of the first quatrain, then achieve brief couplet resolutions, before the final five lines (*deede*) wreathe and unwreathe and rebraid themselves. Often this serpentine wreathing and unwreathing centres on the question of elegy and, by extension, poetry's worth: 'not all our songs, O friend,' writes Swinburne, 'Will make death clear or make life durable' (171–2): about as clear-cut a rejection of elegiac consolation as can be found in the tradition. Yet the need to go on writing affirms itself straightaway: 'At least I fill the place where white dreams dwell / And wreathe an unseen shrine' (175–6). McGann has written well on the 'brilliantly ambivalent' nature of these last two lines, reading 'white dreams' as referring either

[28] Text and translation from Charles Baudelaire, *Selected Poems*, with a plain prose translation, intro. and notes by Carol Clark (London: Penguin, 2004), 145.

[29] Seamus Perry, 'Elegy', in *A Companion to Victorian Poetry*, ed. Richard Cronin, Antony Harrison, and Alison Chapman (Malden: Blackwell, 2008), 130.

to 'the shadow lives of this world' or to 'ghosts like Baudelaire'.[30] One might just add that the ambivalence has a distinctly Shelleyan colouring, recalling the way in which 'unseen' betokens longed-for presence and feared absence in a poem such as 'Hymn to Intellectual Beauty'. Swinburne reaches his own remarkably affecting destination, one virtually the other side of the language he employs with such virtuosic skill, in his final lines, when he consoles the most eloquent of French poets with the thought of an ultimate 'quiet':

> There lies not any troublous thing before,
> Nor sight nor sound to war against thee more,
> For whom all winds are quiet as the sun,
> All waters as the shore.
>
> (195–8)

This is a poetry of sealed assurance that the answer to the question, 'Shall death not bring us all as thee one day / Among the days departed?' (186–7) is 'yes'. In telling Baudelaire to 'Sleep' (177), it denies Shelley's reversal: 'He hath awakened from the dream of life' (*Adonais*, 39. 344). But, as in Shelley's elegy, *Ave atque Vale* imagines places and perceptions beyond the reach of words that can only be gestured towards by words. Death is a predicament for Romantic and Decadent poet alike that prompts continual invention, as in the near-synaesthesia of the close of Swinburne's elegy, which folds into itself the many references to hearing within *Ave atque Vale*, a poem whose sounds finally, in aesthetic terms, offer strange satisfactions to the 'foiled earnest ear'.[31]

5

In his essay on Swinburne, Eliot distinguishes between Shelley as a poet who has 'a beauty of music and a beauty of content', unlike Swinburne in whom 'there is no *pure* content'.[32] He is a poet in whom 'the meaning is merely the hallucination of meaning'. Yet if this sounds hostile, Eliot concedes that 'Only a man of genius could dwell so exclusively and consistently among words as Swinburne'.[33] It is clear that the shifting refrain of Swinburne's 'Itylus' resonated in the hallucinated echo-chamber of *The Waste Land* where, among the 'fragments shored against . . . ruins', we find 'O swallow swallow'.[34] The very way in which 'swallow' in Eliot recalls the reference to 'The change of Philomel' (99) in 'A Game of Chess' shows a powerful

---

[30] McGann, *SEC*, 300–1.

[31] I allude to Paul de Man's famous remark that 'Death is a displaced name for a linguistic predicament', in 'Autobiography as De-Facement', *The Rhetoric of Romanticism* (New York: Columbia University Press, 1984), 81. For recent subtle commentary on this 'predicament', see Mark Sandy, *Romanticism, Memory, and Mourning* (Farnham: Ashgate, 2013).

[32] T. S. Eliot, 'Swinburne as Poet', *Selected Essays*, 3rd enlarged edn. ([1951] London: Faber and Faber, 1976), 325. Hereafter *SP*.

[33] Eliot, *SP*, 327.

[34] T. S. Eliot, *The Waste Land: A Norton Critical Edition*, ed. Michael North (New York: Norton, 2001), 430, 428.

intratextual impulse in *The Waste Land*. Such an impulse comes close to echoing how, for Eliot, Swinburne 'employs, or rather "works", [a] word's meaning'.[35] The 'swallow' is not seen as a swallow in Eliot any more than it is in Swinburne: '[T]he swallow of "Itylus" disappears', writes Eliot with seeming disapproval, yet the disappearance of the word's referential function into its status as literary allusion accounts for the poem's power. We do not read 'Itylus' or *The Waste Land* as ornithologists. We do read them precisely for a reason which Eliot seems to outlaw in his essay on Swinburne, namely that they have the effect of 'statements made in our dreams'.[36]

Simon Jarvis suggestively attacks the idea that he associates with McGann that Swinburne's poetry can be 'figured' as 'the realm of metapoeticality or autoreferentiality themselves'.[37] He 'proceeds, instead, from the hypothesis that no art is really about itself'.[38] But to deny that Swinburne's poetry is latently, subliminally, or explicitly 'about itself', even as it is about other things, may over-insist. Swinburne picks up on Shelley's practice of using words in repeated, alliterated, synaesthetic, near-incantatory groupings, in order to mime, enact, figure, or effect attitudes or shifts of consciousness inseparable from the reader's and poet's (or poem's) sense of being hyper-alert to its own procedures. Passages from Shelley's *Epipsychidion* respond to the poet's assertion of linguistic 'infirmity' (71) through verbal constructions that, like the woman they celebrate, are 'too deep / For the brief fathom-line of thought or sense' (89–90). Thus, Shelley creates a space wherein he can refine, even suspend, the demand for empirical sensory validation: when we read, 'And in the soul a wild odour is felt, / Beyond the sense, like fiery dews that melt / Into the bosom of a frozen bud' (109–11), the poem shows—through such details as its evocation of an 'odour' which 'is felt'—that it is seeking to operate 'Beyond the sense', a word that has been 'worked' throughout the passage until it takes on 'new and quite specific meanings' in McGann's phrase.

These meanings are inseparable from the poem's self-witnessing recognition of its capacity to be, at least in part, 'metapoetic' or 'auto-referential'. In 'Thalassius', thought of by the poet as 'a symbolical quasi-autobiographical poem after the fashion of Shelley or of Hugo', there is a post-Shelleyan fascination with the development in the young poet of 'the soul within the sense' (125).[39] Such a place is the territory of *Epipsychidion*, and Swinbune's poem supplies figuratively oblique representations of autobiography that recall the central section of Shelley's 'idealized history of my life and feelings' (*Letters: PBS*, 2. 434). The terrifying figure of Love who can 'make the night more dark, and all the morrow / Dark as the night as the night whose darkness was my breath' (300–1) has kinship with the False Florimell figure in *Epipsychidion*, of whom Shelley writes: 'The breath of her false mouth was like faint flowers' (258). Swinburne differentiates himself from Shelley by implying that such falsity entwines only too easily with the truth of love, but his very 'working'

---

[35] Eliot, *SP*, p. 325. For thoughtful commentary on the implications of Eliot's idea of ' "working"… [a] word with new and quite specific meanings', see McGann, *SEC*, 137.
[36] Eliot, *SP*, 326.
[37] Simon Jarvis, 'Swinburne: The Insuperable Sea', *The Oxford Handbook of Victorian Poetry*, ed. Matthew Bevis (Oxford: Oxford UP, 2013), 522. Hereafter *SIS*.
[38] Jarvis, *SIS*, 522.   [39] *TPR*, 518. 'Thalassius' is quoted from this edition.

of the word 'dark' and its cognates suggests a Shelleyan root for his song's flowerings. At the same time, the poet of *Songs Before Sunrise*, with his republican, libertarian convictions, also declares allegiance to Shelley (as well as Landor) in his account of the young poet's dedication to 'Liberty' (87).[40] But, in Swinburne as in Shelley, freedom is manifested as a flame that burns most brightly in the regulated, daring movement of the poetry that recognizes no higher authority than itself. It might be said of Swinburne's relationship to Shelley, as Swinburne says of his young poet's relationship with nature, that the Romantic poet's example was able to:

> [...] charm him from his own soul's separate sense
> With infinite and invasive influence
> That made strength sweet in him and sweetness strong,
> Being now no more a singer, but a song.
> ('Thalassius', 471–4)

Shelley's 'invasive influence', welcomed by Swinburne who 'prided himself on the many characteristics he shared with his chief precursor', allowed the younger poet to write an original poetry that seems the embodiment of self-abolishing 'song'.[41]

---

[40] For Shelley's influence on *Songs Before Sunrise* and Swinburne's resistance to Shelley, see Terry L. Meyers, 'Swinburne, Shelley, and *Songs Before Sunrise*', in *The Whole Music of Passion: New Essays on Swinburne*, ed. Ricky Rooksby and Nicholas Shrimpton (Aldershot: Scolar, 1993), 40–51; see also Terry L. Meyers, 'Swinburne's Conception of Shelley', *Pre-Raphaelite Review* 3 (1980): 36–47; for Landor and 'Liberty' in 'Thalassius', see *TPR*, 518.

[41] Catherine Maxwell, *The Female Sublime from Milton to Swinburne* (Manchester: Manchester University Press, 2001), 180.

Coda
A. C. Bradley's Views of Shelley

Critical reception is central to the existence of Romantic legacies, and, in turn, takes on the function of a legacy for subsequent interpreters. In what follows I seek to recover a sense of the contribution made by A. C. Bradley to our understanding of Shelley.[1] Convinced that there is much value in reviewing and re-considering past criticism, which is now relatively neglected, this coda embodies the hope that thinking about the ways in which an author was once considered will involve, at least implicitly, reflection on current critical modes.

1

In a note to his essay 'Shelley and Arnold's Critique of His Poetry', Bradley asserts that 'My plan in preparing the lecture ['a Leslie Stephen Lecture given at Newnham College in 1919'] was to ask myself in what ways my youthful adoration of Shelley and his poetry had been modified in the course of half a century'.[2] Bradley anticipates T. S. Eliot's confession that he 'was intoxicated by Shelley's poetry at fifteen', but he did not react against the poetry, as did Eliot who claimed to 'find it almost unreadable' as an adult (even though the influence of Shelley on his work is evident). With honourable sophistication, Bradley managed to circumvent the stumbling block in the way of Eliot's enjoyment of Shelley, namely the 'question of belief or disbelief' in the poet's 'ideas'.[3]

Mark Kipperman, in his study of the way Shelley's political challenge was absorbed and redefined between 1889 and 1903, argues that, for Bradley, Shelley 'is not a political but a religious moralist'.[4] Yet if Bradley did not see Shelley's politics solely in political terms, he was taking his cue from the poet, since the

---

[1] For acknowledgement of Bradley's importance as a critic, see Susan J. Wolfson's *Formal Charges*, 6. Other critics, notably Harold Bloom (in *Shelley's Mythmaking*) and Donald H. Reiman (in *Shelley's 'Triumph of Life': A Critical Study, Based on a Text Newly Edited from the Bodleian Manuscript* ([1965] New York: Octagon Books, 1979)), have seen Bradley as an insightful commentator on Shelley's *The Triumph of Life*.

[2] A. C. Bradley, 'Shelley and Arnold's Critique of His Poetry', *A Miscellany* (London: Macmillan, 1929), 139.

[3] T. S. Eliot, 'The Use of Poetry and the Use of Criticism (1933)', *Selected Prose of T. S. Eliot*, ed. Frank Kermode (London: Faber, 1975), 86.

[4] Mark Kipperman, 'Absorbing a Revolution: Shelley Becomes a Romantic, 1889–1903', *Nineteenth-Century Literature* 47 (1992): 187–211 (206).

interconnection between aesthetics, spirituality, politics, philosophy, and ethics is a marked feature of Shelley's thinking and multi-layered poetic practice. Indeed Bradley's very manner is at odds with the kind of generalization that Kipperman offers here. As Kipperman himself points out, Bradley was the subject of a hostile attack by Sir Walter Raleigh, who wrote in a letter of 1918 that his Oxford colleague 'treats his text exactly as preachers treat the Bible. Twist it to get the juice out'.[5] Bradley does apply interpretative pressure to Shelley's texts, but he is scrupulously intent on not 'twisting' the poems and prose in the disagreeable sense of 'wrest[ing] the... meaning of' the words (*Shorter OED* III. 3 b *fig*).

Bradley's 'adoration' shifted into a more sobered, even self-divided admiration, yet he remains among the best critics of Shelley because he is always testing his response to the Romantic poet. He does so in, among other places, the essay mentioned above; in the earlier piece, 'Shelley's View of Poetry', included in the *Oxford Lectures on Poetry*, which contains other material on Shelley, principally in the essay 'The Long Poem in the Age of Wordsworth'; in his short pieces (collected in *A Miscellany*) on 'Coleridge-Echoes in Shelley's Poems' and 'Odours and Flowers in the Poetry of Shelley', which contains a cogent footnote doubting the validity of reading *Alastor* as showing that 'the failure of the hero comes from his "self-centred seclusion"';[6] and in his notes on passages in the poetry and prose, and on *The Triumph of Life*.[7] He may have been aware of an element in Oxford disdainful of literary criticism as 'mere chatter about Shelley',[8] but he was not fearful of analysing the Romantic poet's work.

Bradley's quality as a reader of Shelley is evident in one of his 'Notes on Shelley's "Triumph of Life"'. As noted earlier in this book, Bradley singles out, to brood on, Rousseau's wearied comment to the poem's narrator:

> Thou wouldst forget thus vainly to deplore
> Ills, which if ills can find no cure from thee,
> The thought of which no other sleep will quell,
> Nor other music blot from memory.
>
> (327–30)[9]

Bradley observes that 'The lines have a deep and pathetic interest, because they tell us the nature of the thoughts referred to in lines 21–2, thoughts which had kept the poet wakeful through the whole night'. He respects the fact that the detail of those thoughts must remain untold, but he claims that 'They were broodings over, and perhaps self-reproaches concerning, the "ills" of his past years'.[10] So far, so biographical, we might think; but then the note grows more questioning: how,

---

[5] Quoted in Kipperman, 'Absorbing a Revolution', 207.   [6] Bradley, *A Miscellany*, 166n.
[7] For the last two items mentioned in this sentence, see Bradley's 'Notes on Passages in Shelley', *Modern Language Review* 1 (1906): 25–42, and his 'Notes on Shelley's "Triumph of Life"', *The Modern Language Review* 9. 4 (1914): 441-456.
[8] See G. K. Hunter, 'Bradley, Andrew Cecil (1851–1935)', *Oxford Dictionary of National Biography* (Oxford, 2004); online edn October 2005, http://www.oxforddnb.com/view/article/32027, accessed 2 April 2006.
[9] Bradley's quotations from Shelley's poetry are given as he gives them, including in their formatting (452). Elsewhere they are taken from *H*, an edition which Bradley commented on in detail.
[10] Bradley, 'Notes on Shelley's "Triumph of Life"', 452.

asks Bradley, does Rousseau know that Shelley 'is, or has been, deploring such ills at all?' He offers three answers: Rousseau reads the fact in Shelley's face 'and does this with ease because in very important respects (as we readily gather from the poem) Shelley resembles him'; there is an echo of Virgil's ability to read Dante's thoughts; and Shelley might be alluding to 'a mode of being or experience', a kind of collective *déjà vu*, in which he and Rousseau are 'in closer contact than that of two waking men'. Bradley reserves his best all-inclusive but provisional method of tactful surmise to give a sense of this 'mode of being', a mode that is 'other than "life"; pre-existent, perhaps post-existent, possibly somehow subsistent below "life" and even now accessible to some extent'.[11]

These guesses participate in the poem's own activity of similitude and guesswork, keeping hauntingly available to the imagination what cannot be wholly proved or disproved. Even knowing and unknowing blur in the poem; the poem's speaker (Bradley's 'Shelley') 'knew / That I had felt the freshness of that dawn' (33–4), but this conviction does not make understanding of his subsequent experience any easier; conversely, and yet analogously, Rousseau does not know what 'my life had been before that sleep' (332). Probing at a detail, Bradley brings out much that is compelling about the poem. Again, he worries over the qualification, 'ills, which if ills', first offering the obvious answer: namely, that Rousseau does not know enough about the narrator to know whether these ills are ills. But in Bradley's magisterial, self-critical way, that way of adjusting a perception as though he had been handling an instrument not fully focussed, he comments, 'But I am not certain that this answer is right'; he then says something which goes to the heart of Shelley's poetic power in *The Triumph of Life*: 'The words', he writes:

> may imply a doubt on Shelley's own part about the ills that haunted him. Life, he may have felt, is so inexplicable, and so much ill seems to spring from what we once thought good and even superlatively good, that we can have no certainty as to the ultimate ill of what seems, and even haunts us as, ill.[12]

The comment is chasteningly intelligent in its use of a syntax that mimes the work of enigmatic questioning central to the poem and, indeed, other poems by Shelley. Elsewhere, Bradley suggests that 'The best commentary on a poem is generally to be found in the poet's other works'.[13] And, as he notes, Shelley may be 'using the idea' which appears in the 'Conclusion' to *The Sensitive Plant* that 'everything in life except what is "pure" or "divine" is "unreal," or "phantasmal," or a mockery"'.[14] In that Conclusion, Shelley writes:

> It is a modest creed, and yet
> Pleasant if one considers it,
> To own that death itself must be,
> Like all the rest, a mockery.
>
> (126–9)

---

[11] Bradley, 'Notes on Shelley's "Triumph of Life"', 453.
[12] Bradley, 'Notes on Shelley's "Triumph of Life"', 453.
[13] A. C. Bradley, 'Wordsworth', *Oxford Lectures on Poetry*, with introd. M. R. Ridley ([1909] London: Macmillan, 1965), 133.
[14] Bradley, 'Notes on Shelley's "Triumph of Life"', 453.

Here, Shelley mocks himself as he mockingly discovers meaning in the fact that all is 'mockery'. Bradley's comment on the connection between *The Sensitive Plant* and *The Triumph of Life* may not dwell on this vein of 'mockery' in Shelley, but it mines the seam of hope-enabling doubt that runs through the later poetry. Certainly Bradley offers a clue to the nature and value of *The Triumph of Life* by suggesting how Shelley involves the reader in a final lack of 'certainty' about 'what seems, and even haunts us as, ill'. The phrasing, there, captures how what 'seems' ill can, indeed, 'haunt' us as ill, without our ever knowing for sure that it is ill.

At times Bradley himself experiences a lack of certainty about Shelley, a lack related to his doubts about Shelley's own tendency to certainty. In 'The Long Poem in the Age of Wordsworth', Bradley, to begin with, views Shelley in terms that might derive from *The Triumph of Life*: 'The infection of his time was in him', writes Bradley, recalling the Rousseau who confesses 'I / Have suffered what I wrote, or viler pain!' (278–9). Rousseau's declaration reveals a degree of self-awareness that Bradley, here, does not concede to his creator. Bradley presents Shelley as a poet who by the time of his death had only 'half escaped [...] from that bewitching inward world of the poet's soul and its shadowy adventures. Could that well be the world', Bradley goes on to ask, using one of his favoured stylistic mannerisms, 'of what we call emphatically a "great poem"'?[15]

But the rhetorical trick of the question is characteristic because it is not merely rhetorical. As it develops, 'The Long Poem in the Age of Wordsworth' enacts the recoil upon itself of the judging critical mind. At the start of the essay's third section, Bradley concludes that the 'difficulties of the long poem' arise 'from the nature of the intellectual atmosphere which the modern poet breathes', deploying an image at the heart of *Prometheus Unbound*, and he attempts to define that atmosphere, the atmosphere of a 'revolutionary age'.[16] It is Shelley who is 'the typical example of this influence and of its effects'. What follows moves into something not far short of a prose poem as Bradley evokes 'the world of his imagination',[17] and yet it is a prose poem quickened by argument:

> From the world of his imagination the shapes of the old world had disappeared, and their place was taken by a stream of radiant vapours, incessantly forming, shifting, and dissolving in the 'clear golden dawn,' and hymning with the voices of seraphs, to the music of the stars and the 'singing rain,' the sublime ridiculous formulas of Godwin. In his heart were emotions that responded to the vision,—an aspiration or ecstasy, a dejection or despair, like those of spirits rapt into Paradise or mourning over its ruin.[18]

In a mode approximating to that of free indirect discourse, Bradley seeks to evoke the nature of Shelley's 'vision' by means of images, rhythms, and allusions to the poet's work, and to hint at qualifications. The 'clear golden dawn' alludes to Shelley's line in *Epipsychidion*, 'In the clear golden prime of my youth's dawn' (192). Bradley crystallizes the condition of which Shelley speaks while taking from it the specific

---

[15] 'The Long Poem in the Age of Wordsworth', *Oxford Lectures on Poetry*, 187.
[16] 'The Long Poem in the Age of Wordsworth', 195.
[17] 'The Long Poem in the Age of Wordsworth', 196.
[18] 'The Long Poem in the Age of Wordsworth', 196.

precision of 'prime'. The phrase 'singing rain' also alludes to lines from the same paragraph in Shelley's poem: 'And from the rain of every passing cloud, / And from the singing of the summer-birds' (207–8), lines that bring together 'rain', with its associations of sadness as well as renewal, and 'singing', with its suggestions of poetic activity. Tellingly, Bradley refers to a passage concerned with subjective intimations, one central to Shelley's 'idealized history of my life and feelings' (*Letters: PBS*, 2. 434). And, tellingly, too, those subjective intimations will, by the poem's end, not find fulfilment. Shelleyan 'aspiration' will turn into 'dejection' with the speed mimed by Bradley's closing remarks, which refer to Shelley's description in Adonais of Keats's 'quick Dreams' (9. 73) mourning the death of their creator, one of whom the elegist apostrophizes as 'Lost Angel of a ruined Paradise' (10. 88). Again, Bradley's intertextual method conveys an empathy with Shelley. Yet lest we think the passage is uncritically close to Shelley, it is worth noting how we are led, for a moment, to suppose that 'hymning with the voices of seraphs' will be an intransitive construction, until 'hymning' takes as its ironized (though not merely ironized) object 'the sublime ridiculous formulas of Godwin'.[19]

Shelley's development, Bradley tells us, was 'checked and distorted by the hard and narrow framework of [his Godwinian] creed'. At the same time, he was the author of both poetic 'symphonies' and 'songs', and the 'songs' were more perfect than the symphonies because they did not depend upon an 'interpretation of life'; they needed only 'a single thought and mood'.[20] So, Shelley is at his greatest when dealing with single thoughts and moods, as J. S. Mill had argued before Bradley.[21] Yet he is also the poet whose verbal medium is experienced as 'a stream of radiant vapours, incessantly forming, shifting, and dissolving'.[22] It is unsurprising, given these twists, that a footnote turns on the author's comments as 'an exaggerated presentment of a single, though essential, aspect of the poetry of the time, and of Shelley's poetry in particular', and asks us to 'supply corrections and additions' for ourselves; we are also invited to

> observe that Godwin's formulas are called sublime as well as ridiculous. *Political Justice* would never have fascinated such young men as Wordsworth, Coleridge, and Shelley, unless a great truth had been falsified in it; and the inspiration of this truth can be felt all through the preposterous logical structure reared on its misapprehension.[23]

Bradley has, indeed, spoken of 'the sublime ridiculous formulas of Godwin', the lack of a comma turning 'sublime ridiculous' into a near-simultaneous oxymoron, and in his footnote he expands those 'formulas' in to 'a great truth' that has been 'falsified'. In this account of Godwin's influence, Bradley may be tendentious; he may even exaggerate the degree to which Godwin's thinking remains operative for

---

[19] 'The Long Poem in the Age of Wordsworth', 196.
[20] 'The Long Poem in the Age of Wordsworth', 197.
[21] 'It is only when under the overruling influence of some one state of feeling…that he writes as a great poet', J. S. Mill, 'Two Kinds of Poetry' (1833), quoted from *Shelley: Shorter Poems and Lyrics*, ed. Patrick Swinden (Basingstoke: Macmillan, 1976), 58.
[22] 'The Long Poem in the Age of Wordsworth', 196.
[23] 'The Long Poem in the Age of Wordsworth', 197n.

Shelley in his later work; but he homes in on a difficulty which many of the poet's readers have felt, that Shelley put his great verbal gifts at the service of relatively crude revolutionary ideas. It is among the major critical issues raised by Shelley's poems, accounting for the labile dips and leaps in his reputation, and it would be presumptuous to dismiss Bradley's views as simply reactionary. For Bradley, Shelley is a poet of shifting inner divisions: in his words, 'there was something always working in Shelley's mind, and issuing in those radiant vapours, that was far deeper and truer than his philosophic creed'.[24] The position is one which finds support in Shelley's own nuanced poetics as articulated in *A Defence of Poetry*; there, Shelley writes that 'A poet [...] would do ill to embody his own conceptions of right and wrong, which are usually those of his place and time, in his poetical creations, which participate in neither'.[25] Crucially, Bradley is always thinking afresh and urgently about Shelley; considered as the prose is, it gives us the process of critical experience.

2

Shelley is at the heart of Bradley's thinking about Romantic poetry and indeed poetry itself. 'Poetry for Poetry's Sake', the first essay in *Oxford Lectures on Poetry*, cites the opening of 'Stanzas Written in Dejection, near Naples' to prove the inter-involvement of 'meaning or substance' and 'articulate sounds'.[26] Bradley writes: 'If you read the line, "The sun is warm, the sky is clear," you do not experience separately the image of a warm sun and clear sky, on the one side, and certain unintelligent rhythmical sounds on the other; nor yet do you experience them together, side by side; but you experience the one *in* the other' (Bradley's emphasis).[27] 'You experience': by stressing the convergence in the line of meaning and sound, Bradley suggests the pathos created by the countervailing sense it communicates of a separation between speaker and scene. He also quotes from a Shelleyan fragment at the eloquent close of the same essay, as he sets himself the question 'What does poetry mean?': a question he answers by arguing both that poetry involves 'unique expression, which cannot be replaced by any other', and that it 'still seems to be trying to express something beyond itself'.[28] Poetry, for Bradley, must always enjoy aesthetic autonomy, but it can never be merely formalist. Its meaning seems to 'expand into something boundless which is only focussed in it', where an allusion to Julian's hope that 'what we see / Is boundless, as we wish our souls to be' (*Julian and Maddalo*, 16–17) may glimmer, and where a double act of mind suggests itself; 'only' in 'only focussed in it' might mean 'merely' or it might mean 'solely'. The passage from which these words are quoted runs as follows:

---

[24] 'The Long Poem in the Age of Wordsworth', 197.
[25] Quoted from Shelley, *Letters from Abroad, Translations and Fragments*, I. 17.
[26] Bradley, *Oxford Lectures on Poetry*, 14.   [27] Bradley, *Oxford Lectures on Poetry*, 14–15.
[28] Bradley, *Oxford Lectures on Poetry*, 26.

The poet speaks to us of one thing, but in this one thing there seems to lurk the secret of all. He said what he meant, but his meaning seems to beckon away beyond itself, or rather to expand into something boundless which is only focussed in it; something also which, we feel, would satisfy not only the imagination, but the whole of us; that something within us, and without, which everywhere

> makes us seem
> To patch up fragments of a dream,
> Part of which comes true, and part
> Beats and trembles in the heart.[29]

Shelley's lines form a question in their original, the fragment, 'Is it that in some brighter sphere', drafted on the back cover of the Bodleian notebook MS Shelley adds. e. 6, and first published by Richard Garnett in 1862.[30] Bradley's own prose poem turns questions into rhapsodic if tentative assertions.

In 'Shelley's View of Poetry' Bradley begins with an account of Shelley's view of the world and its relation to his 'general view of poetry':

> The world to him is a melancholy place, a 'dim vast vale of tears,' illuminated in flashes by the light of a hidden but glorious power. Nor is this power, as that favourite metaphor would imply, wholly outside the world. It works within as a soul contending with obstruction and striving to penetrate and transform the whole mass.[31]

The technique is one often found in Bradley's criticism: an impressionist and understatedly impassioned survey, quickened by a contact with textual details and shot through with interpretative flair. The 'dim vast vale of tears' recalls Shelley's reclamation of the Christian term for his own purposes in 'Hymn to Intellectual Beauty', where he uses the phrase to describe the world when deserted by Intellectual Beauty (see line 17). 'Power' is a word used frequently in Shelley's poetry and prose for a force ambiguously located inside and beyond human beings, an ambiguity to which Bradley is alert, while the account of a 'hidden but glorious power' may glance at the 'Poet hidden / In the light of thought' (36–7) in 'To a Skylark'. 'A soul contending with obstruction' probably alludes to 'the one Spirit's plastic stress' (43. 381) which in *Adonais* 'Sweeps through the dull dense world' (43. 382), and 'striving to penetrate and transform the world' picks up on the reference in *Epipsychidion* to 'that Beauty' 'Which penetrates and clasps and fills the world' (102, 103). Moreover, the movement of the sentences captures both Shelley's melancholy and his ardent hope for change. In the first sentence, beginning 'The world', the impression is of enduring and suffering; in the second sentence, ending 'the world', the stress is on transforming. As the passage continues, it confirms that Bradley knows well Shelley's texts and characteristic moods and hopes. The paragraph explores Shelley's sense of 'unity in life' and conviction of an all-pervasive spirit or power intent on betterment, and it concludes with the assertion that 'poetry, as the world now is, must be one of the voices of this power, or one tone of its voice'.[32]

---

[29] Bradley, *Oxford Lectures on Poetry*, 26.   [30] See *BSM* V, 360–1.
[31] Bradley, *Oxford Lectures on Poetry*, 152.
[32] Bradley, *Oxford Lectures on Poetry*, 152, 153.

Having sketched with some authority Shelley's 'general view of poetry',[33] Bradley moves on to offer an exposition of *A Defence of Poetry*. His commentary emphasizes two aspects: that Shelley 'is defending [...] something very much wider than poetry in the usual sense',[34] since he defends any activity that shows the operation of creative imagination, and that, for Shelley, the 'imagination' is especially responsive to ideas or images that answer 'perfectly to its nature'. Refining the notion of the imagination, Bradley speaks of 'the imagining soul' as delighting in representations of perfection. Such representations offer the imagining soul 'images or forebodings of its own perfection—of itself become perfect—in one aspect or another'.[35] Bradley touches here on Shelley's ability to make aesthetic use of the Godwinian idea of perfectibility. And Bradley alights on a crucial question raised by Shelley's poetics, one addressed at length by Earl R. Wasserman, among others, when he argues earlier in 'Shelley's View of Poetry': '[...] at first we hear nothing of that perfect power at the heart of things, and poetry is considered as a creation rather than a revelation. But for Shelley, we soon discover, this would be a false antithesis'.[36]

For Bradley, in 'Shelley's View of Poetry', the poet believes 'that the imaginative idea is always [...] beautiful'.[37] He does not annex Shelley metaphysically to an Idealist tradition, in which ideas constitute reality; rather, he dwells on the significance for Shelley of the imagination's capacity for apprehending the beautiful. When Bradley considers Shelley's understanding of poetry 'in the special sense', he brings out the poet's at first sight surprising 'insistence on the importance of measure or rhythm': surprising because Shelley might seem the reverse of a formalist in his emphasis on 'the identity of the general substance of poetry with that of moral life and action'.[38] But, despite this stress on rhythm, Shelley, Bradley asserts, never talks in detail about 'diction'; he does not, unlike Keats, look 'on fine phrases like a lover'.[39] For Shelley, poems, in spite of the evidence proffered by his manuscripts of 'plenty of various readings',[40] are essentially the product of inspiration; hence, in the poems, 'The glowing metal rushes into the mould so vehemently that it overleaps the bounds and fails to find its way into all the little crevices': an expressive characterization of, say, *Laon and Cythna*, and one that draws its images from the Industrial Revolution and Satan's entrance into Eden in *Paradise Lost*, Book IV.[41] Extending a metaphor implicit in Tennyson's account of 'Life of Life' (in *Prometheus Unbound*), 'He seems to go up into the air and burst', Bradley writes dryly yet powerfully that:

---

[33] Bradley, *Oxford Lectures on Poetry*, 152.

[34] Bradley, *Oxford Lectures on Poetry*, 154.   [35] Bradley, *Oxford Lectures on Poetry*, 155.

[36] Bradley, *Oxford Lectures on Poetry*, 153; see, for example, Earl R. Wasserman, *Shelley: A Critical Reading*, on 'Shelley's ambiguous ontology', 217. Wasserman notes that the 'philosophy' of A. C. Bradley's brother, F. H. Bradley, 'is at many points astonishingly like Shelley's' (143), especially in relation to the problem of 'writing off appearances as mere non-existent illusions' (149): Wasserman argues that neither Shelley nor F. H. Bradley does so write off 'appearances'. Though Bradley's debt to his brother's thinking is a complex question, he rarely, if ever, allows poetic thinking to be dictated to by philosophy.

[37] Bradley, *Oxford Lectures on Poetry*, 156.   [38] Bradley, *Oxford Lectures on Poetry*, 157.

[39] Bradley, *Oxford Lectures on Poetry*, 159.   [40] Bradley, *Oxford Lectures on Poetry*, 160.

[41] Satan 'in contempt, / At one slight bound high overleaped all bound / Of hill or highest wall' (ll. 180–2), *John Milton: A Critical Edition of the Major Works*, ed. Stephen Orgel and Jonathan Goldberg (Oxford: Oxford University Press, 1991).

if we are to speak of poems as fireworks, I would not compare *Life of Life* with a great set piece of Homer or Shakespeare that illumines the whole sky; but, all the same, there is no more thrilling sight than the heavenward rush of a rocket, and it bursts at a height no other fire can reach.[42]

Again, the mode is impressionist; but the image is unforgettable, and persists as an authentically vivid response to characteristic lyric effects in Shelley.

The Satan that enters the Eden of Shelley's view of poetry is considered in the third section of 'Shelley's View of Poetry'. For Bradley, it concerns 'the substance of poetry'. 'Substance' is a term of some complexity in Bradley, one he prefers to 'subject', identifies with 'content',[43] and sets in antithetical yet dependent relationship with 'form'. Indeed, Bradley's strongest conviction is that substance cannot be known on its own: 'If substance and form mean anything *in* the poem', he asserts in the same essay, 'then each is involved in the other, and the question in which of them the value lies has no sense' (Bradley's emphasis).[44] Or as he phrases it: 'What you find at any moment of that succession of experiences called *Hamlet* is words'.[45] The sense of experiences in a state of flow is almost Paterian or Humean; but Bradley will not disavow the ethical nor yield up metaphysical questions in despair.

When, then, he comes to discuss the 'substance of poetry' from the viewpoint of Shelley's theory of poetry, it is necessary to see that, for Bradley, the word 'substance' only has a momentary distinctness of identity. Questions may be raised about its presence in Shelley's poetics and, indeed, his poetry. 'Does not his theory', asks Bradley, 'reflect the weakness of his own practice, his tendency to portray a thin and abstract ideal instead of interpreting the concrete detail of nature and life; and ought we not to oppose to it a theory which would consider poetry simply as a representation of fact?' 'To this last question', Bradley replies promptly, 'I should answer No'. Shelley 'did not mean that the *immediate* subject of poetry must be perfection in some form' (Bradley's emphasis).[46] To represent the imperfect may, Bradley contends, be a means of covertly depicting perfection; certainly, for Shelley, a poetic lament about the 'loss of the ideal' is 'indirectly an expression *of* the ideal' (Bradley's emphasis).[47] Again, it is arguable that in treating 'qualities…which are capable of becoming the instruments of evil',[48] the writer is describing a potential for perfection that has gone awry.

Yet, true to his scrupulous weighing of a case, Bradley is not wholly satisfied by aspects of *A Defence of Poetry* with regard to this matter. He detects in some of these aspects 'Shelley's tendency to abstract idealism or spurious Platonism' as he considers and dismisses the 'strange notion' in the Preface to *Prometheus Unbound* 'that Prometheus is a more poetic character than Satan because he is free from Satan's imperfections', or the idea broached in *A Defence* that Homer merely used vice as a costume in which to hide 'the unspotted beauty that he himself imagined'.[49] He goes on to read the two lines 'Life, like a dome of many-coloured glass, / Stains

---

[42] Bradley, *Oxford Lectures on Poetry*, 161.   [43] Bradley, *Oxford Lectures on Poetry*, 13n.
[44] Bradley, *Oxford Lectures on Poetry*, 16.   [45] Bradley, *Oxford Lectures on Poetry*, 17.
[46] Bradley, *Oxford Lectures on Poetry*, 163.   [47] Bradley, *Oxford Lectures on Poetry*, 164.
[48] Bradley, *Oxford Lectures on Poetry*, 165.   [49] Bradley, *Oxford Lectures on Poetry*, 166.

the white radiance of eternity' as showing Shelley's tendency to forget 'the fact that the many colours *are* the white light broken' (Bradley's emphasis).[50] Bradley does not quote the whole sentence of which these lines are part and misses Shelley's awareness of tugs and pulls; indeed, Shelley's lines are conscious that 'the many colours' have their attractions, and that life's stain illuminates beautifully from one perspective, even if it degrades from another. But just as he seems to distance himself from Shelley's views as over-abstract, he suggests that 'Shelley's strength and weakness are closely allied, and it may be that the very abstractness of his ideal was a condition of that quivering intensity of aspiration towards it in which his poetry is unequalled'.[51] There, Bradley's language registers the power of Shelley's own 'intensity of aspiration', and in his shifts of mood and register, composes an essay that dramatizes his strong but complicated response to Shelley.

The essay concludes with reflections on Shelley's dislike, expressed in *A Defence of Poetry*, of what in the Preface to *Prometheus Unbound* he terms 'Didactic poetry', a dislike which Bradley likes. It is not that Shelley means to 'condemn... the writing of a particular poem with a view to a particular moral or practical effect';[52] it is rather, according to Bradley, that he attacks 'the attempt to give, in the strict sense, moral *instruction*, to communicate doctrines, to offer argumentative statements of opinion on right and wrong, and more especially, I think, on controversial questions of the day' (Bradley's emphasis).[53] Bradley's finest qualities emerge and merge when he explains his understanding of Shelley's emphasis on poetry as the work of the imagination; he blends tentativeness with empathy until he adds 'a consideration which is in the spirit of Shelley's',[54] the view that 'poetry [...] is not the *expression* of ideas or of a view of life; it is their discovery or creation, or rather both discovery and creation in one' (Bradley's emphasis). Bradley admires Shelley, as he admires other writers, when, through the imagination, the poet does not seek 'to clothe in imagery consciously held ideas', but to 'produce half-consciously a matter from which, when produced, the reader may, if he chooses, extract ideas'.[55] The essay's last sentences see Shelley, along with Milton, Goethe, Wordsworth, and Tennyson, as a writer whose genius and 'moral virtue' lie not in 'explicit ideas' but in deep feeling and 'intuition'.[56] Bradley celebrates the Romantic poet's 'intuition [...] of the unique value of love', concluding: 'Whatever in the world has any worth is an expression of Love. Love sometimes talks. Love talking musically is poetry'.[57] Shelley's view of poetry has spurred Bradley into talking through the austere music of his prose about his own.

3

Bradley may valorize 'intuition', but he does so with critical intelligence. Indeed, arguing that Arnold was 'somewhat deficient in that kind of imagination which is

---

[50] Bradley, *Oxford Lectures on Poetry*, 167.
[52] Bradley, *Oxford Lectures on Poetry*, 168–9.
[54] Bradley, *Oxford Lectures on Poetry*, 171.
[56] Bradley, *Oxford Lectures on Poetry*, 174.

[51] Bradley, *Oxford Lectures on Poetry*, 167.
[53] Bradley, *Oxford Lectures on Poetry*, 169.
[55] Bradley, *Oxford Lectures on Poetry*, 172.
[57] Bradley, *Oxford Lectures on Poetry*, 174.

allied to metaphysical thought', he seeks to pinpoint the source of Arnold's 'curious failure to appreciate Shelley'.[58] In the later lecture 'Shelley and Arnold's Critique of His Poetry' (collected in *A Miscellany*), Bradley begins by rehearsing Arnold's description of Shelley as 'a beautiful and ineffectual angel, beating in the air his luminous wings in vain'. 'In accordance with Arnold's method', writes Bradley with a touch of hauteur, the 'main point' of this description 'is hammered home by repetition'.[59] Bradley will repudiate Arnold's famous description, but there is a family resemblance between it and the admiration expressed in 'Shelley's View of Poetry' for the poet's 'quivering intensity of aspiration'. Where they differ is that Bradley attaches value to Shelley's struggle towards fulfilment of aspiration.

Bradley looks at two aspects of Arnold's critique: its denial of 'natural magic' to Shelley's handling of language; and its attribution of 'unsubstantiality' to the poetry's representation of the 'moral and spiritual nature of man'.[60] He concedes that Shelley does not provoke the response 'What a master of language he is!' as Keats or Coleridge do. Yet he redefines Arnold's complaint that 'Shelley "strains after"...magical felicity in vain'.[61] A footnote, as often in this critic's work, articulates best the nuanced grasp displayed by Bradley in relation to the issue: 'I think I recognize in *some* of Shelley's poems what Arnold describes as "straining"; but it is not a straining after the happiest word for something easily or distinctly apprehended: it is a straining to find any words at all for something beyond distinct apprehension' (Bradley's emphasis).[62] This comment illuminates some of the finest linguistic triumphs in Shelley: 'Life of Life', say, or the greatest passages in *Epipsychidion*.

Bradley agrees that Shelley does not conjure up pictures of what he sees as do Keats and Coleridge but he argues influentially that Shelley's province is not 'objects at rest', as it often is with Keats, but 'whatever is itself invisible and unpicturable and touches us only through lightning-flashes, or momentary tones, or the agitated motion of things or thoughts or feelings', and that such things are linked, for Shelley, with what is 'for him itself a spirit, if not the spirit of the Universe'. Bradley's prose persuades here by becoming a mirror of and a medium for the qualities it evokes. What 'moves Shelley', in 'To a Skylark', argues Bradley, 'and through his poem moves you, is nothing picturable',[63] where even the shop-worn 'moves' takes on new verbal life because of the passage's celebration of Shelley's fascination with motion. And Bradley goes on to turn to the poet's advantage Shelley's alleged and relative lack of interest in local richness of phrasing; Shelley's language 'is not wrought and kneaded', writes Bradley; 'it flows'. It is, he goes on, 'the common literary language of Shelley's time spoken by an angel'. In using the word 'angel', Bradley declares that he had in mind Garrick's famous account of Goldsmith, 'that he wrote like an angel, though he talked like poor Poll'.[64] But he also rebuts Arnold's description of Shelley as 'a beautiful and ineffectual angel'; as

[58] Bradley, *Oxford Lectures on Poetry*, 127.   [59] Bradley, *Oxford Lectures on Poetry*, 139.
[60] Bradley, *Oxford Lectures on Poetry*, 140, 141.   [61] Bradley, *Oxford Lectures on Poetry*, 142.
[62] Bradley, *Oxford Lectures on Poetry*, 143n.   [63] Bradley, *Oxford Lectures on Poetry*, 144.
[64] Bradley, *Oxford Lectures on Poetry*, 147.

a poet, Bradley implies, Shelley's words have angelic force, a force akin to that power in Goldsmith which makes Bradley say: 'only when you put the book down [do you] become aware that your mind has been moving with perpetual ease and grace'.[65]

Much in what follows addresses the question of Shelley's treatment of 'man's moral and spiritual nature'.[66] Though Bradley refuses to accept that Arnold's distinction between 'the outward world' and 'man's moral and spiritual nature' holds for the Romantics, he does concede much to Arnold in what follows, asserting that Shelley 'fell under the dominion of ideas which at once inspired and half-crippled him'.[67] He describes Shelley's habitual view of life as flawed by its division of the world's inhabitants into two halves: the one contains tyrants and slaves; the other is 'that tiny minority called "the free"'. Bradley agrees with Arnold that this outlook results in an 'unsubstantial' outlook. Furthermore, he questions Shelley's claim (written in Greek in 'the Visitors' book at the Montanvert Inn' in 1816) to be a 'democrat'.[68] By contrast with Mazzini and Whitman, Shelley gives little sense of actually liking and respecting (not just pitying) what Whitman called 'the divine average'. Nor, writes Bradley, can you imagine even the conservative Wordsworth 'writing', as Shelley does (at the end of 'Lines Written among the Euganean Hills', 336), of '"the polluting multitude"'.[69] This assault on Shelley's democratic credentials is penetrating, and anticipates the terms of a fine essay on *Julian and Maddalo* by Kelvin Everest.[70]

Bradley goes on to give short shrift to the idea that Shelley was 'optimistic';[71] he argues that Shelley sold short the present, that the poet merely lamented over rather than found value in its imperfections as he longed ardently for a future perfection. In support of this argument, Bradley again quotes from stanza 52 of *Adonais* (this time lines 460–3), and, again missing Shelley's sense of entangling tensions, sees the lines as proving the poet's need to herd experience into two sealed-off categories: the 'imperfect' and the 'perfect'.[72] But just as Bradley appears to cede much to Shelley's disparagers, something characteristically double has been happening. There is an undertow of self-conflicting argument, always signalled in his criticism through the device of imagined opponents and questions to be answered. Even as he seems to fault Shelley for lacking a tragic vision, for not seeing that 'the greatness of the mind is seen *most* in its power to win good out of evil' (Bradley's emphasis), it transpires that he is not happy with this summation, and he begins his lecture's final section with the words, 'It remains now to glance, in what time remains, at the other side',[73] a move that turns the lecture into a fascinating dialogue that sums up and anticipates many of the central debates provoked by Shelley's poetry. Bradley's opponent is now no longer Arnold, but a part of himself. Defending Shelley, Bradley argues that 'In reality his range of perception

[65] Bradley, *Oxford Lectures on Poetry*, 147.   [66] Bradley, *Oxford Lectures on Poetry*, 148.
[67] Bradley, *Oxford Lectures on Poetry*, 149, 151.   [68] Bradley, *Oxford Lectures on Poetry*, 152.
[69] Bradley, *Oxford Lectures on Poetry*, 153.
[70] Kelvin Everest, 'Shelley's Doubles' in *Shelley Revalued*, pp. 63–88.
[71] Bradley, *Oxford Lectures on Poetry*, 154.   [72] Bradley, *Oxford Lectures on Poetry*, 156.
[73] Bradley, *Oxford Lectures on Poetry*, 155, 156.

and sympathy was wide', as is shown by the portraits of Rousseau and Cenci, both revealing 'psychological subtlety';[74] and that Shelley's view of life is not merely geared towards leaving it behind as the poetry aspires towards the perfection of the One. In fact, Shelley recognizes that there is, in the world, evidence of an 'ultimate spiritual perfection, which is also the ultimate *power*' (Bradley's emphasis).[75] In an evocative passage Bradley captures the elusive yet tenacious conviction in Shelley's poetry that in 'human life which does change and fade and seems so dark, there is still, both behind it and in it, that ultimate Power'.[76] This may underplay Shelley's metaphysical doubt concerning 'ultimate Power', but Bradley's very turns of argument imply recognition of such scepticism, even as he suggests how Shelley seeks to transcend scepticism. Bradley's formulation allows for Shelley's darkness and pessimism, thus quashing any notion of him as sentimentally optimistic, while suggesting the poet's discovery of a force for good not only 'behind' life but also 'in it'. It 'is not only', as Bradley puts it, in ' "some world far from ours" that differences remain and yet unite'.[77]

Bradley again feels the need to posit a distinction between the deepest effects of the poetry and the insistences of Shelley's 'more explicit creed', contending that 'the abstract oppositions of his more explicit creed are softened and harmonized in his poetry, and in the implicit view that it contains'. As evidence of the poet's 'feeling and conviction of the power of the mind', he celebrates the poet's 'faith in science',[78] a faith affirmed by many later critics. Finally, though, Bradley sees Shelley's very melancholy, united with 'the intensity of his aspiration',[79] as the guarantee of a world-view that has its claims upon the reader. As 'the most Shelleyan lines in Shelley', he quotes the following stanza from 'The Zucca', an unfinished lyric from 1822:

> I loved—oh no, I mean not one of ye,
>   Or any earthly one, though ye are dear
> As human heart to human heart may be.
>   I loved I know not what; but this low sphere
> And all that it contains, contains not thee,
>   Thou whom, seen nowhere, I feel everywhere.[80]

These are the 'most Shelleyan lines in Shelley' one might hazard in the slipstream of Bradley's perceptions, not merely because of 'intensity of aspiration', but because 'intensity' is communicated through a syntax and phrasing that bears witness to the poet's intelligence, tact, and awareness of limits and distinctions. Bradley's redefining gloss is affectingly restrained: 'That is aspiration; but so to aspire is to attain'.[81] Shelley's 'sorrow', for Bradley, alluding to *Hyperion*, Shelley's favourite poem by Keats, 'becomes more beautiful than beauty's self' and persuades us that

---

[74] Bradley, *Oxford Lectures on Poetry*, 157, 157–8.
[75] Bradley, *Oxford Lectures on Poetry*, 158.   [76] Bradley, *Oxford Lectures on Poetry*, 159.
[77] Bradley, *Oxford Lectures on Poetry*, 159. Bradley quotes from Shelley's 'To Jane: "The Keen Stars Were Twinkling" ', line 22.
[78] Bradley, *Oxford Lectures on Poetry*, 160.   [79] Bradley, *Oxford Lectures on Poetry*, 161.
[80] Quoted by Bradley, in *Oxford Lectures on Poetry*, 161.
[81] Bradley, *Oxford Lectures on Poetry*, 161.

there is 'something above sorrow and beyond its reach'. This quasi-Mozartian Shelley is permitted election by Bradley to a tragic company at the essay's end:

> If it is true, as in various tongues and divers manners we are told, that except through loss and sorrow, there is no attainment for the spirit of man, does it greatly matter that Shelley did not preach this truth, when his saddest poems make us feel that he had lived it?[82]

Tactfully the phrasing here, however close to Bradley's view of the purposes of 'loss and sorrow', does not turn Shelley into a mouthpiece for the critic's convictions. It implies the applicability to Shelley of his own conviction that 'Poets are the hierophants of an unapprehended inspiration [...] the words which express what they understand not' (*A Defence of Poetry*, 57) with a tough delicacy typical of this critic's dealings with an enduringly complicated and influential Romantic writer.

---

[82] Bradley, *Oxford Lectures on Poetry*, 162.

Bibliography

Allen, Graham. 'Transumption and/in History: Bloom, Shelley and the Figure of the Poet'. 'Shelley Special Issue'. *Durham University Journal* n.s. 35 (1993): 247–56.

Allot, Miriam, ed. *Essays on Shelley*. Liverpool: Liverpool University Press, 1982.

Arnold, Matthew. *Poetry and Criticism of Matthew Arnold*. Ed. A. Dwight Culler Boston: Houghton Mifflin, 1961.

Auden, W. H. *The English Auden: Poems, Essays and Dramatic Writings 1927–1939*. Ed. Edward Mendelson. [1977] London: Faber, 1986.

Auerbach, Eric. *Dante: Poet of the Secular World*. Trans. Ralph Mannheim. Introd. Michael Dirda. 1st pub. in German 1929; New York: New York Review of Books, 2007.

Bagehot, Walter. 'Percy Bysshe Shelley' (1856). *Literary Studies*. 2 vols. London: Dent, 1911.

Baker, Carlos. *Shelley's Major Poetry: The Fabric of a Vision*. [1948] New York: Russell, 1961.

Barcus, James E, ed. *Shelley: The Critical Heritage*. London: Routledge & Keegan Paul, 1975.

Barfoot, C. C., ed. *'A Natural Delineation of Human Passions': The Historic Moment of 'Lyrical Ballads'*. Amsterdam: Rodopi, 2004.

Bate, Walter Jackson. *From Classic to Romantic: Premises of Taste in Eighteenth-Century England*. Cambridge: Harvard University Press, 1946.

Bate, W. Jackson. *The Burden of the Past and the English Poet*. London: Chatto and Windus, 1971.

Baudelaire, Charles. *Les Fleurs du Mal*. Ed. Jacques Dupont. Paris: Flammarion, 1991.

Baudelaire, Charles. *Selected Poems*. Plain prose translation, introd. and notes by Carol Clark. London: Penguin, 2004.

Beatty, Bernard and Vincent Newey, ed. *Byron and the Limits of Fiction*. Liverpool: Liverpool University Press, 1988.

Beddoes, Thomas Lovell. *The Works of Thomas Lovell Beddoes*. Ed. H. W. Donner. London: Oxford University Press, 1935.

Beddoes, Thomas Lovell. *Thomas Lovell Beddoes: Selected Poems*. Ed. Judith Higgens. Manchester: Carcanet Press, 1976.

Beer, Anna. *Milton: Poet, Pamphleteer and Patriot*. London: Bloomsbury, 2008.

Bennett, Andrew. *Romantic Poets and the Culture of Posterity*. Cambridge: Cambridge University Press, 1999.

Berns, Ute. *Science, Politics, and Friendship in the Works of Thomas Lovell Beddoes*. Newark: University of Delaware Press, 2012.

Berns, Ute and Michael Bradshaw, ed. *The Ashgate Companion to the Work of Thomas Lovell Beddoes*. Aldershot: Ashgate, 2007.

Bevis, Matthew, ed. *The Oxford Handbook of Victorian Poetry*. Oxford: Oxford University Press, 2013.

Bielek-Robson, Agata. *The Saving Lie: Harold Bloom and Deconstruction*. Evanston: Northwestern University Press, 2011: 36.

Bieri, James. *Percy Bysshe Shelley, A Biography: Exile of Unfulfilled Reknown, 1816–1822*. Cranbury: Associated University Presses, 2005.

Birch, Dinah. *Ruskin on Turner*. London: Cassell, 1990.

Blake, William. *Blake: Complete Writings*. Ed. Geoffrey Keynes. 1966. Corr. edn. Oxford: Oxford University Press, 1992.

Blank, G. Kim. *Wordsworth's Influence on Shelley: A Study of Poetic Authority*. Basingstoke: Macmillan, 1988.

Bloom, Harold. *Shelley's Mythmaking*. 1959. Ithaca: Cornell University Press, 1969.

Bloom, Harold. *The Visionary Company: A Reading of English Romantic Poetry*. Rev. and enlarged edn. Ithaca: Cornell University Press, 1971.

Bloom, Harold. *The Anxiety of Influence: A Theory of Poetry*. New York: Oxford University Press, 1973.

Bloom, Harold. *Poetry and Repression*. New Haven: Yale University Press, 1976.

Bloom, Harold, ed. *Percy Bysshe Shelley: Modern Critical Views*. New York: Chelsea, 1985.

Bloom, Harold. *The Best Poems of the English Language: From Chaucer through Robert Frost*. Selected and with commentary by Harold Bloom. London: Harper, 2004.

Bloom, Harold. *The Anatomy of Influence: Literature as a Way of Life*. New Haven: Yale University Press, 2011.

Bode, Christoph and Sebastian Domsch, ed. *British and European Romanticisms: Selected Papers from the Munich Conference of the German Society for English Romanticism*. Trier: Wissenschaftlicher Verlag Trier, 2007.

Bone, Drummond, ed. *The Cambridge Companion to Byron*. Cambridge: Cambridge University Press, 2004.

Bornstein, George. *Poetic Remaking: The Art of Browning, Yeats, and Pound*. University Park: Pennsylvania State University Press, 1988.

Bradley, A. C. *A Commentary on Tennyson's 'In Memoriam'*. London: Macmillan, 1901.

Bradley, A. C. 'Notes on Passages in Shelley'. *Modern Language Review* 1 (1906): 25–42.

Bradley, A. C. 'Notes on Shelley's "Triumph of Life"'. *Modern Language Review* 9 (1914): 441–56.

Bradley, A. C. *A Miscellany*. London: Macmillan, 1929.

Bradley, A. C. *Oxford Lectures on Poetry*. Introd. M. R. Ridley. 1909. London: Macmillan, 1965.

Braida, Antonella. *Dante and the Romantics*. Houndmills: Palgrave Macmillan, 2004.

Brewer, William D. *The Shelley-Byron Conversation*. Gainesville: University Press of Florida, 1994.

Bromwich, David. *Hazlitt: The Mind of a Critic*. New Haven: Yale University Press, 1983.

Browning, Robert. *The Oxford Authors: Robert Browning*. Ed. Adam Roberts. Oxford: Oxford University Press, 1997.

Burwick, Frederick and Jürgen Klein, ed. *The Romantic Imagination: Literature and Art in England and Germany*. Amsterdam: Rodopi, 1996.

Burwick, Frederick and Paul Douglass, ed. *Dante and Italy in British Romanticism*. New York: Palgrave Macmillan, 2011.

Bushell, Sally. *Re-reading 'The Excursion': Narrative, Response, and the Wordsworthian Dramatic Voice*. Aldershot: Ashgate, 2002.

Butler, Marilyn. *Romantics, Rebels and Reactionaries: English Literature and Its Background 1760–1830*. Oxford: Oxford University Press, 1981.

Butlin, Martin and Evelyn Joll. *The Paintings of J. M. W. Turner*. 1977. New Haven: Yale University Press, rev. edn, 1984.

Buxton, John. *Byron and Shelley: The History of a Friendship*. London: Macmillan, 1968.

Byron, Lord George Gordon. *Byron's Letters and Journals*. Ed. Leslie A. Marchand. 13 vols. London: Murray, 1973–94.

Byron, Lord George Gordon. *The Complete Poetical Works*. Ed. Jerome J. McGann and Barry Weller. 7 vols. Oxford: Clarendon Press, 1980–93.

Byron, Lord George Gordon. *Lord Byron: The Complete Miscellaneous Prose*. Ed. Andrew Nicholson. Oxford: Clarendon Press, 1991.

Byron, Lord George Gordon. *Lord Byron: The Major Works*. Ed. Jerome McGann. Oxford World's Classics. Oxford: Oxford University Press, 2000.

Byron, Lord George Gordon. *Byron's Poetry and Prose*. Sel. and ed. Alice Levine. New York: Norton, 2010.

Callaghan, Madeleine. *Shelley's Living Artistry: Letters, Poems, Plays*. Liverpool: Liverpool University Press, 2017.

Calvino, Italo. *Why Read the Classics?* Trans. Martin McLoughlin. 1999. London: Penguin, 2009.

Cameron, Kenneth Neill. 'A Major Source of *The Revolt of Islam*'. *PMLA* 56 (1941): 175–206.

Cameron, Kenneth Neill. 'Shelley vs. Southey: New Light on an Old Quarrel'. *PMLA* 57.2 (1942): 489–512.

Cameron, Kenneth Neill, Donald H. Reiman, and Doucet Devin Fischer, gen. eds. *Shelley and his Circle: 1773–1822*. 10 vols to date. Cambridge: Harvard University Press, 1961–.

Cameron, Kenneth Neill. *Shelley: The Golden Years*. Cambridge: Harvard University Press, 1974.

Carlyle, Thomas. *Past and Present*. New York: Colyer, 1843.

Chandler, David. 'A Study of Lamb's "Living without God in the World"'. *Charles Lamb Bulletin*. N.S. 99 (1997): 86–101.

Chaucer, Geoffrey. *The Works of Geoffrey Chaucer*. Ed. F. N. Robinson. 2nd edn. London: Oxford University Press, 1957.

Chernaik, Judith. *The Lyrics of Shelley*. Cleveland: The Press of Case Western Reserve University, 1972.

Chorley, Henry Fothergill. *Memorials of Mrs Hemans: With Illustrations of Her Literary Character from Her Private Correspondence*. 2 vols. London: Saunders and Otley, 1836.

Clairmont, Claire. *The Journals of Claire Clairmont*. Ed. Marion Kingston Stocking. Cambridge: Harvard University Press, 1968.

Clark, Timothy. *Embodying Revolution: The Figure of the Poet in Shelley*. Oxford: Clarendon Press, 1989.

Cochran, Peter. 'Byron and Shelley: Radical Incompatibles'. *Romanticism on the Net* 43 (August 2006) <http://id.erudit.org/iderudit/013589ar>.

Coleridge, Samuel Taylor. *The Poems of Samuel Taylor Coleridge*. Ed. Ernest Hartley Coleridge. London: Oxford University Press, 1912.

Coleridge, Samuel Taylor. *The Friend*. Ed. Barbara F. Rooke, 2 vols. London: Routledge, 1969.

Coleridge, Samuel Taylor. *Biographia Literaria*. Ed. James Engell and Walter Jackson Bate. 2 vols. Princeton: Princeton University Press, 1983.

Coleridge, Samuel Taylor. *Samuel Taylor Coleridge: The Oxford Authors*. Ed. H. J. Jackson. Oxford: Oxford University Press, 1985.

Coleridge, Samuel Taylor. *Table Talk Recorded by Henry Nelson Coleridge (and John Taylor Coleridge)*. Vol. 14. Ed. Carl C. Woodring. 2 vols. *The Collected Works of Samuel Taylor Coleridge*. Gen. ed. Kathleen Coburn. Bollingen Series. Princeton: Princeton University Press, 1990.

Coleridge, Samuel Taylor. *Coleridge's Notebooks: A Selection*. Ed. Seamus Perry. Oxford: Oxford University Press, 2002.

Coleridge, Samuel Taylor. *Coleridge's Poetry and Prose*. Ed. Nicholas Halmi, Paul Magnuson, and Raimonda Modiano. New York: Norton, 2004.

Constable, John. 'Romantic Women's Poetry: Is It Any Good?'. *Cambridge Quarterly* 29 (2000): 133–43.

Cox, Jeffrey N. 'Keats, Shelley, and the Wealth of the Imagination'. *Studies in Romanticism* 34 (1995): 365–400.

Cox, Jeffrey, N. *Poetry and Politics in the Cockney School: Keats, Shelley, Hunt and Their School*. Cambridge: Cambridge University Press, 1998.

Cronin, Richard. *Romantic Victorians: English Literature, 1824–1840*. Basingstoke: Palgrave, 2002.

Crook, Nora. 'Shelley's Jingling Food for Oblivion: Hybridizing High and Low Styles and Forms', forthcoming in *The Wordsworth Circle* (2019).

Cronin, Richard, Antony Harrison, and Alison Chapman, ed. *A Companion to Victorian Poetry*. Malden: Blackwell, 2008.

Curran, Stuart. *Shelley's Annus Mirabilis: The Maturing of an Epic Vision*. San Marino: Huntington Library, 1975.

Curran, Stuart. *Poetic Form and British Romanticism*. New York: Oxford University Press, 1986.

Dante Alighieri. *The Vision; or Hell, Purgatory, and Paradise of Dante Alighieri*. Trans. Henry Francis Cary. 3 vols. 2nd edn corr. with the Life of Dante, Additional Notes, and an Index. London: Taylor and Hessey, 1819.

Dante Alighieri. *Commedia*. Ed. Philip H. Wicksteed. 3 vols. London: Dent, 1904.

Dante Alighieri. *Paradiso*. Verse translation by Robert and Jean Hollander. Introd. and notes by Robert Hollander. New York: Doubleday, 2007.

Day, Aidan. *Tennyson's Scepticism*. Basingstoke: Palgrave, 2005.

De Beer, Gavin. 'An "Atheist" in the Alps'. *Keats-Shelley Memorial Bulletin* 9 (1958): 1–15.

De Man, Paul. *The Rhetoric of Romanticism*. New York: Columbia University Press, 1984.

Delisle, Fanny. *A Study of Shelley's 'A Defence of Poetry': A Textual and Critical Evaluation*. 2 vols. Salzburg: Institut fur Englische Sprache und Literatur, Universitat Salzburg, 1974.

Dickens, Charles. *'American Notes' and 'Pictures from Italy'*. [1865] London: Macmillan, 1903.

Donelan, James. Review of Wayne Deakin, *Hegel and the English Romantic Poets*, *Review of English Studies* (2015), advance access, first published 1 October 2015.

Donner, H. W. *Thomas Lovell Beddoes: The Making of a Poet*. Oxford: Basil Blackwell, 1935.

Duff, David. *Romance and Revolution: Shelley and the Politics of a Genre*. Cambridge: Cambridge University Press, 1994.

Duff, David. *Romanticism and the Uses of Genre*. Oxford: Oxford University Press, 2009.

Dumke, Stephanie Julia. *The Influence of Calderón and Goethe on Shelley in the Context of A. W. Schlegel's Conception of Romantic Drama*. Unpublished PhD thesis. Durham University, 2013.

Eliot, George. *Middlemarch* (1871–2). Ed. W. J. Harvey. Harmondsworth: Penguin, 1965.

Eliot, T. S. *The Complete Poems and Plays*. London: Faber, 1969.

Eliot, T. S. *Selected Prose of T. S. Eliot*. Ed. Frank Kermode. London: Faber, 1975.

Eliot, T. S. *Selected Essays*. 3rd enlarged edn. 1951. London: Faber and Faber, 1976.

Eliot, T. S. *The Waste Land: A Norton Critical Edition*. Ed. Michael North. New York: Norton, 2001.

Eliot, T. S. *The Complete Prose of T. S. Eliot: The Critical Edition: Literature, Politics, Belief, 1927–1929*. Ed. Frances Dickey, Jennifer Formicelli, and Ronald Schuchard. Baltimore: Johns Hopkins University Press, 2015. Online edn.

Ellis, F. S., ed. and comp. *A Lexical Concordance to the Poetical Works of Percy Bysshe Shelley.* London: Bernard Quaritch, 1892.

Engell, James. *The Creative Imagination: Enlightenment to Romanticism.* Cambridge: Harvard University Press, 1981.

Epstein, Andrew. 'Shelley's *Adonais*, Keats, and Poetic Influence'. *Keats-Shelley Journal* 48 (1999): 90–128.

Everest, Kelvin, ed. *Shelley Revalued: Essays from the Gregynog Conference.* Leicester: Leicester University Press, 1983.

Everest, Kelvin. 'Shelley's *Adonais* and John Keats'. *Essays in Criticism* 57 (2007): 237–64.

Feldman, Paula R, ed. *Records of Woman, with Other Poems.* Lexington: University Press of Kentucky, 1999.

Finberg, A. J. *A Complete Inventory of the Drawings of the Turner Bequest.* London: Darling & son, 1909.

Flaxman, John. *Flaxman's Illustrations for Dante's Divine Comedy.* Mineola: Dover, 2007.

Fogle, Richard Harter. 'Dante and Shelley's *Adonais*'. *Bucknell Review* 15.39 (1967): 11–21.

Fogle, Richard Harter. 'John Taaffe's Annotated Copy of *Adonais*'. *Keats-Shelley Journal* 17 (1968): 31–52.

Frye, Northrop. *A Study of English Romanticism.* 1968. Brighton: Harvester Press, 1983.

Fuller, David. 'Shelley and Jesus'. *The Durham University Journal. Percy Bysshe Shelley Special Issue.* Ed. Michael O'Neill 85.2 (1993): 211–33.

Gadamer, Hans-Georg. *The Relevance of the Beautiful and Other Essays.* Trans. Nicholas Walker. Cambridge: Cambridge University Press, 1987.

Gadamer, Hans-Georg. *Truth and Method.* Trans. rev. Joel Weinsheimer and Donald G. Marshall. 2nd edn. London: Bloomsbury, 2013.

Gage, John. *Colour in Turner: Poetry and Truth.* London: Studio Vista, 1969.

Gage, John. *J. M. W. Turner: 'A Wonderful Range of Mind'.* 1987. New Haven: Yale University Press, 1987.

Goethe, Johann Wolfgang von. *Faust: Part One*, trans. David Luke. Oxford: Oxford University Press, 1987: xxxii.

Gowing, Lawrence. *Turner: Imagination and Reality.* New York: Doubleday, 1966.

Haley, Bruce. *Living Forms: Romantics and the Monumental Figure.* Albany: State University of New York Press, 2003.

Hall, Dewey. '"From Steep to Steep": Poetic Indebtedness in Coleridge and Shelley'. *Coleridge Bulletin* 31 (2008): 102–11.

Harding, Anthony John. 'Coleridge as Mentor and the Origins of Masculinist Modernity'. *European Romantic Review* 14 (2003): 453–66.

Hartman, Geoffrey. 'Gods, Ghosts, and Shelley's "Atheos"'. *Literature & Theology*, 24.1 (2010): 4–18.

Hartman, Geoffrey H. *Wordsworth's Poetry, 1787–1814.* Cambridge: Harvard University Press, 1971.

Havely, Nick, ed. *Dante's Modern Afterlife: Reception and Response from Blake to Heaney.* New York: St Martin's Press, 1998.

Hawkes, Terence, ed. *Coleridge on Shakespeare.* Introd. Alfred Harbage. Harmondsworth: Penguin, 1969.

Hawkins, Peter S. *Dante: A Brief History.* Malden: Blackwell, 2006.

Haydon, Benjamin Robert. *Diary.* Ed. Willard Bissell Pope. 5 vols. Cambridge: Harvard University Press, 1960–3.

Haynes, Kenneth. *English Literature and Ancient Languages.* Oxford: Oxford University Press, 2007.

Hazlitt, William. *Complete Works of William Hazlitt*. Ed. P. P. Howe. 21 vols. London: Dent, 1930–4.

Hazlitt, William. *The Spirit of the Age*. Ed. E. D. Mackerness. London: Collins, 1969.

Hazlitt, William. *The Plain Speaker: The Key Essays*. Ed. Duncan Wu; introd. Tom Paulin. Oxford: Blackwell, 1998.

Hazlitt, William. *The Selected Writings of William Hazlitt*. Ed. Duncan Wu. London: Pickering & Chatto, 1998.

Hazlitt, William. *William Hazlitt, The Fight and Other Writings*. Ed. Tom Paulin and David Chandler; introd. Tom Paulin. London: Penguin, 2000.

Heffernan, James A. W. ' "Adonais": Shelley's Consumption of Keats'. *Studies in Romanticism* 23.3 (1984): 295–315.

Heffernan, James A. W. *The Re-creation of Landscape: A Study of Wordsworth, Coleridge, Constable, and Turner*. Hanover: University Press of New England, 1985.

Hemans, Felicia. *The Poetical Works of Mrs Hemans, with Prefatory Memoir, Notes, Etc.* The 'Albion' Edition. London and New York: Warne, 1897.

Hemans, Felicia. *Felicia Hemans: Selected Poems, Letters, Reception Materials*. Ed. Susan J. Wolfson. Princeton: Princeton University Press, 2000.

Hemans, Felicia. *Felicia Hemans: Selected Poems, Prose, and Letters*. Ed. Gary Kelly. Peterborough: Broadview, 2002.

Hickey, Alison. *Impure Conceits: Rhetoric and Ideology in Wordsworth's 'Excursion'*. Stanford: Stanford University Press, 1997.

Hofmann, Michael. 'The State with the Prettiest Name'. *London Review of Books* 40.10 (24 May 2018): 33–4.

Hogg, Thomas Jefferson. *The Life of Percy Bysshe Shelley*. Ed. Edward Dowden. New Edition. London: Kegan Paul, 1909.

Hogle, Jerrold E. *Shelley's Process: Radical Transference and the Development of His Major Works*. Oxford: Oxford University Press, 1988.

Hopkins, David. *Conversing with Antiquity: English Poets and the Classics, from Shakespeare to Pope*. 2010. Oxford: Oxford University Press, 2014.

Hopps, Gavin and Jane Stabler, ed. *Romanticism and Religion: From William Cowper to Wallace Stevens*. Aldershot: Ashgate, 2006.

Howe, Anthony. *Byron and the Forms of Thought*. Liverpool: Liverpool University Press, 2013.

Howe, Tony. 'Shelley and the Development of *Don Juan*'. *Byron Journal* 35.1 (2007): 27–39.

Hughes, Harriet. *Memoir of The Life and Writings of Mrs Hemans, By Her Sister*. Philadelphia: Lea and Blanchard, 1840.

Hunt, Leigh. *Autobiography*. 2 vols. New York: Harpers, 1850.

Hunter, G. K. 'Bradley, Andrew Cecil (1851–1935), literary scholar'. *Oxford Dictionary of National Biography*. 2004–09–23. Oxford University Press. Accessed: 2 March 2018. [http://www.oxforddnb.com/view/article/32027].

Hurley, Michael D. and Michael O'Neill. *Poetic Form: An Introduction*. Cambridge: Cambridge University Press, 2012.

Hyder, Clyde K. *Swinburne: The Critical Heritage*. London: Routledge, 1970.

Jacoff, Rachel. *The Cambridge Companion to Dante*. Cambridge: Cambridge University Press, 1993.

Johnston, Freya. *Samuel Johnson and the Art of Sinking 1709–1791*. Oxford: Oxford University Press, 2005.

Johnson, Samuel. *Johnson's Preface to Shakespeare: A Facsimile of the 1778 Edition*, introd. and commentary P. J. Smallwood. Bristol: Bristol Classical Press, 1985.

Johnson, Samuel. 'Preface' to *The Plays of William Shakespeare. The Major Works*. Ed. Donald Greene. 1984. Oxford: Oxford University Press, 2000.

Jones, Steven E. *Shelley's Satire: Violence, Exhortation, and Authority*. DeKalb: Northern Illinois University Press, 1994.

Jump, John D. *Tennyson: The Critical Heritage*. London: Routledge & Kegan Paul, 1967.

Keach, William. *Shelley's Style*. New York: Methuen, 1984.

Keach, William. *Arbitrary Power: Romanticism, Language, Politics*. Princeton: Princeton University Press, 2004.

Keats, John. *The Letters of John Keats 1814–1821*. Ed. Hyder Edward Rollins, 2 vols. Cambridge: Cambridge University Press, 1958.

Keats, John. *The Poems of John Keats*, ed. Miriam Allott. London: Longman, 1970.

Keats, John. *The Complete Poems*, ed. John Barnard, 3rd edn. London: Penguin, 1988.

Keats, John. *John Keats*. Oxford Authors. Ed. Elizabeth Cook. Oxford: Oxford University Press, 1990.

Kermode, Frank. *An Appetite for Poetry: Essays in Literary Interpretation*. London: Collins, 1989.

Kerrigan, John. *Shakespeare's Originality*. Oxford: Oxford University Press, 2018.

Kipperman, Mark. 'Absorbing a Revolution: Shelley Becomes a Romantic, 1889–1903'. *Nineteenth-Century Literature* 47 (1992): 187–211.

Kraut, Richard, ed. *The Cambridge Companion to Plato*. Cambridge: Cambridge University Press, 1992.

Kucich, Greg. *Keats, Shelley, and Romantic Spenserianism*. University Park: Pennsylvania State University Press, 1991.

Lamb, Charles. *The Letters of Charles Lamb*. Ed. Edward Verrall Lucas. 3 vols. London: Dent, 1935.

Lamb, Charles. *Rosamund Gray 1798*. Introd. and ed. Jonathan Wordsworth. Oxford: Woodstock, 1991.

Lamb, Charles and Mary Anne Lamb. *The Letters of Charles and Mary Anne Lamb*. Ed. Edwin W. Marrs. 2 vols. Ithaca: Cornell University Press 1978.

Landon, Letitia Elizabeth. *Critical Writings by Letitia Elizabeth Landon*. Ed. F. J. Sypher. Delmar: Scholars' Facsimiles and Reprints, 1996.

Landon, Letitia Elizabeth. *Letitia Elizabeth Landon: Selected Writings*. Ed. Jerome McGann and Daniel Riess. Peterborough: Broadview, 1997.

Lang, Cecil Y. ed. *The Pre-Raphaelites and Their Circle*. 2nd edn. Chicago: University of Chicago Press, 1975.

Larkin, Philip. *Collected Poems*. Ed. and introd. Anthony Thwaite. London: The Marvell Press and Faber, 1988.

Larmore, Charles. *The Romantic Legacy*. New York: Columbia University Press, 1996.

Lau, Beth. *Keats's Reading of the Romantic Poets*. Ann Arbor: University of Michigan Press, 1991.

Lau, Beth. *Fellow Romantics: Male and Female British Writers, 1790–1835*. Farnham: Ashgate, 2009.

Leask, Nigel. *British Romantic Writers and the East: Anxieties of Empire*. Cambridge: Cambridge University Press, 1992.

Leavis, F. R. *Revaluation: Tradition and Development in English Poetry*. [1936] Harmondsworth: Penguin, 1972.

Leavis, F. R. *Revaluation: Tradition and Development in English Poetry* Harmondsworth: Penguin, 1964.

Leighton, Angela. *Shelley and the Sublime*. Cambridge: Cambridge University Press, 1984.

Leighton, Angela. *Victorian Women Poets: Writing against the Heart*. New York: Harvester Wheatsheaf, 1992.

Leitch, Vincent B., ed. *The Norton Anthology of Theory and Criticism*. New York, Norton, 2018.

Lessenich, Rolf P. *Romantic Disillusionism and the Sceptical Tradition*. Bonn: Bonn University Press, 2017.

Levine, Caroline. *Forms: Whole, Rhythm, Hierarchy, Network*. Princeton: Princeton University Press, 2015.

Levinson, Marjorie et al., *Rethinking Historicism*. Oxford: Blackwell, 1989.

Lewis, C. S. *Selected Literary Essays*, ed. Walter Hooper. 1969. Cambridge: Cambridge University Press, 2013.

Lindsay, Jack. *Turner: His Life and Work, A Critical Biography*. 1966. Frogmore: Panther, 1973.

Lindstrom, Eric. 'Mourning Life: William Wordsworth and Percy Bysshe Shelley', *Romanticism* 23.1 (2017): 38–52.

Lourie, Margaret A. 'Below the Thunders of the Upper Deep: Tennyson as Romantic Revisionist'. *Studies in Romanticism* 18 (1979): 3–27.

Lowes, John Livingston. *The Road to Xanadu: A Study in the Ways of the Imagination*. 1927. London: Picador, 1978.

Lucas, Edward Verrall. *The Life of Charles Lamb*. 2 vols. London: Methuen, 1921.

Lukács, Gyorgy. *The Theory of the Novel: A Historic-Philosophical Essay on the Forms of Great Epic Literature*. Trans. Anna Bostock. 1915. Cambridge: MIT Press, 1971.

Madden, Lionel, ed. *Robert Southey: The Critical Heritage*. London: Routledge & Keegan Paul, 1972.

Mahoney, Charles, ed. *A Companion to Romantic Poetry*. Malden: Wiley-Blackwell, 2011.

Marvell, Andrew. *The Poems of Andrew Marvell*. Ed. Nigel Smith. Harlow: Pearson, 2007.

Maxwell, Catherine. *The Female Sublime from Milton to Swinburne*. Manchester: Manchester University Press, 2001: 180.

McGann, Jerome J. *Fiery Dust: Byron's Poetic Development*. Chicago: University of Chicago Press, 1968.

McGann, Jerome J. *Swinburne: An Experiment in Criticism*. Chicago: University of Chicago Press, 1972.

McGann, Jerome. *The Poetics of Sensibility: A Revolution in Literary Style*. Oxford: Clarendon, 1996.

McKusick, James C. 'The Politics of Language in Byron's *The Island*'. *ELH* 39 (1992): 839–56.

McMaster, Graham, ed. *William Wordsworth: A Critical Anthology*. Harmondsworth: Penguin, 1972.

Medwin, Thomas. *Conversations of Lord Byron*. London: Colburn, 1824.

Medwin, Thomas. *The Shelley Papers*. London: Whittaker, Treacher, & Co, 1833.

Medwin, Thomas. *The Life of Percy Bysshe Shelley*. London: T. C. Newby, 1847.

Medwin, Thomas. *Conversations of Lord Byron*. Ed. Ernest J. Lovell Jr. Princeton: Princeton University Press, 1966.

Mercer, Anna. *The Literary Relationship of Percy Bysshe Shelley and Mary Wollstonecraft Shelley*. London: Routledge, 2019.

Mellor, Anne K. *Romanticism and Gender*. New York: Routledge, 1993.

Meslay, Olivier. *J. M. W. Turner: The Man Who Set Painting on Fire.* Trans. from the French *Turner L'incendie de la peinture* by Ruth Sharman. 2004. London: Thames and Hudson, 2005.

Meyers, Terry L. 'Shelley's Influence on *Atalanta in Calydon*'. *Victorian Poetry* 14 (1976): 150–4.

Meyers, Terry L. 'Swinburne's Conception of Shelley'. *Pre-Raphaelite Review* 3 (1980): 36–47.

Miller, Christopher R. 'Shelley's Uncertain Heaven'. *English Literary History* 72 (2005): 577–603.

Milton, John. *Milton: Poetical Works.* Ed. Douglas Bush. Oxford: Oxford University Press, 1966.

Milton, John. *The Poems of John Milton.* Ed. John Carey and Alastair Fowler. London: Longman, 1968.

Milton, John. *John Milton: A Critical Edition of the Major Works.* Ed. Stephen Orgel and Jonathan Goldberg. Oxford: Oxford University Press, 1991.

Milton, John. *The Complete Poems.* Ed. John Leonard. London: Penguin, 1998.

Mole, Tom. *What the Victorians Made of Romanticism: Material Artifacts, Cultural Practices and Reception History.* Princeton: Princeton University Press, 2018.

Murray, Les. *Collected Poems.* Manchester: Carcanet, 1991.

Najarian, James. *Victorian Keats: Manliness, Sexuality, and Desire.* Basingstoke: Palgrave, 2002.

Newey, Vincent. 'Shelley and the Poets: *Alastor*, "Julian and Maddalo", *Adonais*'. *Durham University Journal* n.s. 54 (1993): 257–71.

Newey, Vincent. *Centring the Self: Subjectivity, Society and Reading from Thomas Gray to Thomas Hardy.* Aldershot: Scolar Press, 1995.

Newlyn, Lucy. *Paradise Lost and the Romantic Reader.* Oxford: Clarendon Press, 1993.

Norman, Sylva. *Flight of the Skylark: The Development of Shelley's Reputation.* Oklahoma: University of Oklahoma Press; London: Reinhardt, 1954.

Notopoulos, James A. *The Platonism of Shelley: A Study of Platonism and the Poetic Mind.* Durham: Duke University Press, 1949.

O'Gorman, Francis. *Victorian Poetry: An Annotated Anthology.* Malden: Blackwell, 2004.

O'Neill, Michael. *The Human Mind's Imaginings: Conflict and Achievement in Shelley's Poetry.* Oxford: Clarendon Press, 1989.

O'Neill, Michael, ed. and introd. *Shelley.* Longman Critical Reader. London: Longman, 1993.

O'Neill, Michael. 'Cathestant or Protholic?: Shelley's Italian Imaginings'. *Journal of Anglo-Italian Studies* 6 (2001): 153–68.

O'Neill, Michael. 'Fashioned from His Opposite: Yeats, Dante and Shelley'. *Journal of Anglo-Italian Studies* 8 (2006): 149–71.

O'Neill, Michael. *The All-Sustaining Air: Romantic Legacies and Renewals in British, American, and Irish Poetry since 1900.* Oxford: Oxford University Press, 2007.

O'Neill, Michael. 'A. C. Bradley's View of Shelley's Poetry and Poetics'. *Romanticism* 14.1 (2008): 36–46.

O'Neill, Michael. ' "Infinite Passion": Variations on a Romantic Topic in Robert Browning, Emily Brontë, Swinburne, Hopkins, Wilde, and Dowson'. *Romantics Echoes in the Victorian Era.* Ed. Andrew Radford and Mark Sandy. Aldershot: Ashgate, 2008: 175–89.

O'Neill, Michael. ' "Admirable for Conciseness and Vigour": Dante and Romantic Epic'. *Journal of Anglo-Italian Studies* 10 (2009): 15–27.

O'Neill, Michael. ' "Visions Rise, and Change": Emily Brontë's Poetry and Male Romantic Poetry'. *Brontë Studies* 36 (2011): 57–63.

O'Neill, Michael. ' "Altered Forms": Romanticism and the Poetry of Hart Crane'. *Romantic Presences in the Twentieth Century*. Ed. Mark Sandy. Aldershot: Ashgate, 2012: 57–72.

O'Neill, Michael. 'Shakespearean Poetry and the Romantics'. *The Oxford Handbook of Shakespeare's Poetry*. Ed. Jonathan Post. Oxford: Oxford University Press, 2013: 563–81.

O'Neill, Michael. 'The Romantic Bequest: Arnold and Others'. *The Oxford Handbook of Victorian Poetry*. Ed. Matthew Bevis. Oxford: Oxford University Press, 2013: 217–34.

O'Neill, Michael. *Gangs of Shadow*. Todmorden: Arc, 2014.

O'Neill, Michael. 'Anatomizing Casuistry: Shelley's *The Cenci* and the Fate of Analysis'. *Romantic Ambiguities: Abodes of the Modern*. Ed. Sebastian Domsch, Christoph Reinfandt, and Katharina Rennhak. Wissenschaftlicher Verlag Trier, 2017: 169–80.

O'Neill, Michael and Charles Mahoney, ed. *Romantic Poetry: An Annotated Anthology*. Malden: Wiley-Blackwell, 2008.

O'Neill, Michael and Anthony Howe, ed., with the assistance of Madeleine Callaghan. *The Oxford Handbook of Percy Bysshe Shelley*. Oxford: Oxford University Press, 2012.

O'Neill, Michael, Mark Sandy, and Sarah Wootton, ed. *Venice and the Cultural Imagination: 'This Strange Dream upon the Water'*. London: Pickering and Chatto, 2012.

O'Neill, Michael and Madeleine Callaghan. *The Romantic Poetry Handbook*. Hoboken: Wiley-Blackwell, 2018: 321.

Park, Roy, ed. *Lamb as Critic*. London: Routledge & Keegan Paul, 1980.

Paulin, Tom. *The Day-Star of Liberty: William Hazlitt's Radical Style*. London: Faber and Faber, 1998.

Perry, Seamus. *Coleridge and the Uses of Division*. Oxford: Clarendon Press, 1999.

Peterfreund, Stuart. *Shelley among Others: The Play of the Intertext and the Idea of Language*. Baltimore: Johns Hopkins University Press, 2002.

Pindar. *Pindar*. Trans. C. A. Wheelwright. London: Colburn and Bentley, 1830.

Plato. *The Dialogues of Plato*. Translated into English with Analyses and Introductions by B. Jowett. 4 vols. 4th edn. Oxford: Clarendon, 1953.

Plato. *Plato in Twelve Volumes, 'Lysis', 'Symposium', 'Gorgias'*. Trans. W. R. M. Lamb. Cambridge: Harvard University Press, 1975.

Plato. *The Symposium*. Trans. with introd. and notes Christopher Gill. London: Penguin, 1999.

Plato. *The Symposium of Plato: The Shelley Translation*. Ed. and introd. David K. O'Connor. South Bend: St Augustine's Press, 2002.

Pope, Alexander. *Alexander Pope: The Major Works*. Ed. Pat Rogers. [1993] Oxford: Oxford University Press, 2006.

Powell, Cecilia. *Turner*. Norwich: Pitkin, 2003.

Priestman, Martin. *Romantic Atheism: Poetry and Freethought 1780–1830*. Cambridge: Cambridge University Press, 2000.

Quinn, Mary A. 'Shelley's "Verses on the Celandine": An Elegiac Parody of Wordsworth's Early Lyrics'. *Keats-Shelley Journal* 36 (1987): 88–109.

Rawes, Alan. *Byron's Poetic Experimentation* Aldershot: Ashgate, 2000.

Redding, Cyrus with A. & M. Galignani, ed. *The Poetical Works* of *Coleridge, Shelley and Keats 1829*. Otley: Woodstock, 2002.

Redpath, Theodore. *The Young Romantics and Critical Opinion, 1807–1824*. London: Harrap, 1973.

Reiman, Donald H. *Shelley's 'Triumph of Life': A Critical Study, Based on a Text Newly Edited from the Bodleian Manuscript.* 1965. New York: Octagon Books, 1979.

Reiman, Donald H., gen. ed. *Manuscripts of the Younger Romantics: Shelley.* 9 vols. New York: Garland, 1985–97.

Reiman, Donald H., gen. ed. *Bodleian Shelley Manuscripts.* 22 vols. New York: Garland, 1986–97.

Ricks, Christopher. *Tennyson.* 1972. London: Macmillan, 1978.

Ricks, Christopher. *The Force of Poetry.* Oxford: Oxford University Press, 1984.

Ricks, Christopher. *Allusion to the Poets.* Oxford: Oxford University Press, 2002.

Riede, David G. *Swinburne: A Study of Romantic Mythmaking.* Charlottesville: University Press of Virginia, 1978.

Rieger, James. *The Mutiny Within: The Heresies of Percy Bysshe Shelley.* London: George Brazilier, 1967.

Rilke, Rainer Maria. *The Selected Poetry of Rainer Maria Rilke.* Ed. and trans. Stephen Mitchell. 1980. London: Picador, 1987.

Rimbaud, Arthur. *Collected Poems.* Introd. and ed. Oliver Barnard. 1962. rev. edn. London: Penguin, 1997.

Rimbaud, Arthur. *A Season in Hell and Other Poems.* Trans. Norman Cameron. London: Anvil, 1994.

Roberts, Hugh. *Shelley and the Chaos of History.* University Park: Pennsylvania State University Press, 1997.

Robinson, Charles E. *Shelley and Byron: The Snake and Eagle Wreathed in Fight.* Baltimore: Johns Hopkins University Press, 1976.

Roe, Nicholas, ed. *Keats and History.* Cambridge: Cambridge University Press, 1995.

Roe, Nicholas, ed. *Samuel Taylor Coleridge and the Sciences of Life.* Oxford: Oxford University Press, 2001.

Roe, Nicholas. *Fiery Heart: the First Life of Leigh Hunt.* London: Pimlico, 2005.

Rooksby, Ricky and Nicholas Shrimpton, ed. *The Whole Music of Passion: New Essays on Swinburne.* Aldershot: Scolar, 1993.

Rosenblum, Robert. *Transformations in Late Eighteenth Century Art.* 1967. Princeton: Princeton University Press, 1969.

Rossetti, William Michael. 'Notes on the Text of Shelley'. *Essays and Studies.* London: Chatto and Windus, 1875: 184–237.

Rutherford, Andrew, ed. *Byron: Augustan and Romantic.* Basingstoke: Macmillan, 1990.

Ryan, Robert M. *The Romantic Reformation: Religious Politics in English Literature, 1789–1824.* Cambridge: Cambridge University Press, 1997.

Sacks, Peter. 'Last Clouds: A Reading of "Adonais"'. *Studies In Romanticism* 23.3 (1984): 379–400.

Saglia, Diego. ' "A Deeper and Richer Music": The Poetics of Sound and Voice in Felicia Hemans's 1820s Poetry'. *English Literary History* 74.2 (2007): 351–70.

Sandy, Mark. *Politics of Self and Form in Keats and Shelley: Nietzschean Subjectivity.* Aldershot: Ashgate, 2005: 107.

Sandy, Mark. *Romanticism, Memory, and Mourning.* Farnham: Ashgate, 2013.

Sandy, Mark. ' "Lines of Light": Poetic Variations in Wordsworth, Byron, and Shelley'. *Romanticism* 22.3 (2016): 260–8.

Schlegel, A. W. *Lectures on Dramatic Literature and Art* (1809–11). Trans. John Black. London: Baldwin, Cradock, and Joy, 1815.

Schmid, Suzanne and Michael Rossington, ed. *The Reception of Shelley in Europe.* London: Continuum, 2008.

Scrivener, Michael. *Radical Shelley: The Philosophical Anarchism and Utopian Thought of Percy Bysshe Shelley.* Princeton: Princeton University Press, 1982.

Shakespeare, William. *The Norton Shakespeare.* Ed. Stephen Greenblatt and others. New York: Norton, 1997.

Shelley, Bryan. *Shelley and Scripture: The Interpreting Angel.* Oxford: Clarendon Press, 1994.

Shelley, Mary. *The Letters of Mary Wollstonecraft Shelley,* ed. Betty T. Bennett. Baltimore: Johns Hopkins University Press, 1980–8. 3 vols.

Shelley, Mary. *The Journals of Mary Wollstonecraft Shelley, 1814–1844.* Ed. Paula R. Feldman and Diana Scott-Kilvert. 2 vols. Oxford: Clarendon Press, 1987.

Shelley, Mary. *The Mary Shelley Reader.* Ed. Betty T. Bennett and Charles E. Robinson. New York: Oxford University Press, 1990.

Shelley, Percy Bysshe. *Posthumous Poems of Percy Bysshe Shelley.* London: John and Henry L. Hunt, Covent Garden, 1824.

Shelley, Percy Bysshe. *The Works of Percy Bysshe Shelley, with His Life.* 2 vols. London: Ascham, 1834.

Shelley, Percy Bysshe. *Essays, Letters from Abroad, Translations and Fragments.* Ed. Mary Shelley. 2 vols. London: Moxon, 1840.

Shelley, Percy Bysshe. *Shelley's 'Prometheus Unbound': A Variorum Edition.* Ed. Lawrence J. Zillman. Seattle: University of Washington Press, 1959.

Shelley, Percy Bysshe. *The Esdaile Notebook: A Volume of Early Poems.* Ed. Kenneth Neill Cameron. London: Faber and Faber, 1964.

Shelley, Percy Bysshe. *The Letters of Percy Bysshe Shelley,* ed. Frederick L. Jones. 2 vols. Oxford: Clarendon, 1964.

Shelley, Percy Bysshe. *The Complete Works of Percy Bysshe Shelley.* Ed. Roger Ingpen and Walter E. Peck. 10 vols. London: Ernest Benn, 1965.

Shelley, Percy Bysshe. *Percy Bysshe Shelley: Selected Poetry.* Ed. Harold Bloom. New York: Signet, 1966.

Shelley, Percy Bysshe. *The Prose Works of Percy Bysshe Shelley.* Ed. Harry Buxton Forman. 4 vols. London: Reeves and Turner, 1880.

Shelley, Percy Bysshe. *The Complete Poetical Works of Percy Bysshe Shelley.* Ed. Thomas Hutchinson. Oxford: Clarendon, 1904. Issued 1905 and 1934 as Oxford Standard Authors edition; corrected by G. M. Matthews, 1970.

Shelley, Percy Bysshe. *Shelley on Love.* Ed. Richard Holmes. London: Anvil, 1980.

Shelley, Percy Bysshe. *The Poems of Shelley,* ed. G. M. Matthews and Kelvin Everest. 4 vols. London: Longman, 1989–.

Shelley, Percy Bysshe. *Posthumous Poems 1824,* a facsimile reprint. Introd. Jonathan Wordsworth. Oxford: Woodstock Books, 1991.

Shelley, Percy Bysshe. *Percy Bysshe Shelley: Adonais 1821.* Ed. and introd. Jonathan Wordsworth. Oxford: Woodstock, 1992.

Shelley, Percy Bysshe. *The Prose Works of Percy Bysshe Shelley.* Ed. E. B. Murray. Oxford: Clarendon Press, 1993.

Shelley, Percy Bysshe. *Percy Bysshe Shelley: Poems and Prose,* ed. Timothy Webb. London: Dent, 1995.

Shelley, Percy Bysshe. *Shelley's Poetry and Prose.* Ed. Donald H. Reiman and Neil Fraistat, 2nd edn. New York: Norton, 2002.

Shelley, Percy Bysshe. *Percy Bysshe Shelley: The Major Works.* Ed. Zachary Leader and Michael O'Neill. Oxford: Oxford University Press, 2003.

Shelley, Percy Bysshe. *The Complete Poetry of Percy Bysshe Shelley.* Ed. Neil Fraistat, Nora Crook, Stuart Curran, Michael J. Neth, and Michael O'Neill. 3 vols to date. Baltimore: The Johns Hopkins University Press, 2003–12.

Shelley, Percy Bysshe. *Opere Poetiche*. Ed. Francesco Rognoni. Milan: Mondadori, 2018: 1136, 1529.

Southey, Robert. *The Life and Correspondence of Robert Southey*. Ed. Charles Cuthbert Southey. 6 vols. London: Longman, Brown, Green, & Longmans, 1850.

Southey, Robert. *New Letters of Robert Southey*. Ed. Kenneth Curry. 2 vols. London and New York: Columbia University Press, 1965.

Southey, Robert. *Robert Southey: Poetical Works, 1793–1810*. Gen. ed. Lynda Pratt. 5 vols. London: Pickering and Chatto, 2004.

Spender, Stephen. *World Within World*. [1951] London: Faber, 1977.

Spenser, Edmund. *The Poetical Works of Edmund Spenser*. Ed. J. C. Smith and E. De Selincourt. London: Oxford University Press, 1912.

Spenser, Edmund. *The Faerie Queene: Book 1*. Ed. P. C. Bayley, 1966. London: Oxford University Press, 1970 with corrections.

Sperry, Stuart M. *Keats the Poet*. Princeton: Princeton University Press, 1973.

Sperry, Stuart M. *Shelley's Major Verse: The Narrative and Dramatic Poetry*. Cambridge: Harvard University Press, 1988.

Stabler, Jane. *The Artistry of Exile: Romantic and Victorian Writers in Italy*. Oxford: Oxford University Press, 2013.

Stafford, Fiona. *Reading Romantic Poetry*. Hoboken: Wiley-Blackwell, 2012.

Stevens, Wallace. *The Collected Poems of Wallace Stevens*. 1954. London: Faber and Faber, 1955.

Stevens, Wallace. *Collected Poetry and Prose*. Sel. Frank Kermode and Joan Richardson. New York: Library of America, 1997.

Stevenson, Lionel. 'The "High-Born Maiden" Symbol in Tennyson'. *PMLA* 63 (1948): 234–43.

Story, Patrick. 'Pope, Pageantry, and Shelley's *Triumph of Life*'. *Keats-Shelley Journal* 21–2 (1972–3): 145–59.

Sweet, Nanora and Julie Melnyk, ed. *Felicia Hemans: Reimagining Poetry in the Nineteenth Century*. Basingstoke: Palgrave, 2001.

Swinburne, Algernon Charles. *The Swinburne Letters*. Ed. Cecil Y. Lang. 6 vols. New Haven: Yale University Press; London: Oxford University Press, 1959–62.

Swinburne, Algernon Charles. *New Writings*. Ed. Cecil Y. Lang. New York: Syracuse University Press, 1964.

Swinburne, Algernon Charles. *Swinburne as Critic*, ed. Clyde K. Hyder. London: Routledge, 1972.

Swinburne, Algernon Charles. *'Poems and Ballads' and 'Atalanta in Calydon'*. Ed. Kenneth Haynes. London: Penguin, 2000.

Swinburne, Algernon Charles. *Major Poems and Selected Prose*. Ed. Jerome J. McGann and Charles L. Sligh. New Haven: Yale University Press, 2004.

Swinden, Patrick, ed. *Shelley: Shorter Poems and Lyrics*. Basingstoke: Macmillan, 1976.

Taylor, Charles. *Sources of the Self: The Making of Modern Identity*. Cambridge: Cambridge University Press, 1989.

Taylor, Charles H. Jr. *The Early Collected Editions of Shelley's Poems: A Study in the History and Transmission of the Printed Text*. New Haven: Yale University Press, 1958.

Tennyson, Alfred Lord. *In Memoriam*. Ed. Susan Shatto and Marion Shaw. Oxford: Oxford University Press, 1982.

Tennyson, Alfred Lord. *The Poems of Tennyson*. Ed. Christopher Ricks. 2nd edn, incorporating the Trinity College MSS. 3 vols. Harlow: Longman, 1987.

Tennyson, Hallam. *Alfred, Lord Tennyson: A Memoir by his Son*. 2 vols. London: Macmillan, 1897.

Tetreault, Ronald. *The Poetry of Life: Shelley and Literary Form*. Toronto: University of Toronto Press, 1987.

Thomson, James. *The Seasons*. Ed. James Sambrook. Oxford: Clarendon, 1981.

Tucker, Herbert F. *Tennyson and the Doom of Romanticism*. Cambridge: Harvard University Press, 1988.

Tucker, Herbert F. *Epic: Britain's Heroic Muse 1790–1910*. Oxford: Oxford University Press, 2008.

Turner, Paul. 'Shelley and Lucretius'. *Review of English Studies* n.s. 10 (1959): 269–82.

Ulmer, William A. *John Keats: Reimagining History*. Cham, Switzerland: Palgrave MacMillan/Springer, 2017.

Vassallo, Peter. *Byron: The Italian Literary Influence*. London: Macmillan, 1988.

Venning, Barry. *Turner*. London: Phaidon, 2003.

Vicario, Michael A. *Shelley's Intellectual System and Its Epicurean Background*. London: Routledge, 2007.

Vico, Giambattista. *New Science* (1744). Trans. David March. London: Penguin, 1999.

Warrell, Ian, with essays by David Laven, Jan Morris, and Cecilia Powell. *Turner and Venice*. London: Tate Publishing, 2003.

Wasserman, Earl R. *Shelley: A Critical Reading*. Baltimore: The Johns Hopkins University Press, 1971.

Webb, Timothy. *The Violet in the Crucible: Shelley and Translation*. Oxford: Clarendon, 1976.

Webb, Timothy. *Shelley: A Voice Not Understood*. Manchester: Manchester University Press, 1977.

Weinberg, Alan M. *Shelley's Italian Experience*. London: Macmillan, 1991.

Weinberg, Alan. ' "Yet in its Depth What Treasures": Shelley's Transforming Intellect and the Paradoxical Example of Coleridge'. *Romanticism on the Net* 22 (May 2001) <http://id.erudit.org/iderudit/005979ar>.

Weinberg, Alan. 'Shelley's Diversity'. *English* 66 (2017): 6–26.

West, Sally. *Coleridge and Shelley: Textual Engagement*. Aldershot: Ashgate, 2007.

Wilkie, Brian. *Romantic Poets and Epic Tradition*. Madison: University of Wisconsin Press, 1965.

Wilson, Carol Shiner and Joel Haefner, ed. *Re-Visioning Romanticism: British Women Writers, 1776–1837*. Philadelphia: University of Pennsylvania Press, 2004.

Wilson, Ross, ed. *The Meaning of 'Life' in Romantic Poetry and Poetics*. New York: Routledge, 2009.

Wilson, Ross. *Shelley and the Apprehension of Life*. Cambridge: Cambridge University Press, 2013.

Wilton, Andrew. *Turner and the Sublime*. London: British Museum Publications, 1980.

Wilton, Andrew. *Turner in His Time*. 1987. London: Thames and Hudson, 2006 rev. edn.

Winckelmann, Johann Joachim. *Winckelmann: Writings on Art*. Selected and ed. David Irwin. London: Phaidon, 1972.

Wolfe, Humbert, ed. *The Life of Percy Bysshe Shelley, As Comprised in 'The Life of Shelley' by Thomas Jefferson Hogg, 'The Recollections of Shelley and Byron' by Edward John Trelawny, 'Memoirs of Shelley' by Thomas Love Peacock*, introd. Humbert Wolfe, 2 vols. London: Dent, 1933.

Wolfson, Susan J. *Formal Charges: The Shaping of Poetry in British Romanticism*. Stanford: Stanford University Press, 1997.

Wolfson, Susan J. *Borderlines: The Shiftings of Gender in British Romanticism*. Stanford: Stanford University Press, 2006.

Wolfson, Susan J. *Romantic Interactions: Social Being and the Turns of Literary Action.* Baltimore: The Johns Hopkins University Press, 2010.

Wolfson, Susan J. *Romantic Shades and Shadows.* Baltimore: Johns Hopkins University Press, 2018.

Wood, Sarah. *Robert Browning: A Literary Life.* Basingstoke: Palgrave, 2001.

Wordsworth, Jonathan. *The Prelude. A Companion to Romanticism.* Ed. Duncan Wu. Oxford: Blackwell, 1998: 191–205.

Wordsworth, William. *Letters of William Wordsworth: A New Selection.* Ed. Alan G. Hill. Oxford: Oxford University Press, 1984.

Wordsworth, William. *The Excursion.* Ed. Sally Bushell, James A. Butler, and Michael C. Jaye, with the assistance of David García. Ithaca: Cornell University Press, 2007.

Wordsworth, William. *William Wordsworth: The Major Works, including* The Prelude, ed. Stephen Gill, Oxford World's Classics. Oxford: Oxford University Press, 2011.

Wu, Duncan, ed. *Romantic Women Poets: An Anthology.* Oxford: Blackwell, 1997.

Wu, Duncan, ed. *Romanticism: An Anthology.* 3rd edn. Malden: Wiley-Blackwell, 2006.

Yeats, W. B. *The Variorum Edition of the Poems of W. B. Yeats.* Ed. Peter Allt and Russell K. Alspach. New York: Macmillan, 1957.

Yeats, W. B. *Selected Criticism and Prose.* Ed. A. Norman Jeffares. London: Pan in association with Macmillan, 1980.

Yeats, W. B. *Yeats's Poems.* Ed. and annotated. A Norman Jeffares with an Appendix by Warwick Gould. [1989] London: Macmillan, 1991 rev. edn.

Index

Index

Printed and bound by CPI Group (UK) Ltd, Croydon, CR0 4YY